LaunchPad for *Choices & Connections* is where video scenarios, and more are available. See the inside back cover for information or vis

AND TRY THESE FEATURES.

LearningCurve	Advance the Conversation	Advance the Conversation (Video)	Activities
LearningCurve for Ch. 4: Mediated Communication tests your knowledge of competent online messages	"Distorting Online Self-Presentation" helps you handle deceptive practices in online dating (Ch. 2, p. 43)	"Removing an Embarrassing Post" helps you maintain a positive online face (Ch. 4, pp. 112–113)	"Analyzing Your Online Face" provides a chance to self-reflect on your digital identity (Ch. 4, p. 115)
LearningCurve for Ch. 3: Understanding Gender and Culture reviews cultural and gender influences on communication	"Challenging Binary Judgments" confronts preconceived ideas about gender (Ch. 3, p. 72)	"Adapting to Cultural Differences" assesses cultural differences in groups (Ch. 3, pp. 86–87)	
LearningCurve for Ch. 7: Active Listening assesses your understanding of the listening process	"To Multitask or Not, That Is the Question!" tests how you would handle distracting texting practices (Ch. 7, p. 173)		"The 'Noise List'" examines how you can improve your listening skills (Ch. 7, p. 187)
LearningCurve for Ch. 10: Managing Conflict gauges how well you understand approaches to conflicts	"I Wasn't Being Sarcastic!" confronts how to handle misunderstood intentions when online (Ch. 6, p. 154)	"Conflict with a Roommate" explores how roommates can resolve a conflict constructively (Ch. 10, pp. 256–257)	"Choose Your Own Ending" prompts you to reevaluate conflicts you've experienced (Ch. 10, p. 259)
LearningCurve for Ch. 9: Managing Interpersonal Relationships reviews relationship maintenance strategies	"I Didn't Lie!" examines how to manage the fallout of a bad decision in a romance (Ch. 10, p. 248)		"Communication Rules" ponders how you can improve your own relationships (Ch. 9, p. 237)
LearningCurve for Ch. 12: Leadership in Group Communication tests how well you know small group communication skills	"You're Not Funny" deals with handling a group member who is distracting the team (Ch. 11, p. 277)	"Handling Complaints" helps you balance differing opinions in groups (Ch. 12, pp. 310–311)	"Practicing Problem Solving" gives you a chance to be a leader (Ch. 12, p. 313)
LearningCurve for Ch. 17: Persuasive Speaking tests your comfort with guidelines and practices for persuasive speaking	"But the Video Went Viral!" considers how you can handle humor and appropriate examples in speeches (Ch. 14, p. 355)	"Oral Citations" guides you in correctly citing sources in speeches (Ch. 13, pp. 338–339)	"Identifying Rhetorical Proof" asks you to find and evaluate a persuasive speech online (Ch. 17, p. 455)

OUR EDITORIAL BOARD

> *"What we're doing is looking at the language, the content, the imagery, and the presentation in each chapter of the textbook to find out if we can do better with regard to diversity and inclusiveness. I think this should be at the forefront of what we do as educators: being mindful of the population that we serve. Our goal is for the textbook to represent the world that students live in."*

Dorien Martin

S. Lizabeth Martin
Georgia State University, editorial board member

THE STORY

This revision of *Choices & Connections* was developed with the help of eight communication scholars, many of whom have held elected advocacy roles with the National Communication Association (NCA) or with their own institutions. Together, this team of experts helped us revise photos and text examples throughout every chapter with the goal of creating a better, more inclusive experience for students and instructors. They are the Editorial Board for Diversity, Inclusion, and Culturally Responsive Pedagogy:

- **Tenisha Baca**, Glendale Community College
- **Tim Brown**, Queens University of Charlotte
- **Tasha Davis**, Austin Community College
- **Danielle Harkins**, Germanna Community College
- **Tina Harris**, Louisiana State University
- **S. Lizabeth Martin**, Georgia State University (pictured on this page)
- **Rody Randon**, Phoenix College
- **Myra Washington**, University of New Mexico

THE MISSION

To advance and evolve our understanding of diversity, inclusiveness, and culturally responsive pedagogy and to promote their fundamental, not ancillary, place in the development of learning materials.

WHAT DOES THIS MEAN FOR STUDENTS?

Culturally responsive pedagogy promotes self-reflection and critical thinking among students and prepares them for global citizenship, a diverse workplace, and advocacy in various forms.

To learn more about our editorial board, their work, and their mission, visit **macmillanlearning.com/college/us/DICR**

OUR AUTHORS

UAB Honors College

"The words in this text arise not from one voice or two, but from many. I am deeply grateful for this plurality, as the story of Joe's and my book has been inestimably enriched by the insights gifted to us by our editorial board."

Dr. Steven McCornack,
University of Alabama at Birmingham

Steven McCornack ("Steve") has always been fascinated with how people communicate, which led him to pursue undergraduate and graduate degrees in communication, and become a professor. After 27 years at Michigan State University, Steve moved to the South, where he is now Professor and Basic Course Coordinator in Communication Studies at the University of Alabama at Birmingham. Steve has published more than 30 articles in leading communication journals and has received several prestigious awards, including the Amoco Foundation Excellence in Teaching Award, a Lilly Endowment Teaching Fellowship, the MSU Teacher/Scholar Award, the MSU Alumni Excellence in Undergraduate Teaching Award, and the Donald H. Ecroyd Award for Outstanding Teaching in Higher Education. Other than his love of teaching, Steve's principal passions are his family (wife Kelly and three redheaded sons, Kyle, Colin, and Conor), vinyl records and turntables, yoga, karate, mechanical watches, Kona coffee, his "tuner" Subaru WRX, and meditation.

"Input from our editorial board motivated fresh insights to developing a textbook that reflects the diverse range of students sitting in our classrooms and enrolled online."

Joseph Ortiz

Dr. Joseph Ortiz,
Scottsdale Community College

Dr. Ortiz has taught for over 30 years, beginning in 1983 at Clovis Community College (NM). In 1989, he joined the faculty of Scottsdale Community College, where he teaches courses on human communication, interpersonal and small group communication, and digital storytelling. In support of student learning, Dr. Ortiz is heavily involved in the use of classroom assessment tools, service learning, collaborative learning methods, and the use of online technology. A campus leader, he has served as chair of the Fine Arts Division, faculty senate president, and interim Associate Dean of Instruction. Dr. Ortiz holds a B.S. in Speech from Lamar University in Texas, an M.A. in Communication from Eastern New Mexico University, and an Ed.D. in Higher and Adult Education from Arizona State University.

TOMMY

U.S.ARMY

PARK
OPEN 24 HOURS

Zappos

THIRD EDITION

& CHOICES CONNECTIONS

An Introduction to Communication

STEVEN McCORNACK
The University of Alabama at Birmingham

JOSEPH ORTIZ
Scottsdale Community College

bedford/st.martin's
Macmillan Learning
Boston | New York

For Bedford/St. Martin's

Vice President, Editorial, Macmillan Learning Humanities: Leasa Burton
Senior Program Director, Communication and College Success: Erika Gutierrez
Program Manager: Allen Cooper
Development Editor: Will Stonefield
Senior Media Editor: Tom Kane
Associate Editor: Kimberly Roberts
Marketing Manager: Amy Haines
Director, Content Management Enhancement: Tracey Kuehn
Senior Managing Editor: Lisa Kinne
Senior Content Project Manager: Won McIntosh
Senior Workflow Project Manager: Jennifer Wetzel
Production Coordinator: Brianna Lester
Media Project Manager: Emily Brower
Director of Rights and Permissions: Hilary Newman
Permissions Manager: Kalina Ingham
Permissions Editor: Angela Boehler
Photo Researcher: Krystyna Borgen
Director of Design, Content Management: Diana Blume
Interior Design: Jerilyn Bockorick
Cover Design: William Boardman
Composition: Lumina Datamatics, Ltd.
Cover Photos: Klaus Vedfelt/DigitalVision/Getty Images
Title Page Photos: (from left to right) Enrique Castro Sanchez; Gonzalo Fuentes/Reuters; Venturelli/WireImage/Getty Images; Oleksii Sidorov/Shutterstock; AP Images/Bebeto Matthew; David Silverman/Getty Images News/Getty Images; Photo by Sgt. Katryn McCalment/DVIDS/US Department of Defense; Rainmaker Photo/MediaPunch Inc/Alamy Stock Photo; Shannon Fagan/The Image Bank/Getty Images; Ida Mae Astute/ABC/Getty Images; Nicolo' Minerbi/LUZphoto/Redux; Piero Oliosi/Polaris Images/Newscom; Rose Palmisano/ZUMA Press/Newscom; Courtesy of Myriam Sidibe; Henry S. Dziekan III/Getty Images Entertainment/Getty Images; AP Images/Sipa/Carlos Tischler; Betty Kituyi; Brad Swonetz/Redux Pictures
Printing and Binding: King Printing Co., Inc.

ISBN 978-1-319-20116-6 (Student Edition)

ISBN 978-1-319-22738-8 (Loose-leaf Edition)

Manufactured in the United States of America.

4 5 6 24 23 22

For information, write: Bedford/St. Martin's, 75 Arlington Street, Boston, MA 02116 (617-399-4000)

At the time of publication, all Internet URLs published in this text were found to accurately link to their intended website. If you do find a broken link, please forward the information to will.stonefield@macmillan.com so that it can be corrected for the next printing.

NCA Learning Outcomes

In 2018, the National Communication Association (NCA) published learning outcomes for courses within the discipline. Below you can see how coverage in *Choices & Connections,* Third Edition, connects with these learning outcomes.

NCA Outcome	Relevant coverage in *Choices & Connections*
LOC 1 **Describe the communication discipline and its central questions**	Chapter 1 includes an overview of the communication discipline and presents the three main communication models — linear, interactive, and transactional — with illustrated figures. The chapter also provides a brief history of the discipline, from its origins in ancient Greece to its rapid growth after World War II. Coverage centers on the theme of *Choices & Connections:* your communication skills empower you to be your best communicator.
LOC 2 **Employ communication theories, perspectives, principles, and concepts**	The text is grounded in current communication theories and scholarship. Each chapter helps students understand and employ key concepts and theories. These include *self-verification theory* (Ch. 2), *communication accommodation theory* (Ch. 3), *synchronous* versus *asynchronous communication* (Ch. 4), *listening functions* and *listening styles* (Ch. 7), *communication privacy management theory* (Ch. 9), *group roles* (Ch. 11), and the *motivated sequence* and the *elaboration likelihood model* of persuasion (Ch. 17), among many others.
LOC 3 **Engage in communication inquiry**	In each chapter, Advance the Conversation scenario features encourage students to read about the most current scholarly research and then connect that research to a realistic situation as they determine how best to communicate. Advance the Conversation embodies the approach of the entire book: to encourage students to critically interpret and evaluate the research, which allows them to build communication skills that they can apply in their own personal and professional lives.
LOC 4 **Create messages appropriate to the audience, purpose, and context**	Chapter 1 explains that appropriateness is one of the three core components of competent communication, along with effectiveness and ethics. Chapter 13 offers specific advice for conducting audience analysis in the context of public speaking, including guidelines for evaluating audience demographics and one's prior knowledge of the audience.

NCA Outcome	Relevant coverage in *Choices & Connections*
LOC 5 **Critically analyze messages**	Chapter 7 is all about principles of active listening. The chapter includes detailed guidelines for improving one's active listening skills, including how to identify meanings in messages and how to provide mindful and competent feedback. Meanwhile, in LaunchPad, the new video assessment program provides ample opportunity for critical analysis: students and instructors can upload their own speech videos or pull video from anywhere on the web and then engage in conversation.
LOC 6 **Demonstrate the ability to accomplish communicative goals (self-efficacy)**	Each chapter discusses common obstacles to competent communication and provides step-by-step guidelines for overcoming those obstacles. For example, Chapter 2 offers advice for improving self-perception; Chapter 4 contains guidelines for competent mediated communication; Chapters 5 and 6 explain how to achieve competent verbal and nonverbal communication, respectively; Chapter 7 includes tips for active listening; Chapter 13 has guidelines for audience analysis; and Chapter 15 offers detailed advice for overcoming speech anxiety and providing effective feedback on others' speeches.
LOC 7 **Apply ethical communication principles and practices**	Ethics is one of the core components of competent communication introduced in Chapter 1 and discussed throughout the book. Chapter 1 includes the full text of the National Communication Association's Credo for Ethical Communication. Moreover, in every chapter, Advance the Conversation features encourage students to reflect on and actively engage their own values as they decide how to act ethically in challenging communication scenarios.
LOC 8 **Utilize communication to embrace difference**	We recognize that in our globally connected society, students must learn how to communicate competently with people of all cultural backgrounds, gender identities, religions, and sexual orientations. To this end, the entire book has been revised with the help of our Editorial Board for Diversity, Inclusion, and Culturally Responsive Pedagogy, ensuring that a dynamic mix of people are represented in text and photo examples in every chapter. Moreover, Chapter 3 has been completely revised with new coverage of gender, including key concepts like gender polarization, gender fluidity, and the differences between sex and gender. The overhauled chapter, "Understanding Gender and Culture," seeks to help students develop empathy, world-mindedness, and intercultural competence.
LOC 9 **Influence public discourse**	The chapters on public speaking (Chs. 13–17) contain many examples of people speaking to influence public discourse and enact social change. Examples include Scott Harrison, founder of the nonprofit organization charity:water; Emma Watson's leadership role in the United Nations' HeForShe gender equality campaign; and Girls Who Code founder Reshma Saujani. The text emphasizes that students can initiate social change using their communication skills.

Preface

It's a rainy Tuesday morning in Birmingham, Alabama, and Steve has arrived early to his 8:00 a.m. section of Human Communication and Presentational Skills—the basic course in Communication Studies at the University of Alabama at Birmingham—so he can greet his students as they arrive and chat with those who are already there. An hour later and 1,707 miles to the west, Joe does the same in *his* Human Communication class at Scottsdale Community College in Arizona. Although we're separated by geography and time zones, we're united by our in-class experiences. Our students shift their attention away from their devices to the front of the room. Whether they originally enrolled in this class because they wanted to, because they had to fulfill a major requirement, or because an advisor strongly recommended it, they're all here now, at this moment, because they want to be. They've come to realize that what they learn in this class has the potential to transform them. After all, we're teaching our students an invaluable lesson: how to present themselves with confidence and competence. We're teaching them how to sustain healthy, meaningful relationships; how to collaborate successfully within social and professional groups; how to manage interviews with potential employers; and how to inform and persuade audiences to new viewpoints and actions. In sum, we're providing them with the metaphorical keys to the kingdom—*communicative* keys, which they can export into the real world of their complicated lives, opening previously closed doors with new knowledge and skills.

What we teach, and how we teach it, can have a *transformative impact* on our students. This realization not only guides our encounters with our students, it supports everything we have written in this book, *Choices & Connections*, and its associated online learning program, LaunchPad. Our goal with *Choices & Connections* is to empower each student to *be their best communicator*—that is, to learn skills that will help them communicate appropriately, effectively, and ethically in their personal and professional lives. Such a goal is the product of teaching the introductory communication course every semester for decades. Like you, we've seen students' positive transformation through pedagogy when they share their life successes with us, making all our efforts worthwhile. Thomas tells you he passed the medical school admission board interview with flying colors because of the skills you taught him; Tamika, who used your suggestions for speech organization and argument structure to pitch a proposal to a client, is now leading a national corporate marketing campaign; Sean emails you and says he successfully defused a bitter family disagreement with the tips he learned from you regarding constructive conflict management.

For this third edition, we are joined in our effort by our first-ever Editorial Board for Diversity, Inclusion, and Culturally Responsive Pedagogy. This editorial board consists of eight communication instructors from across the United States, each of whom has brought invaluable experience, insight, perspective, and wisdom to the project. Each member of the board has worked diligently to ensure that *Choices & Connections,* Third Edition, welcomes *all* students and instructors, and that the perspectives included in each chapter truly reflect the diversity of students in today's classrooms. You will see the results of the board's efforts in the text, photos, and features throughout the book. We extend our heartfelt thanks to each of the eight members; we could not have achieved this revision without their help.

Whether it's delivered online, face-to-face, or in another format, the introductory human communication course presents unique challenges for us as teachers. How do we distill for students the sheer amount of research and theory the discipline has to offer? How do we create connections between domains that—in many students' eyes—often seem widely disparate? How can we better highlight the practical relevance of this material, thereby boosting student attention *and* retention? What can we do to facilitate their knowledge and skill acquisition, so that they walk away from the class as vastly improved communicators? *Choices & Connections* is designed to meet these challenges in ways that optimize student learning and ease of use for the instructor. Throughout the book, we inspire students to see the connections between seemingly disparate contexts, build adaptive communication skills, and improve their capacity to self-assess.

We have retained the outstanding features from the second edition that instructors love related to active learning pedagogy and student learning outcomes. In the third edition, we have also reimagined two of the features. Now each chapter contains two Advance the Conversation features: one with a video component in LaunchPad and one without video. The first activity presents students with a challenging communication scenario, then prompts them to engage with the most current research and choose how best to respond. Then, at the end of each chapter, students draw on all the skills and concepts they have learned to offer advice to characters in a second scenario with video—and finally, they can go to LaunchPad to watch video of other possible ways the characters in the scenario might have communicated. Through these activities, we systematically guide students through *how* they can apply communication skills and principles to difficult situations and better adapt to daily demands in their own lives.

Beyond the Advance the Conversation activities, the book also includes annotated visuals, sample speech outlines, and two visually annotated sample speeches. LaunchPad supplements the book's coverage with a brand-new video assessment program, which allows students to upload video and receive real-time feedback from classmates and instructors. Further,

LaunchPad includes the complete e-book, the adaptive quizzing program LearningCurve, dozens of interactive videos, additional activities that supplement end-of-chapter coverage, instructor resources, and more.

From the title and chapter content to the online video activities, the book focuses on helping students see the *connections* between various communication contexts. From this, students learn that the knowledge and skills relevant for meeting one type of communication challenge are readily transferable to multiple settings. By helping students better recognize the links that exist between different communication concepts and forms, they will develop greater adaptability and versatility in their communicative skill set. Through features such as Advance the Conversation, we systematically guide students through challenging and thought-provoking communication scenarios, so that they can use their skills to better adapt to life's daily demands.

What you will find throughout *Choices & Connections*, Third Edition, with LaunchPad is a complete digital and print learning program wholly guided by the mission to help every student become their best communicator.

Features

Choices & Connections, Third Edition, is here for *all* students and instructors.

- **The third edition has been extensively revised with the help of our Editorial Board for Diversity, Inclusion, and Culturally Responsive Pedagogy.** This expert team of eight communication scholars has advised the authors and editors throughout the revision to ensure that *Choices & Connections* speaks to *all* students and instructors. With the editorial board's help, we have revised the coverage in all chapters to ensure that diverse people and diverse perspectives are represented in photos and in text examples. *Choices & Connections* has been rebuilt from the ground up to deliver a better, bolder, and more inclusive learning experience.
- **Chapter 3 has been overhauled as "Understanding Gender and Culture" and now incorporates the latest research in gender communication.** The chapter's new gender coverage supplements the existing coverage of culture, which has also been updated with the latest research. This revised chapter is the first in any Introduction to Communication textbook to take an integrated approach to gender and culture, exploring the ways that these two forces intersect and influence one another and how they both work to shape our communication. New topics covered include gender fluidity, transgender and cisgender individuals, gender socialization, and gender identity. Gender coverage throughout all other chapters has also been revised with a more inclusive and non-binary approach.

Choices & Connections, Third Edition, with LaunchPad seamlessly combines print and digital in this introductory text, empowering students to practice competent communication in every situation.

- **Emphasis on making informed and adaptive choices.** The central mission of *Choices & Connections* is to help students understand that communication is an opportunity to *connect* our actions, our speech, and our habits to our fundamental *choice* of who we want to be and what kind of community we want to have. The ability to skillfully adapt their communication to different contexts is an essential skill that students will carry with them throughout their lives.
- **A multifaceted, immersive digital experience.** *Choices & Connections* with LaunchPad was designed from the ground up to use the best aspects of both print and digital to create a superior and individualized learning experience for students. The new video assessment program allows students to easily upload videos and receive immediate, responsive feedback from classmates and instructors. Other videos in LaunchPad bring concepts from the book to life, model speech behaviors, and give students a chance to reflect on their own communication experiences. Students can further master theories and their application through the adaptive and personalized quizzing program LearningCurve. Instructors who choose to adopt LaunchPad have a new and easy way to manage courses online, with content, videos, adaptive quizzing, and activities all in one space. LaunchPad brings it all together; see pp. xiv–xv for more information.
- **An intuitive approach to connecting communication concepts.** Based on decades of experience teaching introductory communication courses, the authors carefully weave together different concepts to provide a holistic view of communication. For example, important cultural and gender influences—a focus of Chapter 3—are integrated in other chapters, videos, and features to give students insight into the complexity of the choices they must consider to competently connect with others. This coverage reinforces the integrated nature of communication.

Choices & Connections, Third Edition, helps students become knowledgeable and adaptable communicators through self-reflection and skills application.

- **Emphasis on practical communication skills and self-assessment that promote student engagement.** Reimagined for the third edition, the two-part Advance the Conversation learning arc in each chapter encourages students to practice and master key skills. Whether giving a speech or resolving a conflict, students are asked to connect cutting-edge research with realistic scenarios that challenge them to draw on the skills they have learned in the chapter. LaunchPad further enhances the Advance the Conversation experience with video, including scenarios that show other possible ways the interaction might have gone if the characters had communicated differently. Combining thought-provoking questions and compelling videos, Advance the Conversation takes students' skill development to a new level.

- **The new video assessment program helps students develop effective public speaking skills.** Students can record speeches directly into their assignment via the Macmillan Mobile Video iOS/Android apps, and instructors and peers can assess the speech live while the student is delivering it. Afterward, students can watch their video paired with feedback to help them start preparing for their next speech. Online students can live-stream a speech while the instructor and classmates give feedback in real time, providing an experience similar to delivering a live speech.
- **LearningCurve creates personalized learning through adaptive quizzing.** Chapter call-outs prompt students to tackle the LearningCurve quizzes to test their knowledge and reinforce learning. Based on cognitive research on how students learn, this adaptive, game-like quizzing program motivates students to engage with course materials. The reporting tools let you see what students understand so that you can adapt your teaching to their needs.

Choices & Connections, Third Edition, offers streamlined coverage, engaging examples, and extensive study tools for students

- **Engaging student experience.** Accessible and appealing, *Choices & Connections* provides streamlined content; built-in study aids to guide reading; a variety of pop-culture and real-life examples; and a clean, eye-catching design.
- **End-of-chapter materials focus on self-review.** Students can test their comprehension of major topics in each chapter's Pop Quiz or go to LearningCurve in LaunchPad to access adaptive quizzes and review further. Chapter Recaps pull out main ideas, while the Activities give students opportunities to self-reflect and try out new skills. Additional Activities for each chapter are also available in LaunchPad.
- **An extensive video collection helps students learn concepts and prepare for their speeches.** LaunchPad's Key Term videos illustrate important chapter concepts, while Sample Speech Resources and other public-speaking clips provide a start-to-finish look at speech preparation, including full-length speech videos and briefer clips.

Available Formats

For more information on these formats, please visit the online catalog at **macmillanlearning.com/choicesconnections3e**

LaunchPad for *Choices & Connections*, Third Edition, is a dynamic platform that enhances teaching and learning. LaunchPad combines the full e-book with our new video assessment program, along with carefully chosen videos, quizzes, activities, instructor's resources, and LearningCurve. LaunchPad offers a student-friendly approach, organized for easy assignability in a simple user interface. Instructors can create reading, video, or quiz assignments in seconds, as well as embed their own videos or custom content. The Gradebook quickly and easily allows you to review the progress for your whole class, for individual students, and for individual assignments. The new video assessment program allows students to upload videos and receive immediate, responsive, and actionable feedback. Meanwhile, Advance the Conversation video scenarios, Key Term videos, and Sample Speech Resources and other video clips enhance every unit of LaunchPad. LaunchPad can be ordered on its own or packaged for free with *Choices & Connections*, Third Edition. Learn more at **launchpadworks.com**

The loose-leaf edition of *Choices & Connections*, Third Edition, features the same print text in a convenient, budget-priced format, designed to fit into any two-ring binder. The loose-leaf version can be packaged *free* with LaunchPad.

The e-book for *Choices & Connections*, Third Edition, includes the same content as the print book and provides an affordable option for students. The e-book comes in a variety of formats, including VitalSource and MOBI.

Resources for Students

For more information on these resources or to learn about package options, please visit the online catalog at **macmillanlearning.com/choicesconnections3e/catalog**

LaunchPad for *Choices & Connections*, Third Edition. Every new copy of *Choices & Connections*, Third Edition, can be packaged with LaunchPad. LaunchPad comes with access to the video assessment program, our new software that allows student to easily receive feedback on videos, such as speeches; as well as **LearningCurve**, an adaptive online learning tool that helps students study, practice, and apply their communication skills. Chapter call-outs in the book prompt students to visit LaunchPad, where they can enhance their learning with quizzes, activities, and more. Learn more at **launchpadworks.com**

When packaged with LaunchPad, *Choices & Connections*, Third Edition, also comes with access to all of the Advance the Conversation video scenarios and over 200 Key Term and Public Speaking videos that define important terms from the text (see the last book page for a list) and provide speech models for students.

***The Essential Guide to Rhetoric,* Second Edition, by Christian O. Lundberg (University of North Carolina, Chapel Hill) and William M. Keith (University of Wisconsin, Milwaukee).** This handy guide is a powerful addition to the public-speaking portion of the human communication course, providing an accessible and balanced overview of key historical and contemporary rhetorical theories. Written by two leaders in the field, this brief introduction uses concrete, relevant examples and jargon-free language to bring concepts to life.

***The Essential Guide to Presentation Software* by Allison Joy Bailey (University of North Georgia) and Rob Patterson (University of Virginia).** This guide shows students how presentation software can be used to support but not overtake their speeches. Sample screens and practical advice make this an indispensable resource for students preparing electronic visual aids.

***Media Career Guide: Preparing for Jobs in the 21st Century,* Twelfth Edition, by Sherri Hope Culver (Temple University) and James Seguin (Robert Morris University).** Practical and student friendly, this guide includes a comprehensive directory of media jobs, helpful tips, and career guidance for students considering a major in communication studies and mass media.

***Research and Documentation in the Electronic Age,* Seventh Edition, by Diana Hacker (Prince George's Community College) and Barbara Fister (Gustavus Adolphus College).** This booklet covers everything students need for college research assignments at the library and on the Internet, including advice for finding and evaluating Internet sources.

***The Essential Guide to Intercultural Communication* by Jennifer Willis-Rivera (University of Wisconsin, River Falls).** This useful guide offers an overview of key communication areas, including perception, verbal and nonverbal communication, interpersonal relationships, and organizations, from a uniquely intercultural perspective. Enhancing the discussion are contemporary and fun examples drawn from real life, as well as an entire chapter devoted to intercultural communication in popular culture.

Resources for Instructors

For more information or to order or download these resources, please visit the online catalog at **macmillanlearning.com/choicesconnections3e/catalog**

Instructor's Resource Manual for *Choices & Connections*, Third Edition, by Laura McDavitt (Jackson State University). This downloadable manual contains helpful tips and teaching assistance for new and seasoned instructors alike. Content includes learning objectives, lecture outlines, general classroom activities, and review questions, as well as suggestions for setting up a syllabus, tips on managing your classroom, and general notes on teaching the course.

Computerized Test Bank for *Choices & Connections*, Third Edition, by Charles Korn (Northern Virginia Community College). The Computerized Test Bank includes multiple choice and essay questions for every chapter. The questions appear in easy-to-use software that allows instructors to add, edit, re-sequence, and print questions and answers. Instructors can also export questions into a variety of formats, including Blackboard, Desire2Learn, and Moodle. The Computerized Test Bank can be downloaded from the "Instructor Resources" tab of the book's catalog page, and the content is also loaded in the Question Picker in LaunchPad.

Lecture Slides for *Choices & Connections*, Third Edition. Available as a download from the catalog page and from LaunchPad, each chapter's slides contain the most important concepts and definitions, including key figures.

iClicker Questions for *Choices & Connections*, Third Edition. If you use iClicker in your classroom, don't miss the brand-new suite of iClicker questions for *Choices & Connections*, Third Edition. These questions test students' knowledge of foundational concepts in each chapter, making it easy for you to assess your students' understanding and progress. The questions come pre-loaded in LaunchPad.

Communication in the Classroom: A Collection of G.I.F.T.S. This new resource is prepared by John S. Seiter, Jennifer Peeples, and Matthew L. Sanders of Utah State University, who have collected over 100 powerful ideas for classroom activities. The guide includes activities designed for various components of the human communication course: public speaking, interpersonal communication, and group communication. All activities have been submitted by real instructors who have tested and perfected them in real classrooms. Each activity includes a detailed explanation and debrief, drawing on the instructors' experiences.

***ESL Students in the Public Speaking Classroom: A Guide for Instructors* by Robbin Crabtree (Fairfield University) and David Sapp (Fairfield University).** As the United States increasingly becomes a nation of linguistically diverse speakers, instructors must find new pedagogical tools to aid students for whom English is a second language. This guide specifically addresses the needs of ESL students in the public-speaking arena and offers instructors valuable advice for helping these students deal successfully with the unique challenges they face.

***Coordinating the Communication Course: A Guidebook* by Deanna L. Fassett and John T. Warren.** This essential resource offers the most practical advice on every topic central to the coordinator/director role. Starting with setting a strong foundation, this professional resource continues with thoughtful guidance, tips, and best practices on crucial topics such as creating community across multiple sections, orchestrating meaningful assessment, and hiring and training instructors. Model course materials, recommended readings, and insights from successful coordinators make this resource a must-have for anyone directing a course in communication.

The Macmillan Learning Communication COMMunity is our online space for instructor development and engagement. Find resources to support your teaching like class activities, video assignments, and invitations to conferences and webinars. Connect with our team, our authors, and other instructors through online discussions and blog posts at **community.macmillan.com/community/communication**

Acknowledgments

We would like to thank everyone at Bedford/St. Martin's who was involved in this project and whose support made it possible, especially Edwin Hill, Vice President, Editorial, Humanities; Erika Gutierrez, Senior Program Director, Communication and College Success; and Allen Cooper, Program Manager, Communication and College Success, who worked with us on the vision for this project and conceived the Editorial Board for Diversity, Inclusion, and Culturally Responsive Pedagogy. A very special thanks goes to Will Stonefield, Development Editor. Your brilliance, energy, acute attention to detail, intellectual honesty, kindness, and expert guidance have truly helped build a more diverse and inclusive community around this book, providing an inspiring model for other publishing programs. Simply put, you rock, and we couldn't have done this without you! Special thanks also goes to Kimberly Roberts, Associate Editor, who coordinated the review programs and contributed greatly to the book and its ancillaries.

This book also would not have come together without the efforts of Tracey Kuehn, Director, Content Management Enhancement; Jennifer Wetzel, Senior Workflow Project Manager; and Won McIntosh, Senior Content Project Manager, who expertly oversaw the book's tight schedule. We would also like to credit our photo researcher, Krystyna Borgen; our copyeditor, Sarah Wales-McGrath; and our permissions team, including Hilary Newman, Director of Rights and Permissions; Kalina Ingham, Permissions Manager; and Angela Boehler, Permissions Editor. Additionally, we are grateful for the dedicated work on LaunchPad for *Choices & Connections*, Third Edition, by Tom Kane, Senior Media Editor; Audrey Webster, Assistant Media Editor; and Emily Brower, Media Project Manager, who made this product a valuable resource for students and instructors. Finally, the enthusiasm and support from the sales and marketing teams are particularly appreciated. Many thanks to Greg David, Senior Vice President of Sales; Amy Haines, Marketing Manager, and the entire sales force of Macmillan Learning.

Throughout the development of this textbook, dozens of human communication instructors voiced their opinions. A special thank-you goes to the dedicated members of the Editorial Board for Diversity, Inclusion, and Culturally Responsive Pedagogy: Tenisha Baca, *Glendale Community College;* Tim Brown, *Queens University of Charlotte;* Tasha Davis, *Austin Community College;* Danielle Harkins, *Germanna Community College;* Tina Harris, *University of Georgia;* S. Lizabeth Martin, *Georgia State University*; Rody Randon, *Phoenix College;* and Myra Washington, *University of New Mexico.* Their thoughtful feedback has allowed us to make the book into a better, more inclusive, and more useful resource for students and instructors in the new edition.

We would also like to thank everyone not named above who participated in the pre-revision review: Leonard Assante, *Volunteer State Community College;* Ray Bell, *Calhoun Community College;* Dennis Blader, *University of New Haven;* Sabryna Cornish, *College of DuPage;* Andrea Davis, *Western New England University;* Sarah Fogle, *Embry-Riddle Aeronautical University;* Mary Staci Fritzges, *University of Central Arkansas;* Amy MacPherson, *Phoenix College;* Shellie Michael, *Volunteer State Community College;* Michelle O'Connell, *Chippewa Valley Technical College;* Tami Phillips, *University of Central Arkansas;* Diane Smith, *University of New Haven;* and Meagan Tomei-Jameson, *Palm Beach State College.*

On a more personal level . . .

Steve McCornack: I would like to thank my parents, Connie and Bruce, for instilling within me a deep and abiding passion for reading and writing; the faculty and administration at the University of Alabama at Birmingham, for valuing the writing of undergraduate textbooks as a worthy professorial pursuit; my sons, Kyle, Colin, and Conor, for their unflagging support of "Dad the author"; and—most of all—Kelly, for simultaneously keeping me grounded yet always lifting me up.

Joe Ortiz: I am deeply grateful to Diana for her love and her ongoing support for this project. Many thanks to my children and grandchildren, who in their own unique ways make every day happy. Finally, I am indebted to my faculty colleagues and students, who stimulate my thinking and animate my teaching.

Finally, no textbook is created by one person. Thank you for the human communication discipline and its students.

Brief Contents

Contents

For videos and LearningCurve quizzing to help you review, go to **launchpadworks.com**

---

3 Understanding Gender and Culture *60*

Venturelli/WireImage/Getty Images

For videos and LearningCurve quizzing to help you review, go to **launchpadworks.com**

Oleksii Sidorov/Shutterstock

For videos and LearningCurve quizzing to help you review, go to **launchpadworks.com**

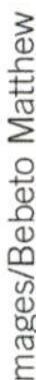
AP Images/Bebeto Matthew

For videos and LearningCurve quizzing to help you review, go to **launchpadworks.com**

6 Nonverbal Communication *138*

David Silverman/Getty Images News/Getty Images

For videos and LearningCurve quizzing to help you review, go to **launchpadworks.com**

7 Active Listening *164*

Photo by Sgt. Katryn McCalment/DVIDS/US Department of Defense

For videos and LearningCurve quizzing to help you review, go to **launchpadworks.com**

PART 2 INTERPERSONAL COMMUNICATION

8 Principles of Interpersonal Communication 188

Rainmaker Photo/MediaPunch Inc/Alamy Stock Photo

For videos and LearningCurve quizzing to help you review, go to **launchpadworks.com**

9 Managing Interpersonal Relationships 214

Shannon Fagan/The Image Bank/ Getty Images

 *For videos and LearningCurve quizzing to help you review, go to* **launchpadworks.com**

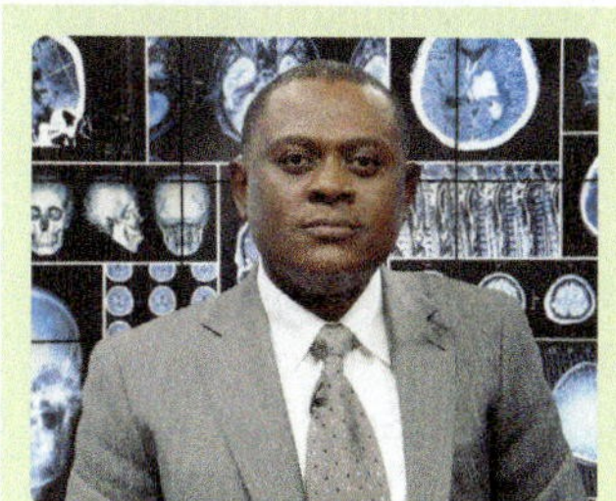

Ida Mae Astute/ABC/Getty Images

 *For videos and LearningCurve quizzing to help you review, go to* **launchpadworks.com**

PART 3 SMALL GROUP COMMUNICATION

11 Small Group Communication 260

Nicolo Minerbi/LUZphoto/Redux

 *For videos and LearningCurve quizzing to help you review, go to* **launchpadworks.com**

12 Leadership in Group Communication 286

Piero Oliosi/Polaris Images/Newscom

 *For videos and LearningCurve quizzing to help you review, go to launchpadworks.com*

PART 4 PUBLIC COMMUNICATION

13 Preparing Your Speech *314*

Rose Palmisano/ZUMA Press/Newscom

 *For videos and LearningCurve quizzing to help you review, go to* **launchpadworks.com**

Courtesy of Myriam Sidibe

 *For videos and LearningCurve quizzing to help you review, go to* **launchpadworks.com**

Appendix Interviewing 456

Brad Swonetz/Redux Pictures

 *For videos and LearningCurve quizzing to help you review, go to* **launchpadworks.com**

& CHOICES CONNECTIONS

An Introduction to Communication

1

Introduction to Communication

It was the World Cup 2018, and Hassan Sedky was in the FIFA fan zone. He had traveled thousands of miles to Yekaterinburg, Russia, to cheer his beloved Egyptian team. But as the match between Egypt and Uruguay unfolded, it would be Sedky—not the game itself—who literally would be lifted into the spotlight, uniting and inspiring people around the world.

A lifelong athlete, Sedky was paralyzed in a car accident in 2011. In the aftermath, he channeled his love of sports into wheelchair basketball, eventually earning a spot on the University of Texas–Arlington "Movin' Mavs" team. In 2017, he helped lead them to a National Championship. As he describes, "Wheelchair basketball changed my life. I want all disabled athletes to be able to experience this in their own way and reach their maximum potential."

On opening day at the World Cup, the fan zone crowd was exuberant. Despite team rivalries, everyone present cheered for everybody else. When Egypt began playing against Uruguay, Sedky's passion was noticed by several Colombian and Mexican fans around him. To honor him, they suddenly lofted him above the crowd, holding him there. As Sedky describes, "It was completely spontaneous. One minute everyone is dancing and the next I was up in the air!"

But the event wouldn't remain a brief moment of connection, communication, and camaraderie. People grabbed their phones and snapped photos. One photo was posted to the "Desmotivaciones Futbol" ("Football Demotivations") Facebook page, where it was shared more than 37,000 times. From there, the photo jumped to the social news aggregation site Reddit and multiple subreddits, from which it was downloaded, tweeted, and retweeted thousands of times. Within a few brief hours, Sedky and those who lifted him skyward had gone viral. Back in the United States, Sedky's coach, Doug Garner, learned about the event when teammates messaged him photo links. "It just shows his spirit," said Garner. "He's seizing the moment to use it as a message that sports are for everybody, sports are inclusive, sports shouldn't exclude people."

Sedky hopes that the photo will unite people of diverse backgrounds and beliefs and, especially, that it will change people's views about the differently abled. "It's an incredible feeling to know that I'm sending a message to the whole world and potentially changing the perspective of other people," he said. "We are not disabled; we're just living a different life, different challenges, different opportunities, and different abilities."

Enrique Castro Sanchez

CHAPTER OUTLINE

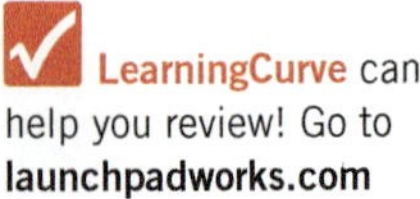

LearningCurve can help you review! Go to **launchpadworks.com**

As Hassan Sedky aptly notes, we all are different from one another. Each of us lives a unique life with particular challenges. But what connects us all to each other is *communication*. Whether you're attending the World Cup or spending a normal day at school, work, or home, you interact with people one-on-one, in groups, and in public. You may tweet, post, text, email, call, or talk face-to-face. You might give a presentation to a small or large audience or interview for a job.

Across all of these types and instances of communication, two things are important to keep in mind. First, *how you communicate connects to the outcomes that follow*. When you communicate well, you increase the likelihood of desirable outcomes, such as successful group projects; compelling presentations; and satisfying, healthy relationships. When you communicate poorly, you are likely to contribute to negative outcomes, such as group dissatisfaction, confused audience members, and relationship turmoil.

Second, *different types of communication are connected to each other in fundamental ways*. Sure, tweeting a photo or texting a close friend is different from sending an email to a work group or giving a speech in front of a class. However, these forms of communication also share similarities. Specifically, they involve presenting yourself to others, planning your messages, and using language to convey your thoughts. Because of these connections, what you learn in every chapter of this book will apply to a wide variety of scenarios. In this chapter, you'll learn:

- What communication is and how the communication process works
- The goals that communication helps you achieve
- How the study of communication developed
- The characteristics of communication competence
- The choices and connections underlying your communication

What Is Communication?

Lots of people believe that communication is just common sense. But people are not born knowing how to communicate well. Instead, they become good communicators by learning about communication concepts and theories, building skills, and practicing in their everyday lives. You can take the first step toward becoming a competent communicator by learning what communication is and why it matters.

When you think about communication and the role it plays in your life, what may leap to mind are the various challenges you face. For instance, "How do I make a good first impression?" "Why don't the other group members listen to my ideas?" or "What can I do to amplify the impact of my presentations?" To answer these questions and meet these challenges, many people rely on intuition. Why? Because they think that communication is "just common sense."

Sanja Bucko/Warner Bros. Pictures/Everett Collection

Whether you're mingling in Singaporean high society like Rachel Chu in *Crazy Rich Asians* or just meeting a friend for coffee, the messages you convey, the context of the situation, and the channel and media through which you interact all have an impact on your conversation.

But there's a gulf of difference between a communicator who relies on intuition and one who is highly trained and educated. Communication is like any other knowledge-based skill set. Think about it: most of us have an intuitive sense of how to kick balls around a field. Does that mean we're all World Cup soccer players? No. When you receive formal education about communication, you learn information based on theory, research, and practice. This empowers you to broaden and deepen your skills as a communicator, allowing you to surpass what you'd be able to do if you relied on intuition alone. Simply put, reading this book and taking this class will train you to become a world-class communicator. Your journey toward this goal begins with this basic question: What exactly *is* communication?

Defining Communication

In this text, we define **communication** as *the process through which people create messages, using a variety of modalities and sensory channels to convey meanings within and across contexts*. This definition highlights the five features that characterize communication: process, messages, modalities, sensory channels, contexts.

First, communication is a *process* that unfolds over time through a series of interconnected actions. Imagine it's the first day of the semester, and the professor asks a question. You raise your hand to demonstrate your attentiveness, but when the professor calls on you, your mind goes blank, and a classmate sitting next to you laughs. Then the next time the professor asks a question, you'll be less likely to raise your hand. Think about the process that unfolded: the professor asked a question; you responded by raising your hand; your mind went blank; a student laughed; your feelings were hurt; and now you're more cautious about sharing your ideas out of fear of ridicule. Thinking of communication as a process means realizing that *everything you and others say and do during encounters shapes what happens in that moment and in the future.*

Second, people engaged in communication ("communicators") use *messages* to convey meaning. A **message** is the "package" of information transported during communication. When people exchange a series of messages, whether face-to-face or online, the result is an **interaction** (Watzlawick, Beavin, & Jackson, 1967).

Third, to convey meaning, communicators choose from many different **modalities**—or forms—for exchanging messages. These include the variety described in our chapter opener: face-to-face interaction, photos, social media posts, tweets, and texting, along with other forms such as email, handwritten notes, or phone calls. Nowadays, many of us seamlessly integrate digital devices with more traditional methods of communication, sometimes using multiple forms simultaneously, like when you chat face-to-face with a roommate while also checking your Instagram. Chapter 4 (Mediated Communication) will further explore how technology influences your communication.

Fourth, people communicate through various sensory channels. A **channel** is the sensory dimension along which communicators transmit information. The most common channels are auditory (sound), visual (sight), and tactile (touch). For example, your professor smiles at you and says, "Great job on your presentation!" (visual and auditory channels), or a friend comforts you with a hug after you learn that you didn't get the job offer you wanted (tactile).

Finally, communication occurs in a seemingly endless variety of **contexts**, or situations. For instance, you communicate with others in class, at parties, at work, and at home. In each context, many different factors affect how you communicate. These factors include how much time you have, how many people are in the situation, and whether the setting is personal or professional. This is why you probably communicate differently with a friend while playing video games than when the two of you are sitting next to each other in class.

Why You Communicate

Why do you communicate? The answer may seem obvious: you communicate to share your thoughts and feelings with others. Although that is true, communication also helps you meet three types of goals (Clark & Delia, 1979).

The first type is **self-presentation goals**, which involve presenting yourself in certain ways so that others will view you as you want them to. For example, Hassan Sedky presented himself as an intensely passionate fan. In fact, he came off as so inspiring that it caused complete strangers surrounding him to literally lift him up. As his friend Mostafa Amin described, Sedky presents himself with such "positive energy" that "we all decided to get him up in celebration of his attitude to life, and to show his example to the rest of the people around us" (Cho, 2018).

The second type is **instrumental goals**—practical objectives you want to achieve or tasks you want to accomplish. We all are constantly communicating in ways that convey who we are to others. But often we have practical purposes as well, that we want to use our communication to accomplish. For instance, following his accident, Hassan Sedky's mother created a foundation to advocate on behalf of disability inclusion, the Al Hassan Foundation. In many of his interviews following the World Cup, Sedky has used his communication to encourage people to donate to the foundation—a practical purpose for his messaging.

The third type is **relationship goals**—building, maintaining, or terminating bonds with others. Communication is our principal vehicle for creating new connections with other people; whether it's friendships, romantic relationships, or coworker collaborations. After Sedky's image went viral, he had dozens of people at the World Cup approach him, introduce themselves, and strike up conversations with him—creating new friendships. Whenever we use our communication to create emotional connections with others, we are pursuing relationship goals.

Communication Models

Think about all the different ways you communicate each day. You text your best friend, saying you're finished with work and are ready to be picked up. You present awards at your volleyball team's end-of-season banquet, acting more animated when you see people's attention start to wander. You spend the evening with your brother, reliving and retelling stories from your childhood.

But how does the communication process differ in each scenario? Sometimes you create messages and send them to receivers (like your text message). Other times you present messages to recipients, and they indicate their understanding and interest (like the audience members at the volleyball banquet). Or you may mutually create meanings with others, with no one serving as "sender" or "receiver" (like you and your brother sharing family stories). These scenarios reflect three different ways of viewing the communication process: the *linear model*, the *interactive model*, and the *transactional model*.

As you continue reading about these models, keep a few things in mind. First, communication scholars developed these models to examine and describe how communication works. Second, the models represent a historical evolution of scholarly thought, from a relatively simple depiction of communication as a linear process (the linear model) to one that views communication as a complicated process that is mutually crafted (the transactional model). Finally, each model doesn't necessarily represent a good or a bad way of thinking about communication. Instead, each offers a different way of identifying the important elements affecting the communication process.

Linear Communication Model. The linear model was the first formal model of communication and was created more than 70 years ago by engineers at Bell Labs to explain how information is transmitted across telephone lines (Shannon & Weaver, 1949). According to the **linear communication model**, communication is an activity in which information flows in one direction, from a start point to an end point. The linear model contains several components. In addition to a *message* and a *channel*, there is a **sender** (or senders)—the individual who generates the information to be communicated, packages it into a message, and chooses one or more channels for sending it. The person (or people) for whom a message is intended is the **receiver**. The transmission of the message is often affected by **noise**—distractions that change how the message is received. Noise may originate outside the communicators—such as lagging or pixelation during Facebook Messenger, Google Hangout, or Skype. Or it can come from the communicators themselves, such as when distracting thoughts cause senders' or receivers' attention to drift. (See Figure 1.1.)

Although the linear model was conceived more than seven decades ago, it still accurately illustrates the broad range of communication forms you experience every day. For example, much of your online communication—including tweets, texts, emails, and social media posts—reflects this model. Certain public-speaking contexts may also fit, especially those in which you present prepared scripts to audience members who are expected to sit quietly and listen without responding to or challenging you. But the linear

FIGURE 1.1

LINEAR MODEL OF COMMUNICATION

Kira Kuznetsova/Shutterstock

model doesn't accurately explain other communication forms, such as face-to-face conversation. For example, when you converse with a friend face-to-face, you may speak in partial sentences and rely on the other person to mentally fill in the missing information. The linear model doesn't account for the back-and-forth flow of such encounters.

Interactive Communication Model. The **interactive communication model** also views communication as a process involving senders and receivers. However, according to this model, communication is influenced by two additional factors: feedback and fields of experience (Schramm, 1954). **Feedback** consists of the verbal and nonverbal messages coming from recipients in response to messages. For example, by nodding and saying "Uh-huh" or "That's right," recipients let senders know they've received and understood messages. Feedback also lets receivers indicate their approval or disapproval of messages. **Fields of experience** consist of the beliefs, attitudes, values, and experiences that each participant brings to a communication event. People with similar fields of experience are more likely to understand each other than are individuals with dissimilar fields of experience. (See Figure 1.2.)

Like the linear model, the interactive model accurately describes a range of communication forms that you experience. For example, while giving a speech in class, you may notice the reactions of your classmates—such as fidgeting or lack of eye contact—and then modify your message on the spot

FIGURE 1.2

INTERACTIVE MODEL OF COMMUNICATION

Kira Kuznetsova/Shutterstock

as needed to capture their attention and get your message across. Classroom instruction, group presentations, and weekly team meetings among coworkers are often viewed as interactive.

Also like the linear model, the interactive model presents communication as a process in which there is a clearly designated and active sender and a receiver. But it overlooks the active role that receivers often play in constructing the meaning of communication events, as well as instances in which people jointly create meaning. At a family reunion, for example, your uncle starts droning on as usual about "kids these days." You and your sister glance at each other and immediately understand the meaning of your shared look. If you were to put words to this meaning, you would both be saying, "Here he goes again." But neither of you is the sender or the receiver in this instance; instead, you *collaboratively* create communication meaning. The transactional communication model can help explain such encounters.

Transactional Communication Model. The **transactional communication model** views communication as multidirectional; that is, participants mutually influence one another's communication behavior (Miller & Steinberg, 1975). According to this model, there aren't senders or receivers. Instead, participants constantly exchange verbal and nonverbal messages and feedback to collaboratively create meanings. (See Figure 1.3.) This may be something as simple as a shared look, as in the preceding example with

FIGURE 1.3

TRANSACTIONAL MODEL OF COMMUNICATION

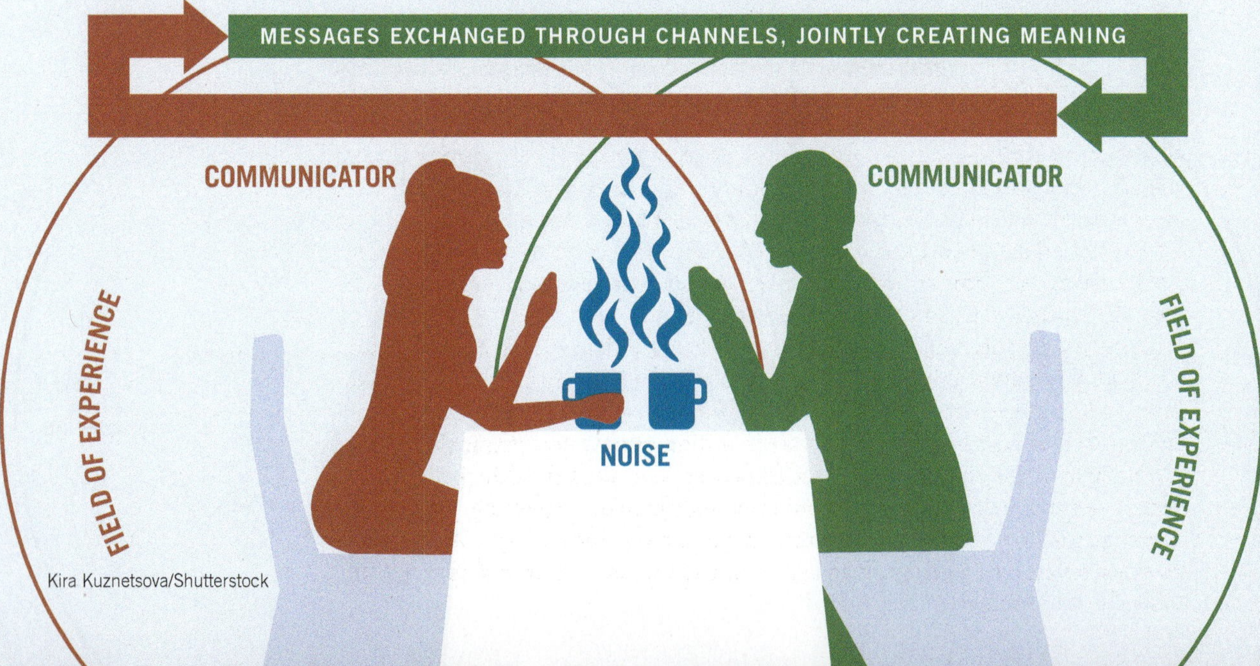

Kira Kuznetsova/Shutterstock

your sister and your uncle. It may be an animated and intense conversation between you and a friend, in which the meanings exchanged go way beyond the words that are said. It may even involve people jointly creating acts of communication. Sociologist Jurgen Streek (1980), in discussing the transactional nature of communication, describes a classroom roll call he once observed. The teacher asked, "Now, where is . . ." and before she could complete her query, a student chimed in "Ernesto?" knowing just who the teacher was seeking. Such instances illustrate how we often build communication collaboratively rather than simply receiving or sending messages.

The transactional communication model intuitively captures encounters that seem interpersonal in nature. These include instances such as you and your romantic partner having a phone conversation in which the words seem secondary to the feelings being conveyed, as well as conversations with close friends, in which a few key words or looks instantly convey a wealth of shared information (we discuss interpersonal communication in more detail in Chapters 8–10). But the transactional model doesn't explain certain types of online communication, such as tweets, texts, emails, and social media posts, in which senders and receivers are more clearly designated; those types of communication are better described as either linear or interactive.

Studying Communication

Now that you have a better understanding of what communication is, let's look at how people have studied communication throughout the ages and at the types of communication that teachers and scholars focus on today. Understanding the past, present, and future of the communication field will help you apply what you learn to your everyday life.

The authors of this book, Steve and Joe, both started college with the goal of becoming lawyers. But their plans—and their lives—changed when they began to study communication. For Joe, the turning point came during an afternoon run with an attorney named Tom Roebuck, who occasionally trained with Joe's university cross-country team. While talking about classes and potential majors, Tom told Joe, "I can't think of any better preparation for law school than a communication degree." The next day, Joe switched his major. As he continued his course work, he grew fascinated with communication as a field of study and ultimately decided to pursue a teaching career instead of going to law school.

Steve's story is similar. As an undergrad, he visited his professor, Mac Parks, during office hours. While chatting about a reading from class, Steve remarked that he had *always* been fascinated by how people communicate, but that he had never pursued this interest because he didn't know how it translated into a collegiate major or profession. Mac then described all of the things that Steve could potentially do with a communication degree: sales, marketing, public relations, publishing, lobbying, consulting, broadcasting, and so forth. When Steve confessed that his *true* passion was the study of romantic relationship problems

COMMUNICATION AT WORK

Studying communication fosters real-life skills that are valuable in the workplace. Whether you're a nurse, an engineer, or an athlete, knowing how to competently communicate can make or break your success.

(Clockwise from top left) Hero Images/DigitalVision/Getty Images; Monty Rakusen/Cultura/Getty Images; John Rhodes/Fort Worth Star-Telegram/Tribune News Service/Getty Images

such as jealousy, betrayal, and deception, Mac asked Steve, "Have you ever thought about going into the field?" Steve admitted that he didn't even know what "the field of communication" was. When Mac told him, "You could spend your life studying and teaching about close relationships," Steve suddenly realized that the field of communication—not the law—was his calling.

For some of you, the communication class you're taking will be your only exposure to the field. For others, this class—and other courses in communication—may inspire you to become communication majors. You might even experience the same thing Joe and Steve did: the realization that you want to devote your life to studying and teaching communication. But regardless of whether you take one communication class, make communication your college major, or build a career involving communication, learning about communication connects you to a scholarly field that dates back thousands of years.

A Brief History of Communication

The field of communication is undeniably modern, with its attention to topics like social media, online relationships, and the effects of video games. But it has ancient roots. By understanding a little about the field's history, you can see how the concepts and practices you'll learn about in this book evolved from the past into their present-day forms.

Communication in Antiquity. Communication is an academic discipline that goes back thousands of years and traverses many different cultures. For example, one of the earliest books ever written—the maxims of the Egyptian sage Ptahhotep (2200 B.C.E.)—offers suggestions for improving your communication (Horne, 1917). In this ancient guidebook, Ptahhotep encourages people to be truthful, kind, and tolerant in their communication. He urges readers to practice active listening, especially in situations in which people lack experience, because "to not do so is to embrace ignorance." He also emphasizes mindfulness in using language, noting that "good words are more difficult to find than emeralds."

Almost 2,000 years after Ptahhotep, the communication tradition known as rhetoric emerged. **Rhetoric** is the theory and practice of persuading others through speech (Dues & Brown, 2004), and it became a formal discipline of study in ancient Greece and Rome (Kennedy, 1999). In Greece, Socrates and his student Plato were among the first to debate the nature of rhetoric. Socrates thought of rhetoric not as a philosophy but as a practical skill that people could gain through experience (Kennedy, 1999). Socrates and Plato also knew that people could use communication skills in either ethical or unethical ways, and they argued strongly against using words to manipulate or exploit others. But it was Aristotle—perhaps the best-known ancient Greek scholar—who taught that ethical persuasion required a speaker to demonstrate credibility, provide logical reasoning, and appeal to the emotions of listeners. As you'll learn in Chapter 17, Aristotle's teachings are still very relevant today in understanding how to develop a persuasive speech.

The study of rhetoric was also a concern of ancient Romans. Statesman and orator Cicero noted three practical objectives of public speaking: to instruct, to persuade, and to honor (Clarke, 1953). These goals are still discussed in modern public-speaking courses as informative, persuasive, and special occasion speeches. Cicero also outlined the five requirements of speech crafting and presentation still in use today: invention (reasoning out truth to make your case compelling), arrangement (organizing the information you want to present), style (selecting suitable words to convey the information), memory (knowing your subject and remembering your words), and delivery (controlling your body and voice when presenting your speech). In Chapters 13–17, you'll learn how these requirements guide the preparation and delivery of speeches.

Communication in the Early Twentieth Century. Throughout the era stretching from ancient Rome to the close of the nineteenth century, communication scholars stayed focused on rhetoric. In the 1900s, however, scholars—stimulated by philosophical interest in the human mind and behavior—began studying forms of communication other than rhetoric, across a broad range of disciplines (Knapp, Daly, Albada, & Miller, 2002). For example, in 1927, political scientist Harold Lasswell detailed the four persuasive aims of governmental propaganda: to create hatred against the enemy, to preserve friendship with allies, to gain the cooperation of neutral parties, and to demoralize the enemy. Harvard business professor Elton Mayo examined the effects of coworker interactions on productivity, giving rise to the human relations movement and the recognition that supportiveness is crucial for competent workplace communication (Roethlisberger & Dickson, 1939). Psychologist Jean Piaget (1926) analyzed the role that children's ability to *perspective-take* (see things from others' viewpoint) played in shaping their communication. By World War II, dozens of scholars in several different disciplines were studying communication and communication-related topics, such as the effect of environments on interaction, empathy, and conflict.

Communication after World War II. Immediately following World War II, interest in the field of communication exploded, mostly owing to the use of mass media propaganda during the war. Countries on each side had harnessed film and radio to send messages on a massive scale to their respective populations, convincing them that their cause was just and that the enemy was "evil." With so many professors wanting to research communication, and so many students wanting to learn about it, universities began creating dedicated communication departments. Some schools housed communication studies researchers alongside rhetorical scholars, creating departments focused on speech communication.

By the early 1970s, dozens of communication and speech communication departments existed in the United States. Colleges and universities taught classes in the traditional areas of public speaking and rhetoric, but they also introduced new areas, such as mass media effects, communication in relationships, group discussion, and organizational communication. As the discipline further diversified, it attracted even more interest among scholars and students. Topics of interest expanded further: by the end of the twentieth century, nonverbal communication, gender and communication, communication across cultures, health communication, and communication technologies became standard offerings in undergraduate curricula at hundreds of U.S. colleges and universities. Institutions outside the United States began to offer communication classes as well.

Today, tens of thousands of students around the world graduate each year with majors in communication, and millions more take communication classes. These students learn about cutting-edge research, examining such things as the impact of gender socialization (Chapter 3), how others' online posts about you influence people's perception of you (discussed in Chapter 4), verbal aggression (Chapter 5), and how to deal with speech anxiety (Chapter 15). Armed with a broad knowledge of communication theory and practical skills, students majoring in communication go on to pursue careers in areas as diverse as human resource management, public relations, sales, marketing, sports broadcasting, media production, news media, advertising, community relations, and political consulting. To see how being skilled in communication may apply to your career path, see Table 1.1.

TABLE 1.1

CAREERS IN COMMUNICATION[1]

CAREER PATH	WHAT CAN I DO?	HOW CAN I GET THERE?
	• Sales • Human Resources • Insurance • Real Estate • Entrepreneur	• Develop strong verbal and written communication, interpersonal, and analytical skills. • Seek leadership roles in other campus organizations. • Learn to work well on a team.
	• Public Relations • Advertising • Marketing • Creative Directing	• Develop excellent writing and public-speaking skills. • Serve as public relations officer of an organization. • Develop a portfolio of writing samples, ad campaigns, and other relevant work.
	• Writing • Editing • Copywriting • Publishing • Broadcasting	• Take courses in journalism, broadcasting, public relations, and advertising. • Develop excellent interpersonal, presentation, and research skills. • Work for campus or local newspaper, radio station, or television station.
	• Community Affairs • Campaigning • Lobbying • Social Services • Prosecution • Defense • Nonprofit or Public Interest	• Develop strong research skills and attention to detail. • Participate in debate or forensic team to hone communication skills. • Take courses in conflict management, and develop negotiation skills.
	• Teaching • Research • Information/Library Science • Administration and Student Support Services	• Develop strong interpersonal communication and public-speaking skills. • Get involved in campus leadership roles in residence halls, student unions/activities, programming boards, orientation, admissions, etc. • Learn to work well with a variety of people.

[1]Table 1.1 data from "What Can I Do with This Major?", retrieved from http://whatcanidowiththismajor.com/major/communication-studies/

Types of Communication

As the preceding history illustrates, communication is a diverse field with a rich past. Although many specific topics are currently being studied and taught (such as doctor–patient communication, information flow within organizations, and deception), the field as a whole can be divided into four broad types: mediated communication (Chapter 4), interpersonal communication (Chapters 8–10), small group communication (Chapters 11–12), and public communication (Chapters 13–17). Throughout this book, we explore the differences and connections between these types.

Mediated communication is separated ("mediated") by some type of technological device. You use mediated communication when you tweet, make phone calls, send text messages or emails, use Facebook Messenger or Skype, and post photos or messages online. As you'll see later in this book, mediated communication is best used to meet certain types of goals. For example, text messaging is fine for planning a meeting location for your study group (instrumental goal). However, you probably wouldn't want to use texting to resolve a disagreement with your romantic partner (relationship goal).

Interpersonal communication is communication between two people in which the messages exchanged have a significant impact on the participants' thoughts, emotions, behaviors, and relationship. Through interpersonal communication, you build, maintain, and end bonds with your friends, family members, lovers, and other relationship partners.

Small group communication involves three or more interdependent persons who share a common identity (such as membership on a team) and who communicate to achieve common goals or purposes. For example, a group might come together to complete a class project, organize a fundraiser, or produce music. Small group communication involves unique challenges, such as the need to coordinate group members' responsibilities, build group unity, clarify expectations, and accommodate members' diverse communication styles.

Public communication is the process of preparing and delivering a message to an audience to achieve a specific purpose (also known as public speaking). An example of this would be a speech you will probably have to give for this class. (This may sound scary, but don't worry—we have advice in Chapter 15 to manage your anxiety.) You might also need to communicate publicly in other situations, such as giving a talk to a youth group or presenting a project idea to your coworkers by videoconference.

These four types of communication differ in terms of their main purpose, the number of people involved, and their nature (linear, interactive, or transactional). Yet they also are *connected* to one another—in history and in current practice. Specifically, in all four types, people use messages to generate meanings. In addition, all four types are affected by the communicators' view of themselves, perceptions of others, cultural background and listening skills, and use of verbal and nonverbal communication. (We will explore these areas together in Chapters 2, 3, 5, 6, and 7.) In addition, you can use the four types of communication to pursue self-presentation, instrumental, and relationship goals.

Perhaps most important, the strength of your communication skills strongly influences the outcomes you experience. When you are able to communicate with skill, you're more likely to get positive outcomes. What does it mean to communicate with skill? We tackle that question in the next section.

DOUBLE TAKE

MEDIATED  PUBLIC COMMUNICATION

Whether you're sending a text or making a speech, different types of communication are often connected. In addition to what is pointed out below, what connections can you make between the different types of communication you participate in each day?

Mediated devices aid in relationship maintenance (interpersonal communication)

Group texts help teammates organize (small group communication)

Klaus Vedfelt/DigitalVision/Getty Images

Presentations can motivate teams to take action (public communication)

Speeches viewed by online audiences can have a global reach (mediated communication)

Hill Street Studios/Blend Images/Getty Images

Communication Competence

Communication is an opportunity. How you phrase your messages, exhibit facial expressions, and even approach a conflict is up to you. Each time you act, you have the opportunity to strive for competence. This can help you set the stage for success in your own life.

Cesar Chavez and Dolores Huerta transformed the lives of thousands by persuading powerful people to act on behalf of the poorest laborers in America.[2] How? They mastered the art of *communication competence*: the ability to consistently interact with others in an appropriate, effective, and ethical fashion. A compelling public speaker, Chavez rallied migrant laborers to organize strikes protesting horrific working conditions in the fields. Huerta, too, demonstrated masterful public communication, coining the slogan "Sí, se puede" (*"Yes, we can"*) as a rallying cry for the labor movement. Both Huerta and Chavez were also skilled at adapting their language to lawmakers, communicating the plight of farmworkers in poignant terms to those who controlled the laws governing them. Although landowners attacked them and their fellow workers with shotguns and dogs, Chavez and Huerta remained committed to ethical communication, never lashing back at those who subjected them and others to violence. Their competence ultimately paid off with a profound outcome: new laws ensuring better working conditions and higher wages for field laborers, and the creation of the United Farm Workers (UFW) organization.

Huerta's and Chavez's communication competence extended to their interpersonal communication as well. For example, after delivering a speech in Washington, D.C., Chavez spied UFW members who had been volunteering to help with the event. He veered toward them, even as his bodyguards tried to force him toward his car. Chavez shook the workers' hands, saying, "I noticed how you stayed here all day and worked so hard. It is because of you there is a movement. I may be the one who does the speaking, but it is you who make the movement what it is!"

Cesar Chavez and Dolores Huerta both received many honors. Huerta earned the Eleanor Roosevelt Award for Human Rights; Chavez was awarded the Águila Azteca, the highest civilian award in Mexico. Both leaders received the U.S. Presidential Medal of Freedom. Their legacy is about justice, nonviolence, and help for the needy. It's also proof that communication can bring about change.

Communication is the means through which you achieve your goals (Burleson, Metts, & Kirch, 2000). But it is the *competence* of your communication that helps determine the *quality* of your outcomes. Competent communicators report higher levels of educational and professional

---

[2]All information regarding Cesar Chavez is excerpted from the California Department of Education (n.d.) and the County of Los Angeles Public Library (n.d.).

Walter Oleksy/Alamy Stock Photo

Cesar Chavez's and Dolores Huerta's ability to adapt their language to connect with both migrant laborers and lawmakers was crucial for their success in the United Farm Workers organization. How does your manner of speaking change according to the person receiving your message?

achievement, more satisfaction with their relationships (including happier marriages), and better psychological and physical health (Spitzberg & Cupach, 2002).

Throughout the book, we explore the knowledge and skills necessary for strengthening your competence in all types of communication. In this chapter, we lay the foundation for your learning by explaining how to achieve communication competence.

Understanding Communication Competence

Communication competence means consistently communicating in ways that are *appropriate* (your communication follows accepted norms), *effective* (your communication helps you achieve your goals), and *ethical* (your communication treats people fairly) (Spitzberg & Cupach, 1984; Wiemann, 1977).

Appropriateness. **Appropriateness** is the degree to which your communication matches expectations regarding how people "should" communicate. In any setting, norms govern what people should and shouldn't say, and how they should and shouldn't act. For example, telling jokes or personal stories about your love life isn't appropriate during a job interview, but it might be appropriate when you're hanging out with close friends who know you and your sense of humor. Competent communicators understand when such norms exist and adapt their communication accordingly.

We judge how appropriate our communication is through **self-monitoring**: the process of observing our own communication and the norms of the situation in order to communicate appropriately. Some individuals closely monitor their own communication to ensure they're acting in accordance with situational expectations (Giles & Street, 1994). Known as *high self-monitors,* they prefer situations in which clear expectations exist regarding how they're supposed to communicate, and they possess both the ability and desire to alter their behaviors to fit into any type of social situation (Oyamot, Fuglestad, & Snyder, 2010). In contrast, *low self-monitors* don't assess their own communication or the situation (Snyder, 1974). They prefer encounters in which they can "act like themselves" by expressing their values and beliefs, rather than abiding by norms (Oyamot et al., 2010). As a consequence, high self-monitors are often judged as more adaptive and skilled communicators than low self-monitors (Gangestad & Snyder, 2000).

One of the most important choices you make related to appropriateness is when to use mobile devices and when to put them away. Certainly, cell phones and tablets allow us to quickly and efficiently connect with others. However, when you're interacting with people face-to-face, the priority should be your conversation with them; if you prioritize your device over the person in front of you, you run the risk of being perceived as inappropriate. *This is not a casual choice*: research documents that simply having cell phones out on a table—but not using them—during face-to-face conversations significantly reduces perceptions of relationship quality, trust, and empathy, compared to having conversations with no phones present (Przybylski & Weinstein, 2012). To avoid such negative judgments, put your mobile devices away at the beginning of the interaction.

Competent communicators also know that overemphasizing appropriateness can backfire. If you *always* adapt your communication to what others want, you may not be acting ethically or effectively. For example, you might give in to peer pressure (Burgoon, 1995). Think of a friend who always does what others want and never argues for his own desires. Is he a competent communicator? No, because he'll probably seldom achieve goals that are important to him. What about the boss who tells employees that their work is fine even when it isn't? Is she competent? No, because she's withholding information her employees need to improve their job performance. Competence means striking a healthy balance between appropriateness and other important considerations, such as achievement of goals and the obligation to communicate honestly.

Effectiveness. **Effectiveness** is the ability to use communication to accomplish the three types of goals discussed earlier (self-presentation, instrumental, and relationship). Sometimes you have to make trade-offs—prioritizing certain goals over others, even if you want to pursue all of them. For instance, to collaborate effectively with groups, you have to know when to stay on task and when to socialize. Say that you and several other students form an intramural softball team to compete in a campus league. At the first team meeting, you may want to come across as athletic, funny, and likable (self-presentation goal) and begin building friendships with others on the team (relationship goal). But if you don't focus your communication during the meeting on creating a practice schedule (instrumental goal), the team won't be ready to play its first game. Chapter 12 discusses how you can be an effective leader and communicator in such situations.

Ethics. **Ethics** is the set of moral principles that guide your behavior toward others (Spitzberg & Cupach, 2002). At a minimum, you are ethically obligated to avoid intentionally hurting others through your communication. By this standard, communication that's intended to erode a person's self-esteem, that expresses intolerance or hatred, that intimidates or threatens others' physical well-being, or that expresses violence is unethical and therefore incompetent (Parks, 1994).

However, to be an ethical communicator, you must go beyond simply not doing harm. During every encounter—whether it's interpersonal, a small group, or a public presentation—you need to treat others with respect and communicate with them honestly, kindly, and positively (Englehardt,

Fremulon, 3 Arts Entertainment, Universal Television/Album/Newscom

In *The Good Place,* Eleanor Shellstrop is an unethical saleswoman who accidentally ends up in "the good place"—the afterlife for morally upstanding people. There, with the help of ethics professor Chidi Anagonye, she learns how to communicate with honesty and respect. What ethical ground rules do you strive to follow in your communication?

2001). As you'll see in Chapter 4, mediated communication presents unique challenges for ethical communication. To help you act ethically in all situations, consider the guidelines in the National Communication Association's Credo for Ethical Communication (1999) in Figure 1.4.

In communication situations that are simple, comfortable, and pleasant, it's easy to behave appropriately, effectively, and ethically. True competence, however, develops when you consistently communicate competently across *all* situations that you face—even ones that are complex, uncertain, and unpleasant. A critical goal of this book is to equip you with the knowledge and skills you need to handle those more challenging communication situations. For example, the Advance the Conversation feature on pages 28–29 asks you to adapt your understanding of communication competence to an unpleasant situation.

FIGURE 1.4

NCA CREDO FOR ETHICAL COMMUNICATION

Questions of right and wrong arise whenever people communicate. Ethical communication is fundamental to responsible thinking, decision making, and the development of relationships and communities within and across contexts, cultures, channels, and media. . . . Therefore we, the members of the National Communication Association, endorse and are committed to practicing the following principles of ethical communication:

- We advocate truthfulness, accuracy, honesty, and reason as essential to the integrity of communication.
- We endorse freedom of expression, diversity of perspective, and tolerance of dissent to achieve the informed and responsible decision making fundamental to a civil society.
- We strive to understand and respect other communicators before evaluating and responding to their messages.
- We promote access to communication resources and opportunities as necessary to fulfill human potential and contribute to the well-being of families, communities, and society.
- We promote communication climates of caring and mutual understanding that respect the unique needs and characteristics of individual communicators.
- We condemn communication that degrades individuals and humanity through distortion, intimidation, coercion, and violence, and through the expression of intolerance and hatred.
- We are committed to the courageous expression of personal convictions in pursuit of fairness and justice.
- We advocate sharing information, opinions, and feelings when facing significant choices while also respecting privacy and confidentiality.
- We accept responsibility for the short- and long-term consequences for our own communication and expect the same of others.

Ecelop/Shutterstock

Putting Competence into Practice

Competent communicators know how to translate their knowledge into **communication skills**—repeatable goal-directed behaviors and behavioral patterns that they routinely practice (Spitzberg & Cupach, 2002). Throughout this book, we provide you with skills you can use in all of the communication challenges you'll face in life, so you can better produce positive outcomes. To illustrate, consider two of the most important skills you'll need in your communication toolbox: knowing when and how to use mediated communication competently, and knowing how to appropriately, effectively, and ethically interact with people whose cultural backgrounds or gender identities differ from your own. Chapter 3 will teach you how to appropriately adapt your communication to other communicators, effectively balance their goals with your own, and treat them with the same dignity and respect that you want for yourself. And as Chapter 4 discusses, using mediated communication competently means making wise choices regarding when to communicate online versus off, recognizing the three Ps of mediated communication (powerful, public, and permanent), and adapting your messages to ensure clarity.

Of course, to use your knowledge and skills to improve your communication, you must also be motivated to do so. If you do not believe your communication needs improvement, or if you believe that competence is unimportant or no more than simple common sense, your competence will be difficult, if not impossible, to refine. But if you are strongly motivated to improve your communication, you can master the knowledge and skills necessary to develop competence.

Choices and Connections

When you're communicating, everything you say and do counts—and is connected to what comes after. There are no "take-backs" or do-overs. That's why it's so important to build communication skills that help you align your actions to who you want to be.

In the 2014 film *Wild* (one of Steve's fave films ever), Reese Witherspoon plays Cheryl Strayed, a woman who solo hikes the Pacific Coast Trail, trying to overcome the emotional devastation of her mother's death. Throughout her journey, Cheryl recalls encounters with her mother, whose choice to adopt an always-cheery attitude was both inspirational and irritating: "What's wrong with you?" "I'm happy—happy people sing!" "Why are you happy—we have *nothing*, Mom, *nothing*!" "We're rich in love!" But toward the end of the film, Cheryl recalls *the* most memorable of her mother's messages: "There is a sunrise and a sunset every day—you can *choose* to put yourself in the way of beauty!"

In *Wild,* Cheryl (Reese Witherspoon) recalls her mother *choosing* to be happy, which reminds Cheryl that she has the *choice* to end the downward spiral her life was on after her mother's death. Similarly, our communication skills empower each of us to *choose* what kind of communicator we want to be.

20th Century Fox/Kobal/Shutterstock

Each of us can set the intention to experience a metaphorical sunrise or sunset every day of our lives—those brief moments of opportunity where we can watch something unfold before us that is breathtaking and awe-inspiring. It can happen when you're having a casual conversation with a new acquaintance and you suddenly sense a special kinship between you—that a deep friendship may emerge. Or it can happen when you're on a team and everything begins to click, and you have the thrill of knowing that you're going to have an incredible, winning season.

But the wisdom of Cheryl's mother—encouraging a focus on the positive when faced with extraordinary adversity—also illustrates the central theme of this book: communication is an opportunity to *connect* our actions, our speech, and our habits to our fundamental *choice* of who we want to be and what kind of community we want to have. Communication empowers our choice.

Communication Skills

How do your communication skills have an impact on you and your life? Take something as simple as how you respond to an angry text message from a family member. If you fire back an equally hostile response, the situation escalates, and the two of you are now fighting. What's more, the conflict will likely spread to other family members, as each person weighs in on what happened and takes sides in the battle. Think about what might happen if you draw on the skills you've learned to respond more competently.

For example, you might use your empathy to craft a message asking why the other person is upset, making sure to avoid sarcastic or accusatory responses. Then you might calmly explain how you see the situation, reassuring him or her of your love and respect. These choices—informed by the skills you'll learn in this course—are far less likely to lead to a fight or involve others in the conflict.

The fact that your communication skills affect your outcomes means your communication is *irreversible*. When you post a message online, send a text or tweet, leave a voice mail message, or express a thought out loud during a group meeting, you influence the outcomes that follow. Once you've communicated something, you can't take it back. That's why it's important to think carefully before you communicate, asking yourself, "Is what I'm about to say likely to lead to outcomes I want?" If the answer is no, then you'll want to revise your message.

Of course, communication (by definition) involves interaction with others, and how *they* act influences your outcomes as well. But you can't control how others behave toward you—only how you behave toward them. Consequently, the best—and only—path you have for improving your outcomes is to consciously practice your communication skills. When you practice these skills, you are empowered to be your best communicator—that is, to communicate appropriately, effectively, and ethically in your personal and professional lives. This book gives you the tools you need to build these and many other skills, which in turn help you be a competent communicator in a wide range of situations—even when others are not.

Communication Connections

In addition to recognizing the link between communication skills, choices, and outcomes, your communication competence will be boosted by learning the connections that exist between the different types of communication. Yes, communicating face-to-face is different from interacting online, just as conversing within a group is different from presenting in front of an audience. Yet many similar skills connect them. Consider, for example, what it means to be a good listener. It matters little whether you're listening to an audience member's question following a presentation or Skyping with your sister who is overseas. The characteristics that constitute being a good listener (discussed in Chapter 7) transcend communication type and context. Becoming a competent communicator means understanding the connections between different forms of communication, as well as the skills that are unique to each.

Throughout this book, we will provide you with numerous examples illustrating the connections between different communication types. For instance, you'll see how determining your communication purpose is important whether you're planning a group meeting or preparing a speech, realize how the skills used for managing interpersonal conflict can help

ADVANCE THE CONVERSATION

TIME FOR PAYBACK?

1 YOUR DILEMMA

You dated Riley for over a year. You were in love and thought the two of you might even get married someday. But last week you discovered that Riley had been cheating on you for the last two months. You were so furious and hurt that you broke it off, and you haven't spoken with Riley since. Riley has been texting and emailing you, begging forgiveness, but you haven't responded.

One night you're studying with your roommate when you get a text from Riley. But instead of being another apology, it's a request. Riley let you borrow a USB drive last week, which apparently contains all of Riley's notes for an important project, and Riley's hard drive just crashed—making the USB drive the only copy of these materials. Riley wants to come by and get it. You're just about to text "OK" when your roommate interjects, "Are you insane!? After what Riley did to you? You should throw it away and tell Riley you can't find it." Just then, Riley texts you again, "Do u have my drive? I really need it. Please text me back."

➔ **How do you feel when your roommate suggests that you throw away Riley's flash drive?**

2 THE RESEARCH

There's no question that betrayal in a close relationship is one of the worst experiences you can have. Some people respond to betrayal by seeking revenge. Revenge comes in many forms, most of which are as unethical and destructive as the behavior triggering the vengeance. Canadian researchers Susan Boon, Vicki Deveau, and Alishia Alibhai (2009) found that vengeful partners commonly exact their revenge online, by posting negative photos of their lovers on Facebook or blogging about their lovers' deficient sexual attributes. In extreme cases, vengeance may involve sabotaging partners at work so that they get fired, or de-enrolling them from their college or university.

Partners who seek revenge report a host of motives for doing so, but the most common involve a desire to "have power over a partner" and "to make the partner suffer" (Boon et al., 2009). People seeking revenge often presume they will feel better once "justice has been served." However, research by communication scholar Stephen Yoshimura (2007) examining the aftermath of revenge suggests that people not only continue to feel angry about the betrayal but also feel remorseful and anxious about repercussions from their vengeful acts. So although you may be tempted to seek vengeance in the wake of a betrayal, keep this in mind: not only is such behavior unethical, but you may suffer even more if you behave in this way.

➔ **Why do you think your roommate suggested throwing away Riley's flash drive? If you follow your roommate's advice, do you think your relationship with Riley will be improved?**

3 YOUR OPPORTUNITY

How will you respond to your roommate? Before you act, consider the facts of the situation and think about the revenge research. Also, reflect on what you've learned so far about communication competence (pp. 18–23), ethics (pp. 21–22), and the ways in which your speech and actions connect to outcomes (pp. 23–27).

➔ **Now it's your turn. Write out a response to your roommate. In your response, be sure to explain how you plan to respond to Riley and why.**

when problems arise in teams, and discover that sharing appropriate and relevant information about yourself (known as *self-disclosure*) is important for both creating small group bonds and establishing rapport with an audience during a speech.

But perhaps even more important than these specific points of connection is the fact that *your communication and your communication skills connect you to other human beings*. Communication is your primary vehicle for exchanging meaning, achieving goals, connecting with others emotionally, and building personal and professional relationships with others.

The importance of communication for connecting you to others makes it essential that you base your communication choices on the best knowledge you have. No one would consider making a decision about a college major, a future career, or major purchases without first gathering the most trustworthy information available. Communication is no different. That's where this book—and the class you're taking—come in. We (your authors: Steve and Joe) will provide you with the best research, theory, and practical skills training that the field of communication has to offer. As you absorb this knowledge and start applying these skills in your own life, you'll position yourself to make the best communication choices. As a result, you'll boost the odds of creating positive outcomes in your personal and professional lives, including healthy and satisfying connections with others.

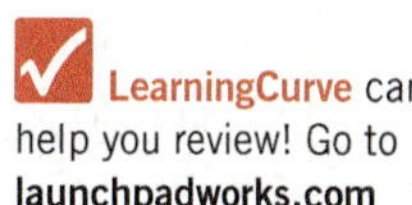
LearningCurve can help you review! Go to **launchpadworks.com**

ADVANCE THE CONVERSATION
Video Activity

COMPETENT CONVERSATIONS

The following scenario will enhance your ability to understand and apply competent communication. Visit LaunchPad at launchpadworks.com to get the full experience with video. As you watch the first video, recall what you've learned about appropriateness, effectiveness, and ethics, and then complete the **Your Turn** prompts. Finally, watch the **Take Two!** video to explore how this scenario could have gone differently.

1 *THE PROBLEM*

Helen's professor assigns her to work with Jacob, her ex-boyfriend's best friend. When Helen and her ex were dating, Jacob was friendly and supportive. But the breakup was ugly, and Jacob hasn't talked to Helen since. As Helen meets with Jacob to brainstorm ideas, there's obvious tension. Helen decides to break the ice and ask him how he's doing. Jacob responds with an icy "Fine, just fine." Then he says, "How are you doing? Destroyed any new lives recently?"

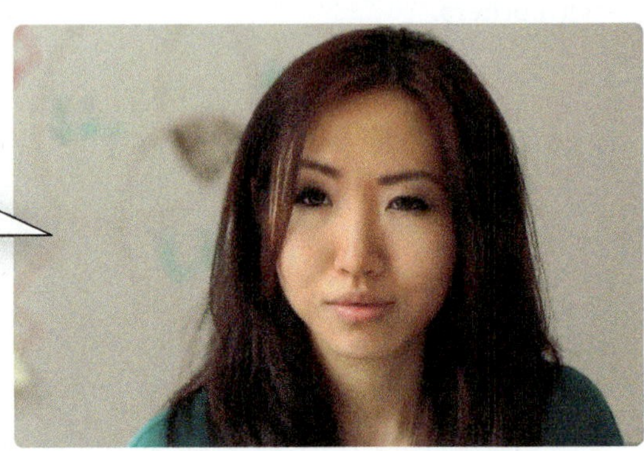

"I don't think this is the right time or place to be talking about that. If you want, I'll hang around after class and maybe we can talk then?"

"I have no interest in talking to you—whether it's now or later."

2 YOUR TURN

Observations. Reflect on how Helen and Jacob communicated in this scenario by answering the following questions:

1. Which character do you identify with more in this situation? How would you feel if you were in their situation?
2. Where were the missed opportunities to practice competent communication?

Discussion. In class or with a partner, share your thoughts about the interaction between Helen and Jacob and work to answer the following questions:

1. Can you understand both perspectives?
2. What could Jacob and Helen have done differently?

Conclusion. Choose one person in the scenario to offer your advice. Based on your analysis, what advice would you give him or her to improve his or her communication competence in this scenario?

3 TAKE TWO!

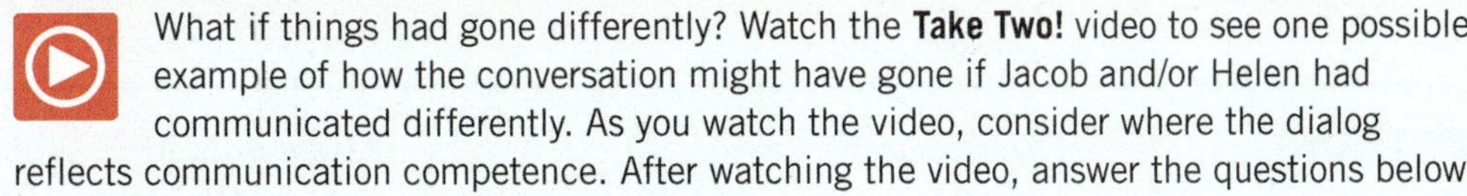

What if things had gone differently? Watch the **Take Two!** video to see one possible example of how the conversation might have gone if Jacob and/or Helen had communicated differently. As you watch the video, consider where the dialog reflects communication competence. After watching the video, answer the questions below:

1. Did Jacob and/or Helen take advantage of opportunities that they missed in the first scenario? Which ones?
2. Did their different actions result in a more productive encounter? Please explain.

CHAPTER 1 REVIEW

CHAPTER RECAP

- **Communication** is the process through which people use **messages** to generate meanings within and across **modalities**, **channels**, and **contexts**.
- You can use communication to help you achieve three types of goals: **self-presentation**, **instrumental**, and **relationship**. Various *communication models* (**linear**, **interactive**, and **transactional**) help you understand how this communication takes place.
- Although the field of communication began with the study of **rhetoric** in ancient Greece, today it is composed of four main types: **mediated**, **interpersonal**, **small group**, and **public communication**.
- **Communication competence** determines the quality of your communication and is a combination of **appropriateness**, **effectiveness**, and **ethics**.
- There are two key axioms to keep in mind when building your **communication skills:** communication empowers our *choice* of who we want to be; and different types of communication are connected to each other in fundamental ways.

LaunchPad for *Choices & Connections* offers unique video scenarios and encourages self-assessment through adaptive quizzing. Go to **launchpadworks.com** to get access.

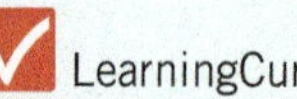

LearningCurve adaptive quizzes

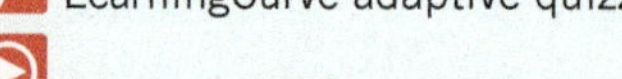

Advance the Conversation video scenarios

Video clips that illustrate key concepts

KEY TERMS

Communication, p. 5
Message, p. 6
Interaction, p. 6
Modality, p. 6
Channel, p. 6
Context, p. 6
Self-presentation goals, p. 6
Instrumental goals, p. 7
Relationship goals, p. 7
Linear communication model, p. 8
Sender, p. 8
Receiver, p. 8
Noise, p. 8
Interactive communication model, p. 9
Feedback, p. 9
Fields of experience, p. 9
Transactional communication model, p. 10
Rhetoric, p. 13
Mediated communication, p. 16
Interpersonal communication, p. 16
Small group communication, p. 16
Public communication, p. 16
Communication competence, p. 19
Appropriateness, p. 19
Self-monitoring, p. 20
Effectiveness, p. 20
Ethics, p. 21
Communication skills, p. 23

POP QUIZ

Looking for more review questions? **LearningCurve** can help you master key concepts from this chapter. Go to **launchpadworks.com**

1. Which of the following is *not* one of the five features that define communication?
   a. Contexts
   b. Ethics
   c. Channels
   d. Modalities

2. If you convince your sister to lend you her car by describing your clean driving record and devotion to speed limits, you are accomplishing what type of goal?
   a. Rhetorical
   b. Relationship
   c. Instrumental
   d. Self-presentation

3. According to this communication model, there aren't senders or receivers; instead, participants constantly exchange verbal and nonverbal messages and feedback to collaboratively create meaning.
   a. Transactional model
   b. Interactive model
   c. Linear model
   d. Instrumental model

4. Which feature of competent communication requires you to treat others with respect and communicate with them honestly, kindly, and positively?
   a. Effectiveness
   b. Ethics
   c. Appropriateness
   d. Modalities

5. Repeatable goal-directed behaviors and behavioral patterns that you routinely practice and that reflect knowledge of competent communication are known as
   a. communication skills.
   b. communication competence.
   c. fields of experience.
   d. feedback.

ACTIVITIES

For more activities, visit LaunchPad for *Choices & Connections* at **launchpadworks.com**

1 Tracking Your Media Meter

As a way to compare how you use different communication media, create a log of your communication patterns across various media for just one day. Track how often you text, tweet, email, post, call, talk face-to-face, and so on. For each communication encounter, include a brief note regarding what it was about. Then, analyze your log based on the following questions: Which communication media did you use most often? Why? What guided your decision in choosing certain media over others? Do certain media seem more intimate or less personal than others? Were some more enjoyable or more demanding? How do you think your choice of communication media influenced the outcomes you experienced?

2 Exploring Competent Communication

Call to mind a recent communication encounter that you found difficult or problematic. This could be a conflict, an awkward interaction, or an instance in which you regretted what you said or someone misinterpreted you. With a partner, recall exactly what you said and what happened as a result. Now, revisit the components of competence discussed on pages 19–22. What aspects of your communication were appropriate, effective, or ethical? Which were not? What could you have done to be more competent in the situation? How would that have changed the outcomes you experienced? What does this tell you about the benefits or limits of competent communication?

2

Self and Perception

For much of her career, she has been number one in the world. She has 23 Grand Slam titles and is far from finished. Now in her thirties, she still hits serves with speeds topping triple digits.[1] But Serena Williams also is a woman who has struggled with negative body image throughout her life and has overcome the prejudiced perception of those who wanted nothing more than for her to quit.

Williams grew up in Compton, California. Rather than encouraging her to compete in the junior tennis tournaments, her father, Richard, trained Serena and her sister Venus in isolation—having them work on tennis fundamentals and practice by hitting against men. When she turned pro at age 14, Serena Williams had power few had ever seen.

Despite her amazing talent, Williams struggled with her self-image, constantly comparing herself against others. "It wasn't easy growing up," she notes, "because I was thicker. Most women athletes are thin. I didn't really know how to deal with it. I had to come to terms with loving myself" (Bronner, 2015).

Williams also has to overcome the prejudice of people who perceive her—an African American woman in a white-dominated sport—primarily through the lens of race, rather than athletic ability. In 2001, she won the prestigious Indian Wells tournament. During the trophy ceremony, many in the mostly white crowd booed and shouted racial slurs. She cried in the locker room after. "I felt I had lost the biggest game ever—the fight for equality," she said. Williams boycotted the tournament for 14 years. And at the 2018 U.S. Open, she smashed her racket in frustration—a behavior common among white male players—and was penalized for doing so. When she called the umpire a "thief," he penalized her again.

When asked whether she thinks Serena Williams is the best player *ever*, Billie Jean King—one of the greatest tennis players herself—said simply, "Yes. I think we all do" (Ledbetter, 2015). In 2015, Williams made the "Daring" list in *Harper's Bazaar* magazine, which celebrates "incredible risk-taking, trailblazing women." In 2018, she launched her own clothing line designed to inspire and empower women, and she advocated on behalf of women suffering postpartum depression. But beneath all the swagger, sadness, complexity, and determination, Williams's strength comes from her capacity for critical self-reflection: "Physically you need to be great, emotionally you need to be stable, and I need to have a good connection with my spirituality. You can be down in life, but you can overcome things based on the way you think and how you set your frame of mind" (Bronner, 2015).

---

[1]Opener adapted from Rodrick (2013).

Gonzalo Fuentes/Reuters

Wilson

CHAPTER OUTLINE

LearningCurve can help you review! Go to **launchpadworks.com**

Few (if any!) of us have the athletic prowess of Serena Williams. But we share with her the ability to critically look within ourselves, see what hampers us, and change our mindsets in ways that optimize our potential. We also have the ability to understand how others perceive us, how we see them, and how these impressions shape our behaviors. By combining these two elements—critical self-reflection and an understanding of perception—you set the stage for successful communication in your own life. In this chapter, you'll learn:

- The nature of self and its impact on communication
- How you present yourself to others, online and off
- The perception process and common errors made in it
- Ways to form impressions of others
- The importance of perception-checking and empathy

The Nature of Self

Your "self" isn't just one thing but many: who you think you are as a person; what your values, attitudes, and beliefs are; and how you feel about your self-worth. Because all of these factors influence how you communicate, the first step to improving your communication is to understand your self.

Who are you? You may answer this question by describing your personality—funny, friendly, or intense—or perhaps by explaining what you do—musician, athlete, or techie. You may even identify the various roles you play—"I'm Grace's daughter," "I'm a nursing student," or "I'm the fry cook at Randy's Grill." Serena Williams sees herself as a "tennis player." As she described in a 2015 *Harper's Bazaar* interview, "Some people are born to do certain things, and I think I was born to do tennis." But who you are—your *self*—isn't a single thing that can be captured in a simple statement. Instead, the **self** is an evolving blend of three components: self-awareness, self-concept, and self-esteem. Your self shapes how you communicate, whether online or off, with friends or in groups, and even before audiences.

Self-Awareness

Self-awareness is the ability to view yourself as a unique person, distinct from your surrounding environment, and to reflect on your thoughts, feelings, and behaviors—in short, asking yourself, "Who am I?" (Rochat, 2003).

But self-awareness isn't only about inward analysis. You also look outward, to others, and compare yourself to them. Through **social comparison**, you assign meaning to others' behaviors and then compare their behaviors against your own. Think of times you've wondered about your own speaking abilities after seeing a classmate deliver a stellar presentation, or pondered your interpersonal skills after watching a sibling comfort a friend. When you stack up favorably against people you admire, you think well of yourself ("I'm as fast as the runner who broke the school record last year!"). When you don't compare favorably, you think less of yourself ("Why can't I be as funny as my brother?"). This was one aspect of Serena Williams's struggle with her own body image: she constantly compared herself to her sister Venus, whom she deeply admired. As she describes, "Especially growing up with Venus, who's so tall and slim and model-like, and me, I'm thick and hips and everything!" (Rodrick, 2013).

When communicating, you are always self-aware, constantly considering your thoughts, feelings, and behaviors. But to improve your communication, you must routinely practice **critical self-reflection**, a special kind of self-awareness that focuses on evaluating and improving your communication. To engage in critical self-reflection, consider these five questions:

1. What am I thinking and feeling?
2. Why am I thinking and feeling this way?
3. How am I communicating?
4. How are my inner thoughts and feelings affecting my communication?
5. How can I improve my thoughts, feelings, and communication?

The goal of critical self-reflection is to enhance your communication. By routinely practicing critical self-reflection when faced with challenging situations, you will achieve a deeper understanding of the factors that influence your communication, allowing you to make better decisions and achieve improved outcomes as a result. For instance, say your brother discloses symptoms of a serious medical condition to you. But when you tell him to see the doctor, he laughingly dismisses your suggestion. You feel your anger rise, and you want to shout that he never listens and he's a stubborn fool! If in such situations you're able to critically reflect on your thoughts, feelings, and behaviors, you'll be more likely to adapt your communication in ways that bring about desired outcomes. In this situation, you might realize, "I'm angry at his response because I'm *worried* about him and want him to be OK." This realization would lead you to say, "I'm sorry; it's just that I love you very much and am concerned. How about *I* call and make the appointment for you, and we can drive over together? What days and times work best for you?"

Self-Concept

If self-awareness asks the question "Who am I?", **self-concept** is the answer—that is, your overall assessment of who you are ("I'm a ____________ person"). Your self-concept is based on the beliefs, attitudes, and values you have about yourself. *Beliefs* are convictions that certain things are true ("I'm a caring person"). *Attitudes* are evaluations ("I'm satisfied with my fitness

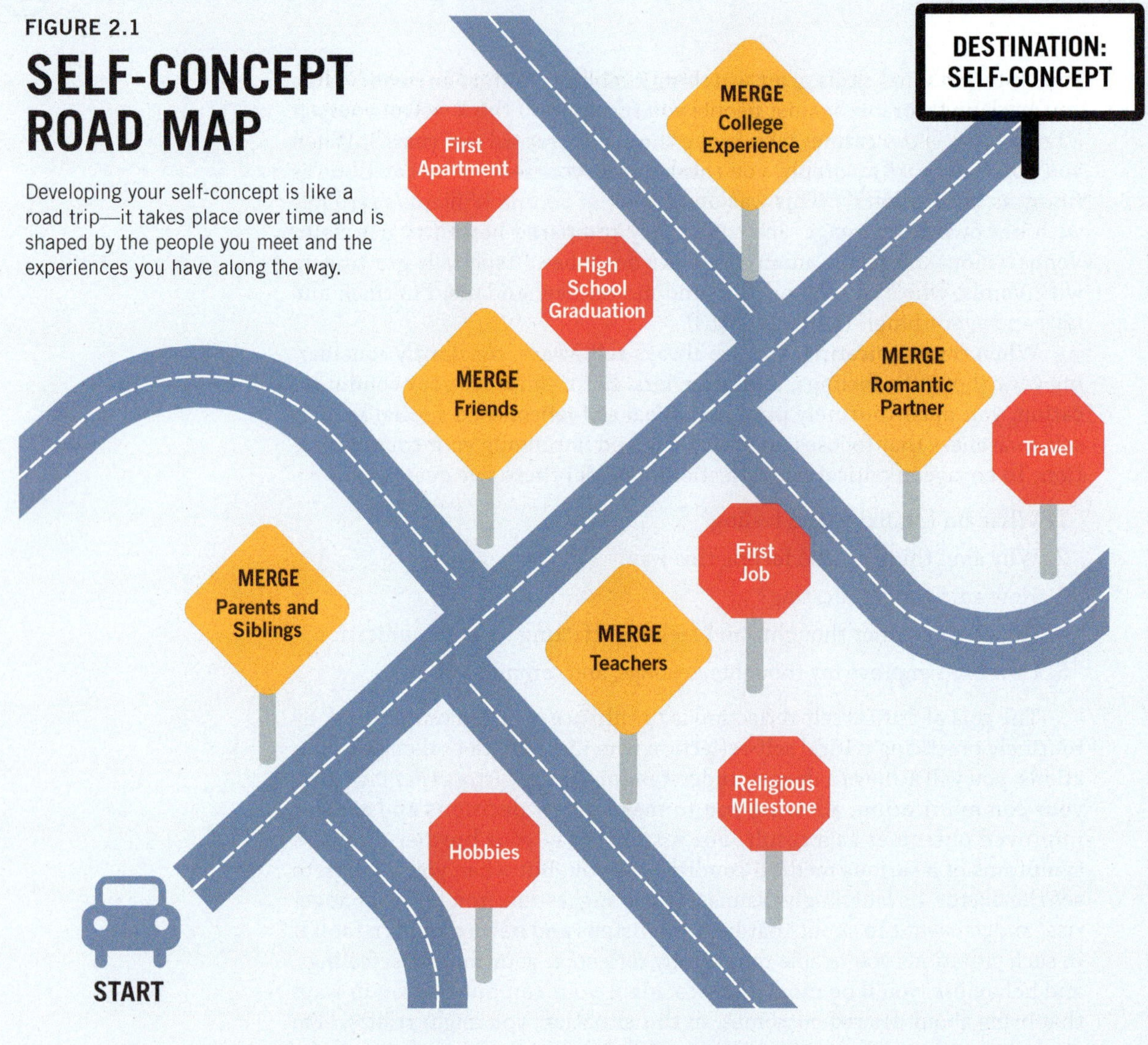

FIGURE 2.1

SELF-CONCEPT ROAD MAP

Developing your self-concept is like a road trip—it takes place over time and is shaped by the people you meet and the experiences you have along the way.

level"). *Values* are enduring principles that guide your behaviors ("I think it's morally wrong to lie"). Your beliefs, attitudes, and values are often intertwined. For example, if you think that communicating honestly is important (value), you likely also view yourself as an honest person (belief) and evaluate your honest communication positively (attitude). Understanding your beliefs, attitudes, and values and how they may differ from those of others helps you adapt your communication to anyone with whom you are interacting.

Early in life, the people who matter most to you—parents, siblings, teachers—help define your self-concept. Their reactions to you serve as a type of mirror in which you begin to see yourself as others see you (Cooley, 1902). For example, when Steve was young, his folks routinely emphasized his musical ability, so he came to think of himself as a musician. In a similar fashion, Joe's parents constantly praised his academic achievements, causing Joe to see himself as a scholar.

As you age, the range of people who help shape and maintain your self-concept broadens to include friends, lovers, and coworkers. In fact, according to **Self-Verification Theory** (Swann, Chang-Schneider, & Angulo, 2007), you often choose your relational partners based on how well they support your self-concept. If you see yourself as an aspiring anime artist, you'll probably choose friends, dating partners, and even roommates who support and reinforce this view—for instance, by praising your work (Swann & Pelham, 2002). This holds true even for negative self-concepts: if you think you're shallow or obsessive, you'll likely be drawn to people who support this view (Swann, Hixon, & De La Ronde, 1992).

Your self-concept often leads to **self-fulfilling prophecies**, predictions you make about interactions that cause you to communicate in ways that make those predictions come true. Say your boss assigns you to a new team whose members strike you as especially creative and intelligent. If you think you're not as talented as they are, you may predict that they'll ignore your contributions to group discussions. As a result of this prediction, you remain quiet during the first team meeting. The other group members interpret your silence as a desire not to contribute and begin excluding you from the discussion. Later, you tell yourself, "See! I knew they wouldn't want my input!" But if you saw yourself as creative and smart, you might predict that the team would welcome your contributions. You would then offer your ideas confidently, and the others would likely make a point of including you in discussions.

Self-Esteem

Self-esteem is the overall value you assign to yourself. Whereas self-awareness asks, "Who am I?" and self-concept is the answer to that question, self-esteem is the follow-up query, "Given who I am, what's my evaluation of my worth?"

Self-esteem strongly shapes our communication, relationships, and general outlook on life. People with high self-esteem report greater life satisfaction, communicate more positively with others, and experience more happiness in their relationships than do people with low self-esteem (Fox, 1997). They also show greater leadership ability, athleticism, and academic performance (Fox, 1992).

According to **Self-Discrepancy Theory**, your self-esteem is determined by how you compare to two mental standards (Higgins, 1987). The first standard is your *ideal self*—all the qualities (mental, physical, emotional, material, spiritual) you want to possess. The second standard is your *ought* *self*—the person you think others want you to be. Ought self stems from expectations of your family, friends, colleagues, and romantic partners, plus the culture you grow up in. You experience high self-esteem when your self-concept matches your ideal and ought selves ("I'm the kind of person I want to be" and "I'm the kind of person others wish me to be"). By contrast, you may suffer low self-esteem if your self-concept is inferior to your ideal and ought selves.

Research documents that self-esteem can change. For instance, studies examining trends across 48 different countries found that self-esteem typically increased from late adolescence to the middle adult years; and this pattern held true for both women and men (Bleidorn et al., 2016). But other than passively waiting for time to pass and yourself to age, what can you do to *actively* improve your self-esteem? You can start by following these steps:

1. *Assess your self-esteem*. List the beliefs, attitudes, and values that make up your self-concept. Review the list, and determine whether you view yourself positively or negatively.
2. *Analyze your ideal self*. Who do you wish you were? If this ideal self is attainable, how could you become this person?
3. *Analyze your ought self*. Who do others want you to be? What would you have to do to become this person?
4. *Revisit and redefine your standards*. If your ideal and ought selves are realistic and reachable, move to step 5. If they're not (e.g., you'd love to

DOUBLE TAKE

IDEAL VS OUGHT SELF

Your self-esteem is determined by how closely your ideal and ought selves align. In which situation do you think the student's ideal and ought selves are more closely matched? Why?

© Hill Street Studios/Blend Images/Veer/Corbis

Lexington Herald-Leader/ZUMA Press/Newscom

be a multimillionaire by age 20, but it's not likely you'll get there), redefine your standards so that they are realistic and reachable. Frame your new standards as a list of goals.

5. *Create an action plan.* List the actions necessary to reach your ideal and ought selves. Establish a realistic time line—perhaps several months or years. Then carry out this action plan, checking your progress as you go.

Gender, Sexual Orientation, Culture, and Self

Engaging in critical self-reflection, pondering your self-concept, and assessing your self-esteem likely aren't new activities. After all, many people spend time looking inward to get a better sense of their selves. But without even realizing it, how you think about your self—and how you communicate that self to others—is shaped by powerful forces, both within and outside of yourself. Three of the most influential of these are gender, sexual orientation, and culture.

Gender and Self. As we'll discuss in detail in our next chapter (Chapter 3), *gender* is the composite of social, psychological, and behavioral attributes that a particular culture associates with an individual's biological sex (American Psychological Association [APA], 2015). Your concept of gender forms over time through interactions with others. Thus, it's distinct from the biological sex organs you are born with, which distinguish you anatomically as male, female, or intersex (having a combination of male and female sex organs).

Immediately after birth, you begin a lifelong process of gender socialization, in which societal norms define and assign appropriate behavior for each gender. Through this process you develop your *gender identity* (discussed in Chapter 3)—your innate sense of yourself as boy, man, or male; girl, woman, or female; or another variation, such as gender-neutral or gender-nonconforming (APA, 2015). Within current culture in the United States, for example, many girls are taught that the most important aspects of self include compassion and sensitivity to one's own and others' emotions (Lippa, 2002). Many boys are taught that the most important aspects of self are assertiveness, competitiveness, and independence. As a result, women and men within the culture form very different views of self (Cross & Madson, 1997). Women tend to see themselves as connected to others; men, as separate from others. However, this doesn't mean that all men and all women think of themselves in identical ways. Many men and women appreciate and embrace both feminine and masculine characteristics in their self-concepts.

Sexual Orientation and Self. Each of us also possesses a **sexual orientation** that strongly impacts our sense of self; that is, an enduring emotional, romantic, sexual, or affectionate attraction to others that exists along a continuum ranging from exclusive homosexuality to exclusive heterosexuality and that includes various forms of bisexuality (APA Online, n.d.). Although sexual orientation exists as a continuum, the full bandwidth of possibilities often is simplified by both scholars and laypersons into three groups: those who are *heterosexual* or *straight* (having an emotional, romantic, or sexual attraction to members of the other sex), those who are *homosexual* or *gay/lesbian* (having an emotional, romantic, or sexual attraction to members of one's own sex), and those who are *bisexual* (having an emotional, romantic, or sexual attraction to both men and women). As the American Psychological Association notes, a range of sexual orientation has been observed across human cultures and history, although the labels people have used to describe it vary widely.

Culture and Self. In this text, we define *culture* broadly and inclusively, as an established, coherent set of beliefs, attitudes, values, and practices shared by a large group of people (Keesing, 1974). Culture includes many types of large-group influences, such as nationality, ethnicity, religion, gender, sexual orientation, physical abilities, and age. You learn your culture from parents, teachers, religious leaders, peers, and the mass media (Gudykunst & Kim, 2003).

Culture influences your communication in many ways, as Chapter 3 discusses in detail. But when it comes to your view of self, whether you grew up in an individualistic or collectivistic culture is highly influential. If you were raised in an *individualistic culture*, you likely learned that individual goals matter more than group goals. By contrast, if you were raised in a *collectivistic culture*, you were probably taught the importance of belonging to groups that look after you in exchange for your loyalty (Hofstede, 2001). (For more information, see page 80 in Chapter 3.)

Presenting Your Self

Anne Burrell is a rock star in the world of chefs. Easily identifiable from her shock of white-blond hair, charisma, humor, and quirkiness, she draws millions of viewers to her Food Network shows *Secrets of a Restaurant Chef* and *Worst Cooks in America*. But in May 2012, her image was challenged when writer and television personality Ted Allen outed her as a lesbian. During an interview on Sirius XM radio, host Romaine Patterson joked to Allen about Burrell, saying, "I have the biggest crush on her . . . whether or not she's a lesbian, I don't care." Allen responded, "I'm not going to put a label on Anne, but she is dating a woman right now. You've got some competition." Afterward, many fans expressed surprise, noting that Burrell had never presented herself publicly as a lesbian. But Burrell herself was quick to embrace the disclosure, releasing a statement confirming her sexual orientation and noting that she is in a committed relationship with another chef, Koren Grieveson (the two subsequently got engaged). Food Network executives supported her "new" self-presentation as well, commenting, "We're always

When celebrity chef Anne Burrell was publicly outed, she had to make a decision about how to reconcile her public and private selves. Are there areas of your private self you would need to reconcile if they became public? How would you manage that?

Angela Pham/BFAnyc/Sipa USA/Newscom

looking to broaden the diversity of our hosts, and we work hard to find talent that has the expertise, charisma, and broad appeal necessary to work on our air."

In addition to your *private self*—the combination of your self-awareness, self-concept, and self-esteem—you also have a *public self*: the self you present to others (Fenigstein, Scheier, & Buss, 1975). You actively create your public self through your communication and behavior.

Sometimes your private and public selves mirror each other. At other times, such as when Ted Allen outed Anne Burrell, it can seem as though your private and public selves are different. But regardless of the nature of your private self, people form impressions about you based on the public self you present. People know and judge the "you" who communicates with them—not the "you" you keep inside. Thus, managing your public self is a crucial part of being a competent communicator.

Creating Faces and Masks

The positive self you want others to see and believe is your **face** (Goffman, 1955). Face doesn't just happen; you actively create and present it through your communication. Your face can be anything you want it to be: perky and upbeat, cool and levelheaded, cynical and detached.

You create different faces for different situations. Sometimes your face is a **mask**: an outward presentation designed to cover private aspects of your self (Goffman, 1955). For example, suppose you have an interview coming up for a new job. The night before, you find out someone close to you has died. When you meet with your potential new boss, you act upbeat, engaging, and competent—even though you want to curl up on the floor and cry. Sometimes you adopt masks to protect others. Paramedics often do this when they talk in calm, comforting tones to keep severely injured accident victims from going into shock.

Losing Face

When you create a certain face (or a mask) and then do something that contradicts it, you *lose face* (Goffman, 1955). People may perceive you as phony and may feel betrayed by your actions. Losing face can also cause you to experience **embarrassment**—feelings of shame, humiliation, and sadness. For example, when Steve was in high school, he competed at a state public-speaking tournament. During the final qualifying round, he suddenly blanked in the middle of his speech. As he stood there silently for several seconds, feeling and looking incompetent in front of his audience, he contradicted his face of "confident, competitive public speaker." The result was embarrassment that he remembers to this day.

Maintaining Face

Losing face is painful for everyone involved, so maintaining face during communication is critical. How can you maintain your face? First, *use words and actions consistent with the face you're trying to create*. If you tell members of a project team that you're excited to hear everyone's input, be sure to demonstrate this by actively listening when each member offers suggestions instead of tuning out and texting your friends. Second, *make sure your communication meshes with others' existing knowledge about you*. If you're giving a speech about the dangers of listening to loud music through headphones and you walked into class blasting music through your earbuds, you won't be able to maintain face. Finally, *try to anticipate and manage events that could contradict your face*. If you tell your dating partner that you haven't been in contact with your ex, you won't want a post from him or her to pop up on your Facebook Timeline.

Of course, everyone falls from grace on occasion. But remember, most people want you to maintain face because your face is the positive, public "you" with whom they're most familiar. So when something happens that causes you to lose face, promptly acknowledge that the event happened, admit responsibility for any of your actions that contributed to the event, apologize for your actions and for disappointing others, and move to maintain your face again. Apologies are fairly successful at reducing people's negative impressions and the anger that may have been triggered—especially

ADVANCE THE CONVERSATION

DISTORTING ONLINE SELF-PRESENTATION

1 YOUR DILEMMA

You recently joined an online matchmaking service. As you craft your profile, your friends encourage you to "spin" your self-presentation. "Make yourself three inches taller," says one, and another encourages you to "change your age and say you have a master's degree." You're unsure, but they say, "Don't worry about it—everyone does it! Besides, do you want to meet people or not?"

After a couple of weeks, you connect with Jordan, who seems to be your soulmate. You two have everything in common, from tastes in movies and music, to religious and political beliefs. Excited to meet offline, you arrange a lunch date.

Jordan proves to be even more desirable in person than online. As you enjoy lunch together, you cover many topics, including your educations, your families, and your life dreams. As lunch ends, you tell Jordan, "I'd really like to see you again." However, Jordan frowns and says, "I'm not sure. Although I've really enjoyed our date, I'm a little confused. You're not exactly how I thought you'd be, based on your profile. As we were talking, you said you are still in school. But that isn't what your description says. Is there stuff you just haven't told me, or did you make things up for your profile?"

How do you feel when Jordan expresses hesitation about seeing you again because of your dishonesty?

2 THE RESEARCH

People often present themselves online in ways that amplify positive characteristics, such as warmth and friendliness, while masking characteristics they think are undesirable or unattractive (Gosling, Gaddis, & Vazire, 2007). This is especially true on online dating sites. More than a quarter of online matchmaking members report having lied in their profiles to present themselves as more attractive (Brym & Lenton, 2001).

Communication scholar Jeffrey Hall and colleagues surveyed over 5,000 online dating service users to examine the specific ways in which they misrepresented themselves (Hall, Park, Song, & Cody, 2010). Although both men and women lied about their ages (making themselves younger), men were more likely than women to lie about income and educational levels, whereas women were more likely to lie about their weight.

Of course, distorting your online self-presentation is ultimately self-defeating if you wish to form offline relationships. Researchers found that 86 percent of dating site users reported having met others who they felt had misrepresented their physical attractiveness (Gibbs, Ellison, & Heino, 2006), and in such situations, they typically felt "lied to" (Ellison, Heino, & Gibbs, 2006). So if your goal is to forge an offline connection, you should present yourself authentically online.

Why do you think Jordan responded in this way? If you were in Jordan's situation, might you have responded the same way?

3 YOUR OPPORTUNITY

How will you respond to Jordan? Before you act, consider what the research tells you about online self-presentation. Also factor in what you have learned about face, embarrassment, and apologies (pp. 41–42, 44).

Now it's your turn. Write out a response to Jordan. Be sure to include an explanation for why you acted the way you did.

when such apologies avoid excuses that contradict what people know really happened (Ohbuchi & Sato, 1994). People who consistently deny their inconsistencies or who blame others for their lapses are judged much more harshly.

Perceiving Others

Along with your view of self, your perception of others determines how you communicate. Although it may seem as though your view of other people is both accurate and objective, it is anything but. Understanding the process of perception will help you avoid errors that might cause you to communicate incompetently.

When communication professor Min Liu first arrived in the United States to work on her PhD, she felt fairly confident about her language skills. After all, she spoke fluent English and had passed a battery of language proficiency exams.[2] But her U.S. students struggled to understand her, and on her teaching evaluations they criticized her as "not speaking English well enough to teach." Such instances are increasingly common, as the majority of U.S. university graduate teaching assistants are now foreign-born (National Foundation for American Policy, 2017), and complaints regarding their communication competence in university classrooms have skyrocketed (Gravois, 2005). But although students place the blame on instructors, is it really poor instructor communication that's the problem, or student perception?

Education and speech communication professor Donald Rubin conducted a series of studies in which U.S. students listened to an audiotape lecture and were told either that the speaker was "John Smith from Portland" (with a photo of a Euro-American instructor) or "Li Wenshu of Beijing" (with a photo of a Chinese instructor). When students were asked afterward to fill in missing words from a printed transcript of the lecture, students who had listened to "Li Wenshu" made 20 percent more errors than students who had listened to "John Smith," despite the fact that *the audiotape was identical*. From this outcome, Rubin concluded that at least some of the difficulty U.S. students experience when communicating with foreign-born instructors is *perceptual*. That is, students often presume that "non-native instructors will be unintelligible" (Gravois, 2005), and this presumption causes them to perceive that the language is difficult to understand—resulting in comprehension difficulties—even though the speakers actually are communicating clearly. As Rubin notes, "All the pronunciation improvement in the world [by foreign instructors] will not by itself halt the problem of students' complaining about their instructors' language" (Gravois, 2005).

The experience of Professor Min Liu and the research of Donald Rubin remind us of the powerful role played by **perception**: the process of selecting, organizing, and interpreting information from your senses. Perception is

---

[2]Information regarding Min Liu is adapted from Gravois (2005).

the gateway to the world around you, and what you "see" through this gateway determines the communication path you'll pursue as you walk through it. But, as we'll also discover, we often see only that which we already believe.

The Perception Process

Perception occurs when you do the following:

1. *Select* information to focus your attention on
2. *Organize* the information into an understandable pattern, such as words, phrases, ideas, or images
3. *Interpret* the meaning of the pattern

Each step in the perception process influences the others: the information you select determines how you organize it, your mental organization of information shapes how you interpret it, and your interpretation of information influences how you mentally organize it. (See Figure 2.2.) Let's take a closer look at each step.

Step 1: Select Information. During the first step of perception, **selection**, you focus your attention on certain sights, sounds, tastes, touches, or smells in your environment. One estimate suggests that even though your senses take in 11 million bits of information per second, you select only about 40 bits to pay attention to (Wilson, 2002). With so much information out there, how do you decide what to select? You're more likely to focus on something when it is visually or audibly stimulating, deviates from your expectations, or is viewed as important (Fiske & Taylor, 1991).

Consider what this means for your communication. If you're attending a presentation and the speaker talks in a dramatic, impassioned way, you're more likely to pay attention than if the presenter had spoken in a monotone and stood passively behind the lectern. If Tom, a team member who's usually talkative, sits silently during a meeting, he'll defy your expectations—so you'll notice him. And if you hear your child start to cry in an adjacent room, you'll likely consider the situation important and focus your attention on it.

Step 2: Organize the Information into a Pattern. Once you've selected something to focus your attention on, you structure the information you receive through your senses into a coherent pattern in your mind. This is the second step of the perception process, known as **organization** (Fiske & Taylor, 1991). For example, once your attention is drawn to Tom (the unusually quiet group member), you begin to observe

FIGURE 2.2

THE PERCEPTION PROCESS

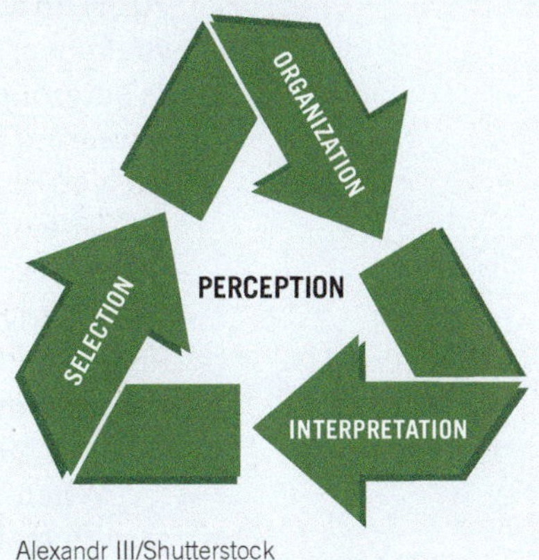

Alexandr III/Shutterstock

all that he is doing—his posture, facial expressions, bodily movements, and lack of comments—and organize it within your mind as a coherent package: "This is how Tom is acting right now."

Step 3: Interpret the Pattern. As you organize the information you've selected into a coherent pattern, you engage in the third step of perception: **interpretation**, or assigning meaning to the information you've selected. You call to mind familiar information that's relevant, and use that information to make sense of what you're hearing and seeing. Borrowing on the previous example, this is the stage of perception in which you would assign meaning to the behaviors of Tom that you have focused your attention on: "When people who are usually talkative are suddenly quiet, they often have something on their minds. Tom is being unusually quiet. Maybe Tom is upset about something."

Perception and Culture

Culture has an enormous and powerful effect on how we select, organize, and interpret information we receive through our senses—especially with regard to other people. Specifically, when you grow up with certain beliefs, attitudes, and values, you naturally perceive those who share these with you as **ingroupers**—people you consider as similar to yourself (Allport, 1954). Individuals from many different social groups can be ingroupers if they share important cultural commonalities with you, such as nationality, political views and/or party affiliation, religious beliefs, ethnicity, age, or socioeconomic class (Turner, Hogg, Oakes, Reicher, & Wetherell, 1987). In contrast, you may view people who aren't culturally similar to yourself as **outgroupers**.

People often feel passionately connected to their ingroups, especially when they reflect central aspects of their self-concept, such as sexual orientation, gender identity, religious beliefs, or ethnic heritage. This feeling of connection means you're more likely to give your money, time, and help to ingroupers than to outgroupers (Castelli, Tomelleri, & Zogmaister, 2008). It also means you're more likely to form positive impressions of people you perceive as ingroupers when you first meet them (Giannakakis & Fritsche, 2011). In addition, when people communicate in rude or inappropriate ways, you're more inclined to form negative impressions of them if you see them as outgroupers (Brewer, 1999). So, if a customer at your job snaps at you, but is wearing a T-shirt advocating your cultural beliefs and values, you're more likely to think, "He's just having a bad day," rather than "What a jerk!"

One of the strongest determinants of ingroup and outgroup perceptions is race. **Race** classifies people based on common ancestry or descent and is judged almost exclusively by a person's physical features (Lustig & Koester, 2006). When we perceive someone's race, we usually—even if unconsciously—assign him or her to ingrouper or outgrouper status (Brewer, 1999) and communicate with him or her based on that status.

When we categorize other people as ingroupers or outgroupers, it's easy to make mistakes. Even if a person seems to be the same race as you (e.g., Asian), she may have a different ethnic, religious, and cultural heritage (you're a U.S.-born Christian; she's from Japan and is Buddhist). Likewise, if someone dresses differently than you do or has a different race or religion, he might nevertheless hold beliefs, attitudes, and values that are similar to your own. If you assume that people are ingroupers or outgroupers based on surface-level differences, you may mistakenly perceive that you don't share anything in common. As a consequence, you might never discover that you do share important qualities and thus could miss out on an opportunity to make a new friend, work productively with a colleague, or form a romantic bond.

Attributions and Perceptual Errors

Following the perception process, you often want explanations for why things are happening the way they are ("Why is Tom not talking during the meeting?"). These explanations are known as **attributions**. Two types of attributions are commonplace. One is that *external* factors or events—things

FUNDAMENTAL ATTRIBUTION ERROR

The morning rush at a coffee shop can be equally frustrating for customers and employees. Think about how their interactions might change if they considered external, rather than internal, attributions for one another's behaviors.

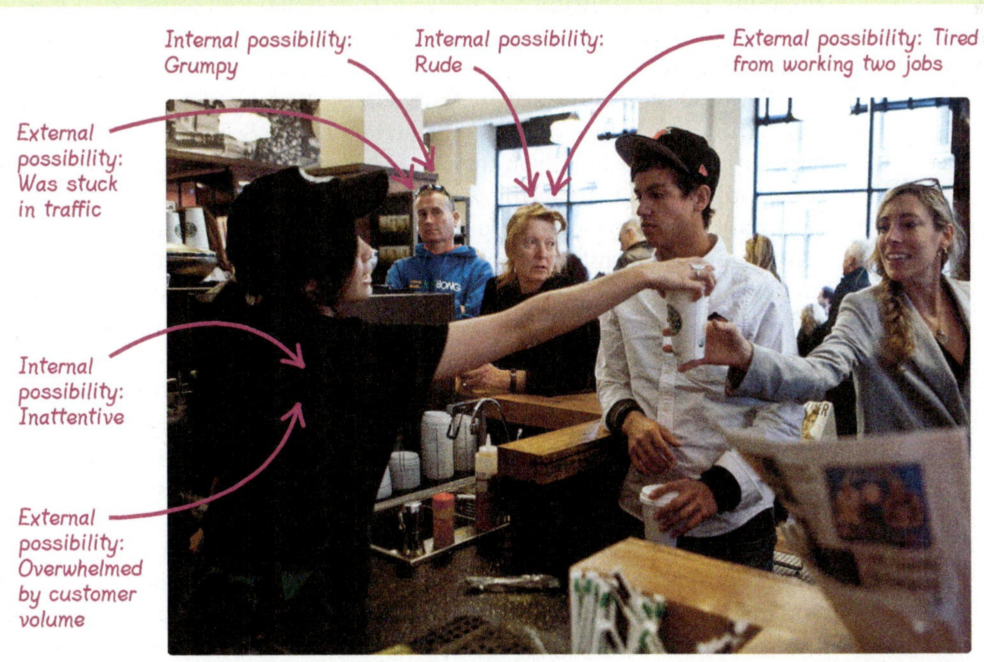

Ramin Talaie/Bloomberg/Getty Images

outside the person—caused the person's behavior ("Tom just heard that his dad is sick, so he's thinking about that instead of taking part in the meeting"). The other is that *internal* factors—personality, character, emotions—caused the person to act as he or she did ("Tom is a moody jerk, and that's why he's not contributing").

Given the number of people you communicate with each day, it's not surprising that you occasionally form invalid attributions. One common mistake is the **fundamental attribution error**, the tendency to attribute others' behaviors to internal rather than external forces (Heider, 1958). You make the fundamental attribution error because when you communicate with others, they—not the surrounding factors that may be causing their behavior—dominate your perception. As a result, when you make judgments about why someone is acting a certain way, you overestimate the influence of the person and underestimate the influence of external factors (Heider, 1958; Langdridge & Butt, 2004).

The fundamental attribution error is the most prevalent of all perceptual errors (Langdridge & Butt, 2004). For example, communication scholar Alan Sillars and his colleagues found that during conflicts between parents and teens, both parties typically fall prey to the fundamental attribution error (Sillars, Smith, & Koerner, 2010). Parents commonly attribute teens' communication to "lack of responsibility" and "desire to avoid the issue," whereas teens attribute parents' communication to "desire to control my life." Similar patterns have been observed during marital conflicts, with spouses typically blaming each other for the fight and attributing negative partner behaviors to internal causes; for example, "He's so stubborn!" and "She's so picky!" (Sillars, Roberts, Leonard, & Dun, 2000).

A related error is the **actor-observer effect**, the tendency to make external attributions regarding your own behaviors (Fiske & Taylor, 1991). During encounters with others, you tend to focus on external factors—especially the people you're interacting with. Therefore, you tend to identify these external factors as causing your behavior. This is particularly prevalent during unpleasant interactions. For example, if you're giving a speech and the audience doesn't pay attention, you might get angry and feel that such anger is a justifiable reaction to audience members' rudeness rather than a lack of self-control on your part.

However, when your actions result in success, you tend to take credit for the success by making an internal attribution ("The audience paid attention because I'm a skilled speaker"). This tendency is known as the **self-serving bias** (Fiske & Taylor, 1991). By crediting yourself for your successes, you feel better about who you are and the skills you possess.

Your attributions directly influence how you communicate with others and the outcomes that result. For example, imagine that your partner forgets to pick up your dry cleaning on the way home from work. If you attribute your partner's forgetfulness to work pressures and a hectic schedule (external causes), you'll probably communicate in a supportive way ("I know how busy you are—I should've texted you a reminder"). But if you make internal attributions ("My partner is self-centered and inconsiderate"), you'll likely communicate in a destructive way ("I'm sure you'd remember if it were *your* stuff that needed picking up!").

Forming Impressions

Whenever you meet people, you paint pictures in your mind of who they are and what you think of them. These images can be positive or negative, long-lasting or subject to change. However, they act as a powerful guide in shaping your communication, for better or for worse.

When Joe (the author of this book) was in college, he was a competitive distance runner. Grueling training runs in the heat and humidity of southeast Texas bonded him and his fellow teammates, helping them overcome differences in their ethnic backgrounds, personalities, lifestyles, and worldviews. But just as they were forming more positive impressions of one another, the runners as a group were perceived differently by other students on campus. At the time, long-distance running was only just starting to gain popularity in the United States. Students who didn't understand the sport viewed the athletes as freaks. Who in their right mind, after all, would run 20 miles a day—in Texas?! The runners' scrawny physiques even led some people to say they were malnourished, creating further skepticism about the sport. Yet many of these same critics were shocked to see how much pizza the runners put away in the dining hall as they loaded up on carbohydrates before a race.

Like those who judged the distance runners, you also use the perception process to form **impressions** of others: mental images of who people are and how you feel about them. All aspects of the perception process shape your impressions: the information you select to focus your attention on, the way you organize this information, the interpretations you make, and the attributions you create.

Because the perception process is complex and everyone organizes and interprets information differently, impressions vary widely. Some take shape quickly: you hear a politician giving a speech and take an immediate dislike to him. Other impressions form slowly, over a series of encounters. Some are intensely positive: "Long-distance runners are amazingly dedicated and disciplined!" Others are neutral. Some are negative: "Long-distance runners are freaks!" Let's look at some ways you form impressions.

Gestalts

One way you form impressions of others is to construct a **Gestalt**, a general impression of a person that's positive or negative. You identify a few traits about the person and then arrive at a judgment ("I like you" or "I don't like you"). For example, audience members begin forming impressions of you the moment you begin a speech. Your clothing, posture, facial expressions, and opening remarks generate an overall impression that can instantly enhance or undermine your credibility.

One way to understand the power of Gestalts is to consider how you feel about controversial public figures. For example, some of us admire pop singer-songwriter Taylor Swift, while others criticize her. Chances are you don't personally know Swift, but you might still have formed a strong Gestalt about her. Consider how this same process works for people you meet in person or online.

AP Images/Evan Agostini

Gestalts form rapidly and require relatively little mental or communicative effort. This makes them useful for encounters in which you must make quick judgments about others based on limited information. Imagine you need to hire someone and have dozens of résumés to review. Although résumés don't reflect the sum total of what the applicants are like, the Gestalts you create based on them will help you decide whom to interview ("This résumé is well crafted, has no typos, and highlights skills relevant to this job. I *like* her already!").

A disadvantage of Gestalts is that they can distort how you interpret information you later learn about people. Think about someone for whom you've formed a strongly positive Gestalt. Now imagine discovering that this person cheated on his taxes. Because of your positive Gestalt, you may dismiss the significance of this behavior ("He probably made an innocent mistake"). This tendency is known as the **halo effect**.

The counterpart of the halo effect is the **horn effect**, the tendency to negatively interpret the behavior of people for whom you've formed negative Gestalts. Call to mind someone you can't stand. Now imagine that this person has cheated on her taxes. Chances are, you'll chalk up her behavior to bad character or lack of values ("I knew she was a cheat!").

Algebraic Impressions

A second way to form impressions is to develop **algebraic impressions**—analyzing the positive and negative things you learn about someone to calculate an overall impression, then updating this impression as you learn new information (Anderson, 1981). It's similar to solving an algebraic equation, whereby you add and subtract different values to compute a final result. However, when forming algebraic impressions, you don't place an equal value on every piece of information you receive. Instead, information that's important, unusual, or negative is usually weighted more heavily than information that's trivial, typical, or positive (Kellermann, 1989). This happens because people tend to believe that important, unusual, or negative information reveals more about a person's "true" character than does other information (Kellermann, 1989).

Of course, other people form algebraic impressions of you, too. So, when you're communicating—whether in person or online, with a friend or in front of an audience—be mindful of what important, unusual, or negative information you share about yourself. This information will have a particularly strong effect on others' impressions of you.

Algebraic impressions are more accurate than Gestalts because you take time to form them and you consider a wider range of information. They're also more flexible. You can update your algebraic impression every time you receive new information about someone. For instance, you discover through Facebook that the cool classmate you went on a date with yesterday has political views much different from your own. Accordingly, you become a bit cautious about pursuing a romantic relationship with this person while remaining open to seeing where things will lead.

Because stereotyping fails to consider the intricate complexities that distinguish individuals from broad group affiliations, it often leads to flawed impressions. To avoid relying on stereotypes, always adapt your communication to the person, not the group.

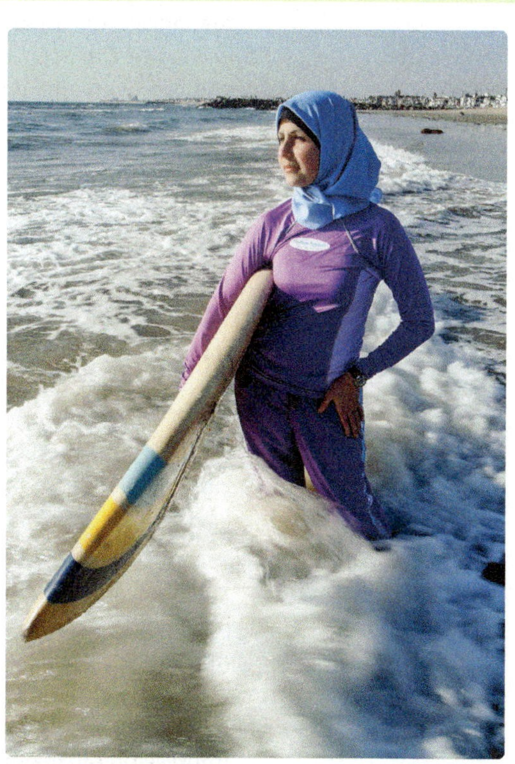

AP Images/Chris Carlson

Stereotypes

A final way to form impressions is to categorize people into a social group (such as their race, age, or gender) and then evaluate them based on information you have related to this group. This is known as **stereotyping** (Bodenhausen, Macrae, & Sherman, 1999). Stereotypes take the subtle complexities that make people unique and replace them with blanket assumptions about their character and worth based solely on their social group affiliations. Stereotyping is difficult to avoid because it's the most common way we form impressions (Bodenhausen et al., 1999). Why? Social-group categories can be the first things you notice about others when you meet them. So you often perceive people in terms of their social group before it's possible to make any other impression (Devine, 1989).

Stereotyping often leads to flawed impressions. In one workplace study, male supervisors who stereotyped women as "the weaker sex" perceived female employees' work performance as deficient and gave women low job evaluations—regardless of the women's actual job performance (Cleveland, Stockdale, & Murphy, 2000). A separate study examining college students' perceptions of professors found a similar biasing effect for ethnic stereotypes. Euro-American students who stereotyped Hispanics as "laid-back" perceived Hispanic professors who set high expectations for classroom performance as "colder" and "more unprofessional" than Euro-American professors who set identical standards (Smith & Anderson, 2005).

Despite claims of being the most democratic and equalizing mass medium, the internet actually enables stereotyping. During online communication, people don't have the nonverbal cues and other information that can distinguish someone as a unique individual. As a result, people communicating online are more likely than those communicating face-to-face to form stereotypical impressions of others (Lea & Spears, 1992; Spears, Postmes, Lea, & Watt, 2001; Wallace, 1999).

Though stereotypes are used to form impressions, they should not reflect rigid attitudes toward groups and their members. This is known as *prejudice* and can cause you to communicate in destructive and unethical ways. See Chapter 3 (pages 77–78) to learn more about prejudice and how you can overcome it.

Improving Your Perception

Even though perception and impression formation occur in specific ways, they are not unchangeable processes. You can improve your perception and impressions by critically questioning your own judgments and routinely considering the feelings, needs, and viewpoints of others.

As we have emphasized throughout this chapter, accurate perception is key if you wish to bolster the competence of your communication. Two skills can help you improve your perception: perception-checking and empathy.

Perception-Checking

Perception-checking is a five-step process for testing your impression of someone and avoiding errors in judgment. (See Table 2.1 on page 54.) Whenever you're in a situation in which having clear, accurate perceptions of others is a must, follow these steps. First, review your knowledge about the person. Your impression of this individual is only as accurate as the information you have. Never presume that you know the "truth" about someone.

Second, assess attributions you've made about this individual. Avoid attributing the person's behavior exclusively to internal causes. Remember that all behavior stems from a blend of internal and external forces.

Third, question your impression. Make sure you're not basing it solely on a Gestalt or a stereotype.

Fourth, share your impression with the individual. Present it as "here's my viewpoint," not as the "right" or "only" perspective.

Fifth, check your impression with the person: "Do you see it the same way?" As communication teachers, we can't count the number of times students have asked us, "Do you think he meant this?" or "Do you think she was trying to . . . ?" We always say, "Why don't you ask them?"

Mastering perception-checking takes practice, but the effort is worthwhile. Perception-checking helps you make fewer communication blunders. It also enables you to tailor your communication to people as they really are. Thus, your messages become more sensitive and effective. Ultimately, others will see you as a more competent communicator if you use perception-checking.

Empathy

Empathy is among the most valuable tools for communicating more effectively with others (Campbell & Babrow, 2004). The word *empathy* comes from the Greek word *empatheia*, meaning "feeling into." When you experience **empathy**, you "feel into" others' thoughts and emotions, making an attempt to identify with them (Kuhn, 2001).

Empathy consists of two components: perspective-taking and empathic concern (Davis, 1994). *Perspective-taking* is the ability to see things from other people's point of view without necessarily experiencing their emotions (Duan & Hill, 1996). *Empathic concern* means becoming aware of how other people are feeling and experiencing compassion for them (Stiff, Dillard, Somera, Kim, & Sleight, 1988). For example, imagine your friend John texts you that his boyfriend just broke up with him. In experiencing empathy for your friend, you would put yourself in his shoes and call to mind instances in which a romantic partner left you. Then you'd envision the emotional pain and turmoil you've felt on such occasions, and use these memories to feel compassion toward John.

We often think of empathy as an automatic process beyond our control, something we either feel or don't feel (Schumann, Zaki, & Dweck, 2014). Consequently, we excuse ourselves from being empathic toward people we dislike or don't get along with. But recent research suggests that whether we feel empathy toward others depends largely on our **empathy mindset**—our beliefs about whether empathy is something that can be developed and controlled (Schumann et al., 2014). People that view empathy as developable and controllable are capable of feeling empathy for a broad range of others—even during challenging communication contexts such as an interpersonal conflict, an argument about political beliefs, or a grief story told

TABLE 2.1

PERCEPTION-CHECKING

SITUATION Imagine that you are working on a group project for your communication class. Your group leader, Heather, doesn't take suggestions from other members and only moves forward with her own ideas. What steps should you take before confronting Heather about her leadership style?

Step	Example
1 Review your knowledge. What do you know about Heather as a classmate?	I know that Heather: • Is a dedicated student • Is on an academic scholarship • Usually works alone
2 Assess attributions. What combination of internal and external attributions may Heather's behavior stem from?	Internal: Heather is controlling. External: Heather has a lot of pressure to succeed academically.
3 Question your impression. Is your conclusion fair?	Is it correct to conclude that Heather is simply a bossy leader?
4 Share your impression. Present your impression to Heather in an open manner to invite conversation.	"To me, it seems the discussions are a little one-sided. I think all the group members would like to contribute."
5 Check your impression. See if Heather understands your viewpoint, and discuss a way to make it better.	"That's my viewpoint. Do you agree? Can we make discussions more inclusive?"

TAKEAWAY Instead of jumping to conclusions, it's important to remember that both internal and external attributions affect a person's behavior. Once you understand that the external pressure to keep her academic scholarship is causing Heather to control the group, you can more competently approach improving communication within the group.

by someone we perceive as completely different from us (Schumann et al., 2014). Those who believe empathy is an uncontrollable, natural response have difficulty experiencing empathy within such challenging encounters.

But experiencing empathy isn't enough. You must also convey your empathy to others. To do so, let others know you're genuinely interested in listening to them ("I'm here to listen if you want to talk"). Tell them you think their views are valid and understandable ("I can totally understand why you would feel that way"). Express your concern about them ("I care about you and am worried that you're not OK"). And finally, share with them your own emotions regarding their situation ("I feel terrible that you're going through this").

When expressing empathy, avoid using "I know" messages ("I know just how you feel"). Even if you make such comments with kind intentions, the other person will likely be skeptical, particularly if they suspect that you don't or can't feel as they do. For example, when people suffer a great loss—such as the death of a loved one—many don't believe that anyone else could feel the depth of anguish they're experiencing. Saying "I know how you feel" isn't helpful under these conditions. To see how you can competently display empathy, see Advance the Conversation: Empathy for a Group Member on pages 56–57.

Competently conveying empathy isn't just something to be strived for as a matter of principle; it's a recommendation packed with practical benefits (Goldstein, Vezich, & Shapiro, 2014). When others perceive you as empathic, they're also more likely to perceive you as someone they can relate to, more likely to like you, and more likely to help you when you are in need.

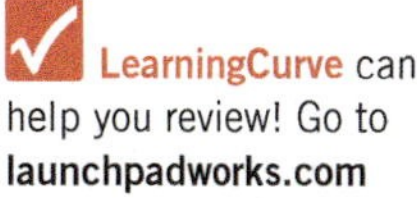

LearningCurve can help you review! Go to **launchpadworks.com**

Trum Ronnarong/Shutterstock.com

When you express empathy to others, be sure you validate their feelings and share your concern for them, but also—perhaps most important—really listen to what they need, and offer to help any way you can. After all, if the roles were reversed, isn't that what you would want from them?

ADVANCE THE CONVERSATION
Video Activity

EMPATHY FOR A GROUP MEMBER

The following scenario will enhance your ability to understand and apply empathy in a conversation. Visit LaunchPad at **launchpadworks.com** to get the full experience with video. As you watch the first video, recall what you've learned about perspective-taking and empathic concern, and then complete the **Your Turn** prompts. Finally, watch the **Take Two!** video to explore how this scenario could have gone differently.

1 *THE PROBLEM*

Paul is assigned to lead a group project for class. One team member, Alex, has missed two of the first three meetings. When Paul meets with Alex to discuss this, he learns that Alex has a 3-year-old she is raising as a single mother. She is working full-time to put herself through school—and, on top of everything else, her boss recently changed her hours. Alex genuinely wants to contribute to the project but is struggling to juggle all of the competing demands in her life. Clearly stressed, she says, "It all works out fine if I just skip sleeping!"

"I can't imagine having to deal with all the stuff that you've got going on. And you know it's totally fine to be stressed, right?"

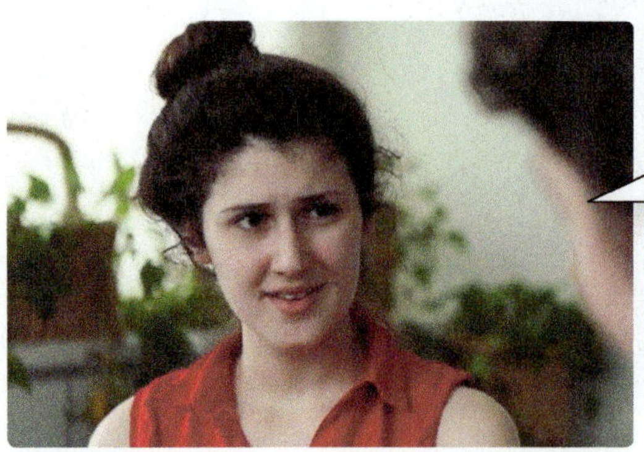

"You've got that right! You can't understand or imagine what I'm going through—and I doubt anyone in the group gets it, either."

2 YOUR TURN

Observations. Reflect on how Paul and Alex communicated in this scenario by answering the following questions:

1. Which character do you identify with more in this situation? How would you feel if you were in their situation?
2. Where were the missed opportunities to practice competent communication?

Discussion. In class or with a partner, share your thoughts about the interaction between Paul and Alex and work to answer the following question:

1. Can you understand both perspectives?
2. What could Alex and Paul have done differently?

Conclusion. Choose one person in the scenario to offer your advice. Based on your analysis, what advice would you give him or her to improve his or her communication competence in this scenario?

3 TAKE TWO!

What if things had gone differently? Watch the **Take Two!** video to see one possible example of how the conversation might have gone if Alex and/or Paul had communicated differently. As you watch the video, consider where the dialog reflects empathy and perspective-taking. After watching the video, answer the questions below:

1. Did Alex and/or Paul take advantage of opportunities that they missed in the first scenario? Which ones?
2. Did their different actions result in a more productive encounter? Please explain.

CHAPTER 2 REVIEW

CHAPTER RECAP

- Your **self** is an evolving blend of three components: **self-awareness**, **self-concept**, and **self-esteem**. These shape how you communicate in all situations and contexts.
- The positive self you want others to see and believe is your **face**; your face is a **mask** when you hide parts of it. To avoid **embarrassment**, work on maintaining your face.
- **Perception** is how you view the world around you. You use **attributions** to explain why things happen.
- There are many ways to form **impressions** of others, including constructing **Gestalts**, forming **algebraic impressions**, and **stereotyping**.
- You can improve your perception by practicing **perception-checking** and **empathy**.

LaunchPad for *Choices & Connections* offers unique video scenarios and encourages self-assessment through adaptive quizzing. Go to **launchpadworks.com** to get access.

 LearningCurve adaptive quizzes

 Advance the Conversation video scenarios

 Video clips that illustrate key concepts

KEY TERMS

Self, p. 34
Self-awareness, p. 34
Social comparison, p. 34
Critical self-reflection, p. 35
Self-concept, p. 35
Self-Verification Theory, p. 37
Self-fulfilling prophecy, p. 37
Self-esteem, p. 37
Self-Discrepancy Theory, p. 37
Sexual orientation, p. 39
Face, p. 41
Mask, p. 42
Embarrassment, p. 42
Perception, p. 44
Selection, p. 45
Organization, p. 45
Interpretation, p. 46
Ingroupers, p. 46
Outgroupers, p. 46
Race, p. 46
Attribution, p. 47
Fundamental attribution error, p. 48
Actor-observer effect, p. 48
Self-serving bias, p. 48
Impression, p. 49
Gestalt, p. 49
Halo effect, p. 50
Horn effect, p. 50
Algebraic impression, p. 50
Stereotyping, p. 51
Perception-checking, p. 52
Empathy, p. 53
Empathy mindset, p. 53

POP QUIZ

Looking for more review questions? **LearningCurve** can help you master key concepts from this chapter. Go to **launchpadworks.com**

1. According to Self-Discrepancy Theory, you are more likely to experience *high* self-esteem if
   - **a.** your self-concept matches your ideal and ought selves.
   - **b.** you prioritize your ought self over your ideal self.
   - **c.** your relational partners disapprove of your self-concept.
   - **d.** you strive for your most idealistic self at all times.
2. Which statement about faces and masks is *true*?
   - **a.** Your face is private, composed of your deeply held beliefs.
   - **b.** A mask covers the private aspects of your self.
   - **c.** You can have only one face but may have several masks.
   - **d.** The best way to recover from embarrassment is to create a new mask.
3. The overwhelming tendency of people to attribute others' behaviors to internal rather than external forces is known as
   - **a.** self-serving bias.
   - **b.** stereotyping.
   - **c.** the actor-observer effect.
   - **d.** the fundamental attribution error.
4. Which of the following impressions forms slowly, over time?
   - **a.** Halo effect
   - **b.** Horn effect
   - **c.** Algebraic impressions
   - **d.** Gestalts
5. Which of the following is *not* one of the five steps of perception-checking?
   - **a.** Review your knowledge about the person.
   - **b.** Compare your impressions with a neutral source.
   - **c.** Question your impressions.
   - **d.** Check your impressions.

ACTIVITIES

For more activities, visit LaunchPad for *Choices & Connections* at **launchpadworks.com**

1 Applying Self-Discrepancy Theory

Revisit Higgins's Self-Discrepancy Theory on page 37, and consider how it applies to you and your feelings about your self. Then, write a brief paper describing your self-esteem. Overall, how do you feel about your self? Briefly explain your self-concept, your ideal self, and your ought self. Where did your ideal and ought selves come from? When you compare them to your self-concept, are there any self-discrepancies? If not, how is the lack of discrepancies related to your self-esteem? If there *are* discrepancies, how might they be overcome? Be specific. If you resolved these discrepancies, would your self-esteem improve? Why or why not?

2 Recovering from Embarrassment

Either individually or in groups, find an example of an embarrassing moment from a TV show, web series, or movie. (You can revisit the discussion of face and embarrassment on pages 41–42.) If possible, find a clip online to share with your class; if not, describe it in detail. How did the character communicate in response to his or her embarrassment? Did he or she maintain face? Now consider the three practices suggested for maintaining face, and the recommendations for recovering from losing face. Based on these, how would you evaluate the character's handling of the situation? What specific advice would you give to him or her on how to better recover from losing face?

3

Understanding Gender and Culture

She's a clothing designer, an actor, an MTV VJ, and the face of Maybelline cosmetics. She's the daughter of a single mother and the goddaughter of Australia's most famous indigenous boxing champion. Above all, she is a human being who self-describes as "gender fluid" rather than as male or female.[1]

In her early childhood, Ruby Rose struggled with her gender identity in a broader Australian culture that largely embraces binary views of gender (two and only two genders, male and female). As she describes, "Growing up, my own understanding was that you had to be either a boy or a girl, and I didn't feel like I fit that mold." This lack of fit with cultural expectations led to feelings of isolation: "I didn't feel like I belonged. I didn't believe I was part of any group or culture." After repeatedly being praised for being a "pretty girl" during her teens, Rose rebelled by shaving her head. This simple act triggered relentless bullying, driving her to depression and attempted suicide. "Guys would say something to me like, 'What are you? You're a girl but you're trying to be a boy!' And if I talked back, I got hit. They'd say, 'I would never hit a girl, but you're not a girl!'"

Despite this abuse, she pursued modeling and was eventually picked up by Maybelline cosmetics. But her dream was to act, so she left for Hollywood. There, her gender fluidity confused casting agents, who couldn't figure out what gendered roles to place her in. Her response was to make her own film, a 2014 short that she released online titled "Break Free" (available on YouTube). In the film, Rose plays a character whose gender expression transforms from very feminine to very masculine through changes in clothing, makeup, and hair. When the film went viral, casting agents began calling, and her acting career took off.

Ruby Rose now has several successful films to her credit, as well as a major role on the hit Netflix series *Orange Is the New Black*. She is a frequent spokesperson for LGBTQ rights and has more than 1.3 million Twitter followers. At the core of her being is her own gender fluidity. As she describes, "Gender fluidity is not really feeling like you're at one end of the spectrum or the other. For the most part, I definitely don't identify as any gender. I'm not a guy; I don't really feel like a woman, but obviously I was born one. So, I'm somewhere in the middle, which—in my perfect imagination—is like having the best of both sexes. Culturally, we're in the middle of something enormous—a transgender movement. I'm just proud to be alive during this massive shift."

[1]Special thanks to Dr. Kelly Morrison for her contributions to gender coverage in this chapter.

Venturelli/WireImage/Getty Images

TOMMY

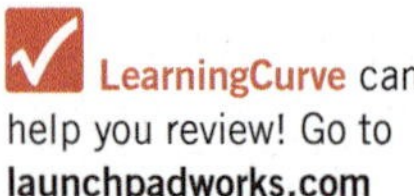
LearningCurve can help you review! Go to **launchpadworks.com**

Our worlds are becoming increasingly diverse. Whether it's online or on campus, not a day goes by without coming into contact with people of varying genders and sexual orientations, as well as diverse cultural beliefs, heritages, and traditions. It may be the classmate who is gender-fluid, like Ruby Rose, or prefers a gendered pronoun different from *him* or *her*. It may be a coworker wearing religious jewelry from another faith, or the instructor who shares samples of recipes from his homeland. In all its myriad forms, diversity surrounds us.

At the same time, when we experience *difference* we often perceive *distance*. When we hear the pronoun, see the jewelry, or taste the spices, our minds focus on the difference. We then assume distance: "This person is nothing like me!" And with perception of distance comes a host of associated judgments and behaviors, including stereotypes, awkward or incompetent communication, and—most destructively—prejudice.

It takes a radical shift in perspective to embrace difference, rather than flinch and turn away from it. Yes, it's true that people differ in their genders, sexual orientations, cultural beliefs, traditions, values, and communication. Such differences are deep, not superficial, and there is much that we can learn from them. But *difference doesn't equal distance*. It just means . . . difference! People who differ from one another may share profound points of commonality, upon which we can build valuable and impactful encounters.

In this chapter, you'll learn:

- The important differences between sex, gender, and gender identity
- How gender shapes our verbal and nonverbal communication
- Suggestions for overcoming gender stereotypes
- The nature of culture
- Important communication differences between cultures
- How you can improve your intercultural competence

What Is Gender?

> **Gender is a complex combination of physical, behavioral, and psychological attributes. Gender is distinct from sex (a person's biological, anatomical characteristics assigned at birth) and from gender identity (a person's deeply felt inner sense of themselves). Each of us undergoes a process of gender socialization and assumes—or rejects—gender roles, as a result of cultural and social forces.**

As Ruby Rose's story illustrates, people across the world are moving away from societies of constructed **gender polarization**, in which individuals are perceptually—and often socially and legally—sorted into binary categories of "male" versus "female." Instead, many people increasingly support the idea of a **gender continuum**, in which individuals are recognized as possessing complex combinations of attributes traditionally thought of as masculine and feminine. This cultural evolution takes many forms, from "all gender" signs on public restrooms to celebrities like Rose who reject binary gender and instead describe themselves as **gender fluid**—that is, not having a fixed gender but instead viewing gender as a dynamic mix of characteristics. The cultural shift is reflected in our language: some people use preferred pronouns such as *per/pers* or *they/them*, rather than *she/her* or *he/him*. And we also see the change within public and professional communities, as illustrated by the American Psychological Association's resolution on gender and sexual orientation diversity for public schools, which asserts that "all persons" are entitled to equal opportunity and a safe environment (see Table 3.1).

Gender Defined

To begin our discussion of gender, we first need to start with vocabulary in order to clarify the meaning of various terms. In particular, let's differentiate sex, gender identity, and gender. Then we'll look at gender roles.

Gender Is Distinct from Sex and Gender Identity. Each of us is born with *anatomical, biological distinctions,* known as our **sex**, which include differences in external genitalia, internal reproductive sex organs, hormones,

TABLE 3.1

PREAMBLE TO THE RESOLUTION ON GENDER AND SEXUAL ORIENTATION DIVERSITY IN CHILDREN AND ADOLESCENTS IN SCHOOLS

WHEREAS people express and experience great diversity in sexual orientation and gender identity and expression;

WHEREAS communities today are undergoing rapid cultural and political change around the treatment of sexual minorities and gender diversity;

WHEREAS all persons, including those who are sexual or gender minority children and adolescents, or those who are questioning their gender identities or sexual orientations, have the right to equal opportunity and a safe environment within all public educational institutions . . .

Resolution on gender and sexual orientation diversity in children and adolescents in schools. Adapted with permission from American Psychological Association & National Association of School Psychologists. (2015). Retrieved from http://www.apa.org/about/policy/orientation-diversity.aspx. Adopted by the Council of Representatives, August 2014. Amended by the Council of Representatives, February 2015.

and chromosomes. At birth we are legally assigned a sex category based on these distinctions: in many countries, birth certificates state "male," "female," or "intersex," which denotes "atypical combinations of features that usually distinguish male from female" (American Psychological Association [APA], 2012). We also see distinctions emerge as we grow older: anatomical males tend to develop greater height and more upper body strength compared to females. Consequently, differences in motor skills exist, such as males' greater grip strength, as well as greater throwing velocity and distance (Hyde, 2005).

In contrast, **gender identity** is *internal* to you: it is your deeply felt awareness and inner sense of being a boy, man, or male; a girl, woman, or female; or an alternative, such as genderqueer, gender-nonconforming, or gender-neutral (APA, 2015; APA & National Association of School Psychologists, 2015). Individuals may identify on the **transgender** spectrum if their gender identity does not correspond to their assigned sex, or they may be described as **cisgender** if their gender identity corresponds to their sex.

As societal awareness of gender diversity expands, we see an increase in illustrative role models. Laverne Cox, a colleague of Ruby Rose on *Orange Is the New Black*, is the first openly transgender person to be nominated for a primetime Emmy acting award. Danica Roem is the first openly transgender person elected to serve in a U.S. state legislature, working in the Virginia House of Delegates (Bruni, 2017). Additionally, some countries have exemplary policies, including the APA resolution previously discussed (Table 3.1) and the U.S. military policy affirming the ability of transgender service members to serve openly and not be discharged based on their gender identity (U.S. Department of Defense, 2016).

Danica Roem, elected to the Virginia House of Delegates in 2017, is the first openly transgender individual to serve in any U.S. state legislature. She campaigned on local issues such as traffic congestion, inadequate teacher salaries, and Medicaid expansion.

AP Images/Steve Helber

At the same time, confusion still exists about the differences between *sex* and *gender*, and you'll likely hear people inaccurately using one term to refer to the other. In part, this is because it wasn't until the late 1960s and early 1970s that social scientists began distinguishing *sex* from *gender* (Unger, 1979; West & Zimmerman, 1987). When they did this, though, many people simply started using *gender* as a *substitute* for *sex*. So, for example, instead of talking about "differences between the sexes," people began to refer to "gender differences."

Although such substitution may be conversationally convenient, it blurs the profound difference in meaning between these two terms. Unlike *sex* or *gender identity*, **gender** is a broader term encompassing all of the *social, psychological, and behavioral attributes that a particular culture associates with your biological sex* (APA, 2015). These attributes may include beliefs about individual characteristics, such as strength, leadership, or emotionality; and about social roles, such as being a parent, teacher, politician, or CEO. Thus, gender encompasses all of the cultural expectancies put upon us to behave and communicate in certain ways.

Consider two examples to help you make sense of these distinctions. Steve's first child was born anatomically male and was given the category assignment of "male" on his birth certificate. Thus his *sex* was established. Immediately after this, Steve and Kelly gave him a "boy name"—Kyle—from a binary list of "boy names" versus "girl names" they had created beforehand. They and all of their relatives then began referring to Kyle as *him* and *he*. These practices—naming and pronoun use—helped define his *gender* as male. As Kyle aged, he himself chose toys, games, and clothes culturally linked with boys, thus further locking down his male *gender*. He also grew into an understanding of his *gender identity*—that is, he thought of himself as, and deeply identified with, being a boy. Hence, Kyle is a *cisgender male*: his sex, gender, and gender identity all match.

Now consider Jazz Jennings, as portrayed on the TLC reality show *I Am Jazz*. Like Kyle, Jazz was born anatomically male and was given the *sex* assignment "male" on her birth certificate. Also like Kyle, she initially was treated like a boy by those around her, defining her *gender* as male. But from the first moments she became aware of her self—that is, from a very young age—she knew herself to be female, despite her physical anatomy. Her family, recognizing the depth and certainty of her female *gender identity*, supported her living a female *gender*: they stopped encouraging her to act "like a boy," and instead supported her growing her hair long and wearing clothes identifying herself as a girl. They also began using *she* and *her* as pronouns, bought her toys and games traditionally associated with girls, and so forth. Hence, Jazz was born with male *sex*, but has a female *gender identity*, and has enacted female *gender*. Thus, she is *transgender female*.

Gender Is Learned. As the former examples illustrate, gender is learned and enforced from a variety of sources, all of which contribute to a lifelong process of **gender socialization**—the cultural training through which we all learn the gender norms that are expected of us. Through advances in ultrasound imaging technology, many people choose to learn the sex of their baby before birth. This allows parents to begin the gender socialization of their child before the child is even born, through selecting masculine or feminine names, baby clothing, toys, and nursery decorations. Some parents even host a "gender-reveal party," during which they reveal to family and friends (and sometimes to themselves!) whether their baby will be a boy

At birth, both Kyle McCornack and Jazz Jennings were assigned the biological sex of "male." As they grew up, their genders and gender identities diverged. Kyle has a male gender identity and enacts male gender, while Jazz has a female gender identity and enacts female gender.

Steve McCornack

Steve McCornack

or a girl. Explore YouTube and you may find more than half a *million* videos of couples at these parties (Hafner, 2017).

After we are born, gender socialization continues and escalates, as parents encourage or discourage behaviors they deem appropriate or inappropriate for the child's gender. Importantly, these behaviors are almost always polarized; that is, there are "boy things" and "girl things" and very little overlap between the two. Such strict separation helps to reinforce the cultural (and stereotypical) notion that boys and girls are polar opposites (i.e., gender polarization).

As they grow, children take a more active role in learning about gender: they voice their preferences for toys, Halloween costumes, and birthday parties. Think back to when you were quite young and may have been involved in planning your birthday parties. Did you plan pink "dress-up" parties? Sports-themed parties? Disney character parties? How did your parents or caregivers respond to your requests? All of these decisions bolster gender. But if such decisions run against societal gender norms, everyone involved feels pressure to conform. For example, if a boy wants to have a Disney Princess party, he and his caregivers may well receive both subtle and direct pushback from salespeople, friends, and relatives insisting that a sports- or superhero-themed party is more appropriate.

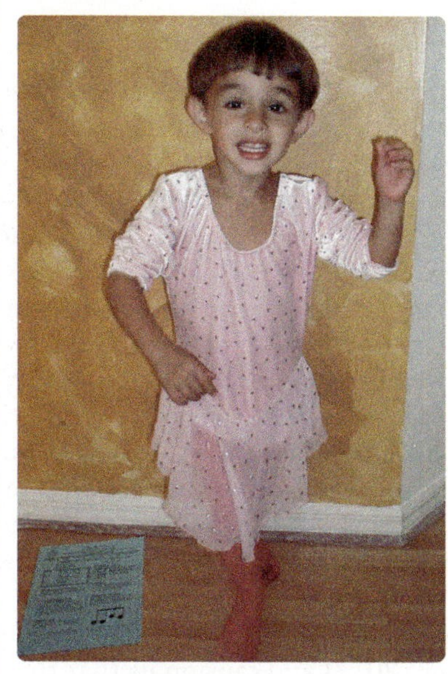

Courtesy of Jeanette Jennings

Emma McIntyre/Unilever/Dove/Getty Images

Gender Roles

As our discussion of gender socialization makes clear, from a very early age we are taught about **gender roles**: the shared societal expectations for conduct and behaviors that are deemed appropriate for girls or women and boys or men. Think back to the gender messages that may have been communicated to you in your youth. Were you taught that big boys don't cry? That it's not ladylike to curse? Were you teased that you throw like a girl or look like a boy? Were you counseled toward or away from particular classes in school or careers? All of these messages are examples of how we create different expectations, or standards, for girls and boys, and how societies instill gender role beliefs by promoting these personality and skill differences (Eagly, Wood, & Diekman, 2000; Eagly & Wood, 2012).

Research indicates that these beliefs take hold early and impact our aspirations for the future. In one study, both 5-year-old girls and 5-year-old boys were likely to link being smart with their own gender—but in the 6-year-old age group, girls were *less* likely than boys to believe that girls are "really, really smart" (Bian, Leslie, & Cimpian, 2017). The researchers further suggest that these beliefs may reduce the range of career options that girls consider, such as pursuing a job in a mathematics-intensive field.

Beliefs about abilities and intelligence aren't the only differences. According to findings from the Global Early Adolescent Study (GEAS), which compiled data on adolescents aged 10 to 14 from 15 countries, girls and boys *across the world* encounter unequal gender expectations and stereotypes (Blum, Mmari, & Moreau, 2017; Chandra-Mouli et al., 2017; Lane, Brundage, & Kreinin, 2017). Researchers stated that "across all study sites, boys are encouraged to be tough, strong, and brave and to demonstrate heterosexual prowess. Girls are taught to be nice, polite, and submissive and to accentuate their physical beauty while maintaining their modesty" (Chandra-Mouli et al., 2017). These gender roles prescribe beliefs that girls are vulnerable and must be protected from boys, who are "trouble." Thus girls' behaviors are often controlled and restricted, while boys are afforded more independence. These inequities are enforced by parents as well as peers, who sanction or tease each other when adolescents stray from these rigid norms.

The GEAS researchers further state that these differences are "socially, not biologically determined" (Blum et al., 2017) and caution us that these prescriptive gender roles have substantial *negative* outcomes. For instance, both girls and boys experience fewer opposite-sex friendships during adolescence than they did when they were younger. Girls experience more tolerance when they bend prescriptive gender norms, such as engaging in "tomboy" behaviors or playing sports; boys who engage in feminine behaviors are routinely mocked and bullied. Moreover, girls may leave school early, become pregnant, experience depression, or be victimized by violence. Boys are more prone to suicide and substance abuse, and as adults have a shorter life expectancy compared to women.

Gender and Communication

Many of us have inaccurate beliefs about men's and women's communication. In fact, there are few real verbal communication differences between men and women. On the other hand, men and women show consistent differences in nonverbal communication, which are influenced by differing social expectations.

Think back to our chapter opener and the story of Ruby Rose. When she was praised for being a "pretty girl," she shaved her head—so that people would see her as more boyish. To this day, she routinely plays with gender displays. As she describes, "I have a lot of characteristics that would normally be present in a guy and then less that would be present in a woman. But then sometimes I'll put on a skirt!" (Mooney, 2015).

Similarly, we *all* "do" gender, every single day (West & Zimmermann, 1987). That is to say, whether or not we actually speak or intend to convey meaning, *how we present ourselves to others conveys a message about our gender identities*. And the principal way in which we express our gender identities is through our verbal and nonverbal communication.

According to communication researchers, men and women have few real differences in verbal communication, but do have some consistent differences in nonverbal communication. Does this research match up with your personal experience? What similarities and differences in communication have you noticed between yourself and people with different genders and gender identities?

Adam Hester/Tetra images/Getty Images

Gender and Verbal Communication

Pause for a moment, and ponder your beliefs about how women and men communicate. Do you believe that they speak differently? Are men more direct or straightforward, clearly stating exactly what they mean, whereas women take longer to get to the point, speaking more indirectly, politely, or carefully? Does one group talk more than another? Interrupt more? Curse more? Use too much detail?

These beliefs about gender and verbal communication are common. If you Google "gender differences in communication," you may discover articles informing you that we are "wired" differently, with women being "emotional" and men more "analytical" (Martinez, 2017). You may find articles that tell you that we have different "purposes," with men "solving problems" and women "using talk to discover how they feel" (Drobnick, 2017). You may find blog posts stating that "women speak about 20,000 words a day" compared to the "7,000 words that men average a day" (New Media and Marketing, 2017).

But what's the scientific truth about differences in verbal communication? The bulk of research suggests a *lack* of gender differences (Canary & Hause, 1993; Dindia & Allen, 1992; Leaper & Smith, 2004). That is, women and men are more *similar* than different in their communication behaviors. When and where differences do exist, the actual differences are small and typically are due to situational factors rather than gender. Put another way, the words you use, and how you use them, are influenced more by who you are talking to, the type of feedback you are receiving, and the topic you are talking about than by your gender. This makes sense, given that gender is socially constructed, flexible, and interactional. In Chapter 5, we will review verbal communication in more detail. For now, let's continue our exploration of gender by examining nonverbal communication.

Gender and Nonverbal Communication

As we will review in more detail in Chapter 6, the scientific research on gender differences in nonverbal communication—the transmission of meaning through nonspoken physical and behavioral cues—suggests several consistent differences, unlike with verbal communication. For example, women tend to be more facially expressive than men (Hall, Carter, & Horgan, 2000) and often use micro-movements in their faces to communicate their emotions. This is a consistent difference, and it's commonly interpreted as supporting the stereotype that women are more emotional than men.

But it's important to ask—given what you now know about gender—is this behavioral difference truly because women are "more emotional" than men, or is it because women are *allowed*, even *expected*, by society to be more facially expressive? For instance, our male students rarely recall being asked to "Smile!" by complete strangers, but our female students frequently report this experience. And research supports the idea that we expect women to smile and men to be angry. In one study, participants were shown photos of

Artist Tatyana Fazlalizadeh is a Brooklyn-based muralist whose series "Stop Telling Women to Smile" attempts to raise awareness around street harassment that women worldwide experience every day. By addressing the act of being told to smile, Fazlalizadeh also opens up a conversation about nonverbal communication norms that women are often expected to adhere to.

Dustin Chambers/© The New York Times/Redux

people with happy, angry, or neutral expressions and were asked to identify the gender of the people in the photos. Participants took longer to match the unexpected pairs; that is, because they expected women to display happy faces and men to display angry faces, it took them longer to categorize photos of angry women as "female" and happy men as "male" (Smith, LaFrance, Knol, Tellinghuisen, & Moes, 2015).

Moving beyond Gender Stereotypes

People who perceive wide gender differences between men and women are also more likely to hold negative, sexist attitudes—especially toward women. As we strive to communicate competently with people of all gender identities, one crucial step is to rethink our ideas about polarized gender.

Given all that we have discussed regarding gender, how do we move forward, leaving stereotypes about polarized gender behind? The answer begins by examining our own attitudes about women and men, as well as our beliefs about gender differences. These two cognitions are connected. A 2016 study found that *the attitudes we hold about women and men are related to how we perceive gender similarity or difference across a range of issues,* such as risk-seeking, self-disclosure, forgiveness, helpfulness, self-esteem, interests in working with other people, and attitudes toward math and science (Zell, Strickhouser, Lane, & Teeter, 2016). Specifically, the researchers found that people who believed in large differences between males and females also were more likely to perceive men as comparatively superior (strong, decisive, brave) and women as comparatively inferior (weak, hesitant, fearful).

What's the takeaway? Belief in polarized gender fuels the perception that others are different from us, and this artificially widens the gulf between us. To build bridges of connection between people of varying genders, we need to begin by challenging the idea of polarized gender. We offer the following suggestions:

1. Reflect on all the ways in which you construct your own gender on a daily basis, and ponder why you do this. Examine your artifacts and purchases, considering not just the product but also how it is advertised. Do your choices say anything about gender roles? What would happen if you made changes in this aspect of your life?
2. Reflect on the media you consume or choose not to consume, including music, print, and social media. Examine how gender is portrayed. Consider exploring different media literacy or advocacy organizations, such as:
   - http://therepresentationproject.org/
   - https://seejane.org/
   - https://www.about-face.org/

ADVANCE THE CONVERSATION

CHALLENGING BINARY JUDGMENTS

1 *YOUR DILEMMA*

Your extended family is having a reunion dinner. You're excited to reconnect with them, especially your cousin Matias. He's a fascinating person with diverse interests and hobbies, and you've always loved talking with him. At the same time, these gatherings have been tough for him over the years, as people (especially his dad) often pick on him. Matias doesn't dress, talk, or behave in ways that men in your culture traditionally do. Some members of your family have not been supportive of him, as your family is *very* traditional—especially with regard to gender roles.

Everyone is crowded around the table, talking, laughing, and eating. Matias arrives late but sees you, smiles, and sits next to you. Before long, however, Matias's father starts in on him: "Matias, you look like a *girl.* When are you going to cut that ridiculous hair?" Everyone at the table laughs, but Matias is obviously hurt.

As the laughter fades and the conversations continue, Matias leans over to you and says, "Sorry about my dad. By the way, I'm not going by *Matias* anymore—my friends call me *Amaris* now, because I think it fits me better." But his dad overhears him. "*Amaris*? Come on, Matias, I'm worried about you. You gotta stop this whole 'pretending to be a girl' thing. You're a *man*, and it's time you start acting like one!" Matias is silent. Then his dad looks at you. "Maybe Matias will listen to you. What do *you* think?"

How do you feel when Matias's dad lashes out at him?

2 *THE RESEARCH*

In the most comprehensive gender research review ever conducted, Professor Janet Shibley Hyde and her colleagues analyzed data from neuroscience, endocrinology, and social and developmental psychology (Shibley Hyde et al., 2018). They found that the vast majority of human brains are not binary "male" or "female," but instead include a "mosaic" of features associated with both sexes. They also discovered that hormone differences between the sexes have been overstated and that hormone levels vary depending on each individual person and on the environment.

Moreover, their study casts doubt on long-presumed psychological differences between men and women. For example, across 242 studies representing over a million women and men, these researchers found no gender difference in math ability. And the researchers found that the vast majority of people expressed interest in *combinations* of traditionally masculine and feminine activities. They concluded that "the multidimensional, complex, interactive, and dynamic nature of gender/sex cannot be captured by only two categories."

What does the research say about your uncle's view of gender? With this research in mind, will you challenge or try to change your uncle's views? Why or why not?

3 *YOUR OPPORTUNITY*

How will you respond to your uncle? Before you act, consider the facts of the situation and think about what the research tells you about sex and gender. Also reflect on what you have learned about gender identity (pp. 63–65), gender stereotypes (pp. 71–73), and power distance (p. 83).

Now it's your turn. Write out a response to your uncle.

3. Reflect on the words you use and contemplate how they may impact others who may have different gender identities and beliefs.
4. Finally, recall if and when you have spoken out against unfair, unjust, or restrictive gender stereotypes, expectations, or roles; and look for opportunities in the future to do so. What prompts you to speak up? Is it easier to let your voice be heard in defense of someone else than for yourself?

What Is Culture?

Whether you realize it or not, your culture affects your communication all the time. More than just your race or ethnicity, cultural traits such as age, physical abilities, socioeconomic class, and even your values and beliefs influence how you view yourself as well as how you perceive others.

The TV show *Modern Family* has remained a hit since 2009 because of the way it reveals the California clan's diverse cultural backgrounds. Euro-American patriarch Jay is married to Gloria, who is originally from Colombia. Jay is stepfather to Gloria's son, Manny, and together he and Gloria have a child, Joe. Jay's children from a previous marriage also have diverse families of their own. Interactions between the characters routinely cross lines of age, gender, ethnicity, and sexual orientation—often at the same time. Not

Mitchell Haddad/ABC-TV/Kobal/Shutterstock

Gloria Delgado-Pritchett, played by Sofia Vergara, is a Colombian woman whose cultural norms often conflict with those of her U.S.-born family members. How do you navigate situations in which culture blurs the line of understanding between yourself and others?

surprisingly, miscommunication often ensues. For example, when a box of baby Jesus figurines is mysteriously delivered to their house, Jay realizes the error: he had told Gloria to call his secretary and order a box of baby *cheeses*.

Shows such as *Modern Family* poke lighthearted fun at cultural differences—but they also reveal that individuals from different cultures can overcome their differences and forge meaningful relationships. Indeed, communicating competently with people from other cultures is an essential skill. In the United States, cultural diversity is rapidly increasing: as of July 1, 2015, more than half the nation's children (50.2% of babies born) are nonwhite—including Latino, Asian, African American, and mixed-raced children (Pew Research Center, 2016). Furthermore, over 1 *million* international students now enroll in U.S. colleges annually (Redden, 2017; Saul, 2017). Plus, smartphones, tablets, and other electronic devices provide easy access to people all over the world. This enables us to conduct business and personal relationships on a global level in a way never possible before. As our daily encounters increasingly cross cultural lines, the question arises: What exactly *is* culture?

Culture Defined

In this book, we take a broad and inclusive view of **culture**, defining it as an established, coherent set of beliefs, attitudes, values, and practices shared by a large group of people (Keesing, 1974). Culture includes many types of influences, such as your nationality, ethnicity, religion, gender, gender identity, sexual orientation, physical abilities, and age. But what really makes a culture a "culture" is that it's widely shared. This happens because cultures are *learned*, *communicated*, *layered*, and *lived*.

Culture Is Learned. You learn your cultural beliefs, attitudes, and values from many sources, including your parents, teachers, religious leaders, peers, and the mass media (Gudykunst & Kim, 2003). This process begins at birth, through customs such as choosing a newborn's name, taking part in religious ceremonies, and selecting godparents or other special guardians. As you mature, you learn deeper aspects of your culture, including the history behind certain traditions—for example, why unleavened bread is eaten during the Jewish Passover or why one should fast dawn-to-sunset during the month of Ramadan. You also learn how to participate in rituals—everything from blowing out the candles on a birthday cake to carving pumpkins on Halloween. In most societies, teaching children to understand, respect, and practice their culture is considered an essential part of child rearing.

Culture Is Communicated. Each culture has its own communication practices (Whorf, 1952). When you communicate with someone from a different culture, this is called **intercultural communication**. Sometimes intercultural communication is seamless because similarities exist across cultures that help us transcend our differences. You may share a love of roots rock with someone from a different background, for instance, and your joint passion quickly connects you. Other times, such interaction can be challenging, especially when cultural communication practices diverge in ways we'll discuss later in this chapter.

Culture Is Layered. Many people belong to more than one culture simultaneously. This means they experience multiple "layers" of culture, as various traditions, heritages, and practices are recognized and held to be important. Steve's Uncle Rick, for example, is originally from Canada but is now a U.S. citizen. Rick is passionate about being an American: he played hockey for a U.S. collegiate team, is deeply patriotic, sings the national anthem at ball games, and celebrates the Fourth of July. But every four years, when the Winter Olympics roll around, his Canadian cultural allegiance emerges, and he cheers the Canadians over and above everyone else—especially when it comes to hockey!

Culture Is Lived. Culture affects everything about how you live your life. It influences the neighborhoods you live in; the transportation you use; and the ways you think, dress, talk, worship, and even eat. Its impact runs so deep that it is often taken for granted. At the same time, culture is often a great source of personal pride. Many people consciously live in ways that celebrate their cultural heritage—through such behaviors as wearing a Jewish yarmulke or Muslim hijab, placing a Mexican flag decal on their car, or greeting others with the Thai gesture of the *wai* (hands joined in prayer, head bowed).

Co-Cultures

In any society, there's usually a group of people who have more **power** than everyone else—that is, the ability to influence or control people and events (Donohue & Kolt, 1992). Having more power in a society comes from controlling major societal institutions, such as banks, businesses, the government, and legal and educational systems. According to **co-cultural communication theory**, the people who have more power within a society determine the *dominant culture*, because they decide the prevailing views, values, and traditions of the society (Orbe, 1998). Consider the United States. Throughout its history, wealthy, heterosexual, cisgender, Euro-American males have been in power. When the country was first founded, the only people allowed to vote were land-owning males of European ancestry. Now, more than 200 years later, Euro-American cisgender males still make up the vast majority of the U.S. Congress and Fortune 500 CEOs. As a consequence, what is thought of as "American culture" is tilted toward emphasizing the interests, activities, and accomplishments of these individuals.

Members of a society whose language, values, lifestyle, or physical appearance differ from those of the dominant culture often form what are called **co-cultures**; that is, they have their own cultures that *co-exist* within a dominant cultural sphere (Orbe, 1998). Co-cultures may be based on age, gender, gender identity, sexual orientation, social class, ethnicity, religion, mental and physical ability, and other unifying elements, depending on the society (Orbe, 1998). U.S. residents who are not members of the dominant culture—people of color, women, members of the LGBTQ community, gender fluid and transgender persons, and so forth—exist as distinct co-cultures, with their own political lobbying groups, websites, magazines, and television networks (such as Lifetime, BET, Univision, Telemundo, and Here TV).

When people from underrepresented groups interact with people from the dominant group, *co-cultural communication* occurs (Orbe & Roberts, 2012). Because members of co-cultures are by definition different from the dominant culture, they develop and use communication practices that help them interact with people in the culturally dominant group (Ramirez-Sanchez, 2008). For example, they might do some of the following:

- Respectfully but clearly express their co-cultural identity through appearance, actions, and words
- Use polite language with individuals from the dominant culture
- Suppress reactions when members of the dominant culture make offensive comments
- Try to excel in their professional and personal lives to counteract negative stereotypes about their co-culture
- Adapt their communication to act, look, and talk more like members of the dominant culture

Intersections of Identity

To this point we've talked about culture and co-cultures in general terms. But what do these mean at the *personal* level, in terms of how we orient to and interact with others? And how does this relate to our prior discussion of gender? Each of us is a complex combination of gender, cultural, and co-cultural identities and experiences, and each of us speaks and perceives from a specific point where all these influences meet. We are each the sum total of our overlapping gender and cultural experiences. For example, say that you are Puerto Rican, Catholic, upper-middle-income, heterosexual, and gender-identify as female. Each of these identities and associated experiences individually impacts your sense of self and perception. But it is the *intersection* of *all* of them that creates a unique and particular "you"—and the perceptual kaleidoscope through which you view the world. When you use that kaleidoscope to look outward at others, the challenge is seeing how *their* identities and experiences also influence *their* perception. All too often we focus our view through just one lens, such as religion, ethnicity, gender, or sexual orientation. But the lens we're using may be one that spotlights difference, whereas a shift to other lenses may allow a similarity to float to the foreground, transforming the entire encounter.

Prejudice

As we discussed in Chapter 2 (pages 51–52), *stereotypes* are a way to categorize people into a social group and then evaluate them based on information we have related to this group. Stereotypes play a big part in how we form impressions about others. This is especially true for characteristics such as ethnicity and gender, since they are among the first things we notice when encountering others. When stereotypes reflect rigid attitudes toward groups and their members, they become **prejudice** (Ramasubramanian, 2010).

When we communicate with others, we must consider their complex "kaleidoscope" of intersecting experiences as well as our own.

Timothy Fadek/Corbis News/Getty Images

Because prejudice is rooted in stereotypes, it can vary depending on whether those stereotypes are positive or negative. According to the **Stereotype Content Model** (Fiske, Cuddy, Glick, & Xu, 2002), prejudice centers on two judgments made about others: how warm and friendly they are, and how competent they are. These judgments create two possible kinds of prejudice: *benevolent* and *hostile*.

Benevolent Prejudice. *Benevolent prejudice* occurs when people think of a particular group as inferior but also friendly and competent. For instance, someone judges a group as "primitive," "helpless," and "ignorant" but attributes their "inferiority" to forces beyond their control, such as lack of education, technology, or wealth (Ramasubramanian, 2010). Thus, although the group is thought of negatively, it also triggers feelings of sympathy (Fiske et al., 2002). People engaging in benevolent prejudice might think that members of a group of people are "inferior" but could improve themselves "if only they knew better."

Hostile Prejudice. *Hostile prejudice* happens when people have negative attitudes toward a group of individuals whom they see as unfriendly and incompetent (Fiske et al., 2002). Someone demonstrating hostile prejudice might see the group's supposed incompetence as intrinsic to the people: "They're naturally lazy," "They're all crazy zealots," or "They're stupid and violent." People exhibiting hostile prejudice often also believe that the group has received many opportunities to improve ("They've been given so much") but that their innate limitations hold them back ("They've done nothing but waste every break that's been given to them").

Overcoming Prejudice. Prejudice, no matter what form, is destructive and unethical. Benevolent prejudice leads to condescending and disrespectful communication. Hostile prejudice is the root of every exclusionary "-ism": racism, sexism, heterosexism, ageism, classism, ableism, and so on, as displayed in Table 3.2.

The root of prejudice is deeply held negative beliefs about particular groups (Ramasubramanian, 2010). If you think you have prejudiced beliefs, your communication skills can help you confront them and permanently give them up. Use the perception-checking and empathy guidelines discussed in Chapter 2 (pp. 53–55) to help you evaluate and change your own beliefs. Also, learn about the cultures and co-cultural groups you have prejudiced beliefs about. Initiate encounters with individuals who have different cultural and gender identities than yours, and listen actively to what they have to say. This will ease the uncertainty and anxiety you may feel around others who are culturally different from you (Berger & Calabrese, 1975). Finally, be open to new people and experiences; this can result in quality relationships that break down prejudicial barriers.

On the other hand, if you've been on the receiving end of prejudice, try not to generalize your experience with that one person (or persons) to all members of the same group. Just because someone of a certain age, gender, ethnicity, religion, or cultural group behaves badly doesn't mean that *all* members of that group do. One of the bitter ironies of prejudice is that it often triggers a reaction of prejudice in the people who have been unfairly treated. This is not to excuse the prejudice or poor communication of others, but to help you avoid adding to the vicious cycle of prejudicial communication.

TABLE 3.2

COMMON FORMS OF HOSTILE PREJUDICE

Racism: Prejudice, discrimination, or stereotyping that unfairly targets people based on their ethnicity or ancestry

Sexism: Prejudice, discrimination, or stereotyping that unfairly targets people based on their sex or gender

Heterosexism: Prejudice, discrimination, or stereotyping against nonheterosexual people based on the premise that heterosexual relationships are superior

Classism: Prejudice, discrimination, or stereotyping that unfairly targets people based on their socioeconomic status

Ageism: Prejudice, discrimination, or stereotyping that unfairly targets people based on their age

Ableism: Prejudice, discrimination, or stereotyping that unfairly targets people based on their physical or mental abilities

Culture and Communication

Your cultural background differs from that of other people in many ways. One way those differences are expressed is through your communication—such as how you deal with power structures and share emotions. Understanding and adapting to such factors will help you communicate more competently.

In chef Eddie Huang's best-selling memoir *Fresh Off the Boat* (the basis for the hit TV series), he recalls the cultural differences he experienced during his childhood. For instance, the first time he saw macaroni and cheese at his friend Jeff's house, Huang mistook the dish for pig intestines. Although Jeff thought the error was funny, Huang viewed it as formative: "Jeff got a taste of macaroni and cheese from *my* eyes, discovering how it felt to be seen as exotic." But the memory that stands out most vividly for Huang is an incident on his first day at a new school. He was standing in the lunch line when the only other student of color at the school called him a racial epithet, pushed him to the ground, and declared "*You're* at the bottom now!" Huang considers the encounter profound, in how it underscored the pervasiveness of cultural difference and the prejudice that often goes with it. At the same time, Huang notes that difference is something we *all* know—and, furthermore, that difference can be a *positive* thing. "The feeling of being different is universal," he says. "We've been fixated way too long on universality and monoculture. It's time to embrace difference and speak about it with singularity."

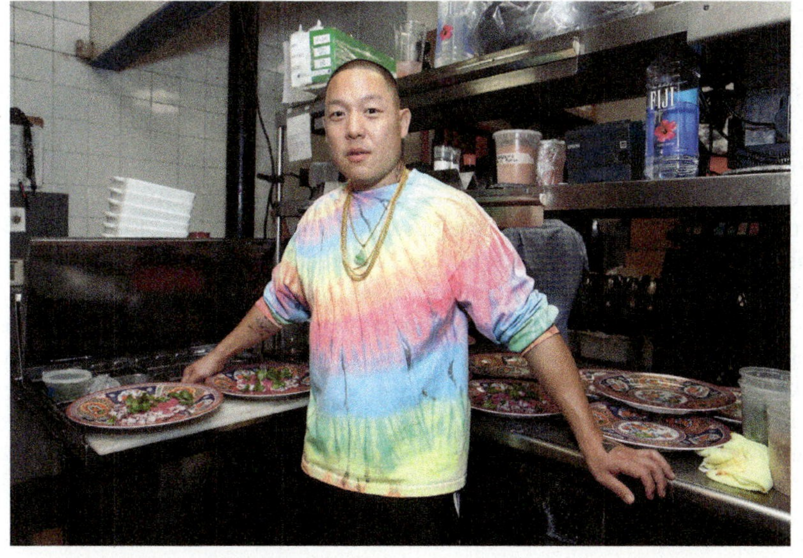

AP Images/Blair Raughley/Invision for Warner Bros. Home Entertainment

Celebrity chef, restaurateur, and *Fresh Off the Boat* author Eddie Huang was born in the United States to Taiwanese parents. Growing up, he sometimes struggled to bridge the cultural differences between his family and his peers. Can you recall a time where you had trouble connecting with someone who seemed very different from you? How did you communicate in that situation?

Dimensions of Difference

As Eddie Huang's book and its TV adaptation illustrate, cultural differences are universally experienced, and these differences and the perceptions associated with them can be profound. Five of the most commonly experienced cultural dimensions are individualism versus collectivism, high and low context, uncertainty avoidance, emotion displays, and power distance.

Although these cultural dimensions traditionally have been thought of as distinguishing between people from different cultures, keep in mind that people *within* particular cultures vary along these dimensions as well. Consequently, as we discuss these dimensions, think about *you* and how your communication practices align with what is being discussed. In particular, consider where you exist on all five dimensions—and the cultural forces that lead you to think and communicate in the ways that make you unique (see Figure 3.1).

Individualistic vs Collectivistic Cultures. In **individualistic cultures**, people tend to value independence and personal achievement. Members of these cultures are encouraged to focus on themselves and their immediate family (Hofstede, 2001), and individual achievement is praised as the highest good (Waterman, 1984). Individualistic countries include the United States, Canada, New Zealand, and Sweden (Hofstede, 2001).

By contrast, in **collectivistic cultures** people emphasize group identity ("we" rather than "me"), interpersonal harmony, and the well-being of ingroups (Park & Guan, 2006). If you were raised in a collectivistic culture, you were probably taught that it's important to belong to groups, or "collectives," that look after you in exchange for your loyalty. In collectivistic cultures, people emphasize the goals, needs, and views of groups over those of individuals and define the highest good as cooperation with others rather than individual achievement. Collectivistic countries include Guatemala, Pakistan, Taiwan, and Japan (Hofstede, 2001).

High and Low Context. Cultures also can be described as *high* or *low context.* In **high-context cultures**, such as in China, Korea, and Japan, people use relatively vague and ambiguous language and even silence to convey important meanings. People in such cultures often talk indirectly (using hints or suggestions) because they presume that members of their ingroup will know what they're trying to say. As a result, they don't feel a need to provide a lot of explicit information.

In **low-context cultures**, people tend *not* to presume that others share their beliefs, attitudes, and values. Thus, they strive to be informative, clear, and direct in their communication (E. T. Hall & Hall, 1987). Many low-context cultures are also individualistic; as a result, people openly express their views and try to persuade others to accept them (E. T. Hall, 1976, 1997a). Within such cultures, which include Germany, Scandinavia, Canada, and the

FIGURE 3.1

YOUR CULTURAL DIMENSIONS

Consider the unique intersection between these five cultural dimensions that defines you and your communication practices. Do you consider some of these dimensions more important to you than others? Are there any other factors that you consider important to your culture?

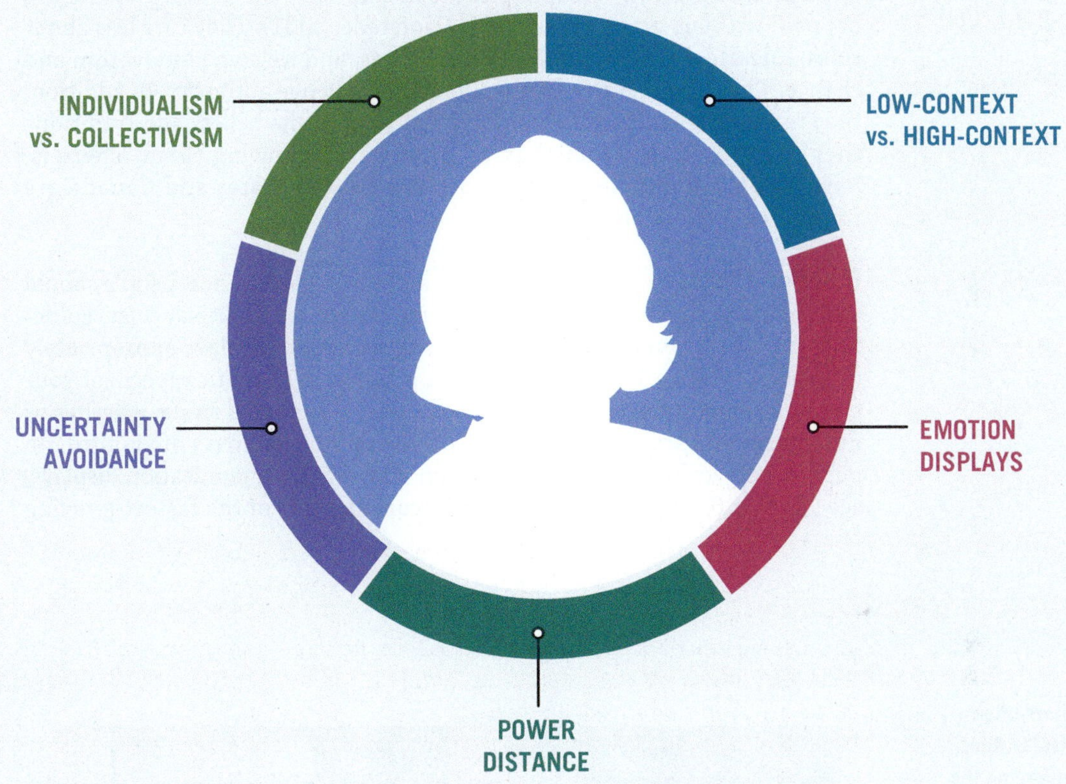

United States, people work to make important information obvious, rather than hinting or implying.

Uncertainty Avoidance. Cultures vary in how much they tolerate and accept unpredictability, known as **uncertainty avoidance**. As scholar Geert Hofstede explains, "The fundamental issue here is how a society deals with the fact that the future can never be known: should we try to control the future or just let it happen?" (Hofstede, 2009a). In *high-uncertainty-avoidance cultures* (such as Mexico, South Korea, Japan, and Greece), people place a lot of value on control. They want structure in their organizations, institutions, relationships, and everyday lives (Hofstede, 2001). Children raised in such cultures are taught to believe in cultural traditions and practices without questioning them.

In *low-uncertainty-avoidance cultures* (such as Jamaica, Denmark, Sweden, and Ireland), people put more emphasis on "letting the future happen" without trying to control it (Hofstede, 2001). They care less about rules, tolerate diverse viewpoints and beliefs, and welcome innovation and change. They also feel free to question and challenge authority. In addition, they teach their children to think critically about the beliefs and traditions they're exposed to rather than automatically following them. There is, however, some middle ground: both the United States and Canada are considered moderately uncertainty avoidant.

Emotion Displays. In all cultures, norms exist regarding how people should and shouldn't express emotion. These norms are called **display rules**: guidelines for when, where, and how to manage emotion displays appropriately (Ekman & Friesen, 1975). Display rules govern very specific aspects of your *nonverbal communication*, such as how broadly you should smile, whether or not you should scowl when angry, and the appropriateness of shouting in public when you're excited. (For more on nonverbal communication displays, see Chapter 6, page 143.) For example, consider two of the fastest-growing

Universal Pictures/Photofest

Comedy writers often play with display rules, purposely enlarging the characters' reactions or going against the norm to create humor. The outlandish expressions and antics from Amy Schumer and Bill Hader in *Trainwreck* are an example. When it comes to display rules, where is the line between funny and wrong?

ethnic groups in the United States: Mexican Americans and Chinese Americans (Zong, Batalova, & Hallock, 2018). In traditional Chinese culture, people prioritize emotional control and moderation; intense emotions are considered dangerous and are even thought to cause illness (Wu & Tseng, 1985). Meanwhile, in traditional Mexican culture, people openly express emotion, even more so than those in Euro-American culture (Soto et al., 2005). For people of Mexican descent, the experience, expression, and deep discussion of emotions provide some of life's greatest rewards and satisfactions.

It's important to be aware of such differences when communicating with others. An emotional expression—such as a loud shout of intense joy—might be considered shocking and inappropriate in some cultures but perfectly normal in others. At the same time, don't presume that all people from the same culture necessarily share the same expectations. As much as possible, adjust your expressions of emotion to match the style of the individuals with whom you're interacting.

Power Distance. The degree to which people in a particular culture view the unequal distribution of power as acceptable is known as **power distance** (Hofstede, 1991, 2001). In *high-power-distance cultures*, it's considered normal and even desirable for people of different social and professional status to have different levels of power (Ting-Toomey, 2005). In such cultures, people give privileged treatment and extreme respect to those in high-status positions (Ting-Toomey, 1999). They also expect individuals of lesser status to behave humbly, especially around people of higher status, who are expected to act superior.

In *low-power-distance cultures*, people in high-status positions try to minimize the differences between themselves and lower-status persons by interacting with them in informal ways and treating them as equals (Oetzel et al., 2001). For instance, a high-level marketing executive might chat with the cleaning service workers in her office and invite them to join her for a coffee break.

Power distance influences how people communicate in close relationships, especially families. In traditional Mexican culture, for instance, the value of *respeto* emphasizes power distance between younger people and their elders (Delgado-Gaitan, 1993). As part of *respeto*, children are expected to defer to elders' authority and to avoid openly disagreeing with them. In contrast, many Euro-Americans believe that once children reach adulthood, power in family relationships should be balanced, with children and their elders treating one another as equals (Kagawa & McCornack, 2004).

Communication Accommodation

Given the significant real-world differences that exist between people with different cultural backgrounds, how can you better bridge cultural divides when communicating with those from different cultures? According to **communication accommodation theory** (Giles, Coupland, & Coupland, 1991), one of the most important things you can do is adapt to other people's communication preferences (Bianconi, 2002). During interactions, notice how long a turn people take when speaking, how quickly they speak, how direct they are, and how much they appear to want to talk compared to you. You may also need to learn and practice cultural norms for nonverbal behaviors, including eye contact, head touching, and handshaking. Research documents that people who use communication accommodation are perceived as more competent communicators (Coupland, Giles, & Wiemann, 1991; Giles, Coupland, & Coupland, 1991).

You can even do this during public presentations. For example, find out about your listeners' preferences during your audience analysis, and try to adapt your communication accordingly while developing your speech. If you'll be speaking to an audience whose first language is not English, avoid slang; your listeners may not understand it. At the same time, avoid imitating other people's dialects, accents, or word choices. Most people consider such imitation inappropriate and insulting.

Creating Intercultural Competence

Even when you understand what culture is, how co-cultures work, and the ways culture influences communication, it can still be difficult to communicate with people from different cultural backgrounds. To work toward competence, be mindful of the differences discussed so far, actively seek to understand other cultures, and adapt your communication.

When you consider all that we have covered in this chapter, two things are readily apparent. First, in a world that is increasingly diversifying, we all need to be able to competently communicate with others who are different from ourselves. Second, each of us—and everyone with whom we interact—exists at an intersection of various identities, making them (and us) complex.

But overlaying all of this lies a fundamental fact: human beings have a deep and abiding tendency to prefer people who seem similar to themselves (ingroupers) over and above people whom they perceive as different (outgroupers). We *all* make judgments regarding outgroupers that lead us to perceive them as distant, different, and sometimes even inferior. At the same time, we also all have the capacity to be liberated from these perceptions and prejudices and to form lasting bonds with people who are different from ourselves. The gateway to such connections is **intercultural competence**: the ability to communicate appropriately, effectively, and ethically with people from diverse backgrounds. How can you achieve intercultural competence? You can start by routinely striving to practice *world-mindedness* and *attributional complexity*.

World-Mindedness

When you possess **world-mindedness**, you demonstrate acceptance and respect toward beliefs, values, and customs that are different from your own

(Hammer, Bennett, & Wiseman, 2003). You can practice world-mindedness in three ways. First, accept others' expression of their gender, culture, and/or co-culture as a natural element in their communication, just as your communication reflects your identities and background (Chen & Starosta, 2005). Second, avoid any temptation to judge others' beliefs, attitudes, and values as "better" or "worse" than your own. Third, treat all people with respect.

This can be especially challenging when the other person's beliefs, attitudes, and values conflict with your own. But practicing world-mindedness means more than just tolerating differences you find perplexing or problematic. Instead, treat all people with respect by being kind and courteous in your communication. You can also preserve others' personal dignity by actively listening to and asking questions about viewpoints that may differ from yours.

World-mindedness is the opposite of **ethnocentrism**, the belief that one's own cultural beliefs, attitudes, values, and practices are superior to those of others. Ethnocentrism is not the same thing as pride in your cultural heritage or patriotism. You can be culturally proud or nationally patriotic and not be ethnocentric. Instead, ethnocentrism is a *comparative evaluation*. Ethnocentric people view their own culture or co-culture as the standard against which all other cultures should be judged, and they often have contempt for other cultures (Neuliep & McCroskey, 1997; Sumner, 1906). Consequently, such people tend to see their own communication as competent and that of people from other cultures as incompetent.

Attributional Complexity

When you practice **attributional complexity**, you acknowledge that other people's behaviors have complex causes. To develop this ability, observe others' behavior and analyze the various forces influencing it. For example, rather than deciding that a classmate's reserved demeanor or limited eye contact means she's unfriendly, consider the possibility that these behaviors might reflect cultural differences in communication.

Also, learn as much as you can about different cultures and co-cultures, so you can better understand people's communication styles and preferences. Experiencing other cultures through observation, travel, or interaction is a great way to sharpen your intercultural communication competence (Arasaratnam, 2006).

In addition, routinely use *perception-checking* to avoid attributional errors, and regularly demonstrate *empathy* to identify with others. In situations in which the cultural gaps between you and others seem wide, try to see things from their perspectives, and consider the motivations behind their communication. Avoid making statements such as, "I know that people like you act this way because you think that . . ."; you'll only come across as presumptuous. Instead, examine how people from diverse backgrounds make decisions, and compare their approaches to yours. Finally, ask others to explain the reasons for their behavior, and then accept and validate their explanations ("That makes sense to me") rather than challenging them.

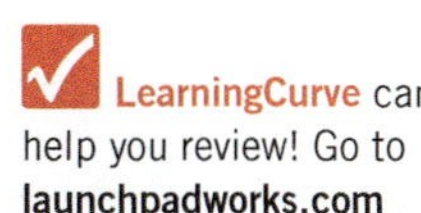

ADAPTING TO CULTURAL DIFFERENCES

The following scenario will enhance your ability to understand and apply competent communication in a group setting. Visit LaunchPad at launchpadworks.com to get the full experience with video.

As you watch the first video, recall what you've learned about communicating with people from diverse cultures, and then complete the **Your Turn** prompts. Finally, watch the **Take Two!** video to explore how this scenario could have gone differently.

1 THE PROBLEM

Paul is assigned to a group project with several classmates who come from collectivistic cultures. The group chooses one of them, Lily, as group leader. At your first meeting, Lily starts by suggesting a topic for the project. All the other group members immediately agree. This annoys Paul, who has a different idea that he was excited about and wanted the group to pursue—but he also doesn't want to alienate the other group members. Lily notices his hesitation and says, "Paul, you're quiet. What do you think?"

"I like the idea for the project. It's smart, and there's a general consensus, so I want to do what the group wants to do."

"Paul, don't let my position as group leader hold you back from expressing your opinion. Tell me: what do you really think about my idea?"

2 YOUR TURN

Observations. Reflect on how Paul and Lily communicated in this scenario by answering the following questions:

1. Which character do you identify with more in this situation? How would you feel if you were in his or her situation?
2. Do you think that both characters are communicating competently? Why or why not?

Discussion. In class or with a partner, share your thoughts about the interaction between Paul and Lily and work to answer the following questions:

1. Can you understand both perspectives?
2. What could Lily and Paul have done differently?

Conclusion. Choose one person in the scenario to offer your advice to. Based on your analysis, what advice would you give him or her to improve his or her communication competence in this scenario?

3 TAKE TWO!

What if things had gone differently? Watch the **Take Two!** video to see one possible example of how the conversation might have gone if Lily and/or Paul had communicated differently. As you watch the video, consider where the dialog reflects communication competence. After watching the video, answer the questions below:

1. Did Lily and/or Paul take advantage of opportunities that they missed in the first scenario? Which ones?
2. Do you think Paul and Lily communicated more competently or less competently in this version than in the original scenario? Why? Please explain your answer.

CHAPTER 3 REVIEW

CHAPTER RECAP

- **Gender** encompasses all of the social, psychological, and behavioral characteristics associated with a person's biological sex. Gender is distinct from both **sex**—a person's biological and anatomical characteristics assigned at birth—and **gender identity**, which is a person's deeply felt inner sense of themselves.
- Each individual undergoes a lifelong process of **gender socialization**, in which they learn the **gender roles** expected of them.
- Men and women have few real differences in verbal communication, but they do have consistent differences in nonverbal communication as a result of gender socialization.
- A **culture** is a set of widely shared beliefs, attitudes, values, and practices; cultures are learned, communicated, layered, and lived. In most societies, **co-cultures** exist alongside a *dominant culture.*
- When we use stereotypes to make overly broad, uninformed, and inaccurate judgments about groups and their members, we engage in **prejudice**.
- You can strengthen your **intercultural competence** through communication accommodation, **world-mindedness**, and **attributional complexity**.

LaunchPad for *Choices & Connections* offers unique video scenarios and encourages self-assessment through adaptive quizzing. Go to **launchpadworks.com** to get access.

 LearningCurve adaptive quizzes

 Advance the Conversation video scenarios

 Video clips that illustrate key concepts

KEY TERMS

Gender polarization, p. 62
Gender continuum, p. 62
Gender fluid, p. 63
Sex, p. 63
Gender identity, p. 64
Transgender, p. 64
Cisgender, p. 64
Gender, p. 65
Gender socialization, p. 65
Gender roles, p. 67
Culture, p. 74
Intercultural communication, p. 74
Power, p. 75
Co-cultural communication theory, p. 75
Co-culture, p. 75
Prejudice, p. 77
Stereotype Content Model, p. 77
Individualistic culture, p. 80
Collectivistic culture, p. 80
High-context culture, p. 80
Low-context culture, p. 80
Uncertainty avoidance, p. 81
Display rules, p. 82
Power distance, p. 83
Communication accommodation theory, p. 83
Intercultural competence, p. 84
World-mindedness, p. 84
Ethnocentrism, p. 85
Attributional complexity, p. 85

POP QUIZ

Looking for more review questions? LearningCurve can help you master key concepts from this chapter. Go to **launchpadworks.com**

1. What is the term for a person's anatomical, biological distinctions, including external genitalia, internal reproductive organs, hormones, and chromosomes?

   a. gender
   b. sex
   c. gender identity
   d. gender expression

2. The process by which children and teens learn about cultural expectations for their gender is known as gender

   a. roles.
   b. polarization.
   c. fluidity.
   d. socialization.

3. According to co-cultural communication theory, the *dominant culture* within any society is determined by the people with the most

   a. ethnocentrism.
   b. world-mindedness.
   c. prejudice.
   d. power.

4. In this type of culture, people tend not to presume that others share their beliefs, attitudes, and values; thus, they strive to be informative, clear, and direct in their communication.

   a. individualistic culture
   b. low-context culture
   c. high-context culture
   d. collectivistic culture

5. Which of the following is *not* a way to achieve intercultural competence?

   a. practicing attributional complexity
   b. employing benevolent prejudice
   c. using communication accommodation
   d. considering cultural influences on communication

ACTIVITIES

For more activities, visit LaunchPad for *Choices & Connections* at **launchpadworks.com**

1 Exploring Cultural Identity

We all exist as multiple layers of cultural influences—including gender, age, class, nationality, ethnicity, sexual orientation, and religion. To better understand how your varied gender, cultural, and co-cultural identities impact your communication, list what you think are your most important identities (e.g., "I'm an upper-middle-class, cisgender, Evangelical, Latina woman from the Southwest United States"). Then, write a brief comment (no more than one to two sentences for each cultural marker) explaining how you think each identity affects your communication with others and the ways in which others perceive you—both positively and negatively.

2 Gender and Culture in the Media

Many TV shows and movies base their jokes on stereotypical communication problems between men and women or between people from different cultures. For example, think about how shows like *Fresh Off the Boat* or movies like *Trainwreck* get a lot of their laughs. With a partner, find an example from the media that uses gender and communication and/or culture and communication in this way. Discuss how the example does or does not reflect principles discussed in this chapter. How could the media better represent communication between people with different gender identities and between people from different cultures?

4

Mediated Communication

Sitting at an Arizona Diamondback baseball game, the Alpha Chi Omega sorority sisters were doing something commonplace in this day and age: holding their phones at arm's length, taking selfies while posing with hotdogs and churros. But this ordinary act drew extraordinary interest from the sportscasters commentating on the game. For almost two minutes, the television cameras switched between the selfie-shooting women and the play on the field. And when the focus was on the women, the broadcasters made mocking remarks, such as:[1]

"Do you have to make faces when you take selfies?"

"That's the best one of the 300 pictures I've taken of myself today."

"Can we do an intervention?"

The video footage quickly went viral, prompting tweets, blog postings, and national news coverage. Opinions about the selfie session were varied. Many social media postings reflected harsh stereotypes, often rooted in sexist attitudes—suggesting, for instance, that the women were vain and self-centered, and didn't appreciate the game of baseball.

But they also had a host of defenders. One sports editor, Tanya Bondurant (2015), directly chastised the *sportscasters* for engaging in selfie-shaming, writing:

> Welcome to 2015, gentlemen. Everyone is on their phone all the time. Baseball is a game with a lot of breaks and using that downtime to capture a fun moment with your friends shouldn't make you the topic of a two-minute call-out. It just makes you a human in the 21st century.

Indeed, posting selfies has become a common practice for maintaining an online presence. In 2019, the hashtags #me and #selfie accompanied nearly 400 million Instagram photo postings. Celebrities and sports figures fill their social media feeds with selfies as a way of letting fans into their lives. Actor James Franco (2013) believes selfies are meaningful "tools of communication." He goes on to observe:

> I am actually turned off when I look at an account and don't see any selfies, because I want to know whom I'm dealing with. In our age of social networking, the selfie is the new way to look someone right in the eye and say, "Hello, this is me."

Although selfies are an integral part of how we communicate online, the act of taking and posting selfies influences perceptions others may form of us and our messages. Just as the Arizona Diamondbacks' broadcasters misperceived the young women at the game, we, too, can be misunderstood. Communicating through text messages, tweets, video chat, and the many other ways available to connect with others online presents unique challenges.

In the wake of the controversy, Alpha Chi Omega turned what could have been an enduring embarrassment into a charitable triumph. When the Diamondbacks offered the sorority free tickets to a future game, they politely declined. Instead, they asked that the tickets be donated to a local nonprofit supporting victims of domestic violence. They were then invited to appear on *The Ellen DeGeneres Show*, where Ellen surprised the women with a $10,000 donation to support their charity work.

---

[1]Content that follows adapted from White and Hwang (2015).

Oleksii Sidorov/Shutterstock

LearningCurve can help you review! Go to **launchpadworks.com**

We won't all go viral or be invited onto *The Ellen DeGeneres Show* for shooting selfies with friends at a game. But like the women of Alpha Chi Omega, we live our lives immersed in technology, and the devices we use play a major role in how we communicate with others. Understanding how various media affect your communication will help you communicate more competently. In this chapter, you'll learn:

- The functions and characteristics of mediated communication
- Ways to present your identity through mediated communication
- The challenges of using mediated communication
- Guidelines for competently using mediated communication

What Is Mediated Communication?

Technology is so prevalent in our lives, it is easy not to think about it much. Phone, laptop, app—what does it matter? Indeed, technology helps with everything from family chats to late-night study sessions, but it also has unique considerations of its own. For starters, technology changes your communication, including what kind of feedback you receive and how you process it.

Think about all the ways you communicate each day. How much do you talk to other people in person or on the phone? How many texts and tweets do you send? How often do you check in or post selfies and comments to social networking sites? Chances are, you do most of your communicating through communication technologies—texting, Instagram, Snapchat, Twitter, FaceTime, WhatsApp, or any of the hundreds of sites, apps, and tools that become available each day (and that often disappear just as quickly!).

Many of your waking hours are likely spent on the phone and computer—often at the same time. When you use these technologies to talk, text, post, tweet, email, and chat, you engage in **mediated communication**: communication with others that is separated, or "mediated," by some type of technological device.

Types of Mediated Communication

The phrase *mediated communication* may make you think about "the media"—that is, online news and entertainment sites, video games, television channels, movies, radio stations, newspapers, and magazines. These are examples of **mass media**: mediated communication vehicles that involve the sending of messages from content creators to huge, relatively anonymous audiences (Chaffee & Metzger, 2001). The content in such media is created for public consumption and is mostly one-directional; that is, you

USING MEDIATED COMMUNICATION

Every text, tweet, post, video, pin, or note you send through mediated channels (whether personal, professional, or for fun) is as much an act of communication as the words you use in a face-to-face conversation. How much do you consider the functions and characteristics of your messages before sending them?

(Clockwise from top left) Csondy/iStock/Getty Images; Take A Pix Media/AGE Fotostock; PYMCA/Universal Images Group/Getty Images

don't directly interact with the content creator while reading or watching this content.

Although mass media are an important area of research for communication scholars, this chapter focuses on **social media**, which enable communicators to directly send and receive messages in real time or across time intervals to manage their personal and professional relationships. At work, for instance, most interactions take place over email, texts, or phone calls. Many businesses use Skype (or other videoconferencing systems) to conduct employment interviews. Daily communication with friends, family, and romantic partners happens through social media—dropping parents a quick "Hi" by text message or catching up with friends through Snapchat or video call. As a student, you might participate in online discussion groups and make online presentations for classes. For an overview of the differences between mass media and social media, see Table 4.1.

TABLE 4 .1

DIFFERENCES BETWEEN MASS MEDIA & SOCIAL MEDIA[2]

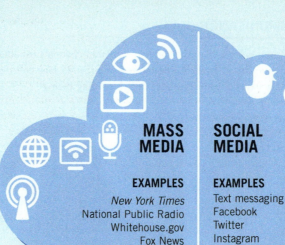

MASS MEDIA	SOCIAL MEDIA
EXAMPLES	**EXAMPLES**
New York Times National Public Radio Whitehouse.gov Fox News	Text messaging Facebook Twitter Instagram
COMMUNICATION FLOW	**COMMUNICATION FLOW**
One-way	Two-way
PURPOSE	**PURPOSE**
Information (news) Entertainment Advertising Public service	Information Self-presentation Relationship building Managing work tasks Alleviating boredom
FAMILIARITY WITH THE AUDIENCE	**FAMILIARITY WITH THE AUDIENCE**
Mostly unknown	Mostly known
CONTENT CONTROL	**CONTENT CONTROL**
Source provider	Senders and receivers
TYPE OF FEEDBACK	**TYPE OF FEEDBACK**
Viewer ratings and comments, page view counts	Immediate and/or delayed responses or replies

[2]Information from Chaffee & Metzger (2001).

VLADGRIN/Shutterstock

Functions of Mediated Communication

Even though the specific platforms, sites, and apps you use to communicate via social media change constantly, the goals they serve are the same as those discussed previously in Chapter 1:

- *Instrumental goals* are the practical objectives you want to achieve or tasks you want to accomplish. This includes using social media to find information, coordinate schedules, and confirm reservations. For example, college students find social media to be the easiest way to get information about upcoming social events (Quan-Haase & Young, 2010).

- *Relationship goals* include how you build, maintain, or terminate bonds with others. This is a popular way to use social media, allowing you to get in touch with people you haven't spoken to in a while, share your own news, and even block people you aren't close to anymore. Such tools are often at the center of our social lives. For instance, young adults use Snapchat to communicate in highly personal ways in their important relationships (Vaterlaus, Barnett, Roche, & Young, 2016).
- *Self-presentation goals* involve presenting yourself in certain ways so that others view you as you want them to. Through photos, updates, posts, and comments, you create a public self. As Chapter 2 discusses, a *public self* is the self you present to others (Fenigstein, Scheier, & Buss, 1975). In this chapter, we'll explore how you use *online self-presentation* to create that self.

In addition to fulfilling such goals, mediated communication serves two other important functions:

- *Participating in professional and public communities* means you can engage with people outside your intimate networks of family and friends. For example, you could use emails or tweets to express your concerns about proposed new laws to government officials. Or you could deliver a virtual presentation to work team members at offsite locations. (We'll discuss more about delivering speeches online in Chapter 15.) Using social media in a community-based fashion includes heightening public awareness of important causes, a practice known as **hashtag activism**. One notable example is #MeToo, which calls public attention to sexual harassment and sexual assault at work.
- *Alleviating boredom* through social media is a common experience (Quan-Haase & Young, 2010). People often seamlessly integrate mediated communication into the less stimulating moments of their lives. You might text with coworkers during slow work shifts ("Are you as bored as I am?") or Snapchat with friends when you need a break from studying.

Characteristics of Mediated Communication

Since mediated communication serves different functions, you have choices in the types of media you use to communicate with others. Imagine that you've just received a great job offer. Would you share the good news with your roommate in person or through a text message? In either format, your message is essentially the same: "I got the job!" But the characteristics of your communication—including how you interact with your roommate, the nonverbal cues exchanged, and how long your message endures—will differ depending on the media device or app you choose.

Synchronous versus Asynchronous Communication. When you talk with someone face-to-face, you're engaged in **synchronous communication**: a back-and-forth exchange of messages that occurs in real time. Some media devices enable synchronous communication, including phone conversations, instant messages, and videoconferences. By contrast, in **asynchronous communication**, time lapses exist between messages. When you use email, send a text message, or post to a social media site, a delay occurs before a response arrives or you may get no response at all.

Synchronous communication is best used when you're communicating difficult or complicated messages. For example, you may want to use the phone or video chat to tell your family that you won't be coming home for the holidays as planned. If you text them with the news, they may think you're insensitive or incompetent ("What kind of daughter cancels holiday plans through a text?"). However, synchronous communication requires all the communicators to be available at the same time. That's not always possible, especially when people live in different time zones or have conflicting work or life schedules. In these situations, asynchronous communication may be your only choice for sending and receiving messages. It is also appropriate for non-urgent, quick, and simple messages, such as letting a friend know you're running a few minutes late for a lunch date.

Restriction of Nonverbal Information. Communicating face-to-face with others provides immediate access to *nonverbal* cues, such as facial expressions and tone of voice, which help you understand other people's thoughts and feelings. When your roommate responds with a smile and a high-five after you tell her you got a new job, she clearly feels happy for you. As Chapter 6 explains, nonverbal behaviors are undeniably an important part of your communication with others.

In mediated communication—especially those forms that involve text only—you get little or no nonverbal information. According to the **cues-filtered-out model**, in this type of communication, many of the cues vital for making sense of messages are not available; they are "filtered out" (Culnan & Markus, 1987). This makes mediated communication more difficult to understand than face-to-face communication. If you're emailing or texting with someone, it's almost impossible to tell if he or she is being sarcastic or sincere. In one study, 27 percent of respondents agreed that email is likely to result in miscommunication of the senders' intended meaning, and almost 54 percent agreed that it's relatively easy to misinterpret an email message (Rainey, 2000). To help minimize such confusion, communicators use acronyms (LOL, SMH) or emoji to convey their intent more clearly. But even these symbols are a poor substitute for the nonverbal cues available when communicating face-to-face.

The fact that nonverbal information is restricted during most mediated communication doesn't necessarily mean that the interaction is less important or personal. According to **social information processing theory** (Walther,

To help mitigate the cues-filtered-out model, a common practice is to use emoticons or emoji (like the ones shown here) to provide some nonverbal cues about the message's intent. In what types of scenarios do you use such images to clarify the meaning of your text messages?

1992), people communicating through social media compensate for the lack of nonverbal cues by taking more care when choosing their words. The result is that mediated communication, though "cue filtered," can be just as personal as face-to-face interaction (Walther & Parks, 2002).

Message Life Span. A basic principle of communication is that there are no "take-backs" or do-overs. Everything you say becomes part of the permanent record of your relationship with others. So when you say something rude to your parents or insert a tasteless joke into a speech, you can't turn back time and erase your error.

This is especially true in mediated communication. Every time you send a digital message (text, email, tweet, video, or post), it stays in your account *and* in the accounts of those who received it. It also stays in the servers of companies hosting the accounts. Deleting a text, an email, a post, or the entire account doesn't make the information go away. Anyone with the right access can find it. Even apps that promote disappearing messages or pictures (like Snapchat) can be easily saved with a little know-how.

Digital messages thus have a long life span and are easily searchable, retrievable, and replicable (boyd, 2007). Why does this matter? One reason is because many employers check job applicants' social media profiles to get a sense of what the applicant is really like. One poll of more than 2,000 hiring managers and human resource professionals across different industries revealed that over 70 percent of them searched applicants' social media presence as part of the hiring process (CareerBuilder, 2017). Be mindful when sending text messages and emails or posting online, because you're creating an enduring record of your communication that is easy to find and to share.

Self-Presentation and Mediated Communication

Take a moment to think about how you're dressed today. Are you wearing casual clothes or something more professional? You select your clothing to make a specific impression, based on what you'll be doing and who you'll be seeing. Likewise, when you select photos, post updates, and share information online, you create an impression that influences how others see you.

If you have a social media account, look at your profile and feed: the photos, status updates, links you've posted, and your list of friends or followers. What does all this say about you? Are you fun and outgoing? A hard partier? Deeply philosophical? A humanitarian? A shopaholic? In a study of almost 400 Facebook profiles, researchers found that 92 percent of users posted personal photographs, 83 percent made their wall public, and 55 percent indicated their sexual orientation (Nosko, Wood, & Molema, 2010). You could learn a lot about someone from that information alone!

DOUBLE TAKE

ONLINE FACE & SELF-PRESENTATION

Imagine you saw the images below posted to two new acquaintances' Instagram pages. Based on the photos, what would you perceive about the online face each is presenting? Why?

ED JONES/AFP/Getty Images

Ross Gilmore/Redferns/Getty Images

Whenever you use social media, you make decisions about how you want to present your self. However, the particular social media platform you use may influence how closely you pay attention to your *self-presentation goals* (DeVito, Birnholtz, & Hancock, 2017). For example, you may be less thoughtful about your self-presentation when communicating with friends on Snapchat, and you might pay closer attention when you edit and post a selfie of your recent vacation on Instagram.

Creating Your Online Face

Scholars studying mediated communication suggest that three elements largely determine your online face: your posted content, your usernames, and your friends and professional connections.

Posted Content. Everything you post online communicates information about who you are and how you wish to be seen. This is particularly true when you use *asynchronous* mediated communication, such as an Instagram post, which provides you the opportunity to be much more selective in how you present yourself and your messages (Walther, 2007). A status update like, "Hiked Camelback in 1 hr. 38 min.—gonna beat my record next week!" or a tweet that reads, "$1 oysters until 7 pm at Harpers—come hang with the gang!" communicates powerful messages about your tastes, interests, and social identity (you're an avid hiker; you're a foodie). The same goes for posting, sharing, and tagging photographs and videos.

Online faces are far from objective, however. People are motivated to post content that highlights their positive characteristics such as warmth, friendliness, and extraversion (Vazire & Gosling, 2004). Before posting selfies, people will commonly crop the photo or use filters in order to present themselves in the most positive light possible. One study found that women put more time than men do into editing their selfies before posting (Fox & Vendemia, 2016). Because women often face societal pressures to place a high value on their physical appearance, the researchers posited that the difference may be motivated by concerns about body image or a desire to earn "likes." Interestingly, when other women view a selfie that they believe is edited, they tend to judge the woman who posted the edited selfie to be dishonest (Ohio State University, 2018). This finding suggests that people view self-generated posts—like selfies and profile descriptions—with doubt, unless the posts are supported by what other people say about you online.

Research shows that when friends, family members, coworkers, or romantic partners post information about you, their content shapes others' perceptions of you even more powerfully than your own postings do—especially when their postings contradict your self-description (Walther, Van Der Heide, Kim, Westerman, & Tong, 2008). Why do others' posts have so much power? When evaluating someone's online description, you consider the **warranting value** of the information presented—that is, the degree to which the information is supported by other people and outside

Public figures, such as former first lady Michelle Obama, carefully curate the photos and other content that they post on their social media feeds. Although most of us don't have 22 million Instagram followers like Michelle Obama does, we *all* communicate messages about ourselves, our interests, and our personalities whenever we post content online. How do your posts support your online face?

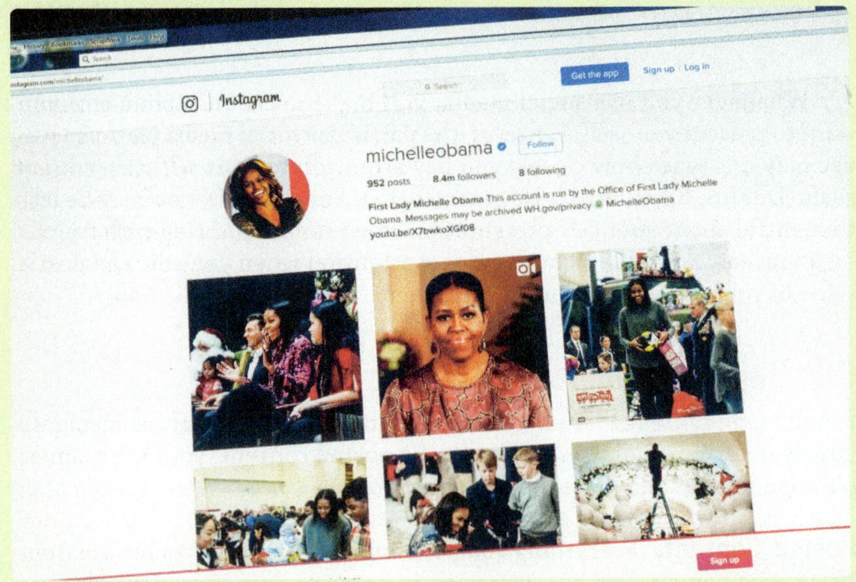

sjscreens/Alamy Stock Photo

evidence (Walther, Van Der Heide, Hamel, & Schulman, 2009). Information that was obviously crafted by the person, that isn't supported by others online, or that can't be verified offline has *low warranting value*. For example, people may not trust an online profile in which you describe yourself as fun and outgoing when there are no posted comments from others to support your description. But your profile information has *high warranting value* if the social media feed has photos of you in social settings and relevant posted comments from others ("*You were SO MUCH fun to hang with last night!*") (Walther et al., 2009).

The research on warranting value suggests that you need to manage online content posted by others that contradicts the self you want to present—even if you think such content is cute or funny. If anyone posts information about you that doesn't match how you want to be seen, politely ask that person to delete it. For more on managing your online face, see Advance the Conversation: Removing an Embarrassing Post on pages 112–113.

Usernames. The name you use for your email address and online profiles tells others how you want to be perceived (Baym, 2010). The username you choose will usually depend on the platform and the audience. People often use pseudonyms on sites where personal privacy is important, such as in forums related to mental health or addiction recovery (van der Nagel, 2017). Pseudonyms also are appropriate when you want to project a casual, even fun, identity. For example, Joe (the author of this book) is known as joeStros13 in his fantasy baseball forums. Steve (the other author) belongs to online audio circles that celebrate turntables, vinyl records, and tubed amplifiers: there, he is The Analog Kid (in honor of one of his favorite Rush songs).

Although pseudonyms can serve useful purposes, they are not helpful when you want to project a professional image. This is especially true when using email for academic and business purposes. For example, it isn't a good idea to use an email pseudonym, such as skywalker999@email.com, on a job application. A creative email pseudonym from an unknown person may lead the recipient to make assumptions about the sender's age, biological sex, and race based solely on the username (Heisler & Crabill, 2006). Rather than risk projecting an unprofessional image, create email usernames that contain a minimum of your first initial and last name.

Friends and Professional Connections. Your followers on Instagram and Twitter, your Facebook friends, and your professional connections on LinkedIn can also give impressions about your social status, political ideology, and other interests (Donath & boyd, 2004). For example, if you follow people who post frequently about animal rights, someone looking at your profile might assume that this cause is important to you, too. Even the physical appearances of your friends can impact judgments about you. In one study, research participants perceived a Facebook profile owner as more attractive when the owner had attractive friends (Walther et al., 2008). Additionally, Utz (2010) found that photos of friends at a party posted on your social media wall or feed can lead others to judge you as friendly and socially desirable.

Managing Your Online Face

Given how much communication occurs through social media, it's essential to competently manage your online face. This can be especially challenging if your social media followers are a diverse mix of family, coworkers, friends, and perhaps even professors (Rui & Stefanone, 2013). Keeping in mind the three Ps of mediated communication—*powerful*, *public*, and *permanent*—can help you do just that.[3]

Mediated communication is *powerful* in shaping others' impressions of you. When you communicate with others through social media, they're more likely to think that your communication reflects your "true" self than they would be if you communicated face-to-face (Shedletsky & Aitken, 2004). For example, if you email a job application to a potential employer and don't include a proper subject line, greeting, or message, they could conclude that you're unprofessional.

Mediated communication is *public*. Always assume that the self you present to others through social media is going to be viewed by a much larger audience than you intended. Emails, texts, tweets, photos, videos, comments, and status updates can be downloaded, saved, edited, copied,

---

[3]Personal communication with authors, May 13, 2008. This material was developed specifically for this text and published with permission of Dr. Malcolm Parks; it may not be reproduced without written consent of Dr. Parks and the authors.

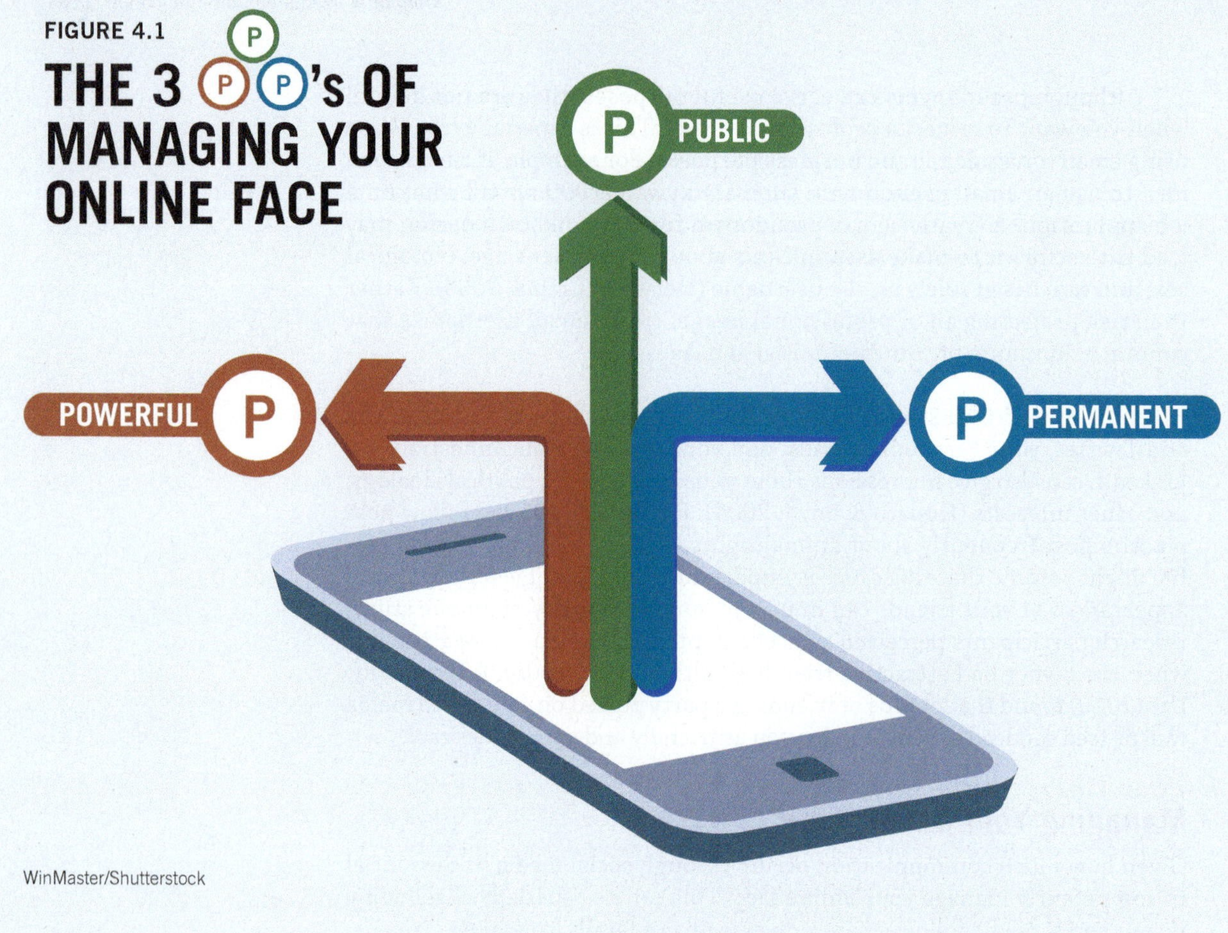

WinMaster/Shutterstock

captured, and forwarded by recipients to others. Even if you have privacy settings enabled, there's nothing stopping authorized friends from downloading posts and photos and distributing them to others.

Mediated communication is *permanent*. Blog posts, status updates, tweets, photos, and emails don't "go away" when you send or delete them; they are saved by recipients and stored on servers and can be retrieved later. Assume that anything and everything you and others post about you online may still be available long into the future.

Keeping the three Ps of mediated communication in mind will help you create and maintain the online face you want others to see. Additionally, there are unique challenges for maintaining positive face when you communicate online in work groups—known as *virtual teams*—and when you deliver online presentations. Chapter 11 (Small Group Communication) considers specific skills for communicating in virtual teams, and Chapter 15 (Delivering Your Speech) addresses steps for making online presentations.

Mediated Communication Challenges

Although mediated communication can be a convenient way to stay connected with others, it has drawbacks. Excessive use of social media can impact your well-being. And sometimes mediated communication makes it easier to send sarcastic or harassing messages and forget how such messages can affect the person receiving them.

Imagine volunteering to give up mobile devices for one whole month. No viewing of your favorite celebrity's posts on Instagram. No texting with your friends. Removing your Twitter app from your phone, which effectively eliminates quick access to breaking news. Could you do it?

Georgetown University professor and author Cal Newport invited followers of his work to disconnect from their mobile devices for one month as part of his research for a book he was writing. Expecting that around 50 people would agree to participate, Professor Newport was surprised that over 1,600 signed on to the challenge. But not all made it through the month. Some, like Kristi Kremers, quickly gave in to the urge to check the news online, to use Facebook to coordinate birthday plans, and to check social media to keep tabs on her favorite NFL team (Cochran, 2018).

Professor Newport's challenge reveals that mediated communication is so entwined in our daily lives that it can be difficult to go without it. The negative impact of using mobile phones and social media can be equally difficult to see. Specifically, when we spend too much time on digital devices, we are more likely to experience feelings of loneliness. Additionally, sometimes people use mobile devices and social media to send messages that are disruptive to others.

Perceived Social Isolation

Excessive use of social media is linked to feelings of loneliness and envy. Specifically, people who spend over two hours a day on their social media are more than twice as likely to report feeling lonely than people who use these apps for less than 30 minutes a day (Primack et al., 2017). Feeling socially isolated is especially likely when you passively scroll through other people's posts without engaging with them (Verduyn, Ybarra, Résibois, Jonides, & Kross, 2017). Likewise, passively consuming social media can lead you to compare your life to others, which may cause you to feel envious (Lin, van de Ven, & Utz, 2018). You may feel excluded, for example, if you come across Instagram photos of your friends at the club, and you weren't invited.

To reduce feelings of isolation and envy that may be associated with social media use, try doing two things. First, be intentional in monitoring the amount of time that you spend on social media. Several apps, such as Moment and BreakFree, are available to help you track your usage and

In one episode of the dystopian TV series *Black Mirror*, Bing Madsen and Abi Khan live in a world where almost every surface is covered with computer screens and digital devices, leading them to feel increasingly socially disconnected. Have you ever felt lonely or isolated after spending too much time online?

CHANNEL 4/ZEPPOTRON/Album/Alamy Stock Photo

screen time, and even set alerts for when you're approaching a predetermined time limit. Freeing up some time from the technology has benefits: participants in Professor Newport's challenge reported that they read more, picked up new hobbies, and enjoyed improved sleep (Cochran, 2018). Second, make *active* rather than *passive* use of social media. By posting status updates, sharing links, and commenting on your friends' posts, you may gain access to both useful information and social support, as well as build stronger relationships (Verduyn et al., 2017). These outcomes won't happen if you're spending most of your time passively scrolling through social media.

Online Disinhibition

When using mediated communication, especially text-only social media, people often feel free to say things—good and bad—that they'd never say to someone face-to-face. This effect is known as **online disinhibition** (Suler, 2004). As noted earlier, much of mediated communication is *asynchronous*—you don't interact with others in real time but exchange messages that are read and responded to later. This can make you more willing to openly express emotions that you might otherwise conceal if you knew you'd get an immediate response.

Contributing to the online disinhibition effect is the sense of invisibility afforded by mediated communication. When you're not sharing physical space with your communication partners, you feel as if they can't really see or hear you. This makes you feel detached from the consequences of your messages. A sense of invisibility is enhanced when you have usernames or identities that aren't traceable to your offline self.

Another contributing factor to online disinhibition is the restriction of nonverbal cues when using mediated communication, making it hard to experience empathy. As Chapter 2 discusses, *empathy* is the ability to "feel into" others' thoughts and emotions. During face-to-face encounters, you constantly track feedback from others as you watch their facial expressions, eye contact, and gestures, and listen to their tone of voice. This feedback enables you to feel empathy for them—to imagine what they're thinking and feeling about your communication. But communicating via text, email, tweeting, or posting online limits your access to the other person's nonverbal feedback during the communication. If you can't perceive others' immediate nonverbal feedback, you can't experience empathy and adjust your communication accordingly (Goleman, 2007).

This dramatic reduction in your ability to experience the other person's feelings is known as an **empathy deficit**. When you have an empathy deficit, you may express yourself in blunt, tactless, and inappropriate ways—like "shouting" by using capitalized words or communicating things you'd never say over the phone or face-to-face. Imagine that you invite your roommate to watch a marathon session of the TV series *Game of Thrones,* and you are confused by the text she sends in response: "oh, great ;)". In this situation, you are less able to *perspective-take*—that is, to see the situation and your communication from your partner's point of view. Is your roommate excited? Sarcastic? Annoyed? You assume that your roommate's text means she's dismissing your idea for a *Game of Thrones* marathon, and you text her back: "FINE! You don't have to be involved!!!" Complicating matters further, people on the receiving end of your communication have the same deficit. Their online messages are less sensitive and less tactful as well, even if they don't mean it any more than you do.

Because mediated communication is often asynchronous, it creates a sense of invisibility, and it makes empathy difficult. Individuals can be unconstrained and even hostile when communicating with others. The online disinhibition effect can lead to four disruptive types of communication: flaming, trolling, online harassment, and cyberbullying.

Flaming and Trolling. If you've ever received mediated messages that are insulting or profane, you know they can be hurtful. When people say vicious and aggressive things online that they would never say in person, they are **flaming**. Flaming is a direct outcome of online disinhibition: when you feel little empathy toward others and also feel comparatively "invisible," you're more likely to communicate in inappropriate, destructive ways.

To reduce the likelihood of flaming in your own mediated communication, draft text messages, emails, and posts and then reread them before sending, asking yourself, "Would I say the same thing to this person's face?"

If your answer is no, then don't send the message. Instead, delete it and consider more constructive ways to express your thoughts.

Some people post flame messages on purpose to start fights, a practice known as **trolling**. People troll for their own enjoyment or because they're bored (Donath, 1999). Read the comments for popular YouTube videos, and you'll see trolling at work ("My 3-year-old sings and plays better than this sucky band!"). Trolls can be very disruptive to online communities because their intent is to cause discord, and they will often continue to post until disruption is achieved. When a hostile comment is posted online, it's not unusual to see the acronym *DNFTT* (Do not feed the trolls) soon follow, as a warning not to "take the bait." The best response to trolls is to ignore them.

Online Harassment and Cyberbullying. Some texts, emails, or posts constitute **online harassment**: mediated messages perceived by the recipient as disturbing, threatening, or obsessive (Walker, Sockman, & Koehn, 2011). For instance, your roommate—much to your embarrassment and against your direct requests not to—repeatedly Snapchats pictures of you drinking at parties. Or a coworker forwards emails with sexist humor and images to you at work, even after you ask him to stop. People under the age of 30 and those who identify as gay, lesbian, or bisexual are more likely to report witnessing or experiencing online harassment (Lenhart, Ybarra, Zickuhr, & Price-Feeney, 2016). If you are the target of online harassment, never ignore this kind of communication. Instead, directly and clearly ask the person to remove the post or to stop sending the emails. If the person refuses, contact people in positions of authority (managers, resident advisers, professors, parents) and ask for advice on what to do.

Online harassment can turn into **cyberbullying** if the communication patterns become persistent and are used to exert power over you (Walker et al., 2011; Wolak, Mitchell, & Finkelhor, 2006). Much like face-to-face bullying, cyberbullying is intended to cause social embarrassment, inflict emotional pain, or damage a person's reputation. Its impact can be devastating. Such was the case with Phoebe Prince—a high school student in Massachusetts—who killed herself in 2010 following repeated acts of verbal aggression by her fellow female students via text messages, Facebook posts, and face-to-face encounters. Sadly, hundreds of similarly cyberbullied children attempt suicide every year.

Although cyberbullying is most common among teens, it can also happen in the workplace in the form of threatening emails or voice mails and sexually charged material (White, 2010). If you believe you're being cyberbullied, firmly tell the bully to stop, and keep written records or screenshots of the offending messages. If the bullying doesn't stop, meet with an authority figure (such as a school or human resources administrator) to describe what's taking place and to ask for help. Most important, if the bullying has you fearing for your physical safety, immediately report it to local law enforcement. Many states have laws to protect victims of cyberbullying. If you need help with handling cyberbullying, refer to www.stopbullying.gov.

Digital Deception

A real concern when developing a new relationship in an online forum is determining whether the person is being truthful about his or her identity and motives. Anyone who sends messages that intentionally mislead or create a false belief in recipients is committing **digital deception** (Hancock, 2007). Digital deception can take several forms. One form is **identity-based digital deception**, whereby someone falsely misrepresents his or her identity or gender (Hancock, 2007). Such deception is common on dating apps, where people exaggerate their education and income levels and lower their weight and age (Hall, Park, Song, & Cody, 2010).

Another form of digital deception is **message-based digital deception**, which is the manipulation of information with the intent of misleading recipients (Hancock, 2007). This type of deception can include **butler lies**, which people use to avoid conversation, prevent embarrassment, or simply be polite (Hancock & Toma, 2009). For example, you ignore a friend's text but later reply saying, "just got your message." Message-based digital deception also includes serious lies that can devastate personal, social, and work relationships (DePaulo, Kirkendol, Kashy, Wyer, & Epstein, 1996). Examples include texting your spouse that you're in a work meeting to cover up an affair, or emailing a professor that you missed an assignment due to illness when in fact it's just because you were unprepared.

Using Mediated Communication Competently

> You probably spend a lot of time playing with the various features of a new phone or tablet, but it's just as important to learn how to communicate competently using technology. Otherwise, you might make some missteps—like sending lengthy text messages when a phone call would've been easier, or sounding more aggressive than you intended.

Among the news media that covered the Alpha Chi Omega selfie controversy described in our chapter opener was AZCentral.com, the premier online source for Arizona news and information. The website encourages readers to comment on and discuss news stories posted on its site. But there's one catch. You must use your Facebook account to post comments to AZCentral news stories. Why? Because the news staff wants to remove invisibility and discourage readers from posting flaming comments. And to prevent trolls from creating fake Facebook accounts, AZCentral requires readers to have a profile photo and at least four friends before comments are made visible on its site.

ANCE THE ONVERSATION

FRIENDS DON'T LET FRIENDS TEXT AND TALK

1 YOUR DILEMMA

Cruz is a good friend, but he spends a lot of time on his phone. Any time you're talking, Cruz has the habit of glancing at incoming notifications. Sometimes he'll even interrupt you to reply to a message. Usually you ignore or joke about his behavior, but today is different.

Since Cruz is one of your best friends, you want his advice about whether you should accept a promotion at work. Sitting at your favorite coffee shop, you begin to explain that you think the added job responsibilities might interfere with your course load at school. At first, Cruz appears interested and asks questions. But he's quickly distracted by the sound of a text notification. You're interrupted a few more times by Cruz's phone notifications, and each time he looks at his phone, weighing the importance of the text. He soon gets a text from your mutual friend, Mara. Picking his phone up, he says: "Hey, it's Mara. She wants to know what I'm up to. Should I ask her to meet up here?" It's now clear that you've lost Cruz's attention.

How does Cruz's frequent checking of his phone notifications make you feel?

2 THE RESEARCH

Mobile phones are an integral part of face-to-face interactions. When friends are together, they often use phones as a source of entertainment by looking at memes, viewing videos, or taking group photos. But when a friend uses a phone to interact with others who aren't present, it can lead the other person to feel unimportant—or worse, that the friendship is not being taken seriously (Miller-Ott & Kelly, 2017). Even the *mere presence* of a phone during conversation can negatively impact perceptions of trust and relationship quality (Przybylski & Weinstein, 2012). This is especially true when you are discussing a personally meaningful topic.

How might you respond when a friend's phone use is disrupting the conversation? Miller-Ott and Kelly (2017) found that young adults often tolerate the distraction if the offending friend offers a disclaimer, apology, or explanation for the interruption ("It's my boss; I need to reply to this"). Some research participants said that they might respond to such behavior by looking at their own phone, confronting the person directly ("Would you mind getting off your phone?"), or putting their own phones away hoping that the friend gets the hint to stay off his or her phone.

Are there any situations in which you would consider Cruz's habit of frequently checking his phone acceptable? Why or why not?

3 YOUR OPPORTUNITY

How will you respond to Cruz? Before you act, consider the facts of the situation and the research on mobile phone interruptions. Also, reflect on what you've learned about mediated communication challenges (pp. 103–107) and the guidelines for competent mediated communication (pp. 107–111).

Now it's your turn. Write out a response to Cruz.

AZCentral and other reputable news agencies want to ensure that public commentary on news stories meets standards for online competence: that the posts are respectful and free of personal attacks. You can demonstrate competence when using social media by observing the following suggestions.[4]

1. *Know when to use mediated communication versus face-to-face.* In many situations, mediated communication is more time efficient than in-person communication. For instance, messaging a friend to remind her of a coffee date makes more sense than dropping by her workplace, and it's probably quicker and less disruptive than calling her. But mediated communication is not the best approach for giving in-depth and lengthy explanations, detailing problems, or conveying important decisions. This fact is intuitively known by young adults, who recognize that communicating through mobile devices is less personal and more likely to cause misunderstandings than communicating face-to-face (Pettegrew & Day, 2015).

   Since it isn't practical (or necessary) to interact face-to-face on every issue, consider these guidelines in determining the best medium for your message. First, *consider the message itself.* Handle emotional messages face-to-face. If this isn't possible, use synchronous communication (a phone call or video chat) so that you can better monitor and respond to the other person's reactions. With complex and difficult messages, consider using more than one medium. For example, hold a meeting to explain work policy changes and then follow up by emailing a summary of your main points or additional details to the meeting attendees. Second, *consider the recipient of your message.* Does he or she prefer certain means of communication? If so, adapt your format accordingly.
2. *Remember the three Ps.* Always remember that mediated communication is *powerful*, *public*, and *permanent*. The things you say and do online endure. Old emails, photographs, videos, messages, and blogs may still be accessible years after you first send them. Think before you post.
3. *Practice creating drafts.* Because mediated communication makes it easy to flame, many of us impulsively fire off messages that we later regret. Instead, get into the habit of saving posts, texts, and email messages as drafts. Then revisit the drafts later and edit them as needed for appropriateness and effectiveness. You may be surprised at how a little time can give you perspective on a message. And don't forget that sometimes the most competent mediated communication is none at all. If you are reviewing a draft and realize it's only going to cause unnecessary damage, delete it.

---

[4]Material for the first four points is published with permission of Dr. Malcolm Parks; it may not be reproduced without written consent of Dr. Parks and the authors.

FIGURE 4.2

PRACTICING COMPETENT COMMUNICATION ONLINE

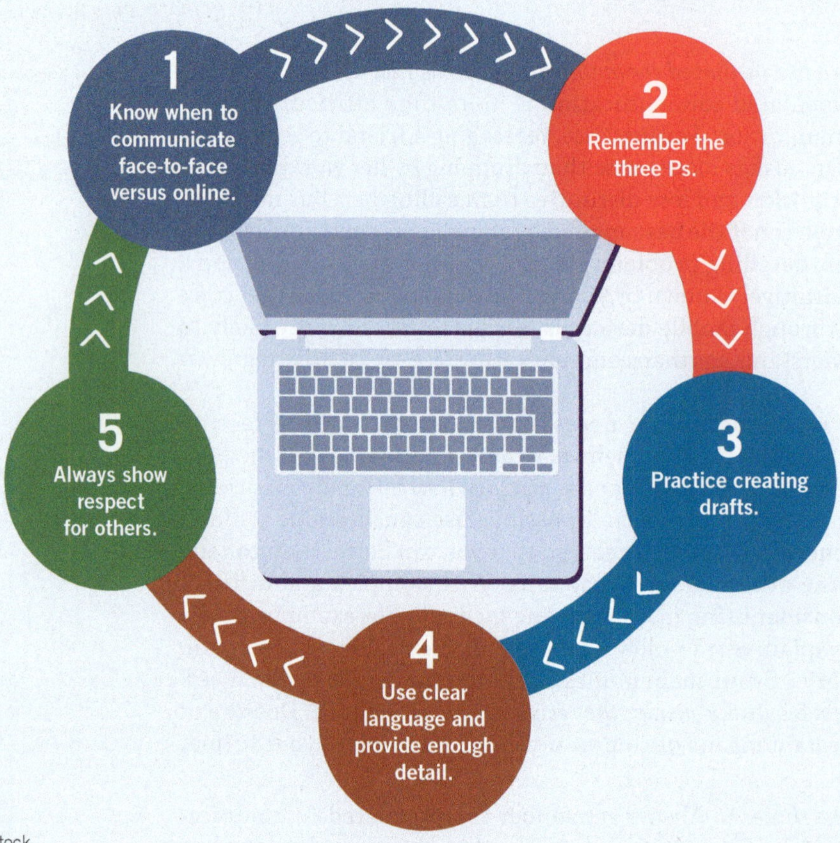

Bplanet/Shutterstock

4. *Use clear language and provide enough detail.* Without feedback, people often misinterpret mediated messages. To avoid misunderstandings, try to use the clearest words possible. Avoid slang, jargon, and abbreviations unless you know the receiver will understand them and interpret them correctly. This is especially true when giving online presentations or participating in videoconference meetings, when it is important that your audience understand your messages clearly.

   In addition, provide enough detail in your messages. In the rush of texting, we often resort to the simplest, shortest messages possible. Take a bit more time to provide enough detail so that the other person has some context for your message. If you text your spouse "home

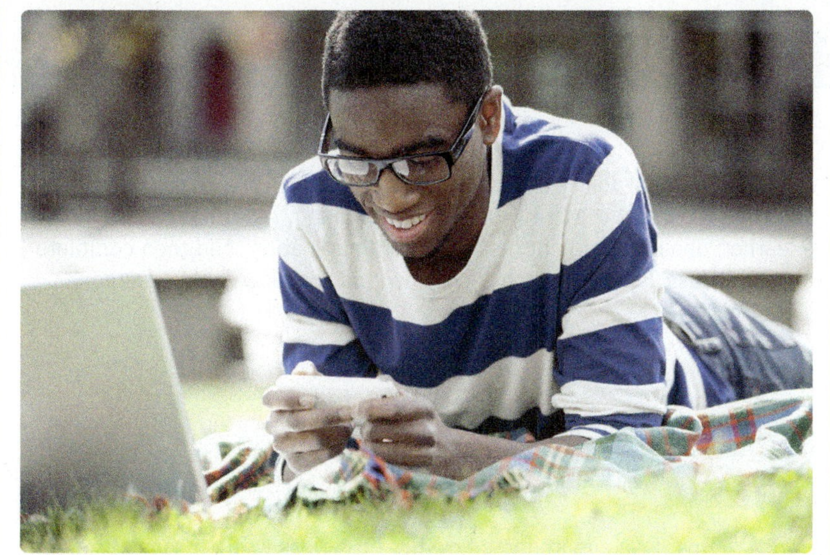

Fancy Collection/SuperStock

The convenience of mediated communication sometimes makes it easy to forget its specific challenges and the time it can take to use it competently. Before sending out your next quick text or multitasking between several apps, take a moment to be sure you are sending the message you intend.

2 hrs late," he might wonder if something bad has happened. If your text says, "Still working. Be home 2 hrs late," he can relax, knowing that you're OK. For more on how to create understandable messages, see Chapter 5, pages 122–124.

5. *Always show respect for others*. Empathy deficits can make it hard to communicate in sensitive, respectful ways. So when you're communicating through social media, put extra energy into *perspective-taking*, or seeing things from other people's point of view, and *empathic concern*—becoming aware of how other people are feeling and experiencing compassion for them. As Chapter 2 explains, this will help you experience and express *empathy* for other people. Demonstrating kindness, caring, and concern in every form of mediated communication will go far to reduce tensions, build rapport, and create more positive outcomes in all your communication.

LearningCurve can help you review! Go to **launchpadworks.com**

ADVANCE THE CONVERSATION
Video Activity

REMOVING AN EMBARRASSING POST

The following scenario will enhance your ability to manage your online self-presentation. Visit LaunchPad at **launchpadworks.com** to get the full experience with video. As you watch the first video, recall what you've learned about competent mediated communication, and then complete the **Your Turn** prompts. Finally, watch the **Take Two!** video to explore how this scenario could have gone differently.

1 THE PROBLEM

While hanging out with friends, Danielle imitates how her boss flirts with customers, totally unaware that her friend Tim is shooting a video of her performance. The next day, Danielle is horrified to discover that Tim has posted the video online. She asks to meet with him right away, and asks him to take the video down. But Tim doesn't understand why she's upset. "Come on," he says. "Get over yourself—you were great!"

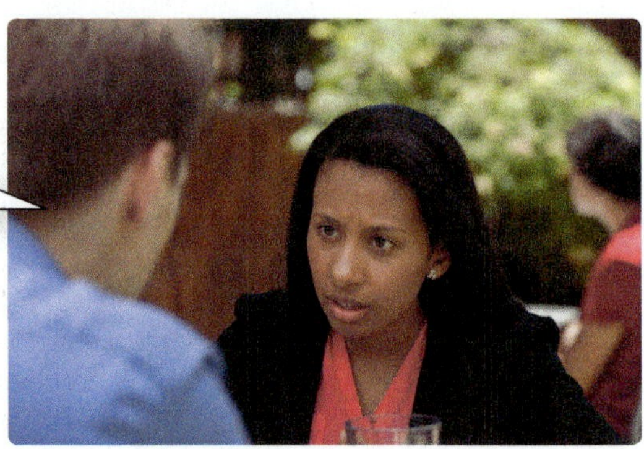

"Look, I know you mean no harm by it, but I'd like for you to remove it. Would you please do that for me right now?"

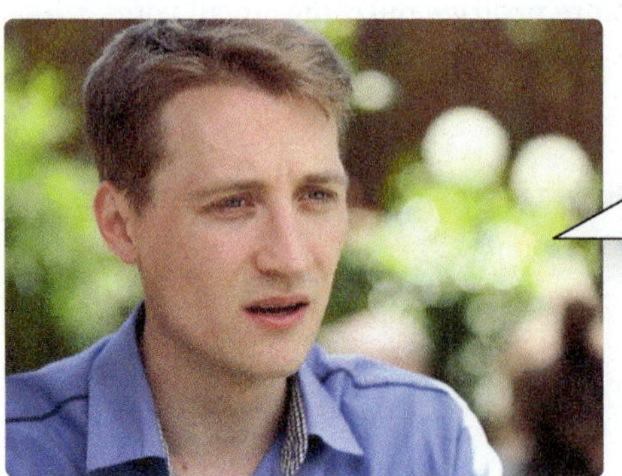

"I don't see why you're so mad about it. Nobody knows who you're imitating, and it's funny! Look—it's got a whole bunch of new comments."

2 YOUR TURN

Observations. Reflect on how Danielle and Tim communicated in this scenario by answering the following questions:

1. Which character do you identify with more in this situation? How would you feel if you were in his or her situation?
2. Where were the missed opportunities to practice competent communication?

Discussion. In class or with a partner, share your thoughts about the interaction between Danielle and Tim and work to answer the following questions:

1. Can you understand both perspectives?
2. What could Tim and Danielle have done differently?

Conclusion. Choose one person in the scenario to offer your advice to. Based on your analysis, what advice would you give him or her to improve his or her communication competence in this scenario?

3 TAKE TWO!

What if things had gone differently? Watch the **Take Two!** video to see one possible example of how the conversation might have gone if Tim and/or Danielle had communicated differently. As you watch the video, consider where the dialog reflects communication competence. After watching the video, answer the questions below:

1. Did Tim and/or Danielle take advantage of opportunities that they missed in the first scenario? Which ones?
2. Did their different actions result in a more productive encounter? Please explain.

CHAPTER 4 REVIEW

CHAPTER RECAP

- There are two types of **mediated communication**: **mass media** and **social media**. Social media help you meet your instrumental, relationship, and self-presentation goals.
- Since social media can limit the amount of nonverbal information you receive, the **social information processing theory** suggests that you compensate for this by taking more care with the words you use.
- When creating and managing your online face, remember the three Ps of mediated communication: any content you post is *powerful*, *public*, and *permanent*.
- One possible negative effect of mediated communication is perceived social isolation. **Online disinhibition** and **empathy deficits** are two causes of other mediated communication challenges, such as **flaming**, **trolling**, **online harassment**, **cyberbullying**, and **digital deception**.
- Knowing how to competently use mediated communication can help you improve your relationships, your work life, and your online presentation skills.

LaunchPad

LaunchPad for *Choices & Connections* offers unique video scenarios and encourages self-assessment through adaptive quizzing. Go to **launchpadworks.com** to get access.

 LearningCurve adaptive quizzes

 Communication Lab video scenarios

 Video clips that illustrate key concepts

KEY TERMS

Mediated communication, p. 92
Mass media, p. 92
Social media, p. 93
Hashtag activism, p. 95
Synchronous communication, p. 96
Asynchronous communication, p. 96
Cues-filtered-out model, p. 96
Social information processing theory, p. 96
Warranting value, p. 99
Online disinhibition, p. 104
Empathy deficit, p. 105
Flaming, p. 105
Trolling, p. 106
Online harassment, p. 106
Cyberbullying, p. 106
Digital deception, p. 107
Identity-based digital deception, p. 107
Message-based digital deception, p. 107
Butler lie, p. 107

POP QUIZ

Looking for more review questions? LearningCurve can help you master key concepts from this chapter. Go to **launchpadworks.com**

1. If you want to have an important conversation with a family member, you should first try to engage in a real-time conversation, or
   a. asynchronous communication.
   b. synchronous communication.
   c. public communication.
   d. nonverbal feedback.

2. When evaluating information posted online, which of the following is part of the content's warranting value?
   a. Whether the content has relevant comments from other people
   b. Whether the content can be verified by alternative sources
   c. Whether the content was obviously crafted by the person posting it
   d. All of the above are correct.

3. Which of the following is the cause of empathy deficits online?
   a. Cyberbullying
   b. Perceived social isolation
   c. Lack of nonverbal feedback
   d. Use of identity-based digital deception

4. Which phenomenon occurs when people say negative things online that they would never say in person?
   a. Flaming
   b. Butler lies
   c. Cyberbullying
   d. Deception

5. Which of the following is *not* one of the chapter's suggestions for competently using mediated communication?
   a. Avoid misunderstandings by using clear language and appropriate amounts of detail.
   b. Create message drafts and revisit them later before sending.
   c. Use perspective-taking and empathic concern when communicating online.
   d. Limit mediated communication to a few messages per day.

ACTIVITIES

For more activities, visit LaunchPad for *Choices & Connections* at **launchpadworks.com**

1 Analyzing Your Online Face

Open your profile on a social media site. Working with a classmate, use the three Ps of mediated communication—powerful, public, and permanent—to evaluate each other's profiles. What online face do you perceive your partner to have? Does this online face match his or her in-person face? Based on what your partner perceived about *your* online face, how can you improve your profile?

2 Flaming and Trolling in Action

Look at the discussion thread in the comment section of a recent online news article about a controversial topic (e.g., find articles at www.washingtonpost.com or www.nytimes.com). Identify any instances of flaming, trolling, or harassment, and analyze how other commenters responded to these posts. Work with a small group of classmates to prepare a group report on how these comments worked with or violated the guidelines for mediated communication competence suggested in this chapter. Present the report in class.

5

Verbal Communication

As a poet, motivational speaker, and actor, Ed Mabrey spends his life carefully crafting his words. His hard work has paid off. Mabrey is a four-time winner of the Individual World Poetry Slam Championship (2007, 2012, 2013, and 2016).[1] In this annual competition featuring dozens of the world's best performance poets—each of whom is a champion in his or her home region—Mabrey and others get to show off their unique talents. Mabrey's recent victories have cemented his status as one of the finest performance poets ever.

Poetry slam is the competitive art of performance poetry. Unlike written poetry, which is designed to be read, performance poetry is created to be spoken in front of a live audience. At poetry slams, judges assess poets and award them points. Although slams vary in their rules, most require that the poems be brief and that poets perform without props, costumes, or musical instruments. Poets are judged solely on their choice of words and the emotion with which these words are communicated to the audience.

The poetry performed at slams varies widely in topic—everything from comedy to social commentary, inner reflection to outward expression of love. Champion Ed Mabrey's poetry focuses on his view of world events, his close relationships, and even casual encounters. His poem "Pursuit of Happyness," for example, is about a conversation with a homeless person at a Subway restaurant.

Many slam poets incorporate aspects of their gender and cultural identities into their works. For example, Mwende "FreeQuency" Katwiwa, who identifies as a "26-year-old Kenyan, Immigrant, Queer Womyn writer and speaker," incorporates her activism on behalf of Black Lives Matter and LGBTQ advocacy into her writings and performances. In 2018 she won the Women of the World Poetry Slam (WOWps)—a four-day festival and competition featuring 96 of the world's top female-identifying slam poets—with a poem describing harrowing scenes of police brutality and suicide.

But despite the diversity among poets and poetic content, the common theme that runs throughout performance poetry is the importance of carefully choosing clear, honest, and understandable language packed with powerful meaning. Poets seeking to win slams can't just craft language into small, elegant poems. They must verbally communicate their creations to audiences in a competent fashion. Although poetry slams are highly competitive—poets intensely vie with one another for points and tenths of points—they are ultimately about celebrating the communicative power of the spoken word. As poet Allan Wolf describes, "The points are not the point; the point is poetry."

[1]All content that follows adapted from Poetry Slam, Inc. (www.poetryslam.com), and Seattle Poetry Slam (2013).

AP Images/Bebeto Matthew

LearningCurve can help you review! Go to **launchpadworks.com**

You may not be a performance poet like Ed Mabrey or Mwende Katwiwa, facing audiences and judges who evaluate you through points, but you are judged just the same, every single day, on the words you use. If you competently communicate to others, you're awarded "points" in the form of people liking you, being influenced by you, or judging you to have desirable skills—like being "an amazing speaker" or "a skilled conversationalist." Regardless of your rhyme or reason, your words pack a potent punch in shaping others' impressions of you. As a consequence, it's important to understand the power of verbal communication and how to use it competently. In this chapter, you'll learn:

- The four defining features of language
- Strategies for creating understandable messages and taking responsibility for your words
- How to use language that avoids gender bias and is mindful of cultural differences
- Ways to manage the challenging aspects of verbal communication

The Nature of Verbal Communication

Whenever you write, speak, sign, tweet, or text, you're using language to convey meaning to others. But your words also communicate powerful messages about who you are in relation to your listeners. Understanding how verbal communication works will help you use language more competently in every area of your life.

Your days are filled with verbal communication. You speak with your professor during her office hours, then text your roommate to see if you can get a ride home. You email group members about an upcoming project, then give a presentation in front of your communication class. You chat with coworkers after your shift, then FaceTime with your partner stationed overseas. Through all of these exchanges, you employ **verbal communication**—the use of spoken or written language to interact with others. Because language is the basis of verbal communication, understanding the nature of language is key for improving your verbal communication skills. Language has four defining features: it is symbolic, it is governed by rules, it conveys meaning, and it is intertwined with culture.

Language Is Symbolic

When Steve was in sixth grade, his friend Ed would play an annoying word game with people. Ed would point to a table and say, "What's that?" The unwitting victim would answer, "It's a table, duh!" Ed would say, "No, that's just the *word* we use to represent it. What is it *really*?" The person would pause, then respond, "Oh, I see. OK, it's wood and metal and plastic." "No,"

Ed would laugh, "those are just *words* that we use to *represent* what it is. What is it *really*?"

Ed's game illustrates the first defining feature of language: it is symbolic. When items are used to represent other things, they are considered **symbols**. In verbal communication, words are the primary symbols used to represent people, objects, events, and ideas (Foss, Foss, & Trapp, 1991). Thus, the word *table* refers to an object with a flat surface and legs to support it. You could just as well call it a "cotknee" or some other term. If you did, nothing about the actual object would change—just its name. As psychologist Erich Fromm noted, words only point to our experience of the world; they are not the experience. All languages are collections of symbols in the form of words people use to communicate.

Language Is Governed by Rules

Two types of rules govern the use of language. The first type is **constitutive rules**, which define words' meanings. Constitutive rules tell you what words stand for what objects (Searle, 1965). For example, in the English language, *dog* represents a four-legged domesticated animal that is a common household pet. In Spanish, the word *perro* represents this same animal. Constitutive rules involving informal or metaphorical expressions can make things challenging when you're trying to learn a new language. For example, someone new to English may get confused when a friend says, "My dogs are tired," if the speaker really means, "My feet hurt."

The second type comprises **regulative rules**, which control how you use language. Regulative rules guide everything from spelling to grammar to conversational structure. Examples in the English language include "Add an *s* or an *es* to a noun to create its plural form" and "When someone asks you a question, you should answer."

Language Conveys Meaning

Language enables you to convey meaning to others in two ways. The first is the literal meaning of your words, as agreed on by members of your culture. These are known as **denotative meanings**. Such meanings are what you find in dictionaries; for example, *family* means "a group of individuals related through common ancestry, legal means, or other strong emotional or social bonds."

But the word *family* evokes different meanings for different people. Some may hear the word and immediately think, "Individuals I can count on for love and support." Others may hear it and think, "People who are always judging me!" Such variations represent **connotative meanings**—the meanings you associate with words based on your life experiences. What does the word *family* mean to you?

Denotative and connotative meanings can create confusion if you don't manage them carefully. For example, suppose your friend aces an exam that you flunked. You text her, "I hate u!" The denotative meaning suggests

DOUBLE TAKE

CONNOTATIVE MEANINGS: THIS  THAT?

Depending on your personal experiences, the word *gambling* can have vastly different connotative meanings. When a friend says she is going gambling, do you think that sounds fun, boring, wasteful, or something else entirely?

© Tim Pannell/Corbis

Fuse/Corbis/Getty Images

you feel hatred toward your friend. But the connotative meaning—your real message—is "I'm envious but proud of you." If you and your friend have a history of communicating with each other in this way, your friend will probably read your message as you intend. But with a person you don't know as well, an "I hate u!" text could backfire. To use verbal communication competently, choose your words carefully and clarify connotative meanings if there's a chance someone could misunderstand your message.

Language and Culture Are Intertwined

Members of a culture use language to communicate their thoughts, beliefs, attitudes, and values with one another, and thereby reinforce their collective sense of cultural identity (Whorf, 1952). Consequently, the language you speak (English, Spanish, Mandarin, Urdu), the words you choose (proper, slang, profane), and the grammar you use (formal, informal) all announce to others: "This is who I am! This is my cultural heritage!"

Each language reflects distinct sets of cultural beliefs and values. However, a large group of people within a particular culture who speak the same language may (over time) develop their own variations on that language, known as **dialects** (Gleason, 1989). Dialects may include unique phrases, words, and pronunciations (such as accents). Dialects reflect the shared history, experiences, and knowledge of people who live in a particular geographic region (the American Midwest or the Deep South), share a common socioeconomic status (urban working class or upper-middle-class suburban), or possess a common ethnic or religious ancestry (Irish English or Yiddish English) (Chen & Starosta, 1998).

People often judge those who use dialects similar to their own as ingroupers and are thus inclined to make positive judgments about them (Delia,

1972; Lev-Ari & Keysar, 2010). As Chapter 3 discusses, this is a cultural influence; ingroupers are people you perceive to be culturally similar to you. In a parallel fashion, people tend to judge those with dissimilar dialects as outgroupers (people who are culturally dissimilar to you) and make negative judgments about them. Keep this tendency in mind when you're speaking with people who don't share your dialect, and resist the temptation to make negative judgments about them. For additional ideas on managing ingroup or outgroup perceptions, see Chapter 3.

Verbal Communication Skills

Even though people use language all the time to verbally communicate, not everyone does so skillfully. Knowing the difference between words that are understandable, inclusive, and respectful, and those that aren't—and putting this knowledge to use when speaking with others—is essential to competent verbal communication.

Students in the 2018 graduating class at the University of Southern California Annenberg School for Communication and Journalism might have walked into the auditorium expecting to hear a formulaic keynote address extolling "the importance of being successful" and "having a competitive edge." But Oprah Winfrey—philanthropist, media executive, and cultural icon—didn't give the usual graduation speech. Instead, she said, "If you can capture the humanity of the people in the stories you're telling, you get that much closer to your own humanity." She talked about the importance of seeking truth and bringing clarity to a world that often seems divided and conflicted. As Winfrey spoke, the crowd quieted. Students and parents alike stopped texting and chatting and began listening. In a dramatic moment in her speech, Winfrey declared:

> Here's what you have to do: you make the choice every day, every single day, to exemplify honesty, because let me tell you something about the truth: the truth exonerates and it convicts. It disinfects and it galvanizes. The truth has always been and will always be our shield against corruption, our shield against greed and despair. The truth is our saving grace.

Students and family members applauded Winfrey throughout her speech—and when she

Oprah Winfrey's commencement speech shows how powerful language can impact an audience. Have you ever been similarly affected by a speech? Why?

Marcus Ingram/WireImage/Getty Images

finished, everyone rose to cheer and give her a standing ovation. Immediately after, people in the stadium began texting and chatting again. But this time, their messages and comments were uniform: "That was an amazing speech!"

Undoubtedly, the profound nature of Winfrey's topic helped make her speech memorable. But a person can talk about important things in vague, wordy, or distorted ways that make listeners tune out. In Winfrey's case, it was her *choice of words* that created the biggest impact: understandable, honest, and inclusive language that crossed gender and cultural boundaries. Winfrey made an audience of thousands feel as though they were joined together in something bigger and better than simply sitting in a stadium, listening to a speech.

How can you harness the power of language in similar ways when you communicate verbally? Try four things: (1) create understandable messages; (2) use "I" and "we" language; (3) avoid gender-based presumptions; and (4) be mindful of cultural differences.

Create Understandable Messages

As noted in our chapter opener, performance poets like Ed Mabrey or Mwende Katwiwa can't win poetry slams just by crafting small, elegant

Brian Cahn/ZUMA Press, Inc./Alamy Stock Photo

Grand Slam poets like Mwende "FreeQuency" Katwiwa must choose their words carefully to ensure that the audience understands their intended message. Can you recall a time when someone misunderstood what you were trying to say? Do you think you could have done anything differently to make your message more understandable?

poems. Instead, they must verbally communicate their creations in an understandable fashion to audiences. But what makes messages *understandable*?

In his exploration of language and meaning, philosopher Paul Grice noted that in order for people to optimally understand your communication, you should strive to abide by the **cooperative principle**: making your verbal communication as *informative*, *honest*, *relevant*, and *clear* as required for a particular situation (Grice, 1989).

Be Informative. Being *informative* means presenting all the information that is appropriate and important to share. It also means not providing information that isn't appropriate or important. For example, suppose your sister is getting married and you are in the wedding party. When you make a toast at the reception following the ceremony, everyone will expect you to comment on how the couple met and how their love for each other is inspiring. To *not* say these things would be remiss. On the other hand, you won't want to be *too* informative by sharing inappropriate details (such as stories about their sex life) or unimportant details (such as what was on the menu at the restaurant where they first met).

Be Honest. **Honesty** is the single most important characteristic of competent communication because other people count on the fact that the information you share with them is truthful (Grice, 1989). Being honest means not sharing information you're uncertain about and not presenting information as true when you know it's false. For example, let's say that during a meeting, someone asks you a question you're unable to answer. Rather than fumbling through a potentially incorrect response, acknowledge that you don't know the answer, and determine a way to get the required information. Dishonesty in verbal communication violates standards for ethical behavior and leads others to believe false things (Jacobs, Dawson, & Brashers, 1996).

Be Relevant. You are *relevant* when you present information that's responsive to what others have said and applicable to the situation. As examples of responsiveness, when people ask you questions, you provide appropriate answers. When they make requests, you explicitly grant or reject those requests. Dodging questions or abruptly changing topics is uncooperative and may be seen as deceptive. In the wedding toast scenario, a relevant speech would cover the couple's relationship. Going off on tangents regarding your own relationships would be irrelevant ("Seeing them together reminds me of my own love life; just last week I . . .").

Be Clear. Using *clear language* means presenting information in a straightforward fashion rather than framing it in vague or ambiguous terms. This was one of the most impressive aspects of Winfrey's commencement speech: she used clear, concise language that everyone easily understood:

"The truth is our saving grace." (Check out Chapter 15 for suggestions on how to use clear language in your own speeches.)

At the same time, using clear language doesn't mean being brutally frank or dumping offensive or harmful information on others. When you find yourself in situations in which you have to deliver bad news ("Your project report needs serious revision"), tailor your message in ways that consider others' feelings ("I'm sorry for the inconvenience this may cause you"). Similarly, you'll improve the likelihood of positive outcomes during conflicts by expressing your concerns clearly ("I'm really upset") while avoiding language that attacks someone's character or personality ("You're such an idiot") (Gottman & Silver, 1999).

Misunderstandings. Of course, just because you use informative, honest, relevant, and clear language doesn't guarantee that others will understand you. When one person misperceives the meaning of another's verbal communication, **misunderstanding** occurs.

Misunderstanding occurs frequently online, owing to the lack of nonverbal cues that help clarify intended meaning. One study found that 27.2 percent of respondents agreed that email is likely to result in miscommunication of intent, and 53.6 percent agreed that it is relatively easy to misinterpret an email message (Rainey, 2000). The tendency to misunderstand communication online is so prevalent that scholars suggest the following practices: *if a particular message must be absolutely error-free or if its content is controversial, don't use email or text messaging to communicate it*. Whenever possible, conduct high-stakes encounters, such as important attempts at persuasion, face-to-face. Never use emails, texts, or social media posts for sensitive actions, such as professional reprimands or dismissals, or relationship breakups (Rainey, 2000). To learn how to create understandable messages and avoid misunderstandings during conflicts, see Advance the Conversation: Disagreement with Family on page 134.

Mediated communication platforms like FaceTime and Skype help eliminate the possibility of misunderstanding someone when you're not able to talk in person. How does the language you use when interacting via webcam differ from the language you use when texting?

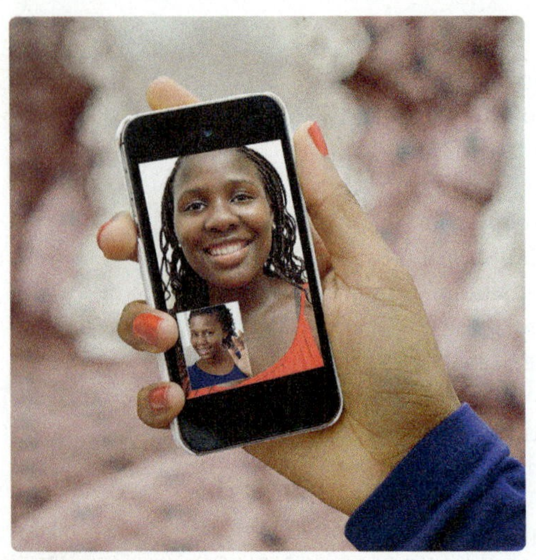

David Malan/The Image Bank/Getty Images

Use "I" and "We" Language

When verbally communicating, avoid using **"you" language**—phrases that place the focus of attention and blame on other people, such as "You let me down" or "You make me so angry!" Instead, use **"I" language**—phrases that emphasize ownership of your feelings, opinions, and beliefs. "I" language makes it clear that you're expressing your own perceptions rather than stating unquestionable truths, making it less likely to trigger defensiveness in others (Kubany, Richard, Bauer, & Muraoka, 1992). For instance, imagine you're involved in a group project, and some group members are working harder than others. If you bring up this topic with the group, saying "I think it's important that the workload be evenly distributed" will seem less threatening than "You people aren't doing your fair share!"

At the same time, strive to build solidarity through **"we" language**—phrases that both emphasize inclusion and enhance feelings of connection and similarity (Honeycutt, 1999). In the group project example, you might say "We all want this project to be a success" in order to emphasize how the whole group is working together. One study found that married couples who used "we" language maintained more positive emotions during disagreements and had higher overall marital satisfaction than couples who did not (Seider, Hirschberger, Nelson, & Levenson, 2009). To compare and contrast the differences between "you," "I," and "we" language, see Table 5.1.

TABLE 5.1

"YOU," "I," AND "WE" LANGUAGE

SITUATION	"YOU" LANGUAGE	"I" LANGUAGE	"WE" LANGUAGE
A friend blows up at you when you cancel dinner plans.	"You really hurt my feelings."	"I'm feeling really hurt."	"We need to work harder on not hurting each other's feelings."
A classmate forgets to make a main point during a group presentation.	"You totally messed up our presentation."	"I feel like our presentation had some mistakes."	"Although we made some mistakes in our presentation, we totally rocked the paper."
A coworker isn't filling out order sheets correctly.	"You need to do a better job on your order sheets."	"I think the order sheets could be done a bit better."	"We can improve the quality of our order sheets with better inventory management."

VoodooDot/Shutterstock

Avoid Gender-Based Presumptions

Many people believe that men and women have different verbal communication preferences and practices. Specifically, they assume that women use and prefer "indirect" and "flowery" language, whereas men use and prefer "direct, clear, and concise" language (Spender, 1990). But scientific research has found that men and women are actually more similar than different when it comes to language. For example, after reviewing data from more than 1,000 gender studies, researchers Dan Canary, Tara Emmers-Sommer, and Sandra Faulkner (1997) found that if you consider all the factors that influence communication and compare their impact, only about 1 percent of people's verbal communication behavior is related to gender. The researchers concluded that during verbal communication, "men and women respond in a similar manner 99% of the time."

So why do people think that men and women use language differently? Perception. Because people *believe* that men and women are different, they *perceive* differences in their communication—even when such differences don't exist. In a well-known study documenting this effect, researchers gave two different groups of participants a copy of the same speech (Mulac, Incontro, & James, 1985). One group was told that a man had authored and presented the speech; the other group, that a woman had authored and presented it. Participants who thought the speech was female in origin perceived it as having a more "artistic quality" and complimented the language for being "pleasing, sweet, and beautiful." Participants who were told that a man had authored the speech viewed it as having more "dynamism" and complimented the language as "strong, active, and aggressive." Yet both groups read the same speech.

The lesson? You don't need to adjust your verbal communication to your listeners' or readers' gender. Men and women appreciate language that is informative, honest, relevant, and clear. Everyone prefers talking with people who avoid placing blame through "you" language and who use "I" language to take responsibility for their own actions and feelings. Additionally, using "we" language creates a sense of unity with others, regardless of their gender.

Be Mindful of Cultural Differences

As Chapter 3 discusses, different cultures often have different ideas about what constitutes competent verbal communication. To help you communicate competently with people from other cultures, consider the following guidelines.

First, adjust your verbal communication to match others' speech rates and desired balance of "turn taking" (Bianconi, 2002; Coupland, Giles, &

Wiemann, 1991). Observe how rapidly the person you're talking with speaks, and how long a turn he or she takes when talking. Then match the person's speech rate, and use similar turn lengths. Monitor any feedback while you're conversing (such as nodding or fidgeting) to see whether your conversation partner wants you to continue or stop. (For more details on accommodating, see pages 83–84 in Chapter 3.)

Second, and even more important, don't change your language or voice in substantial ways just because you're speaking to someone from another culture. For example, many Euro-American college students switch to simplistic language and talk slower and louder when interacting with Asian and Asian American students, as if they were talking with small children. This change in speech behavior is viewed as both patronizing and insulting by recipients (Jimenez & McCornack, 2011).

Verbal Communication Challenges

> **"Sticks and stones may break my bones, but words can never hurt me." Nonsense. The words you use have the power to cause grievous injury to the emotions and self-esteem of others. But by learning to identify and avoid destructive forms of language—and constructively respond when others use them—you can become a more competent verbal communicator.**

He is the most prejudiced, verbally aggressive, deceptive, and slanderous character ever to show up on television screens. He has been described as

***South Park*'s Eric Cartman is the cartoon definition of how *not* to communicate. His unabashed bad behavior is shocking but also shows viewers the consequences of poor communication skills. How do you handle any real-life "Cartmans" you run into?**

"a bundle of pure, unadulterated evil." He's *South Park*'s Eric Cartman—a boy plagued by greed, hatred, and an unquenchable thirst for power. Through hundreds of episodes across more than 22 seasons, Cartman has tried to reignite the Civil War, feigned disability, tricked another boy into eating his own parents at a chili cook-off, and released an almost endless anti-Semitic verbal assault on his classmate Kyle.

Cartman's terrible communication often has disastrous outcomes. His manipulation of and cruelty to others only occasionally nets him happiness, and he never learns from his mistakes. This makes him endearing in a strange way: his communicative failings make viewers feel good about their capacity to change and improve. So whether you love Cartman or loathe him, laugh at his offensive antics or recoil from them, he reveals an essential truth about the dark side of verbal communication: when you use prejudiced, aggressive, deceptive, or defamatory language, you sow the seeds of your own destruction.

Prejudiced Language

As Chapter 3 discusses, *prejudice* means presuming negative things about other people based on their group affiliation (ethnicity, religion, age, gender, sexual orientation). It is a negative form of *stereotyping*. People who use **prejudiced language** speak in ways that display contempt, dislike, or disdain for a group or its members. In *South Park*, for example, Cartman uses anti-Semitic prejudiced language almost constantly when he talks with his friend Kyle.

There are as many types of prejudiced language as there are groups. A person can use language that's prejudiced toward men or women (*sexist language*) or toward gays, lesbians, bisexuals, or transgender persons (*homophobic language*). It can also be used to criticize various ethnicities (*racist language*), people of different ages (*ageist language*), and even socioeconomic groups (*classist language*). Some people use prejudiced language when discussing physical or mental disabilities, political affiliations, social or religious groups, and even college majors.

Most of us readily recognize racist, sexist, and disability-related slurs. But prejudiced language can be less obvious—for example, when people use ethnic and gender-specific modifiers to describe others, even when such descriptors are unnecessary to the point they're making ("the Hispanic doctor" or "a male nurse"). Prejudiced language also shows up in the use of such expressions as "That's so gay," to mean that something isn't cool or acceptable. Such expressions are hurtful and perpetuate negative stereotypes.

What can you do if another person's language is prejudiced and offensive? As we discuss in Chapter 10 about managing conflict, confronting others is rarely easy, but it can be done. Consider the following suggestions:

- Determine the risk of confrontation. Is the person likely to be open to your point of view? A friend, family member, or peer may be willing to listen. However, if it's a stranger or someone with power over you (like your boss), it might be best to ignore the comments or to leave the situation.

- If you choose to confront the person, avoid an approach that causes the person to lose face, creating embarrassment. Instead, talk with the person privately, and open with an affirming statement ("I know that you probably mean no harm when you say, 'That's so gay, but . . .'").
- Next, state your feelings about the prejudiced language, and politely ask the person to revise his or her language ("I feel uncomfortable with this phrase because I have a brother who's gay; I would appreciate it if you didn't use it").
- Finally, listen to and acknowledge what the person says in response. If necessary, reassert your request that the prejudiced language be avoided ("I understand that you mean nothing by it, but I would still appreciate it if you didn't use it").

Verbal Aggression

Verbal aggression is the use of language to attack someone's personal attributes, such as their weight, looks, intelligence, or physical ability (Infante & Wigley, 1986). Verbal aggression is distinct from prejudiced language in three respects: the goal is to intentionally injure a particular person's feelings, the attack targets unique personal attributes rather than group affiliation, and the message often includes profanity. Verbal aggression can happen in face-to-face conversation, or it can take the form of *cyberbullying*: habitually attacking a person using the internet or social media. (For more information about cyberbullying, see pages 106–107 in Chapter 4.)

Why are people verbally aggressive? Sometimes the behavior is triggered by a temporary state of stress, anger, or exhaustion. Other times it's in reaction to real or perceived slights. Still others act aggressively because they believe that using profanity, insults, and threats will get them what they want, like Cartman from *South Park.*

It's hard to communicate competently with verbally aggressive people. Imagine giving a speech in a public forum, such as a student union meeting, and having someone stand up and yell, "Shut up, you loser!" What would you say and do? To manage verbally aggressive individuals, researcher Dominic Infante (1995) offers three suggestions:

- Avoid communicating in ways that may trigger aggression in the first place, such as teasing, baiting, or insulting others.
- If you know someone who is *chronically verbally aggressive*—meaning he or she is verbally aggressive most of the time—avoid or minimize contact with that person.
- If you can't avoid such interactions, try to remain polite and respectful. Don't interrupt the aggressive person. Stay calm, and acknowledge the

TABLE 5.2

HOW TO HANDLE VERBAL AGGRESSION ONLINE

If you receive a text, email, or online post that is aggressive or hostile toward you, try the following steps to respond competently and not escalate the situation:

1. Consider the intent of the message carefully to help you determine whether you should respond. Is the sender intentionally trying to provoke you? Did the sender just get carried away with emotion? Is the sender aware of the tone of the message?
2. If you choose to respond, create a draft message first, save it, and then revisit it in a few hours. Do not send the message yet.
3. Later, check your response. Is it informative, honest, relevant, and clear?
4. Did you avoid "you" language and use "I" and "we" language where appropriate to minimize defensiveness and bridge your differences?
5. Make sure your message is respectful and polite, avoiding any hint of personal attack or retaliation.
6. Only once you are sure the message fits these requirements should you send it.

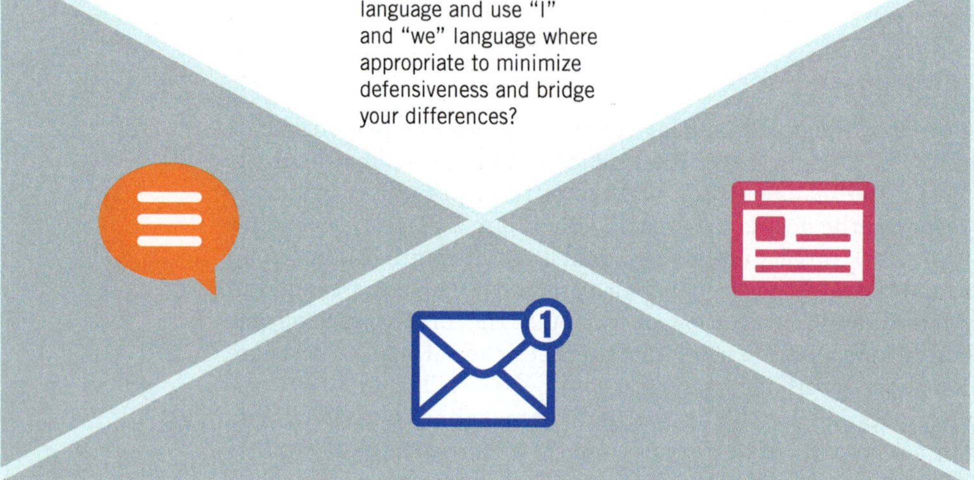

VLADGRIN/Shutterstock

other person's perspective if possible. Avoid retaliating with personal attacks of your own; they'll only escalate the aggression.

For ideas on how to handle verbal aggression online, see Table 5.2.

Deception

Deception is the deliberate use of uninformative, untruthful, irrelevant, or vague language for the purpose of misleading others. Deception takes many forms. People may be overly vague in what they say, trying to "veil" the truth. They may dodge a question or change the topic to avoid embarrassing or problematic disclosures. The most common form of deception is *concealment*: leaving important and relevant information out of messages

(McCornack, Morrison, Paik, Wisner, & Zhu, 2014). Table 5.3 explains other types of deception, including avoidance, lying, and being vague.

Deception is especially commonplace online. People can easily hide and distort information in chat or email messages, and recipients of messages have little opportunity to check accuracy. Some people provide false information about their backgrounds, professions, appearances, and gender online to amuse themselves, to form relationships unavailable to them offline, or to take advantage of others through online scams (Rainey, 2000). However, most people provide accurate information on social networking sites like Tumblr or Instagram because close friends will hold them accountable for what they post (Back et al., 2010).

Whether it's face-to-face or online, deception is unethical, impractical, and destructive. It exploits the message recipients' belief that speakers are communicating cooperatively by tricking them into thinking that the messages are informative, honest, relevant, and clear (McCornack, 2008). Deception is unethical because it denies others information they may need to make personal or professional decisions, and it demonstrates disrespect (LaFollette & Graham, 1986). Deception is impractical because a lie typically leads to more lies (McCornack, 2008). Even something as simple as telling

TABLE 5.3

TYPES OF DECEPTION

AVOIDANCE	CONCEALMENT	LYING	VAGUE
Changing the topic to avoid revealing troublesome information	**Responding with partial truth—but leaving out important information**	**Presenting a message that is entirely false**	**Answering questions with ambiguous language, designed to hide the truth**
Example: A coworker asks if you've heard anything about layoffs, and you shift the topic to sports ("Speaking of layoffs, did you hear about the baseball strike?") to avoid telling him that he's going to be fired.	**Example:** Your dentist asks if you've been flossing and you say, "Yes, I have"—but you conceal the fact that you've flossed only twice in the last month.	**Example:** You give an informative speech telling your class about "your summer working on a ranch," but the whole story is made up, based on a post you saw on Reddit.	**Example:** Your friend asks your opinion about a new dress that she obviously loves, and you say, "It's so unique!" to hide the fact that you think it looks horrible on her.

Adrian Niederhaeuser/Shutterstock

ADVANCE THE CONVERSATION

PROTECTING A FRIEND FROM HARM

1 YOUR DILEMMA

Kevin is your best friend on campus. He is funny, athletic, and hardworking. He's also painfully shy; it's often difficult for him to meet new people.

It's a Friday night, and you and Kevin decide to head to a nightclub to celebrate the end of a tough week. You both take turns as the designated driver, and tonight is your turn to drive. Shortly after arriving at the club, Kevin orders a couple of drinks, approaches a woman, and asks her to dance. You are excited that he took the initiative to meet someone new, but you're not sure if the woman is Kevin's type. When you express your concern to Kevin, he laughs and says, "I've had classes with her before—she's fine. Her name is Aliana."

As the hours slide by, it's clear that as Kevin continues to drink, he is acting far outside his normally reserved demeanor and is starting to embarrass himself in front of other people at the club. He is making a serious play for Aliana, and he's feeding her drinks, one after the next, so now both of them are wasted. You decide to intervene, but when you tell Kevin it's time to go, he says he's going home with Aliana. When you tell him you don't think that's a good idea, Kevin snaps, "Don't tell me what to do! You're not my mother!"

 **How do you feel when Kevin lashes out at you?**

2 THE RESEARCH

Researchers Lisa Menegatos, Linda Lederman, and Aaron Hess (2010) looked at college students' verbal communication strategies for trying to stop drunken friends from hooking up with strangers. They found that college students in such situations commonly use one of three strategies to intervene:

- *Persuasion:* They try to convince their friend not to go home with the other person, emphasizing the potential health and social consequences, such as the risks of pregnancy and sexually transmitted infections, and regrets that may be experienced in the morning.
- *Deception:* They trick their friend into not leaving with the other person. For example, they might tell their friend that they'll provide a ride to the hookup's house but drive to a restaurant to get something to eat instead.
- *Confrontation:* They verbally or physically discourage their friend from leaving with the other person by assertively telling the friend that it's time to leave the club or even physically removing the friend from the club, if necessary. Alternatively, they might confront the person who is pursuing the hookup, telling him or her to leave their friend alone.

Of these three communication approaches, which would you most likely try in dealing with Kevin? Would you consider any other approaches? Do you think you have an ethical obligation to stop Kevin?

3 YOUR OPPORTUNITY

Before you act, consider the facts of the situation, and think about what the research tells you about communicating with an intoxicated friend who is engaging in risky behavior. Also reflect on what you have learned about deception (pp. 130–131), verbal aggression (p. 129), and verbal communication skills (pp. 121–127).

 **Now it's your turn. Write a response to Kevin.**

a friend that you like his new jacket when you don't can get you into trouble. From then on, when you're with your friend, you would have to remember to always praise the jacket rather than criticize it. Otherwise, he will discover your lie. Finally, deception is destructive; when discovered, it has unpleasant personal and professional consequences (McCornack & Levine, 1990), such as conflicts among friends or romantic partners, loss of trust from an audience, or even dismissal from a job.

Defamation

Defamation is intentionally false communication that harms a person's reputation. In written form, defamation is called *libel*; in spoken form, it's *slander*. Defamation isn't just ineffective verbal communication; it can result in legal charges against the person who commits it. But whether such charges will stick depends largely on whether the target of the defamation is a public figure (politician, celebrity, famous athlete) or a private citizen. For public figures, the legal system counts criticism as "free speech." To have defamation charges upheld, public figures must demonstrate that those who made the statements *acted with malice* and *knew that their claims were false.*

In cases involving private citizens, such as gossip or online rumors, legal action is more likely. Private citizens don't have the same access as public figures to media outlets that can counter defamatory statements; they also don't open themselves up to criticism by being a public figure. Consequently, private citizens' rights to protect their reputations outweigh free-speech rights to criticize and defame.

What does this mean in practical terms? When communicating with others—especially online (which is permanent) or in a speech (which is public)—don't write or say anything that could harm a private citizen's reputation. For example, blogging about a coworker engaging in sexual harassment, or giving a speech in which you denounce a local businessman as racist, may result in someone filing a lawsuit against you. Although you have free-speech rights to (fairly) criticize public figures, you do *not* have the right to publicly assail private citizens in ways that damage their reputations. When it comes to verbal communication, the old adage is true: if you don't have something nice to say about someone, don't say anything at all.

ADVANCE THE CONVERSATION
Video Activity

DISAGREEMENT WITH FAMILY

The following scenario will enhance your ability to use verbal communication skills to navigate a disagreement with a family member. Visit LaunchPad at launchpadworks.com to get the full experience with video. As you watch the first video, recall what you've learned about competent verbal communication, and then complete the **Your Turn** prompts. Finally, watch the **Take Two!** video to explore how this scenario could have gone differently.

1 THE PROBLEM

Reynaldo's mom, Bobbie, decides that a great way for their family to reconnect is to take a two-week road trip next summer, driving across the country to see the grandparents. Bobbie sends Reynaldo and his siblings an email, highlighting the sights they'll see and how much fun it will be. Everyone is excited—except Reynaldo. He had planned on working full-time over the summer to earn money to pay for the next semester's tuition. He meets with his mom as soon as possible to talk about their plans for the summer—and as he expected, she isn't thrilled. "Reynaldo," Bobbie says sternly, "we're already counting on you coming. It's been so long since we've all been together. I already told your grandparents, and they are so excited!"

"I know how excited everyone is about the trip, especially you. But I just can't take two weeks off from work."

"You know what, Reynaldo? This may come as a shock to you, but the whole world doesn't revolve around you and your work schedule. You need to make a decision what's more important: your work or your family."

2 YOUR TURN

Observations. Reflect on how Reynaldo and Bobbie communicated in this scenario by answering the following questions:

1. Which character do you identify with more in this situation? How would you feel if you were in his or her situation?
2. Where were the missed opportunities to practice competent communication?

Discussion. In class or with a partner, share your thoughts about the interaction between Reynaldo and Bobbie, and work to answer the following question:

1. Can you understand both perspectives?
2. What could Reynaldo and Bobbie have done differently?

Conclusion. Choose one person in the scenario to offer your advice. Based on your analysis, what advice would you give them to improve their communication competence in this scenario?

3 TAKE TWO!

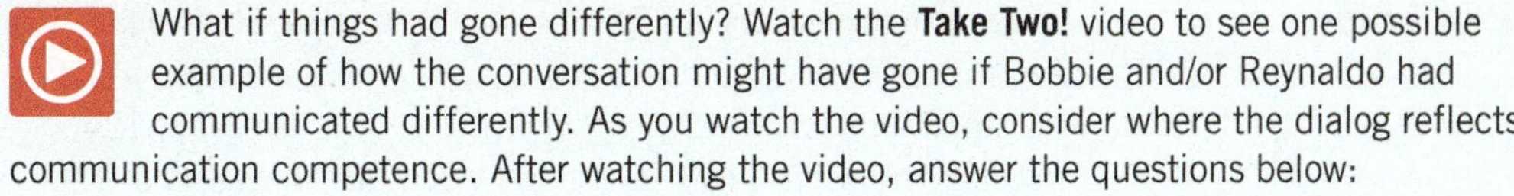

What if things had gone differently? Watch the **Take Two!** video to see one possible example of how the conversation might have gone if Bobbie and/or Reynaldo had communicated differently. As you watch the video, consider where the dialog reflects communication competence. After watching the video, answer the questions below:

1. Did Bobbie and/or Reynaldo take advantage of opportunities that they missed in the first scenario? Which ones?
2. Did their different actions result in a more productive encounter? Please explain.

CHAPTER 5 REVIEW

CHAPTER RECAP

- **Verbal communication** is the use of written or spoken language to interact with others. Language is symbolic, is governed by rules, conveys meaning, and is intertwined with culture.
- You can increase your verbal communication skills by creating messages that adhere to the **cooperative principle** and by using **"I" language** and **"we" language**.
- Although there are many common stereotypes about how men and women communicate, studies show that men's and women's verbal communication is more similar than different.
- Consider how cultural factors like preferred speech rates and desired balance of turn-taking can influence interactions, and adapt as best you can.
- Avoiding verbal communication pitfalls such as **prejudiced language**, **verbal aggression**, **deception**, and **defamation**—and learning how to handle situations when others use them—will help you improve your communication competence.

LaunchPad for *Choices & Connections* offers unique video scenarios and encourages self-assessment through adaptive quizzing. Go to **launchpadworks.com** to get access.

LearningCurve adaptive quizzes

Advance the Conversation video scenarios

Video clips that illustrate key concepts

KEY TERMS

Verbal communication, p. 118
Symbols, p. 119
Constitutive rules, p. 119
Regulative rules, p. 119
Denotative meaning, p. 119
Connotative meaning, p. 119
Dialect, p. 120
Cooperative principle, p. 123
Honesty, p. 123
Misunderstanding, p. 124
"You" language, p. 124
"I" language, p. 124
"We" language, p. 125
Prejudiced language, p. 128
Verbal aggression, p. 129
Deception, p. 130
Defamation, p. 133

POP QUIZ

Looking for more review questions? LearningCurve can help you master key concepts from this chapter. Go to **launchpadworks.com**

1. You and your sister using the phrase "blue moon" to signal to each other when your mom is in a bad mood is an example of

   a. regulative rules.
   b. constitutive rules.
   c. connotative meanings.
   d. denotative meanings.

2. Which of the following is *not* one of the four characteristics of understandable language, according to the cooperative principle?

   a. Honest
   b. Symbolic
   c. Clear
   d. Informative

3. Phrases that both emphasize inclusion and enhance feelings of connection and similarity are known as

   a. "we" language.
   b. "you" language.
   b. "I" language.
   d. the cooperative principle.

4. According to researcher Dominic Infante, how can you competently communicate with verbally aggressive people?

   a. Avoid teasing, baiting, or insulting others.
   b. Minimize contact with people who are chronically verbally aggressive.
   c. Remain polite and respectful, and don't retaliate with your own attacks.
   d. All of the answers are correct.

5. According to Table 5.3, Types of Deception, which of the following refers to revealing part of the truth while leaving out important information?

   a. Vague
   b. Avoidance
   c. Lying
   d. Concealment

ACTIVITIES

For more activities, visit LaunchPad for *Choices & Connections* at **launchpadworks.com**

1 What Went Wrong?

Think of a recent conflict or unpleasant encounter you've had. It can be with anyone: a professor, a friend, a roommate, a family member, a coworker. Write out exactly what you and the other person said, to the best of your recollection. If it was a text-based interaction, use the emails, texts, or tweets for reference. Now, look at the language that you and your partner used. How did specific things that each of you said contribute to the unpleasantness of the interaction? Revisit the coverage of the cooperative principle and "I" and "we" language on pages 124–125. What could you have said differently to help the situation be more positive or to better explain your point of view?

2 Just a Little White Lie

With a partner, discuss the definitions and differences between the types of deception outlined in Table 5.3: avoidance, concealment, lying, and vague. Do you consider some of these types worse or more deceptive than others? When, if ever, is it acceptable to use these forms of deception? Is it ever ethical to deceive? Provide examples and rationales.

6

Nonverbal Communication

Serene smiles. Goofy grins. Contorted grimaces. Giant posters of people making such faces have been popping up all over the globe for the last several years—from southern Sudan to the Standing Rock Indian Reservation in North Dakota. Most are pasted illegally onto the sides of buildings, bridges, and walls; on public staircases; and even on trains and buses. Who's behind these displays? Renegade French artist JR.[1] When asked about the meaning of his work and what he is hoping to achieve through it, he notes that his work can change people's perceptions of one another in powerful, positive ways. How? When you see these people making faces, you also see their humor, personalities, and willingness to poke fun at themselves. You see them using nonverbal behaviors to communicate. Suddenly, people who might have seemed strange and different from you seem silly, similar, and likable.

JR's art installations are collaborative group projects. For a project entitled *Face2Face*, JR photographed Israelis and Palestinians who did the same jobs—taxi drivers, lawyers, and cooks. He then pasted the images side by side in various Israeli communities. As he describes, "The experts said no way—the people will not accept it. But they did. When you paste an image it's just paper and glue. People can tear it, tag on it, the people in the street are the creator. The rain and the wind will take them [the images] off anyway. They're not meant to stay. But it's now four years after, and most of them are still there. *Face2Face* demonstrated that what we thought was impossible was possible."

Wherever they are pasted, JR's installations are immediately recognizable, because they focus on close-up images of the human face. JR uses a wide-angle lens to photograph his subjects, which requires him to stand just a few inches away from them—an intimate distance requiring trust. He then has people "make faces" that represent themselves—communicating vivid and intense messages of identity and emotion. As he describes, "I ask people to make a face as a sign of commitment—not a smile that really doesn't tell who you are or what you feel."

In 2011, JR received the prestigious TED Prize, which recognizes "an extraordinary individual with a creative and bold vision to spark global change" (TED .com, n.d., *The TED Prize*). One of his latest projects, *Inside Out* (insideoutproject.net) involves people submitting self-portraits, which he then prints on enormous posters and sends back, so that contributors can paste them wherever they want. Inherent to *Inside Out* is JR's ongoing recognition of the power of nonverbal communication to impact people's impressions. As he notes, "The idea is that you have to stand for what you care about. It is easy on Facebook to say 'I love this' or 'I'm against that.' But to stand for your own image in the street? That's another level."

[1]All content that follows adapted from Khatchadourian (2011) and JR (2011).

David Silverman/Getty Images News/Getty Images

BM 8

CHAPTER OUTLINE

LearningCurve can help you review! Go to **launchpadworks.com**

As the artwork of JR spotlights, your nonverbal communication powerfully impacts people's impressions of you. Something as simple as a grin or a scowl can make the difference between people liking or not liking you, approaching or avoiding you. This makes learning about, taking control of, and improving your nonverbal communication incredibly important. When you take the time to better understand nonverbal communication and strengthen your skills, the potential payoff is enormous. Nonverbal communication ability is related to higher levels of self-esteem and life satisfaction, perceptions of attractiveness and popularity, greater interpersonal influence in situations requiring persuasive ability, and higher relationship satisfaction (Burgoon & Hoobler, 2002; Carton, Kessler, & Pape, 1999; Hodgins & Belch, 2000). In this chapter, you'll learn:

- The characteristics that define nonverbal communication
- How to use different types of nonverbal communication
- The functions of nonverbal communication
- Ways to improve your nonverbal communication skills

Characteristics of Nonverbal Communication

Although the words you choose are important, your nonverbal communication has more impact because it conveys more meaning. Thus, your nonverbal communication is the most important tool in your communication competence toolbox. The starting point for using this tool skillfully is understanding the characteristics that define it.

Nonverbal communication is the transmission of meaning through an individual's nonspoken physical and behavioral cues (Patterson, 1983, 1995). This includes instances in which you intentionally mean to communicate—such as rolling your eyes to convey annoyance when arguing with your sister—and times when you unintentionally send a message, such as yawning during class. You may just be tired that day, but your teacher could interpret it as a sign that you're bored by her lecture. In addition to being both intentional and unintentional, nonverbal communication has several distinguishing features: it uses multiple channels, conveys more meaning than verbal communication, blends with verbal communication to create meaning, and is influenced by gender and culture.

Nonverbal Communication Uses Multiple Channels

Nonverbal communication conveys information through multiple channels, including auditory, visual, and tactile. Consider what happens when a classmate presents an idea during a discussion. As she speaks, you listen to and interpret the meaning of her words (verbal communication). But at the same time, you're noticing various nonverbal channels—her vocal pitches and tones (auditory); her facial expressions, gestures, postures, and appearance (visual); and possibly physical contact (tactile), such as if she's sitting next to you and happens to touch you. You receive all this information simultaneously and use it to interpret her meaning: Is she excited about her idea? Unsure? Tired? Her nonverbal communication helps you make sense of the words she says and the meaning she intends.

Nonverbal Communication Conveys More Meaning Than Verbal Communication

Because it uses multiple channels, nonverbal communication conveys more meaning than verbal. This is especially evident when people send **incongruent messages**, in which their verbal and nonverbal behaviors contradict each other—for example, saying "I'm fine" while frowning. In such situations, people overwhelmingly trust the nonverbal messages more than they trust the verbal (Burgoon & Hoobler, 2002). An essential part of competent nonverbal communication is producing **congruent messages**, in which your verbal and nonverbal communications match. Congruent messages are perceived as direct and honest, and they create less confusion for others. For example, if you're mad at your sister, you scowl instead of smile when saying, "Yes,

DOUBLE TAKE

INCONGRUENT  CONGRUENT MESSAGES

When your verbal communication ("I'm so happy for you!") doesn't match your nonverbal behavior, people are more likely to believe your nonverbal communication. In the following photos, which woman is sending congruent messages?

Andrew Hobbs/Photodisc/Getty Images

Diego Cervo/Veer

I'm angry!" Or when you're giving a speech, you reinforce the strong statement "Incidents like this cannot happen again!" by pounding your fist on the lectern rather than standing there motionless.

Nonverbal Communication Blends with Verbal Communication

When interacting with others, you don't just use either verbal or nonverbal communication. Instead, you blend both to create and interpret messages (Birdwhistell, 1970; Jones & LeBaron, 2002). You can do this in five ways:

- *Replace* verbal expressions with nonverbal, such as shrugging your shoulders and turning your palms upward instead of saying, "I don't know."
- *Repeat* verbal messages—for instance, saying, "It's up there" and then pointing upward.
- *Contradict* verbal messages with nonverbal communication deliberately—for example, using sarcasm by telling a friend "I love that song" while rolling your eyes, to indicate that you really don't like the song at all.
- *Enhance* the meaning of verbal messages, such as telling a cousin about a professor who kept blinking her eyes while lecturing—and blinking your own eyes repeatedly to demonstrate the teacher's nervous behavior.
- *Spotlight* certain parts of verbal messages—for example, elevating the volume of your voice on a single word: "I did *not* mean it that way!"

Nonverbal Communication Is Influenced by Gender

As noted previously in Chapter 3, gender stereotypes suggest that women and men communicate nonverbally in different ways. Women are often thought to be submissive or meek, whereas men are conceived of as powerful and aggressive. But these are just beliefs. What are the *facts* about gender and nonverbal communication? Data from hundreds of studies suggest four consistent differences between the sexes, none of which align with the stereotypes (Hall, 1998; Hall, Carter, & Horgan, 2000). First, women are better than men at communicating nonverbally in ways receivers can correctly interpret and are more accurate than men in interpreting others' nonverbal expressions. Second, women show greater facial expressiveness than men, and they smile more. Third, women gaze at others more than men do during interpersonal interactions, especially during same-sex encounters. Indeed, women are more likely than men to find speakers persuasive when the presenters maintain eye contact with them (Bailenson, Beall, Loomis, Blascovich, & Turk, 2005). Fourth, men are more territorial than women in terms of personal space. Men maintain more physical space between themselves and others while talking, tolerate intrusions into their personal space less than women do, and are less likely to give way to others if space is scarce. Correspondingly, women enjoy closer proximity during same-gender encounters than men, prefer side-by-side seating more than men do, and perceive crowded situations more favorably.

Of course, not all women and men show these differences. Understanding that such differences *may* exist can help you improve your cross-gender nonverbal communication. For example, if you're hosting a presentation in which the audience is largely male, arrange the seating to provide ample space between audience members. When you're talking with a female friend, she may desire shared gaze and prefer to sit in close proximity to you.

Nonverbal Communication Is Influenced by Culture

The culture in which you were raised plays an enormous role in molding your nonverbal communication behaviors (Matsumoto, 2006). Different cultures have very different *display rules*—guidelines for when, where, and how to appropriately express emotion (Ekman & Friesen, 1975). Cultures also vary in the degree to which they emphasize close physical space, shared gaze, and physical contact during interaction. People from *high-contact cultures* prefer frequent touching, shared gaze, close physical proximity, and direct body orientation (facing each other while talking). Those from *low-contact cultures* prefer infrequent touching, little shared gaze, larger physical distance, and indirect body orientation (angled away from each other during interaction). For more information, see pages 83–84 in Chapter 3.

Types of Nonverbal Communication

Your use of body movement, voice, touch, personal space, appearance, and environmental features work together to create your nonverbal communication. This influences how others perceive your messages, who you are, and how you feel. Understanding the different types of nonverbal expression and how they work will help you make sure these impressions are the right ones.

At age 16, Tyra Banks began doing fashion shows in Europe for designers such as Chanel, Valentino, and Fendi. She subsequently appeared in *Elle* and *Vogue*, and she was the first African American woman to grace the cover of *GQ*. But what catapulted her to the top of the global modeling industry was not just her beauty—it was also her unique self-awareness of, and control over, the various types of nonverbal communication. For example, Banks distinguishes 275 different smiles she uses when modeling that reflect specific emotions or situations, from anger to surprise. One of these smiles uses body posture and movement—specifically, shifting her shoulder position sideways and downward, and turning her head toward the listener. Another smile, which Banks has famously coined the *smize*, doesn't involve the mouth at all, just the eyes. The smize has been one of the most difficult

Tyra Banks believes that just a simple manipulation of your eyes and smile can cause a drastic change in the attitude you portray to the world. How do you use nonverbal communication to express your emotions?

Kevin Mazur/Child11/Getty Images

and elusive expressions for aspiring models to emulate and has inspired videos and online tutorials on how to do it correctly.

Tyra Banks has built a media empire from her uncanny ability to manipulate her nonverbal communication to create unique expressions on fashion runways, on television, and in photographs. But the types of nonverbal communication she uses—and coaches other models how to modify—are the very same ones you use in your daily life. Scholars of communication identify six such types: body movement, voice, touch, personal space, appearance, and environmental features. Although you experience these collectively as a whole, understanding how each type influences your own and others' communication can make the difference between successful and unsuccessful interactions.

Body Movement

Communication scholars refer to body movement as **kinesics**, from the Greek word *kinesis*. This broad category encompasses most of the cues people typically think of as nonverbal communication: facial expressions, eye contact, gestures, and body postures.

Facial Expressions. Think back to the story of French artist JR in our chapter opener. Why would he focus on people's faces as the centerpieces of his art installations? Because of all the behaviors people display when communicating, facial expressions have the most impact (Knapp & Hall, 2002). Everything from the arch of an eyebrow to the curl of a lip can convey information about mood and emotion (Ekman, 2003). Facial expressions are so important that you may feel compelled to use emoticons (e.g., ☺ ☹) when texting to clarify your intentions. In fact, one of the reasons for the popularity of Skype, FaceTime, videoconferencing, and video chat is that these technologies allow people to see and interpret their communication partners' facial expressions.

Eye Contact. You use eye contact to show attention, interest, affection, and even aggression. Looking directly at your audience while giving a speech, for example, conveys concern for their reactions and affiliation with them. Eye contact conveys the same message within group and interpersonal settings as well. When you look at people directly, you're attentive to them, and when you avoid eye contact, you signal that you're disinterested, bored, or ready for the encounter to end. Of course, eye contact can also be used aggressively. When you want to convey dominance over someone—something we talk about later in this chapter—you may try to "stare them down" (Matsumoto, 2006). Since eye contact can show a variety of emotions and intentions, it can be challenging to make sure you perceive others' communication correctly. For ideas on how to handle such situations, see Advance the Conversation: Perceiving Nonverbal Messages on pages 160–161.

Gestures. People use four types of *gestures* (hand motions) to communicate nonverbally:

- **Emblems** substitute for verbal statements—for example, waving your hand at a friend to communicate "Hi!"
- **Illustrators** accent verbal messages—for example, holding your hands a certain distance apart while saying, "The fish I caught was this big."
- **Regulators** help control turn-taking during interpersonal encounters, group discussions, and question-and-answer sessions following presentations. You may point your finger, hold your palm up, or twirl your hands to "tell" people to keep talking, repeat something, hurry up, or wait longer before beginning their turn.
- **Adaptors** are touching gestures that serve a psychological or physical purpose, such as rubbing your chin when thinking about a tough question or playing with a paper clip when you're bored during a long meeting.

Keep in mind that different gestures—and especially emblems—may have very different meanings across cultures. As just one example, in the United States, the thumbs-up gesture is positive ("Good job!" or "Way to go!"), whereas in Greece, the Middle East, and Western Africa, it is grossly offensive. When traveling abroad, always acquaint yourself with nonverbal customs rather than risk an inappropriate gesture.

Body Postures. The straightness of your back (erect or slouched), your body lean (forward, backward, or vertical), the straightness of your shoulders (firm and broad or slumped), and your head position (tilted or straight up) all communicate information to the people with whom you're interacting. For example, Steve's karate instructor interviewed convicted muggers regarding what they looked for in potential victims. The most popular response? Body posture. The muggers perceived people who walked with shoulders slumped, back slouched, and heads drooping as "weak" and "good targets." They saw people who walked with shoulders back, spines erect, and heads up as "confident and strong," and avoided them. The ability of your posture to make such strong impressions is important to remember, not only when you are making a presentation, as it will influence how the audience perceives you, but also when you are interviewing for a job, as the interviewer will take your nonverbal communication into account when forming an impression of you.

Voice

Vocal characteristics used to communicate nonverbal messages are known as **vocalics**. We can use four qualities of voice—tone, pitch, loudness, and speech rate—to create distinct impressions for listeners in any interaction.

Tone. *Tone* stems from the resonance and breathiness of your voice. You can create a rich vocal tone—conveying authority and confidence—by allowing your voice to resonate deep in your chest and throat. Alternatively, restricting your voice to your sinus cavity ("talking through your nose") creates a whiny tone—often judged as unpleasant. How much you breathe while speaking also affects tone. If you expel a great deal of air when speaking, you may convey sexiness. If you constrict airflow when speaking, you create a thin, hard tone, which may communicate nervousness or anxiety.

Pitch. *Pitch* is the frequency range of your voice—how high or low it is. People tend to associate lower pitches with strength and competence, and higher pitches with weakness (Spender, 1990).

Loudness. *Loudness* is the volume of your voice. You can increase loudness to emphasize certain words, phrases, or points. When texting, tweeting, or posting online, people indicate loudness (i.e., shouting or yelling) with CAPITAL LETTERS.

Speech Rate. *Speech rate* is how quickly you speak. Although it is commonly believed that talking at a moderate and steady rate is the best choice, research

In the hit singing competition TV series *The Voice*, each season begins with "blind auditions" in which the judges sit facing away from the singers. The judges claim that listening solely to the contestants' voices, without any other messages, allows them to more effectively evaluate each singer. Can you recall a time when you gained important information from someone's vocalics that was *not* conveyed in their body language or in their actual words?

NBC/Photoshot

shows that speaking fast or slow by itself doesn't seem to determine speech effectiveness (Krause, 2001). Instead, it's whether you correctly pronounce and clearly articulate your words. Keep this in mind if you are making a public speech; if you're a fast talker, take care not to slur or blur your words.

Touch

Communication scholars refer to touch as **haptics**, from the ancient Greek word *haptikos*. The meaning of such physical contact with others depends on the duration, part of the body being touched, strength of contact, and surrounding context (Floyd, 1999). For example, *functional-professional touch* is used to accomplish some type of task, such as touch between physicians and patients during examinations, or between coaches and athletes while "spotting" a workout activity. *Social-polite touch* derives from social norms and expectations, the most common form being the handshake, which has served as a form of greeting for over 2,000 years (Heslin, 1974). You use *friendship-warmth touch*—for example, gently grasping a friend's arm and giving it a squeeze—to express liking for another person. *Love-intimacy touch*—cupping a romantic partner's face tenderly in your hands, giving him or her a big, lingering hug—lets you convey deep emotional feelings. *Sexual-arousal touch*, as the name implies, is intended to physically stimulate another person. Finally, *aggressive-hostile touch* involves forms of physical violence, such as grabbing, slapping, and hitting—behaviors designed to hurt and humiliate others.

People differ widely in their personal preferences for giving and receiving touch, with some liking less contact than others. For example, both Steve and Joe are low-contact people: Joe isn't much of a hugger, and Steve dislikes handshakes. Yet both have family members who are high-contact and enjoy sharing lots of touch. This makes for interesting—and occasionally awkward—interactions at family get-togethers, where the parties involved struggle with whether hugs and handshakes should be shared or avoided. Keep such individual preferences in mind when you interact with others, and adapt your touch behaviors to match their desires.

Personal Space

How close or far away you position yourself from others while communicating is known as **proxemics**, from the Latin word *proximus*, meaning "near." Proxemics often illustrates the nature of the encounter and how you feel about the people with whom you're interacting. There are four different zones for physical distance (see Figure 6.1), and each is used in specific kinds of settings (Hall, 1963):

- *Intimate space* ranges from 0 to 18 inches. Most people use this only with people to whom they feel extremely close.
- *Personal space* ranges from 18 inches to 4 feet and is often used during encounters with friends.

FIGURE 6.1

SPATIAL DISTANCE

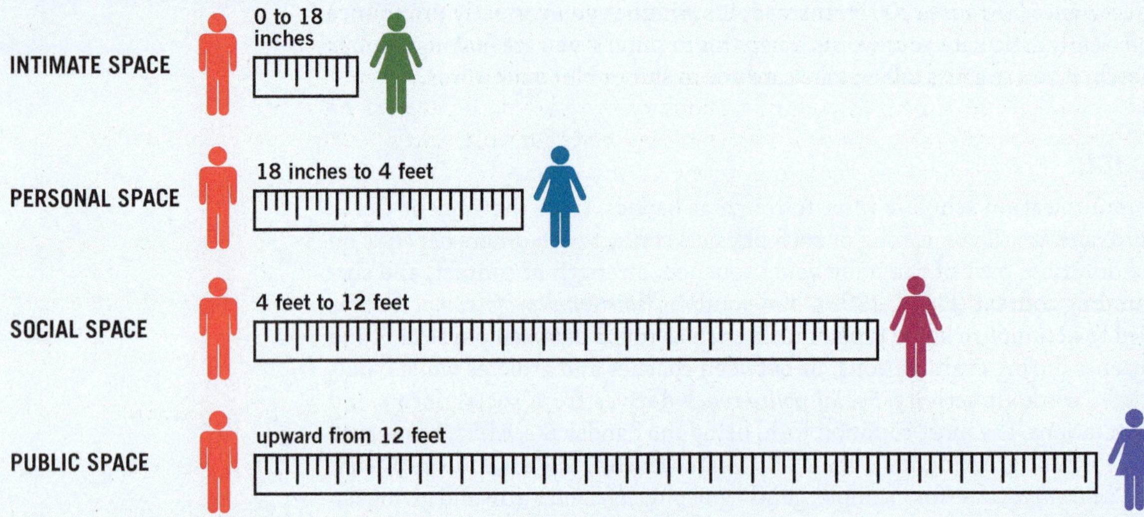

Michael D. Brown/Shutterstock.com

- *Social space* ranges from about 4 feet to 12 feet. Many people use it when communicating in the workplace or with acquaintances and strangers.
- *Public space* ranges upward from 12 feet—including great distances—and is used during formal occasions, such as public speeches or college lectures.

Of course, these distances aren't absolute; different people have different preferences for space. You may feel crowded if people sit closer than two feet from you, whereas your best friend may be perfectly comfortable sitting shoulder-to-shoulder with others. Space preferences also vary widely across cultures (Chen & Starosta, 2005). For example, during casual conversations, most North Americans feel comfortable an arm's-length distance apart. Latin Americans, North Africans, and those from the northern and western Middle East tend to prefer a closer distance. Japanese and Chinese tend to keep a larger distance. Failure to appreciate these differences can cause awkwardness and anxiety during cross-cultural encounters. People from cultures emphasizing closer distance may keep edging closer to their conversation partner and may judge the other person as aloof and standoffish if he or she keeps backing away. Correspondingly, people from cultures emphasizing larger distances will be baffled by and uncomfortable with perceived invasions of their space. Because violations of space expectations can cause discomfort, try to adjust your use of space in accordance with others' preferences whenever possible.

Appearance

The way you look speaks volumes about who you are because people use your *physical appearance*—visible attributes such as hair, clothing, body type, and other features—to make judgments about you. For example, people who judge you as attractive may also see you as intelligent, persuasive, poised, sociable, warm, powerful, and successful (Hatfield & Sprecher, 1986). Such perceptions are made online as well. If your friends post attractive photos of themselves on your Facebook page, people will perceive you as more physically and socially attractive. If your friends post unattractive photos, you'll seem less attractive to others (Walther, Van Der Heide, Kim, Westerman, & Tong, 2008).

NONVERBAL COMMUNICATION IN CONTEXT

Whether it's through body language, facial expressions, or environmental features, all forms of nonverbal communication influence your perception of a situation. What do the nonverbal cues in the photos tell you about each workplace?

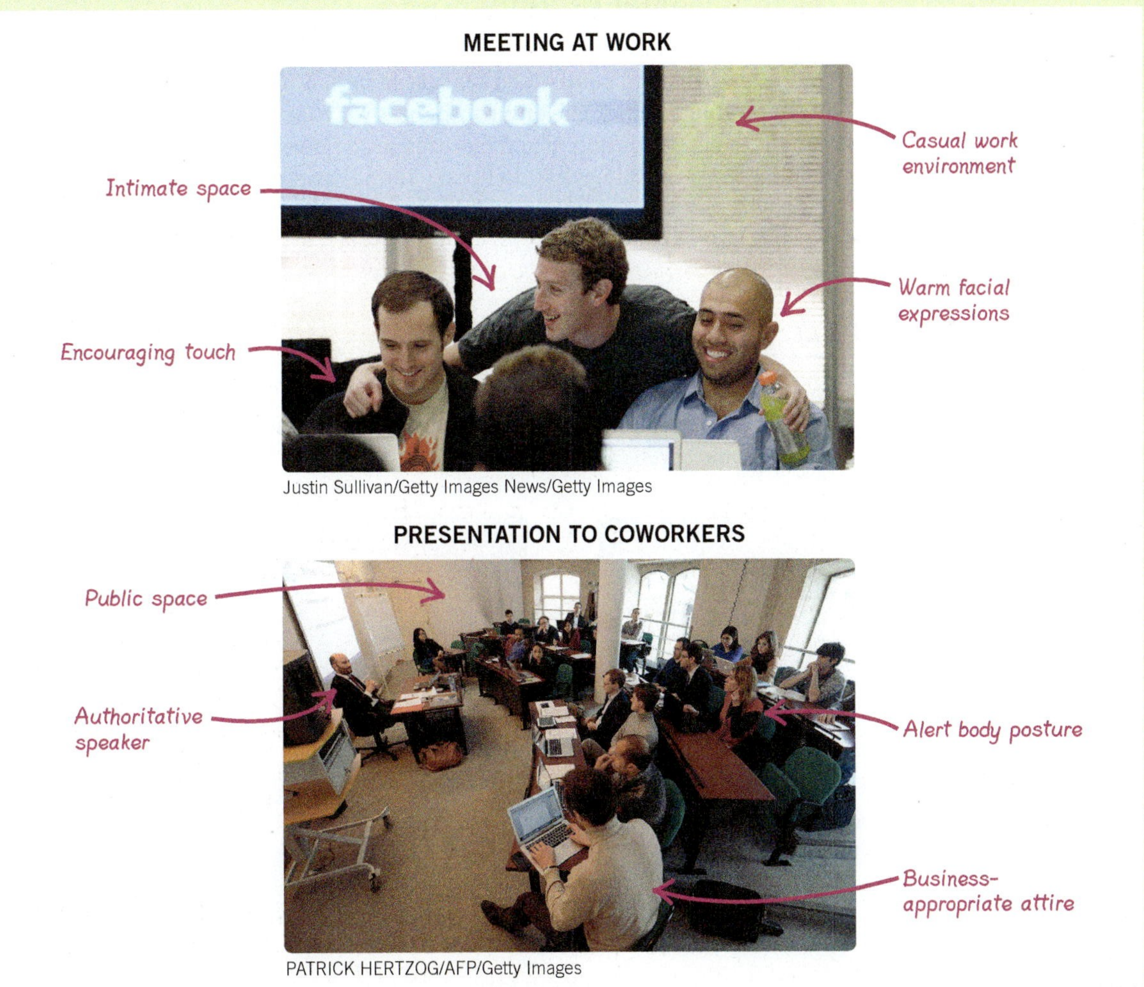

Justin Sullivan/Getty Images News/Getty Images

PATRICK HERTZOG/AFP/Getty Images

Clothing plays a large role in your physical appearance. People draw conclusions about your profession, level of education, socioeconomic status, and even personality and values based solely on what you're wearing (Burgoon, Buller, & Woodall, 1996). So before leaving the house, ask yourself whether your outfit is appropriate for your plans and whether your clothing will convey the image you want it to convey. If you want a job interviewer to see you as socially skilled and highly motivated, wear something business appropriate to the interview (Gifford, Ng, & Wilkinson, 1985). Your clothing choices include **artifacts**—objects you possess to communicate your identity to others, such as watches, jewelry, and handbags. Artifacts can communicate your affluence, influence, and attractiveness (Burgoon et al., 1996). Men in the United States, for instance, typically don't wear much jewelry, so a man who wants to stand out may sport a large expensive watch to convey power and wealth.

Environmental Features

Two types of environmental features shape nonverbal communication: fixed features and semi-fixed features (Hall, 1981). *Fixed features* are relatively stable parts of the environment—for example, walls, ceilings, floors, and doors in a building. Fixed features send powerful nonverbal messages to others. For example, what do luxury homes and cars share in common with first-class seating in airplanes? *Bigger size*. Simple differences in the fixed

ENVIRONMENT IN CONTEXT

Consider how environmental features in these two living rooms send nonverbal messages. What do you perceive about the people who live there based on the fixed features and semi-fixed features? What messages are you trying to send through environmental spaces you have control over?

PlusONE/Shutterstock.com

pics721/Shutterstock.com

features of room size, ceiling height, and (in the case of cars and airplanes) seat size and legroom convey greater wealth and prestige. People recognize this and use such features to nonverbally communicate stature to others (by driving big cars, building huge houses, and so forth).

Semi-fixed features are impermanent and usually easy to change. They include things like furniture, lighting, and color. Hard, uncomfortable furniture shortens interactions, just as soft, plush seating encourages relaxed, lengthy encounters. Bright lighting is associated with action-filled environments, whereas soft lighting goes with calm, intimate environments. Color also makes a difference; people experience blues and greens as relaxing, yellows and oranges as arousing and energizing, reds and blacks as sensuous, and grays and browns as depressing (Burgoon et al., 1996).

You can make choices about fixed and semi-fixed factors to send a nonverbal message. For example, if you want to convey a sense of formality while conducting your monthly sales meeting, have attendees sit at a large, rectangular conference table in rigid high-backed chairs, in a room adorned with portraits of the company founders. If you want to convey a sense of creativity and relaxation, have the meeting at a local coffee shop, where salespeople can lounge in comfy chairs in front of a fireplace.

Functions of Nonverbal Communication

Although nonverbal communication seems like something that just happens, it isn't random, nor is it a pointless companion to verbal messages. Instead, it is purposeful and serves many functions. By understanding these functions, you can better match your nonverbal communication to the demands of different situations.

At the 1968 Summer Olympics, U.S. sprinter Tommie Smith won the men's 200-meter gold medal, and teammate John Carlos won the bronze. During the medal ceremony that followed, neither athlete said a word. But their nonverbal communication spoke volumes. Instead of standing with heads up, eyes open, and hands over hearts as the U.S. national anthem played, both runners closed their eyes, lowered their heads, and raised black-gloved fists. Smith's right fist represented black power, and Carlos's left fist represented black unity (Gettings, 2005). The two fists, raised next to each other, created an arch of black unity and power. Smith wore a black scarf around his neck for black pride, and both men wore black socks with no shoes, representing African American poverty. These kinesics (gestures, posture, eyes) and clothing choices (gloves, socks, scarf) combined to communicate the runners' protest of racial injustice and their sense of solidarity with the African American community. Nearly 50 years later, in 2017, NFL football players mirrored the messages of Smith and Carlos by using nonverbal communication—kneeling rather than standing during the national anthem—to wordlessly convey concern regarding police brutality.

Tommie Smith and John Carlos's protest at the 1968 Olympics and NFL players' protests in 2017 reveal the power of nonverbal communication to drive the national conversation. Can you recall a time when someone's nonverbal communication had a powerful impact on you?

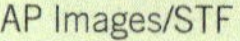
AP Images/STF

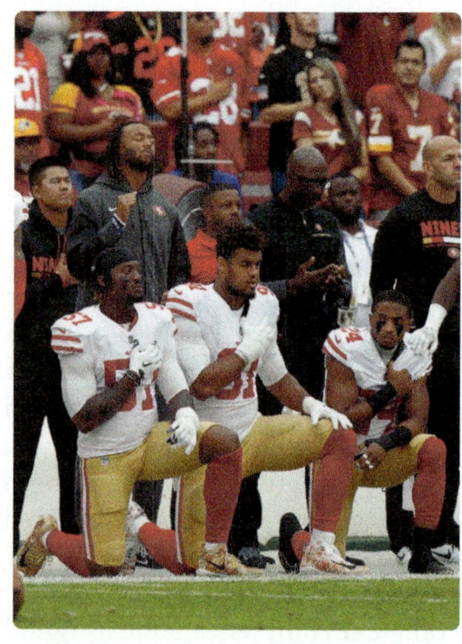

Lee Coleman/Icon Sportswire/Getty Images

Whenever we nonverbally communicate, the messages we use can directly convey meanings. Socks without shoes can mean poverty, just as arms raised in an arch can mean unity. But in addition to communicating meanings, our nonverbal communication serves other functions as well. We can express emotions, present ourselves in specific ways, manage interactions, and define relationships, all through how we nonverbally communicate. Let's take a closer look at all of these functions.

Conveying Meaning

Nonverbal communication conveys meaning both directly and indirectly. Sometimes you directly communicate, such as flashing a thumbs-up sign to a friend who performed well during a play. At other times, your nonverbal communication is comparatively indirect—for example, wearing black to signal sadness or grief rather than openly crying.

Although you regularly use nonverbal communication to convey meaning, be careful about presuming particular meanings from the nonverbal displays of others. Consider deception, for example. Around the world, people believe that liars fidget nervously, play with their hair or clothes, and smile too much (Global Deception Research Team, 2006). The most commonly believed deception cue is *eye contact*: "Liars can't look you in the eye," or so we're told by movies, TV shows, websites, books, and magazines. But these beliefs are *false*. Across hundreds of scientific studies

FIGURE 6.2

NONVERBAL BEHAVIORS

When communicating, you combine different nonverbal behaviors to provide specific functions. Depending on the interaction and your communication goals, you adjust these behaviors. For example, what other nonverbal behaviors might you employ (or avoid) in each situation listed below to achieve your communication goals?

COMFORT A FRIEND
Lowered voice pitch
Furrowed brow
Nodding
Sharing more touch
Takeaway:
Nonverbal behaviors can convey emotional support
CELEBRATE AN ANNIVERSARY
Leaning in closer
Expelling air when speaking
Smiling more
Sharing more gaze
Takeaway:
Nonverbal behaviors can communicate intimacy
CONFRONT A SIBLING
Direct gaze and staring
Larger-than-life claiming of space
Speaking loudly
Scowling
Takeaway:
Nonverbal behaviors can convey dominance
GIVE A PRESENTATION
Watching for head nods
Using regulators
Standing with your shoulders back
Posture shifts
Takeaway:
Nonverbal behaviors can help manage interactions

1. VoodooDot/Shutterstock.com; 2. ekler/Shutterstock.com; 3. tele52/Shutterstock.com; 4. Introwiz1/Shutterstock.com

involving tens of thousands of participants, not a single nonverbal behavior has been found that consistently indicates deception (DePaulo et al., 2003; Sporer & Schwandt, 2006). So, if someone doesn't look you in the eye while speaking, don't presume that it means deception—the person could simply be shy or come from a culture in which direct eye gaze is viewed as inappropriate.

Expressing Emotion

You also use nonverbal communication for **affect displays**: intentional or unintentional behaviors that depict actual or feigned emotion (Burgoon et al., 1996). Affect displays are presented primarily through the face and voice. You communicate hundreds, if not thousands, of real and faked emotional states with your face. You may grin in amusement, grimace in

ADVANCE THE CONVERSATION

I WASN'T BEING SARCASTIC!

1 YOUR DILEMMA

Chelsea is the top student in your public speaking class. Although she is brilliant and talented, she knows it and goes out of her way to show off. You admire her, but her arrogance irks you.

Your professor assigns Chelsea to critique your first in-class speech. Chelsea must analyze a video of your speech, then send comments to you and the professor. Your speech goes well, but you're worried that Chelsea—who is a perfectionist—might be harsh in her assessment. When you read her review, though, you see that her comments are complimentary, detailed, fair, and extremely insightful. Since your shift at work starts in five minutes, you send her a hasty message to thank her: "Just wanted to say I REALLY appreciate your BRILLIANT and INSIGHTFUL comments!"

After work, you find another message from Chelsea. It reads, "You know, I always thought you were kind of a loser. But I gave you the benefit of the doubt and approached your speech with an open mind. I spent two hours on my review. The least you could have done was thank me straight up, instead of being sarcastic. I guess my initial impression was right after all. Don't bother writing back."

 **How do you feel when you read Chelsea's message?**

2 THE RESEARCH

To understand sarcasm, people rely primarily on nonverbal communication (Bryant & Fox Tree, 2005). Facial expressions (smirking), eye movements (rolling eyes), and vocal cues (varying pitch) all indicate that speakers mean the opposite of their spoken words.

Because sarcasm is conveyed nonverbally, dealing with sarcasm online can be tricky (Eisterhold, Attardo, & Boxer, 2006). Researchers Whalen, Pexman, and Gill (2009) found that college students use sarcasm in only 7.4 percent of their email. However, when sarcasm is used, it is almost always marked by online nonverbals, such as capped letters, emoticons (winks), or parenthesized statements ("not!" or "sarcasm!").

Whalen et al. (2009) warn that regardless of such markers, using sarcasm online is risky because of the potential for misunderstanding. Despite this, people typically have high confidence that their online messages will be understood correctly (Kruger, Epley, Parker, & Ng, 2005).

What aspects of your message triggered Chelsea's attribution of sarcasm? If you were in Chelsea's shoes, would you have interpreted your message in the same way?

3 YOUR OPPORTUNITY

How will you respond to Chelsea? Before you act, consider the facts of the situation and think about the sarcasm research. Also, reflect on what you've learned about characteristics of nonverbal communication (pp. 140–143) and functions of nonverbal communication (pp. 151–156).

 **Now it's your turn. Write a response to Chelsea.**

disgust, furrow your brow in concern, or lift one eyebrow in suspicion. Your voice also conveys emotions. For instance, most people express emotions such as grief and love through lowered vocal pitch, and hostile emotions such as anger and contempt through loudness (Costanzo, Markel, & Costanzo, 1969).

Presenting Self

Consider all the ways you can use nonverbal communication to present different aspects of your self to others. You can wear religious artifacts to convey your spiritual beliefs. You can select clothing to present your self as Goth, hipster, preppy, or punk. You can walk slouched and hunched over to communicate dismay, or stand with your head up and shoulders back to demonstrate confidence. Smiling presents you to others as friendly and approachable, while scowling presents you as threatening. An important part of being a competent nonverbal communicator is recognizing the demands of the situation (formal/informal; intimate/impersonal), then shifting your nonverbal communication quickly to present your self in appropriate ways.

Managing Interactions

Your nonverbal communication helps you manage interactions. For example, during conversations or question-and-answer sessions following presentations, you use regulators (such as pointing to the person you want to hear from next), eye contact, touch, smiling, nodding, and posture shifts to signal who gets to speak and for how long (Patterson, 1988). You also read your partner's or audience's nonverbal communication while you're speaking—watching for eye contact, smiles, and head nods to ensure that they're listening and engaged. If someone raises an eyebrow after you make a statement, you may pause to see if the listener has a question or comment.

Defining Relationships

A final function that your nonverbal communication serves is to help define two important interpersonal dynamics in your relationships with others: the level of intimacy that you share, and the power balance—that is, who is dominant and who is submissive (Burgoon & Hoobler, 2002; Kudoh & Matsumoto, 1985). Let's explore each of these dynamics individually.

Intimacy. The feeling of bonding or union between yourself and others is known as **intimacy** (Rubin, 1973). Nonverbal communication helps convey and confirm intimacy during interpersonal encounters. Think about how your nonverbal communication differs depending on whether you're interacting with a romantic partner or a close family member—versus an acquaintance. Chances are, with your intimate relationship partner, you likely share more touch (and more intimate forms of touch), sit closer together, share more gaze, use more relaxed postures, lean in toward each other more, smile more, and (of course) share more time with that person than you do with acquaintances (Floyd & Burgoon, 1999; Floyd & Morman, 1999).

Power Balance. In any encounter, communication partners negotiate the balance of power in two ways. **Dominance** involves behaviors used to exert power and influence over others (Burgoon & Dunbar, 2000). To nonverbally communicate your dominance, you would use direct gaze and staring, frowning, and scowling; larger-than-normal claiming of space; invasion of others' space; and indirect body orientation. In contrast, **submissiveness** is the willingness to allow others to exert power over you. To communicate submissiveness, you would smile more, look down and away, take up as little space as possible, and allow others to invade your space without complaint or protest.

Nonverbal communication of dominance or submissiveness sends messages about how you perceive the power balance between you and others. Displays of dominance are most appropriate when you're in a position of power (such as group leader, manager, or team captain) and when you're trying to actively assert your authority to control the behavior of others. Dominance is inappropriate when dealing with people who have power over you or those who are equal to you (e.g., friends, coworkers, and romantic partners). Similarly, be wary of conveying submissiveness to those whom you are supposed to be leading, as it will foster impressions of weakness and incompetence. Submissiveness is most appropriate when faced with others who have authority over you, such as law enforcement officers, military unit leaders, or upper-level managers.

Strengthening Your Nonverbal Communication Skills

Using nonverbal communication competently is as much about learning to better express your intentions as it is about suppressing inappropriate responses. Knowing when to employ nonverbal behaviors, when to control them, and how to better interpret others' use of them will lead you to more competent communication.

Nonverbal communication often seems automatic, something that just naturally occurs while interacting with others. But communicating nonverbally is just as controllable as communicating verbally if you invest the time and energy into learning how to do so. Focusing on three areas will strengthen your nonverbal communication skills: enhancing your nonverbal expressiveness, inhibiting your nonverbal behaviors when necessary, and checking your nonverbal attributions (Riggio, 2006).

Enhancing Your Nonverbal Expressiveness

Nonverbally expressive people accurately convey their feelings and attitudes through their nonverbal communication (Riggio, 2006). You know when they are happy, worried, or excited, because they smile, wrinkle their brows, or increase their speech rate. On the other hand, people who have trouble expressing themselves nonverbally are difficult to read and may often be misunderstood. For instance, if you have a blank facial expression during a romantic crisis, your partner may conclude that you don't care about what's happening. Or if you fail to gesture decisively and speak loudly enough while making a sales pitch to potential clients, they may assume that you're not enthusiastic about the product you're selling.

To improve nonverbal expressiveness, strengthen your awareness of your own behavior (Knapp & Hall, 2002) by soliciting feedback from others and observing yourself. For example, ask a trusted friend, mentor, or teacher how your nonverbal behavior comes across when you're communicating interpersonally, in small group settings, or while giving a speech. Do you project confidence or seem nervous? What does your posture say about your level of involvement with the conversation, the other person, or the

PictureLux/The Hollywood Archive/Alamy Stock Photo

The 2018 horror film *A Quiet Place* follows a family struggling to survive in a world overrun with predatory creatures that are drawn to sound—*any* sound. Because any noise could put them in grave danger, the family members rely entirely on nonverbal cues—including facial expressions, body language, and hand signals—to communicate information to each other. Can you recall a time when you have used nonverbal communication to convey an important message?

topic of your presentation? How does your voice sound, and what messages does it send? If you are giving a speech, you can improve your expressiveness by rehearsing in front of a mirror or by viewing video of your performance. Chapter 15 explores specific nonverbal behaviors to use when you're giving a presentation.

Inhibiting Your Nonverbal Behaviors

To communicate competently, you sometimes need to *inhibit*, or control, your nonverbal behaviors. Many contexts and cultures require that you limit nonverbal expression of intense emotions. For example, leaders during crisis situations are expected to demonstrate calm instead of openly displaying their anxiety or fear (Riggio, 2006). A calm leader is less likely to trigger panic in his or her followers during a crisis. Imagine how you'd feel if the president of the United States, during a national crisis, gave a speech while nervously looking around, fidgeting uncontrollably, and gesturing with trembling hands. It wouldn't matter what was said; your confidence would be swiftly eroded simply by the lack of nonverbal control. Keep this in mind whenever you occupy leadership positions. Similarly, many cultures—especially those emphasizing collectivism (such as China)—have *display rules* discouraging direct expressions of powerful emotions, such as anger. Within such cultures, you'd want to suppress those kinds of expressions, such as the urge to scowl, shout, or shake your fist in response to a group member's argument.

The key to learning nonverbal inhibition is to practice *critical self-reflection*. Identify situations that evoke strong emotional reactions in you. Perhaps these include job interviews, class presentations, and interactions with difficult family members. Then, reflect on how your thoughts and feelings affect your nonverbal communication in these situations. What is it that sets you off in these encounters? How might you think about each situation differently, and what changes could you make to get better results?

For instance, suppose you dread spending time with your brother because you think he resents your success and is therefore angry with you. This fear triggers nervous behaviors—such as avoiding eye contact and fidgeting with your hair—when you get together with him. The behaviors in turn create a sense of distance between you. How might you think about the situation differently to control this fear and avoid unwanted nonverbal behaviors? Perhaps you could envision your brother's attitude toward you as stemming from pain, not resentment. If you reframe the situation that way, you may feel less fearful when you're with your brother and more compassionate instead—an emotion that's less likely to trigger nervous behaviors. Then you could practice actively making changes to your nonverbal behaviors to increase intimacy, such as making more eye contact. Mastering this process can help you inhibit nonverbal emotion displays when it's important to do so.

Checking Your Nonverbal Attributions

Another valuable nonverbal communication skill is correctly interpreting the meaning and intent behind others' nonverbal communication—in other words, making accurate nonverbal attributions. To do this, carefully consider the context as well as factors that may be influencing the other person's behaviors. Always keep in mind the most important rule of attributional accuracy: *People's behavior rarely, if ever, stems from just one simple cause*. For example, many people believe that crossed arms indicate a closed, defensive person. This attribution is touted as truth on TV talk shows and in self-help and advice blogs. But for many people, crossed arms is a relaxed posture. For others, this behavior could simply mean that they're cold. Similarly, if you're conducting a performance evaluation with an employee who makes little eye contact with you, does that mean he's lying? Not necessarily. It could be a culturally learned behavior indicating deference or respect for authority.

Rather than trying to attribute specific meanings to isolated behaviors, consider the cultures and genders of the people involved as well as the communication context. If you're confused about someone's behavior, or if it's important to make accurate attributions about another person's nonverbal communication, practice *perception-checking*. As Chapter 2 explains, figuring out the meaning behind someone else's nonverbal communication can be as simple as asking the person about it. For example, if your roommate comes home and goes straight to her room without greeting you—an unusual behavior for her—you could later ask her, "I was confused by your quietness this afternoon; are you OK?" Rather than assuming she was mad at you about something, you can share your observation of her nonverbal behavior with her, and ask her to clarify what the behavior meant.

LearningCurve can help you review! Go to **launchpadworks.com**

ADVANCE THE CONVERSATION
Video Activity

PERCEIVING NONVERBAL MESSAGES

The following scenario will enhance your ability to understand and apply competent nonverbal communication. Visit LaunchPad at **launchpadworks.com** to get the full experience with video. As you watch the first video, recall what you've learned about appropriateness, effectiveness, and ethics, and then complete the **Your Turn** prompts. Finally, watch the **Take Two!** video to explore how this scenario could have gone differently.

1 *THE PROBLEM*

Erika is Skyping with Danielle, her long-distance friend. Erika has recently started dating a new romantic partner, Amy, and she is excited to tell Danielle about her new relationship. But as Erika is telling a story about Amy, Danielle frowns, rolls her eyes, and looks down at the floor. Erika isn't sure how to interpret these nonverbal messages.

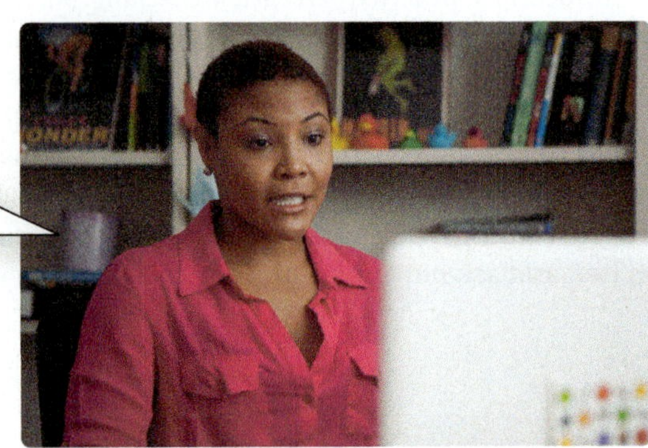

"I get the impression that I've been talking too much about Amy. Is it a problem, or do you have to go someplace right now?"

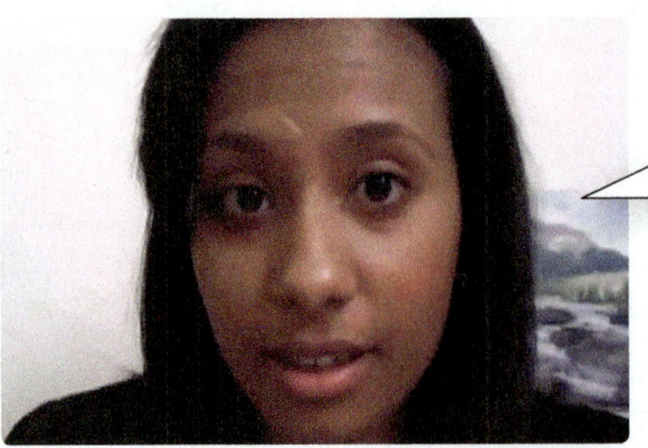

"What? No, I just . . . I had something in my eyes. You know what? I just noticed the time. I'm going to be late for my shift."

2 YOUR TURN

Observations. Reflect on how Erika and Danielle communicated in this scenario by answering the following questions:

1. Which character do you identify with more in this situation? How would you feel if you were in their situation?
2. Where were the missed opportunities to practice competent communication?

Discussion. In class or with a partner, share your thoughts about the interaction between Erika and Danielle and work to answer the following questions:

1. Can you understand both perspectives?
2. What could Danielle and Erika have done differently?

Conclusion. Choose one person in the scenario to offer your advice. Based on your analysis, what advice would you give him or her to improve his or her communication competence in this scenario?

3 TAKE TWO!

What if things had gone differently? Watch the **Take Two!** video to see one possible example of how the conversation might have gone if Danielle and/or Erika had communicated differently. As you watch the video, consider where the dialog reflects communication competence. After watching the video, answer the questions below:

1. Did Danielle and/or Erika take advantage of opportunities that they missed in the first scenario? Which ones?
2. Did their different actions result in a more productive encounter? Please explain.

CHAPTER 6 REVIEW

CHAPTER RECAP

- Because it uses multiple channels, **nonverbal communication** conveys more meaning than verbal communication. However, it also works with verbal communication to create messages.
- According to some studies, men and women actually do differ in their use of nonverbal expression. Similarly, *display rules* vary from culture to culture, and *high-* and *low-contact cultures* have varying degrees of comfort with regard to touch, space, and shared gaze.
- The different types of nonverbal communication include **kinesics**, **vocalics**, **haptics**, **proxemics**, appearance, and environmental features.
- Nonverbal messages serve a host of functions: conveying meaning; presenting **affect displays**; creating self-presentations; managing interactions; and defining levels of **intimacy**, **dominance**, and **submissiveness**.
- Knowing how to use nonverbal behaviors, when to control them, and how to interpret others' use of them will help you communicate competently in any situation.

LaunchPad for *Choices & Connections* offers unique video scenarios and encourages self-assessment through adaptive quizzing. Go to **launchpadworks.com** to get access.

 LearningCurve adaptive quizzes

 Advance the Conversation video scenarios

 Video clips that illustrate key concepts

KEY TERMS

Nonverbal communication, p. 140
Incongruent messages, p. 141
Congruent messages, p. 141
Kinesics, p. 144
Emblems, p. 145
Illustrators, p. 145
Regulators, p. 145
Adaptors, p. 145
Vocalics, p. 146
Haptics, p. 147
Proxemics, p. 147
Artifacts, p. 150
Affect displays, p. 153
Intimacy, p. 155
Dominance, p. 156
Submissiveness, p. 156

POP QUIZ

Looking for more review questions? **LearningCurve** can help you master key concepts from this chapter. Go to **launchpadworks.com**

1. People from which type of culture prefer frequent touching, shared gaze, and close physical proximity?
   - **a.** low-contact cultures
   - **b.** individualistic cultures
   - **c.** collectivistic cultures
   - **d.** high-contact cultures

2. Gestures that substitute for verbal statements—for example, giving a thumbs-up to communicate "Good job!"—are known as
   - **a.** emblems.
   - **b.** illustrators.
   - **c.** regulators.
   - **d.** adaptors.

3. In terms of nonverbal communication, you can express your identity, affluence, and influence through your use of
   - **a.** artifacts.
   - **b.** personal space.
   - **c.** social-polite touch.
   - **d.** fixed features.

4. Which of the following is *not* a way to show dominance through nonverbal communication?
   - **a.** Directly staring
   - **b.** Frowning or scowling
   - **c.** Looking down
   - **d.** Invading others' space

5. One way to improve your nonverbal competence is to evaluate the accuracy of your attributions through
   - **a.** inhibition control.
   - **b.** perception-checking.
   - **c.** submissiveness.
   - **d.** affect displays.

ACTIVITIES

For more activities, visit LaunchPad for *Choices & Connections* at **launchpadworks.com**

1 Communicating Deception

Write down four facts about yourself and your background (hometown, major, profession, personal interests and activities, family history, significant memories). Two of these facts should be true, and two should be false (i.e., two "facts" are made up or lies). In a small group, present these facts to your classmates. While others in your group are presenting, note which facts you think are truths and which are lies based on the presenters' nonverbal communication. Afterward, check the accuracy of your observations as well as which facts about you your classmates thought were false. What nonverbal signals seemed more deceptive? Were there any common deceptive expressions in the group? How did your observations align with the chapter content on deception and nonverbal communication (pages 152–153)?

2 Eye Contact and Intimacy

To test how intimacy is fostered by nonverbal communication, pair up with a classmate you don't know. This activity is timed, so have a phone or watch ready to count 60 seconds. Stand face-to-face, two to three feet from each other. At the start, stare directly into each other's eyes. Hold this direct mutual gaze, without speaking, for the entire 60 seconds. Afterward, discuss your impressions with your partner. How intimate did the shared gaze feel? Did this activity change how intimate or familiar you feel with others? How? What does this illustrate about intimacy and nonverbal expression?

7

Active Listening

On March 30, 2012, hundreds gathered at Fort Bragg, North Carolina, to celebrate the retirement of Command Sergeant Major Joseph Allen. He had served in the U.S. Army for 37 years, having played pivotal roles in Operation Desert Shield and Operation Desert Storm during his multiple tours in Iraq. General Lloyd Austin, Commanding General of United States Forces-Iraq, summed up Allen's service to his country by saying, "I've never known a more courageous and selfless individual in my 36-plus years in uniform." But it wasn't just Allen's courage and selflessness that was celebrated. He had long been a proponent of active listening as a critical component of military command. As he describes, "listening is a powerful tool for leaders, and it's a big part of [my] approach to dealing with service members." He was known to tell his troops, "I work for you; if there's something I need to do, you need to tell me" (Dey, 2010).

Although many civilians may assume that interactions in the U.S. military consist only of commands and assents, the emphasis that Allen places on actively listening to others is far from unique. Officers increasingly stress listening as the cornerstone of communication. In fact, Navy admiral Mike Mullen describes the three Ls of leadership as "listening, learning, and leading" (Garamone, 2011). Of course, it isn't just U.S. military officers who feel this way. The NATO (North Atlantic Treaty Organization) guide on leadership and command specifically mentions that listening skills are essential for successful military command around the world (Febbraro, McKee, & Riedel, 2008).

During combat operations, active listening can mean the difference between life and death. Soldiers must be able to hear, understand, and respond immediately to commands so that everyone takes the actions needed to come out of the engagement safely. The benefits of active listening are not solely tactical, however. In helping soldiers recover from combat-related injuries or deal with depression, *the* most important communication skill family and friends can display is a willingness to listen.

Willingness to listen defined Command Sergeant Major Allen's service. As Allen himself notes, "Everyone has something significant going on in their lives that might affect them. Sometimes people just need an ear; they just need somebody to listen to their problems." And those who served under him, including First Sergeant Demetrius Johnson, deeply appreciated this approach. "I have deployed with [Allen] twice," says Johnson, "and he always made himself available anytime a service member, regardless of rank, had an issue that they needed a compass check on. And he would always have an answer."

Photo by Sgt. Katryn McCalment/DVIDS/US Department of Defense

ALLEN
U.S.ARMY

CHAPTER OUTLINE

LearningCurve can help you review! Go to **launchpadworks.com**

Being a good listener is hard work. Whether you're in the military or a civilian, in a public or a private setting, it takes a lot of mental energy to remain focused on other people, follow what they are saying, and make sense of it. Yet many people think of listening as something that just happens. Nothing could be further from the truth. People spend more time listening than engaging in any other type of communication activity (Jalongo, 2008). Moreover, the ability to listen actively has been shown to improve academic success (Brigman, Lane, Lane, Lawrence, & Switzer, 1999) and can increase your ability to provide emotional support to others (Bodie & Fitch-Hauser, 2010). Employers also value listening skills, identifying them as a key consideration when making decisions about pay raises and promotions (Janusik, 2002). Learning to improve your *active listening* skills can have a significant impact on all areas of your life. In this chapter, you'll learn:

- How the listening process works
- Why people use different listening styles
- The barriers to active listening
- Ways to strengthen your active listening skills

The Listening Process

Before you can strengthen your listening skills, it's important to explore the foundation of listening: how you listen, why you listen, and the potential pitfalls of multitasking when trying to listen.

When you listen to someone, you're not engaged in a single act. Instead, you are taking part in a process—a series of separate yet linked actions. As you'll see in the text that follows, how you listen is guided by your motives for listening. What's more, each step of the listening process can be disrupted if you try to engage in other tasks while listening.

Stages of the Listening Process

The process of **listening** involves six stages: hearing, understanding, interpreting, evaluating, remembering, and responding to others' communication. As you learn about each stage, consider why it is critical to becoming a more active listener.

Hearing. Listening begins with **hearing**: physically processing the sound that others have produced, and mentally focusing your attention on it. Hearing occurs when sound waves enter your inner ear, causing your eardrum to vibrate. These vibrations travel along special nerves to your brain, which interprets them as words and sounds. For people who are hearing impaired or deaf, "hearing" means visually noticing that someone else is communicating by seeing either the person's lips move or the person's hands gesture in signs (if they are using American Sign Language). In such cases, you can hear with your eyes rather than with your ears.

PictureLux/The Hollywood Archive/Alamy Stock Photo

Kimmy, the title character on the hit Netflix series *The Unbreakable Kimmy Schmidt*, often struggles to correctly listen to and engage with the people she encounters—a fact largely explained by the fact that she spent 15 years in an underground cult, apart from society. Whether with her roommate Titus, her landlady Lillian, or strangers on the street, Kimmy often doesn't interpret messages correctly—usually with comical results. How can you improve your own listening skills?

During this stage of the listening process, the mental side of hearing also begins, as you actively concentrate your attention on the sounds or signs of the other person. If you don't notice the person's messages, or if you are distracted and not paying attention, you can't go on to understand, interpret, evaluate, remember, and respond. Being distracted often happens when you are multitasking (something we'll discuss in more detail later) or when you have a low interest in what someone is saying.

The link between hearing and attention implies a critical truth about listening: *if you want to become an active listener, you need to give people your undivided attention when they are speaking* (Beall, 2010). To boost your attention level, try to recognize the forces that negatively affect it. Throughout the day, notice how your ability to pay attention naturally strengthens and weakens, depending on what's happening within or around you. For example, when you're hungry or under a lot of stress, you may have a harder time paying attention to what someone is saying. You can also try to control the factors that make it harder to focus your attention. Avoid situations that call for careful listening when you are overly stressed, hungry, ill, or fatigued—all of which can leave your brain foggy. If you've noticed that you have higher energy levels in the morning or early in the week, schedule attention-demanding activities, meetings, and encounters during those times.

Understanding, Interpreting, and Evaluating. After hearing, the next three stages of the listening process take place almost simultaneously. You begin **understanding** what you've heard; that is, you recognize the literal (or *denotative*) meaning of the words the other person has said. At the same time, you work on **interpreting** the full meaning of the message. You identify any

THE LISTENING PROCESS

Listening involves a series of stages that work together. Consider how the entire process is interrupted when one stage isn't completed, like if you get distracted and fail to correctly interpret what was said to you.

Hearing includes both recognizing spoken words and any gestures or lip movements that communicate meaning.
Understanding, interpreting, and evaluating happen almost simultaneously.
Remembering provides context for what you hear.
Responding completes the listening process and lets others know you've heard them.

Monkey Business Images/Shutterstock.com

implications (or *connotative meanings*) suggested in the person's words, and consider what action the person is trying to perform (Is she asking you a question? Issuing a command? Cracking a joke?). To interpret the full meaning of something you've heard, you consider nonverbal cues, such as the speaker's tone of voice, posture, and facial expression. You also take into account the situation and the background knowledge that you and the speaker share.

Even as you're understanding and interpreting the meaning of a message, you're also **evaluating** it: comparing the newly received information against your past knowledge to check its accuracy and validity. Evaluating the message helps you draw conclusions, such as "He's lying" or "She knows what she's talking about."

How do these three stages happen so quickly yet simultaneously? Consider the following example. A student in your class gives a speech on class warfare in politics. At one point in his presentation, he laughs and says, "Most homeless people are that way by choice; why don't they just get a job!?" Once you *hear* this comment (you process the sound of his voice and focus your attention on his message), you immediately do three things. You *understand* the literal meaning of his words, "Most/homeless/people/are . . ." You also *interpret* his intended meaning: Is he serious? Joking? Being sarcastic? At the same time, you *evaluate* the validity of what he said: Is it true that homeless people are that way by choice?

This example highlights an important insight regarding how you understand, interpret, and evaluate messages while listening. *Your mental processing of messages—and eventual responses—are influenced by your own knowledge, attitudes, beliefs, and values*. You don't listen objectively; instead, your listening is guided by what you already think. For instance, if you believe that homeless people aren't homeless by choice and that your classmate was ridiculing homelessness, you might take offense.

How can you use this insight to improve your understanding, interpretation, and evaluation of messages? Use the *critical self-reflection* and *perception-checking skills* we discuss in Chapter 2 (pages 35 and 52). First, practice critical self-reflection while listening. Specifically, get into the habit of asking yourself the following questions: What am I thinking and feeling in response to what is being said? Why am I thinking and feeling this way? How am I listening? How are my thoughts and feelings affecting my listening—especially my understanding, interpretation, and evaluation of the message? Then, perception-check your conclusions by asking yourself the most important question of all: Is my understanding, interpretation, and evaluation of the message accurate? When in doubt, don't hesitate to ask the source of the message to verify your assessment ("I may be completely off, but my interpretation of what you said is this . . . Is that right?").

Remembering. Once you've understood, interpreted, and evaluated a message, it gets stored in your memory. Later, you can call it back into your conscious mind, a process known as **remembering** (or *recalling*). Remembering is a crucial part of the listening process. Just imagine not being able to remember anything you've heard others say. Merely carrying out daily tasks would be virtually impossible—you couldn't remember a teacher's instructions on how to complete an assignment or even what time your roommate said she would be home. When you can accurately recall information after you've heard, understood, interpreted, and evaluated it, then you've successfully listened to the message (Thomas & Levine, 1994). Indeed, almost every scientific measure of listening uses remembering to measure listening effectiveness.

How can you boost your ability to remember? One way is to use **mnemonics**—devices that aid memory. Mnemonics are abbreviations, words, simple phrases, ideas, or images associated with what you're trying to recall. Alternatively, you might think of an image, an idea, or a song that goes with what you're trying to remember. When creating mnemonics, follow two simple rules: *keep it simple*, so the information is easy to remember, and *repeat the device often*, so you lock it down. For instance, when Steve teaches yoga classes, he needs five items: music to accompany and inspire the class, water to stay hydrated, keys to open the stereo system and equipment rooms at the health club, his yoga mat, and his book with choreography notes. For the first year he taught, however, he would inevitably forget one of these items, causing chaos before his classes. Finally, after much frustration, Steve created a simple mnemonic: "music-water-keys-mat-book." He said this again and again until it was firm in his mind. Now, every time he has to teach, he says "musicwaterkeysmatbook" out loud to himself before leaving his house—then checks to make sure he has each item.

Responding. The outcome of listening is **responding**—communicating your attention and comprehension to the speaker. Skillful listeners do more than simply attend and comprehend; they convey the results of their listening to speakers by using verbal and nonverbal behaviors known as *feedback*. Scholars distinguish between two kinds of feedback: positive and negative.

When you use **positive feedback**, you look directly at the person who is speaking, smile, position your body so that you're facing him or her, and lean forward. You might also offer *backchannel cues*. These are verbal and nonverbal behaviors, such as nodding and making comments ("Uh-huh," "Yes"), signaling that you're paying attention to and comprehending specific comments. All of these behaviors combine to show speakers that you're listening.

In contrast, people who use negative feedback send a very different message—namely, that they're not listening to the speaker. **Negative feedback** behaviors include avoiding eye contact, turning your body away, looking bored or distracted, and not using backchannel cues.

Feedback can have a powerful effect on speakers. For example, if you're giving a presentation, receiving positive feedback from your listeners can enhance your confidence, generate positive emotions within you, and convince you that your audience members are skilled listeners (Purdy & Newman, 1999). Negative feedback can cause you to hesitate, make mistakes, or stop talking in order to figure out why your audience members aren't listening.

Motives for Listening

As noted in our chapter opener, active listening can mean the difference between life and death for soldiers serving in combat. The reason for actively listening in such settings are obvious: soldiers must accurately understand each other so that everyone comes out of the engagement safely. But listening to comprehend is not the only motive for listening within military settings. Military mechanics often listen carefully to the sound of machinery to ensure that it's operating smoothly. Soldiers often listen to relaxing music between missions to help them unwind. And when managing the grief associated with the loss of fallen friends, the most important reason for listening is to support.

In a similar fashion, we all listen for a variety of reasons when communicating with others. These different purposes are known as **listening functions**, and they powerfully shape how you choose to listen in specific situations. There are five common listening functions:

- When you *listen to comprehend*, you focus on accurately interpreting and storing the information you receive, so that you can correctly recall it later.
- When you *listen to provide support*, you take in what someone else says without evaluating it, and openly express empathy in response.
- When you *listen to analyze*, you carefully evaluate and critique the messages you're receiving.

- When you *listen to appreciate*, you concentrate on enjoying the sights and sounds you're experiencing.
- When you *listen to discern*, you focus your attention on distinguishing specific sounds—for instance, trying to figure out whose phone is ringing at a large and noisy party.

These five functions are not mutually exclusive: you might use two or more within the same encounter, or shift suddenly from one to another as circumstances change. In fact, you *should* demonstrate such flexibility. A key step in becoming an active listener is learning how to adapt your listening to the situation in which you find yourself (Teo, 2005). For example, while at a concert you may listen to appreciate until your campus newspaper editor texts you a reminder that your review of the show is due the next morning—at which point you'll listen to analyze. (See Table 7.1 for examples of how different listening functions can work together.)

TABLE 7.1

MATCHING LISTENING FUNCTION TO SITUATION

LISTENING SITUATION	APPROPRIATE LISTENING FUNCTION
A friend texts you to cancel your dinner plans because he has the flu.	comprehend support
Your manager gives a presentation detailing an upcoming project and how to best approach the client.	comprehend
A classmate challenges your position on a controversial topic during a group discussion.	comprehend support analyze
Your romantic partner, who is very insecure about his or her singing ability, sings your favorite song for you at your birthday party.	support appreciate
A classmate with whom you're delivering a class presentation inquires as to whether her voice "still sounds funny" after she received Novocain during a dental checkup.	support analyze discern

acequestions/Shutterstock.com

To strengthen your ability to adapt your listening function, practice noticing the listening demands that different situations call for. Routinely ask yourself, "What is my purpose for listening?" Keep in mind that in some situations, certain types may be inappropriate or even unethical—like listening to analyze when your friend is clearly seeking emotional support.

Multitasking and Listening

Many forms of social media—especially on phones—create hard-to-ignore distractions that make it difficult to stay focused on listening when someone else is speaking. For example, when you're sitting in class and receive a text message, what do you do? If you're like a lot of students, you stop listening to your professor so you can read and respond to the message. This situation is not unique to texting. You may also be tempted to check Twitter, Snapchat, or Instagram; play online games; or use other apps while chatting with a friend, family member, or coworker. However, the research on multitasking is clear: people who **multitask**—that is, shift their attention back and forth between many different things at once—suffer a number of negative outcomes. For example, students who habitually multitask have difficulty focusing their attention on any single task for more than five minutes at a time (Rosen, Carrier, & Cheever, 2013). They also suffer substantially lower overall GPAs than do students who limit their multitasking (Juncoa & Cotten, 2012).

Multitasking also has a devastating effect on listening. Habitual multitaskers are poor listeners and are more likely to mishear messages or miss

It's easy to multitask when using various media—for example, watching a video lecture while checking your Twitter feed, or texting during a conversation. But shifting your attention between media makes it more likely that you will misunderstand or not hear messages. What problems have you encountered while trying to listen and multitask?

Cultura Limited/Superstock

ADVANCE THE CONVERSATION

TO MULTITASK OR NOT, THAT IS THE QUESTION!

1 YOUR DILEMMA

You're attending a weekend seminar for a professional certificate. To obtain the certificate, you must pass a test, which involves listening to a presentation and answering questions. Once you pass this test and acquire the certificate, you will receive an immediate pay raise.

The test session is off to a smooth start: the presenter is great, and much of the material is familiar, so you breeze through the first set of questions. As the presenter continues speaking, you find time to text your family for updates on your sister Danielle's softball game. Her team is playing in a tournament, and if they win, she'll pitch in the finals that night. As you sit in the auditorium, Danielle's team is up by one, but she loads the bases with no outs in the last inning. You're freaking out when suddenly you hear the instructor call your name. Looking up, you see her staring at you. She snaps, "This content is essential for your certification. Please tell me you're not sitting there texting while you're supposed to be listening!"

➔ How do you feel when the instructor calls you out for not listening?

2 THE RESEARCH

One of the most important ways you can improve your listening is to limit the amount of time you spend multitasking—especially shifting your attention back and forth between different forms of technology, each of which feeds you unrelated streams of information (Ophir et al., 2012). Stanford psychologist Clifford Nass has found that multitaskers are extremely confident in their ability to perform well on the tasks they juggle (Glenn, 2010). Their confidence, however, is misplaced. Multitaskers perform substantially worse on tasks compared with individuals who focus their attention on only one task at a time (Ophir et al., 2012).

Why is limiting multitasking important for improving listening? Because multitasking erodes your capacity for sustaining focused attention (Jackson, 2008). Cognitive scientists discovered that our brains adapt to the tasks we regularly perform, an effect known as brain plasticity (Carr, 2010). In simple terms, we train our brains to be able to do certain things through how we live our daily lives. People who spend too much time shifting attention rapidly between multiple forms of technology train their brains to focus attention only in brief bursts. They lose the ability to focus attention for long periods of time on just one task (Jackson, 2008). Limiting your multitasking and spending at least some time each day focused on just one task (such as reading, listening to music, or engaging in prayer or meditation), with no technological distractions, helps train your brain to sustain attention—and you to listen more effectively.

➔ If you were in the presenter's shoes, what attribution would you have made about your behavior? Would you have reacted in the same way?

3 YOUR OPPORTUNITY

Before you act, consider the facts of the situation and think about the multitasking research. Also, reflect on what you've learned so far about listening and multitasking (pp. 172–174), listening functions (pp. 170–172), and feedback (p. 170).

➔ Now it's your turn. Write a response to the presenter in which you explain your situation.

them completely (Ophir, Nass, & Wagner, 2012). This is true even if they think they are skilled multitaskers; people who consider themselves good at multitasking are just as bad as everyone else when they try to listen while multitasking (Ophir et al., 2012).

Why does multitasking so dramatically impact listening? Because it disrupts all aspects of the listening process. Think about it: because you fail to hear, understand, interpret, and evaluate information correctly in the first place, you can't accurately remember or competently respond to it after the fact. In simple terms, if you multitask, you won't be able to listen well; and if you don't listen well, you can't recall and respond well. This is especially crucial for settings such as college classes and workplace presentations, in which you receive lots of important information very rapidly—all of which needs to be remembered.

Fortunately, a simple solution to this dilemma exists: *resist the urge to multitask while listening.* Whenever you're in an environment in which you need to be able to hear, understand, interpret, evaluate, remember, and respond to information, turn your phone off (don't just put it on vibrate or silent), put away other work, close your laptop or shut off your tablet, and actively focus on the person who is speaking.

Listening Styles

Everyone has preferred ways of listening. Do you like listening to long stories told by friends, or do you urge them to "get to the point"? Do you ask for detailed instructions on how to complete tasks at work, or do you just want a brief overview? Your preferred listening style determines how you listen and is shaped by both your gender and your culture.

> *"If the person you are talking to doesn't appear to be listening, be patient. It may simply be that he has a small piece of fluff in his ear."*[1]

He is a billion-dollar-a-year industry, and one of the few fictional characters to have a star on the Hollywood Walk of Fame. His insights have been used to help introduce Taoism to Western cultures. Books about him have been translated into 34 languages. He is such a popular character in Poland that residents of Warsaw have named a street after him. But at the heart of the stories about Edward Bear—or, as he is commonly known, Winnie-the-Pooh—is a cast of characters who have very different listening styles.

In the original books by playwright and poet A. A. Milne, Christopher Robin is a young boy who is presented as a consistently empathic listener. All the other characters turn to him for comfort and a compassionate ear. Whenever Pooh worries about his own ineptitude ("I am a bear of no brain at all"), Christopher Robin listens sympathetically and offers emotional support:

---

[1]The quote and information that follows are adapted from the following sources: A. A. Milne (1926, 1928) and J. Milne (2007).

"You're the best bear in all the world." Pooh tries desperately to adopt Christopher Robin's listening style but instead finds himself nodding off or daydreaming about honey (his favorite treat) when someone comes to him with problems.

In contrast to Pooh, Owl is Mr. Analytical. He prides himself on being wise and encourages others to bring detailed information and dilemmas to him, even if he often doesn't know the answers. (He's good at pretending he does, though!) Meanwhile, Rabbit just wants people to get to the point so he can act on it. He tends to interrupt them if they stray from what he considers the purpose of the conversation, sometimes even asking, "Does it matter?" Tigger, for his part, though extremely good-natured, never seems to have the time to listen. For instance, when the group goes adventuring, Tigger can't help but run around in circles excitedly, urging the others to "Come on!" Then he leaves without waiting to hear their responses. Though these characters are fictional, they each demonstrate a listening style that people use in real life.

Though characters from children's books, Pooh and his friends illustrate the different styles of listening. Do you know people in your life who characterize the styles in similar ways? Which style best represents you?

Advertising Archive/Everett Collection

Four Listening Styles

Like the characters in Milne's beloved tales, each of us tends to listen in a way that is consistent across all situations. A habitual pattern of listening behaviors, which reflects your attitudes, beliefs, and predispositions about listening, is known as a **listening style** (Barker & Watson, 2000). In general, there are four different listening styles.

People-oriented listeners view listening as an opportunity to establish bonds between themselves and others. When asked to identify the single most important aspect of competent listening, people-oriented listeners say that it's empathy for other people's emotions (Barker & Watson, 2000). Because of their ability to empathize, others perceive them as being caring and concerned.

Content-oriented listeners prefer to be intellectually challenged by the messages they receive. They thoroughly evaluate what's been said before they draw conclusions, and they enjoy hearing all sides of an argument.

Action-oriented listeners (or task-oriented listeners) like focused and organized information, and they want clear, to-the-point messages from others. They use that information to quickly make decisions and plot courses of action.

Time-oriented listeners prefer brief encounters. They tend to let others know in advance exactly how much time they have available for each conversation. Individuals using this style are more likely to interrupt speakers and signal lack of interest through negative feedback than people using other styles (Barker & Watson, 2000).

Listening styles are learned early in life, from watching and interacting with parents and caregivers, gender socialization (learning about how men and women are "supposed" to listen), and cultural values regarding what counts as skilled listening (Barker & Watson, 2000). Through constant practice, your listening styles become deeply entrenched in your communication routines. As a consequence, you may rely on one or two styles for all your interactions, and resist switching from your dominant styles—even when those styles are inappropriate for the situation (Chesebro, 1999). This may result in people perceiving you as an inflexible and even incompetent communicator. To be an active listener, you have to use all four styles and strategically deploy them as needed. If you need to provide emotional support—perhaps a friend is going through a breakup—you should use a people-oriented listening style (Barker & Watson, 2000). But if you are listening to a professor present lecture recaps for a midterm, you would want to use an action-oriented style to quickly pick out the information you will need to study.

FIGURE 7.1

WHAT'S YOUR LISTENING STYLE?

When a friend comes to you with a problem, do you . . .

A
focus on her emotions?
You have a **people-oriented** listening style.

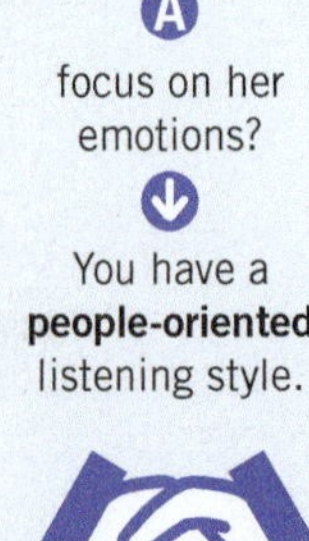

B
try to imagine the situation from all angles?
You have a **content-oriented** listening style.

C
try to find the clearest solution?
You have an **action-oriented** listening style.

D
listen as best you can before you have to leave?
You have a **time-oriented** listening style.

1. Introwiz1/Shutterstock.com; 2. WonderfulPixel/Shutterstock.com; 3. Fenton one/Shutterstock.com

Gender and Listening Styles

As with other aspects of communication we've discussed, many people are *stereotyping* when they think that women and men have very different listening styles. Women are presumed to be people-oriented listeners; men, action-oriented listeners (or sometimes unable to listen at all!). But interestingly, this is one of those rare instances in which stereotypes contain a kernel of truth. Research comparing male and female preferences suggests that men show a *small* preference for action-oriented listening, while women show a *strong* preference for people-oriented listening (Bodie & Fitch-Hauser, 2010). Among individuals who use more than one style, men tend to favor action- and time-oriented styles; women favor people- and content-oriented styles.

These findings have led researchers to conclude that men (in general) tend to have a task-oriented and hurried approach to listening, while women perceive listening as more of a relational activity. Keep these differences in mind during interpersonal interactions, group discussions, and presentations. When interacting with men, observe the listening styles they display, and adapt accordingly. Don't be surprised if time- or action-oriented styles emerge the most. When conversing with women, follow the same pattern, and be prepared to quickly shift to more people- or content-oriented styles if needed. On the other hand, don't automatically assume that just because someone is female or male she or he will always listen—or expect you to listen—in certain ways. Instead, take your cue from the person you are talking with.

Culture and Listening Styles

Because research suggests that culture influences thought (Janusik & Imhof, 2017) it follows that culture also powerfully shapes how we listen and how we think about listening. What's considered competent listening by one culture is often perceived as ineffective by others, something you should always keep in mind when communicating with people from other cultures. For example, in *individualistic cultures* such as the United States and Canada (and particularly in U.S. workplaces), time- and action-oriented listening styles dominate. People often approach encounters with an emphasis on time limits ("I have only 10 minutes to talk" or "I'm going to keep this presentation short and to the point"). Many people also feel and express frustration if others don't communicate their ideas efficiently ("Just say it!"). By contrast, individuals living in *collectivistic cultures* often emphasize people- and content-oriented listening styles.

When you communicate with people from other cultures, adapt your listening style accordingly. If you're communicating with someone from a collectivistic culture, try to adopt a people-oriented listening style, and provide positive feedback while the person is speaking. Express interest in his or her feelings, opinions, and concerns, and emphasize points of commonality.

More than anything, avoid hurrying the interaction. Similarly, if you're communicating with someone from an individualistic culture, be prepared to embrace a time- or action-oriented approach to listening. Expect quicker, blunter reactions, and less patience with extended explanations. Of course, always match your style to the individual, and don't assume someone will have a certain listening style just because he or she has certain cultural affiliations.

Barriers to Active Listening

Being a good listener isn't easy—it's hard work. Numerous challenges exist that can drive you away from active listening and toward incompetence. Overcoming these challenges is essential to improving your listening skills.

Years ago, Steve and his wife, Kelly, went car shopping. Kelly had left her job as a marketing rep and was starting graduate school, so she needed to replace the company car she used previously. Upon entering the showroom, a salesperson approached Steve and said, "How can I help you today?" When Steve clarified that *Kelly* was the buyer, the salesperson nodded but said to Steve again, "So, what exactly are you looking for?" Steve then said, "No, *Kelly* is the buyer!" more emphatically, pointing to Kelly. The salesperson nodded, put her hand lightly on Steve's arm, and said, "Why don't you take a look at our best-selling model . . ." At this point, Steve said, "I think we're done here," and he and Kelly walked toward the door. But the salesperson blocked them. "What's wrong?" she inquired. Kelly responded, "Do you *really* want to know?" "Yes," the salesperson said, acknowledging Kelly's presence for the first time. Drawing on her years of sales experience, Kelly then provided a reasoned critique of how the salesperson hadn't listened and had mishandled the encounter. With every point Kelly raised, however, the salesperson lashed back, still not listening: "That's ridiculous!" she said. "What makes *you* an expert!?" Finally, after several extremely awkward minutes, Steve and Kelly made their escape.

We all have had encounters in which people failed to actively listen. Perhaps audience members were texting while you were giving a presentation. Maybe you were politely pretending to listen during a group discussion but were actually tuned out. Or maybe, like Kelly and the car salesperson, someone invited criticism but then seemed more interested in lashing back at you than listening to what you had to say. In this chapter so far, we've discussed a number of listening pitfalls, including failing to identify the right purpose for listening, multitasking, and neglecting to adapt listening style to the situation. But in this section, we focus on three of the most common and substantial barriers to active listening—selective listening, pseudo-listening, and aggressive listening—and how you can overcome them.

Selective Listening

Perhaps the greatest challenge to active listening is overcoming **selective listening**—taking in only bits and pieces of information from a speaker (those that attract your attention the most) and dismissing the rest. This was the problem with the salesperson's listening: she perceived "married couple," stereotypically presumed "male buyer," and tuned out Steve's repeated assertions that Kelly was the customer. When *you* selectively listen, like the salesperson who missed out on a potential sale, you lose out on the opportunity to learn information from others that may affect important personal or professional outcomes.

Selective listening is difficult to avoid because it is the natural result of fluctuating attention. To overcome selective listening, you shouldn't strive to listen to everything all at once. Instead, try to slowly and steadily broaden the range of information you can actively attend to during your encounters with others. You can do this by practicing the suggestions for enhancing attention discussed earlier in this chapter (page 167). The most important technique is to avoid multitasking with mediated communication—such as phone calls and text messages—which splits your attention when listening to others.

Pseudo-Listening

You were up most of the night, prepping for an important exam. Now the test is over and you're sitting outside, tired, when you get a call from your best friend. As he tells you about his latest romantic woes, you find your attention wandering. But because you don't want to embarrass yourself or your friend you do your best to act the part of an active listener—saying "Uh-huh" and "Oh, that's too bad," when needed.

In such a scenario, you're engaging in **pseudo-listening**—behaving as if you're paying attention though you're really not. Pseudo-listening is an incompetent way to listen because it prevents you from really attending to or understanding information coming from other people. Thus, you can't accurately recall the encounter later. Pseudo-listening is also somewhat unethical because it's deceptive. Although occasional instances of pseudo-listening to veil fatigue or protect a friend's feelings (such as in our example) are understandable, if you continually engage in pseudo-listening, people will eventually realize what's going on and may conclude that you're dishonest or disrespectful.

Aggressive Listening

People who engage in **aggressive listening** attend to what others say solely to find an opportunity to attack their conversational partners. (This is also known as *ambushing*.) For example, your friend may routinely ask for your opinions regarding fashion and music, but then disparage your tastes whenever you share them with her. Or a guest lecturer may encourage questions and comments following his presentation, but then mock your opinions when you volunteer them.

The costs of aggressive listening are substantial. People who consistently use listening to ambush others typically think less favorably of themselves (Infante & Wigley, 1986), experience lower marital satisfaction (Payne & Sabourin, 1990), and may experience more physical violence in their relationships (Infante, Chandler, & Rudd, 1989).

If you find yourself habitually listening in an aggressive fashion, you can combat it by discovering and dealing with the root cause of your aggression. Often, external pressures such as job stress, relationship challenges, or family problems can play a role, so be careful to consider all possible causes and solutions for your behavior. Don't hesitate to seek professional assistance if you feel it would be helpful. If you're in a personal or professional relationship with someone who uses aggressive listening against you, limit your interactions when possible, be polite and respectful, and use a people-oriented listening style. Avoid retaliating by using aggressive listening yourself, because it will only escalate the person's aggression.

Improving Your Active Listening Skills

Although it sounds like a cliché, improving your active listening skills will improve your life. If you're a skilled listener, people will perceive you as a more competent communicator overall, and you'll benefit both professionally and personally as a result.

We all go through our lives "listening" to others. Listening is our most common communicative activity. But when we *actively* listen, we transcend simply hearing and processing what people say and instead make the people in our lives feel valued and respected. How can you listen in such powerful, positive ways? At the heart of active listening are three skills: managing your nonverbal and verbal feedback, adapting your listening to speakers and situations, and recognizing the value of silence.

Manage Your Feedback

The starting point for active listening is making people feel as though you're really listening to them. Regardless of your listening style, listening function, or the situation, active listening always includes attentiveness to the speaker (Purdy & Newman, 1999). When speaking, you look for nonverbal and verbal signs that your listeners are paying attention, such as those that signal positive feedback. When listening, you can provide speakers with the same signals. For example, eye contact is an especially powerful indicator of active listening. In fact, if you break eye contact while someone else is talking, that person is likely to assume that you've stopped listening. He or

US State Department/Alamy Stock Photo

Successful interviewers, like Stephen Colbert, engage in active listening (and sometimes humor!) to make people feel comfortable. When people feel you are truly listening to them, they are more likely to respond in kind, strengthening your relationships and ability to achieve your own communication goals.

she may even stop and say something like, "Am I boring you?" or "Do you need to leave?" (Goodwin, 1981).

To improve your listening skills, you can manage your feedback by following four guidelines. First, *make your feedback positive*. Lean forward, sit or stand in a position that lets you directly face the speaker, and use your facial expressions to mirror the emotions of what's being discussed. Above all else, look at the speaker while he or she is talking. Avoid behaviors that might be mistaken as negative feedback. For example, something as simple as glancing at your cell phone or someone who's walking by could give the impression that you're bored or that you want the encounter to end.

Second, *make your feedback obvious*. No matter how attentively you listen, unless speakers notice your feedback, they won't know you're listening. To ensure that speakers can perceive your feedback, make sure your vocal feedback ("Uh-huh," "Yes") is loud enough for them to hear, and that your visual feedback (smiling, head nodding) is visible to them.

Third, *make your feedback appropriate*. Some situations call for intense, almost aggressive feedback—for example, a musician urging the audience to participate during a concert, or a coach trying to pump her team up before a big game. In situations like these, you're expected to use dramatic behaviors—clapping, jumping up and down—to show that you're interested and paying attention. In other settings, it's more appropriate to use gentler feedback, such as sustaining eye contact when listening to a romantic partner or nodding when listening to a group member describe the budget for a fund-raising dance.

Finally, *make your feedback immediate*. Always provide feedback as soon as you can. If you wait too long to provide the feedback, the speaker may not recognize the response as feedback, or may even infer that you're not listening (such as when you say, "Uh-huh, yeah," several seconds after he or she has finished talking). To see how managing your feedback and other active listening skills can influence an encounter, go to Advance the Conversation: Active Listening on pages 184–185.

Adapt Your Listening

A key theme that runs throughout this chapter is the importance of quickly and flexibly adapting your listening styles and functions, depending on the speaker to whom you're listening and the demands of the situation. When it comes to listening actively, one size (or approach) does *not* fit all. For example, and as discussed earlier, people of different genders or from different cultures often have very different expectations about what counts as competent listening. This is why it's important to take these differences into consideration when communicating, and adapt your listening as needed.

In addition, situational demands are dynamic, not static. Communication encounters are always changing, and with these changes come varying demands in what is expected of your listening. For instance, imagine that you're having a group meeting, and the discussion is focused on critiquing the research the group is including in the final presentation. Suddenly, one of the group members, who has been grinning throughout the meeting, says, "Hold on a second. I can't stand it anymore. I just have to tell you guys: I got engaged last night!" Continuing to listen in an analytical fashion at this point (saying, "That's nice, but let's stick to assessing the research. There's a problem with . . .") would be completely inappropriate. Instead, you instantly shift to *listening to provide support* and *a people-oriented style* ("I am so excited for you! Congratulations!"). To be an active listener, be mindful of the situational demands, the purpose of the encounter, and the needs and wants of the speaker—and then adapt your listening skills accordingly. For additional hints on how to be an active listener, see Table 7.2 on page 183.

Recognize the Value of Silence

A final, often unappreciated, quality of being an active listener is recognizing the value of silence. Sometimes people just want someone to quietly listen so that they can share their thoughts, feelings, and emotions—a sympathetic ear or a shoulder to cry on. If you're listening to someone who has this need, maintain good eye contact, as always, but avoid frequent use of more obvious forms of positive feedback, such as comments like, "I know what you mean" or "I can see why you're upset." For someone who just wants an ear or a supportive shoulder, these behaviors could come across as intrusive.

TABLE 7.2

ACTIVE LISTENING

To be a more active listener, try these strategies:

Concentrate on important aspects of encounters, and control factors that impede your attention.

Communicate your understanding to others in competent and timely ways by providing polite, obvious, appropriate, clear, and quick feedback.

Improve your recall abilities by using mnemonics or linking new information to other senses, visuals, or features.

4

Develop an awareness of your primary listening functions in various situations.

Practice shifting your listening style quickly, depending on the demands of the encounter.

gst/Shutterstock.com

In fact, research on grief management has found that the two listening behaviors identified as most helpful by people who are grieving are quietly allowing the griever to vent, and providing a sense of presence and attentiveness while the griever talks (Bodie & Fitch-Hauser, 2010). In such situations, it's not just a matter of adopting a people-oriented listening style and listening to provide comfort. In addition, you must dial down your conversational participation so that the other person feels free to fill the silence with what he or she wants to say. By listening in this way, you'll not only help the person work through his or her grief but also make it clear that you're there for him or her.

LearningCurve can help you review! Go to **launchpadworks.com**

ADVANCE THE CONVERSATION
Video Activity

ACTIVE LISTENING

The following scenario will enhance your ability to understand and apply active listening skills. Visit LaunchPad at launchpadworks.com to get the full experience with video. As you watch the first video, recall what you've learned about active listening, and then complete the **Your Turn** prompts. Finally, watch the **Take Two!** video to explore how this scenario could have gone differently.

1 *THE PROBLEM*

Reynaldo asks his close friend Mirirai for her feedback on an informative speech he is preparing for class. However, during their practice session, Reynaldo breaks down emotionally, confessing that his father—who has been increasingly forgetful—has recently been diagnosed with Alzheimer's. Reynaldo is deeply shaken by the diagnosis. When Mirirai asks how he is holding up, he replies, "I don't know. It's just all so new, you know?"

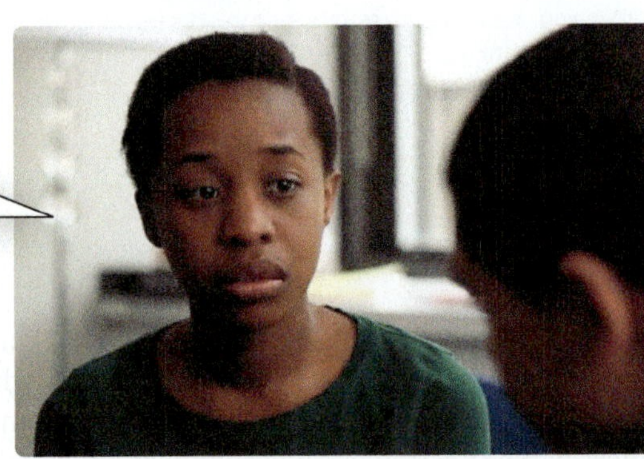

"Of course. What can I do to help?"

"There's nothing you can do to help. There's nothing anybody can do to help."

2 YOUR TURN

Observations. Reflect on how Mirirai and Reynaldo communicated in this scenario by answering the following questions:

1. Which character do you identify with more in this situation? How would you feel if you were in his or her situation?
2. Where were the missed opportunities to practice competent communication?

Discussion. In class or with a partner, share your thoughts about the interaction between Mirirai and Reynaldo and work to answer the following questions:

1. Can you understand both perspectives?
2. What could Reynaldo and Mirirai have done differently?

Conclusion. Choose one person in the scenario to offer your advice. Based on your analysis, what advice would you give him or her to improve his or her communication competence in this scenario?

3 TAKE TWO!

What if things had gone differently? Watch the **Take Two!** video to see one possible example of how the conversation might have gone if Reynaldo and/or Mirirai had communicated differently. As you watch the video, consider where the dialog reflects strong active listening skills. After watching the video, answer the questions below:

1. Did Reynaldo and/or Mirirai take advantage of opportunities that they missed in the first scenario? Which ones?
2. Did their different actions result in a more productive encounter? Please explain.

CHAPTER 7 REVIEW

CHAPTER RECAP

- The process of **listening** involves six stages. In addition to **hearing** a message, you also **understand**, **interpret**, and **evaluate** it, before **remembering** and **responding** to it.
- Although knowing how the different **listening functions** work and how to switch between them is important, try not to **multitask** when listening, or you might completely miss information.
- Your **listening style** is influenced by your personal preference, gender, and culture. However, being an active listener means using all four styles as needed.
- Though common, try to avoid listening pitfalls, such as **selective**, **pseudo-**, and **aggressive listening**.
- By managing your feedback, adapting your listening, and recognizing the value of silence, you can improve your active listening skills.

LaunchPad for *Choices & Connections* offers unique video scenarios and encourages self-assessment through adaptive quizzing. Go to **launchpadworks.com** to get access.

 LearningCurve adaptive quizzes

 Advance the Conversation video scenarios

 Video clips that illustrate key concepts

KEY TERMS

Listening, p. 166
Hearing, p. 166
Understanding, p. 167
Interpreting, p. 167
Evaluating, p. 168
Remembering, p. 169
Mnemonics, p. 169
Responding, p. 170
Positive feedback, p. 170
Negative feedback, p. 170
Listening functions, p. 170
Multitask, p. 172
Listening style, p. 175
People-oriented listeners, p. 175
Content-oriented listeners, p. 175
Action-oriented listeners, p. 175
Time-oriented listeners, p. 176
Selective listening, p. 179
Pseudo-listening, p. 179
Aggressive listening, p. 179

POP QUIZ

Looking for more review questions? **LearningCurve** can help you master key concepts from this chapter. Go to **launchpadworks.com**

1. During which stage of the listening process do you compare new information against your existing knowledge?

   a. Evaluating
   b. Understanding
   c. Interpreting
   d. Responding

2. If your sister is giving you detailed directions to her new apartment during a phone call, you are listening to

   a. analyze.
   b. appreciate.
   c. comprehend.
   d. discern.

3. During which of the following activities are you most likely to mishear messages?

   a. Positive feedback
   b. Negative feedback
   c. Interpreting
   d. Multitasking

4. Which of the following types of listeners view listening as an opportunity to establish bonds between themselves and others?

   a. Content-oriented
   b. Action-oriented
   c. People-oriented
   d. Time-oriented

5. Though possibly caused by stress, people who use this type of listening may think less favorably about themselves and experience lower marital satisfaction.

   a. Aggressive listening
   b. Selective listening
   c. Pseudo-listening
   d. Action listening

ACTIVITIES

For more activities, visit LaunchPad for *Choices & Connections* at **launchpadworks.com**

1 The Impact of Negative Feedback

Recall an encounter in which you were saying something important but the other person gave you negative feedback. Perhaps the person made fun of what you were saying or clearly ignored your message via text or email. Write a brief paper explaining what happened and how the negative feedback affected your communication during the interaction. Did this influence any other communication between the two of you? Is negative feedback ever competent? If so, when?

2 The "Noise List"

To examine how your attention wavers when listening, choose two people—a classmate, a friend, a family member, a coworker, a romantic partner—and engage each of them in a conversation of at least 10 minutes. Afterward, record as many details as you can about each conversation—whom it was with, topics covered, time of day, and location. Then come up with a "noise list," detailing the distractions you faced in each conversation. What impeded your ability to actively listen? Did you multitask during either of the conversations? Did you experience similar noise challenges in both conversations? How could you overcome such distractions, or noise, during future conversations?

Principles of Interpersonal Communication

Without fail, every season of *The Bachelor* (and its spin-off show, *The Bachelorette*) is touted as the "most controversial" ever. Kaitlyn Bristowe, the 11th season bachelorette, triggered vicious online "slut-shaming" after she had sex with a contestant early in the season. And in Season 22, bachelor Arie Luyendyk Jr. caused fan shock and outrage (and received huge media coverage) when he proposed to contestant Becca Kufrin, only to suddenly break up with her a few weeks later—with cameras rolling—so he could be with rival contestant Lauren Burnham. But apart from the silliness, drama, and carefully marketed "controversy" of contestant decision making, *The Bachelor* illustrates deeper truths about what drives us to be attracted to some people and not to others, the expectations that enfold us when we forge connections with others, and the dynamic and ever-changing nature of close relationships.

The Bachelor is a dating game show that matches a single man with more than two dozen female contestants.[1] The women are eliminated over a series of episodes, based on the bachelor's interactions with them. The show's goal is to have the bachelor propose marriage in the final episode to the "winner" (though not all seasons end with a proposal).

The show involves strong expectations regarding communication and relationships. The bachelor evaluates each contestant's potential as a spouse based on physical attractiveness, similarity, strength of attraction toward him, and how well she rises to such challenges as bungee jumping and swimming with sharks. Because the goal of the show is for the bachelor to find love, there is an expectation that some of the relationships will progress steadily through the stages of development, with one eventually culminating in marriage. The creation of closeness is fostered by relentless pressure on contestants to openly share their thoughts and feelings with the bachelor.

Though the contestants are competing with one another for the chance to "win," they also live together and are expected to form friendships. Those who don't act like a friend—who don't share their thoughts and feelings with and provide emotional support to other contestants—invite scorn from both their rivals and the viewers. This is the main reason viewers hated Courtney Robertson in season 16—she refused to communicate supportively toward the other women. Instead, she treated them competitively, going so far as to taunt them with snarky remarks, such as "Winning!" when she received a rose, which guaranteed her protection from elimination.

The Bachelor is one of the most successful reality shows in television history and has licensed spin-off shows in more than 20 other countries, including India, Vietnam, Russia, and Japan. But though *The Bachelor*, in all its forms, is framed as a show about finding love, at its heart it's about what happens when people are thrown together, attraction sparks, and relationships form and disband. What's at the core of all these processes? *Interpersonal communication.*

[1]All information that follows is from Rice (2011).

Rainmaker Photo/MediaPunch Inc/Alamy Stock Photo

PARK
OPEN
24
HOURS

CHAPTER OUTLINE

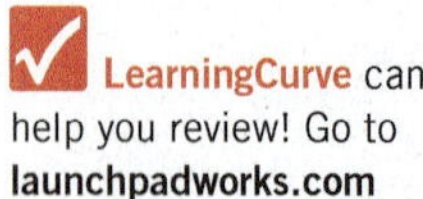
LearningCurve can help you review! Go to **launchpadworks.com**

Reality shows like *The Bachelor* and *The Bachelorette* aren't reality. Instead, they're heavily edited forms of entertainment, dressed up to look like real life. At the same time, these shows mirror the communication and relationship dramas that many people face. Watching them provides a reflection of how our own communication choices directly correspond to the relational outcomes that follow—whether for good or bad. They are also reminders of the importance of positive, healthy relationships—not only with romantic partners but also with friends, family members, and coworkers (Myers, 2002).

This chapter is the first of three exploring the primary tool you use to create, maintain, and end your relationships—*interpersonal communication*. This chapter covers its basic principles. Chapter 9 provides a close look at how to manage and sustain the relationships you build during your life. Finally, Chapter 10 offers strategies for managing conflict in interpersonal relationships. In this chapter, you'll learn:

- The defining characteristics of interpersonal communication
- What compels you to form relationships in the first place
- Four types of relationships and their key characteristics
- The stages relationships may progress through

What Is Interpersonal Communication?

As the name implies, interpersonal communication is "inter-person," or between two people. But what makes interpersonal communication "interpersonal" goes way beyond numbers. Interpersonal communication is how you connect with other human beings in meaningful ways; it's what makes up the moments that matter.

Interpersonal communication is communication between two people in which the messages exchanged significantly impact the thoughts, emotions, behaviors, and relationships of the people involved. As this definition highlights, one difference between interpersonal communication and other communication types is that it is **dyadic**—that is, it involves pairs of people, or *dyads*. For example, when you text back and forth with your roommate between classes, FaceTime with a long-distance cousin, or chat with a coworker when on break, you are engaging in interpersonal communication.

In addition, interpersonal communication is your primary tool for building, maintaining, and ending relationships. These relationships include friends, family members, coworkers, and romantic partners, but they also include anyone with whom you have meaningful interactions, such as classmates or group members. (In Chapters 11 and 12, we discuss communication between team members in small groups.) Because interpersonal communication impacts relationships, sharpening your interpersonal communication skills is one of the best ways to improve your relationship

INTERPERSONAL RELATIONSHIPS

Interpersonal communication can help you forge meaningful bonds with others—whether friends, coworkers, romantic partners, or family.

(Clockwise from top left) Sam Edwards/OJO Images/Getty Images; Hill Street Studios LLC/DigitalVision/Getty Images; Tim Klein/Getty Images; PictureIndia/Superstock

health and happiness. To enhance your skills, it's helpful to first understand the four defining characteristics of interpersonal communication.

Interpersonal Communication Is Transactional

Typically, interpersonal communication is *transactional*: both parties contribute to the meaning created during the communication. As Chapter 1 explains, this covers everything from a shared glance to an intense conversation. For example, if you and your brother spend an evening together, talking about your shared past, you will both likely chime in with contributions and thus construct the stories together. This is very different from most linear forms of communication, such as public speaking, in which a speaker creates and presents messages to audience members who receive and interpret them.

However, interpersonal communication can also be linear, depending on the situation. For instance, suppose you know that a coworker is feeling sad about a recent breakup. You send her a consoling text message in the middle of the workday ("So sorry about what happened. I'm here if you need anything"). You don't expect her to respond because you know she's busy—and she doesn't. In this communication, there is a sender (you), a message (your expression of support), and a receiver (your coworker). It is a linear encounter, but it's also interpersonal because it's dyadic, and it makes your coworker feel supported and therefore strengthens your connection with her.

Interpersonal Communication Is Dynamic

Interpersonal communication also differs from such events as formal group presentations and public speeches because it's *dynamic*—that is, constantly changing. When you interact with others, your communication and everything that influences it—your perceptions, thoughts, feelings, and emotions—are continually shifting.

For this reason, no two moments within the same interaction will ever be identical. Imagine that your friend starts a conversation by sharing exciting news about receiving a job offer. The encounter starts on a positive note but changes when you learn that it's the same job you wanted—making you happy for your friend but also sad and envious that you didn't get it.

Moreover, because interpersonal communication is dynamic, no two interactions with the same person will ever be identical. So although you were comfortable talking with your father last Sunday on the phone, things may feel more awkward the next time you talk because he seems preoccupied.

Interpersonal Communication Is Relational

Interpersonal communication is relational because it builds bonds with others—easing the distance that naturally arises from differences between people. Philosopher Martin Buber (1965) argued that you can make that distance seem "thinner" by embracing the fundamental similarities that connect you with others, trying to see things from others' points of view, and communicating with honesty and kindness. You don't have to agree with everything another person says and does, but you do need to approach that individual with an open mind, giving the person the same attention and respect you expect for yourself. According to Buber, only then can you build a meaningful relationship with that person. When you forge relationships in this way, you view your connections to others as **I-Thou**.

Contrast this with when people focus on their differences with others, refuse to accept or even acknowledge others' viewpoints as legitimate, and communicate in ways that emphasize their own supposed superiority over others. This approach views interpersonal connections with others as **I-It**—regarding people as "objects which we observe, that are there for our use and exploitation" (Buber, 1965, p. 24). The more you see others as objects, the more likely you'll communicate with them in disrespectful, manipulative, or exploitative ways. By treating others this way, you can't build meaningful, healthy relationships with them.

Interpersonal Communication Is Impactful

Interpersonal communication *impacts* the thoughts, emotions, behavior, and relationships of the people taking part in it. When you communicate interpersonally with others, it matters. As a result of the interaction, you may change how you feel and think about yourself and others; alter others' opinions of you; and create, maintain, or dissolve relationships. Interpersonal communication contrasts sharply with **impersonal communication**—exchanges that have a negligible perceived impact on your thoughts, emotions, behaviors, and relationships. For example, you lean over to a classmate and ask her what time it is, and she shows you the display on her phone. Although you are glad to have found out the time, this exchange has no further influence on you, your classmate, or your relationship with this person.

Why Form Relationships?

Whether it is one of life's big moments or an everyday encounter, interpersonal communication is how you share experiences with others and form the bonds that anchor any relationship. Knowing how and why you create such relationships is the first step toward understanding how you communicate within them.

Think about all the people you interact with and meet, online and off, every day—acquaintances, neighbors, service providers, lovers, family members, classmates, friends, coworkers. Across all these encounters, how many people do you make the effort to get to know well? How many would you consider "relationship worthy"? It's likely that only some of these people reach such a status and that you feel "close" to even fewer.

What leads you to form relationships with only a select few individuals, given the vast number of people you interact with every day? To answer this question, let's first define relationships.

The hit Netflix series *Stranger Things* centers on a ragtag group of misfits who, each season, find themselves drawn into a series of supernatural events. But amid all the otherworldly drama, the friendships and romantic crushes among the young protagonists are the true heart of the show, and they represent many of the common factors that lead people to form relationships—including proximity, similarity, attraction, and reciprocal liking. How much have each of these factors influenced recent relationship developments in your own life?

Netflix/Everett Collection

Interpersonal relationships are the emotional, mental, and physical involvements that you forge with others through communication. Scholars suggest that five factors influence whether these interpersonal relationships form or not: proximity, resources, similarity, reciprocal liking, and physical attractiveness (Aron et al., 2008). These factors influence your relationship choices regardless of gender or sexual orientation (Felmlee, Orzechowicz, & Fortes, 2010).

Proximity

The first factor influencing relationship development is one of the most obvious yet often overlooked: proximity. You're more likely to pursue relationships with people with whom you have frequent contact, whether face-to-face or online. This phenomenon is known as the **mere exposure effect** (Bornstein, 1989). For example, a coworker who works in a cubicle near yours is more likely to become a friend or romantic partner than is one who works on a different floor. Similarly, if you have a cousin whose activities you regularly follow on Twitter, you'll be more likely to think of her as a close family member than a distant relative you see only at annual family gatherings.

Resources

Another factor that compels you to pursue relationships with others is their **resources**—the valued qualities people possess. Resources range from personality traits and physical skills to social status and material wealth. Most people consider certain resources—such as a sense of humor, intelligence, kindness, supportiveness, and whether the person seems fun—to be valuable regardless of gender or sexual orientation (Felmlee et al., 2010).

What leads you to view a particular person's resources as desirable? According to **social exchange theory**, you'll feel drawn to individuals who offer you substantial *benefits* (positive things you like and want) with few *costs* (negative things demanded of you in return). So, you'll be interested in a potential lover who is smart, is attractive, has lots of money, and knows many interesting people as long as this person isn't also jealous, demanding, possessive, and untrustworthy. In addition, social exchange theory predicts that you will pursue a particular relationship with someone if you think that person offers you rewards you believe you deserve, but only if those rewards seem better than rewards you can get elsewhere (Kelley & Thibaut, 1978). For example, in choosing which neighbor to befriend in your apartment complex, you're more likely to pursue a relationship with one who is funny and friendly than one who is aloof.

Similarity

Research suggests that people seek romantic partnerships, close family involvements, friendships, and coworker relationships with those whom they see as similar to themselves (Miller, Hefner, & Scott, 2007). This is known as the **birds-of-a-feather effect** (from the saying "Birds of a feather flock together"). Say that you have two sisters. Both of them have lived with you since birth (proximity), and both have many attributes that you appreciate (resources). But one sister has interests and personality traits very similar to yours. The birds-of-a-feather effect suggests that you'll feel closer to this sister than you will to your other sister.

At the same time, differences in surface-level tastes and preferences, such as foods, music, and movies, won't hurt your relationship as long as you and the other person are similar in other, more important ways (Neimeyer & Mitchell, 1988). For example, Steve loves the band Radiohead so much that he even had a RADIOHD vanity plate on his car for a number of years. His close friend Mac doesn't like the band. However, they have other musical tastes in common (John Coltrane, Death Cab for Cutie), and—more important—they have very similar personalities, senses of humor, and political views; thus, their friendship endures.

Reciprocal Liking

If someone you're interested in makes it clear that he or she is also interested in you, this is known as **reciprocal liking** (Aron et al., 2008). Reciprocal liking increases the chance that you and the other person will forge a

TABLE 8.1

INFLUENCES ON RELATIONSHIP FORMATION

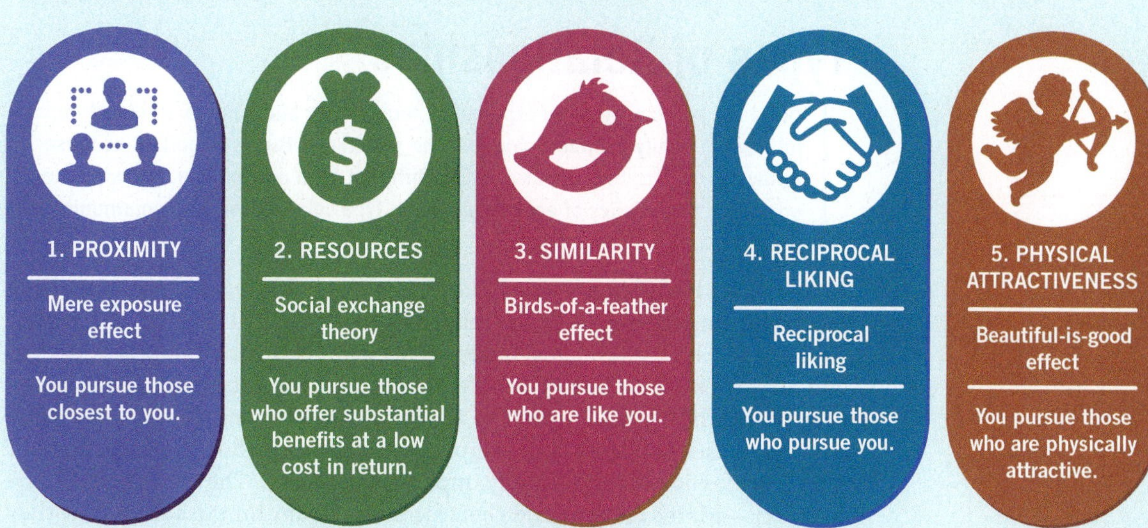

1. PROXIMITY	2. RESOURCES	3. SIMILARITY	4. RECIPROCAL LIKING	5. PHYSICAL ATTRACTIVENESS
Mere exposure effect	Social exchange theory	Birds-of-a-feather effect	Reciprocal liking	Beautiful-is-good effect
You pursue those closest to you.	You pursue those who offer substantial benefits at a low cost in return.	You pursue those who are like you.	You pursue those who pursue you.	You pursue those who are physically attractive.

Domofon/Shutterstock.com; WinMaster/Shutterstock.com; Introwiz1/Shutterstock.com; jossnat/Shutterstock.com relationship. For example, you're much more likely to become friends with a coworker who strikes up conversations with you and laughs at your jokes—showing that she likes you—than with a coworker who expresses no interest in you. When it comes to romantic involvements, studies examining people's narrative descriptions of "falling in love" have found that reciprocal liking is *the* most commonly mentioned factor leading to love (Riela, Rodriguez, Aron, Xu, & Acevedo, 2010).

Physical Attractiveness

Finally, you're more likely to get involved with people you perceive as physically attractive. Although it might seem obvious that people would naturally be drawn to beauty and good looks, there is another reason for its appeal. Attractive people are often assumed to offer other valued resources, such as competent communication skills, intelligence, and well-adjusted personalities—a phenomenon known as the **beautiful-is-good effect** (Eagly, Ashmore, Makhijani, & Longo, 1991). At the same time, being perceived as exceptionally physically attractive by others may actually create relationship instability for some people. In a series of four studies, Harvard psychologist Christine Ma-Kellams and her colleagues documented that people who were perceived as more physically attractive by others had shorter marriages and higher divorce rates than their less-attractive counterparts (Ma-Kellams, Wang, & Cardiel, 2017). Why? Because highly attractive people have a broader range of alternative partners who strongly desire them, making their current relationship less unique and necessary. They also are more likely to receive "poaching attempts"—that is, have numerous potential partners "hit on" them and try to lure them away from their current lovers (Schmitt & Buss, 2001).

Types of Relationships

Of all the relationships you experience, four usually stand out as the most impactful: lovers, family members, friends, and coworkers. But as important as these involvements are, they are also widely different from one another. Knowing the unique characteristics of each relationship type can improve your communication within them.

In Kaui Hart Hemmings's novel *The Descendants* (2007), attorney Matt King faces daunting challenges in the relationships that fill his life. On the professional front, he must make a business decision involving billions of dollars and affecting thousands of people. As the descendant of native Hawaiian royalty and the controlling heir to a massive land holding, Matt must decide whether to sell the land to developers or preserve it. But the decision isn't purely professional; it has family implications as well. The other heirs to the property—Matt's cousins and their families—want him to sell so that they can share in the profits. What's more, they make it clear that if he doesn't sell, there could be a permanent rift in the family. Meanwhile, on the home front, Matt's wife, Joanie, has suffered a devastating brain injury while boat racing and is in an irreversible coma. Suddenly a single parent, Matt must try to reconnect emotionally with two daughters from whom he has long been detached. He must also let friends and family members know that Joanie is dying. Complicating matters further, he discovers that Joanie—whom he had considered his best friend, sparring partner, and closest confidante—had been cheating on him before the accident and was planning to divorce him. In the climactic scene of the book, he puts the pain of her betrayal to rest:

> I bow my head and speak to Joanie softly. "I'm sorry I didn't give you everything you wanted. I wasn't everything you wanted. You were everything I wanted. Every day. Home. There you are. Dinner, dishes, TV. Weekends at the beach. You go here. I go there. Parties. Home to complain about the party." I can't think of anything else. Just our routine together. "I forgive you," I say. Why is it so hard to articulate love, yet so easy to express disappointment? (Hemmings, 2007, pp. 235–236)

Kaui Hart Hemmings, author of *The Descendants,* explores many types of interpersonal relationships through her protagonist, Matt King, who adapts his communication as he interacts with his daughters, extended family, friends, and business associates. When you consider your own communication, how does it differ depending on the type of relationship you have with the other person?

ZUMA Press Inc/Alamy Stock Photo

Throughout *The Descendants*, Matt King juggles the love and pain he feels toward his dying wife, the demands of being a single parent, his encounters with friends and family members, and his dealings with business partners. Similarly, all our lives are filled with these same relationship types: romantic, family, friendship, and workplace.

These relationships differ in many respects, but they share one critical point of commonality: *interpersonal communication*. It may sound clichéd, but interpersonal communication is the lifeblood of all your relationships, no matter the type. It's how you initiate relationships, build and sustain them, and end those that have run their course. No matter the variety of channels used to interact within them—online, over the phone, and face-to-face—the focus is always interpersonal.

Given the central role of interpersonal communication in your relationships, let's explore each type of involvement and its defining characteristics.

Romantic Relationships

Romantic relationships are interpersonal involvements in which the participants perceive the bond as romantic. As this definition suggests, romantic relationships are rooted in *perception*: a romantic relationship exists whenever the two partners believe that it does. As perceptions change, so, too, does the relationship. For example, a couple may consider their relationship "casual dating" but still define it as romantic (rather than friendly). But if one person feels romantic and the other does not, they don't have a romantic relationship (Miller & Steinberg, 1975).

In addition to being affected by the partners' perceptions, romantic relationships can vary in terms of the emotions that the partners feel toward each other.

Liking and Loving. Being in love is arguably the biggest distinction between romances and other relationship types, which center more on liking. What does it mean to be "in" love, and how does this differ from liking?

Most scholars agree that liking and loving are separate emotional states, with different causes and outcomes (Berscheid & Regan, 2005). **Liking** is a feeling of affection and respect that we often have for our friends, extended family members, and coworkers (Rubin, 1973). *Affection* is a sense of warmth and fondness toward another person, while *respect* is admiration for another person, regardless of how he or she treats or communicates with you.

Loving is a more intense emotional connection, consisting of intimacy, caring, and attachment (Rubin, 1973). *Intimacy* is a feeling of closeness and "union" between you and another person (Mashek & Aron, 2004). *Caring* is the concern you have for another person's welfare and the desire to keep him or her happy. *Attachment* is a longing to be in another person's presence as much as possible; in romantic involvements, this often takes the form of sexual desire. Although we may experience intimacy, caring, and attachment with close friends and family members, within romantic relationships, these feelings have a special intensity.

Passionate and Companionate Love. Many people believe that to be in love, you have to feel constant and consuming sexual attraction toward a partner. In fact, the experience of romantic love covers a broad range of emotions. At one end of the spectrum is **passionate love**, a state of intense emotional and physical longing for union with another (Hendrick & Hendrick, 1992). Passionate love is experienced across cultures, genders, and ages. Men and women in all cultures report experiencing this type of love with equal frequency and intensity. Moreover, for adults, passionate love is integrally linked with sexuality and sexual desire (Berscheid & Regan, 2005). In one study, undergraduates were asked whether they thought there was a difference between "being in love" and "loving" another person (Ridge & Berscheid, 1989). Eighty-seven percent of respondents said that there was a difference and that sexual attraction was the critical distinguishing feature of being in love. However, passionate love is *negatively* related to relationship duration. Like it or not, the longer you're with a romantic partner, the less intense your passionate love will feel (Berscheid, 2002).

At the other end of the romantic spectrum is **companionate love**: an intense form of liking defined by emotional investment and the close intertwining of two people's lives (Berscheid & Walster, 1978). Many long-term romantic relationships begin as passionate love and then slowly evolve into companionate love, as the "fire" of passion cools with age and familiarity. For example, in *The Descendants*, Matt reflects on how his love for Joanie changed over the course of their relationship from passionate to companionate: "At weddings we roll our eyes at the burgeoning love around us, the vows that we know will morph into new kinds of promises: I vow not to kiss you when you're trying to read; I will tolerate you in sickness and ignore you in health; I promise to let you watch the stupid news show about celebrities" (Hemmings, 2007, p. 46).

Family Relationships

Families today are incredibly diverse. Between 1970 and 2010, the percentage of households composed of married couples with biological children in the United States declined from 40 percent to just 20 percent (Tavernise, 2011), and of those married-couple-with-children households, only 23 percent were "traditional" families with a stay-at-home parent (U.S. Census Bureau, 2017). Similar trends have been observed in Canada (Statistics Canada, 2012). Couples are increasingly living together rather than getting married, and rising divorce and remarriage rates have led to blended arrangements featuring stepparents and stepchildren. Adding to this complexity, individual families are constantly in flux, as children leave home, then move back in with parents while looking for work; as grandparents

DOUBLE TAKE

PASSIONATE VS COMPANIONATE LOVE

At opposite ends of the spectrum, passionate and companionate love are just two of the types of love you may experience in your romantic relationships. How would you describe other types of love? What experiences do you have with how love can change over the course of a relationship?

Goran Bogicevic/Shutterstock.com

Monkey Business Images/Shutterstock.com

join the household to help with day care or receive care themselves; and as spouses separate geographically to pursue job opportunities (Crosnoe & Cavanagh, 2010).

To embrace this diversity, we use a broad and inclusive definition of family. A **family** is a network of people who share their lives over long periods of time and are bound by marriage, blood, or commitment; who consider themselves a family; and who share a significant history and an anticipated future of functioning in a family relationship (Galvin, Brommel, & Bylund, 2004). This definition highlights three characteristics that distinguish families from other relationship types: shared identity, multiple roles, and emotional complexity.

Shared Identity. Families possess a strong sense of shared identity: "We're the MacTavish clan, and we've always been adventurous" or "We Singhs have a long history of creative talent." This sense of shared identity is created by three factors, the first of which is how the family communicates (Braithwaite et al., 2010). The stories you exchange and the way members of your family deal with conflict and talk with one another all contribute to a shared sense of what your family is like (Tovares, 2010). For instance, our friend Lorena's great-grandparents emigrated from their farm in Sicily to the United States. To build a life in their adopted country, they learned English, worked in textile mills, and eventually bought their own home. But they also endured taunts and mistreatment from people who looked down on immigrants. Lorena remembers attending multigenerational family dinners at their home on Sundays, where everyone recounted stories about how tough and resilient her "Nana and Nano" had to be to succeed in America—and how they had passed on these same qualities to the next generations.

In addition to how a family communicates, genetic material can further foster a sense of shared identity (Crosnoe & Cavanagh, 2010). This can lead to shared physical traits—such as distinct hair colors, body types, and facial characteristics—as well as similar personalities, mental abilities, and ways of relating to others.

Finally, a common history can also help create a sense of shared identity (Galvin et al., 2004). Such histories can stretch back for generations and may feature family members from a broad array of cultures. In *The Descendants*, for instance, Matt King's family is incredibly diverse but bonded by their heritage as native Hawaiian royalty. The history you share with your family is created jointly as you go through time together. For better or worse, everything you say and do becomes a part of your family history.

Multiple Roles. Family members constantly juggle multiple roles (Silverstein & Giarrusso, 2010). When you're a lover, a friend, or a coworker, you're just that: lover, friend, or coworker. Within your family, however, you're not just a daughter or a son—you may also be a sibling, a spouse, and an aunt or an uncle. By the time you reach middle age, you may simultaneously be parent, spouse, grandparent, daughter or son, *and* sibling. Each of these roles carries its own expectations and demands, forcing you to learn how to communicate effectively in each one, often at the same time.

Emotional Complexity. It is commonly thought that people should feel only positive emotions toward their family members (Berscheid, 2002). As psychologist Theodor Reik (1972) notes, people are "intolerant of feelings of resentment and hatred that sometimes rise in [them] against beloved persons—we feel that such an emotion has no right to exist beside our strong affection, even for a few minutes" (pages 99–100). Yet members of the same family typically experience both warm and antagonistic feelings toward one another (Silverstein & Giarrusso, 2010). That's because family members get into conflicts, just as do people in any other type of relationship. Personality differences, contrasting interests and priorities—all of these can create tensions that fuel resentment and other unpleasant emotions among family members. But if you believe you're not *supposed* to feel angry or frustrated with your family, this sense of wrongness can make these emotions seem even more intense. Two things you can do to improve your family relationships are to realize that it's perfectly normal to not always get along, and to accept the complexity of emotions that will naturally occur within such involvements.

Will Smith and Jada Pinkett Smith may be best known for their successful acting careers, but being an entertainer is an identity shared by their children, Jaden and Willow Smith, who also perform in the music and film industries.

AP Images/Evan Agostini

Friendships

Friendships play a crucial role in your life. In addition to being one of the most common types of relationships you experience, they are also an important source of emotional security and self-esteem (Rawlins, 1992). They provide a sense of belonging when you're young, help you solidify your identity during adolescence, and provide satisfaction and social support when you're elderly (Miller et al., 2007).

What exactly are friendships? **Friendships** are voluntary interpersonal relationships characterized by intimacy and liking (McEwan, Babin Gallagher, & Farinelli, 2008). Whether casual or close, short or long term, friendships have three distinguishing characteristics: they are based on liking, they are created by choice, and their bonds are strengthened through shared interests.

Liking. People feel affection and respect for their friends; in other words, friends are people whom you *like* (Rubin, 1973). You also enjoy spending time with them (Hays, 1988). At the same time, because friendships are rooted in liking rather than love, you're not as emotionally attached to your friends as you are to your romantic partners, and you don't put as many emotional demands on them. Indeed, many people assume that they should be more loyal to and more willing to help romantic partners and family members than their friends (Davis & Todd, 1985). Imagine a friend calls you at work, in tears because her boyfriend has just dumped her. She's extremely depressed, and you're worried about her, but you hesitate to leave work early to see her. If it had been your sister who called in the same predicament, you might have been more willing to leave work to make absolutely sure she was OK.

Choice. You have more freedom in choosing your friendships than you do in any other relationship category (Sias et al., 2008). Whether you decide to become friends with someone is a pretty straightforward process: if you both want to be friends, you form a friendship. It's not always that simple in romantic, family, and workplace involvements. For example, in some cultures, people can choose whom they date or marry. But in others, there may be rules governing such matters—including arranged marriages. In your family, you may be bound to others through involuntary ties, including birth, adoption, or the creation of a stepfamily. In the workplace, you have to work with certain people, whether you like them or not.

Shared Interests. Similarity in interests is the primary force that draws you to your friends (Parks & Floyd, 1996), no matter what your age, gender, sexual orientation, or ethnicity. As a result, friendships are less stable, more likely to change, and easier to break off than family or romantic relationships (Johnson, Wittenberg, Villagran, Mazur, & Villagran, 2003). Why? When your interests and activities change, your friendships may change, too. If you adopt different political or religious beliefs or suffer an injury that prevents you from playing a beloved sport, friendships that were built on previous similarities may evaporate. Of course, some friendships will endure—if you and your friend find new points of commonality—but others will fade away. Indeed, a change in shared interests is one of the most common reasons friendships end (Miller et al., 2007).

Workplace Relationships

Affiliations you have with professional peers, supervisors, subordinates, or mentors are **workplace relationships**. These involvements vary along three dimensions: *status*, *intimacy*, and *choice* (Sias & Perry, 2004). First, most workplaces are structured hierarchically in terms of status, with some people ranked higher or lower than others in organizational position and power. Thus, a defining feature of workplace relationships is the equality or inequality of relationship partners. For example, you may work side by side every day with your coworker Katelyn, doing food prep, inventory, and cleanup in a restaurant. But if Katelyn is also your supervisor—she decides whether you keep your job and whether you get promotions and raises—she has power over you. That affects how you and she communicate. If Katelyn asks you to stay late or do additional work, it isn't simply a request:

ADVANCE THE CONVERSATION

WHEN A GOOD FRIEND CHANGES

1 YOUR DILEMMA

Raisa has been your friend for years. She's a first-generation Guatemalan American, and her family is very strict. Growing up, Raisa prioritized grades over play, but the payoff came when she was admitted to elite universities. Thrilled, her family now wants her to attend law school.

You've always liked Raisa, because although she's kind of uptight (perfectly groomed and ridiculously polite), she's also very supportive. She's the one friend you can always count on for good advice, whether you're fighting with a family member or suffering a romantic breakup.

Raisa recently traveled to Guatemala to build houses with Habitat for Humanity. Although you initially stay in touch with her by Skype, as the months pass, it becomes too much of a hassle to schedule chats, and so you switch to occasional emails. You still feel close to her, but you also can tell from the tone of her messages that her experiences there are having a substantial impact on her.

When Raisa returns, you pick her up at the airport because her parents are working. Raisa is unrecognizable. She's lost 15 pounds, and her hair is wild. There's a gleam in her eye, and she greets you with a big hug. As you drive home, she talks nonstop about her passion for her culture and how she wants to work full time for Habitat. She also tells you that her family doesn't approve, and that they have complained that she has "become a hippie." After a while, Raisa notices your silence. "I know I've changed," she says, "but I've finally figured out who I am. My family can't accept this. Can you?"

How do you feel about this change in Raisa's self-presentation?

2 THE RESEARCH

An essential part of building and sustaining close relationships is providing support for *valued social identities*: the aspects of your self you consider most important in defining who you are—musician, nurse, athlete, charity worker, teacher, mother, and so on. Within close relationships, communicating in ways that convey understanding, acceptance, and support for these identities is crucial, even if these identities change over time.

Scholars Carolyn Weisz and Lisa Wood (2005) studied friendships across a span of four years, looking at the impact that identity support, amount of communication, and general emotional support had on these relationships. They found that friends who reported high levels of identity support at the beginning of their study were more likely to describe each other as *best* friends four years later. In fact, identity support proved to be the strongest determinant of closeness—even more so than how often people communicated with each other.

Put yourself in Raisa's shoes. How would you feel if you were in her position, facing family opposition? What does she want from you?

3 YOUR OPPORTUNITY

Before you act, consider the facts of the situation and think about the identity support research. Also, reflect on what you've learned so far about why you form relationships (pp. 193–196) and the characteristics of friendships (pp. 201–202).

Now it's your turn. Write out a response to Raisa.

WORKPLACE RELATIONSHIPS

No matter the type of work environment, the relationships you have at work are defined by status, intimacy, and choice.

Intimacy: Open office environments can provide more opportunities for you to get to know your coworkers.
Status: Coworkers of equal standing can collaborate on new ideas before presenting them to a supervisor.
Choice: You must work with all your colleagues, but who becomes your friend is entirely up to you.

AP Images/Robert Schlesinger

it's a professional demand. However, you can't make similar demands of her because you don't have the same level of authority.

Workplace relationships also vary in intimacy. Some remain strictly professional, with interpersonal communication restricted to work-related concerns. Others become deeply intimate. If you spend three nights a week sharing the same shift with Erin and Dante, you'll likely get to know them both. But if you share the same tastes, attitudes, beliefs, and values only with Dante—not Erin—you may end up forming a deeper bond with Dante than with Erin.

Finally, workplace relationships are defined by varying degrees of choice—the degree to which participants willingly engage in them. As noted earlier, you don't get to pick your coworkers. This can be especially challenging when you're expected to work closely and productively with people you don't like or don't get along with. On the other hand, you *do* get to choose which coworkers become your friends—and sometimes, even which become romantic partners.

Relationship Stages

Although there's no set rule for how relationships progress, most go through certain stages, marked by differences in communication and intimacy. Sometimes these are positive—such as when good friends become best friends. Other times they're less pleasant, such as when you break off a romance. Knowing about these stages will help you recognize the status of your own relationships and communicate better within them.

Think back to *The Bachelor* TV show, which we discussed in our chapter opener. On that show, relationships between the women and the man grow closer or further apart depending on what each learns about the other and how they perceive their interactions. Relationships among the female contestants also change, evolving into strong friendships or unraveling into heated conflicts depending on how they communicate with each other.

In those regards, *The Bachelor* mirrors real life. As people spend more time together communicating and interacting, relationships develop as well as decay. Most relationships—including romantic, family, friendships, and workplace involvements—go through various stages. At each stage, the partners' communication, thoughts, and feelings demonstrate distinctive patterns. Communication scholar Mark Knapp (1984) identified 10 relationship stages, five of them related to "coming together" and five of them related to "coming apart."

Coming Together

Knapp's stages of coming together illustrate one possible flow of relationship development. As you read about the stages, keep in mind that these suggest benchmarks or turning points in relationships and are not fixed rules for how involvements should progress. Your relationships may go through some, none, or all of these stages. They may skip stages, jump backward or forward in the sequence, or follow a completely different trajectory.

Initiating. During the **initiating** stage, you size up a new person to decide whether you want to get to know that person better. You consider how attractive or interesting he or she seems by drawing on any information you can find, such as an online profile or impressions from other people who know him or her. You also work out an appropriate way of greeting the individual. You might do this in person—for instance, walking up to a classmate and saying, "Hi, I'm Jonas; would you like to get a coffee sometime?" Or you might do it online, such as when you connect with a long-lost family member through a genealogy website like Ancestry.com. People interested in initiating romantic relationships often use online dating sites to meet new partners (Heino, Ellison, & Gibbs, 2010).

FIGURE 8.1

COMING TOGETHER

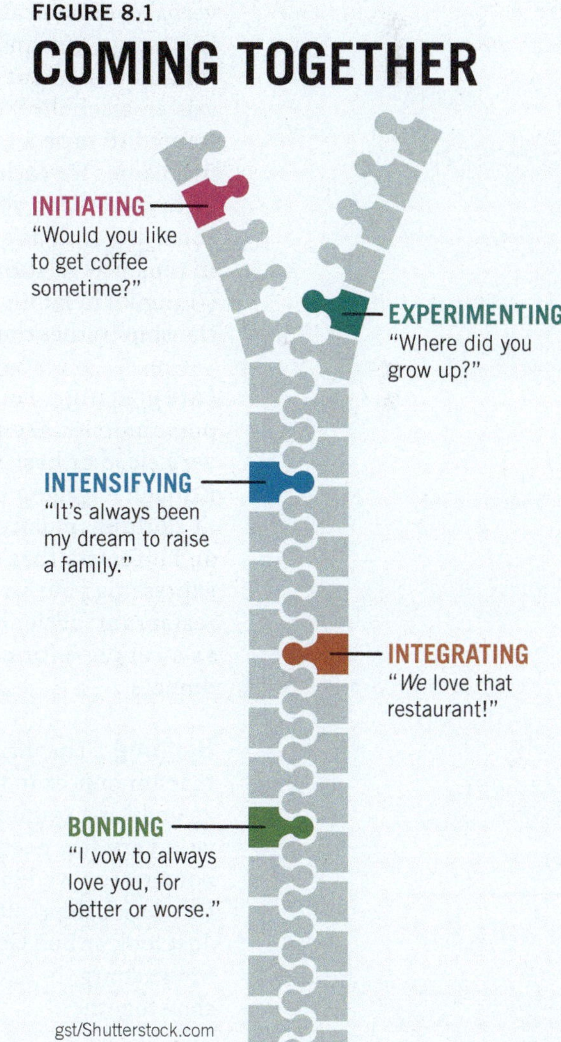
INITIATING
"Would you like to get coffee sometime?"
EXPERIMENTING
"Where did you grow up?"
INTENSIFYING
"It's always been my dream to raise a family."
INTEGRATING
"*We* love that restaurant!"
BONDING
"I vow to always love you, for better or worse."

gst/Shutterstock.com

Experimenting. Once you've initiated an encounter with someone, you enter the **experimenting** stage: exchanging demographic information (names, majors, hometowns). As you disclose these details, you look for points of commonality to foster further interaction. For instance, meeting a distant cousin for the first time at a family gathering, you might say, "You were an Army brat? So was I! Wasn't it tough to keep changing schools?" In a romance, this is the "casual dating" phase; in a friendship, it's the "making an acquaintance" stage. Most involvements never progress beyond this stage. You are likely to go through life experimenting with many people but forming deep connections with relatively few of them.

Intensifying. Occasionally, you'll find yourself feeling strongly attracted to or interested in another person. When this happens, your verbal and nonverbal communication becomes increasingly intimate. During this **intensifying** stage, you and the other person begin to share much more personal information about yourselves, such as secrets from your past ("My father was an alcoholic") or your most cherished dreams and goals ("I've always wanted to raise a family"). Within friendships, you might develop private nicknames for each other (e.g., calling your friend Benjamin "BangBang"). With coworkers, you begin discussing challenges you've faced in your personal life, such as a failed marriage or family tragedy (Sias & Cahill, 1998). In romantic relationships, you may begin expressing commitment verbally ("I think I'm falling for you") and online (marking your status as "in a relationship" rather than "single").

Integrating. During the **integrating** stage, your and your partner's personalities seem to blend. Twins may experience this stage, as do very close or best friends. In romantic relationships, partners integrate through engaging in sexual activity and sharing belongings, such as items of clothing, music, and photos. You and your partner engage in activities and interests that clearly join you together as a couple and use language expressing your new identity—"*Our* favorite movie is . . . ," "*We* love that restaurant!" Friends, colleagues, and family members begin treating you as a couple—for example, always inviting the two of you to parties or dinners.

Bonding. The ultimate stage of coming together is **bonding**, a public ritual that announces to the world that you and a relationship partner have made an enduring commitment to each other. Bonding is something you'll share with very few people during your lifetime. The most obvious example of bonding is a wedding or commitment ceremony with a partner in a romantic relationship, but bonding can happen in nonromantic relationships, too. Just look at Bob Goodpaster and Chico Mbanu, two lifelong best friends in Brownsburg, Indiana, who cemented their bond when they opened a bagel shop together.

Chico Mbanu and Bob Goodpaster exemplify bonding in a nonromantic friendship. The two men have been best friends since their days at Purdue University in the 1990s. After college, they worked together for 20 years, played hoops together, and later became "uncles" to the each other's children. In 2018 they opened a bagel and coffee shop together—appropriately named Best Friends Coffee and Bagels—thus making their long-standing friendship into a legal business collaboration.

Coming Apart

In most of your relationships, you will also experience stages of coming apart—getting less intimate with your relationship partners. One study of dating couples found that across a three-month period, as many as 30 percent of the couples broke up (Parks & Adelman, 1983). Friendships are even less stable than romantic relationships (Johnson et al., 2003). Why? Consider the differences in depth of commitment between friendships and romantic attachments. Friendships are rooted in shared interests, but people's interests frequently change. So, if you switch your major from biology to music, it's likely you will grow apart from the friends you made in your biology lab, as you no longer share the same academic interests or take the same classes. In comparison, romantic relationships are forged from more powerful bonds, such as deep emotional and sexual attachment.

Like coming together, coming apart unfolds over stages marked by changes in the partners' thoughts, feelings, and communication. Many romantic partners, family members, friends, and coworkers experience some of these stages at various points in their relationships. Again, your relationships may go through some, none, or all of these stages. In fact, not all relationships that begin to come apart result in a permanent ending of the relationship. Sometimes, with enough effort, people can resolve their differences. Other times, ending the relationship is the right thing to do because the people involved have either grown apart or permanently lost interest in each other. No matter the situation, the stages of coming apart often involve intense emotional pain that can make it difficult for the individuals involved to communicate competently with each other. This is why it is important to know and understand these relationship stages, so you can better handle them as they come up.

Differentiating. In all relationships, partners share differences as well as similarities. But during the first stage of coming apart, **differentiating**, the beliefs, attitudes, and values that distinguish you from your partner come to dominate your thoughts and communication ("I can't *believe* you think that!" or "We are *so* different!").

Most healthy relationships experience occasional periods of differentiating. These moments can involve arguing over what the partners see as conflicting viewpoints, tastes, or goals. But you can move your relationship through this difficulty—and thus stop the coming-apart process—by openly discussing your points of difference and working together to resolve them.

Circumscribing. If one or both of you respond to problematic differences by ignoring them and spending less time talking, you enter the **circumscribing** stage of coming apart. You actively begin to restrict the quantity and quality of information you exchange in the relationship, creating "safe zones" in which you discuss only topics that won't provoke conflict. Common remarks made during circumscribing include "Don't ask me about that" and "Let's not talk about that anymore."

Stagnating. If circumscribing becomes so severe that you and the other person have almost no safe topics to talk about, communication slows to a standstill, and the relationship enters the **stagnating** stage. You both presume that communicating is pointless because you believe it will only lead to further problems. People in stagnant relationships often experience a sense of resignation; they feel stuck or trapped. However, some stay in the relationship for months or even years. Why? They may believe that it's better to leave things as they are than to put in the enormous effort needed to end or try to rebuild the relationship, or they simply may not know how to repair the damage done to their earlier bond.

Avoiding. During the **avoiding** stage, one or both of you decide that you can no longer be around the other, and you begin distancing yourself physically. Some people communicate avoidance directly and verbally ("You are no longer my son, and I want no further contact with you!" or "We're no longer friends"). Others may do it by spending more and more time away from their partner—for example, by avoiding family get-togethers or moving out of a shared apartment because "I need some space to myself." Some avoid the other person indirectly—for example, screening the individual's calls, ignoring his or her texts, changing their Facebook status from "in a relationship" to "single," or "de-friending" or "un-following" someone.

Terminating. In ending a relationship, some people want to come together for a final encounter that gives a sense of closure and resolution. During the **terminating** stage, former partners might discuss the past, present, and future of the relationship. They often describe their past relationship by making accusations ("No one has ever betrayed my friendship as much as you have!") or expressing sadness over what's been lost ("I'll never be able to find someone as perfect as you"). Their verbal and nonverbal behaviors reveal a lack of intimacy—for instance, standing far apart and making little eye contact. The partners may also discuss the future status of their relationship. Some may agree to end all contact going forward; others may choose to maintain some type of contact, like an occasional phone call, even though the relationship is officially over.

Many people find terminating a relationship painful or awkward. It's hard to tell someone that you no longer want to be involved with him or her, and it's equally painful to hear it. But by drawing on all you've learned about communication, you can survive this dreaded moment. Use skills from Chapter 2, such as *empathic concern*—being aware of how your partner is feeling and experiencing compassion for him or her—and *perspective-taking*—the ability to see things from your partner's point of view—to handle the situation competently. See Advance the Conversation: Ending a Relationship on pages 210–211 for additional advice on handling a breakup conversation. You may also find it useful to remind yourself that relationship endings are a kind of death and that it's normal to experience grief, even when terminating is the right thing to do. The suggestions offered in the section on supportive communication in Chapter 9 can help you manage this aspect of termination (see pages 231–233).

LearningCurve can help you review! Go to **launchpadworks.com**

FIGURE 8.2

COMING APART

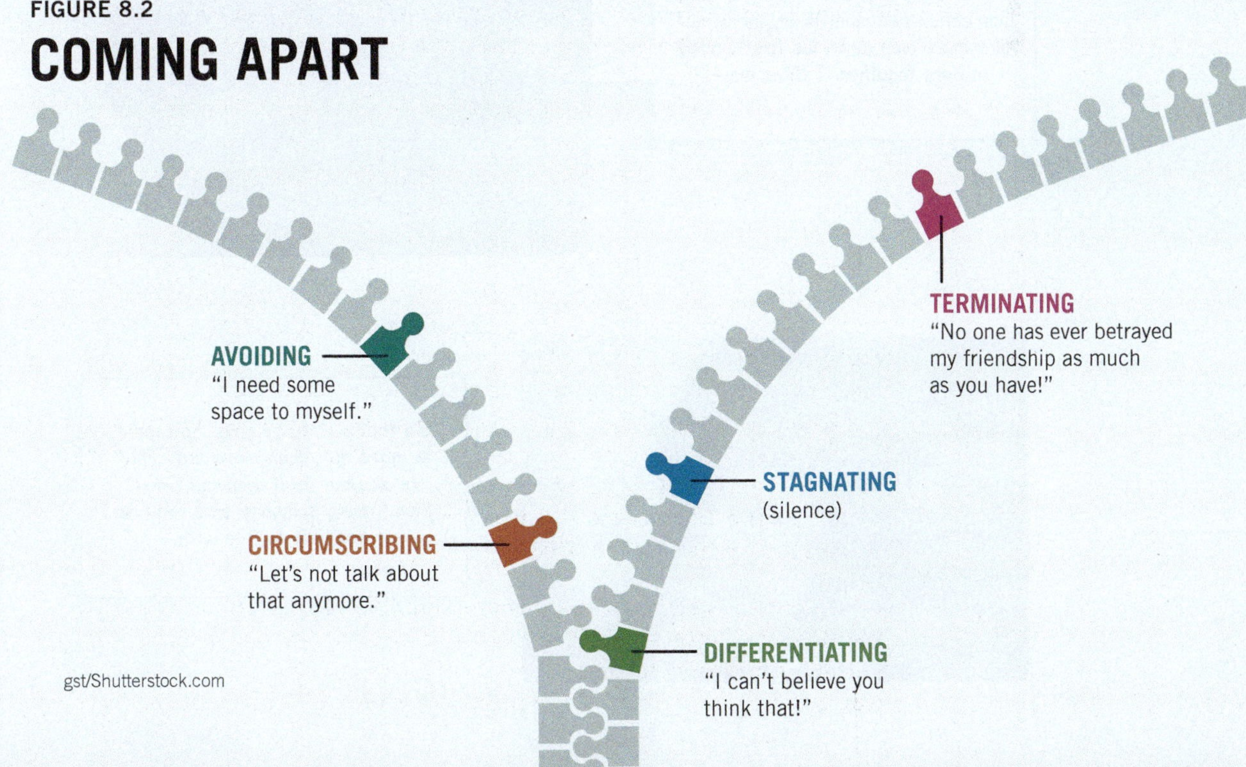
AVOIDING
"I need some space to myself."
CIRCUMSCRIBING
"Let's not talk about that anymore."
STAGNATING
(silence)
DIFFERENTIATING
"I can't believe you think that!"
TERMINATING
"No one has ever betrayed my friendship as much as you have!"
gst/Shutterstock.com

ADVANCE THE CONVERSATION
Video Activity

ENDING A RELATIONSHIP

The following scenario will enhance your ability to understand and apply competent communication. Visit LaunchPad at **launchpadworks.com** to get the full experience with video. As you watch the first video, recall what you've learned about the stages of coming apart, and then complete the **Your Turn** prompts. Finally, watch the **Take Two!** video to explore how this scenario could have gone differently.

1 THE PROBLEM

The close connection that once existed between Mirirai and her roommate, Alex, has faded. Mirirai feels that the two of them no longer share anything in common, and they argue more than they get along. Mirirai wants to end their relationship and sees an opportunity to do so when their lease is up. When Alex gets home from work, Mirirai breaks the news: "I'm going to look for another place to live. I mean, on my own."

"I just don't feel that there's a solid connection between us anymore, not like there was when we first moved in here together. I think we—"

"So that's it, huh? Fine. You want to move out, then move out. This is all your fault anyway! Good luck finding someone else. You're impossible to live with."

2 YOUR TURN

Observations. Reflect on how Mirirai and Alex communicated in this scenario by answering the following questions:

1. Which character do you identify with more in this situation? How would you feel if you were in her situation?
2. Where were the missed opportunities to practice competent communication?

Discussion. In class or with a partner, share your thoughts about the interaction between Mirirai and Alex and work to answer the following questions:

1. Can you understand both perspectives?
2. What could Alex and Mirirai have done differently?

Conclusion. Choose one person in the scenario to offer your advice. Based on your analysis, what advice would you give her to improve her communication competence in this scenario?

3 TAKE TWO!

What if things had gone differently? Watch the **Take Two!** video to see one possible example of how the conversation might have gone if Alex and/or Mirirai had communicated differently. As you watch the video, consider where the dialog reflects communication competence. After watching the video, answer the questions below:

1. Did Alex and/or Mirirai take advantage of opportunities that they missed in the first scenario? Which ones?
2. Did their different actions result in a more productive encounter? Please explain.

CHAPTER 8 REVIEW

CHAPTER RECAP

- **Interpersonal communication** is **dyadic** and is your primary tool for building, maintaining, and ending relationships.
- The four defining characteristics of interpersonal communication are that it is transactional, dynamic, relational, and impactful.
- Scholars suggest that five factors influence how people form interpersonal relationships: proximity, **resources**, similarity, **reciprocal liking**, and physical attractiveness.
- Though each type is unique, people build and maintain their relationships—**romantic**, **family**, **friends**, and **workplace**—through interpersonal communication.
- Many relationships progress through certain stages, marked by differences in communication and intimacy. These turning points can be positive—**initiating**, **experimenting**, **intensifying**, **integrating**, and **bonding**—or negative—**differentiating**, **circumscribing**, **stagnating**, **avoiding**, and **terminating**.

LaunchPad

LaunchPad for *Choices & Connections* offers unique video scenarios and encourages self-assessment through adaptive quizzing. Go to **launchpadworks.com** to get access.

 LearningCurve adaptive quizzes

 Advance the Conversation video scenarios

 Video clips that illustrate key concepts

KEY TERMS

Interpersonal communication, p. 190
Dyadic, p. 190
I-Thou, p. 192
I-It, p. 192
Impersonal communication, p. 193
Interpersonal relationships, p. 194
Mere exposure effect, p. 194
Resources, p. 194
Social exchange theory, p. 194
Birds-of-a-feather effect, p. 195
Reciprocal liking, p. 195
Beautiful-is-good effect, p. 196
Romantic relationships, p. 197
Liking, p. 198
Loving, p. 198
Passionate love, p. 198
Companionate love, p. 198
Family, p. 200
Friendships, p. 201
Workplace relationships, p. 202
Initiating, p. 205
Experimenting, p. 206
Intensifying, p. 206
Integrating, p. 206
Bonding, p. 206
Differentiating, p. 208
Circumscribing, p. 208
Stagnating, p. 208
Avoiding, p. 208
Terminating, p. 208

POP QUIZ

Looking for more review questions? **LearningCurve** can help you master key concepts from this chapter. Go to **launchpadworks.com**

1. According to philosopher Martin Buber, when you embrace the fundamental similarities that connect you with others and try to see things from others' points of view, you're communicating in what fashion?
   a. Dyadic
   b. Loving
   c. I-Thou
   d. I-It

2. Studies have found that *the* most commonly mentioned factor leading to love is
   a. proximity.
   b. resources.
   c. physical attractiveness.
   d. reciprocal liking.

3. The stories that family members exchange, the way they deal with conflict and talk with one another, and their common history all contribute to a sense of
   a. shared identity.
   b. shared interests.
   c. emotional complexity.
   d. companionate love.

4. Which of the following is *not* a factor in determining how workplace relationships develop?
   a. Attachment
   b. Choice
   c. Intimacy
   d. Status

5. During this stage, you become so close to someone else that your personalities seem to blend.
   a. Bonding
   b. Integrating
   c. Experimenting
   d. Intensifying

ACTIVITIES

For more activities, visit LaunchPad for *Choices & Connections* at **launchpadworks.com**

1 Interpersonal vs Impersonal

Working with a partner, come up with your own definition of interpersonal communication based on how you use it daily. Include what distinguishes it from impersonal communication. Then, discuss how mediated forms of communication, such as social media, emails, and texts, can be interpersonal and how they can be impersonal. What makes the difference? Does the number of people impact whether an encounter is interpersonal? How? Come up with examples for each, and discuss how the technology can influence whether the communication is interpersonal or impersonal.

2 Love, Hollywood Style

Identify three of the most romantic movies you've seen (e.g., *The Notebook*, *The Fault in Our Stars*, *Love Actually*, *Brokeback Mountain*). For each, assess how passionate love and companionate love are depicted. Is passionate love depicted as superior to companionate love? How do the movies deal with love over time? How do these depictions contrast with your own views of passionate and companionate love? What factors of loving and liking are shown, and which are ignored? What effect does this have on the portrayal of "real" romantic relationships in the movies?

9

Managing Interpersonal Relationships

What will make you happy? This seems to be a simple question, with obvious answers: Fame. Being remembered as someone who did something great. Or perhaps fortune. In one survey of college students, 75 percent of respondents rated "being very well off financially" as their top goal in life, and 78 percent said, "It's important to have a beautiful home, a new car and other nice things."[1]

Thinking about what makes you happy is important, because happiness matters. Studies show that happy people are healthier, more energized, more confident, and more socially connected than are unhappy people. Moreover, the pursuit of happiness is the driving force behind most people's decisions: they choose colleges, majors, and careers based on what they believe will help them become happier. But there's a catch: what people *think* will satisfy them often doesn't.

What *really* makes people happy? Psychologist David Myers has devoted much of his career to gathering and interpreting scientific findings on enduring joy. What he has found is both obvious and surprising. Decades of research involving hundreds of studies and thousands of people in dozens of countries show that human beings are happier when they have meaningful activities to consume their time (challenging jobs, passionate hobbies), exercise regularly, have spirituality in their lives, and get sufficient sleep. It turns out that age, gender, parenthood status (whether you have kids or not), and physical attractiveness have little impact on happiness. What else *doesn't* guarantee happiness? Money. As Myers describes, "Wealth is like health: its utter absence breeds misery, but having it doesn't ensure happiness."

But among all the factors that shape enduring joy, one leaps out as the most important in Myers's analysis: *the quality of interpersonal relationships*. Consider these facts: the happiest college students are those who have satisfying romantic relationships, family bonds, friendships, and workplace attachments. People who report close interpersonal relationships are better able to cope with life's inevitable stresses, which can range from unemployment and illness to the deaths of loved ones. In the previously noted survey of college students, most reported financial gain as their top goal; however, when asked, "What is *necessary* for your happiness?" they answered, "Satisfying interpersonal relationships."

[1]All findings and quotes that follow adapted from Myers (2000, 2002, 2004, 2013).

Shannon Fagan/The Image Bank/Getty Images

CHAPTER OUTLINE

LearningCurve can help you review! Go to **launchpadworks.com**

Your life is filled with relationships—so many that you often don't give them a second thought. Maybe you have a neighbor whom you wave to on your way to school and occasionally chat up, a barista who makes your morning coffee, a checkout clerk at the grocery store who has rung up your purchases every Sunday for years. Then there's your inner circle of lovers, family members, friends, and coworkers—the people you consider to be close to you, and with whom you interact every day. Collectively, your connections to all these people directly determine how you feel as you go through your life. When these relationships are harmonious, your days are filled with joy and laughter. When they fracture, your days darken with pain and sadness.

Given that satisfying interpersonal relationships are essential for your life happiness, it's important to know how to manage these relationships in a way that best sustains them. In this chapter, you'll learn:

- Ways to use self-disclosure to build relationships
- How to manage relationship tensions
- Successful strategies for sustaining your relationships
- How to support your relationship partners in times of need

Self-Disclosure in Relationships

When you share private information with others, you open up your innermost self to them. Such sharing, known as self-disclosure, is the foundation for intimacy in a relationship. But it's not as simple as "sharing equals closeness." Instead, you must know what, why, and when to disclose in order to build happy and enduring relationships.

In season 2 of the Golden Globe–winning Showtime series *The Affair* (Steve's favorite show), Cole and Luisa become romantically involved. Cole is a "local boy" who grew up in Montauk, Long Island. Following the death of his young son, Cole's wife, Alison, leaves him to pursue "the affair" that gives the show its name. Luisa is an Ecuadoran immigrant who meets Cole while working in Montauk as a bartender and housekeeper. A few weeks into their relationship, Luisa discloses her true feelings—telling Cole, "Te Amo" (I love you). Still struggling with the emotional aftermath of losing both son and wife, Cole responds, "*What* did you say!?" then walks out of the room. Later, when Luisa confronts him as to why he reacted the way he did, Cole says, "Do you want muffins? I'm starving!" and then picks a fight with her, accusing her of stealing money. She is so offended by the accusation that she leaves. That night, fearful of losing yet another person he loves, Cole seeks Luisa out and shares his feelings:

> It's been a while since I've had someone I care about, so I wanted to come here and apologize. I was *trying* to hurt you; I was *trying* to get you out of my house; and as soon as you walked out that door, I wanted you back. Look, I can't promise that I'll be the best thing that ever happens to you,

Mark Schafer/Showtime/Everett Collection

In *The Affair*, Cole must share his past struggles with Luisa in order for their relationship to grow and deepen. How have such personal disclosures influenced relationships with lovers, friends, and coworkers in your life?

> but I promise that I will never hurt you like that again, and I am good for my word, Luisa, you can ask anyone! There's one other thing: *Te amo tambien* (I love you too). (Season 2, Episode 7)

We've all been in situations in which people have shared information with us that clarified who they are and how they feel. Similarly, we've all had the experience of feeling compelled to seek people out and share with them our innermost selves. Such instances illustrate the essential role of interpersonal communication in creating and sustaining relationships. When people disclose their innermost thoughts to each other, they forge a strong emotional bond, and sometimes, like Cole and Luisa, find their way to the realization of mutual love.

Self-Disclosure and Relationship Development

Revealing private information about your self to others is known as **self-disclosure** (Wheeless, 1978). Self-disclosure is a key part of building and sustaining relationships (Reis & Patrick, 1996). When you disclose to someone, you reveal aspects of your self that you previously kept hidden. Psychologists Irwin Altman and Dalmas Taylor (1973) think of self-disclosure as similar to peeling back layers of an onion. According to their **social penetration theory**, the self is an "onion-skin structure" consisting of three sets of layers. The *outermost (or peripheral) layers* of your self are demographic characteristics, such as your birthplace, age, gender, and ethnicity (see Figure 9.1). When you meet someone for the first time, you typically focus the conversation on these characteristics: What's your name? What's your major? Where

FIGURE 9.1

THE LAYERS OF SELF-DISCLOSURE

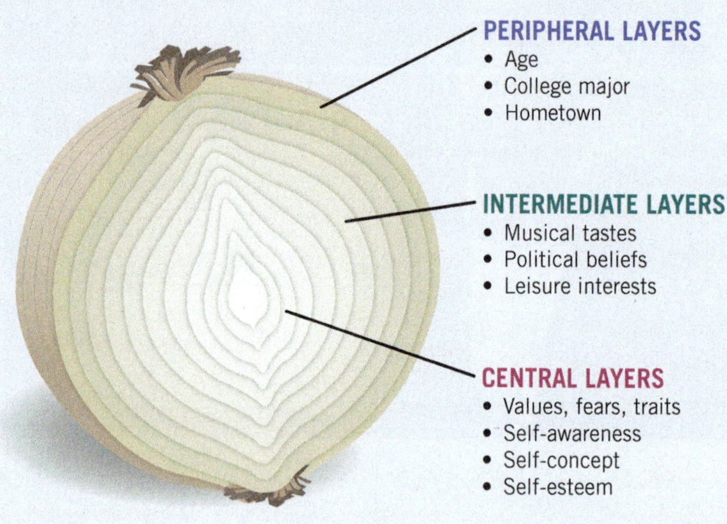

are you from? The *intermediate layers* contain your attitudes and opinions about things like music, politics, food, and entertainment. Deep within the onion are the *central layers* of your self—core characteristics such as self-awareness, self-concept, self-esteem, personal values, fears, and distinctive personality traits. As Chapter 2 discusses, this is what makes up your *self*.

This notion that the self consists of layers helps explain how to distinguish between casual and close involvements. As relationships progress, partners start peeling down to the deeper layers of the onion, disclosing increasingly personal information to each other. But in addition to *depth*, the revealing of selves that occurs during relationship development involves *breadth*—sharing more aspects of your self at each layer. For example, when you're sharing your attitudes and opinions (the intermediate layers of your self), you would be demonstrating breadth if you covered a relatively wide range of topics instead of discussing in detail only your taste in music.

The deeper and broader self-disclosure becomes, the more it fosters **intimacy**—feelings of closeness between you and others (Mashek & Aron, 2004). Intimacy is self-perpetuating: the more intimacy you feel, the more you disclose; and as you disclose more, feelings of intimacy deepen (Shelton, Trail, West, & Bergsieker, 2010). But for self-disclosure to create intimacy, several conditions must be met (Reis & Shaver, 1988). For one thing, *both* partners must disclose. If one person shares previously private thoughts and feelings, and the other person doesn't, the relationship isn't intimate—it's one-sided.

The partner who is listening to someone self-disclose must also respond supportively. Have you ever shared something deeply personal with a friend, who then commented with something like "I can't believe you did something so stupid!" If so, how did this response make you feel? Chances are it created a feeling of distance rather than one of closeness between the two of you.

Finally, to foster feelings of intimacy with others, it's important to disclose information that people view as appropriate. Sharing information that is perceived as problematic or peculiar can damage relationships (Planalp & Honeycutt, 1985). Imagine that a coworker tells you he's obsessed with serial killers. You probably won't feel closer to him—unless you share the same obsession!

Communicating Self-Disclosure

Researchers have conducted thousands of self-disclosure studies over the last 40 years (Tardy & Dindia, 1997). These studies suggest five important facts about self-disclosure. First, self-disclosure appears to promote mental health and relieve stress (Tardy, 2000). When information is especially troubling, keeping it inside can lead to obsessing about the secret, as you constantly monitor what you say so you don't disclose it (Kelly & McKillop, 1996). This can raise stress levels, causing immune-system problems, ulcers, and high blood pressure (Pennebaker, 1997).

Second, people self-disclose more during online interactions than during face-to-face exchanges. During most online encounters, you can't see the people with whom you're interacting, so you don't notice the consequences of your disclosures (Joinson, 2001). As a result, online interactions and relationships can seem more intimate than they really are. Even when you can see others—via FaceTime, Skype, webcam, or videoconference—the quality of the video or delays in the streaming can make it difficult to accurately perceive their responses. As Chapter 4 discusses, you can better manage your online interactions by remembering the three Ps of mediated communication—that it is powerful, public, and permanent (see pages 101–102).

Third, despite common beliefs, little evidence exists supporting the stereotype that men can't share their feelings in relationships. In close same-gender friendships, for example, both men and women disclose deeply and broadly (Shelton et al., 2010). In cross-gender romantic involvements, men often disclose at levels equal to or greater than those of their female partners (Canary, Emmers-Sommer, & Faulkner, 1997). However, studies do suggest that both men and women feel more comfortable disclosing to females than to males (Dindia & Allen, 1992).

Fourth, in all cultures, people vary widely in the degree to which they self-disclose. Some people naturally share more of their thoughts and feelings, whereas others don't (Jourard, 1964). Trying to force someone with a different idea of self-disclosure to match your style—for example, to open up or to share less information—not only is unethical but also can damage the relationship by causing resentment (Luft, 1970).

Dating is a common example of social penetration theory. On first dates or in initial online chats, people tend to disclose only their outermost layers. If the relationship continues, the intermediate and central layers are revealed as the couple progresses through the experimenting, intensifying, and integrating stages.

Beau Lark/Corbis

Fifth, different cultures have distinct overall patterns for self-disclosure. For instance, Chinese college students tend to disclose less than do Euro-American students (Chen, 1995). In fact, Euro-Americans generally tend to disclose more frequently than do almost any other cultural group, including Asians, Hispanics, and African Americans (Klopf, 2001).

Self-Disclosure Skills

Given the importance of self-disclosure in building your interpersonal relationships, putting energy into strengthening your self-disclosure skills is enormously worthwhile. These practices can help:

- *Know your thoughts and feelings.* When you disclose to others, you affect their lives and relationship decisions. Consequently, you're ethically obligated to be certain about the truth of information before you share it. This is especially important when disclosing intimate feelings, such as romantic interest. For instance, don't tell someone you are dating that you love him or her unless you're sure that's how you really feel.
- *Know your audience.* Whether it's a text message or an intimate conversation, think carefully about how others will perceive your disclosure and how it will impact their thoughts and feelings about you. If you're unsure about a disclosure's appropriateness, don't disclose. Instead, talk more generally about the issue or topic first, gauging the person's level of comfort with the conversation before deciding whether to disclose. For example, suppose you decide that you *do* love your new boyfriend,

but you're not sure how he feels about you. Instead of blurting out, "I love you!" broach the subject gently, by saying something like, "I've really been enjoying spending time with you. We seem to have so much in common, and I have to admit—I'm starting to have some strong feelings for you." If he seems happy to hear this, it may be OK to say, "I love you." If he appears uncomfortable, you may want to hold off disclosing your love.

- *Don't make assumptions about gender.* Just because someone is a woman doesn't mean she will disclose freely, and just because a person is a man doesn't mean he's incapable of discussing his feelings. Even though men *and* women tend to feel more comfortable disclosing to women, don't assume that when you're talking with a woman, she'll expect you to share your innermost self. Instead, be aware of how individual people respond to your disclosures, and adjust accordingly.
- *Be sensitive to cultural differences.* When you're interacting with people from cultural backgrounds different from yours, disclose gradually to test their responses. Don't make assumptions about what another person will disclose based on his or her ethnicity. For example, just because a new acquaintance is Italian American doesn't mean she will want to openly share her innermost thoughts and feelings. Likewise, just because someone is Chinese American doesn't mean he will be reluctant to disclose.
- *Don't force others to self-disclose.* Though it's perfectly appropriate to let someone know you're available to listen, it's unethical and destructive to try to make others share personal information with you if they don't want to. People have reasons for not wanting to share certain things about themselves—just as you have reasons for protecting your own privacy.

FIGURE 9.2

SELF-DISCLOSURE SKILLS

1
Know your thoughts and feelings.
2
Know your audience.
3
Don't make assumptions about gender.
4
Be sensitive to cultural differences.
5
Don't force others to self-disclose.
6
Actively listen & express empathy to others' disclosure.

Matej Kotula/Shutterstock.com

ADVANCE THE CONVERSATION

I DON'T WANT TO HEAR THIS!

1 *YOUR DILEMMA*

Growing up, your parents fought constantly, and the bitterness of their relationship tore you apart because you love each of them dearly. Now they are divorced, and you live with your mom, who bad-mouths your dad all the time. You try to be a supportive listener, but it's hard because you love your dad, and her comments are so toxic.

The situation escalates when your mom starts dating John. She and John get along really well, but the contrast between their relationship and your parents' former marriage makes things worse. When you visit your dad, he says horrible things about your mom and John, and your mom is still slandering your dad. There seems to be no escape from the negativity, and you're stressed, exhausted, and unhappy.

One night you're at your mom's, and she's on the phone with John. After she hangs up, she says to you, "I'm so glad to have John in my life. He supports me in ways your father never did. And he's a better lover and friend than your father ever was. I can't believe I wasted all those years with your dad!" Listening to her, you feel sick to your stomach. Noticing your reaction, she says, "I'm sorry for always dumping this stuff on you. It's just I've felt so out of control recently. And you're such a good listener—it means so much to me to be able to tell you everything!"

How is your mom making you feel? What challenges do you face in explaining your feelings to her?

2 *THE RESEARCH*

Communication scholars Tamara Afifi, Tara McManus, Susan Hutchinson, and Birgitta Baker (2007) studied divorced parents' *inappropriate disclosures* to their children: comments that insulted the other parent; were age inappropriate; or placed the child in an uncomfortable position as mediator, counselor, or friend.

The most frequent type of inappropriate parental disclosure was insults. Parents who slandered one another to their children often felt justified saying such things to support "their side of the story" regarding the breakup. Parents who believed their lives were out of control were more likely to dump inappropriate information on their kids.

Parents' inappropriate disclosures had destructive effects on their children. Kids who said, "My parent tells me negative things that my other parent has done" or "My parent tells me things that a child shouldn't have to hear" reported poorer physical and mental health, less psychological well-being, and increased stress.

What can you take away from this research? Although self-disclosure is essential for building and sustaining intimacy, sharing inappropriate *negative* information can be devastating. When you are in a position to share negative information, consider what is appropriate, effective, and ethical given the situation and relationships involved.

If you were in your mom's place, would you be thinking and talking in similar ways?

3 *YOUR OPPORTUNITY*

Before making a communication choice, consider the facts of the situation, and think about the inappropriate disclosure research. Also, reflect on what you've learned so far about self-disclosure in relationships (pp. 216–223) and the dynamics of family relationships (pp. 199–201).

Now it's your turn. Write out a response to your mom.

- *When others disclose to you, actively listen and express empathy.* In situations in which people opt to share personal information with you, be sure to treat their disclosures with the same respect you expect from others when you share such information. Show them that you're listening by providing *positive feedback* and using a *people-oriented listening style*, as discussed in Chapter 7. You can demonstrate that you care about what they're saying by expressing *empathy*—trying to see things from their perspective and showing compassion for them (see Chapter 2 for more tips on empathy).

Managing Relationship Tensions

Self-disclosure can create positive outcomes, including a sense of trust and increased intimacy. But it also brings with it challenges, such as how to avoid feeling vulnerable and how to retain a sense of your separate self as you get closer to others. Learning how to resolve such tensions is critical for maintaining healthy, happy interpersonal relationships.

As you engage in relationships, competing impulses or tensions often arise in your feelings toward your relational partners. These tensions are known as **relational dialectics** (Baxter, 1990). For example, you may want to "bare your soul" to your partners, but you don't want to be vulnerable. Or, though you want to feel close, you also want to remain independent. Sometimes you want your partners to be predictable, but then again, you don't want things to get boring. Such dialectics aren't necessarily bad for relationships; rather, they occur naturally as you become more intimate. At the same time, competently managing these tensions will help you better sustain your relationships.

Relational dialectics take three common forms: openness versus protection, autonomy versus connection, and novelty versus predictability. Let's consider how each develops and how you can deal with them.

Openness vs Protection

The first relational dialectic is *openness versus protection*. As we discussed earlier in this chapter, when you mutually share private information with others, relationships naturally develop. Most of us enjoy the feeling of connection and mutual insight that such self-disclosure creates. But although people want to be open with their relationship partners (whether lovers, family members, friends, or coworkers), they also desire to keep certain aspects of their selves—such as their most private thoughts and feelings—protected. Too much openness can give people an uncomfortable sense that they've lost their privacy, which can make them feel vulnerable.

According to **communication privacy management theory** (Petronio, 2000), individuals create *information boundaries* by carefully choosing the kind of private information they reveal and the people with whom they share it. These boundaries are constantly shifting, depending on the degree of risk associated with disclosing information (Afifi & Steuber, 2010). The more comfortable people feel disclosing, the more likely they are to reveal sensitive information. Inversely, people are less likely to share when they expect negative reactions to the disclosure.

Think about how people manage information boundaries in romances and friendships. Over time, most lovers and friends learn that it's best not to talk about certain issues, topics, or people; otherwise, conflicts may occur (Dainton, Zelley, & Langan, 2003). As a result, partners negotiate **communication rules**—conditions governing what they can (and can't) talk about, how they can discuss such topics, and who else should have access to this information (Petronio & Caughlin, 2006). Such rules can be perfectly healthy as long as both people agree on them and as long as the avoided issues aren't central to the relationship's survival.

For example, when Steve and his wife, Kelly, were engaged but living in different cities, Kelly would go out dancing with her friends on the weekends. Often, she and her friends would meet handsome, charming, and funny men, and spend the evening chatting and dancing with them. Kelly—being scrupulously honest—would then call Steve and tell him all about it. But Steve was stressing about getting his graduate school work done, so hearing details about these men would make him mad, and the conversation would sour. After several of these unpleasant encounters, they negotiated a new rule: when Kelly goes out dancing with her friends, just tell Steve whether the evening was fun or not, and leave it at that. Because Steve trusted Kelly, he was fine with her providing a general assessment while leaving out the details that would spark his jealousy.

Now consider how communication rules governing openness versus protection are negotiated within families. In some families, members feel free to talk about any topic, at any time, and in any situation. In other families, discussion of sensitive topics—such as politics, religion, or money—may be considered appropriate only in certain settings. For instance, some parents might discuss their finances with a child planning how to pay for college but would not discuss such matters with their younger children. In other families, people never, under any circumstances, talk about topics the family has defined as completely off-limits, such as sex, recreational drug use, legal or financial woes, or serious health problems. Breaking a family communication rule by forcing discussion of a "forbidden" topic can cause intense emotional discomfort among other family members. It may even prompt the family to exclude the "rule breaker" from future family interactions. Keep this in mind before you force discussion of an issue that other family members consider off-limits. If you believe that breaking a communication taboo in your family is essential for a family member's health, consider doing it with the help of a mediator, such as a family therapist or a family-intervention specialist.

Kevin Mazur/Getty Images Entertainment/Getty Images

Reality TV shows that feature families, like *Keeping Up with the Kardashians*, often reveal the intimate communication that takes place between parents and children as well as between siblings. The Kardashians stand out even among reality TV families because they have almost no communication rules: they discuss all topics with one another and, thus, share these disclosures with viewers. How do you think having so much openness can affect family communication?

Managing openness versus protection through communication rules is also essential within the workplace. Communication rules in the workplace govern whether communications are formal or informal, whether they are personal or impersonal, and even which channels (email, instant messaging, texting, printed memos, face-to-face conversations) are the most appropriate for use among coworkers.

Autonomy vs Connection

The second relational dialectic is *autonomy versus connection.* People form close relationships mostly out of a desire to bond with other human beings. Yet if you come to feel *so* connected to your partners that your own identity seems to dissolve, you may choose to pull back and reclaim some of your autonomy, or independence.

The tension between autonomy versus connection is especially pronounced in romantic and family relationships. When you're in a romantic relationship and enter the *integrating* stage (see Chapter 8), family members, friends, and colleagues start treating you as a couple—for example, always inviting the two of you to social events. This may cause you to start wondering if you have an identity separate from that of your partner. As a student of ours once told his partner when describing this feeling, "I'm not me anymore; I'm *us*."

As with openness versus protection, honest discussion of the issue and relationship rules can help people better balance autonomy versus connection. For instance, a couple may establish a weekly "date night" to reinforce their connection to each other as well as a weekly "me night," during which each person can get together with other friends or spend time on a hobby or another interest.

Within families, managing autonomy versus connection is even harder. As children move through their teen years, they begin to assert their independence from parents (Crosnoe & Cavanagh, 2010). Their peers eventually replace parents and other family members as having the most influence on their interpersonal decisions (Golish, 2000). This pulling away from the family can be difficult for parents or other caregivers, who have come to count on the connection with their children.

Connections with family can also cause stress when family members seem blind to who you really are. For example, suppose your mother still treats you as the baby of the family when you get together with older siblings during the holidays—even though you're in your twenties or thirties. In this case, you may want to try spending some time alone with her, discussing your latest professional achievements. This will help remind her that you're not only "her baby" but also an independent, successful adult.

Novelty vs Predictability

The final relational dialectic is the tension between people's need for excitement and change and their need for stability—known as *novelty versus predictability.* We all like the security that comes with knowing how our lovers, family members, friends, and coworkers will behave, how we'll behave, and

DOUBLE TAKE

AUTONOMY VS CONNECTION

Spending time with friends can be one of life's great joys. Even though you choose friends based on your similarities and shared interests, spending time pursuing personal hobbies can help you maintain your separate sense of self.

manley099/iStock/Getty Images

Rob Tringali/SportsChrome/Getty Images

how our relationships will unfold. For example, romances are more successful when partners act in predictable ways that reduce uncertainty (Berger & Bradac, 1982). However, predictability can also trigger boredom. As you get to know people better, the excitement you felt when the relationship was new wears off, and things can start to feel boring. Reconciling the desire for predictability with the need for novelty is one of the most profound emotional challenges facing relationship partners, especially those involved in romances.

No one perfect solution exists for maintaining a balance between novelty and predictability. But your best bet for dealing with this dialectic is to share novel experiences with your partner—activities that keep your relationship from growing stale. For example, you might go on an adventurous vacation once a year that requires learning new skills together, such as scuba diving. Or you might seek out different activities to share with a friend or sibling, such as hiking, a road trip, or a baking class. Regardless of the particulars, the key is exposure to interesting, new experiences that you can share with each other.

Sustaining Your Relationships

Some relationships make it, and some don't, and there's not much you can do about it, right? Wrong. Relationships don't survive because of fate or magic; they survive because people invest time and energy into making them work. You can help your relationships endure by learning relational maintenance tactics and by providing support when others need it.

In the spring of 2015, Steve and his wife, Kelly, accepted faculty positions at the University of Alabama, Birmingham (UAB). But they faced a dilemma. Although their two oldest sons, Kyle and Colin, were both in college (Kyle at the University of Chicago; Colin at Michigan State), their youngest son, Conor, was still in high school. Not wanting to uproot Conor from his friends and the only community he had ever known (East Lansing, Michigan), they made a radical choice. Until Conor graduated, Steve would teach on-site at UAB, and Kelly would stay in East Lansing and teach her UAB classes online. This meant that the family was geographically splintered: Steve in Birmingham; Kyle in Chicago; and Kelly, Colin, and Conor in East Lansing. But despite the distance, they remained close. Steve, Kelly, and Conor Skyped nightly; and Steve and Kelly texted thoughts, feelings, and updates throughout the day. Steve, Kyle, Colin, and Conor exchanged Facebook posts and emails multiple times weekly—about music, politics, religion, and current events. And every holiday—and for a week in the summer—the five reunited, reaffirming the in-person bonds they'd kept solid through technology.

Many people believe that relationships just happen—that love affairs, family bonds, friendships, and professional affiliations arise on their own, run their natural course, and then succeed or fail according to fate. But a core principle of this book is that *you control the destiny of your relationships through the communication choices you make.* When you use all available means—online and off—to communicate positively, assure partners of your commitment, share your feelings, and support partners in times of need, your relationships thrive. When you communicate negatively, keep partners guessing about your degree of commitment, hide your feelings, and fail to support partners, your relationships wither.

Relational Maintenance

Relational maintenance refers to the use of communication behaviors to keep a relationship strong and to ensure that each party continues to draw satisfaction from the relationship (Stafford, Dainton, & Haas, 2000). Across years of research, communication scholar Laura Stafford has observed three strategies that help romantic partners, family members, friends, and coworkers maintain their relationships: *positivity*, *assurances*, and *self-disclosure* (Stafford, 2010).

Positivity. Arguably the most powerful maintenance tactic in sustaining healthy relationships is **positivity**—communicating in a cheerful and optimistic fashion, doing unsolicited favors, and giving unexpected gifts (Stafford, 2010). Cross- and same-gender partners involved in romantic relationships, as well as family members, friends, and coworkers, all routinely cite positivity as the most important maintenance tactic for ensuring happiness (Dainton & Stafford, 1993; Haas & Stafford, 2005; Stafford, 2010). You use positivity when you[2]

- Try to make interactions with others enjoyable
- Make an effort to build others up by giving them compliments
- Strive to be fun, upbeat, and optimistic with others

You undermine positivity when you

- Constantly look for and complain about problems in your relationships with others without offering solutions
- Whine, pout, and sulk when you don't get your way
- Criticize favors and gifts you've received from others

How can you implement positivity in your interpersonal relationships? Start doing favors for your relationship partners without being asked, and surprise them with small gifts that show you care. Invest energy into making each encounter enjoyable. Avoid complaining about problems that have

---

[2]All bulleted items that follow adapted from the revised relationship maintenance behavior scale of Stafford (2010).

no solutions, ridiculing others, whining or sulking when you don't get your way, and demanding favored treatment from others. Show appreciation when someone does something nice for you. Positivity can be especially helpful at work, since it can help offset the stresses you and your coworkers will inevitably face. (See Table 9.1 on page 231.)

Assurances. Another powerful maintenance tactic in boosting relationship satisfaction is the use of **assurances**—messages that emphasize how much your relationship partners mean to you, point out how important the relationships are to you, and show that you see a secure future together. You use assurances when you

- Regularly tell your partners how important they are to you
- Talk about future plans and events that you'll share together
- Do and say things to demonstrate the depth of your feelings

You undermine assurances when you

- Suggest that other relationships and things in your life are more important than your relationship partners
- Tell your partners not to count on anything long term
- Systematically avoid expressing any type of enduring relationship commitment to your partners

EmirMemedovski/E+/Getty Images

Spending time on mobile devices while on a date—or in any situation where you are expected to interact face-to-face with another person—can place significant strain on the relationship. Can you recall a time when you or someone you know communicated negative messages by using mobile devices inappropriately?

In romantic relationships, family relationships, and friendships, one of the most powerful ways to convey assurances to relationship partners is to *prioritize them as the focus of your attention, in situations where the principal activity is sharing time together*—such as when on a romantic date, sharing a meal with family members, or hanging out with friends. Research on intimacy and technology usage clearly documents that both men and women distinguish between time spent "casually hanging out together" versus "quality time"; most people believe that mobile phone usage is acceptable during the former but off-limits during the latter (Miller-Ott & Kelly, 2015). More specifically, partners consider mobile phone usage during encounters where attention "should be" focused on them to be a substantial violation of expectations, one that communicates powerful messages about the *lack* of importance placed on the relationship and undermines relational satisfaction (Kelly, Miller-Ott, & Duran, 2017).

Self-Disclosure. As we discussed earlier, *self-disclosure* is the revealing of private information about yourself to others in interpersonal communication. Self-disclosure can foster intimacy with another person—for example, when you share increasingly personal information with a new friend as you get closer to him or her.

However, when you use self-disclosure as a relational maintenance tactic, the focus is on creating a climate of security and trust with others. You want to help your relationship partners feel that they can disclose their fears and other feelings to you without you judging, criticizing, or rejecting them. To encourage others to self-disclose, you must behave in ways that are predictable, trustworthy, and ethical. Over time, such behavior convinces your relationship partners that you'll welcome personal information from them. You use self-disclosure for relational maintenance when you

- Tell your partners about your own fears and vulnerabilities
- Share your thoughts and emotions with them
- Encourage them to disclose their thoughts and feelings, and offer them empathy in return

You undermine self-disclosure when you

- Make fun of or criticize your relationship partners' perspectives
- Routinely hide important information from them
- Betray them by sharing confidential information about them with others

To foster disclosure with your lovers, family members, and friends, routinely make time just to talk. Encourage them to share their thoughts and feelings about issues that matter to them, whether it's online, face-to-face, or by phone. When they share their feelings and concerns with you, respond in a respectful way by both showing that you've heard and understood them and not interrupting or letting other events distract you from listening. Avoid betraying secrets that your relationship partners have confided in you, and don't hide relevant information from them.

TABLE 9.1

STRATEGIES FOR MAINTAINING RELATIONSHIPS

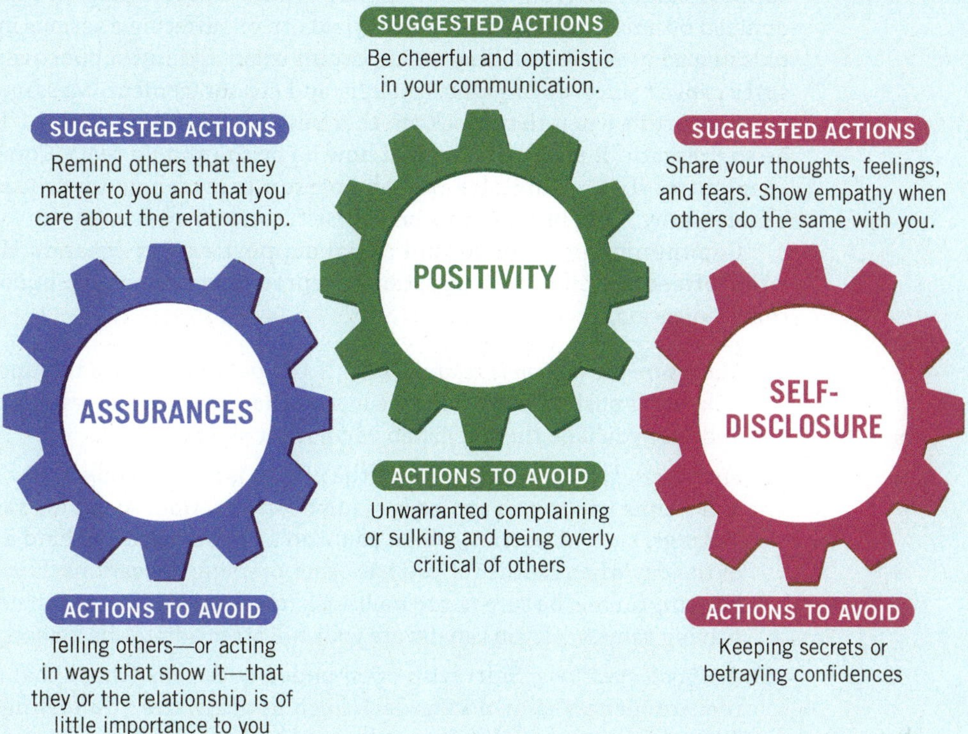
SUGGESTED ACTIONS
Be cheerful and optimistic in your communication.
SUGGESTED ACTIONS
Remind others that they matter to you and that you care about the relationship.
SUGGESTED ACTIONS
Share your thoughts, feelings, and fears. Show empathy when others do the same with you.
POSITIVITY
ASSURANCES
SELF-DISCLOSURE
ACTIONS TO AVOID
Unwarranted complaining or sulking and being overly critical of others
ACTIONS TO AVOID
Telling others—or acting in ways that show it—that they or the relationship is of little importance to you
ACTIONS TO AVOID
Keeping secrets or betraying confidences

In your workplace relationships, you can use self-disclosure to create feelings of trust between you and your colleagues. This means following through on your promises, respecting confidences, and demonstrating honesty and integrity in your behavior. (See Advance the Conversation: Relationship Maintenance at Work on pages 234–235.)

Supportive Communication

As noted at the beginning of the chapter, the quality of our interpersonal relationships is the most powerful predictor of our life happiness. When our relationships are healthy, we tend to be happy; and when they're not, we aren't. The techniques we just discussed—positivity, assurances, and self-disclosure—are powerful tools for sustaining interpersonal relationships, thereby fostering happiness. But sometimes you need to do more. When you provide **supportive communication**, you express emotional support and offer personal assistance to lovers, family members, friends, or coworkers who need it (Burleson & MacGeorge, 2002). The need for such support can arise from a wide range of events—everything from being dumped by a romantic partner, getting laid off, or suffering a serious injury, to losing a loved one or failing an important exam. Skillful supportive messages convey sincere sympathy, concern, and encouragement. Messages are not supportive when they mock another person's need for support ("Don't be so dramatic"), tell the individual how he or she should feel ("Come on, snap out of it!"), or indicate that the person is somehow inadequate or blameworthy ("You brought this on yourself, you know").

Communication scholar and social support expert Amanda Holmstrom offers the following suggestions for providing competent supportive communication[3]:

1. *Make sure the person is ready to talk.* If the person appears too upset to talk, don't push it. Instead, make it clear that you care and want to help, and that you'll be there to listen when he or she needs you.
2. *Find the right place and time.* Once the person is ready to talk, find a place and a time where you can have a quiet conversation. Avoid distracting settings, such as parties, where you won't be able to focus. Find a time of the day when neither of you has other pressing obligations. If you are chatting online, be sure not to multitask (checking Twitter or WhatsApp, playing games), so you can devote your full attention to the person.
3. *Ask good questions.* Start with open-ended questions (those that don't require just a yes or no answer), such as "How are you feeling?" or "What's on your mind?" Then follow up with more targeted questions, such as "Are you eating and sleeping OK?" (If the person says no, that may indicate depression.) Don't assume that because you've been in a similar situation, you know what someone is going through. Resist any urge to say "I know just how you feel."
4. *Legitimize, don't minimize.* Don't dismiss the problem or the significance of the person's feelings by saying things like "It could have been worse" or "Don't worry; you'll find someone else!" Research shows that these comments are unhelpful. Instead, let the person know that whatever he or she is feeling is OK ("It's terrible that you are going through this and completely understandable that you are upset").
5. *Listen actively.* Drawing on your listening skills from Chapter 7, show interest in what the person is saying. Make eye contact, lean toward the individual, and provide feedback—such as "Uh-huh" and "Yeah"—when appropriate.
6. *Offer advice cautiously.* Everyone wants to help someone who is suffering, so you may feel compelled to jump right in and start offering

---

[3]Content that follows provided to the author by Dr. Amanda Holmstrom and published with permission. The authors thank Dr. Holmstrom for her contribution.

advice. But often that's not helpful, and it may not be what the person wants. He or she may only need a sympathetic ear at the moment. Only give advice when the individual asks you for it, if you have relevant expertise or experience, and if it suggests an action that the person can actually take. When in doubt, ask if the person would like your advice—or just hold back until asked.

7. *Show concern and give praise.* Let the person know you genuinely care and are concerned about his or her well-being ("I am *so* sorry for your loss" or "You're really important to me"). Build the person up by praising his or her strength in handling this challenge ("You've got a lot going on, and you've done so well dealing with it"). Showing care and concern helps connect you to the person, and giving praise can help him or her feel better and gather strength that will be needed to tackle the problem at hand.

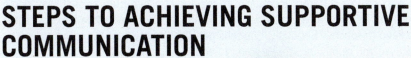

LearningCurve can help you review! Go to **launchpadworks.com**

FIGURE 9.3

STEPS TO ACHIEVING SUPPORTIVE COMMUNICATION

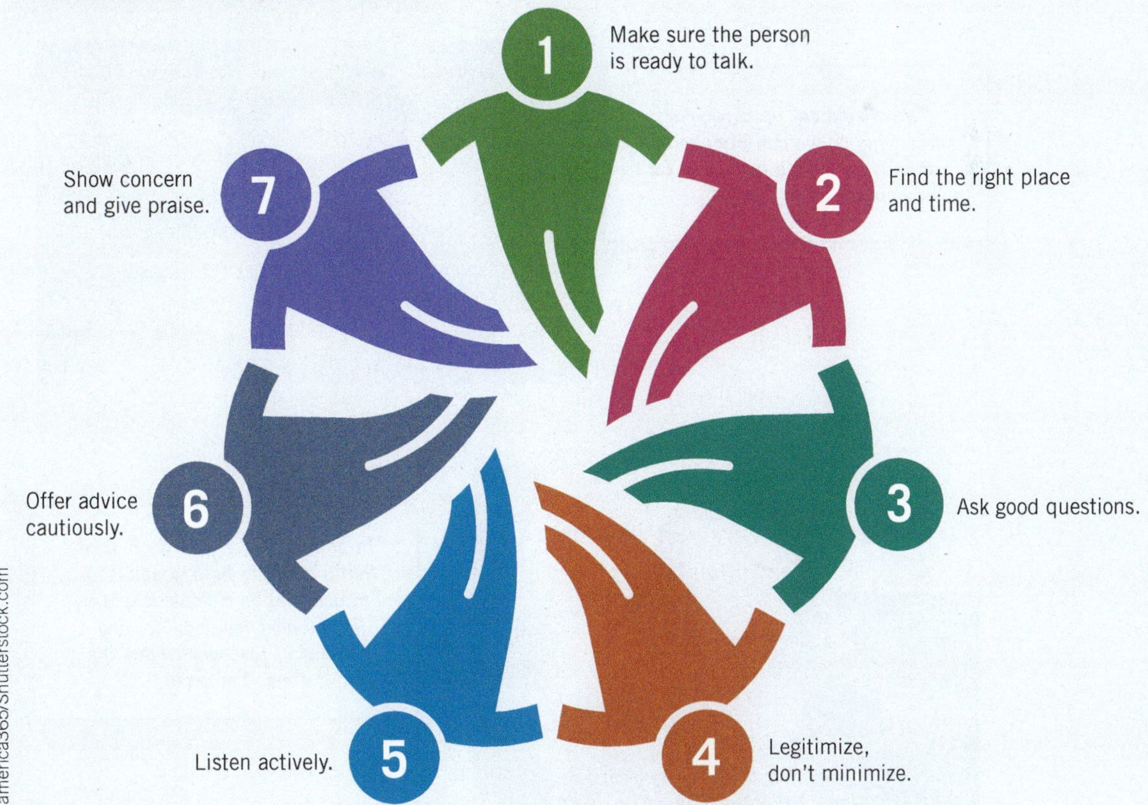
1
Make sure the person is ready to talk.
2
Find the right place and time.
3
Ask good questions.
4
Legitimize, don't minimize.
5
Listen actively.
6
Offer advice cautiously.
7
Show concern and give praise.

america365/Shutterstock.com

ADVANCE THE CONVERSATION
Video Activity

RELATIONSHIP MAINTENANCE AT WORK

The following scenario will enhance your ability to manage an interpersonal relationship with a friend at work. Visit LaunchPad at launchpadworks.com to get the full experience with video. As you watch the first video, recall what you've learned about managing relationship tensions, relationship maintenance, and supportive communication. Then complete the **Your Turn** prompts. Finally, watch the **Take Two!** video to explore how this scenario could have gone differently.

1 THE PROBLEM

For the last two years, Tim has worked side by side with Hannah. She is his closest friend at work, and she's funny, smart, and supportive. Recently, Hannah was promoted. Starting next week, she will be working in a different location. Tim is happy for her, but sad that they won't get to hang out together as often anymore. He meets with Hannah in her office and suggests a way for them to keep in touch. "Seriously," he tells her, "you're my best friend here. Don't think that just because you're moving, that's going to end."

"We should set up a regular lunch thing so we can stay caught up on each other's lives. Maybe every other week?"

"In all honesty, I just don't think that's going to be a possibility. I'm going to be ridiculously busy in the next few months, and I probably just won't have the time. I'm sorry."

2 YOUR TURN

Observations. Reflect on how Tim and Hannah communicated in this scenario by answering the following questions:

1. Which character do you identify with more in this situation? How would you feel if you were in his or her situation?
2. Where were the missed opportunities to practice competent communication?

Discussion. In class or with a partner, share your thoughts about the interaction between Tim and Hannah and work to answer the following questions:

1. Can you understand both perspectives?
2. What could Hannah and Tim have done differently?

Conclusion. Choose one person in the scenario to offer your advice. Based on your analysis, what advice would you give him or her to improve his or her communication competence in this scenario?

3 TAKE TWO!

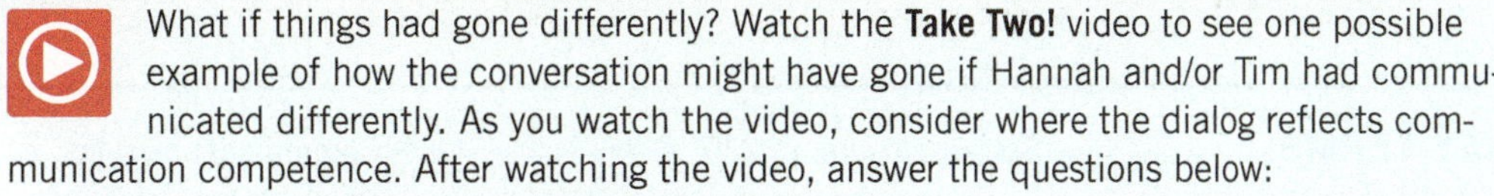

What if things had gone differently? Watch the **Take Two!** video to see one possible example of how the conversation might have gone if Hannah and/or Tim had communicated differently. As you watch the video, consider where the dialog reflects communication competence. After watching the video, answer the questions below:

1. Did Hannah and/or Tim take advantage of opportunities that they missed in the first scenario? Which ones?
2. Did their different actions result in a more productive encounter? Please explain.

CHAPTER 9 REVIEW

CHAPTER RECAP

- According to **social penetration theory**, people use **self-disclosure** to reveal themselves to others.
- Self-disclosure builds **intimacy** in relationships. Intimacy is self-perpetuating: the more intimacy you feel, the more you disclose; and as you disclose more, feelings of intimacy deepen.
- Though **relational dialectics** can bring challenges to relationships, competent communication can help you manage these tensions.
- You can sustain your relationships through **relational maintenance**, which includes **positivity**, **assurances**, and self-disclosure.
- Providing competent **supportive communication** can help you convey sincere sympathy, concern, and encouragement to your interpersonal relationship partners.

LaunchPad

LaunchPad for *Choices & Connections* offers unique video scenarios and encourages self-assessment through adaptive quizzing. Go to **launchpadworks.com** to get access.

 LearningCurve adaptive quizzes

 Advance the Conversation video scenarios

 Video clips that illustrate key concepts

KEY TERMS

Self-disclosure, p. 217
Social penetration theory, p. 217
Intimacy, p. 218
Relational dialectics, p. 223
Communication privacy management theory, p. 223
Communication rules, p. 224
Relational maintenance, p. 228
Positivity, p. 228
Assurances, p. 229
Supportive communication, p. 231

POP QUIZ

Looking for more review questions? LearningCurve can help you master key concepts from this chapter. Go to **launchpadworks.com**

1. Which of the following is *not* true about how people communicate self-disclosure?
   - **a.** People disclose more online than in person.
   - **b.** Women tend to disclose more than men.
   - **c.** Disclosure can help relieve stress.
   - **d.** People in different cultures disclose at different rates.
2. In close relationships, partners often negotiate conditions governing what they can (and can't) talk about. This is known as
   - **a.** communication rules.
   - **b.** intimacy.
   - **c.** communication privacy management theory.
   - **d.** supportive communication.
3. Which relational dialectic do families frequently experience when children grow up and become less dependent on their guardians for emotional support?
   - **a.** Novelty vs. predictability
   - **b.** Openness vs. protection
   - **c.** Autonomy vs. connection
   - **d.** Passiveness vs. argumentativeness
4. Constantly criticizing someone or complaining about problems but not offering solutions undermines
   - **a.** self-disclosure.
   - **b.** assurance.
   - **c.** positivity.
   - **d.** intimacy.
5. The feeling of closeness between you and others is known as
   - **a.** self-disclosure.
   - **b.** relational dialectics.
   - **c.** communication rules.
   - **d.** intimacy.

ACTIVITIES

For more activities, visit LaunchPad for *Choices & Connections* at **launchpadworks.com**

1 Communication Rules

With a partner, revisit the discussion of the openness versus protection relational dialectic and communication privacy management theory on pages 223–225. Discuss how you think this applies to romantic relationships. First, identify topics or issues that "must" be talked about (i.e., topics about which romantic partners must be open). Then, consider more complicated topics, as well as topics that "should absolutely not" be discussed (attraction to a coworker, flirting with strangers, sexual infidelity). Finally, analyze how these categories affect communication in relationships. How does keeping things from a partner impact intimacy? How would you deal with differences in topics that must or should not be discussed?

2 Relationship Reflection

Write a brief reflection paper analyzing how you engage in relationship maintenance. Pick a close relationship in your life (romance, family member, or friendship), and describe typical interactions that you have with that person. How often do you communicate in ways that bolster and undermine positivity, assurances, and self-disclosure? Provide specific examples. How does this communication impact the relationship—positively and negatively? How can the relational maintenance tactics help you improve your relationship?

10

Managing Conflict

When forensic pathologist Bennet Omalu examined a dead football player's brain, he had no idea that his story would soon become the Hollywood movie *Concussion* or that his findings would place him in conflict with professional peers and a multibillion-dollar sports industry.[1] But what he saw while sitting in his lab, looking through his microscope, stunned him: the deceased player's brain tissue was deeply damaged, in ways similar to, yet distinct from, Alzheimer's disease. His first thoughts went to naming the condition. What came to mind was *chronic* ("long-term"), *traumatic* ("associated with trauma"), and *encephalopathy* ("a bad brain"). And CTE was born.

But discovering and naming CTE immediately placed Omalu in conflict with those supportive of football, including his professional peers and the NFL. When Omalu submitted his results to a scientific journal for publication, the journal had more than *18* scholars criticize his paper, rather than the usual practice of just two reviewers. What's more, the NFL hired a group of doctors to publicly denounce his research as "fraud." One doctor even implied that Omalu was practicing "voodoo" instead of science—an insult related to Omalu's Nigerian background. As he fought to defend his integrity, Omalu grew weary: "I told my younger sister that I'm getting tired, and she called me out immediately, saying, 'No, Bennet. You think it's by chance that this is happening? Everybody has a calling, and God gives you a cross to bear because he knows you can bear that cross. With your knowledge, you can help these people!'"

Eventually, numerous scholars corroborated Omalu's CTE findings, and he was vindicated. In the aftermath, CTE became recognized worldwide as a legitimate medical condition, and everyone from little leagues to the NCAA began taking steps to combat it. As neuropathologist and Alzheimer's researcher Peter Davies noted, "The credit must go to Bennet Omalu, because he first reported this and nobody believed him, and I'm included in that. But when I looked at the stuff, he was absolutely right."

Omalu himself always believed that the goal should be collaboration toward forging a cooperative solution, rather than adversarial competition. His goal now is to work with the football industry to create a diagnostic instrument and cures for CTE, while players are still alive. "Why not?" he says. "You pop a pill before you play, a medicine that prevents the damage. This is how we now need to talk. Not this back-and-forth of human selfishness."

[1]All content in this section is adapted from Kirk (2013).

Ida Mae Astute/ABC/Getty Images

LearningCurve can help you review! Go to **launchpadworks.com**

Dr. Omalu's story mirrors conflicts we all have experienced in our own lives. Each of us has experienced situations in which our goals or actions were perceived by others as attacking their interests, provoking a clash. Many of us also have had people lash out at us defensively or wield power in an attempt to get us to give up what we want. And in such situations, we often end up feeling a sense of despair, as Omalu did before his sister inspired him to continue. Yet conflicts don't have to be hopeless, because we're not helpless. Each of us has the ability to use our communication skills to manage conflicts constructively.

In this chapter, we explore interpersonal conflict and how best to manage it. You'll learn:

- What conflict is and how it unfolds as a process
- The role power plays in conflict
- Which approaches to managing conflict are least—and most—competent
- How the conflict-management approach you use affects the outcomes that result
- What barriers exist to managing conflict well, and how they can be overcome

Defining Conflict

> **How do the conflicts in your life happen? Are they "out of nowhere" blowups? Do they contain heated language? Do you avoid them at all costs? No matter the type, all conflicts are a process involving people who perceive incompatible goals or actions. Knowing what conflicts are empowers you to recognize them when they exist, and manage them more constructively.**

Consider all the things that have triggered conflict in your life: jealousy, betrayal, stress, perceived slights, sex, time, money, work, politics, religion, personal habits—or even combinations of these. Now think about the people with whom you've shared these disputes: family, friends, coworkers, classmates, roommates, neighbors, strangers, romantic partners. And don't forget the setting. You've likely clashed with others while chatting online or texting, during phone calls, while engaged in face-to-face group discussions, or perhaps even during formal talks or presentations. Yet despite the seemingly limitless variation in causes, participants, and contexts, all conflicts have surprisingly similar defining elements. A **conflict** is a communication process between people who perceive incompatible goals or interference in achieving their objectives (Wilmot & Hocker, 2010). Almost all conflicts you'll experience follow this definition: they begin with perception, involve clashes between goals or actions (or both), and are processes that unfold over time.

Conflict Begins with Perception

Conflict doesn't begin with communication. It doesn't even begin when goals or actions collide. Instead, conflict begins when people *perceive* incompatible goals or actions (Roloff & Soule, 2002). Because conflict begins with perception, the perceptual errors and biases Chapter 2 discusses play an active role in shaping how conflicts unfold. For example, during conflicts, you're more likely to place blame on others than on yourself, perceive others as uncooperative and yourself as helpful, and believe you're acting reasonably and others are behaving irrationally. These self-enhancing perceptual errors may lead you to communicate incompetently when managing the conflict.

Conflict Involves Clashes between Goals or Actions

At the heart of conflicts are clashes between people's goals or actions. Some conflicts revolve around goal disputes, ranging from disagreements between group members (whether or not a presentation should start with a funny story) to arguments between romantic partners regarding relationship desires (whether or not they should be exclusive). Other conflicts break out when the actions of certain people interrupt or interfere with the actions of others: someone takes the parking space you were waiting for, or a roommate repeatedly texts you while you're trying to study.

DOUBLE TAKE

DEALING WITH CONFLICT IN PERSON  ONLINE

Understanding and managing a conflict with a friend can change dramatically depending on whether it occurs face-to-face or through a mediated form of communication. In the images below, how might the setting influence perceptual errors or the conflict process?

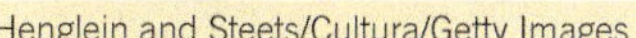

Henglein and Steets/Cultura/Getty Images

Peter Cade/The Image Bank/Getty Images

Conflict Is a Process

Conflicts often seem as if they're single, isolated events: "I had a terrible fight with my mom this weekend" or "Our group meeting turned into an all-out war last night." Sure, a single act of communication, such as a comment, text message, email, or social media post can *trigger* conflicts. But conflicts are never just one event. Instead, they are a communication process that unfolds over time. Most conflicts proceed through several stages, each involving actions that influence the direction of the conflict.

Selecting an Approach to Conflict

When conflict erupts, you can deal with it in several ways. You may avoid the issue, accommodate the wishes of others, compete to get what you want, or collaborate to solve the problem. Each approach has consequences, and the approach you take will affect whether the conflict endures, escalates, or is resolved.

Prince T'Challa is a powerful man. Not only is he the heir to the throne of Wakanda—a prosperous and technologically advanced kingdom—he also is the "Black Panther," gifted with superhuman strength and speed. And he has seen more than his share of conflict. When his father, the king, is killed, T'Challa faces multiple challengers who want to seize the throne for themselves: first M'Baku, the leader of the Jabari tribe; and then the ruthless Erik Killmonger, T'Challa's cousin. Unfortunately, T'Challa has only one choice for dealing with these challengers, given the traditions of Wakanda regarding how to resolve succession disputes: ritual combat. That is, T'Challa must physically fight each claimant to the throne, one-on-one, beneath a sacred waterfall—and whoever prevails will be crowned king.

Few (if any) of us will ever face a situation in which we must compete with rivals for succession to a throne—much less ritually fight them! But perhaps more importantly, unlike T'Challa in *Black Panther*, when we face the disagreements that populate our daily lives, we can take a range of different approaches to manage them. In this section, we discuss four common approaches to conflict—avoidance, accommodation, competition, and collaboration—and the outcomes that commonly ensue when each approach is used.

Avoidance

When you practice **avoidance**, you approach a conflict by *not* managing it. You ignore or avoid talking about the conflict, or you communicate about it in indirect ways, by dropping hints, cracking jokes, or making sarcastic

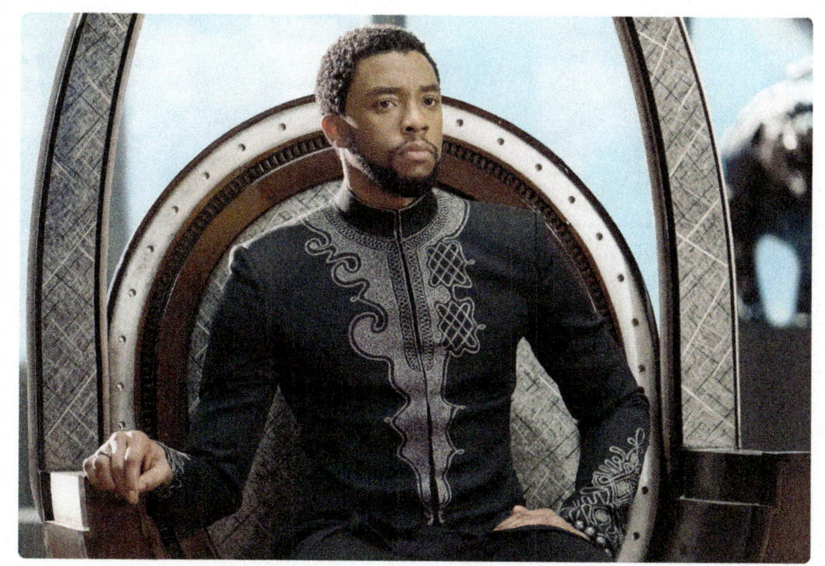

Matt Kennedy/Marvel/Walt Disney Studios Motion Pictures/Everett Collection

In *Black Panther*, T'Challa must navigate conflicts with challengers to the throne. What conflict approaches have you used recently in your own life?

remarks. Avoidance is the most frequent approach to conflict (Sillars, 1980). People often use it because it seems easier and safer than directly engaging in disputes with others.

Although people opt for avoidance because it seems safe, it actually poses substantial risks (Afifi, McManus, Steuber, & Coho, 2009). First, routinely avoiding conflict can create **cumulative annoyance**, in which your repressed resentment grows as your mental list of complaints about other people builds up (Peterson, 2002). Eventually, cumulative annoyance overwhelms your ability to suppress it, and you explode. Imagine you're working on a group project, but the other members reject every suggestion you make. You manage this by not saying anything; after all, you don't want your group to think you're difficult to work with. But your irritation intensifies. Then, when planning the group's final presentation, you realize the perfect way to hook your audience's attention. When you suggest it to the group, they shoot you down yet again. "That's it! I don't care what you all do; I'll handle my part by myself," you say. Such an angry outburst may destroy any possibility of working further with the group. Perhaps it's no surprise, then, that people who use avoidance are less satisfied with their relationships than people who engage more directly in conflict (Caughlin & Golish, 2002).

Second, avoidance raises the risk of **pseudo-conflict**, the perception that there's a conflict between you and others when there really isn't. For

TABLE 10.1

TYPES OF POWER

	 RESOURCE	 EXPERTISE
DESCRIPTION	Power derived from material things, such as money, property, and food	Power based on special skills or knowledge
EXAMPLE	Most bosses have resource power over employees, since they control workers' employment and compensation.	People with specialized degrees or a lot of experience in an area—like software developers or nurses—have power, since they know things others don't or can do things others can't.

1. WinMaster/Shutterstock.com; 2. Fenton one/Shutterstock.com;

example, you think your new manager at work dislikes you because she never tries to make conversation with you. Since you assume she doesn't like you, you worry that she'll give you a negative performance review (or worse, fire you). So you start searching for a new job. But the manager actually *does* like you; she's just stressed out by her new job demands. If you never bother to talk with her about this ("Gayle, I was wondering why we never chat"), you might end up leaving a much-loved job because of your misperception.

Despite the risks, avoidance can be a wise choice for managing conflict in situations in which emotions run high (Berscheid, 2002). If you and the other person involved are angry to the point where neither of you can control your emotions, you risk saying things that will permanently hurt the relationship if you continue the interaction. To prevent that unhappy outcome, it's best to leave the room, hang up, or hold off on responding to texts or emails until your temper has cooled. If you choose this route, be sure to provide a brief explanation for your departure ("I'm sorry, but I've got to leave for a while and sort out my thoughts"), and give an approximate time when you will contact the person again ("I'll call you tonight" or "I will text you in a half hour to let you know how I'm doing"). This lets the person know that you aren't abandoning him or her and are planning on returning. When you've calmed down, you can reestablish contact and try another approach.

Accommodation

If you use **accommodation**, you manage conflict by abandoning your own goals or actions and giving in to others' desires. Similar to avoidance, accommodation may result in positive or negative outcomes, depending

SOCIAL NETWORK	 PERSONAL	 INTIMACY
Power that comes from having an extensive network of friends, family, acquaintances, or business partners with substantial influence	Power based on desirable personal characteristics, such as beauty, intelligence, charisma, communication skills, or sense of humor	Power acquired from a close and unique bond with another person
People with lots of connections have power if they can help others get access to jobs, schools, material goods, and so on.	Social butterflies or other charming people have power when their personalities or other social skills attract others to them.	Accommodating to or doing favors for close family members or romantic interests that you wouldn't do for other friends demonstrates power based on intimacy.

1. Introwiz1/Shutterstock.com; 2. andromina/Shutterstock.com; 3. jossnat/Shutterstock.com

on the situation and your relationship with the others involved. For example, accommodating close relational partners is a hallmark of healthy relationships (Hendrick & Hendrick, 1992). Putting their needs before your own, at least on occasion, shows them that you love them and you're willing to make sacrifices to ensure their happiness. But if accommodation runs in only one direction—one person always giving in to the other, never the other way around—the person who always gives in will probably build up resentment and grow dissatisfied with the relationship (Sprecher, 2001).

Whether you use accommodation depends in part on your **power** in the situation and the relationship—that is, your ability to influence or control important resources, people, and events (Donohue & Kolt, 1992). Powerful people can choose whether they wish to accommodate others or not, without fear of reprisal. People without power often accommodate those who have power—if they don't, they could suffer harmful consequences. For example, suppose you work as a barista at a coffee shop and are an "at-will" employee, meaning that your manager has the authority to fire you at any time, for any reason, without cause or notice. Your manager has enormous power over you, so when he asks you to stay late and work an extra shift, you'll probably accommodate his request—even if you have to give up your plans for the evening. After all, if you don't accommodate him, you might lose your job. Correspondingly, if *you* are the manager—and have the power—you have the freedom to pick and choose whether you want to accommodate employees who ask favors of you (such as a night off), without fear of repercussion from your decision. People have different types of power that they can use in various ways. For an overview of the different types of power, see Table 10.1.

Competition

Another way to approach conflict is **competition**—confronting others and pursuing your own goals to the exclusion of theirs. This was the approach forced upon T'Challa by tradition in *Black Panther*: he *had* to fight if he wished to claim the throne that rightfully was his. Competition has two defining characteristics: open and clear discussion of the conflict, and pursuit of one's own goals without regard for others' goals (Sillars, 1980).

As with accommodation, whether you'll engage in competition depends in large part on your power in the situation and the relationship. Simply put, if you have power, you'll be more likely to use competition than if you don't (Peterson, 2002). Because powerful people control important resources, they can withhold those resources from others to serve their own desires. Consider how this works between parents and children. If parents wish to vacation at one destination, but the kids want to go somewhere else, the parents can just say, "Too bad, we're going where *we* want to go," and the matter is finished. After all, they control the money needed to fund the trip.

The competitive approach raises the risk of **escalation** in a conflict—a dramatic rise in emotional intensity and unproductive communication. If you and the others involved in the conflict refuse to back down from the dispute, the conflict becomes a test of wills, virtually guaranteeing that tensions will escalate. Even conflicts that start out as minor can quickly explode into major disputes. When this happens, conflicts can intensify into something called **kitchen sinking** (from the expression "throwing everything at them but the kitchen sink"), in which combatants hurl assorted accusations at each other that have little to do with the disagreement at hand: "You didn't like my presentation? Well, nobody here at work can stand you! We all wish you'd quit!" The goal of kitchen sinking is to hurt the other person's feelings in whatever way you can, rather than manage the conflict constructively. The result is often irreparable damage to the relationship.

Technology can inadvertently foster escalation in conflicts. When we communicate through social media, we can't see or hear our communication partners and their reactions (Shedletsky & Aitken, 2004). This lack of feedback makes it harder to understand what others are feeling. Known as *empathy deficits*, this puts us at risk for incompetent communication. When we are unaware of the full impact our communication has, it's easier to bully others or use hostile personal attacks that escalate the conflict. Also, as Chapter 4 explains, people on the receiving end of our communication experience the same empathy deficits. Their online messages are less sensitive and less tactful as well, even if they don't mean them to be.

Collaboration

The most constructive approach for managing conflict is **collaboration**—treating conflict as a mutual problem-solving challenge. Often, the result of using a collaborative approach is *compromise*, in which everyone involved modifies his or her individual goals to come up with a solution to the conflict. (We discuss compromise more on page 250.) You're most likely to use collaboration when you respect the other people involved and are concerned about their desires as well as your own (Keck & Samp, 2007; Zacchilli, Hendrick, & Hendrick, 2009).

When collaborating, try to meet face-to-face, rather than through mediated channels, if at all possible. Meeting in person makes it more likely that the people involved will seek constructive solutions and consider everyone's goals and desires (Frisby & Westerman, 2010). If this isn't an option, arrange a phone call instead.

To manage conflict through collaboration, try the following four suggestions (Wilmot & Hocker, 2010). First, *attack problems, not people*. When talking about the conflict, keep your language courteous, respectful, and positive—avoiding personal attacks. Treat the source of the conflict as separate from the people who are involved, using *"I"* and *"we" language* to emphasize this: "*I* can see that this disagreement is bothering us; let's try to figure out how *we* can solve it." As Chapter 5 explains, avoid *"you" language*, which can place blame on others.

Second, *focus on common interests and long-term goals* ("I know we all want this group project to be a success"). Arguing over positions ("I want this" or "I want that!") may just escalate things, as the conflict becomes a test of wills about who will back down first.

Third, *create options before arriving at decisions*. Identify different possible routes for resolving the conflict, and then combine the best parts of them to come up with a solution. Don't get bogged down searching for the one "perfect" solution—it may not exist.

Fourth, *critically evaluate your solution*. Carefully consider this question: Is it equally fair for everyone involved?

Because collaboration focuses on respectful and ethical communication, and on satisfying everyone's interests rather than just one person's, it tends to net more positive outcomes than the other approaches to conflict. Collaboration increases people's relationship satisfaction (Frisby & Westerman, 2010), and individuals who regularly use collaborative approaches are more likely to resolve their

FIGURE 10.1
COLLABORATION

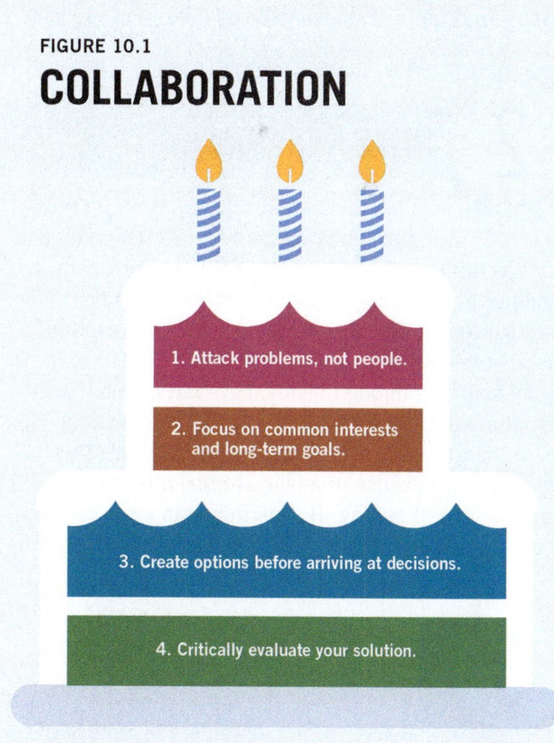
1. Attack problems, not people.
2. Focus on common interests and long-term goals.
3. Create options before arriving at decisions.
4. Critically evaluate your solution.

pking4th/Shutterstock.com

ADVANCE THE CONVERSATION

I DIDN'T LIE!

1 YOUR DILEMMA

You're dating Casey, whom you love very much. Even though you've been together for over a year, Casey continues to express jealousy toward your ex, Jaden. You are still close friends with Jaden, and you tease each other about everything, including your relationships. This has gotten you into trouble with Casey, who recently saw a text message from Jaden to you that joked, "When are you going to dump Casey and come back to me?" Casey was livid and wanted you to end all contact with Jaden, but you convinced Casey that wasn't necessary since you don't have feelings for Jaden anymore. Even so, Casey doesn't fully trust you.

It's Wednesday night, and Casey is working, so you head to the library to get a head start on an upcoming paper. You send a text telling Casey this. Then you get a message from Jaden: "Huge party at my place!" You decide to skip the paper and head to Jaden's. Not wanting to trigger a fight, you don't text Casey about your change in plans. Jaden's party is awesome, and you end up staying until early in the morning.

Heading home, you find your phone is flooded with missed calls and texts from Casey. One of Casey's friends took videos of you and Jaden dancing at the party and posted them on Snapchat. Casey is furious, saying that you lied and that it's over between the two of you.

How do you feel when Casey lashes out and announces that it's over? If you were Casey, would you have interpreted the situation in the same way?

2 THE RESEARCH

Communication scholars Brandi Frisby and David Westerman (2010) studied conflict within romantic relationships—specifically, whether partners communicated face-to-face or through technology, and the outcomes that resulted. Nearly two-thirds of their participants reported managing conflicts through technology (texts, email, and social media). The most common tool was texting; more than half the sample dealt with conflicts this way, usually because of a lack of proximity and the convenience of texting. But participants also reported that face-to-face conflict "is so much better" because they could see the other person and read his or her nonverbal communication.

The choice of medium for communicating about conflict substantially influenced the participants' approaches to conflict and their outcomes. Those who chose to manage conflicts via technology were more likely to compete. In contrast, those who met face-to-face were more likely to use collaboration and were substantially happier with their relationships afterward.

What challenges do you face in reaching out to Casey and explaining your side of the story? How can they be overcome?

3 YOUR OPPORTUNITY

Before you act, consider the facts of the situation and think about the research on technology and conflict. Reflect on what you've learned about conflict approaches (pp. 242–249) and escalation (pp. 245–246). You might also want to review the section on mediated communication challenges in Chapter 4 (pp. 103–107).

Now it's your turn. Write out a response to Casey in which you explain your side of the story.

conflicts and experience shorter and fewer disputes overall (Caughlin & Vangelisti, 2000). For an example of a situation where two people might benefit from collaboration, check out Advance the Conversation: Conflict with a Roommate on pages 256–257.

Conflict Endings

When you're in the middle of a conflict, it seems to last forever. But conflicts do end. The approach you take in dealing with a conflict affects not only your future communication with those involved but also the type of ending that will occur.

Conflicts take many forms. Some go on for a long time, as was the case for Dr. Bennet Omalu in our chapter opener, whose opponents in the NFL attacked him for years, even after he published his ground-breaking paper about CTE. Other conflicts are brief. But most conflicts eventually reach some sort of conclusion. And since conflicts usually occur between people who are close—whether group members, friends, lovers, family members, or coworkers—these conclusions are necessary for the relationships to continue (Benoit & Benoit, 1990; Malis & Roloff, 2006). Most conflicts end in one of five ways: separation, domination, compromise, integrative agreements, or structural improvements (Peterson, 2002).

Separation

Some conflicts end when one or more of the people involved terminate communication contact, known as **separation**. Separation can take many forms. It might be *technological*: you ignore texts, turn your phone off, and delete incoming emails. It might be *physical*, such as when you stop showing up for team meetings or avoid family reunions. Or it might be *communicative*, such as when you are still living with a roommate but refuse to talk to each other.

Separation ends conflict encounters but doesn't solve them. Although you might feel better—having detached yourself from the source of stress—the conflict isn't resolved; it's just temporarily on hold. On the other hand, separation isn't always negative. As noted in the *competition* discussion, if your conflict has escalated to the point that you or others might start kitchen sinking, it's probably best to separate. Temporary separation may help everyone cool off; then you can regroup later and consider how to collaborate.

Domination

When one person or group of people gets others to abandon their own goals and instead do what the person or group wants, **domination** has occurred. Conflicts that end with domination are often called *win-lose solutions*. The people who get their way "win," while the ones who accommodate "lose." The strongest predictor of domination is the power balance between the people involved. In cases in which one person or group has substantial power and opts to use competition, others with less power will likely back down, allowing those with power to dominate.

Domination isn't always destructive, however. Consider, for example, medical or military decisions. During emergency situations in which multiple parties are disputing options, having people in positions of authority enforce decisions while other people accommodate solves conflict efficiently, enabling swift action.

Compromise

Conflicts end in **compromise** when the parties involved change their goals and actions to make them compatible. This typically results from people using a collaborative approach and is most effective in situations in which people have relatively equal power and the clashing goals aren't especially important.

In cases in which everyone considers their goals important, however, compromise tends to foster resentment and regret (Peterson, 2002). Why? Imagine that you're leading a meeting in which a team of nurses will plan next month's work schedule. If everyone comes to the meeting open to working days or nights and weekdays or weekends, you can all collaborate and easily compromise on who works when. But if people have strong preferences about their schedule ("I absolutely cannot work Friday nights"), then compromising on these plans will most likely lead to bitterness as team members compare who got their way and who sacrificed the most.

Integrative Agreements

When people in conflict forge **integrative agreements**, they generate creative solutions that enable all sides to keep and reach their original goals. Such agreements are commonly called *win-win solutions*, and people can arrive at them only through collaborative approaches. To create integrative agreements, the parties remain committed to their individual goals but are flexible in how they achieve them (Pruitt & Carnevale, 1993). Borrowing from the previous example, imagine that you and a coworker both want the same night off. Rather than arguing about who has to sacrifice their night-out plans, you could work together to find two other nurses who are qualified to cover for both of you.

Structural Improvements

Sometimes conflicts end with **structural improvements**: the parties involved change their relationship rules to prevent further disputes. For example, Steve and his wife, Kelly, used to fight whenever he neglected to tell Kelly about Facebook messages he received from his ex, Michelle. After several clashes, they created a new agreement: *Whenever Michelle contacts Steve, he must tell Kelly*. Now they both know the ground rules regarding Michelle's messages, and this prevents further arguments.

In structural improvement cases, the conflict itself becomes a vehicle for reshaping relationships in positive ways—clarifying rules (as with Steve and Kelly), improving the balance of power, or redefining expectations about who will play what roles (for instance, members of a student organization deciding to divide authority between co-presidents after two candidates tie in the presidential election). But as with compromise and integrative agreements, you and others can arrive at structural improvements only by choosing to manage your conflicts through collaboration.

Barriers to Constructive Conflict

It's not easy to resolve conflicts. There are powerful barriers that get in the way—and they are often ones you create: blaming others but not yourself, using words as weapons, and failing to recognize cultural differences. Overcoming such challenges will help you improve your conflict-management skills.

By this point, you might think that constructive conflict management is simple. You adopt a collaborative approach and work with those involved to forge healthy compromises, satisfying integrative agreements, and positive structural improvements. But it's not that easy. Instead, a wide range of barriers keeps us from choosing effective approaches. Three of the toughest barriers are attributional errors, destructive messages, and cultural differences.

Attributional Errors

Recall the most recent serious conflict you've had. Who was to blame? Who behaved cooperatively? When you said or did something negative, what caused your behavior?

If you're like many people, your answers to these questions will be self-serving—designed to make you feel better about yourself. As we discuss in Chapter 2, this happens because human perception is subjective, not objective: people see what they want to see, not what is really true. This frequently leads to errors in your *attributions*: the explanations you create for why things are happening the way they are. Consequently, when conflicts erupt, you don't judge yourself, others, or the situation objectively. Instead, you perceive these things subjectively, in ways that paint yourself in a positive light and make others look bad (Sillars, Roberts, Leonard, & Dun, 2000).

During a conflict, it is easy to blame other people for causing it and consider yourself faultless (Schutz, 1999). At the same time, the individuals with whom you're fighting do the exact same thing—think *they're* in the right and *you're* in the wrong. Such one-sided blaming is an attributional error, because in most conflicts, one person isn't the sole cause. Instead, conflicts are mutually created by two or more people, based on differing goals, opinions, or desires. For example, most marital conflicts stem from differing opinions regarding money, housework, sex, or child care (Schutz,

3 ARTS ENTERTAINMENT/Album/Alamy Stock Photo

Like many comedy shows, *Broad City* builds its conflicts, resolutions, and laughs around attributional errors. The two main characters, friends Abbi and Ilana, frequently misunderstand one another's intentions: Ilana is oblivious to how her actions affect others, and Abbi often finds herself unwillingly dragged into Ilana's schemes. Such scenarios—though entertaining—could be greatly helped if the characters engaged in perception-checking more often.

1999). Yet spouses don't attribute mutual blame for these conflicts ("We created this dispute because we disagree on this issue"). Instead, they typically blame each other for causing the conflict. What's more, they even blame each other for their *own* negative remarks made during the fight. Thus, when terrible things are said during the heat of battle, participants rarely think, "I said that horrible thing because I was angry and out of control." Instead, they typically think, "*You* provoked me into saying it!" Spouses also consistently attribute their own communication to "good intentions" and describe their partner's communication as "irrational" and "inconsistent."

Of course, such attributional errors aren't limited to romantic partners. Everyone makes attributional errors during disagreements, which in turn prevent participants from using collaborative approaches. For example, people typically perceive those they are in conflict with as uncooperative and themselves as cooperative (Sillars et al., 2000). This comparison discourages collaboration. Moreover, people tend to attribute conflicts to long-term differences that can't be overcome ("You've never understood me, so why bother even talking about it?"). Such attributional errors are especially likely to happen—and to amplify the perception of division—when you're in conflict with someone you view as an *outgrouper* (see pages 46–47 in Chapter 2). So, for example, if you perceive someone as having a different ethnicity, religion, sexual orientation, socioeconomic class, or political party than yourself—or perhaps all of the above at the same time!—the likelihood that you will perceive the distance as unbridgeable and the conflict as unresolvable will be amplified.

TABLE 10.2

TIPS FOR MANAGING CONFLICT ONLINE

Nearly two-thirds of college students (61.2%) use mediated channels to engage in conflicts, most commonly via text messaging (Frisby & Westerman, 2010). While managing conflicts offline reduces attributional errors and boosts empathy, that isn't always possible or desirable. When you must deal with a conflict online, try these suggestions (Munro, 2002):

WAIT AND REREAD. When you receive a message that provokes you, don't respond right away. Instead, take a break and then reread it. This gives you a chance to reassess it and reply when you are calmer.

ASSUME THE BEST AND WATCH OUT FOR THE WORST. Presume that the sender meant well but didn't express himself or herself competently. Remember all the challenges of online communication, such as *online disinhibition* and *empathy deficits*. At the same time, realize that some people enjoy conflict. Firing back a nasty message may be what the person wants.

SEEK OUTSIDE COUNSEL. Before responding, discuss the situation (ideally, face-to-face) with someone whose opinion you trust. Having an additional viewpoint will enhance your ability to perspective-take and will help you communicate competently.

WEIGH YOUR OPTIONS CAREFULLY. Choose cautiously between engaging or avoiding the conflict. Consider the likely consequences associated with each option.

COMMUNICATE COMPETENTLY. Use "I" language, incorporate appropriate emoticons, express empathy and perspective-taking, encourage the other person to share relevant thoughts and feelings, and make clear your willingness to collaborate. Importantly, start and end your message with positive statements that support rather than attack the other person.

To improve your conflict-management skills, practice *perception-checking*. Analyze the attributions you're making and adjust them to compensate for any potential errors. Get into the habit of asking yourself three questions:

- Is my partner *really* being uncooperative, or am I just imagining it?
- Is my partner *really* the only one to blame, or have I also done something to cause the conflict?
- Is this conflict *really* due to ongoing differences between us, or is it due to temporary factors, such as stress or fatigue?

Destructive Messages

The problem with attributional errors is that they don't just stay inside your head; you express them. When you perceive others as uncooperative and blame them for the conflict (as well as your own bad behavior), you may say things that make them feel bad, escalate the conflict further, and damage the relationship. Known as destructive messages, these usually take one of three forms: *sniping*, *sudden-death statements*, and *dirty secrets*.

During conflicts, some people resort to **sniping**—communicating in a negative way and then leaving the encounter. When you snipe, you shoot a remark at others and immediately hide, so the others can't shoot back. For example, your dad waits until he knows you're too busy to answer your phone, then leaves you a voice mail filled with complaints about how you've been neglecting him. Needless to say, sniping is disrespectful, unethical, and destructive. It serves no purpose other than to hurt; thus, it only fuels conflicts.

If conflicts spiral out of control, **sudden-death statements** can occur: spontaneous declarations that the relationship is over, even though the people involved did not consider termination a possibility before the conflict. A fight between romantic partners about "friending" an ex on Facebook morphs into, "Maybe we should date other people!" A disagreement between roommates about who's responsible for which household chores escalates into, "Fine—I'm moving out!" Or a dispute over how best to approach a group project results in, "Forget it—we'll all just work separately on our own ideas!" A person can "walk it back" after issuing a sudden-death statement, but this is hard to do without looking foolish and impulsive and may result in *losing face* or experiencing *embarrassment* (see also page 42). For that reason, many people stand behind their threatening statements, even if there are unintended consequences.

But of all the destructive things that can come out during conflicts, the worst (in terms of personal and communicative costs) are **dirty secrets**—messages that are honest in content but have been kept hidden to protect someone's feelings. Examples of dirty secrets include criticism of a romantic partner's physical appearance ("You'll never be as hot as my ex!"), a revelation about workplace attitudes ("Don't you know that most people here think you are terrible at your job?"), and lack of maternal feelings ("I wish you'd never been born!"). Like sniping, dirty secrets are designed to hurt. But they do far worse damage because the content is true. They have the power to permanently damage recipients' feelings and destroy relationships. Although you may be tempted to reveal a dirty secret in the heat of the moment, it's not worth it. Instead, leave the encounter and return later, after you've cooled down.

Cultural Differences

A final consideration in competently managing your conflicts involves cultural differences. People from individualistic and collectivistic cultures perceive and approach conflicts in radically different ways. Specifically, people raised in *collectivistic cultures* often view direct discussion of the causes behind a conflict as personal attacks and see such discussion as disruptive to the "harmony" of encounters (Kagawa & McCornack, 2004). Consequently, they

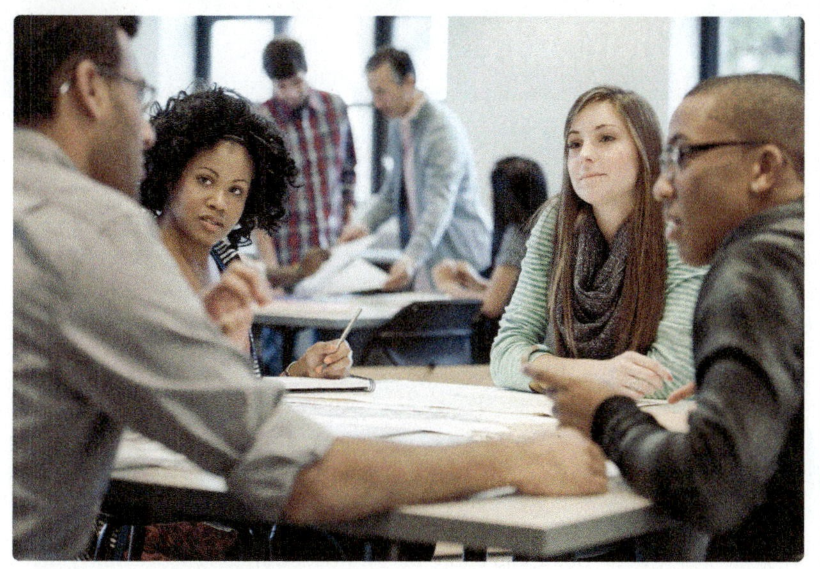

Troy House/Corbis NX/Getty Images

Working on group projects can be difficult—balancing personalities, workload, time constraints, and leadership responsibilities. Having to manage conflicts as well makes the experience even more complicated. In such situations, remember to consider any cultural differences affecting the communication. For example, how can you help everyone feel comfortable while being respectful of differing opinions?

may approach conflict through avoidance or accommodation. In contrast, many people raised in *individualistic cultures* feel more comfortable openly discussing disputes and don't necessarily perceive such arguments as personal affronts (Ting-Toomey, 1997). As a result, they often compete or collaborate.

Given these differences, how can you manage conflict competently across cultures? If you're an individualist embroiled in a dispute with people from collectivistic cultures, consider these suggestions (Gudykunst & Kim, 2003):

- Maintain the face of everyone involved. Avoid humiliating or embarrassing anyone, especially in public.
- Use indirect verbal messages more than you usually do. For example, sprinkle your comments with "maybe" and "possibly," and avoid blunt responses, such as an outright "no."
- Recognize that collectivists may prefer to have a third person mediate the conflict. Mediators allow those in conflict to manage their disagreement without direct confrontation. This lack of confrontation helps maintain harmony in the group or relationship.

If you're a collectivist in contention with someone from an individualistic culture, the following tips may help:

- Manage conflicts when they arise, even if you'd rather avoid them.
- Use an assertive style and be more direct than you usually are. For example, use "I" messages, and directly state your opinions and feelings.
- Recognize that individualists often separate conflicts from people. Just because you're in conflict doesn't mean that the situation is personal.

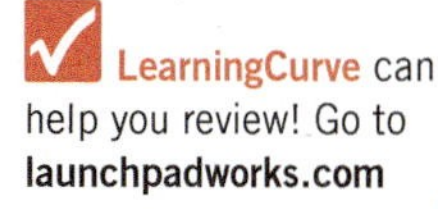

LearningCurve can help you review! Go to **launchpadworks.com**

ADVANCE THE CONVERSATION
Video Activity

CONFLICT WITH A ROOMMATE

The following scenario will enhance your ability to manage a conflict with a roommate. Visit LaunchPad at **launchpadworks.com** to get the full experience with video. As you watch the first video, recall what you've learned about selecting an approach to conflict and barriers to constructive conflict. Then complete the **Your Turn** prompts. Finally, watch the **Take Two!** video to explore how this scenario could have gone differently.

1 THE PROBLEM

Connor's roommate, Tim, hasn't been doing his share of the housework. He leaves dirty dishes and clothes lying around and never helps with the cleaning. It's been a source of frustration for Connor, who walks into the kitchen and sees—yet again—that Tim has created a mess. Even worse, Connor has friends coming over soon and is embarrassed by the state of the apartment. He decides that he has finally had enough and confronts Tim directly. "I'm really frustrated by how messy things are," Connor begins.

"We need to work on keeping this place looking more presentable. Look, if we divide up the housework, we could easily keep it clean."

"I'll take care of my room. You can take care of everything else. You're better at cleaning anyway. It's not a big deal to me."

2 YOUR TURN

Observations. Reflect on how Connor and Tim communicated in this scenario by answering the following questions:

1. Which character do you identify with more in this situation? How would you feel if you were in his situation?
2. Where were the missed opportunities to practice competent communication?

Discussion. In class or with a partner, share your thoughts about the interaction between Connor and Tim and work to answer the following questions:

1. Can you understand both perspectives?
2. What could Tim and Connor have done differently?

Conclusion. Choose one person in the scenario to offer your advice. Based on your analysis, what advice would you give him to improve his communication competence in this scenario?

3 TAKE TWO!

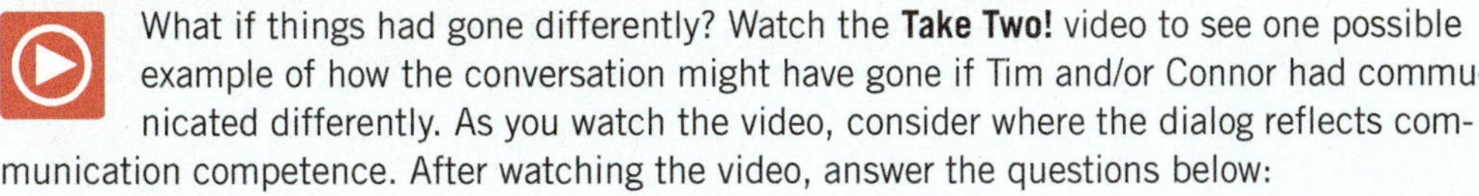

What if things had gone differently? Watch the **Take Two!** video to see one possible example of how the conversation might have gone if Tim and/or Connor had communicated differently. As you watch the video, consider where the dialog reflects communication competence. After watching the video, answer the questions below:

1. Did Tim and/or Connor take advantage of opportunities that they missed in the first scenario? Which ones?
2. Did their different actions result in a more productive encounter? Please explain.

CHAPTER 10 REVIEW

CHAPTER RECAP

- A **conflict** is a communication process between people who perceive incompatible goals or interference in achieving their objectives.
- The most common approaches to conflict are **avoidance**, **accommodation**, **competition**, and **collaboration**.
- The ways in which we approach conflict are influenced by many factors, including the **power** of those involved and whether the people involved are willing to collaborate.
- Most conflicts end in one of five ways: **separation**, **domination**, **compromise**, **integrative agreements**, or **structural improvements**.
- Managing any conflict runs the risk of dealing with attributional errors, destructive messages, or cultural differences. You can minimize these obstacles by practicing *perception-checking* and *empathy*.

LaunchPad

LaunchPad for *Choices & Connections* offers unique video scenarios and encourages self-assessment through adaptive quizzing. Go to **launchpadworks.com** to get access.

 LearningCurve adaptive quizzes

 Advance the Conversation video scenarios

 Video clips that illustrate key concepts

KEY TERMS

Conflict, p. 240
Avoidance, p. 242
Cumulative annoyance, p. 243
Pseudo-conflict, p. 243
Accommodation, p. 244
Power, p. 245
Competition, p. 246
Escalation, p. 246
Kitchen sinking, p. 246
Collaboration, p. 246
Separation, p. 249
Domination, p. 249
Compromise, p. 250
Integrative agreements, p. 250
Structural improvements, p. 250
Sniping, p. 254
Sudden-death statements, p. 254
Dirty secrets, p. 254

POP QUIZ

Looking for more review questions? LearningCurve can help you master key concepts from this chapter. Go to **launchpadworks.com**

1. A pseudo-conflict may result if you engage in
   a. avoidance.
   b. accommodation.
   c. competition.
   d. collaboration.

2. When you respect the other people involved in a conflict and are concerned about their desires as well as your own, you're more likely to engage in
   a. avoidance.
   b. accommodation.
   c. competition.
   d. collaboration.

3. Some conflicts end with creative solutions that enable all sides to reach their goals. These are known as
   a. separations.
   b. integrative agreements.
   c. competitions.
   d. compromises.

4. Of all the destructive things that can be communicated during conflicts, the type that is most likely to permanently damage a relationship or all future communication is
   a. kitchen sinking.
   b. dirty secrets.
   c. sniping.
   d. sudden-death statements.

5. Which of the following is *not* likely to be an effective strategy for handling a conflict with a person from a collectivistic culture?
   a. Maintain the face of everyone involved.
   b. Use indirect verbal messages.
   c. Use "I" messages, and directly state your opinions and feelings.
   d. Involve a third person to mediate the conflict.

ACTIVITIES

For more activities, visit LaunchPad for *Choices & Connections* at **launchpadworks.com**

1 Checking Your Attributions

To see how attributional errors can influence conflicts, write a brief essay describing a recent conflict you experienced, and answer these questions: Who was to blame? Who behaved cooperatively? When you said or did something negative, what caused your behavior? Then, analyze your answers and communication by responding to these prompts: Are you apportioning blame equally, or is some bias apparent? What impact did your judgments have on your communication? How might different attributions have led you to communicate differently in the conflict?

2 Choose Your Own Ending

With a partner, determine a common but important conflict you both experience (e.g., conflicts with roommates over room rules or with parents over family obligations). Then, decide what each type of conflict ending (see pages 249–251) would look like for this example. For instance, given your conflict, what would a structural improvement look like? How would a compromise work out? Once you've identified each ending, which ones are optimal? Why? Which approaches would result in those endings? What does this tell you about approaches and endings for different conflict situations?

11

Small Group Communication

She's the spry, sharp-talking fashion designer that has become a favorite among fans of Pixar's *The Incredibles* franchise. Edna Mode is the brainchild of Pixar writer-director Brad Bird, who conceived of her to answer this one important question: How do superheroes get their costumes? It's Edna's job to create them.

Although Brad Bird envisaged Edna Mode, it took the team-based production process that defines Pixar Studios to integrate her persona into the *Incredibles* movies. As the industry leader in telling animated stories, Pixar has achieved success largely due to its small teams of employees who take ideas — like a family of superheroes and their eccentric costume designer — and turn them into films that capture the hearts and imaginations of children and adults alike.

According to Ed Catmull (2014), Pixar cofounder and former president, an outstanding team can turn even a mediocre idea into a meaningful and memorable story. Everyone who works on a Pixar film — illustrators, animators, producers, technicians, directors, and more — is responsible for some part of the creative effort. Catmull suggests that getting people to work together improves story ideas and the development of characters, like Edna Mode. When all team members have a stake in the success of the film, they are more likely to support one another, provide useful feedback, and come together to help solve problems.

Even the design of the Pixar campus encourages teamwork. The campus has a large central atrium, which contains employees' mailboxes, meeting rooms, the cafeteria, the main bathrooms, and a game area. Cofounder Steve Jobs, who believed it was important to have a physical space that encourages employees to interact, played a leading role in designing the atrium. As Brad Bird puts it: "The atrium initially might seem like a waste of space. . . . But Steve realized that when people run into each other, when they make eye contact, things happen" (Lehrer, 2011).

Because of its commitment to teamwork, Pixar consistently produces innovative films that set new standards for technical, creative, and financial success. *Incredibles 2* broke the all-time opening weekend record for an animated film, earning over $180 million (Rubin, 2018). And Pixar characters like Edna Mode remain popular with people of all ages, all over the world.

Nicolo Minerbi/LUZphoto/Redux

LearningCurve can help you review! Go to **launchpadworks.com**

Pixar is not the only company to score great successes by using small groups (or *teams*, as they are often called in the workplace) to conduct its business. Most businesses rely on small groups to manage key assignments and tasks, including designing smartphone apps (product development), improving customer experiences (customer relations), creating and delivering presentations about new products to potential customers (sales), and organizing sponsorships of local charity events (fund-raising) (Kozlowski & Bell, 2003). Yet small groups aren't limited to the workplace; they exist in many different areas of your life. For instance, you might meet with your family to decide where to go on vacation next year, or work with a group on a class project. Maybe you're part of a homeowners' association or a town council. In all of these cases and countless more, you are communicating in small groups. To generate the most value from these experiences, you need to know how small groups operate and how to best communicate within them. In this chapter, you'll learn:

- The defining characteristics and various types of small groups
- How effective small groups communicate
- How individual characteristics affect small groups
- Ways to address the challenges of participating in virtual small groups

Defining Small Groups

Participating in groups can help you accomplish tasks that would be difficult to do on your own. But working in groups is not always easy. In order to increase the chances for a group's success, it helps to know why small groups form and what stages they go through.

What makes a collection of individuals a *small group*? Would three friends planning a going-away party constitute a small group? What about parents talking outside a dance studio as they wait for their children's lesson to end? Although it may seem as though the people in both of these situations would be considered a small group, only the former matches how communication scholars define the term. A **small group** is three or more interdependent people who share a common identity and who communicate to achieve common goals. Let's take a closer look at the defining characteristics of small groups, the different types, and the phases of small group development.

Characteristics of Small Groups

A small group has four defining characteristics. First, it is made up of interdependent persons. This means that each person's behavior influences the entire group. If one person doesn't follow through on an assigned job, the other members could fall behind schedule or fail to accomplish their shared goals. For example, planning a friend's going-away party requires

Whether you're working on a project in person, planning a trip with friends virtually, or coming together to create music like the K-pop band BTS, it is important that all members share an identity as a group. When have you been part of groups or teams that had a strong identity? How did members create this sense?

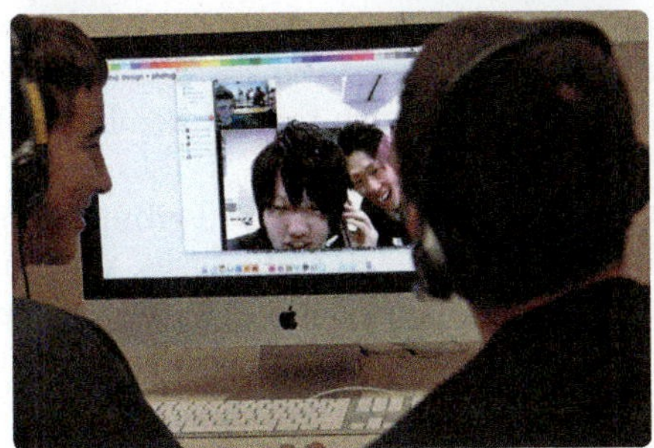

(Clockwise from top left) track5/Getty Images; The Star-Ledger/Matt Smith/The Image Works; Debbie Noda/Modesto Bee/ZUMAPRESS.com/ Alamy Stock Photo

coordinating various responsibilities. One person forgetting to order the cake causes a problem for the whole group.

Second, small groups have at least three people. After that, scholars disagree about when a group is no longer considered "small." For example, communication scholar Thomas Socha (1997) suggests that a small group is 3 to 15 people. In practice, however, the upper limit on the number of people in a small group depends on how the communication changes as the group gets larger. Imagine that 30 people will be attending the going-away party. It would be very hard — even messy — to involve all 30 attendees in planning the event. Instead, you'd want to have a smaller group take over the effort, then share the plan with the other attendees. For the purposes of this book, we will say that a group must be small enough to allow all members to have input in coordinating its activities (Socha, 1997).

Third, members of a small group share a common identity — they see themselves as a group. This makes small groups different from a random assortment of people — say, seven strangers standing together and chatting while waiting to cross a street. After being together for a while, small groups develop rituals, inside jokes, and stories that further strengthen their identity. A friend planning the going-away party might say, "I spoke to Mr. Bowtie today about the menu, and he said . . . ," evoking laughter from other group members who share knowledge of the food caterer's fondness for wearing bowties. As a group develops, unique verbal and nonverbal codes emerge that reflect its common identity and give members a strong sense of belonging and pride (Adelman and Frey, 1994).

Finally, members in a small group communicate to achieve common goals. Suppose a handful of friends are waiting for a yoga class to start. If they're communicating to pass the time ("How's your week going?"), they're not a small group. But once they decide to plan the going-away party together, they've created a common purpose and would be considered a small group.

Today, digital technology makes it increasingly likely that you will work in a team that rarely or never meets in person. A team of three or more people who rely on *mediated communication* to achieve common goals is known as a **virtual small group**. This could include working with classmates on a project for an online course or planning a vacation with family members who reside in different states or countries.

Two additional characteristics are unique to virtual small groups. First, team members are separated by physical distance; in some cases, they may be on entirely different continents (Bell & Kozlowski, 2002). Second, virtual small groups rely mainly on digital technology to manage information, data, and personal communications (Bell & Kozlowski, 2002). If you primarily use discussion boards and web-based software, like Google Docs, to develop a course project with a few classmates, you're in a virtual small group.

Types of Small Groups

There are two basic types of small groups. **Primary groups** are the individuals who meet your basic life, psychological, and social needs. For instance, your family and friends protect you from harm and loneliness. (Or at least you hope they will!) Interpersonal communication skills — such as self-disclosure and relational maintenance — are important for developing and maintaining primary group relationships.

Secondary groups consist of people with whom you want to achieve specific goals or perform tasks. Some secondary groups have a short life, such as neighbors brainstorming ideas for a Fourth of July block party. Other secondary groups work together over long periods of time, like the teams at Pixar. Table 11.1 lists different types of secondary groups you might be part of at school, in your community, or at work. In this chapter, we explore the concepts and skills you need to communicate competently in secondary groups.

Development of Small Groups

When you first join a group, it's natural to wonder how the group will work together. How will it decide on a plan? How will members get to know one another? How will the group handle disagreements? What will

TABLE 11.1

TYPES OF SECONDARY GROUPS

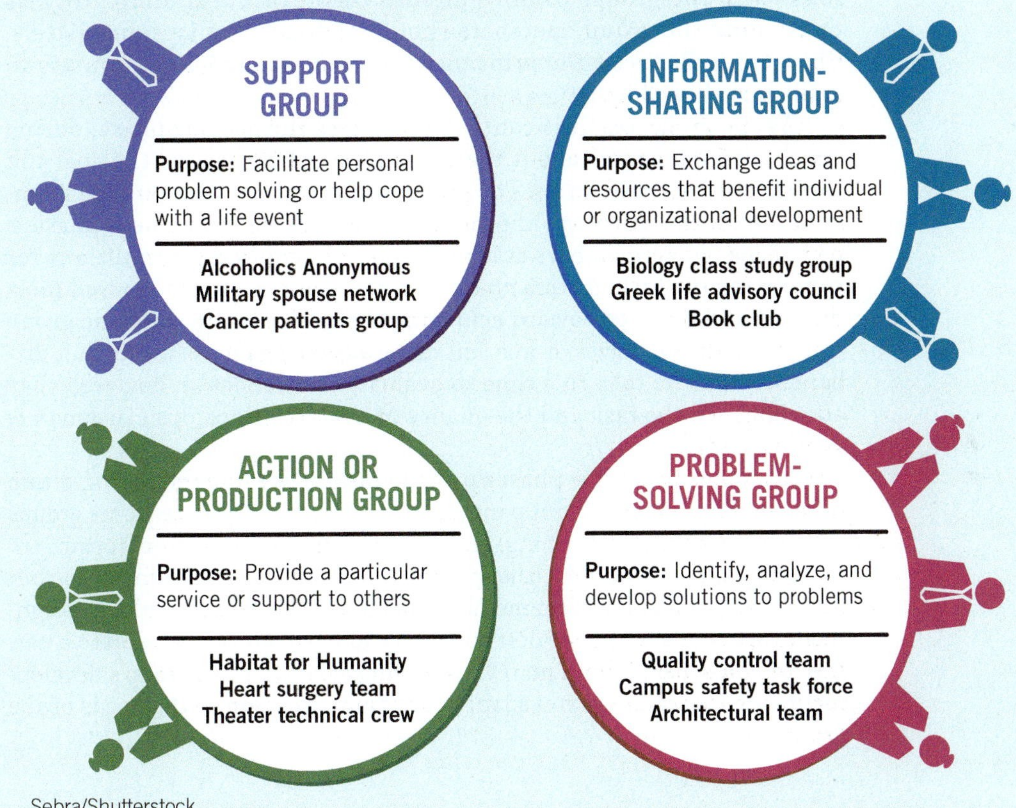

SUPPORT GROUP
Purpose: Facilitate personal problem solving or help cope with a life event
Alcoholics Anonymous
Military spouse network
Cancer patients group
INFORMATION-SHARING GROUP
Purpose: Exchange ideas and resources that benefit individual or organizational development
Biology class study group
Greek life advisory council
Book club
ACTION OR PRODUCTION GROUP
Purpose: Provide a particular service or support to others
Habitat for Humanity
Heart surgery team
Theater technical crew
PROBLEM-SOLVING GROUP
Purpose: Identify, analyze, and develop solutions to problems
Quality control team
Campus safety task force
Architectural team

Sebra/Shutterstock

be the group identity? Although each group is unique, groups generally go through five phases — forming, storming, norming, performing, and adjourning (Tuckman, 1965; Tuckman & Jensen, 1977). You can tell what phase a group is in by how members communicate with one another, which changes over time.

A small group starts in the **forming** phase — during which members become acquainted with one another and seek to understand the task. When a group first comes together, there is a high level of uncertainty. Group members relieve this by getting to know one another and sharing any relevant personal background — such as prior experiences or interests — related to the task as well as their expectations. This knowledge helps the group begin to focus its attention on discussing goals for the task (Bushe & Coetzer, 2007).

As the group becomes familiar with its task and with one another, it moves to the **storming** phase, when members express different ideas about how to approach the task and who will take on leadership roles. This is when personality differences and power struggles may surface, creating tension in the group. To prevent such clashes from stalling progress or dividing the group, members should address conflict immediately. Chapter 12 discusses the principles and skills group leaders can use to manage such conflict.

As the group resolves conflicts, it enters the **norming** phase, during which members agree about the plans for working toward the goal and the various responsibilities. The group's unity is expressed through members' commitment to one another and the team goal. The next phase is **performing**, when members actually make the required contributions for completing the task. At this phase, group members' efforts are well coordinated and directed toward achieving the goal. Finally, once the group completes its objectives, it may enter the **adjourning** phase, in which it disbands. Members take this time to evaluate and reflect on how well they accomplished the task and the quality of their relationships (Tuckman & Jensen, 1977).

Although these five phases provide insight for understanding group development, not every group moves in this orderly sequence. Some groups will have no conflict (storming) and will move immediately from forming to norming and performing. Other groups will be at the performing phase but revert to storming if a team member fails to follow through with an assignment. Occasionally, groups don't officially adjourn but continue on to a new task or just separate with no review. Paying attention to a group's developmental phases can help you adapt your communication to the needs of the group.

How Small Groups Communicate

Groups achieve their stated goals when members communicate in a cooperative and productive fashion. You can help the group build and maintain positive relationships by understanding how group roles work and adapting your communication to foster group unity.

As the chapter opener illustrates, Pixar Studios relies on teamwork to produce movies. These teams produce good stories by fostering competent communication and participation. Each member of the project, including the director (or leader), communicates as part of a team, with scriptwriters, visual artists, and animators performing clear tasks and contributing throughout the production process so that the film will be ready on time for distribution in theaters.

One way that Pixar encourages team communication is by scheduling meetings known as "dailies." Dailies are meetings during which animators show work in progress, often leading to script rewrites and drawing revisions. These meetings include some fun, such as singing '80s songs and playful teasing, but most importantly, dailies involve honest and specific feedback on project ideas (Catmull, 2014). While some parts of dailies may

Hero Images/Getty Images

Like the teams at Pixar, many successful small groups meet frequently not only to share ideas and assess in-progress work, but also to build supportive relationships among team members. The way that group members communicate with each other influences how successfully they reach their goal. When you have been part of a group or team, how has members' communication contributed to the success—or failure—of your goals?

seem silly, these activities build supportive relationships. Because the team gives equal attention to building relationships and to communicating about tasks, Pixar ensures a climate of creativity and excellence.

The success or failure of any small group is largely attributable to how members communicate with one another. Setting the stage for competent communication can be accomplished in five ways: balancing group roles, building cohesiveness, establishing positive norms, sharing leadership responsibilities, and managing physical space.

Balancing Group Roles

Within a small group, members fulfill different types of roles. **Formal roles** are assigned positions that members take on by appointment or election (Myers & Anderson, 2008). For example, a director is the "leader" of a film production team. Other small groups, like project teams, often have formal roles — such as "chairperson" and "meeting recorder" — that bestow members with unique responsibilities, such as leading meetings and taking notes on group decisions.

In addition to formal roles, there are **group roles** (also known as *informal roles*) — specific patterns of behavior and communication that members develop from interacting over time. Group roles are classified in two ways: *task roles* support the group in achieving its goals; *maintenance roles* help strengthen and secure relationships among group members. Unlike formal roles, both task and maintenance roles emerge naturally in groups. Various group members fulfill these roles as needed, depending on the situation.

Task Roles. When you're exchanging information about duties or goals important to your group, you are fulfilling **task roles**. For example, an interior designer who's remodeling a hotel lobby might share the following information during a design meeting: "The blueprints show that the lobby is 2,250 square feet." Another member of the group could ask, "Do you know how much natural lighting is available in the lobby entrance?" This exchange of messages about the task at hand helps the group carry out its work (see Table 11.2). Individuals serving task roles may provide ideas, clarify points, summarize discussion, and coordinate information.

Maintenance Roles. Through **maintenance roles**, group members communicate to build trusting and appreciative interpersonal relationships. Teams can achieve high levels of performance when members trust one another and feel personally valued (Campany, Dubinsky, Druskat, Mangino, & Flynn, 2007). Group members can create this environment by listening to one another, appropriately self-disclosing, and managing conflict. For example, some group members may be good at noticing when others are unusually quiet during a discussion and try to involve them ("Analise, what do you think about this proposal?"). Or perhaps another member knows how to spot and deal with tension in the group ("I think we've been at this too long. How about we take a break?"). Members who fill maintenance roles can sustain harmony and satisfaction within the group.

Group Role Emergence and Flexibility. When you are part of a group, you may find that the roles members take on in the group can depend on their personality. Extraverted individuals tend to naturally fall into maintenance roles, and group members who are conscientious assume task roles with greater ease (Kozlowski & Ilgen, 2006). By practicing *critical self-reflection* (Chapter 2), you increase your self-awareness of the various roles you can play in a small group.

It is important to remember that group roles are not fixed. Instead, each member may take on different roles as the group develops. For example, during the forming phase of a group project, you might be the person who makes sure everyone is acquainted by engaging in small talk (maintenance role). Later on, you might ask questions about decision alternatives (task role). During a stressful situation, someone in the group might say something funny to relieve the tension (maintenance role) but then try to bring the group back to a productive conversation (task role).

In order for a group to be effective, there must be a balance of task and maintenance roles. Neglecting one or the other can create problems. If members focus only on getting the task done, they can exhaust themselves, which erodes morale. On the other hand, if they spend all their time building strong interpersonal bonds, they'll soon fall behind in completing tasks.

TABLE 11.2

TYPES OF GROUP ROLES

ROLES	EXAMPLES	IMPACT ON THE GROUP
TASK		
• Coordinator • Information giver • Researcher • Critical thinker • Note taker	*"I think we should . . ."* *"What additional research do we need?"* *"Let's consider the pros and cons."*	Directs group toward goal achievement
MAINTENANCE		
• Supportive listener • Encourager • Peacemaker • Mood observer • Gatekeeper	*"That's a great idea."* *"I can see your point."* *"You've been quiet."*	Helps build group relationships
EGOCENTRIC		
• Aggressor • Dominator • Withdrawer • Side talker • Joker	*"I'm cool with whatever."* *"Don't be ridiculous."* *"Let me tell you what happened last night."*	Creates delays and/or disharmony for the group

Information from Mudrack and Farrell (1995)

Appropriately balancing task and maintenance role behaviors helps a group become more productive and draw more satisfaction from working together.

Egocentric Roles. Successful groups also watch for and address the emergence of **egocentric roles**, which occurs when one team member's communication disrupts the group's efforts (see Table 11.2). For example, an overly aggressive group member can make others afraid to offer their ideas. One common egocentric role is the teammate who relies on other members to do all the work, a phenomenon known as **social loafing** (Harkins, 1987). This can spark resentment among other group members. For ideas on how to handle such behavior, see Advance the Conversation: Conflict with a Group Member on pages 282–283.

Members of a small group can neutralize egocentric roles by establishing positive expectations for behaviors when the group first forms (this is known as *norms*; we discuss them later in the chapter) and by directly confronting disruptive behaviors (Druskat & Wolff, 2001). So if a teammate's constant joking becomes a distraction, someone in the group needs to tell that person that the behavior is keeping the group from doing its work. Otherwise, the group could lose focus, and members could become upset, making it harder for the group to achieve its goals (Druskat & Wolff, 2001).

Building Cohesiveness

One reason people join groups is that they fulfill a human need to belong (Baumeister & Leary, 1995). This need is best met when you are part of a **cohesive group**, in which members like one another and have a sense of camaraderie. In highly cohesive groups, members feel a strong sense of unity and commitment to the group's work. In groups that lack cohesion, members may feel disconnected from the group and have difficulty committing to group goals (Johnston, 2007). Members of a small group can build cohesiveness by appropriately self-disclosing to promote trust, constructively managing conflict to overcome dissatisfaction, and reserving time for external activity (such as having lunch together) to become better acquainted.

Establishing Positive Norms

Norms are the expectations about behavior within a group. For example, your work team may expect everyone to be on time for meetings and to arrive prepared. To have the most impact, norms should be clearly communicated. Members can establish positive norms by following a few simple steps:

- *Create ground rules.* When the group first comes together, take time to develop *ground rules*, or written expectations about behavior. For example, "Notify the group if you're going to miss a meeting, silence your phone during meetings, and don't interrupt when someone else is talking."
- *Begin and end meetings on time.* Waiting for everyone to arrive before you start a meeting sends a message that it's OK to arrive late. Similarly, regularly allowing meetings to go over their scheduled time is frustrating for group members with busy schedules.
- *Confront problem behaviors immediately.* Use the conflict-management skills discussed in Chapter 10 to confront behaviors that disrupt the group's interpersonal relationships or goals. For example, avoid making hurtful attacks ("Quit acting like such a baby!"), and focus on collaboration.
- *Evaluate the group regularly.* To ensure the group is adequately working toward its goals, conduct regular evaluations (e.g., at the end of each meeting or month). Members can do this by openly identifying what's going well in the group and what needs to be changed. For instance, a group may be meeting its project deadlines, but if members are arguing over workload and responsibilities, that problem needs to be addressed.

Sharing Responsibility

As our Pixar example illustrates, everyone involved in the creation of a film — directors, scriptwriters, visual artists, and actors — plays an important role in its success (or failure). In addition to their specific task roles, members are also committed to the group's mission: producing a film that will entertain audiences and bring in money for the company as a whole.

Barry Wetcher/© Warner Bros. Pictures/Everett Collection

In *Ocean's 8*, a dysfunctional group of thieves, hustlers, and hackers must work together to pull off an elaborate heist. Although a heist movie may seem unrelated to small group communication, the characters take on a variety of roles—both maintenance and task—throughout the film, while also establishing norms and sharing leadership responsibilities in order to fulfill their goal: steal the precious necklace known as the Toussaint.

For example, during the production of *Incredibles 2*, one team member suggested that a male villain might be better cast as a female villain, which gave rise to the character Evelyn Deavor, an important contribution in developing the narrative (Acuna, 2018). When group members behave in this way, it is known as *shared leadership*; members influence one another's work, and they each feel a sense of ownership about their contributions and the group's goals. To encourage a sense of shared leadership, the formal leader of a small group should communicate in ways that help members accomplish their tasks, maintain strong interpersonal bonds, and encourage all members to engage in honest (but respectful) dialog. Chapter 12 explores the concept of shared leadership in more detail.

Managing Physical Space

In any interaction, the physical environment affects the communication process. In small group situations, *semi-fixed features* of the environment—those that can be easily moved or changed, such as chairs and other furniture—influence how group members communicate with one another (Sommer, 1965). For example, members of highly cohesive groups tend to sit closer together than do those in less cohesive groups. Additionally, those who occupy seats at the head of a table or in a center position are more likely to be perceived as leaders.

To manage physical space in ways that support communication, teams should look for a space that fits their needs, such as a quiet, comfortable environment for meetings, or a room with whiteboards, so they can list ideas generated during brainstorming sessions. In a virtual small group, members should make sure everyone can be seen on videoconference and has access to a microphone. If you plan accordingly, the physical space you meet in can positively influence your group's communication.

The Self's Influence on Small Group Communication

Your self-concept shapes how you communicate in small groups. Everything, from your personality to your gender and cultural background, affects your communication and other group members' perceptions of you. By enhancing your self-awareness, you can communicate more competently in small groups and teams.

Your group might be in the depths of the earth trying to find your way back to the surface, or you might be spies on a classified mission. Adding to the pressure, you must complete your task in under 60 minutes. These and other escape the room adventures have become increasingly popular entertainment in the United States and across the world. A typical adventure

As of this writing, over 2,000 companies in the United States offer "escape the room" adventures. This unique type of entertainment—which involves hands-on puzzle-solving in thematic physical rooms—has exploded in popularity, in large part because it fosters cooperation and creative problem solving as a group. Have you ever visited an escape room? If so, did your team succeed in overcoming the obstacles and achieving their goal?

Zoltan Balogh/EPA/Shutterstock

consists of a series of physical rooms, each set up with clues and riddles that a small group — usually four to ten people — must solve within a preset time limit in order to "escape" from the room. In her description of a spy-themed adventure that she experienced, journalist Tessa Berenson recalls that her nine-person group quietly worked alone trying to solve the clues in the room without much verbal communication. Then, with only 25 minutes to go and not much progress made, the group started communicating. Knowing that solving riddles is not her strong suit, Berenson encouraged verbal communication with other group members to reveal each member's knowledge and insights, which allowed the group to successfully escape the room (Berenson, 2015).

Although all small group members work toward a common goal, each person brings his or her own unique self, experiences, and communication preferences to the group. In an escape the room adventure, group members must openly communicate their knowledge and experiences in order to overcome the challenge within the time limit. But some group members may be naturally comfortable speaking up, while others may be quiet and reserved. Knowing how certain factors — such as your own communication traits, gender, and culture — influence small group behavior will help you communicate more competently within groups.

Communication Traits

You possess certain enduring traits that affect your communication no matter what the situation. For example, if you are an extravert, you are generally social and outgoing and tend to seek out interactions with people, whether you are chatting with your sister or making a speech (Littlejohn & Foss, 2010). However, when it comes to small groups, there are two communication traits that are especially important: communication apprehension and argumentativeness.

Communication Apprehension. Have you ever been afraid to speak up and say what's on your mind? If so, you may have experienced **communication apprehension** — fear or anxiety about real or anticipated communication (McCroskey, 2008). Most people experience a small amount of communication apprehension from time to time — for example, when giving a speech. (We discuss how to handle speech anxiety in Chapter 15.) But some individuals experience apprehension on such a regular basis that it becomes part of how they communicate. Known as *high communication apprehension*, this can be so paralyzing that it prevents a person from communicating in everyday situations, such as chatting with coworkers. Naturally, this can result in negative consequences. For example, college students with high communication apprehension experience less academic success in classes that require a lot of discussion compared to students who aren't as fearful about communication (McCroskey & Andersen, 1976). In groups, someone who's nervous and silent may appear to other members as aloof, stiff, withdrawn, or restless

(McCroskey, Daly, & Sorensen, 1976). As a result, the other members may wrongly assume that the apprehensive person doesn't care about the group's goals, and they may stop trying to elicit contributions from him or her.

If you experience communication apprehension in groups, you can try to reduce your fear with focused practice. Start by asking simple questions to clarify points made during group discussions. Provide brief comments of support for others when it's appropriate ("Yes, I think that's a good idea"). Try to anticipate what topics may be under discussion or what questions might be asked, and prepare messages you can contribute in advance. Knowing what to say ahead of time will make it easier to speak up. If you believe your communication apprehension is really holding you back, find the courage to talk with an instructor who can direct you to resources that may help.

Argumentativeness. Whereas high communication apprehension can make small group communication challenging, a trait that can enhance it is argumentativeness. **Argumentativeness** is the willingness to take a stance on controversial issues and verbally refute others who disagree with you (Infante & Rancer, 1982). Although the word *argument* carries negative connotations, it can be a positive form of communication in small groups. That's because argumentativeness fosters the exchange of ideas, which is

DOUBLE TAKE

ARGUMENTATIVENESS 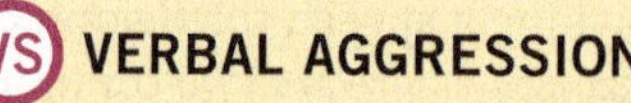 VERBAL AGGRESSION

Group projects can often lead to conflicts among members. It's important to know how to vocalize your different opinions because there's a big difference between being argumentative and being verbally aggressive. Which of these scenarios do you think ended on better terms? Why?

Westend61/Getty Images

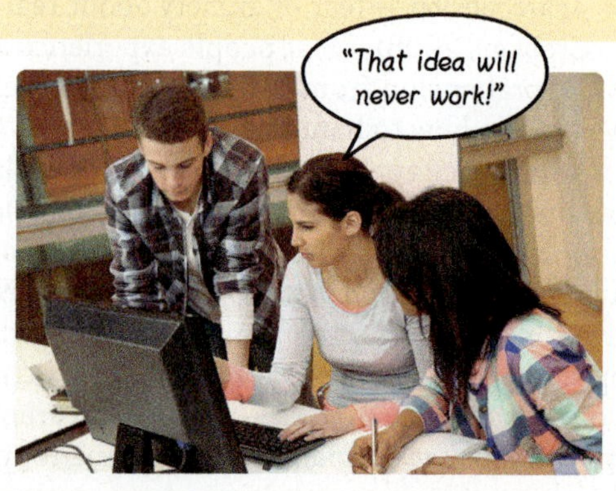

goodluz/Shutterstock

valuable for group decision making. Being highly argumentative is not the same as being *verbally aggressive*, which is characterized by hostile personal attacks on others (Infante, 1987). Instead, someone who is argumentative openly disagrees with ideas without making it personal. If you disagree with your teammate and say, "I see where you're coming from, but I'm not sure that clue is going to give us the combination of the lock," you are showing argumentativeness. But if you say, "That's a stupid idea! Don't you have any understanding of how to read this clue?", it's verbal aggression. Since highly argumentative individuals separate issues from people, they tend to communicate well in groups and often emerge as group leaders (Limon & La France, 2005).

Argumentativeness encourages groups to think through and debate ideas, something the Pixar teams do when creating their successful films. This boosts the chances that a group will end up choosing the best possible ideas to act on. Constructive arguing also strengthens bonds in a group. When group members are argumentative, they are more likely to be satisfied with the group relationship and to believe that the group has reached consensus on decisions (Anderson & Martin, 1999). Despite the advantages of argumentativeness, there's a constructive way to argue and a not-so-constructive way, which can lead to unproductive conflict. Chapter 12 presents strategies for effectively dealing with conflicts in small groups.

Gender

Popular stereotypes suggest there are big differences in how men and women communicate. According to these, men are unemotional, dominant, and achievement oriented, whereas women are nurturing, caring, and emotional. However, men and women actually communicate similarly in many ways, including levels of talkativeness, assertive speech, and self-disclosure (Cameron, 2009; Hyde, 2005).

So what does this mean for communication within a small group? As recommended in Chapter 3, you need to move beyond gender stereotypes when interpreting your teammates' communication behaviors. People have a tendency to negatively judge men and women who communicate in ways that defy gender stereotypes (Hyde, 2005). For example, you might dismiss an overly emotional male teammate during a heated debate if you think he's not acting the way a man "should" act. Conversely, you may decide that a female team member who doesn't smile often or talk much is cold because women are "supposed" to be warm and open with their feelings. If you think gender-based stereotypes might be affecting your perception of team members, use *perception-checking* to form more accurate impressions. As Chapter 2 discusses, you can do this by reviewing your knowledge about the other person, assessing any attributions you've made about the individual, and questioning your impression to make sure you're not basing it solely on a stereotype.

Culture

Your culture affects all your communication, but three factors are especially relevant when interacting within small groups (see Figure 11.1). The first is whether you see your individual needs as more or less important than the group's needs. As Chapter 3 discusses, people raised in an *individualistic culture* (e.g., the United States and Australia) will place greater importance on their individual achievement and personal happiness than will those from a *collectivistic culture* (e.g., China and several West African cultures). People with a collectivistic orientation place greater importance on group goals, and they especially value cooperation and interpersonal harmony.

A second important cultural dimension is *power distance*, the degree to which people expect inequality between persons of low and high power (Hofstede, Hofstede, & Minkov, 2010). In high-power-distance cultures (such as Mexico and Saudi Arabia), an individual of low power wouldn't disagree with a leader during a discussion. In low-power-distance cultures (including the United States and Canada), many people expect leaders to treat those below them with respect and to invite everyone's input on certain decisions.

FIGURE 11.1

CULTURE AND SELF-AWARENESS

In groups, it is important to be aware of how cultural preferences affect all members' communication, even your own.

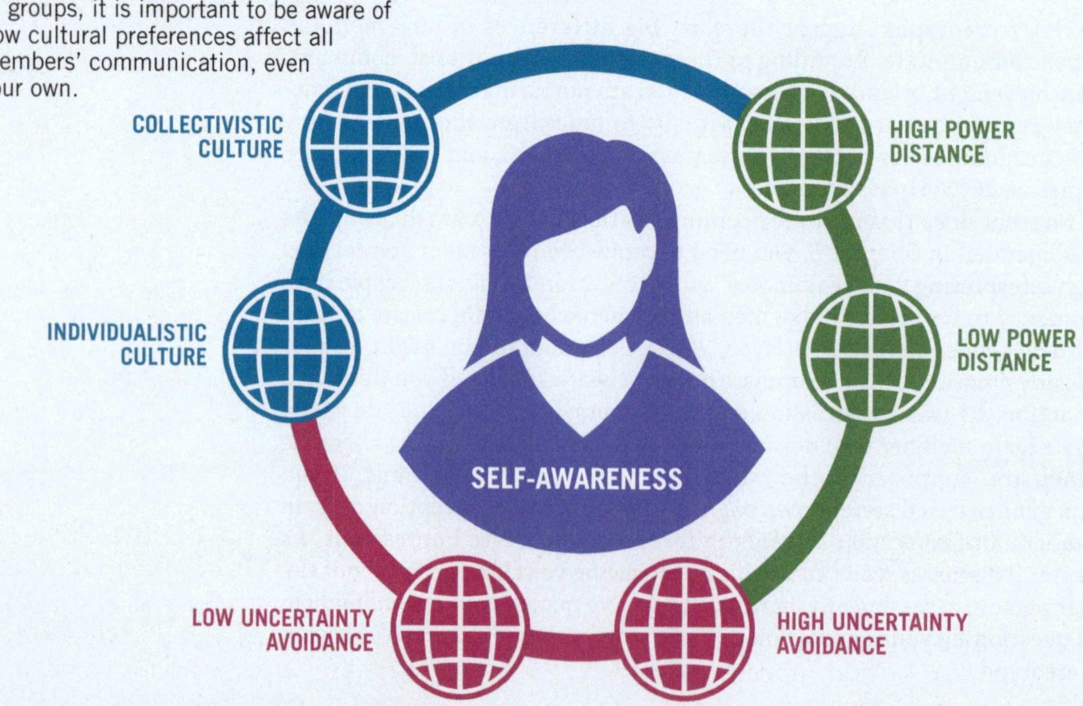

Max Griboedov/Shutterstock; VoodooDot/Shutterstock

ADVANCE THE CONVERSATION

YOU'RE NOT FUNNY

1 YOUR DILEMMA

You had a bad feeling when you learned that Professor Bradley had assigned Derek to your sociology project group. Since the first day of class, Derek has been "that sometimes funny but annoying guy" in class.

Sure enough, during your first group meeting, Derek distracts from the task by talking about his favorite show, *Rick and Morty*. Two other group members, Jamie and Greg, laugh along with Derek, reciting lines from a recent episode. Since you don't watch the show, you feel left out. Sylvia, your other group member, is quiet, too.

Trying to refocus the discussion, you say, "OK, enough about *Rick and Morty*. Who's read the assignment?" Derek replies, "I didn't download it. Anyway, did you guys see the episode when Rick . . ." Unsure of what to say next, you silently review the assignment while making notes. Sylvia is now preoccupied with looking over the assignment, too.

Realizing that today's discussion is going nowhere, you decide to leave. As you get up, you say, "For our next meeting on Thursday, let's read the assignment requirements and come with some ideas. See you later."

Driving home, you worry about how Derek's behavior will impact the group's performance. You give serious thought to asking Professor Bradley to move you to another group.

➔ **How do you feel when Derek derails the discussion? Do you think you have an ethical obligation to remain in the group and not abandon the other members?**

2 THE RESEARCH

One exciting aspect of group work is encountering others with different personalities. But some communication behaviors cause stress and lead to divisive conflict (Felps, Mitchell, & Byington, 2006). Known as *bad apple behaviors*, these include withholding effort, displaying excessive negativity, and violating interpersonal norms (Felps et al., 2006). If bad apple behaviors aren't promptly dealt with, they can negatively affect team motivation and performance.

Felps and colleagues (2006) identified three ways team members respond most often to bad apple behaviors:

1. *Motivation intervention* is an attempt to change the negative behavior through verbal persuasion ("C'mon, Derek, we need to focus on the assignment"). Individuals will likely respond this way when they believe the person can control the disruptive behavior.
2. *Rejection* involves ignoring the bad apple behavior. Group members would most likely take this route when efforts to change the behavior through verbal persuasion have failed.
3. *Defensiveness* is communicating in a manner that protects your sense of self, including physically withdrawing or being verbally aggressive toward the offending party. When direct or indirect attempts to change bad apple behavior are unsuccessful, or when you have limited power in the group, you may respond defensively.

➔ **What do you gain and risk by responding to Derek in each of these three ways?**

3 YOUR OPPORTUNITY

Before you act, consider the facts of the situation and think about the research. Also, reflect on what you've learned so far about group roles (pp. 267–269), cohesiveness (p. 270), norms (p. 270), and communication traits (pp. 273–275).

➔ **Now it's your turn. Write out a response to Derek. As you write, think about whether or not you will ask your professor to move you to a different group.**

A final cultural factor affecting small group communication is *uncertainty avoidance*, or how much tolerance people have for risk (Hofstede et al., 2010). In cultures with high uncertainty avoidance (such as Germany and Finland), individuals expect structure and rules. In those with low uncertainty avoidance (including the United States and China), people feel more comfortable with change and with having relatively few rules.

Understanding how your cultural orientation affects your communication in small groups is a component of your *self-awareness*. Let's say you have been oriented to collectivistic ways of thought and embrace a high power distance. In this case, you may avoid disagreeing with a group leader or offering a dissenting opinion during a discussion. Or suppose you have high uncertainty avoidance; you might become frustrated when a group lacks clear goals or ground rules. By knowing how cultural factors influence your own group behavior, you can be mindful of communicating your ideas in ways that maintain the self-worth, or face, of culturally different teammates (Oetzel & Ting-Toomey, 2003). For example, if you're part of a group in which many members are from a high-power-distance culture and you disagree with something the senior person in the group said, how would you handle it? Voicing your opinion mid-meeting may cause other team members embarrassment. Instead, you could approach the high-status person during a break and ask, "Are you open to hearing another opinion?" Choosing to raise your objection privately shows respect for the senior person and avoids a potentially embarrassing situation.

Virtual Groups and Teams

Social media and videoconferencing help virtual groups organize their work and communicate. However, as with all online interactions, remember that the three Ps of mediated communication—powerful, public, and permanent—from Chapter 4 still apply. Your self-presentation matters just as much (if not more) when you're working in virtual small groups as it does when you're communicating online with close friends and family.

In our technology-saturated culture, it's easy to think that communicating online with virtual groups should be second nature to us all, but that isn't always the case. For example, Jason Walker, vice president of sales at software company iLinc, was sharing his screen while delivering a virtual presentation to his managers when a message unexpectedly appeared on his screen: "I love you Teddy Bear." The message was from Walker's significant other and, embarrassingly, all five remote attendees saw it on his shared screen. Walker never lived it down: his colleagues teased him and called him "Teddy Bear" for months afterward (Mattioli, 2008).

Professionals are increasingly working on teams that have members all over the country—even around the globe. Perhaps not surprisingly, an entire industry has sprung up to teach people how to avoid embarrassing situations like the one "Teddy Bear" found himself in. With almost any career you choose — from video game design to public relations — or any class project you participate in, you could be working in a virtual small group. A *virtual small group* is any team of three or more individuals who work together to achieve a common goal and who communicate primarily through technology instead of face-to-face encounters. Working in a virtual small group presents both challenges and advantages. In this section, we discuss pitfalls to watch out for and suggest strategies for improving communication in your next virtual group experience — so you can avoid your own "Teddy Bear" moment.

Challenges of Virtual Groups

Lack of face-to-face interactions presents virtual small groups with several challenges. First, the physical distance separating members restricts their nonverbal communication. If you can't see your team members' facial expressions and body postures, you don't know if they're smiling and nodding in agreement or if they're confused or bored. This lack of feedback makes it hard to know how the team feels about what is being said. Even when using videoconferencing and webcams, people can still feel cut off from the group, which can lead to their getting caught up in other activities during a virtual meeting that disrupt their concentration, such as eating or checking social media feeds (Mattioli, 2008).

Second, it's hard to build cohesion in a virtual team. In interviews with members of a virtual group working for a travel company, one study found that the group experienced mistrust, limited rapport, and feelings of isolation (Kirkman, Rosen, Gibson, Tesluk, & McPherson, 2002). To offset these problems, virtual team members should occasionally meet face-to-face if at all possible. These interactions are essential for building interpersonal relationships and strengthening cohesion. When it's not possible to arrange face-to-face meetings, virtual teams can benefit from icebreaker activities early in a meeting, such as introducing themselves by self-disclosing a fact that others may find surprising (Nunamaker, Reinig, & Briggs, 2009) or engaging in small talk in later meetings once everyone knows one another.

Third, it's difficult to communicate complex information and to make decisions during online meetings. Even with lots of different resources to enable interaction — including instant messaging and videoconferencing systems — groups can suffer from missed or delayed messages, misinterpretations, and other issues. Some media are better than others for overcoming these challenges. Table 11.3 considers the advantages and disadvantages of common tools intended to support virtual small group communication. Use this table to determine the best way to reach out to other members of a virtual group, depending on your communication goals.

Finally, team members may vary greatly in their ability to use the group's chosen communication technology. Perhaps a member lacks access

TABLE 11.3

COMMON TOOLS FOR VIRTUAL SMALL GROUP COMMUNICATION[1]

EMAIL
(e.g., Gmail & Microsoft Outlook)

Advantages

Easily accessible

Free or low cost

Useful for exchanging routine information

Disadvantages

Lacks nonverbal information

Less effective for conveying complex information

TELECONFERENCE
(e.g., conference calls)

Advantages

Easily accessible

Useful for exchanging routine information and increasingly complex information

Disadvantages

Lack of visual nonverbal information (i.e., facial expressions and gestures)

Difficult to maintain team members' attention and engagement

VIDEOCONFERENCE
(e.g., Skype & Cisco WebEx)

Advantages

Provides access to verbal and nonverbal information

Useful for communicating complex information and decisions

Disadvantages

Requires all team members to have the same technology

Subject to technical difficulties (user error or equipment failure)

PROJECT MANAGEMENT TOOLS
(e.g., Google Docs & wikis)

Advantages

Free or low cost

Useful for compiling research findings and collaborating on reports

Disadvantages

Requires moderate training

Team members must continually check the site to contribute and view others' contributions (Nunamaker, Reinig, & Briggs, 2009)

[1]Except where noted, information in this table is from Bell & Kozlowski (2002).

VLADGRIN/Shutterstock; Domofon/Shutterstock; Vector/Shutterstock; Marish/Shutterstock

to high-speed internet, or another member's computer crashes during a web conference. All virtual groups need backup plans in case such problems occur. They should also make sure that every member knows how to participate in any conferencing programs, such as those developed by WebEx or Citrix. If you're forming a virtual team, take steps early on to see that everyone has both access to and the ability to use any necessary technology.

Improving Communication in Virtual Small Groups

If you're part of a virtual small group, consider the following guidelines to help improve communication:

1. *Determine the best communication method.* Virtual teams often use different technologies for communicating and sharing information. Large teams with members working in different locations rely heavily on electronic messaging, like email and instant messaging (Timmerman and Scott, 2006). File-hosting websites like Dropbox and Google Docs allow virtual teams to share meeting notes and reports. Phone calls, videoconferencing, and collaborative platforms are appropriate for discussing complex matters and making decisions. Team members should understand what technologies to use for handling routine communication, managing group documents, and conducting meetings. Importantly, be sure that every team member has the proper login details and the capability to use the technologies.
2. *Provide specific directions before meetings.* Take time-zone differences into account when scheduling a meeting. If group members are from vastly different time zones, schedule meetings so that members take turns being inconvenienced. It's not fair to expect any one person to always be available during very early morning or very late evening hours. Also identify the purpose, expectations, and desired outcomes of each meeting (Nunamaker et al., 2009).
3. *Involve all group members.* Make sure all participants have a chance to contribute to group discussions and meetings. You can do this by asking everyone to share something at the start of a meeting or by asking each person to give a response to questions posed at different points in the meeting (Nunamaker et al., 2009).
4. *Use the cooperative principle.* It's especially important to craft informative, honest, clear, and relevant messages when you're taking part in a virtual group interaction. That's because team members have few or no nonverbal cues to interpret your communication. (See Chapter 5 for more on the cooperative principle.)
5. *Attend to the group's social needs.* If virtual teams are able to meet face-to-face occasionally, this will promote team identity and foster group cohesion (Siebdrat, Hoegl, & Ernst, 2009; Timmerman & Scott, 2006). When costs, time, or distance get in the way of such gatherings, help your team develop other ways of attending to members' social needs. Make time for conversations about things other than work, such as group members' interests or hobbies. Or create a team website that contains pictures of each member and information about their backgrounds and interests. Getting to know one another can help team members feel more of a social connection.

LearningCurve can help you review! Go to **launchpadworks.com**

ADVANCE THE CONVERSATION
Video Activity

CONFLICT WITH A GROUP MEMBER

The following scenario will enhance your ability to communicate with a group member who is being difficult. Visit LaunchPad at **launchpadworks.com** to get the full experience with video. As you watch the first video, recall what you've learned about social loafing, egocentric roles, and competent small group communication. Then complete the **Your Turn** prompts. Finally, watch the **Take Two!** video to explore how this scenario could have gone differently.

1 *THE PROBLEM*

As an assignment for her human communication course, Maeve is part of a group that is making a 15-minute presentation explaining the cultural factors that influence communication. One group member, Paul, did not prepare his slides for the meeting in which the group is putting together the final presentation. Maeve is irritated that Paul doesn't seem to be doing his share of the work, so she decides to confront him. "Hey, Paul," she begins. "You got a minute?"

"Last meeting, we all agreed that we were going to have our parts of the presentation ready for today. You didn't have your slides. What happened?"

"Just a lot of stuff. Um, listen, can you text me, because I've got to go to class?"

2 YOUR TURN

Observations. Reflect on how Maeve and Paul communicated in this scenario by answering the following questions:

1. Which character do you identify with more in this situation? How would you feel if you were in his or her situation?
2. Where were the missed opportunities to practice competent communication?

Discussion. In class or with a partner, share your thoughts about the interaction between Maeve and Paul and work to answer the following questions:

1. Can you understand both perspectives?
2. What could Paul and Maeve have done differently?

Conclusion. Choose one person in the scenario to offer your advice. Based on your analysis, what advice would you give him or her to improve his or her communication competence in this scenario?

3 TAKE TWO!

What if things had gone differently? Watch the **Take Two!** video to see one possible example of how the conversation might have gone if Paul and/or Maeve had communicated differently. As you watch the video, consider where the dialog reflects communication competence. After watching the video, answer the questions below:

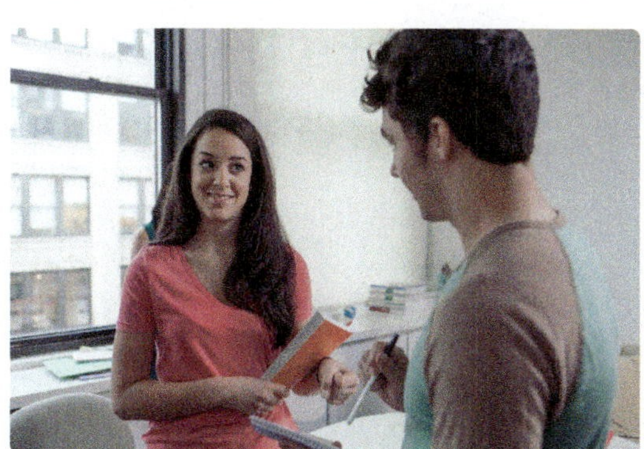

1. Did Paul and/or Maeve take advantage of opportunities that they missed in the first scenario? Which ones?
2. Did their different actions result in a more productive encounter? Please explain.

CHAPTER 11 REVIEW

CHAPTER RECAP

- A **small group** is composed of three or more interdependent persons who share a common identity and come together to achieve a common goal.
- Small groups develop in stages, which include **forming**, **storming**, **norming**, **performing**, and **adjourning**.
- To achieve their goals, members of small groups balance group *roles*, build *cohesiveness*, establish **norms**, share responsibility, and manage physical space.
- Your *self* influences how you communicate in a group, specifically your levels of **communication apprehension** or **argumentativeness** and even your culture and gender.
- **Virtual small groups** are increasingly common at work and school. Though they come with specific challenges, you can overcome them by carefully planning the tools and messages you employ.

LaunchPad for *Choices & Connections* offers unique video scenarios and encourages self-assessment through adaptive quizzing. Go to **launchpadworks.com** to get access.

 LearningCurve adaptive quizzes

 Advance the Conversation video scenarios

 Video clips that illustrate key concepts

KEY TERMS

Small group, p. 262
Virtual small group, p. 264
Primary group, p. 264
Secondary group, p. 264
Forming, p. 265
Storming, p. 265
Norming, p. 266
Performing, p. 266
Adjourning, p. 266
Formal role, p. 267
Group role, p. 267
Task role, p. 268
Maintenance role, p. 268
Egocentric role, p. 269
Social loafing, p. 269
Cohesive group, p. 270
Norms, p. 270
Communication apprehension, p. 273
Argumentativeness, p. 274

POP QUIZ

Looking for more review questions? **LearningCurve** can help you master key concepts from this chapter. Go to **launchpadworks.com**

1. Which phase of group development occurs when members of a small group agree about the plans for working toward the group's goals?
   a. Forming
   b. Norming
   c. Storming
   d. Performing

2. Which of the following is an example of a task role?
   a. Serving as president of a debate team
   b. Mediating an argument between two group members
   c. Collecting and distributing contact information for all members
   d. Consistently telling jokes to add humor to meetings

3. All of the following can help establish positive norms *except*
   a. starting each meeting with an icebreaker activity.
   b. making sure to always begin meetings on time.
   c. asking members to not multitask during meetings.
   d. identifying what is going well in the group and what isn't.

4. If group members have different levels of __________, they may have varying expectations for how much structure the group should have.
   a. self-awareness
   b. power distance
   c. uncertainty avoidance
   d. argumentativeness

5. Members of virtual groups may experience __________ if they are unable to see one another's nonverbal behaviors, such as smiles, nods, or looks of confusion.
   a. restricted small talk
   b. a limited sense of cohesion
   c. difficulty making decisions
   d. a lack of feedback

ACTIVITIES

For more activities, visit LaunchPad for *Choices & Connections* at **launchpadworks.com**

1 What's Your Role?

Choose a small group to which you belong (student club, community organization, or work group), and identify the formal and group roles you take on when you participate in the group (task, maintenance, or egocentric). In a one-page paper, explain when you take on different roles in the group, and how your role behaviors impact the group.

2 Defining Group Norms

In a small group (in person or online), brainstorm a list of ground rules that would be appropriate for a school study group. For example, "Be on time." As a group, agree to the five most important ground rules. Present and critique the final lists with the rest of the class. What seems to be common in the lists? Did any group have a ground rule that you found surprising?

12

Leadership in Group Communication

Quiet, introverted people are often misunderstood in small groups. They may be seen as uninterested, dull, and certainly not leaders. Susan Cain is working to change this perception. How? After publishing her book *Quiet: The Power of Introverts in a World That Can't Stop Talking*, Cain started the "quiet revolution," a mission-based business that aims to transform attitudes about introverted personalities. NASA and Proctor & Gamble are among the companies that are asking Cain to help them develop the team leadership potential of introverted employees.

Her "quiet revolution" is especially important in the United States, where verbal skill is a highly valued leadership quality. As Cain (2013) observes,

> The more a person talks, the more other group members direct their attention to him, which means that he becomes increasingly powerful as a meeting goes on. It also helps to speak fast; we rate quick talkers as more capable and appealing than slow talkers. (p. 51)

Because we pay attention to outspoken and verbally fluent group members, quiet members are less likely to emerge as leaders in groups. But Cain (2013) provides evidence of quiet people who were strong leaders, including Mahatma Gandhi, Eleanor Roosevelt, and Rosa Parks. A more contemporary example is Marissa Mayer, a self-described introvert and one of the most powerful technology leaders in the world. Among the first programmers hired at Google, Mayer made a name for herself by leading the development of Google Search, Google Maps, and Gmail. She has gone on to provide innovative leadership in the artificial intelligence industry. Mayer developed her leadership capability through rigorous academic preparation and a tireless work ethic.

However, working in small groups does not come easy for Mayer. She is often perceived as cold and detached. In meetings, Mayer gives tough feedback on ideas, making her seem like an "art teacher correcting first-semester students" (Holson, 2009). As a Stanford undergraduate, she grew impatient with chatty study groups, reminding them to get back on task (Carlson, 2015). She was even less likely to socialize with them after their study sessions. Despite her social unease, Mayer still inspires teams with her technical skills, vision, high expectations, and decisiveness.

Even though Mayer and other introverted leaders are sometimes perceived as cold and detached, Cain's "quiet revolution" now challenges perceptions about introverts and their leadership capability. She answers the question of *why* they're so quiet by revealing the nature of introverts' thinking and decision making. Rather than being disconnected from group discussions, introverts prefer to think matters through before speaking up. They prefer quiet settings to noisy settings and take time making decisions rather than acting too quickly. Time with others can be exhausting; time alone recharges their energy. When introverts are in leadership positions, they are less likely to dominate the discussion but instead listen more closely to ideas. In fact, scholars have found that highly motivated teams produce better outcomes when leaders talk less and listen more (Grant, Gino, & Hofman, 2011).

Piero Oliosi/Polaris Images/Newscom

CHAPTER OUTLINE

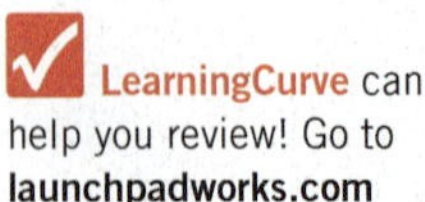

Through school, work, and community life, you've undoubtedly had experiences with various leaders. Some may have been loud and outspoken, while others were more quiet, leading by their actions. What all leaders have in common is the capacity to positively impact others around them. When it comes to small group communication, we define **leadership** as the ability to influence and direct others to meet group goals. Many small groups have a designated leader who has been appointed or otherwise chosen to serve in that position. However, even when a group has a designated leader, other members can still provide leadership within the group. That's because *the ability to influence and direct* stems from communication behaviors — which anyone in a group can either initiate or foster in others. Since no one person can provide a group with everything it needs in all situations, other group members must also step up as leaders. With **shared leadership**, each group member has the capacity to influence and direct the group in achieving its goals (Pearce & Conger, 2002).

Developing your leadership capacity is certainly important for being a competent designated leader, but small groups benefit when all members possess and exercise leadership skills. In this chapter, you'll learn:

- Different perspectives on understanding leadership
- Ways to encourage productive communication in a group
- Strategies for leading group problem solving
- How to support effective group decision making
- Ideas for planning, running, and evaluating meetings

Perspectives on Leadership

> **Who are leaders? Are leaders born to lead, or are they created in crisis? Are they tough? Compassionate? Laid back? Powerful speakers? All of the above? By understanding how researchers study and view leadership, one thing becomes clear: leaders are not one thing but a mix of different communication skills and styles.**

Before exploring how leadership operates in groups, it is important to have a basic understanding of what leadership really is. Scholars have long explored questions about leadership: What personal qualities do effective leaders have? What distinctive behaviors do they demonstrate? Why do some leadership approaches work in some situations but not others? The research resulting from such questions reflects four primary ways to look at leadership — the traits view, the style view, the situational view, and the functional view. Together, these perspectives clarify what it means to be a leader in a variety of group situations.

Traits View

As the chapter opener stated, we often view leaders as having strong verbal skills. If someone asked you to identify other defining characteristics of

VARIATIONS IN LEADERSHIP STYLES

Examples of competent leaders abound in real life and in the media. Former PepsiCo CEO Indra Nooyi, activist and nonprofit founder Van Jones, and Ethiopian president Sahle-Work Zewde all carry themselves differently but still assert themselves as strong leaders. Their different but effective leadership styles exemplify the notion that there is no one formula for being a successful leader.

Rick Davis/Splash News/Newscom; REUTERS/Jonathan Ernst; Tom Maruko/Pacific Press/Alamy Stock Photo

a good leader, you might say things like "smart," "decisive," "sociable," and maybe even "physically attractive" or "tall." A **traits view of leadership** assumes that all talented leaders share certain personal and physical characteristics. For instance, a CareerBuilder.com interview with business professionals suggested that effective leaders are honest, passionate, confident, caring, engaging, humble, fearless, genuine, and supportive (Farrell, 2011). Other studies have shown that in the business world, successful leaders possess drive, knowledge of the business, self-confidence, and integrity (Kirkpatrick & Locke, 1991).

Although the traits view helps us think about the desirable qualities we look for in leaders, a person who has the "right" leadership traits may still not perform well as a leader. For example, extraversion (being sociable and outgoing) is a quality found in many leaders (Judge, Ilies, Bono, & Gerhardt, 2002). But an extravert who is unable to make decisions may have trouble being a group leader. Similarly, as the chapter opener points out, it's just as likely that a person who is quiet or shy—traits not normally associated with leaders—could be a valuable leader if he or she has expertise crucial to the group's goals. Friendliness and attention to detail are important traits for leading teams on routine tasks, but creative and dynamic work teams need leaders who are imaginative and open to taking risks (De Hoogh, Den Hartog, &

Koopman, 2005). It's important to remember that the traits view is useful for describing qualities of effective leaders, and each member of a group may possess different traits that contribute leadership in certain situations.

Style View

The **style view of leadership** focuses on the distinctive behaviors leaders use to influence others. This perspective identifies three basic behavioral styles. Someone who exhibits an **autocratic leadership style** directs others, telling them what to do. Leaders displaying this style accept limited input from others in the group. Think of a community theater director. For each production, she might choose a script, cast actors in roles, and determine how the actors should interpret the script, with no input from anyone else. Although the cast members are critical for a production's success, the director retains ultimate authority over the play.

On the other end of the spectrum are leaders who provide little direction or structure to their teams. Their behavior reflects what is known as the **laissez-faire leadership style**. When leaders exhibit this style, the group maintains control of what happens. If the theater director has a laissez-faire leadership style, she might let cast members make production decisions, such as how the costumes will look or where each actor should stand during particular scenes (Kramer, 2006).

Finally, leaders who invite input from group members and encourage shared decision making are exercising a **democratic leadership style**. A theater director with a democratic style might start production planning by asking the cast and crew for ideas about set design and other matters related to the play. As the production unfolds, the director may remain open to suggestions and feedback.

The style view of leadership gives us a way to talk about leaders. For example, if you tell your dad that the new director is "really autocratic," he'll probably know what you mean. This view can also help you think about the type of leader you'd enjoy working with. Do you like a leader who is laid-back, forceful, or somewhere in between? If a leader is democratic in his or her approach, how does he or she handle a group that is reluctant to give input when planning an event? The style view provides a convenient vocabulary for describing leaders.

Like the traits view of leadership, the style view has limitations. First, it suggests that a leader's style is unchanging. But you may find yourself in some groups where you feel like you need to take charge and direct others (autocratic), and there may be other times when you want others to have more direction over you (democratic or laissez-faire). Moreover, the style view doesn't address the type of leadership that a group might need in certain situations. Sometimes groups may need more structured, autocratic leadership while other groups do not require such control. The situational view of leadership, which we cover next, can help us understand how leadership styles fit in with the needs of groups.

Situational View

Imagine a group that has been together for a long time and has a lot of experience with, say, raising funds for a local charity. The group would probably need a different style of leadership than a group with little experience or motivation. The **situational view of leadership** maintains that effective leadership is determined by the group's readiness to take on a task, including its motivation and individual group members' experience and knowledge (Hersey & Blanchard, 1988). A charity team that has just been assembled and that has little experience with fund-raising would benefit from a leader with a *telling*, or autocratic, style. The leader would need to establish structure, provide specific direction about the task, and give frequent feedback to the group about performance. When a group has a moderate degree of experience and motivation with fund-raising, a *selling* style might be the best leadership choice. The leader would give encouragement to group members while maintaining control over how the work is done. As experience and motivation with fund-raising increases within a group, a leader's style may become more *participating*, encouraging shared decision making and providing less specific direction. Finally, a team with a lot of fund-raising experience and motivation would likely require a leader who leads by *delegating*, whereby group members have complete responsibility for organizing and doing the work.

The situational view of leadership explains two important things. First, a leader must adapt his or her skills and style to fit the needs of the group. For example, an autocratic leadership style can be successful in some

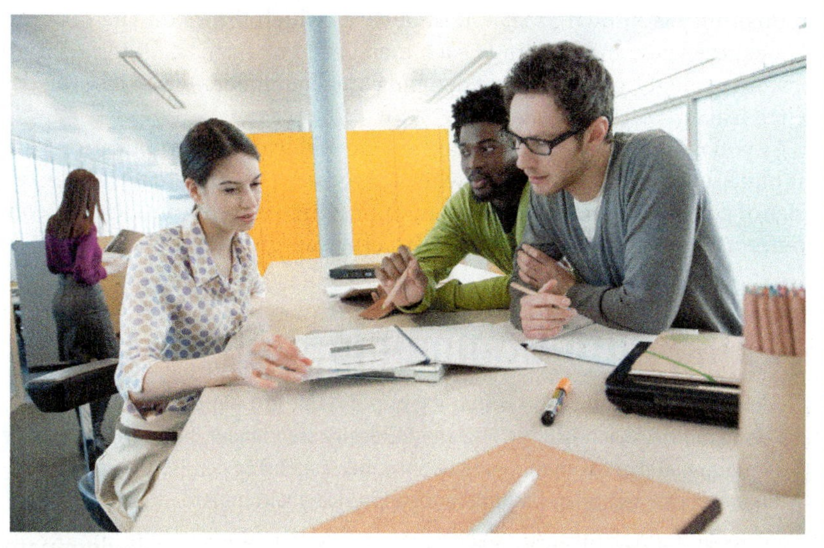

Eric Audras/ONOKY/Getty Images

The relationship you have with fellow group members is a big factor in deciding the most effective leadership style to use. Do you take charge differently with friends than you do with classmates? How do shared experiences and motivations affect the way you lead?

situations (if the group is new) and fail miserably in others (if members are used to having more control over tasks). Second, as Tuckman's model points out (Chapter 11), groups change over time as motivation fluctuates, conflicts occur, or members gain confidence with the task at hand. Effective leaders adapt their style to changing circumstances.

A limitation of the situational view is that — much like the traits and style views — it focuses on *characteristics* and *approaches* of individuals who are leading others. Each of these views asks a common question: What do effective leaders look like? But none of the three views can account for how *communication* helps a group share responsibility in leading the group. Instead, members in any small group can make contributions that help lead the group at a particular moment. The next view of leadership considers the role communication plays in influencing and directing groups.

Functional View

The **functional view of leadership** considers the types of communication behaviors that help a group work toward its goal (Morgeson, DeRue, & Karam, 2010). As Chapter 11 explains, in any group, some communication behaviors help get the job done (*task roles*), while others help build interpersonal bonds within the group (*maintenance roles*). In the functional view, all of these communication behaviors count as a form of leadership because they are all helping the group succeed. For example, if you volunteer to put together the slide deck for a group presentation, you are providing useful task leadership. If another group member steps in to help resolve a conflict between two team members, he or she is bringing valuable maintenance leadership to the group.

The functional view sees leadership as the responsibility of each group member rather than a quality that's inside a single person or position. This responsibility is known as *shared leadership*, which draws on the different skills, experiences, and talents of each member to manage tasks and relationships. Accordingly, group success depends on all members — not just the designated leader.

As you read the rest of this chapter, you will learn communication skills that build leadership capacity. So whether you are the appointed (or elected) leader of a group or simply a member, improving your communication competence in these areas will contribute to effective group leadership.

Leading with Communication

Competent communication within a group doesn't just happen; it takes work. This is not the responsibility of a single, designated leader, however. Instead, if all group members communicate openly and respond to conflicts competently, the group can create and maintain a supportive environment.

Chef Niki Nakayama knows pressure. As a female in the male-dominated culinary world, she has battled stereotypes and dismissive attitudes for over

20 years. A Japanese customer once left her sushi bar without eating, believing that she couldn't be making "real sushi" (Fontoura, 2014). Even Nakayama's family saw her culinary interest as a hobby rather than a career (Fontoura, 2014). But now foodies pay as much as $185 for a 13-small-course meal at her Los Angeles restaurant, n/naka. Considered to be the only female chef serving *kaiseki* — an ancient Japanese method of preparing carefully sequenced servings of light and heavy foods using seasonal ingredients — Chef Nakayama relies on a small team committed to delivering a high-quality dining experience.

Chef Nakayama inspires her team with her vision, coordinates various tasks, and, most important, creates a setting in which the team shares responsibility for serving uniquely tailored dishes for each guest. Her kitchen and serving team help in menu planning by keeping records of everything customers eat so that when they return to n/naka, they don't eat the same dish twice. Servers and kitchen staff have ongoing communication to maintain a rhythm to the meal, which can span over two hours. Working closely in leading the team is Carole Iida, who is also Chef Nakayama's wife. Chef Nakayama describes Iida as organized and attentive to details, unlike herself. The two women are partners both in the workplace and in life, and their skills complement one another. Together they lead a culinary team

The obstacles Chef Niki Nakayama faced in her culinary career did not diminish her ambition. At n/naka, Chef Nakayama (right) leads a team — including her wife, sous chef Carole Iida (left) — that must have impeccable communication, because they are responsible for creating a unique, "extraordinary" dining experience for each guest. Without strong leadership, even the most dedicated teams can struggle to complete a given task.

that one food critic described as "perfectly calibrated" and "extraordinary" (Rodell, 2013).

If you watch television shows like *Hell's Kitchen, The Great British Baking Show*, or *Cake Boss*, you know that culinary teams are unnecessarily stressed when their communication and leadership are poor. Whether it's a culinary team or any other group, competent leadership requires careful attention to maintaining satisfying relations among members while monitoring and evaluating progress toward completing the given task (Morgeson et al., 2010). To foster a satisfactory working relationship among members, group leaders should make every effort to support gender and cultural diversity, create a supportive climate, prevent groupthink (see page 297), and help group members constructively work through the conflicts that will inevitably arise.

Supporting Gender and Cultural Diversity

Gender and cultural differences within a team can make it challenging to work as a cohesive unit. Ignoring these differences — or worse, allowing stereotypes to guide your perception — will lead to poor communication, uneasiness, and a general lack of trust within a group (Phillips, 2014). For example, assumptions about appropriate gender behaviors can negatively affect perceptions of women and men in designated leader positions. When women leaders exhibit assertive and competitive behaviors, they risk being disliked (Koenig, Mitchell, Eagly, & Ristikari, 2011). On the other hand, men are perceived as weak leaders if they display qualities that are viewed as feminine, such as expressing empathy and vulnerability (Mayer, 2018). But as the traits view discussed earlier illustrates, there is no single set of characteristics that describes a competent leader. Qualities that are stereotypically labeled as "feminine" (empathy and vulnerability) or "masculine" (assertiveness and competitiveness) can all be important in providing competent leadership, regardless of the leader's gender.

Additional challenges surface when team members have cultural differences. Chapter 11 emphasizes how self-awareness can help you adapt your communication to differences related to *individualistic and collectivistic cultures*, *power distance*, and *uncertainty avoidance* in small groups. For example, a team member who insists on highly structured discussions might bother you, but it is possible that this team member may have higher uncertainty avoidance than you or other team members. Awareness of such differences can prevent you from expressing irritation and help you adapt your communication as needed. In a study of work teams in 80 countries, one thing was clear about leadership and culture: leaders who are friendly and attentive and who adapt to the needs of others promote higher team cohesion (Wendt, Euwema, & van Emmerik, 2009).

Finally, we can practice competent communication with people of different genders and cultures in three additional ways. First, we can simply recognize that a socially diverse team enhances creative and critical thinking about the task (Phillips, 2014). If group members are too similar in their life experiences, they are less likely to express alternative points of view. Second, we can express *empathy* (see Chapter 2) to experience issues from another person's point of view. This skill is especially important the more different a group member seems to you. Third, we can practice *world-mindedness* (see Chapter 3). Accept that others will express beliefs, values, and attitudes that may conflict with your own. Demonstrating respect for gender and cultural differences helps establish a supportive communication climate, which is discussed in detail in the next section.

Creating a Communication Climate

Take a moment to consider your recent experiences as a member of a group. What emotions did you have when you were with the group? Did you feel defensive and concerned about what the other members thought of your ideas? Did you feel supported, even when you disagreed with other group members? Your answers to these questions describe the group's **communication climate**, or the emotional tone established within the group (Forward, Czech, & Lee, 2011; Gibb, 1961). Every group develops a communication climate, and that climate influences all aspects of the group — from how productive the group is to how well its members get along.

The communication climate arises from the verbal and nonverbal messages group members exchange. For example, if members insult one another's ideas, promise to handle a task and then don't follow up, or gossip behind each other's backs, they create a *defensive communication climate*. In such a climate, team members see the group as threatening (Forward et al., 2011; Gibb, 1961). This can damage group cohesion.

In contrast, members of a group can create a *supportive communication climate* by exchanging respectful and supportive verbal and nonverbal messages. When groups communicate this way, they create an environment of *psychological safety* in which team members feel free to speak up and experience high levels of mutual respect and trust. This environment in turn allows members to focus on the ideas being expressed rather than the individuals expressing them (Forward et al., 2011; Edmondson & Lei, 2014). Even during disagreements, members of the team strive to generate ideas that everyone can support instead of shutting down conversations or taking sides in the dispute. To learn more about dealing with disagreements productively, see Advance the Conversation: Handling Complaints on pages 310–311.

TABLE 12.1

SUPPORTIVE AND DEFENSIVE COMMUNICATION

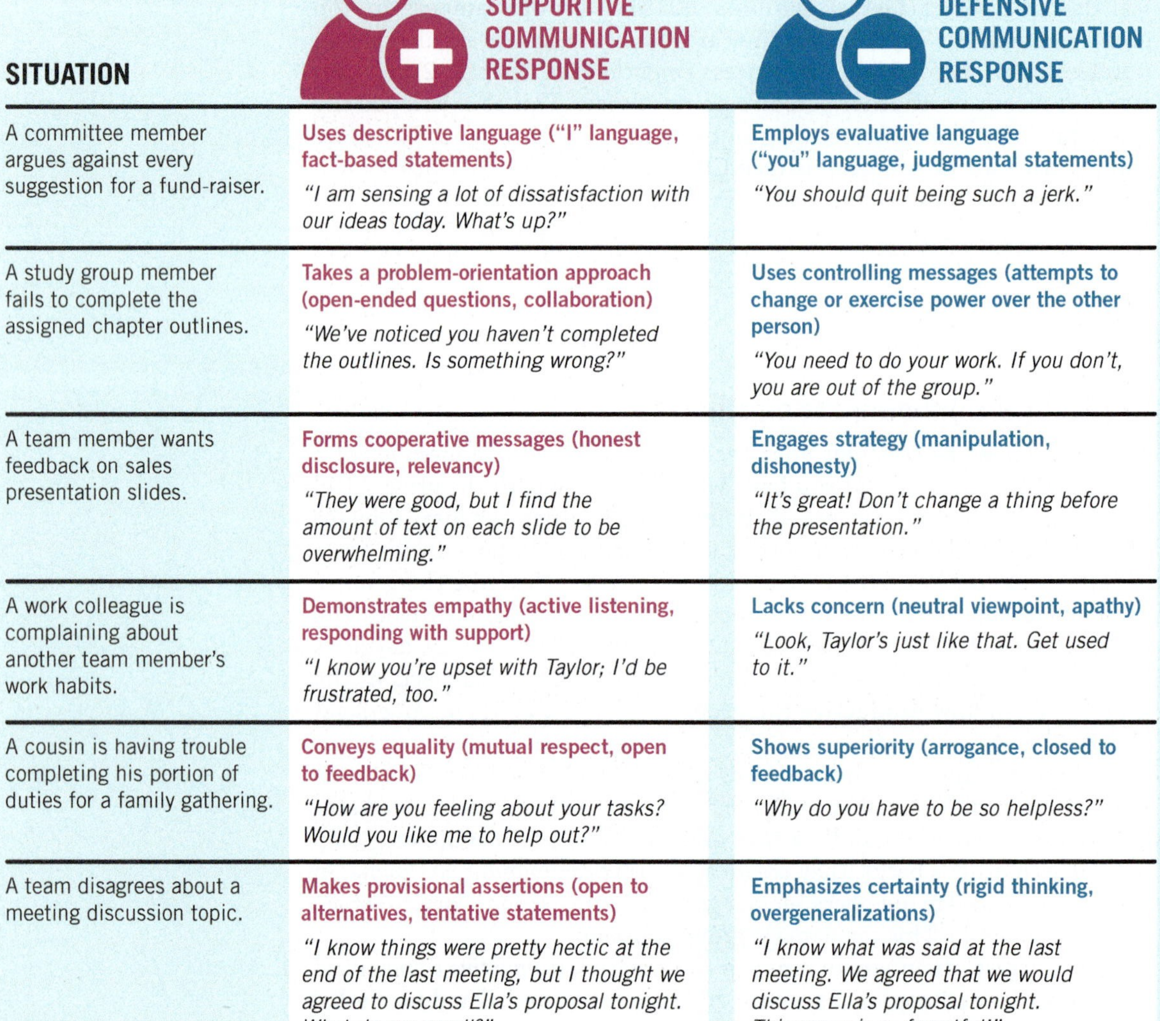

SITUATION	SUPPORTIVE COMMUNICATION RESPONSE	DEFENSIVE COMMUNICATION RESPONSE
A committee member argues against every suggestion for a fund-raiser.	**Uses descriptive language ("I" language, fact-based statements)** *"I am sensing a lot of dissatisfaction with our ideas today. What's up?"*	**Employs evaluative language ("you" language, judgmental statements)** *"You should quit being such a jerk."*
A study group member fails to complete the assigned chapter outlines.	**Takes a problem-orientation approach (open-ended questions, collaboration)** *"We've noticed you haven't completed the outlines. Is something wrong?"*	**Uses controlling messages (attempts to change or exercise power over the other person)** *"You need to do your work. If you don't, you are out of the group."*
A team member wants feedback on sales presentation slides.	**Forms cooperative messages (honest disclosure, relevancy)** *"They were good, but I find the amount of text on each slide to be overwhelming."*	**Engages strategy (manipulation, dishonesty)** *"It's great! Don't change a thing before the presentation."*
A work colleague is complaining about another team member's work habits.	**Demonstrates empathy (active listening, responding with support)** *"I know you're upset with Taylor; I'd be frustrated, too."*	**Lacks concern (neutral viewpoint, apathy)** *"Look, Taylor's just like that. Get used to it."*
A cousin is having trouble completing his portion of duties for a family gathering.	**Conveys equality (mutual respect, open to feedback)** *"How are you feeling about your tasks? Would you like me to help out?"*	**Shows superiority (arrogance, closed to feedback)** *"Why do you have to be so helpless?"*
A team disagrees about a meeting discussion topic.	**Makes provisional assertions (open to alternatives, tentative statements)** *"I know things were pretty hectic at the end of the last meeting, but I thought we agreed to discuss Ella's proposal tonight. What do you recall?"*	**Emphasizes certainty (rigid thinking, overgeneralizations)** *"I know what was said at the last meeting. We agreed that we would discuss Ella's proposal tonight. This group is so forgetful!"*

VoodooDot/Shutterstock

You can provide leadership in a group by creating an open exchange of ideas among group members and encouraging constructive rather than destructive communication. For a comparison of supportive and defensive communication behaviors, see Table 12.1. To foster a supportive communication climate in a group, focus on mastering the behaviors described in the middle column and avoiding the defensive behaviors listed in the last column.

Preventing Groupthink

Chapter 11 notes that a key feature of small groups is the degree of *cohesiveness*, or sense of unity, a team achieves. When a group has trouble building cohesiveness, members may not feel committed to the group's tasks or to one another (Aubert & Kelsey, 2003). As a result, they may not follow through on assigned tasks or help out other group members. But *too* much cohesiveness can be just as risky because group members may hesitate to critically evaluate one another's ideas and decisions. In an overly cohesive group, people want to maintain harmony more than anything else, so they avoid challenging one another's ideas, a phenomenon known as **groupthink** (Janis, 1982). Highly cohesive groups become particularly vulnerable to groupthink when they have a long history of success, are under time pressure, or have a high-status or particularly persuasive individual on their team. In the interest of not rocking the boat, group members hold back potentially conflicting opinions and information. This prevents the group from gathering the diverse views and knowledge it needs to make smart decisions.

Though all groups need cohesion, leaders must also look for and promptly address symptoms of groupthink (Janis, 1982). When groupthink occurs, members may believe that the group is invincible and can do no wrong. They may come to quick agreement on decisions and ignore information or opinions that go against what has been decided. Or members may put pressure on dissenters to "just go along" — for example, by staring disapprovingly at someone who questions a decision or telling the person to "let it go."

If a team seems to be slipping into groupthink, leaders need to take action — fast. The following steps can help:

1. *Encourage input from everyone.* Ask all members to contribute ideas and opinions. Pay particular attention to quiet members, who may be reluctant to express their feelings ("Peter, you haven't said much; what do you think about this idea?").
2. *Appoint a devil's advocate.* Have someone in the group take responsibility for expressing dissenting points of view ("I sense we're all ready to move on this, but what are the potential drawbacks of this decision?").
3. *Delay the decision.* If at all possible, encourage the group to take time to gather more information or to reflect on the decision in question before committing to a final course of action ("I don't feel comfortable deciding on this until we see more data").

Dealing with Conflict

Just as in any interpersonal relationship, conflict is an inevitable part of working in teams. Small groups experience two forms of conflict. **Substantive conflict** revolves around disagreements about the group's tasks, procedures, or decision options (Rahim, 2002). **Affective conflict** stems from interpersonal, gender, or cultural differences between members; power struggles; or simply bad feelings (Rahim, 2002). A moderate amount of substantive conflict can help prevent groupthink, but when groups experience too much substantive conflict or get embroiled in affective conflict, it's time for a group member to assume leadership and manage the situation.

As noted in Chapter 10, there are several possible approaches to dealing with conflict. Choosing the right approach depends on the nature and severity of the conflict. In situations involving unethical behaviors or clearly "right" courses of action, consider using a *competitive* approach, in which you pursue your own goals to the exclusion of others (Rahim, 2002). For example, your class group might want to ignore an assignment requirement they think is "unimportant." Rather than avoiding a conflict and going along with the group, a leader using a competitive approach would openly listen to the group but ultimately insist that the assignment requirement be met.

In instances with too much substantive or affective conflict, a *collaborative* approach may be best. This approach gives everyone a say in the resolution, so they tend to view the outcome as fair. Taking a collaborative approach to managing a conflict involves applying the following practices:

- Focus on common ground rather than proving who's right ("Gina and Yasmine, you both care about meeting the deadline; you're just disagreeing about how to get there").
- Use *active listening skills* from Chapter 7 by asking questions and paraphrasing what you've heard someone else say ("So, Martin, it sounds like you're concerned that this option is going to cost too much. Is that correct?").
- State your point of view clearly, using "I" and "we" language" ("I'm not comfortable with this plan because it lacks specifics. Can we take time to talk more about who's responsible for getting the supplies?").
- Be congruent in your verbal and nonverbal messages ("I'm not comfortable with this plan") rather than sending mixed messages ("This plan has problems, but if everyone else is OK with it, I guess we can do that . . .").
- Stick to the issue at hand, and avoid bringing up unrelated matters ("We need to stay focused on the problems in the plan").

In general, avoiding a conflict is not productive unless the issue is insignificant ("You're sitting in my chair!").

ADVANCE THE CONVERSATION

THE BEARER OF BAD NEWS

1 YOUR DILEMMA

"We nailed it!" Clayton exclaims as the team exchanges enthusiastic nods and smiles. As the outreach director for the Silver City Parks Department, you and three local college interns—Desiree, Clayton, and JC—just finished presenting to department staff a website redesign to market after-school recreation programs.

You think back to the interns' first week together. At that time, you weren't sure they would ever be a cohesive team. Clayton was outgoing but self-absorbed. Desiree—although shy—came highly recommended by her graphic design teacher. JC was ambitious but preoccupied with family troubles. You invested a lot of time getting the students to work as a team, and the website redesign played a key role in bringing them together.

"Do you think the staff liked the design?" JC asks.

"Hard to tell," you reply, "but I meet with Mr. Jackson on Monday. I'll let you know what he says."

Monday morning brings bad news. "The staff hated it," Mr. Jackson tells you in his office. "Here's a list of things you need to fix ASAP before the site goes live." When you tell Mr. Jackson that the interns are now on spring break, he replies, "Not a problem. Have Hernandez help you."

"But the students put a lot of time into the design. I'd like to . . ." you begin to protest. Mr. Jackson interrupts, "Send them an email. Tell them it was a good effort, but we're going in a different direction. It happens." Stunned and angry, you leave the office.

→ **What responsibility do you have to immediately share the feedback with your interns?**

2 CONNECT THE RESEARCH

Among the difficult tasks of a leader is giving feedback to group members about their work. In order to competently communicate unpleasant messages, a leader must balance two goals: (1) help group members maintain a positive face, and (2) convey trustworthiness. To do this, a leader should carefully consider how to form the message and which communication channel to use (Kingsley, Westerman, & Westerman, 2010).

Face-saving messages frame unpleasant messages in a way that softens the impact ("Perhaps the design expectations weren't entirely clear, but the new website design needs additional work"). Such messages are more likely to be perceived as nonthreatening than would a message that is too direct.

Second, the communication channel (face-to-face or online) matters. When leaders give unpleasant feedback in person, they are seen as more competent, and the message is perceived as less threatening. This may be because face-to-face communication includes nonverbal cues that are important for empathic concern and for giving the recipient an opportunity to ask clarifying questions.

→ **What are the potential consequences if you share the feedback with the students via email? What do you risk by waiting until they return from spring break?**

3 YOUR OPPORTUNITY

Before you act, consider the facts of the situation and think about the research on managing impressions and communication channels. Also, reflect on what you've learned so far about leadership styles (p. 290) and communication climates (p. 295–297).

→ **Now it's your turn. Write out a response to the interns. Be sure to specify which communication channel you are using.**

Leading Problem Solving

A common reason for being part of a small group is to solve a problem. But even with such a direct task, groups still need leaders to provide structure to the process. To lead a group in problem solving, you need to fully understand the problem and thoughtfully consider all possible solutions.

If you've ever had a magnetic resonance imaging scan (MRI), you know how disturbing it can be to lie perfectly still in a dark tunnel while a very large and loud machine scans images of your body. Now imagine the procedure from a child's point of view. Although parents go to great lengths to reduce the child's fears ("It won't hurt," "I'll be here the whole time with you"), it can still be a terrifying experience for a young patient. Doctors often calm children by sedating them, which increases the risk of medical complications. General Electric (GE) — a producer of MRI equipment — tackled the problem of how to make the procedure less frightening and reduce the need for medical sedation.

With that goal in mind, a GE team met with child development experts, music therapists, and even child museum curators to redesign the MRI experience (Kapsin & Hess, 2013; Kelley & Kelley, 2012). Out of dozens of meetings spanning several months, the team created story-themed imaging rooms. Instead of a cold and scary medical procedure, pediatric patients are invited into fully scripted deep-sea dive or pirate ship adventures. The MRI technicians assume roles as adventure guides, following carefully crafted scripts ("We need your help in trying to find the treasure chest").

Known as the GE Adventure Series, the redesign of the MRI experience for children has substantially reduced the need for sedation and has led to higher parent satisfaction ratings (Kapsin & Hess, 2013). Encouraged by this success, GE has begun to implement the design in hospitals around the nation.

Small groups organize for lots of different purposes, including sharing information, providing support or services to others, and — like the General Electric team — solving a specific problem. A *problem* is a gap between a current situation (children fear MRI procedures, and often need to be sedated) and a desired condition (reduce the need to sedate MRI pediatric patients). Some problems require only an individual with the right expertise working alone — like a qualified mechanic fixing a car. Other problems are more complex — like how to make the MRI experience less scary for children. Addressing these complex problems requires the collective thought and input of a team. Problem-solving teams generally use two approaches when searching for a solution: structured problem solving and group brainstorming.

Structured Problem Solving

Groups use a *structured approach* to examine and solve a problem. This helps groups maintain a focused and orderly discussion about the problem. To apply the **structured problem-solving approach**, teams collect information

DOUBLE TAKE

PROBLEMS VS PROBLEM SOLVING

These pictures illustrate how successful, collaborative problem solving at General Electric has improved the way children experience an MRI procedure. What other situations can you think of in which groups using the problem-solving method completely changed a situation for the better?

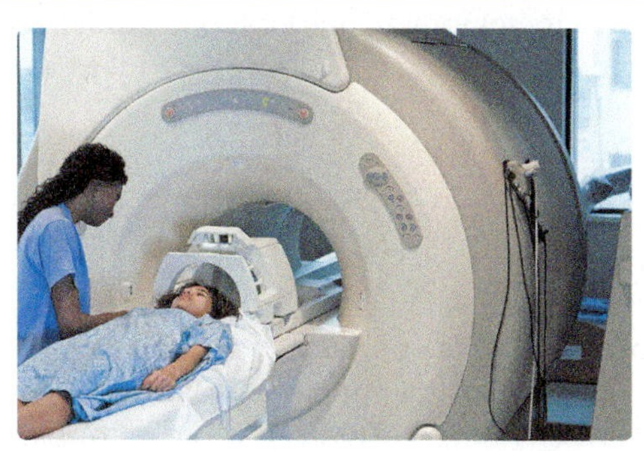

Erproductions/Ltd./Blend Images/Corbis

GE Healthcare

on the nature and scope of the problem facing them. Then they systematically search for a solution (Dewey, 1933). Although there is some variation to this method, a structured approach generally follows these steps:

1. *Define and analyze the problem.* Gather information to understand the nature, scope, causes, and effects of the problem. The General Electric team did this when it gathered information from child development and museum specialists. Group leaders are responsible for making sure the team gathers enough information about the problem and critically analyzes that information.
2. *Establish criteria for a solution.* Define the criteria that an acceptable solution must meet. For example, what is the deadline? What results must the solution produce? What is the maximum cost the solution can incur? The General Electric team identified "reduce need for sedation" as a criterion for its solution.
3. *Generate possible solutions.* Suggest a number of potential solutions. If necessary, conduct additional research to understand how similar problems have been solved. More research can also shed light on unintended consequences of the solutions your group is considering. To design the Adventure Series, the General Electric team identified and analyzed many different sketches and story ideas.
4. *Choose the best solution.* Using the solution criteria and the discussion about possible solutions, identify the solution that seems optimal.

Watch out for overly quick agreement on a solution; this could suggest that your team is falling victim to groupthink.

5. *Implement the solution, and evaluate the results.* Try out the solution, and assess the results to determine whether it is effectively solving the problem. Don't assume that just because a solution is in place the work is done. The General Electric team tested its solution in one location — Children's Hospital of Pittsburgh — and then continued refining its ideas as it expanded into other medical facilities.

Group Brainstorming

Through **group brainstorming**, a team focuses on generating as many ideas as possible to solve a defined problem. This approach is often integrated with step 3 of the structured problem-solving process described in the *structured approach* section. Brainstorming is also used when an outside person or organization asks a group for input in solving a problem. For example, a college administrator may attend a student organization meeting to seek ideas for increasing student participation in a semiannual blood drive. Brainstorming can help groups think creatively when coming up with solutions. First introduced in his book *Applied Imagination*, advertising executive Alex Osborn (1953) provided four guidelines for effective brainstorming:

- *Encourage wild ideas.* Even far-fetched ideas can spark creative, workable solutions. For example, during a brainstorming session about increasing campus blood-drive participation, one student might suggest a vampire theme, including a live bat exhibit.
- *Avoid judging ideas.* Strive to generate as many ideas as possible without judging them. Premature judging — "That's crazy; don't you know bats carry diseases?" — can discourage group members from offering additional thoughts that could be valuable. In brainstorming, the goal is to keep coming up with suggestions.
- *Quantity is important.* The more ideas a group can generate, the greater raw material it has as the basis for designing a good solution.
- *Combine and elaborate on ideas.* Blend together ideas offered by group members, and build on them to generate new ideas. For instance, another student might build on the vampire theme by recommending that the blood drive be scheduled in late October to include a Halloween theme (minus the live bats!).

Building on Osborn's original recommendations, recent studies have shown that a group brainstorming session can be enhanced if the individual members write their ideas privately before the discussion and then post them for other teammates to view. This helps trigger additional thoughts in the other members, too, which they can contribute during the group brainstorming discussion (Brown & Paulus, 2002).

Group brainstorming does, however, have some limitations. If team members feel overwhelmed by the volume of ideas being offered, they may stop expressing their own ideas. Or if they're afraid others will judge them or their ideas, they may avoid making contributions. In some cases, individuals might just be lazy and let others do all the thinking (Sawyer, 2007).

If you're leading or taking part in a brainstorming group, you can help combat these potential downfalls. How? Share Osborn's four guidelines with the entire group before starting a brainstorming session. If you hear any criticism occurring during a brainstorming session, remind group members that the goal is to generate lots of ideas *without judging them.* Finally, encourage all members to participate to avoid *social loafing* during the session.

Leading Decision Making

Small groups make tons of decisions—everything from who should be in the group to how to achieve its goals. How do members make such decisions? Should the leader decide for everyone? Should there be a vote? Or should the group discuss choices until everyone agrees? Depending on the group's goals, the leadership style, and the decision being made, it could be any of these options.

It was a simple ad with a big impact. The 2013 NFL Super Bowl came to a screeching halt when the power went out in the New Orleans Superdome. As players, coaches, sportscasters, and fans were left idling for 34 agonizing minutes, the social media team for Oreo went to work. Seizing the opportunity to create a timely and relevant ad, the 15-person group created, approved, and posted an image of an Oreo cookie to Twitter with this simple caption: "Power out? No problem. You can still dunk in the dark" (Watercutter, 2013). The group did all this in about 10 minutes—an exceptionally fast turnaround in terms of designing and publishing an ad. The team was able to move so quickly because the designated leaders—in this case, brand managers for Oreo—made fast and firm decisions, enabling the rest of the team to execute the plan immediately. The result was a highly regarded and memorable ad—and proof that a group with clear decision-making processes can achieve great success.

Small groups make a series of decisions at various points in their work together. Everything from deciding when the group should meet to determining whether to sign an agreement is subject to **decision making**—the process of making choices among alternatives. Groups commonly rely on three methods for decision making: decision by authority, decision by vote, and decision by consensus.

The quick decisions made by the marketing team at Nabisco allowed the company to capitalize on an "at the moment" event during the Super Bowl XLVII blackout.

Oreo Cookie
@Oreo
Follow
Power out? No problem. pic.twitter.com/dnQ7pOgC
1:48 AM - 04 Feb 13
YOU CAN STILL DUNK IN THE DARK
16,071 RETWEETS 6,182 FAVORITES
Considered the most creative response to the blackout, the ad's simple coloring mimicked what was happening at the game.
Datasift.com said the ad reached a potential audience of 13.3 million, making it hugely successful for a tweet.

Decision by Authority

Some groups use *decision by authority*, in which an expert or a designated leader makes decisions on behalf of the group. Relying on an authority is appropriate when a group must make a decision quickly or when an individual member has expertise that's especially critical for solving the problem at hand. For example, emergency-department physicians determine treatment priorities for incoming patients, while nurses and other support staff follow those decisions and provide little or no input. Decision by authority also can be suitable when the matter to be decided is of little consequence ("What food should we order for the lunch meeting?").

However, this method has its drawbacks. For example, team members who disagree with a decision may feel pressured to go along with it. If a team member sees serious flaws in the thinking behind a decision but doesn't speak up loudly enough, disaster can result. If you are leading a group and making a decision by authority, it is still helpful to listen to any questions or concerns of your group members to ensure that your decision is as informed as possible.

Decision by Vote

To use the *decision by vote* method, leaders identify two or more options, and all members of the group vote or poll the members. In most groups, the option that receives the most votes is declared the winner. This is a common and familiar way to make decisions in groups. Since leaders pick only a few choices for members to vote on, this method can be efficient—particularly in larger groups, in which discussion of various options can take up a lot of time. However, this is not a good approach to use when a group needs to make a quick decision, as in the situation the Oreo branding team faced during the Super Bowl.

One possible consequence of using this approach is that voting divides a group into winners and losers. Those who voted for an option that "lost" may feel that they wasted their time or that their input wasn't valued.

Therefore, they may not feel committed to following through on what the group decided.

Decision by Consensus

When a group is responsible for not only making a decision but also putting that decision into action, leaders may want to strive for *decision by consensus*. Achieving **consensus** on decisions means that all members support a given course of action. For example, your class group may be picking a service-learning project to complete as part of a course requirement. Rather than risk fragmenting the group by voting, a consensus decision secures all group members' commitment to the chosen project. Even group members who have concerns about the decision will still support it (Johnson & Johnson, 2008). In most cases, groups that decide by consensus report greater member satisfaction with the decision than groups relying on majority rule (Sager & Gastil, 2006). This happens because the discussion encourages input from all group members and helps build cohesiveness in a team.

To promote decision by consensus, leaders must encourage open discussion. It takes considerable time to get everyone to agree on a course of action, but the resulting group cohesiveness is well worth it. To help set group members' expectations, leaders should clearly explain that decisions will be made by consensus (Sager & Gastil, 1999). Team members, for their part, must strive to actively listen to all ideas as they are proposed. Leaders should also make sure that team members don't feel pressured to simply go along with the group. Saying something like, "If anyone here feels uncomfortable with the decision we're moving toward, please speak up and let us know your concerns. We want everyone's input here," will help minimize that outcome.

Each decision-making approach has its pros and cons and is best used under specific circumstances. Regardless of which approach is used, it's important for the leader to clarify the approach for the group. Otherwise, leaders' actions can sometimes seem arbitrary and unpredictable, which can erode group morale and satisfaction.

Leading Meetings

> **Small groups do much of their work in face-to-face and virtual meetings. But when meetings are poorly planned or managed, people get frustrated, and time is wasted. When leading a group, you can ensure that meetings run smoothly by developing an agenda, encouraging participation during meetings, and following up afterward.**

Have you ever sat in a meeting that had no apparent purpose? What about a meeting in which people talked on and on about a topic but never arrived at a decision, or a meeting that got derailed by one person and never got back on track? If you've had these experiences, you're not alone. Although meetings are critical for conducting group work, all too many are hugely unproductive.

What are the culprits behind such meetings? Studies of business professionals identify these common meeting problems: (1) participants get off subject, (2) there is no clear agenda, (3) meetings take too long, (4) team members come unprepared, and (5) no definitive action is taken after the meeting (Romano & Nunamaker, 2001; Allen et al., 2012). To combat these problems and get the most out of group meetings, leaders must take responsibility for planning, conducting, and following up on/evaluating meetings.

MEETINGS GONE WRONG

Whether it's because they're out of touch, bad-tempered, or just plain bizarre, the leaders in *Superstore*, *Brooklyn Nine-Nine*, and *Silicon Valley* demonstrate how meetings with coworkers or team members can go wrong. When you are leading a meeting or a group discussion, what factors are most important for making sure it goes well?

(Clockwise from top left) NBC/Photofest; 3 Arts/Judgemental Inc/Kobal/Shutterstock; Fox Broadcasting/Photofest

Planning Meetings

Like speeches, the most useful meetings begin with a plan. What is the first step in that plan? Defining the purpose of the meeting. Meetings that don't have a clear purpose waste everyone's time. Teams meet for many different purposes. In *information briefings*, participants get updated on key developments of an event or a situation. For example, Joe's oldest son attends monthly sales meetings at his job to learn about new products and sales incentives. *Problem-solving meetings* address an undesirable situation, such as when microchip engineers gather to analyze defects in their company's manufacturing process and generate ideas for remedying the problem. *Decision-making meetings* entail making a choice about something, such as when your French club meets to choose a date for the annual picnic.

Most meetings incorporate a bit of all three — information briefing, problem solving, and decision making — though one of these purposes may be paramount. Whatever the purpose, identifying it (or them) helps leaders develop the **meeting agenda** — a structured, written outline that guides communication among meeting participants by showing which topics will be discussed, in what order, and (often) for how long. Without an agenda, team members may start talking about different subjects at the same time or go off on tangents. (See Table 12.2 for a sample meeting agenda.)

Identifying a meeting's purpose and developing an agenda help leaders decide who should attend the meeting and what materials participants will need to prepare for and take part in the meeting. Leaders can then make sure to distribute in advance any readings, reports, or other materials that will be discussed in the meeting, so participants can come prepared.

Conducting Meetings

If you're conducting a meeting, start by clarifying its purposes and anticipated outcomes. Ensure that participants are acquainted with one another and that they understand each member's role and responsibilities. If you're conducting a virtual meeting by videoconference or telephone, make sure to introduce everyone involved so that all participants know who is attending and can identify anyone who speaks.

In addition, carefully manage the group's communication so that everyone sticks to the agenda. If the discussion starts veering away from the agenda, redirect attention back to the plan. Watch or listen for people who are dominating the discussion, and encourage quieter members to provide their input. Pay attention to how much time the group is spending on each agenda item, and keep the discussion moving forward so that all items get covered. If a particular task needs more detailed conversation, suggest covering it in a separate meeting. Designated meeting leaders ensure a satisfying meeting experience by encouraging the group to help manage the

TABLE 12.2

SAMPLE MEETING AGENDA

STUDENT LEADERSHIP TEAM

Monday, November 3
2:00–3:00 pm
Location: South Conference Room 211

ITEM	PERSON RESPONSIBLE	REQUIRED ACTION	TIME
1. Discuss personal reflection on last month's service project.	All	None	15 minutes
2. Decide on two applications for new student organizations.	Jean	Vote	20 minutes
3. Brainstorm spring retreat locations.	Jean	Identify top two, and assign person to conduct research to present at next meeting.	20 minutes
4. Confirm time and place for next meeting.	Sarah	Follow-up email with reminder about time and place.	5 minutes

discussion (Lehmann-Willenbrock, Allen, & Kauffeld, 2013). Group members can do this by keeping track of time, speaking up when the discussion gets off topic, and offering to take notes.

Finally, end the meeting by summarizing key decisions, identifying actions that must be taken, and clarifying who will be responsible for carrying out those actions. Taking time to do this is a type of *perception-checking* (Chapter 2), which clarifies points of confusion or misinterpretation.

Following Up On/Evaluating Meetings

Once a meeting ends, team members tend to go about their personal and work lives. They may forget all about the action items and decisions that came out of the meeting. To counteract this tendency, follow up on agreed-upon actions, and evaluate the outcome of the meeting.

Within 24 hours of a meeting, send a written record of the discussion, actions, and decisions — often called the **meeting minutes** — to everyone who attended the meeting as well as anyone who needs to know what happened. Include any information that was missing from the meeting or materials that were requested during the meeting.

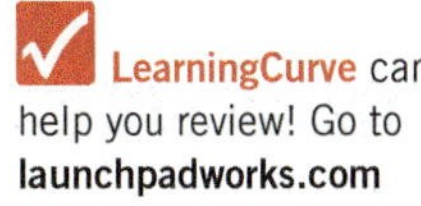

LearningCurve can help you review! Go to **launchpadworks.com**

Then spend some time reflecting on what worked well in the meeting and what could be improved upon at the next meeting. For example, did a number of people come to the meeting unprepared because they didn't have enough time to review the materials you sent ahead of time? If so, consider sending required reading even earlier the next time.

ADVANCE THE CONVERSATION
Video Activity

HANDLING COMPLAINTS

The following scenario will enhance your ability to communicate competently with a team member who has a negative attitude. Visit LaunchPad at launchpadworks.com to get the full experience with video. As you watch the first video, recall what you've learned about creating a supportive communication climate and dealing with conflict in a group. Then complete the **Your Turn** prompts. Finally, watch the **Take Two!** video to explore how this scenario could have gone differently.

1 THE PROBLEM

Danielle is leading a group at work that is in charge of launching a new line of juices targeted at busy moms. This is her first leadership position at work, and there have been a lot of delays in the project, which is stressing Danielle and her teammates. During a weekly status meeting, the team is trying to decide which juice flavors they should use at launch. Danielle goes over the data they have and then makes a suggestion, to which Tim, another group member, responds negatively.

"What about another market test for the multiberry?"

"We've been going back and forth on these berry flavors for months. It's a waste of time to do more analysis, especially since I've done a lot of work on this and you've completely ignored it!"

2 YOUR TURN

Observations. Reflect on how Danielle and Tim communicated in this scenario by answering the following questions:

1. Which character do you identify with more in this situation? How would you feel if you were in his or her situation?
2. Where were the missed opportunities to practice competent communication?

Discussion. In class or with a partner, share your thoughts about the interaction between Danielle and Tim and work to answer the following questions:

1. Can you understand both perspectives?
2. What could Tim and Danielle have done differently?

Conclusion. Choose one person in the scenario to offer your advice. Based on your analysis, what advice would you give him or her to improve his or her communication competence in this scenario?

3 TAKE TWO!

What if things had gone differently? Watch the **Take Two!** video to see one possible example of how the conversation might have gone if Tim and/or Danielle had communicated differently. As you watch the video, consider where the dialog reflects communication competence. After watching the video, answer the questions below:

1. Did Tim and/or Danielle take advantage of opportunities that they missed in the first scenario? Which ones?
2. Did their different actions result in a more productive encounter? Please explain.

CHAPTER 12 REVIEW

CHAPTER RECAP

- Scholars generally agree on four leadership perspectives—the **traits view**, the **style view**, the **situational view**, and the **functional view**—to help clarify how leadership works in small groups.
- In addition to establishing a **communication climate**, productive leaders help prevent **groupthink** and deal with **substantive** and **affective conflict** in a group.
- Two of the most common approaches used for solving problems in groups are **structured problem solving** and **group brainstorming**.
- Groups commonly rely on three methods for **decision making**: decision by authority, decision by vote, and decision by consensus.
- To get the most out of group meetings, leaders must take responsibility for planning, conducting, and following up on/evaluating meetings.

LaunchPad for *Choices & Connections* offers unique video scenarios and encourages self-assessment through adaptive quizzing. Go to **launchpadworks.com** to get access.

 LearningCurve adaptive quizzes

 Advance the Conversation video scenarios

 Video clips that illustrate key concepts

KEY TERMS

Leadership, p. 288
Shared leadership, p. 288
Traits view of leadership, p. 289
Style view of leadership, p. 290
Autocratic leadership style, p. 290
Laissez-faire leadership style, p. 290
Democratic leadership style, p. 290
Situational view of leadership, p. 291
Functional view of leadership, p. 292
Communication climate, p. 295
Groupthink, p. 297
Substantive conflict, p. 298
Affective conflict, p. 298
Structured problem-solving approach, p. 300
Group brainstorming, p. 302
Decision making, p. 303
Consensus, p. 305
Meeting agenda, p. 307
Meeting minutes, p. 309

POP QUIZ

Looking for more review questions? LearningCurve can help you master key concepts from this chapter. Go to **launchpadworks.com**

1. How does the concept of shared leadership apply to small group communication?
   a. It prevents groupthink.
   b. It reflects the traits view of leadership, since members have different skills.
   c. It allows all group members to influence and direct the group.
   d. It avoids affective conflict.

2. In the situational view of leadership, a group that has high amounts of motivation and experience may benefit the most from which leadership style?
   a. Telling
   b. Participating
   c. Delegating
   d. Selling

3. A potential outcome of a defensive communication climate within a group is
   a. the avoidance of destructive communication.
   b. a weakening of group cohesion.
   c. a demonstration of empathy.
   d. the formation of cooperative messages.

4. Which of the following is *not* a step in the structured problem-solving approach?
   a. Evaluate the implemented solution.
   b. Establish criteria for a solution.
   c. Discuss possible solutions.
   d. Determine the cheapest solution.

5. A potential drawback to this type of decision is that members who lost may not feel committed to the group decision.
   a. Decision by vote
   b. Decision by consensus
   c. Decision by authority
   d. Decision by function

ACTIVITIES

For more activities, visit LaunchPad for *Choices & Connections* at **launchpadworks.com**

1 Leading Hollywood

Watch a film featuring strong leaders, such as *Selma*, *Lincoln*, *The Help*, *The Post*, or *The Devil Wears Prada*. How did the leaders in the film embody one or more of the views of leadership? Give specific examples. Did they adapt their styles to certain situations or people? How successful were their leadership styles? How do you think their leadership styles could be improved?

2 Practicing Problem Solving

Working with a small group of classmates, choose a campus problem—such as student parking, food services, or student health services—and apply the structured problem-solving approach to identify a potential solution. Share your solution with the rest of the class, and then analyze how well the group worked together using the structured problem-solving approach and what you would do differently in the future.

13

Preparing Your Speech

What needs to happen to get a speaker ready to step into the red circle? If you've watched a TED (Technology, Entertainment, Design) talk online, you may have noticed that presenters stand inside a red circle on a small stage when they present their speech. Getting ready to stand in that red circle involves rigorous preparation of the message to be communicated to the audience. Social scientist Noah Zandan describes preparing for his TED talk as a "long journey" where it's impossible to succeed by just "winging it."[1]

Zandan has always been passionate about human behavior, interested in how we act in different situations and why. In 2012 he founded Quantified Communications, a company that helps people improve their communication skills by using data to evaluate their speech and body language. When TED invited Zandan to give a talk, he was thrilled for the opportunity to share his research with a larger audience. He decided to focus his TED talk on how to effectively handle disagreements in close relationships—a topic with which he had considerable experience, and also one that he felt would interest his audience of diverse professionals at TED. He spent a few months researching and developing his talk, and then he went to New York for a rehearsal.

Rehearsing in front of approximately 20 TED employees, Zandan had to be open to feedback. When the TED team suggested that he take his topic (and all the preparation he had done) in a totally different direction, he was disheartened. But as Zandan observes, "Despite my own nerves and frustrations, this was an opportunity to trust the TED curation and coaching process, and to really think about what the audience (both live and on TED.com) could take away from my point of view."

The feedback prompted more brainstorming and discussion, which eventually led to his final presentation topic: how to speak like a visionary leader. Excited by this new direction, Zandan plunged himself into additional research, preparation, and rehearsal. He estimates that he spent over 300 hours preparing to step into that red circle.

Zandan's determination and careful preparation led to a presentation that supports TED's mission: "Ideas worth spreading." TED talks often go viral online, thanks in large part to the careful steps that TED presenters take to make their speeches as engaging as possible.

[1]Opener adapted from Zandan (2018).

Rose Palmisano/ZUMA Press/Newscom

41

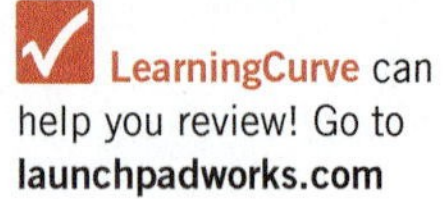
LearningCurve can help you review! Go to **launchpadworks.com**

Relatively few people deliver a TED talk, but in the course of your life, you will inevitably give presentations. Knowing how to properly prepare for such occasions will help you achieve success.

Public speaking is the process of preparing and delivering a message to an audience to achieve a specific purpose. Perhaps you'll deliver a project-status briefing in a Skype meeting with clients, or make a presentation asking a group of parents to volunteer for after-school activities at your child's school. At the very least, you will likely give a speech for this class. This idea makes many people nervous, even though the speech may be days or weeks away. Don't worry if you're feeling unsettled at the mere idea of giving a speech; even experienced TED presenters feel this way! We'll help out by discussing strategies for coping with public-speaking anxiety (pages 385–388). For now, try to relax, and take comfort in the fact that you already know many of the communication principles and skills that support strong speech preparation. In this chapter, you'll learn:

- The five steps of speech preparation
- How to select your speech topic
- Ideas for analyzing your audience and adapting your topic to them
- How to develop a strategy for researching your speech
- Ways to conduct your research and evaluate your resources

Preparing Your Speech: Five Steps

Think about the speeches you've heard during your lifetime. Some were probably very good, holding your interest and providing useful information. Some were probably not so good—perhaps they were boring or forgettable or both. What's the difference? Preparation. Public speakers who carefully prepare their speeches engage their audiences the most.

As TED talks demonstrate, skilled speakers carefully prepare their messages to engage and inspire their audiences. To do the same, follow the five steps of speech preparation: think, investigate, compose, rehearse, and revise. (See Table 13.1.)

First, **think** about your audience and speech topic. Determine the purpose of your speech, choose the topic, and consider how to adapt it to your audience. When working through this step, it will be important to develop *accurate perceptions*, or knowledge, of your listeners so that you can deliver an understandable speech.

Second, **investigate** resources to use in developing your presentation. This includes planning your research strategy, conducting your research, and evaluating the resources you find.

TABLE 13.1

FIVE STEPS IN SPEECH PREPARATION

THINK	**INVESTIGATE**	**COMPOSE**	**REHEARSE**	**REVISE**
Choose your topic, adapt to your audience	Plan your strategy, conduct your research, evaluate your sources	Develop your speech structure and supporting materials, prepare your visual aids	Create speaking notes, practice aloud, work on delivery	Process feedback from others and self-reflection, write a final outline and speaking notes

edel/Shutterstock

Third, **compose** your presentation, outlining your ideas and planning any visual support. You will prepare an introduction to capture your audience's attention, identify your main points, and decide how to conclude the speech. Successful public speakers use the *cooperative principle* (from Chapter 5) in preparing their message by making their words informative, honest, relevant, and clear. They also use "we" language to better connect to and build solidarity with their audience.

Fourth, **rehearse** your presentation. TED talks look easy because of the extensive time the presenters spend rehearsing. In this step, you practice your presentation on your own and in front of others, inviting feedback for improvements. This is also the time to work on your *nonverbal skills*—including eye contact, gestures, and facial expressions—to further engage your listeners.

Fifth, **revise** your presentation, adapting it based on the feedback you received while rehearsing. You can further improve your speech content and delivery by being *critically self-reflective*—honestly assessing your communication and considering ways to improve it. You can also use any feedback you receive after the presentation to prepare for your next public-speaking occasion.

In this chapter, we focus on the first two steps: *thinking about your speech* and *investigating your sources*. We discuss steps 3, 4, and 5 in Chapters 14–15.

Choosing Your Speech Topic

The first part of step 1: think is to identify why you are giving a speech and choose a speech topic. Although you will want to choose a topic that is appropriate for the situation, it should also be a topic that excites you. You will be spending a lot of time working on the speech, so you might as well enjoy the topic.

The chapter's opening story makes the point that TED presenters go to great lengths to prepare memorable presentations. Although the purpose of each presentation is to convey innovative ideas, a lot of things happen when you watch a TED talk. You may learn about new technologies and how they work. You may be entertained with musical performances or stories. A presenter may passionately argue that a new scientific advancement can change the way we live. But TED talks aren't random. They are guided by a clear sense of purpose.

Since its founding in 2006, the nonprofit organization charity:water has helped fund over 20,000 charitable projects in dozens of countries. Founder Scott Harrison is able to deliver powerful speeches to his audiences because he cares about helping people access clean water and feels a sense of purpose. When giving a speech, what topic would you speak about that would give you a similar sense of purpose?

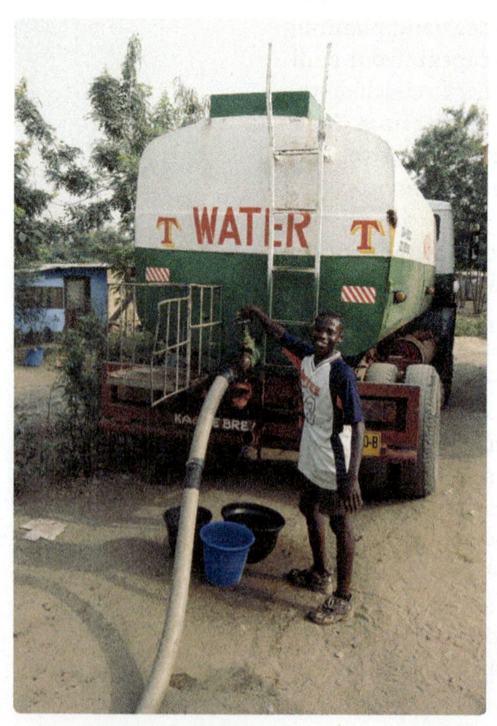

Jesper Jensen/Alamy Stock Photo

Similarly, Scott Harrison, the founder of charity:water, has a sense of purpose when he talks with audiences about clean water. Harrison was a successful New York nightclub promoter when he grew tired of his life of excess and felt he needed a change. He eventually began volunteering in Liberia aboard a floating hospital that offered free medical care. Seeing the hardship and disease caused by unclean water in Liberia and other countries, Harrison was moved to take action. He left his nightclub business to found charity:water, a nonprofit that supports drilling water wells and filtration in developing nations. Now he tells his personal story in presentations to persuade audiences of the importance of clean water and to move them to help those in need.[2]

What Scott Harrison and other competent public speakers have in common is a sense of purpose as they prepare their presentations. Your speech preparation begins in the same way: by thinking carefully about the general purpose of your speech and considering what topic to discuss.

[2] charitywater.org/about/mission.php

Identifying Your General Purpose

When preparing a speech, you should first determine your **general purpose**—your reason for giving the presentation. Speeches typically have one of three purposes:

1. *To inform* your audience. **Informative speeches** educate your audience about a topic, describe an object, demonstrate how something works, or explain a concept.
2. *To persuade* your audience. **Persuasive speeches** reinforce or change listeners' attitudes and beliefs and may motivate them to take certain actions.
3. To recognize or celebrate a *special occasion*. **Special-occasion speeches** entertain, celebrate, commemorate, or inspire. These include introducing someone at an event, accepting or giving an award, commemorating an event or a person, or giving a toast.

For the speeches you'll be giving in your communication course, your instructor will probably assign the general purpose. For example, he or she might require you to give an informative or a persuasive speech (or both). When you give speeches in other settings, you will determine your general purpose. For instance, suppose you work as a drug rehabilitation counselor. If you were going to talk to parents of high school students, you could plan an informative speech to explain the warning signs of teen drug use, since that topic would be of interest to the parents. But if you were speaking directly to the teens, you might adapt your plan to give a persuasive speech about why they should resist pressure to use illegal drugs.

However, your general purpose is not always so straightforward. Consider the technology company Apple, which often delivers presentations to inform audiences about new products (informative). Such presentations may include stories and music to entertain attendees (special-occasion), but the presentations are ultimately designed to promote the Apple brand (persuasive). Sometimes, like Apple, you may blend purposes.

Considering Speech Topics

Once you know the general purpose of your speech, it's time to choose your **speech topic**—the specific content you will present. In your course, the instructor may allow you to select a topic appropriate to the assignment. When you give a speech outside the classroom, the setting usually determines your topic. If you are invited to speak to student groups about competent conflict resolution, your topic is defined by the invitation; you can't show up and talk about how to design mobile apps instead!

When you have the freedom to choose your own topic, the choice can seem overwhelming. So how do you decide what to talk about? With some careful thought, you can come up with a topic that both interests you and will engage your audience. Let's explore three ways for coming up with topic ideas: reflecting on your personal interests and experiences, brainstorming, and developing a concept map.

Interests and Experiences. One of the first things to think about is what interests you. If you have a passion for a certain hobby, cause, or subject, that is a great place to start. Also consider personal experiences, such as vacations, jobs, or volunteer work. One of our students worked as a limousine driver and used his experience to prepare a speech on when and how to properly tip service workers.

Other ideas for speech topics can be drawn directly from your academic studies. For example, perhaps you learned about eating disorders or social media addiction in a psychology course. Your speech assignment provides the opportunity to share what you've learned with others.

Basing a speech topic on personal interests and experiences has some advantages. Your direct involvement gives you credibility with your audience and opportunities to tell engaging stories. If you feel passionately about your topic, you are more likely to inspire your audience. After all, when audience members see you excited about an issue or a hobby, they can't help but feel curious and interested, too.

Brainstorming. **Brainstorming** is a creative problem-solving strategy that involves coming up with as many ideas as possible in a defined period of time. This is similar to *group brainstorming*, which, as Chapter 12 discusses, is often used in small group communication settings. The most common approach to brainstorming is *freewriting*, or *listing ideas*: writing down all the ideas that come to mind, without judging them, during the allotted time—say, 15 minutes. Some experts maintain that the wilder the ideas are during the brainstorming period, the better the final ideas may be (Kelley & Littman, 2001). After the brainstorming period ends, review your list of ideas and eliminate any that don't interest you. Look over the remaining ideas to see which ones intrigue you the most. This shorter list provides a base for you to further develop your topic by narrowing broad interest areas into more specific ideas. For example, if your brainstorming list has *food* and *health*, you could think further along those lines to *fad diets*, *fast food*, *farm-to-table dining*, or *organic foods*.

Concept Map. Another way to explore ideas is by creating a **concept map**: a drawing showing connections among related ideas. A concept map helps you expand on one idea with more specific topics. (In contrast, brainstorming helps you generate multiple ideas.) If you came up with a broad topic that interests you during brainstorming but are having trouble narrowing it down, a concept map can help you be more specific. For instance, if you're interested in giving a speech about computers, your concept map may look something like Figure 13.1.

FIGURE 13.1

SAMPLE CONCEPT MAP

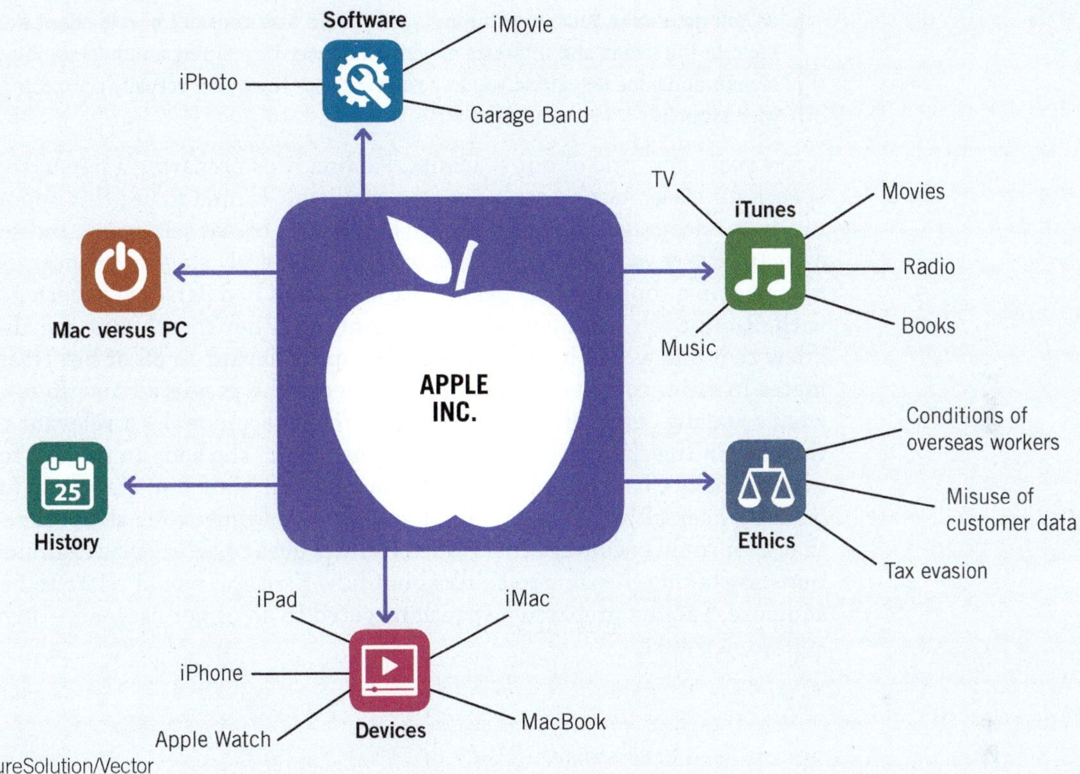

PureSolution/Vector

Deciding on Your Topic

After you identify a possible topic, ask yourself whether the topic could serve as the basis for a successful speech. The answer could be yes if you find the topic personally or socially important. You want to be interested in and challenged by the topic, since you'll be spending considerable time preparing your speech. You'll also want to consider whether you could complete your speech in the time allotted. For a classroom speech, check whether your topic is acceptable. Your instructor might veto your proposed topic if it's been overdone or is inappropriate (such as gun control, abortion, or the legalization of recreational marijuana).

Finally, think about whether you will be able to find quality information about your topic. Later in the chapter we cover how to research your topic, but it's important to think now about whether you'll be able to locate and use sources on your topic. If you have any doubts, check with a librarian or your instructor.

Analyzing Your Audience

As you determine your speech topic, you should also consider how to adapt the topic to the needs and interests of your audience. Developing an understanding of your audience will guide you in narrowing your topic and actually composing your speech.

A few years ago, one of our students, Paolina, was preparing a persuasive speech for class. As a breast cancer survivor, she wanted to use this opportunity to encourage women to engage in monthly breast self-exams and see a doctor every year, common ways to detect the early stages of cancer. By focusing on a topic she was passionate about and had personal experience with, Paolina felt confident about the content of her speech. But she also knew that she would have to make her topic relevant to all of her classmates in order to deliver a successful speech. She pondered how to take what's usually considered a women's health issue and make it relevant to the men in the class. While researching her topic, she kept an eye out for ways to make that connection and discovered that men, too, are at risk for breast cancer, although in smaller numbers than women. She also realized that men could encourage the women in their lives to get regular examinations. By taking the time to think about how her topic would relate to her audience, Paolina prepared a speech targeted to *all* of her listeners—men and women alike.

Part of delivering a successful speech is making sure all audience members, not just one demographic, engage with the topic. Paolina's speech was one example of this. But what if the speaker is someone you wouldn't typically associate with the topic? Consider how an audience analysis would help actor Ricardo Chavira connect with his mostly female audience at a breast cancer research fund-raising rally.

Linda Spillers/Race for the Cure/Getty Images

Understanding Your Audience

By thinking about how her topic would connect with her audience, Paolina was using **audience analysis**—a process of identifying important characteristics about audience members, and using this information to prepare a speech.

Audience analysis fulfills three purposes. First, the more you analyze your audience, the better you can adapt your topic to their needs and interests. This is why Paolina's speech on breast cancer awareness addressed men as well as women.

Second, analyzing your audience helps you relate supporting materials and factual details to your audience's lives and viewpoints. For example, using statistics on local breast cancer rates (as opposed to national or global rates) can make the issue seem more real to listeners.

Third, audience analysis helps shape your nonverbal delivery and language style. Consider how a medical doctor speaking to breast cancer patients about treatment options would use a different manner and vocabulary than when she's explaining the same thing to medical students.

To better understand your audience, you can explore several factors, including demographics; attitudes, beliefs, and values; knowledge; and type.

Audience Demographics. Your listeners' **demographics** include their age, sex, education level, group memberships (religious or political associations), socioeconomic status, family status (single, married, divorced, partnered, with or without children), and cultural background. Depending on your speech topic, some demographic characteristics of your audience will be more relevant than others. For example, imagine that you represent a nonprofit agency and speak frequently to local community groups. The ages and socioeconomic status of your listeners will be important factors to consider as you prepare each speech. College students on a budget may be more interested in learning about volunteering for your agency than donating money, so your speeches to campus clubs would emphasize such opportunities. On the other hand, local business professionals may be willing to donate both service and financial support. You would adjust your speeches to them accordingly.

Although it's important to take your listeners' demographic characteristics into account when preparing your speech, there are some things you need to consider. As Chapters 2 and 3 describe, people often engage in *stereotyping*—categorizing people into a social group and then forming impressions about them based on information they possess about the group. When conducting your audience analysis, recognize that stereotypes based on demographic characteristics—such as age and sex—can be flawed. For example, Paolina didn't stereotype men in her class as being disinterested in the issue. Instead, she found ways to broaden the focus of a "women's health issue" to include the men in her audience. Demographics are best used to develop a sense of possible shared characteristics among your audience that may reflect on their knowledge or interest in your topic. But be careful not to overgeneralize about your audience because each listener possesses unique attitudes, beliefs, and values that may shape how he or she reacts to your speech.

Audience Attitudes, Beliefs, and Values. Your listeners are not just a collection of demographics; each one also interprets your speech through his or her sense of self. This *self-concept*—or who each perceives him- or herself to be—influences how individual audience members will respond to your message. As Chapter 2 explains, self-concept is based on the attitudes, beliefs, and values you have about yourself. An **attitude** is an evaluation that makes a person respond favorably or unfavorably toward an issue, a situation, or a person. If your friend says, "I love Mexican food," she is expressing an attitude.

A **belief** is a conviction regarding what is true and untrue. People develop their beliefs from many sources, including their family, religious or community authorities, education, and life experiences. "There is absolutely life on other planets" is a belief.

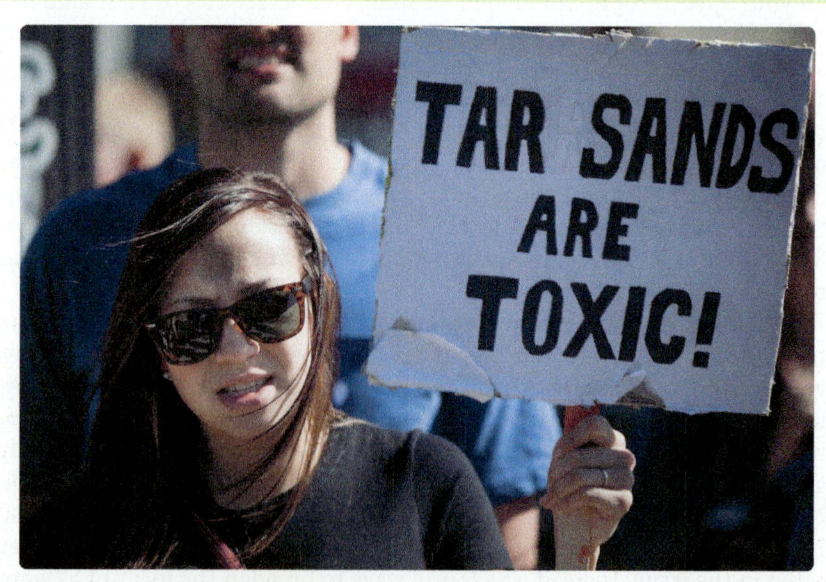

Julie Dermansky/Getty Images

Each member of your audience has his or her own *self-concept*, which includes individual attitudes, beliefs, and values. All of these affect the way the person perceives incoming information. If you were giving a speech to the rally-goers pictured here, how would you interpret their values, and how could that influence your delivery?

Strongly held beliefs that guide our behaviors are known as **values**. How people answer the question, What's important to me? reveals their values. Is it family? Equal rights for all people? Money? Values are strongly shaped by culture—for example, valuing individual freedoms (*individualistic cultures*) over group concerns (*collectivistic cultures*), or vice versa.

By understanding your audience's attitudes, beliefs, and values, you can better adapt your speech topic to connect with them. If you are dealing with controversial social issues, such as gun laws, urban poverty, or environmental racism, you'll need to demonstrate respect for your audience's attitudes, beliefs, and values regarding your topic, as these may vary from your own. Even when you take a strong stand on a contentious topic, you will need to present your ideas in a way that is civil, is ethical, and doesn't degrade others. You can do this by acknowledging your audience members' views and explaining why you want to present your topic from a particular perspective. For more ideas on accounting for your audiences' attitudes, beliefs, and values, see Advance the Conversation: Speaking Your Mind on page 327.

Audience Knowledge. Another part of your audience analysis is to consider your listeners' existing level of knowledge about your speech topic. You can make educated guesses about how much your audience members already know or what kind of information they need by reflecting on their demographics (age, education) and their attitudes, beliefs, and values. So although a class of college students will likely know a lot about Twitter or Snapchat, a group of senior adults may be less likely to know about such technologies.

When possible, directly poll your audience while preparing your speech to gauge their knowledge, and adapt your presentation accordingly. Let's say you have video production experience and want to talk about editing video. From an informal poll of your class, you discover that most of your classmates record short videos but have no editing experience. This tells you that you'll need to explain and define basic video editing terminology in your speech.

Audience Type. Audiences come in various types. Sometimes you'll be addressing a **captive audience**, meaning that your listeners are required to attend the presentation. Your class is a captive audience because students enrolled in the course have to listen to one another's speeches. Think about how you feel when you're *required* to listen to something versus *choosing* to listen. In general, being forced to listen to a presentation makes you less receptive to its message. So when you're addressing a captive audience, give listeners a reason to pay attention by explaining early in the presentation how they'll benefit from the information you're providing.

In contrast, a **voluntary audience** attends out of self-interest or to fulfill some personal need. These individuals are motivated to listen and may already have some knowledge about your topic. Suppose you go to a tile-laying demonstration at your local home-improvement store because you want to tile your patio. The person conducting the demonstration doesn't need to devote much time explaining the benefits of laying your own tile. You're already aware of those benefits; that's why you're there!

Developing Your Audience Analysis

To develop an audience analysis, ask basic questions about your audience, and keep the answers to those questions in mind (or preferably in written notes) while preparing your speech. For example, let's say you're planning a classroom speech. You'll want to make informal observations about your listeners on demographic factors that may be relevant in adapting your topic and speech content: What's the age range? Various ethnic and gender identifications? You've probably learned things about your classmates through class activities and discussions, other speech assignments, or any profiles posted online to a course site. You can also informally poll your class: "How many of you have hiked Copperhead Trail?" You could also distribute a written or an online questionnaire to help you identify your listeners' knowledge, attitudes, and beliefs about your topic.

Analyzing a non-classroom audience is trickier. You can briefly interview the person who asked you to make the presentation, to get his or her sense of the audience's demographics; their attitudes, beliefs, and values; and their existing knowledge. You can also ask the person the following questions: What's the purpose of the meeting or event? How many people will attend? Are they required to attend? What other speakers or topics has the group heard recently? What is the group expecting to gain from my presentation? Are there specific needs or challenges you want me to address in my speech? Getting answers to these inquiries will help you narrow your speech topic and determine what content to cover.

Writing Your Specific Purpose Statement

Now that you have your general purpose, a speech topic, and your audience analysis, you're ready to write a specific purpose for your speech. A **specific purpose statement** is one complete sentence summarizing the goal of your speech. It indicates whether you intend to inform or persuade your audience, reflects a narrowing of your speech topic, and is influenced by your audience analysis.

You want to complete your audience analysis before writing your specific purpose statement because what you learn in your analysis will influence your statement. For example, suppose you're preparing a speech to inform your audience about the topic of bullying. Through informal polling,

ADVANCE THE CONVERSATION

SPEAKING YOUR MIND

1 YOUR DILEMMA

While attending a campus rally about immigration reform, you watch, with disappointment, as protesters with opposing views quickly turn the rally into a screaming match and begin trading insults. The turmoil spills over to social media, where students post misinformed and racist comments. Over the next few days, tensions on campus rise as everyone becomes more devoted to his or her point of view, including you. Your parents immigrated to this country before you were born, and you have strong feelings about the issue.

Seeking to encourage an open and respectful debate, your sociology professor, Dr. Levine, asks you to make a speech at a campus forum. The forum speeches will provide different perspectives about immigration reform. You would be one of four people to speak at the event, after which Dr. Levine will moderate a discussion with all four speakers.

Given your respect for Dr. Levine and your passion about the topic, you want to make the presentation, but you don't want to say something disrespectful, causing you to lose face with the audience or offend someone.

What are your ethical obligations to an audience when presenting a controversial topic?

2 THE RESEARCH

When presenting to audiences with views different from your own, you can still connect with them by creating *goodwill*. Establishing goodwill increases the likelihood of maintaining positive face (believability and likability) as a speaker (McCroskey & Teven, 1999). Even political candidates who demonstrate goodwill with voters are more likely to be viewed favorably (Teven, 2008).

Demonstrating goodwill starts with preparation. Maintain fairness and objectivity when conducting your research. By carefully examining all sides of the issue, you'll broaden your *perspective-taking* and understanding of opposing views. When developing your own position, avoid *polarizing language* (e.g., "those people") and labels (e.g., "conservatives" or "liberals"), which can cause your audience to become defensive.

During the speech, use your opening remarks to express genuine *empathy* for your listeners' views. For example, say something like, "I know many of you may disagree with me about this issue, and I respect your viewpoint. But today I'm going to explain why I feel the way *I* do." Be sincere in expressing your respect and goodwill. Audiences are more open to your messages when you show authentic caring, empathy, and fairness (McCroskey & Teven, 1999). Explaining how the information benefits your listeners can also sway those who may initially dislike your views.

In addition to expressing goodwill verbally, avoid defensive nonverbal communication (limited eye contact, crossed arms, stiff posture, stern voice). Instead, appropriate smiling, vocal variety, gesturing, and purposeful movement around the room will express caring and goodwill to your listeners (Teven & Hanson, 2004).

Do you think it's possible to create goodwill with your audience while being firm in your viewpoint? Why or why not?

3 YOUR OPPORTUNITY

Before you act, consider the facts of the situation and think about what the research says about establishing goodwill. Also, reflect on what you've learned so far about audience analysis (pp. 325–328) and preparing speeches in general.

Now it's your turn. What are you going to do when preparing your speech? Be sure to mention any specific strategies you plan to use.

you discover that many of your audience members have experienced or witnessed bullying in the workplace, rather than in school. Therefore, you would want to emphasize that fact in your specific purpose statement: "I want to inform my audience about how to effectively handle bullying in the workplace."

Your specific purpose statement will help you prepare your speech, but it isn't set in stone; you may decide to adjust it while researching your speech. For example, let's say your specific purpose is "I want to persuade my audience to take steps to manage their privacy online." While researching this topic, you discover interesting information about identity theft, including stories of college students as victims. As a result, you could change your specific purpose statement to "I want to persuade my audience to take steps to protect themselves from identity theft."

Planning Your Research Strategy

During step 2: investigate, you begin looking for sources for your speech. Although many resources are easily available, not all of them will help you prepare a good speech. After all, Googling your topic is likely to result in thousands of hits. Taking the time to plan a proper search can help you develop a factual speech.

Once you have crafted your specific purpose statement, you may be tempted to start researching your speech. But this could generate more information than you can possibly sift through, and you may not be sure of exactly what to look for. To manage your time effectively and focus on finding relevant information, plan a strategy for conducting your research. A successful *research strategy* includes (1) identifying your information needs, (2) drawing on your personal knowledge, (3) talking with librarians, and (4) determining how to document and file your research findings.

Identifying Your Information Needs

Your information needs will change as you learn more about your topic and think about your audience. Start by finding general information about your topic, then search for more specific content. Use these questions to guide your research process:

- *What background information will my audience need?* Depending on your audience analysis, you may need to provide historical background or definitions of key terms in your presentation. If you're giving an informative speech about the benefits of qigong, for example, you should probably provide some history on this ancient Chinese meditative practice. If you don't already have such knowledge about your topic, look for trustworthy resources that provide it, such as organizational websites and dictionaries.

- *What specific information is appropriate for my audience?* Your audience analysis should determine how much expertise your listeners have with your speech topic. A communication professor presenting her research to professional peers would include more technical details on her methods and findings than she would when presenting the same research to a lay audience.
- *How current does my information need to be?* Some speeches cover topics for which the information is fairly stable, such as a speech on the uses of penicillin. For others, information is changing fast—such as a speech on the use of DNA evidence in murder investigations. If your speech topic falls into the latter category, use recent online articles, newspapers, magazines, academic journals, and experts for your research.
- *What requirements, if any, does the assignment have about information resources?* Your instructor may have defined the number and types of resource materials you can use to develop your speech. For instance, some instructors may require you to use only sources acquired from your campus library databases. If you are not sure about the requirements, ask your instructor what is acceptable.

FIGURE 13.2

YOUR INFORMATION NEEDS CHECKLIST

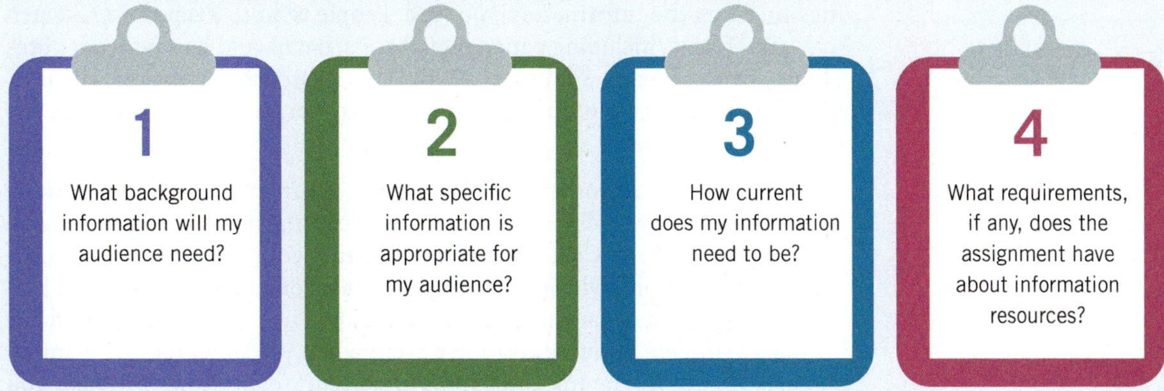
1
What background information will my audience need?
2
What specific information is appropriate for my audience?
3
How current does my information need to be?
4
What requirements, if any, does the assignment have about information resources?

Fenton one/Shutterstock.com

Drawing on Your Personal Knowledge

Although quality research strengthens a speech, don't discount your own knowledge or experiences regarding your topic. Personal stories often make presentations more memorable. Let's say that you recently completed a self-defense class and are preparing a speech to persuade your audience to do the same. Your self-defense training experience is a rich source of relevant information, as are any print materials, websites, or videos provided during your training.

If you are developing a speech based on recent papers or projects you completed for other classes, the reference lists you created are a good place to start your research. If you choose a topic that's currently getting a lot of media attention, any news sources or reputable blogs you regularly view could make good starting places for your research.

Talking with Librarians

Meet with a librarian at your campus or local library. Many college libraries even have 24/7 online chat support. Librarians are specially trained to help you find the quality information you need. By talking with a librarian about your specific purpose, you can get ideas for where to start your research and which search terms to use in library databases. Libraries also have extensive collections of print resources, media, and special collections that may not be available online.

Documenting Your Research Findings

Your research strategy should include how you'll document and file your findings. This will help you organize your research and avoid committing *plagiarism*—misrepresenting others' works as your own.

Organizing Your Research. Develop a consistent approach to documenting and filing the information you find. People tend to keep their research in several forms, including paper, digital apps, email, and handwritten notes (Jones, Bruce, Foxley, & Munat, 2006). This approach can make it difficult to find specific pieces of information. To better organize your research, follow these guidelines:

1. *Know the documentation style required.* Your instructor will usually require that you document your sources in a standard format, such as APA, MLA, or Chicago. Before you start your research, look up the proper citation style, and develop the habit of collecting complete bibliographic information for every source you use. If your library's databases provide a source citation option when you download or print an article, use it. Having consistent and accurate citations will help you when you write the reference page for your speech outline.

2. *Create a filing system.* Whether for maintaining handwritten notes, printed articles, or online sources, you will need a way to organize your findings. Create a digital or print folder system with meaningful subfolders, so you can easily find the materials you'll need:

General Folder	SpeechStuff
Subfolder	Backgrd_Info (documents with background information)
Subfolder	Stat_Info (documents with statistical information)
Subfolder	Quotes_Ex (documents with useful quotes and examples)
Subfolder	VisAid (graphs and charts)

   You can also keep notes, documents, and online sources organized in note management apps like Evernote (evernote.com), Google Keep (google.com/keep), or Microsoft OneNote (onenote.com).

3. *Use online bookmarking systems.* To organize information you find on the web, use **social bookmarking**—free web-based services that let you save, organize, and keep brief notes about your online resources. Useful social bookmarking services for academic work are Delicious (delicious.com), CiteULike (citeulike.org), and Diigo (diigo.com).

Avoiding Plagiarism. Documenting your research will also help you avoid plagiarism, a serious academic, ethical, and legal error. **Plagiarism** is misrepresenting others' works as your own. You commit plagiarism when you use exact words from someone else's work or summarize a unique idea without crediting the source. You have an ethical and a legal responsibility to credit any work that has been created by others, including written texts and spoken words. When you write a paper, you include source information to let your readers know where you found specific information or ideas. In a similar fashion, you must do this for speeches by orally citing your sources during a presentation. Even if you unintentionally use others' ideas without proper credit, you're still committing plagiarism. Plagiarizing can have terrible consequences, including receiving a failing grade, being put on academic probation, or—in the professional world—losing a job.

You are more likely to plagiarize when pressed for time and when your source materials are disorganized. To reduce your chances of plagiarizing, use the following strategies:

- *Start early on the assignment.* Rushing to prepare a speech can lead you to make mistakes in documenting and orally citing your research sources.
- *Document everything.* Develop the habit of putting clear source documentation on all your research findings. Do this even if you're just summarizing ideas. You don't want to face a situation in which you have great information to include in your speech but can't recall where you got it.
- *When in doubt, drop it.* Don't include information in your speech if you've lost the source documentation.

FIGURE 13.3

TIPS TO AVOID PLAGIARISM

1
Start early on the assignment.
2
Document everything.
3
When in doubt, drop it.

SoleilC/Shutterstock

To be an ethical communicator, you want to clearly credit your sources during your speech. Advance the Conversation: Oral Citations on pages 338–339 shows how to orally cite sources effectively. When you are unsure about whether to orally cite the source of an idea, it is better to err on the side of caution and give a citation rather than risk plagiarism. Additionally, when preparing your speech, you can ask your instructor for direction if you're confused about whether a particular idea in your speech requires an oral citation.

Conducting Your Research

Once you have determined your research strategy, the next part of step 2: investigate is to conduct your research. This includes gathering relevant data from a combination of print resources, websites, electronic databases, and conversations with people.

An essential part of responsible and ethical public speaking is making sure the information in your speech is accurate and trustworthy. Some audience members may be inclined to use their mobile devices to quickly fact-check your claims. (Think of how often politicians get called out for making false claims in their speeches.) Conducting comprehensive research ensures that your presentation is truthful and helps build your credibility with the audience.

Primary and Secondary Resources

There are two types of research resources. **Primary resources** are direct accounts, straight from the original source. These include scientific reports, eyewitness descriptions of events, diary writings, photographs of events, congressional-hearing transcripts, and speech manuscripts.

Secondary resources are works that analyze and interpret primary resources. For example, a web posting that summarizes the results of a study on how treadmill exercise affects the heart rates of people with diabetes and includes additional opinions on the topic is a secondary resource. (The original study published in a medical journal is the primary resource.) Additional examples of secondary sources include magazine articles, biographies, textbooks, and newspaper articles. Secondary resources can help you interpret complex statistical information and gather alternative opinions.

Whether you use primary or secondary resources depends on your topic and your specific purpose statement. Many classroom speech topics can be developed using only secondary resources. For example, if your specific purpose is to persuade your classmates to vote, you can draw from websites and magazine articles that examine the benefits of voting. But if you want to spotlight low turnout among young adult voters in local elections, you might seek a primary resource, such as a report on voter turnout from your local government office.

Internet Resources

You will probably conduct the majority of your research online (whether at home or in a library). But conducting research online involves more than just Googling your topic and seeing what pops up. Instead, get the most out of your online research by knowing the types of resources available online and how to best use them (see Table 13.2).

Although a search engine such as Google helps you find information quickly, it can also create *information overload*. For instance, if you are planning to persuade your audience to improve their sleep habits and you enter the search term "sleep habits" into Google, you'll get more than 120 million links. How do you know where to start? Evaluate the information quality of the links, choosing only those sources that have real value for your speech. For example, among the links produced by the Google search, many are selling medication or books. Avoid such sites; if the site is selling you something, it is likely to include biased information. Sites ending in .com can provide quality information if they are objective, such as articles from reputable newspapers and magazines.

Sometimes the most popular sites (those that appear at the top of the search results) aren't the best to use for research purposes. For example, Wikipedia's popularity is driven by the vast amount of material available on the site as well as its high visibility through search engines (Rainie & Tancer, 2007). It is often the first stop for many people doing research online. However, Wikipedia has its critics, especially in college and university settings. Some academic departments even ban its use for student assignments (Educause, 2007). Before using any website in your research, make sure it meets the requirements of the assignment.

TABLE 13.2

HELPFUL ONLINE RESEARCH SOURCES

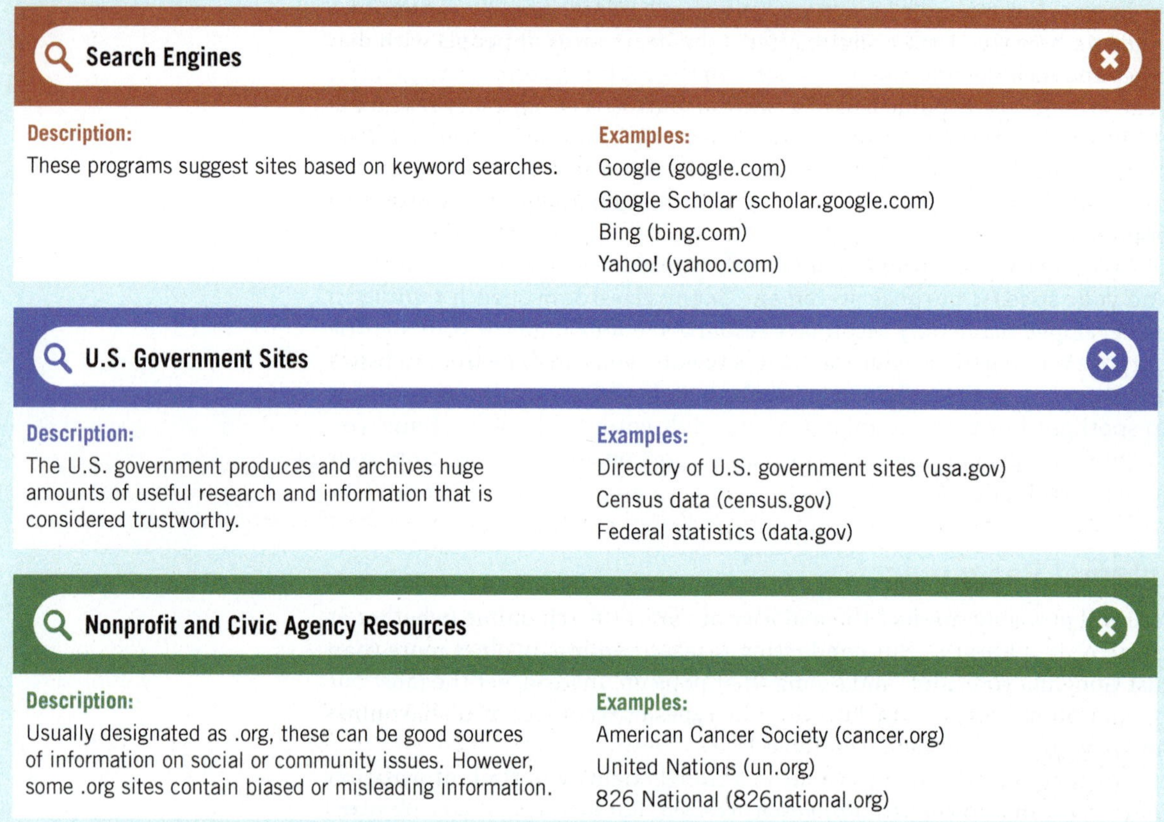

Source	Description	Examples
Search Engines	These programs suggest sites based on keyword searches.	Google (google.com) Google Scholar (scholar.google.com) Bing (bing.com) Yahoo! (yahoo.com)
U.S. Government Sites	The U.S. government produces and archives huge amounts of useful research and information that is considered trustworthy.	Directory of U.S. government sites (usa.gov) Census data (census.gov) Federal statistics (data.gov)
Nonprofit and Civic Agency Resources	Usually designated as .org, these can be good sources of information on social or community issues. However, some .org sites contain biased or misleading information.	American Cancer Society (cancer.org) United Nations (un.org) 826 National (826national.org)

Library Resources

A typical academic library invests thousands of dollars annually to provide students with online resources for conducting research. Some popular online library resources include EBSCOhost, LexisNexis Academic, and ProQuest. These databases enable you to search newspapers; primary source documents; periodicals; scholarly journals; government, business, and legal documents; and even televised news transcripts. Moreover, most academic databases allow you to search for photographs, graphs, and other images you may want to use in your speech.

Libraries also offer print and online versions of generalized and specialized encyclopedias and dictionaries. Dozens of subject-specific encyclopedias and dictionaries exist, ranging from *Ancient Europe, 8000 B.C.*

to A.D. *1000: Encyclopedia of the Barbarian World* to *The Dictionary of Cell and Molecular Biology*. Many encyclopedia entries reference other key sources you can use while researching your speech, such as related books and articles.

Finally, many college libraries subscribe to two popular and useful online resources for persuasive speech assignments: *CQ Researcher* and *Opposing Viewpoints in Context*. *CQ Researcher* is a database of reports developed by journalists on specific themes, ranging from health care to the economy. Each report provides background on the topic, an objective examination of different perspectives on the topic, and a bibliography. *Opposing Viewpoints in Context* takes several of the best primary and secondary sources available on controversial social issues and organizes them by topic. Each of these resources is a good starting point for gaining a broad perspective on a social issue.

Interpersonal Resources

Although it may not be the first thing that comes to mind, talking with people one-on-one can provide useful information on your speech topic. Faculty members on your campus or experts in your community can provide insights, explanations, and stories different from online and print resources. For example, interviewing an organ-donor recipient produces a powerful personal story about the importance of organ donation.

If you decide to talk with someone as part of your research, you will need to plan an **information interview**—a meeting in which you ask questions to gain knowledge or understanding about a particular topic. To conduct a successful interview, you will need to arrange an appointment and indicate how much time you will need with the person. Show respect for your interviewee's time by sticking to the agreed-upon time frame and having questions prepared in advance. When you interview the person, maintain a friendly but professional manner. For more details about how to conduct an information interview, check out pages A-10–A-13 in the appendix.

Evaluating Your Resources

Today, anyone can publish a book, an article, or a website given a little time and the right computer apps. So it's a good idea to maintain a healthy skepticism about the sources you find for your speech. No matter where your research is from, you need to evaluate it by considering these five factors: relevancy, currency, authority, objectivity, and consensual validation.

Relevancy. Consider the degree to which your source is related to your speech's specific purpose. You can waste a lot of time sifting through and reading material that barely touches on your topic. Take, for example, an informative presentation for your art history class about the use of color in French impressionist paintings. Your research could lead you to hundreds of books, articles, and online materials about French impressionism. To eliminate irrelevant resources, stay focused on your specific purpose—the use of color in such art.

Currency. For some speech topics, it's critical to have the most current information available. Publication dates of magazines, newspapers, articles, and books are relatively easy to determine, but some websites present a different challenge. Try to determine when a site was last updated—check for timely commentary, copyright dates on the home page, or dates of individual posts. Avoid relying on information from any website that hasn't been updated in several months. Any site with broken hyperlinks is probably outdated.

Authority. For each resource you find, ask yourself, What are the author's credentials? To determine this, find out qualifications the creator brings to the work, such as personal experience, a prolonged professional career, or relevant academic degrees from a respectable educational institution. You can usually find information about an author's credentials within the first few pages of a book or in a footnote or biographical note in an article or another document.

For an online source, consider the reputation of the sponsoring organization. For example, information found on the American Medical Association (AMA) website has authority because of the AMA's reputation as a medical organization. You should also look for footnotes or works-cited listings. Check out those sources to see if they look valid. Often, an online post will link to more information about the author, providing you a chance to check out his or her credentials. Finally, use your instincts to judge the look and feel of the site. Although appearance should never be the sole indicator of authority, mistakes and sloppiness suggest a lack of authority.

Objectivity. You want to use *objective* research sources—those based on facts, not bias. Of course, all sources have some degree of bias. But you want to avoid blatantly one-sided or propaganda-like resources, whose sole purpose is to convey the author's point of view or a particular ideology.

If the resource is a website, click on the "About" link, which should take you to a page describing the mission and purpose of the group or organization that publishes the site. Review this information to see if the site is pushing a particular agenda. Also, examine any external links on the site to see what types of organizations the group associates with. Do these associations suggest possible bias? Finally, don't over-rely on commercial websites (.com); these sites usually exist to sell or promote some product or service.

Consensual Validation. A resource has **consensual validation** when other sources agree with or use the same information you're considering using. Consensual validation suggests that the information (especially that found on the web) is reliable. For instance, imagine you're researching drinking in college. You come across a website that defines binge drinking as men drinking five consecutive alcoholic drinks or women consuming four consecutive alcoholic drinks. You ask yourself, What kind of alcohol, and over what period of time? What's the original source of this information? As you research a bit further by consulting library databases, you find several studies conducted at Harvard that use the same definition of binge drinking but that provide more details that answer your questions. You now have confidence in the original information as well as additional details to use in your speech.

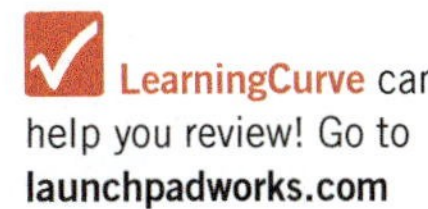
LearningCurve can help you review! Go to **launchpadworks.com**

ADVANCE THE CONVERSATION
Video Activity

ORAL CITATIONS

The following scenario will enhance your ability to use effective oral citations of sources in your speech. Visit LaunchPad at launchpadworks.com to get the full experience with video. As you watch the first video, recall what you've learned about citing sources in your speech. Then complete the **Your Turn** prompts. Finally, watch the **Take Two!** video to explore how this scenario could have gone differently.

1 *THE PROBLEM*

For his communication class, Reynaldo is giving a speech about why it's important to develop good sleep habits. His professor wants him to incorporate at least three academic sources. Reynaldo knows how to write source citations for research papers, but he isn't sure how to go about crediting his sources in a speech. The first time he rehearses his speech, he makes a few common mistakes in his citations.

Cognitive Impairment
"Before continuing, I would like to say that my sources for this next part of my speech include the Center for Disease Control, the National Institute for Health, and the University of Georgia's health center."

"The National Heart, Lung, and Blood Institute, which is part of the National Institute for Health, a division of the U.S. Department of Health and Human Services, a government agency, published a brief PDF . . ."

2 YOUR TURN

Observations. Reflect on how Reynaldo orally cited his sources in the rehearsal by answering the following questions:

1. Overall, do you think Reynaldo's oral citations were effective?
2. What did Reynaldo do well? What can he improve on?

Discussion. In class or with a partner, share your thoughts about Reynaldo's oral citations and work to answer the following questions:

1. How might Reynaldo listing all of his sources together affect his audience's understanding of the speech?
2. How might Reynaldo's audience react when he includes many details about one source: the National Heart, Lung, and Blood Institute?

Conclusion. Based on your analysis, what advice would you give Reynaldo to improve his oral citations in this scenario?

3 TAKE TWO!

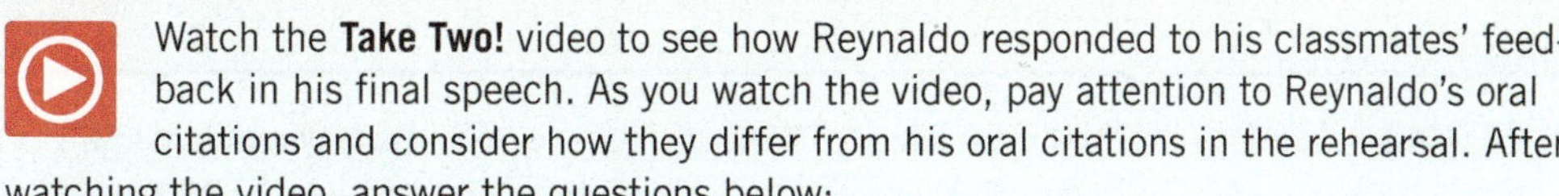

Watch the **Take Two!** video to see how Reynaldo responded to his classmates' feedback in his final speech. As you watch the video, pay attention to Reynaldo's oral citations and consider how they differ from his oral citations in the rehearsal. After watching the video, answer the questions below:

1. How did Reynaldo revise his oral citations from the rehearsal to his final speech? Identify specific examples.
2. In your opinion, are Reynaldo's oral citations in his final speech more effective? Why or why not?

CHAPTER 13 REVIEW

CHAPTER RECAP

- By following the five steps of speech preparation—**think**, **investigate**, **compose**, **rehearse**, and **revise**—you can create compelling public speeches that engage and inspire audiences.
- After determining your **general purpose**, you can select your **speech topic** by reflecting on your personal interests and experiences, **brainstorming**, or developing a **concept map**.
- By conducting an **audience analysis**, you explore several factors, including your listeners' **demographics**; **attitudes**, **beliefs**, and **values**; knowledge; and type.
- To manage your time effectively and focus on finding relevant information, plan a research strategy. This not only helps you find and organize information but also helps you avoid **plagiarism**.
- When researching your speech, gather relevant data from a combination of print resources, websites, electronic databases, and **information interviews**, and don't forget to evaluate your sources.

LaunchPad for *Choices & Connections* offers unique video scenarios and encourages self-assessment through adaptive quizzing. Go to **launchpadworks.com** to get access.

 LearningCurve adaptive quizzes

 Advance the Conversation video scenarios

 Video clips that illustrate key concepts

KEY TERMS

Public speaking, p. 316
Think, p. 316
Investigate, p. 316
Compose, p. 317
Rehearse, p. 317
Revise, p. 317
General purpose, p. 319
Informative speech, p. 319
Persuasive speech, p. 319
Special-occasion speech, p. 319
Speech topic, p. 319
Brainstorming, p. 320
Concept map, p. 320
Audience analysis, p. 323
Demographics, p. 323
Attitude, p. 324
Belief, p. 324
Values, p. 325
Captive audience, p. 325
Voluntary audience, p. 326
Specific purpose statement, p. 326
Social bookmarking, p. 331
Plagiarism, p. 331
Primary resources, p. 332
Secondary resources, p. 333
Information interview, p. 335
Consensual validation, p. 337

POP QUIZ

Looking for more review questions? LearningCurve can help you master key concepts from this chapter. Go to **launchpadworks.com**

1. During which step of the speech preparation process can you use critical self-reflection to improve your content and delivery?
   a. Think
   b. Compose
   c. Rehearse
   d. Revise

2. During your audience analysis, you may consider your listeners' demographics in adapting your speech as needed. However, it is important to avoid ___________ during this process.
   a. brainstorming
   b. captive audiences
   c. stereotyping
   d. voluntary audiences

3. Your specific purpose statement is influenced by all of the following *except*
   a. research strategy.
   b. general purpose.
   c. audience analysis.
   d. speech topic.

4. When planning your research strategy, consider which background content—such as definitions or historical context—your audience may need explained. This is part of
   a. evaluating your resources.
   b. documenting your research findings.
   c. drawing on your personal knowledge.
   d. identifying your information needs.

5. While researching your speech, check that your sources are ___________ to ensure that they aren't providing biased information.
   a. accurate
   b. objective
   c. current
   d. relevant

ACTIVITIES

For more activities, visit LaunchPad for *Choices & Connections* at **launchpadworks.com**

1 Comparing Concept Maps

Working with a partner, choose one of the following topics. Work independently for 10 minutes to draw your own concept maps of the same topic. Compare your efforts, and discuss what the differences illustrate about selecting a speech topic.

a. Music
b. Washington, DC
c. Sports
d. Social media
e. Health

2 Clarifying Specific Purposes

Each of the following specific purpose statements fails to fulfill the guidelines specified in the chapter. For each one, identify the problem, and then rewrite the statement using the guidelines for specific purpose statements on pages 326 and 328.

a. I want to talk about how to succeed in college.
b. Explain the difference between a curve ball and a slider.
c. Eliminating world hunger.
d. My audience will appreciate classical music and be encouraged to enroll in private music lessons.
e. Pros and cons of starting your own business.

14

Composing Your Speech

When Dr. Myriam Sidibe speaks to audiences, her message is one that parents tell children every day: wash your hands.[1] But unlike most parents, she has a PhD in public health and handwashing, and she's on a mission to ensure children live healthy, normal lives. Dr. Sidibe knows too well the health risks involved when children neglect to wash their hands. They are more likely to contract flu, pneumonia, respiratory illnesses, and diarrhea. In some parts of Asia and Africa, these preventable diseases can be a death sentence for young children who don't have adequate medical care. When she speaks to audiences, Dr. Sidibe makes a clear point: handwashing with soap is one of the most cost-effective ways of saving children's lives.

Speaking at a TED conference in New York City, Dr. Sidibe made her point about the importance of handwashing in several dramatic ways, first by opening her talk with a horrifying scenario:

> So imagine that a plane is about to crash with 250 children and babies, and if you knew how to stop that, would you? Now imagine that 60 planes full of babies under five crash every single day. That's the number of kids that never make it to their fifth birthday. 6.6 million children never make it to their fifth birthday.

Dr. Sidibe then developed her talk by introducing supporting material—statistics, stories, and visual graphics—to show that many childhood diseases are preventable through handwashing with soap. To further engage her listeners, she asked them to shake hands with the person sitting next to them. Her audience erupted in nervous laughter afterward when she stated that four out of five persons globally don't wash their hands when coming out of a restroom.

Even when soap is available, it is used for other purposes. For example, soap can be found in 90 percent of households in India, but many don't use it for handwashing. To illustrate why, Dr. Sidibe displayed a photograph of a young boy named Mayank and explained:

> Why is it that Mayank, this young boy that I met in India, isn't washing his hands? Well, in Mayank's family, soap is used for bathing, soap is used for laundry, soap is used for washing dishes. His parents think sometimes it's a precious commodity, so they'll keep it in a cupboard. They'll keep it away from him so he doesn't waste it.

Dr. Sidibe urged her listeners—most of whom were global health and wellness experts—to realize that soap is "the most beautiful invention in public health" and to be advocates of using it for proper handwashing. She also encouraged their support for Global Handwashing Day, an awareness campaign that is celebrated annually on October 15.

In a speech lasting less than 12 minutes, Dr. Sidibe shared stories, provided scientific research, and involved her listeners. When it was over, the audience understood that the habit of handwashing with soap saves lives, and that a carefully composed speech can be an event to experience and remember.

[1]Opener crafted from Sidibe (2014).

CHAPTER OUTLINE

LearningCurve can help you review! Go to **launchpadworks.com**

Even when you know the specific purpose for your speech, determining exactly how to achieve it can be difficult. Dr. Sidibe had an important message to share with her audience, but deciding how to present her message took work. This process of determining your speech thesis and main ideas and arranging them into a coherent and engaging presentation is the third step of the speech preparation process: **composing**. (See Table 13.1 on page 317 for the Five Steps in Speech Preparation.) In this chapter, you'll learn:

- How to develop your speech thesis
- Ways to identify and arrange your speech's main points
- Ideas for keeping your audience engaged
- Strategies for introducing and concluding your speech
- How to write preparation and delivery outlines

Developing Your Speech Thesis

At this point in your speech preparation, you've spent considerable time thinking about your audience, narrowing your topic, and finding quality information to use in your presentation. Now it's time to begin step 3: compose by putting all this information together in the central idea—the thesis—of your speech. This will help you structure your presentation.

Your **speech thesis** is one complete sentence that identifies the central idea of your presentation for your audience. This statement is the foundation for composing your speech. Everything from what points you make and which visual aids you use to how you draft your conclusion will relate to it. You will eventually share the speech thesis with your audience as part of the speech's introduction. A compelling speech thesis answers the question, What is the overall point or position I want to convey to my audience? Dr. Sidibe's speech thesis was "Handwashing with soap is one of the most cost-effective ways of saving children's lives." This central idea helped her compose her main points, stay on topic, and inform her audience about what she wanted them to know.

A good speech thesis meets three requirements. First, it evolves from your specific purpose statement. You adapt the idea based on what you discover during your research and to be more specific to your actual speech. Second, the speech thesis clearly demonstrates to the audience your overall point or position on the topic. Finally, the thesis provides clues as to how your main points will develop. Consider how these requirements are met in the following example:

Specific purpose: I want to inform my audience how to effectively handle bullying in the workplace.

Speech thesis: Workplace bullying is an intolerable situation that can be effectively curbed through specific actions.

Although the speech thesis and specific purpose may seem similar, there is an important difference: the speech thesis is stated directly during the introduction of your presentation, whereas the specific purpose guides your research.

Identifying and Supporting Your Main Points

The speech thesis reflects your point of view or position on the topic. But simply stating your thesis isn't enough; you need evidence to back up your ideas. You do this by identifying your main points and providing appropriate supporting materials. Without such evidence, it is hard to build credibility with your audience.

With your speech thesis drafted, you can begin to structure your speech—that is, determine what you will say in each part of your presentation. Most speeches have three parts:

- *Introduction:* You lay the groundwork for your speech by connecting with your audience, disclosing your speech thesis, establishing your credibility, and previewing your main points.
- *Body:* You develop your speech thesis with main points and supporting evidence. This is the heart of your presentation.
- *Conclusion:* You summarize your main points and share any final thoughts on your topic.

We will go over all three sections in this chapter, but let's start with the body of the speech. Identifying and supporting your main points will help you figure out what to say in your introduction and conclusion.

Identifying Your Main Points

The **main points** of your speech are the key statements or principles that support your speech thesis and help your audience understand your message. These are the ideas that build the case for why your thesis statement is true.

One way to identify your main points is to ask yourself what essential information is necessary to support your thesis. For example, if you were composing a speech about the dangers of texting while driving, your audience might need to understand why that behavior is dangerous. Let's say that your research uncovered information about the different types of distractions caused by texting. These distractions could make up the first main point of your speech.

You also can identify main points for your thesis by looking for themes in your research. Suppose you have information from your state's department of public safety showing that texting-related traffic accidents have been increasing over the past two years. In addition, you interviewed a state police officer who told you that many of the accidents he investigates now are caused by distracted drivers. Taken together, this information could be used to write a second main point for your speech: accidents caused by texting while driving have been increasing.

Additionally, you might discover that there are several general ideas that will support your thesis. However, you'll want to include only those that are relevant to your audience. If your *audience analysis* (see Chapter 13, pages 322–328) shows that your listeners are unaware of proposed laws to prohibit texting while driving, you might decide it is important to explain them in detail. This could also lead you to conclude that the audience could benefit from information about how to change their personal behavior and encourage others to do the same. These two final main points are important because they have a direct bearing on the audience. Table 14.1 reviews how the speech thesis and main points work together.

When developing main points, remember these guidelines:

- *A speech should contain a small number of main points, usually two to five.* You want to keep your information manageable, making it easier for listeners to understand your speech.

TABLE 14.1

IDENTIFYING MAIN IDEAS

Speech thesis:

Stopping the dangerous practice of texting while driving must be addressed through new legislation and personal behavior change.

Note:

Speech Preparation step 3: composing starts with writing the thesis statement. You will mention it in your speech, usually during the introduction.

Main points:

I. Texting while driving presents three types of distractions.

II. Traffic accidents caused by texting while driving have been increasing.

III. New legislation is needed to control the problem.

IV. Individuals must also take responsibility for changing their behaviors.

Note:

Your main points directly support your speech thesis. You will use the supporting materials from your research to fully develop each of the points during the speech.

- *Each main point must support your thesis statement.* You don't want to distract from your speech thesis by including a point that is unrelated to it. A focused presentation increases your chances of keeping the audience's attention.
- *Each main point should focus on only one idea.* If a point introduces a new idea, then it should appear as a separate main point. As an example, consider how many main points are included in the following sentence: Texting while driving presents three types of distractions, and you can take steps to stop the practice. (The answer is two; each idea—types of distractions and steps to stop the practice—should be developed as a separate main point.)

Finally, some main points may need to be further divided into **subpoints**, specific principles derived from breaking down main points. Subpoints are especially useful if a main point can be broken down into parts or steps. For example, main point I in Table 14.1 could have three subpoints:

I. Texting while driving presents three types of distractions.[2]

   A. Visual distraction

   B. Manual distraction

   C. Cognitive distraction

By using subpoints, you can explain a main point better, and your audience will have an easier time listening to the overall idea. When creating subpoints, make sure they all relate to the main point to avoid confusing your audience.

Supporting Your Main Points

All your main points and subpoints require *supporting materials* to clarify the ideas and make them memorable for your listeners. Supporting materials include definitions, statistics, examples, and testimony—the proof you need to back up your claims. You can't just tell the audience that texting while driving causes three types of distractions and expect them to take your word for it. Instead, you need to explain what each type is and how that information relates to your thesis. Providing adequate supporting materials lets your audience know that the information you are providing is trustworthy.

How do you know what type of supporting materials you need? When conducting your audience analysis, consider questions like the following: How familiar is your audience with your topic? Will they need terms defined or other background information? Do you need to include stories and examples that illustrate your points? These types of questions will help you choose appropriate supporting materials that will inform and interest your audience. Although you can base much of your supporting materials on your audience analysis, you might also need to do additional research to fill in any gaps.

---

[2]distraction.gov/stats-research-laws/facts-and-statistics.html/

Definitions. When composing your speech, be aware of when you may have to define terms for your listeners. After all, as Chapter 5 on verbal communication discusses, differences in language use can cause misunderstandings. *Connotative meanings*, for instance, are the meanings you associate with words based on your life experiences. But you can't assume that all members of your audience will share those references. Also, your *dialect*—which reflects the language variations you use based on where you live, your socioeconomic status, or your ethnic or religious ancestry—can be a source of misunderstandings if you and your audience use terms differently.

Even within a culture, these differences can cause people who share the same language to misunderstand each other. For example, what comes to mind when you hear the term *civility*? When presenting a talk on the societal impact of artificial intelligence, technology writer Steve Lohr (2016) started by defining the term *civility* to make sure his audience understood it in the same way he did:

> The definition of civility typically revolves around the rules, mores and assumptions for how we deal with each other. (p. 8)

During your audience analysis, get a realistic sense of terms or concepts you may need to define for your audience. This way, you can provide them with all the information they need but not waste time defining words they already know.

Statistics. A **statistic** is a number that summarizes a formal observation about a phenomenon. Statistics can help you make a compelling point, as business executive Jo Ann Jenkins (2017) did in a speech about the increasing age of the U.S. population:

> Here in the U.S., there are about 75,000 Americans aged 100 or older. In fact, people 100 and over represent the second fastest growing age group in the country. The fastest? People over 85. Three out of five 65-year-olds today will live well into their 90s. (p. 120)

When using statistics, keep a few things in mind. First, think about using a visual chart or graph to summarize statistical information. Seeing the numbers in addition to hearing them will help your audience make sense of them. Second, round off large numbers. For example, instead of listing the exact number of Americans over the age of 100, Jenkins said, "about 75,000." Third, when possible, place statistics in a context that your audience will find meaningful. Jenkins could've said that 75,000 people is comparable to the population of a specific local city or the number of fans that can fit into a professional sports stadium. Finally, although statistics can bring attention to your point, use them sparingly. Listeners can get confused trying to understand a lot of abstract statistical information. Try to use statistics only when doing so will have an impact on your audience.

Examples. Main points are made vivid and clear when you use **examples**, or specific references that illustrate ideas. *Real examples* are drawn from actual events or occurrences. Consider how this speaker uses a real example to show how the United States has been a leader in space exploration:

> America is still the only nation to successfully land a spacecraft on Mars. When our latest Mars spacecraft, MAVEN, arrived last September to study the Red Planet's upper atmosphere, it joined a fleet of orbiters and rovers that we already had on the surface—and have had on the surface since Viking I and II landed in the 1970s. (Bolden, 2015, p. 209)

Sometimes you'll develop a *hypothetical example*—an imagined event or occurrence—to make a point. This type of example is helpful when you have difficulty finding an appropriate real example. In a speech about the early warning signs of dating violence, you could develop a hypothetical example to illustrate intentional embarrassment by saying, "Imagine that you're out with friends and your partner starts criticizing your appearance in front of them. This is an act of intentional embarrassment." You should indicate the use of hypothetical examples by using phrases like "Imagine that . . . ," "Suppose . . . ," or "Let's say that . . ." so that your audience knows you're not giving real examples. When developing a hypothetical example, it is important to create one that is realistic and believable. If it is out of the ordinary, your audience may ignore it as an exception.

A special type of example is an **analogy**, which compares something that is familiar to your audience with something that is unfamiliar to them but that you want them to understand. Analogies are useful for illustrating a particularly difficult main point. Here, a speaker uses an analogy to explain the versatility of mobile phones:

> The smartphone, akin to a Swiss Army Knife, can replace a PC, watch, alarm clock, camera, hand-held GPS, flashlight, transistor radio, portable music player, TV, even plastic credit cards, keeping a lot of material out of landfills. (Hesse, 2015, p. 150)

When using an analogy, be sure that the comparison you're making is clear and will make sense to your audience. If necessary, point out the similarities between the two unlike things, and explain why the comparison works.

Testimony. Relying on the words or experience of others by using **testimony** is a common way that speakers support main points. Speeches incorporate two types of testimony. *Expert testimony* comes from those who, by way of their academic study, work experience, or research, have special knowledge about your topic. *Layperson testimony* is derived from those who have personal experience with the topic. For example, in a persuasive speech on stiffening the laws related to drunk driving, a speaker may draw on testimony from police officers who enforce the laws (experts), survivors of alcohol-related traffic accidents (laypersons), or both.

Testimony can be presented in your speech through **direct quotation**. A direct quotation uses the exact words of a person to make your point. In a speech about expanding opportunities in business for women, United Parcel

FIGURE 14.1

SUPPORTING YOUR MAIN POINT

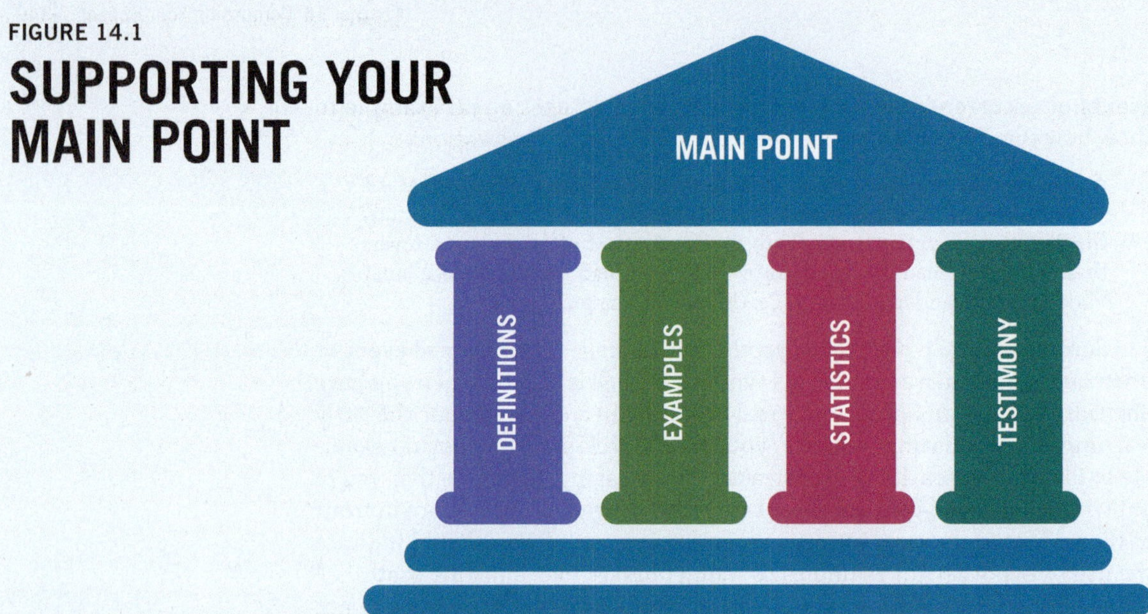

artizarus/Shutterstock

Services executive Romaine Seguin (2017) quotes a line from the movie *Hidden Figures*:

> I can't talk about the quotes that led to insights without talking about the ones that triggered some real introspection. One in particular . . . Mary's saying, "I'm not gonna entertain the impossible," was a reality check. (p. 306)

When using a direct quotation, you have an ethical responsibility to accurately convey the words of the person. Don't change the words or take the quote out of context. Be clear in citing the source from which you got the quote, and if necessary, provide some background about the person, such as the professional or personal experience that makes the quote relevant.

Another way of presenting testimony is by **paraphrasing**, or providing your own summary of another person's words or experience. Paraphrasing is useful when the original words are too complicated, too long, or too confusing to quote directly. When paraphrasing, do not alter the original meaning of what the person said or experienced. You have the same ethical responsibility to properly cite the source when paraphrasing as you do when quoting.

Organizing Your Speech

Considering all the time and energy you put into finding supporting materials for your speech, you want your audience to get the most out of it. One of the best ways to do that is to clearly organize your speech. This will help audience members understand your points and stay engaged while listening.

As our chapter opener mentioned, Dr. Sidibe delivered a speech on the importance of handwashing. Her speech held her audience's attention in part because of the thought-provoking topic, but also because the speech was easy to follow and understand. She chose a clear organizational pattern (the *problem-solution pattern*, discussed on page 352) and structured her speech accordingly. But you don't need to be a leading innovator or scientist like Dr. Sidibe to make a speech with a similar effect. You just need to develop a clear organization for your speech, transition smoothly throughout the presentation, and keep your audience engaged.

Selecting an Organizational Pattern

For your audience to follow the development of your speech thesis, you need to arrange your main points into a logical pattern. There are five common organizational patterns: topical, chronological, spatial, cause-effect, and problem-solution.

Topical. Use a **topical pattern** when your main points can be organized into categories or subtopics. You can arrange the topics in any order—such as least to most important, most to least common, or type (e.g., types of movies: comedy, drama, action, adventure, documentary). Just be sure your order is logical and supports your thesis statement. For example, in a speech about composing photographs with your phone camera, you could arrange your main points from the most simple to the most complex techniques:

Speech thesis: Keeping three techniques in mind will help you compose beautiful photographs with your phone camera.

Main points:

I. Ensure that your phone is steady.
II. Apply the rule of thirds in framing shots.
III. Find the leading lines in your shots.

Chronological. When your main points suggest a time sequence or a series of steps, you can organize them using a **chronological pattern**. Speeches about a process or how to do or make something often use this pattern:

Speech thesis: Brewing your own delicious kombucha tea can be done in five easy steps.

Main points:

I. Start by gathering the right equipment and supplies.
II. Next, you want to assemble the necessary ingredients.
III. Make the tea base by mixing the ingredients.
IV. Add the symbiotic culture of bacteria and yeast to your tea base (scoby) to enact the first period of fermentation.
V. Remove the scoby and bottle the tea for the final period of fermentation.

Spatial. The **spatial pattern** shows listeners how things are related within a physical space. For example, if you were briefing a group on packing a backpack for a hiking trip, you might arrange the main points in the following way:

Speech thesis: Properly packing your backpack will give you easy access to your gear and provide you with maximum comfort on your hike.

Main points:

I. Spread out your gear to determine size and weight of items.

II. Pack the bottom of your pack with gear that will be needed once you reach your destination.

III. Maintain proper balance to your backpack by placing heavier items at the center.

IV. Place essential items at the top of the backpack for easy access while you're on the trail.

Cause-effect. The **cause-effect pattern** enables you to show how events or forces will lead to (or did lead to) specific outcomes:

Speech thesis: Sleep deprivation can have a serious impact on your physical health, your mental functioning, and your relationships.

Main points:

I. Sleep deprivation makes you vulnerable to colds, flu, and other illness.

II. Sleep deprivation decreases mental alertness and memory.

III. Sleep deprivation affects moodiness, which can lead to interpersonal conflict.

Problem-solution. The **problem-solution pattern** helps you motivate listeners to take action to address a challenge. In this arrangement, you describe a problem and then present a solution:

Speech thesis: Taking personal action can prevent hate speech on college campus.

Main points:

I. Incidents of hate speech on college and university campus have been increasing.

II. Hate speech on campus creates a hostile environment that impacts psychological and physical safety.

III. You can take steps to discourage hate speech on campus, in person, and on social media.

Using Connectives

Once you've arranged your main points in an organizational pattern, think about how **connectives**—words and phrases that link your ideas together—will help you move from one idea to the next. Connectives will help your audience accurately receive and understand your speech because they show how your ideas are related. As we will discuss later in the chapter, you should write connective phrases into the outline of your speech. Doing so will help you think through the relationship of your ideas and the flow of your speech. There are four types of connectives: internal previews, internal summaries, transitional phrases, and signposts.

Internal Previews. Sometimes you will want to provide your listeners with a first look at the information you're about to cover with statements known as **internal previews.** These statements let your audience in on what you are going to tell them before you actually do. Consider this internal preview in a speech about why students drop out of school:

> Three factors contribute to student dropout. These are a lack of academic readiness, financial need, and poor advisement. Let's look at each of these in turn.

When a main point has subpoints, an internal preview can help your audience follow along as you develop each subpoint.

Internal Summaries. **Internal summaries** provide a short review of information you've discussed within a section of the speech. This connective is especially useful when you have covered a main point with multiple aspects, as in the speech about student dropout rates:

> As you just heard, poor academic preparation, inadequate finances, and misguided advice prior to enrollment are contributing causes to student dropout rates.

Providing your listeners with internal summaries will solidify the most essential information about the main point before you move on.

Transitional Phrases. When you want to indicate that you're shifting to another point or idea, you can use **transitional phrases.** These phrases provide a verbal signal that you are moving on:

> *Now that we've examined* the reasons for student dropout, *let's focus* on what you can do to prevent it.

These simple phrases can keep your audience from getting lost when you begin to make a different point.

Signposts. **Signposts** are brief words—often numbers—that quickly introduce a new idea. Words like *First*, *Second*, *Next*, *Additionally*, and *Finally* are signposts, as in the following:

> *Additionally*, students can take action to control the forces causing them to drop out.

These are most helpful when you are covering several steps or examples that your audience will need to keep track of.

Samantha Bee's infectious energy and humorous spin on current events and pop culture are two reasons for her popularity as a host and a comedian. Though her banter and comments are meant for entertainment, how might you use similar methods in your own speeches to make them memorable and relevant?

Jessica Miglio/© TBS/Everett Collection, Inc.

Keeping Listeners Engaged

Even when your audience wants to listen to your speech, it is easy for them to get distracted by other people or by their phones, or for their minds to simply wander. To combat such obstacles, present information in a way that stimulates your listeners' senses and provides new or unexpected ideas (Fiske & Taylor, 1991; Medina, 2008). When planning your organizational pattern and use of connectives, also think about ways to keep your audience engaged:

- *Integrate novelty*. People pay attention to information that is *novel* (new), different, or unusual (Silvia, 2008). Look for ways to tell your audience something they don't already know. You may recall that Dr. Sidibe had her listeners shake hands, and then she told them that four out of five people don't wash their hands when coming out of a restroom. You also achieve novelty by having a mix of statistics, testimony, and examples to support your points.
- *Use appropriate humor*. A funny story or joke invites attention and is memorable. After all, most people like to laugh. But use humor sparingly, and make it relevant (Gruner, 1985). Never use humor that is obscene, racist, sexist, or insulting to any group—you'll only offend your audience.
- *Tell a story*. Stories engage listeners and create the sense of a shared experience. They also support your speech thesis by clarifying your main points. Stories work best when they use descriptive language, evoke emotion, and, of course, are relevant to the points you're making.
- *Integrate presentation aids*. Your audience will pay the most attention to what they *see* (Medina, 2008). Consider how charts, graphs, images,

ADVANCE THE CONVERSATION

BUT THE VIDEO WENT VIRAL!

1 *YOUR DILEMMA*

You're sitting at your desk when your roommate, Eliza, walks in the door and greets you: "How's it going? Still working on your speech?"

You reply, "Yeah. I found this hilarious video that I want to use, but I'm not sure."

"Can I see it?" Eliza asks.

"Sure. It's here on YouTube." The video features talk-show host Jimmy Kimmel, who challenged viewers to prank kids with terrible Christmas gifts and record their reactions. Among the prank gifts are a rotten banana, a half-eaten sandwich, and a battery. Without fail, every child is stunned and then melts into disappointment or an outright tantrum. Eliza watches quietly, laughing just a few times.

When the video ends, Eliza remarks, "I think it's cruel how parents lied to their kids."

"C'mon," you say, "they were just teasing . . . the class will crack up when I show it. I have a heavy topic." You tell Eliza the specific purpose of your speech—to convince the class to give money or time to a charity during the holidays. You believe the video will support a main point in your speech: the holidays are a time when many people think more about themselves than others.

Eliza responds, "That is a serious topic, but there's got to be other ways to make your point. My dad used to pull practical jokes like that, and I hated it."

How do you feel when Eliza reacts negatively to the video? Does her reaction surprise you?

2 *THE RESEARCH*

Humor, thoughtfully integrated in speeches, can enhance speaker credibility and persuasiveness (Lynch, 2002). Comic relief can also motivate interest in a message. After reviewing decades of research related to humor and public speaking, Charles R. Gruner (1985) came up with the following suggestions:

- Small amounts of relevant and appropriate humor can lead an audience to see you as likable and trustworthy.
- Humor directed at yourself can enhance your image with the audience. Listeners appreciate speakers who are able to poke fun at themselves.
- Humor may be unnecessary when you have other interesting forms of support, such as suspenseful or engaging stories.
- Excessive humor or inappropriate humor (sick, racist, or sexist) may cause your message to be rejected. Don't assume that others will share your sense of humor or see offensive humor as "just a joke."
- Sarcastic or disparaging humor toward opposing views may annoy or offend your audience when you're trying to persuade them. It's more effective to make your case using well-reasoned claims.

What other forms of supporting material (humorous or not) could you use to support your main point: that the holiday season is a time when many people think more about themselves than others?

3 *YOUR OPPORTUNITY*

Before you act, consider the facts of the situation, what you know about supporting materials, and the research on using humor in speeches. Also, reflect on what you've learned so far about composing a speech, including supporting your main points (pp. 349–352) and keeping your listeners engaged (pp. 356–357).

Now it's your turn. Write a response to Eliza. Be sure to mention whether or not you will include the video in your speech.

video, animations, and other materials can be brought into your presentation to support a point. We'll take a closer look at how to use presentation aids in Chapter 15.

Keeping your listeners engaged is important even when giving short talks, such as *elevator speeches*, in which you must convey a lot of information in a small amount of time. For more on how you can successfully handle such a situation, see Advance the Conversation: Elevator Speeches on pages 362–363.

Introducing and Concluding Your Speech

How your speech begins and ends can make or break its success. Your introduction is your chance to grab your audience's attention, and your conclusion has the final impact on how your audience responds to your overall message.

Liz Dozier is the founder and CEO of Chicago Beyond, a community activist organization that provides counseling and professional development services for disadvantaged Chicago students. When she spoke in 2018 at SXSW EDU—a conference promoting innovation in education—she started her presentation by greeting the Texas audience with a "Hey, y'all!" (Dozier, 2018). She then emphasized the common ground she shares with her listeners as educators and, further, she promised that her talk would include scandal, intrigue, and some laughter. Her central point was that *every* student, especially those with academic and behavioral problems, can achieve an education. After previewing her main points, Dozier moved skillfully through the body of her speech, making compelling arguments for programs like adult mentoring, socio-emotional learning, and anger management classes. Finally, she concluded her presentation by challenging her listeners to look inside themselves and question their own assumptions about underprivileged students and how educators and community leaders can help them.

By starting her speech with a friendly greeting, expressing common interests in education, and offering to share something scandalous, Dozier connected immediately with her listeners and gained their attention. Then in her conclusion, she challenged the audience to take specific action in how they view troubled students. Let's look at how you can create equally strong and memorable introductions and conclusions for your speeches.

Introducing Your Speech

Your speech introduction is your first chance to connect with your audience and prepare them for what you will say. During this time, you want to gain listeners' attention, disclose your speech thesis, establish credibility, connect to listeners' needs and interests, and preview your main points. Although other information might be included—like brief background

Jeff Schear/Getty Images Entertainment/Getty Images

Well-crafted introductions and conclusions that work together—as in Chicago Beyond founder Liz Dozier's speech at SXSW EDU 2018—bring a power to your presentation that your main points cannot do alone. How can you make sure your introductions and conclusions come with a punch?

about the topic—speech introductions often begin with gaining your listeners' attention and end by previewing your main points.

Gain Listeners' Attention. More than anything else, your introduction tells the audience what type of speech you are going to give. If you start your speech with overused phrases like "Hi, my name is . . . and today I'm going to talk about . . . ," you are telling your audience that your speech is going to be boring. Instead, create anticipation for what you have to say with a more creative introduction. Here are some ways to do that:

- *Ask a real question.* Posing a real question is a way to involve your audience immediately. For example, "By a show of hands, how many of you have public social media accounts?" Exercise caution if you encourage verbal responses because lengthy answers will sacrifice your speech time. Be prepared to step in and cut off responses if things get out of hand.
- *Ask a rhetorical question.* Rhetorical questions prompt your listeners to silently reflect on an issue. Dr. Sidibe used this technique when she opened her speech with, "So imagine that a plane is about to crash with 250 children and babies, and if you knew how to stop that, would you?" This can also work especially well if you are delivering your speech online and can't see or hear the responses of your audience.
- *Make a startling or suspenseful statement.* Start with a fact or statistic that raises your listeners' curiosity or challenges their worldview. For example, "One in three of you in this class will get it at some point in your lives. It's known as the 'silent killer.'"

TABLE 14.2

INTRODUCTION CHECKLIST

Gain listeners' attention

Disclose your speech thesis

Establish credibility

Connect to listeners' needs and interests

Preview your main points

file404/Shutterstock

- *Tell a story*. Begin your introduction with a compelling, relevant story. When telling a story, keep it brief. You don't want the story to become the speech itself.
- *Use a brief quotation*. Alert your audience to the speech's theme, and grab their attention with a relevant quote. For example, "Gandhi said, 'You must be the change you want to see in the world,'" or "I'm an adopted child, and my mother always told me, 'We chose you.'"
- *Reference the occasion or recent events*. Comment on common ground between you and your audience. For example, "Tonight is a wonderful opportunity for all of us to reflect on the significance of 50 years of marriage as we honor Lawrence and Charlene."

Disclose Your Speech Thesis. After grabbing your audience's attention, you reveal the subject matter of your speech by clearly stating your speech thesis. For example, "You can reduce the likelihood of falling victim to cyberstalking by taking steps to protect your privacy online." Sometimes you will need to provide background information or definitions to make sure your audience understands your thesis. In a speech about cyberstalking, you may need to define the term in your introduction so that there is no confusion about what you mean.

Establish Credibility. As you introduce a speech, the audience may wonder about your qualifications or experience with the topic. Listeners are more receptive to your message if they perceive you as credible or trustworthy. Although *credibility* is a key component in persuasive speaking, you also want to be trustworthy and ethical when giving informative and special-occasion speeches. How do you establish your credibility during the speech introduction? Briefly tell listeners about any relevant personal experience, or explain why you're interested in the topic. For example, "Last October I discovered that I had a cyberstalker."

Of course, you must maintain your credibility throughout the entire speech. We discuss how to do this in Chapter 17.

Connect to Listeners' Needs and Interests. People pay more attention to a speech when they think the topic is relevant to their needs and concerns. But it's not always apparent to your listeners how they can benefit from listening to your speech. This is why it is important to clearly state "what's in it for them" during your introduction. For instance, "I know that many of you have Instagram, Twitter, and other social media accounts. What I have to share with you today can lower your chances of becoming a victim of cyberstalking."

Preview Your Main Points. End your introduction by highlighting the main points of your presentation. This signals to your audience that you are transitioning from the introduction to the body of your speech: "I will first discuss the common types of cyberstalking that occur online. Then I'll go over some steps you can take to protect yourself."

Concluding Your Speech

Your conclusion indicates that you have finished presenting your main points and are approaching the end of your speech. Plan your conclusion carefully—it's your last chance to make sure your audience understands your main points. An effective conclusion signals the end of your speech, summarizes your main points, and has a memorable impact on your audience.

Signal the End. To signal that your speech is coming to a close, provide your listeners with a signpost or transition. Simple phrases like "In summary" or "Before I close" tell the audience that you're about to end the speech. This transition also gives inattentive audience members one last chance to hear your main points.

Summarize Your Main Points. An age-old saying about how to make a speech is "Tell them what you're going to tell them, tell them, and tell them what you told them." In your conclusion, a quick review of your main points helps your audience remember and understand them. But remember that you're only summarizing. Don't repeat extensive details about your main points. Instead, express each main point in one sentence, and avoid introducing any new material in your conclusion.

Have a Memorable Impact. Just as you opened your speech with an attention-getting

TABLE 14.3

CONCLUSION CHECKLIST

1 Signal the end

2 Summarize your main points

3 Have a memorable impact

file404/Shutterstock

statement, your parting words should also be memorable. Some of the same strategies used to gain listeners' attention also work for closing your speech—including asking questions, using quotations, or telling a brief story. Another possibility is to introduce your presentation by telling a story but leave the audience in suspense about its ending. You can then finish the story in the conclusion of your speech.

Take time to compose a final statement that leaves a lasting impression. Instead of trailing off by saying, "Well, I guess that's it," there should be a clear indication to your audience that you are done.

Putting It All Together: Speech Outlines

The end result of step 3: composing is a written outline. All the time you devote to thinking about your topic, researching it, writing a thesis, drafting your main points, and organizing your ideas is reflected in written outlines that you will use in delivering your speech.

Watch any major awards show, such as the Oscars or the Grammys, and you're bound to see some celebrities take the stage completely unprepared to accept their awards. Fumbling through their acceptance speeches, they make classic mistakes—like forgetting to thank someone or rambling on endlessly. Only on rare occasions do you see celebrities reach into a pocket for prepared notes and speak eloquently and appreciatively about the award. Such planning is crucial for any successful speech.

The last task in composing your speech is to develop your written outlines. A **preparation outline** details your presentation's overall structure. Similar to outlines for essays or research papers, a preparation outline helps you plan the order, flow, and logic of your speech, ensuring that there are no weaknesses or missing elements. A **delivery outline** helps you keep track of your ideas while you're actually presenting your speech to an audience. This section provides general guidelines for developing both types of outlines. However, since outline formats often vary, be sure to check with your instructor regarding any specific outline requirements for your class.

Preparation Outline

Your preparation outline details your speech's introduction, body, and conclusion. It also lists the references you used to develop your speech and your specific purpose and speech thesis statements. This outline is a great way to keep track of all the information in your speech. You will likely make several drafts of it as you practice your speech and add or delete information as needed. Be sure to keep your outline up to date, so that it reflects your latest thoughts about the speech's structure. You can find an example of a preparation outline on pages 364–367. When creating your preparation outline, keep the following principles in mind:

- Use a consistent set of symbols and indentation. Typically, section headings show the parts of your speech—the introduction, body, and conclusion. Roman numerals (I, II, III) designate your main points for each section; uppercase letters (A, B, C) indicate your subpoints. Additional indentation levels (arabic numbers and lowercase letters) can be used if needed—for example, if you want to include the exact wording for testimony you will quote in the speech. Consistency in symbols and indentation helps you see the relationships among your ideas and makes sure those relationships are logical.

- Identify each main point using one complete sentence. This forces you to determine the best way to communicate each point.
- Make certain that all subpoints support the main point they sit under. Known as the **principle of subordination**, this practice ensures that you're making valid arguments and that your claims are well supported and logical.
- Write your connective words and phrases in the outline, but set them off in parentheses ( ) so that they don't get confused with your main points or subpoints. Adding these phrases will help you determine whether your ideas are flowing smoothly.
- Include a works-cited or references section at the end of your outline. This should encompass all the information you'll cite in your speech as well as sources you consulted while preparing the speech. Talk with your instructor about any specific content and formatting requirements for this section.

Delivery Outline

Whereas the preparation outline helps you think through your speech's structure before you give the speech, your delivery outline acts as your "speaker notes" during the actual presentation to remind you of main points and key phrases. Create your delivery outline after you have practiced your speech several times using your preparation outline. Whether you prepare your delivery outline on note cards, sheets of paper, or an iPad, there are some features that are common to all good delivery outlines (see pages 367–369):

- Write your delivery outline using keywords or phrases. Since the purpose of the delivery outline is to jog your memory while you're presenting, include only words or phrases that trigger the larger ideas you want to convey.
- Type your notes, and use a font (typeface) that is large enough for you to read easily. If you must handwrite your notes, make sure your writing is legible. You don't want your audience to see you struggling to read your own notes!
- Put in time codes (e.g., 4:00, meaning 4 minutes) and side notes (e.g., Pause briefly) to guide your delivery. Time codes help you stay on track, so you don't rush through your speech or go too slowly. Also, include reminders to use your nonverbal communication skills, such as smiling, looking around the room, and speaking slowly and clearly. Since you are the only one who will see your delivery outline notes, use them in any way that helps you deliver an effective, memorable speech.

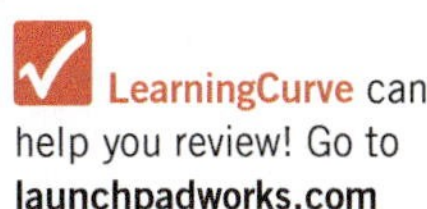
LearningCurve can help you review! Go to **launchpadworks.com**

ADVANCE THE CONVERSATION
Video Activity

ELEVATOR SPEECHES

The following scenario will enhance your ability to communicate competently in impromptu speech scenarios. Visit LaunchPad at **launchpadworks.com** to get the full experience with video. As you watch the first video, recall what you've learned about keeping listeners engaged. Then complete the **Your Turn** prompts. Finally, watch the **Take Two!** video to explore how this scenario could have gone differently.

1 *THE PROBLEM*

Lily is a graduate student research assistant working with Bobbie, a marine biology professor. Lily is studying how small fish transport carbon dioxide from the air and ocean surface into the deep sea. One day, Lily and Bobbie unexpectedly run into Dr. Mike Snyder, the college president, in the hallway of their department building. Dr. Snyder is on his way to a meeting, but he asks Lily to briefly explain her research. "Well," Lily says excitedly, "this semester we've been running data correlating CO_2 levels and its negative impact on the atmosphere, which then in turn is directly related to global warming. I mean, the data isn't definitive, but we're optimistic that the small fish that consume the excess CO_2 on the ocean's surface can lead to finding a more natural solution to correct the imbalance." Dr. Snyder looks slightly confused. "So," he asks, "you're looking for ways to reduce climate change?"

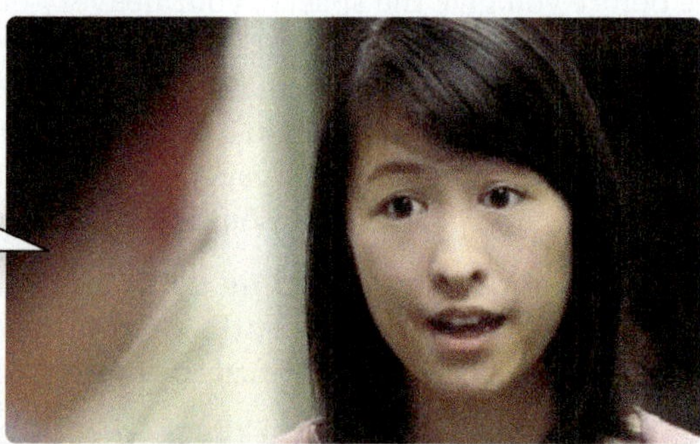

"Ultimately—or that's the hope, anyways. As a matter of fact, there have been a lot of encouraging projections recently regarding this."

"Yes, well, thank you, Lily. I wish I could stay and hear more, but I see I'm needed at the moment."

2 YOUR TURN

Observations. Reflect on how Lily and Dr. Snyder communicated in this scenario by answering the following questions:

1. Which character do you identify with more in this situation? How would you feel if you were in his or her situation?
2. Where were the missed opportunities to practice competent communication?

Discussion. In class or with a partner, share your thoughts about the interaction between Lily and Dr. Snyder and work to answer the following questions:

1. Can you understand both perspectives?
2. What could Lily and Dr. Snyder have done differently?

Conclusion. Choose one person in the scenario to offer your advice. Based on your analysis, what advice would you give him or her to improve his or her communication competence in this scenario?

3 TAKE TWO!

What if things had gone differently? Watch the **Take Two!** video to see one possible example of how the conversation might have gone if Lily and/or Dr. Snyder had communicated differently. As you watch the video, consider where the dialog reflects communication competence. After watching the video, answer the questions below:

1. Did Lily and/or Dr. Snyder take advantage of opportunities that they missed in the first scenario? Which ones?
2. Did their different actions result in a more productive encounter? Please explain.

Sample Preparation and Delivery Outlines

Preparation Outline

SPEECH TITLE: PROTECT THE LARGEST ORGAN IN YOUR LIFE

By: Jessica Bordonaro, Scottsdale Community College

• *Write your specific purpose and thesis as part of the outline heading to keep the central idea of your speech in mind as you develop your outline.*

Topic: Reducing Skin Cancer Risks
Specific purpose: To persuade my audience to take precautionary steps to reduce the risks of skin cancer and other skin-related health issues. •
Speech thesis: By protecting yourself adequately from overexposure to the sun, you lessen your risk of skin damage and skin cancers.

• *Section headers are used to identify the introduction, body, and conclusion of the speech. This helps you see the overall speech organization.*

• *The outline includes all five components for an effective introduction.*

• *The preview statement links the introduction to the body of the speech.*

INTRODUCTION: •

I. Gain attention: "By a show of hands, how many of you always protect yourselves when you know you are going to be in the sun for a significant amount of time?"

II. Speech thesis: By protecting yourself adequately from overexposure to the sun, you lessen your risk of skin damage and skin cancer.

III. Establish credibility: I have firsthand experience with the negative effects the sun can have on people. •

  A. Two family friends died in the past three years from skin cancer.
  B. I am very passionate about wanting people to know how to protect themselves from overexposure to the sun.

IV. Connect listeners' need: Living in Arizona, you have exposure to the sun all year round.

V. Preview main points: I am going to discuss how not protecting yourself from overexposure to the sun can contribute to skin-health problems, such as sunburn, premature aging, and skin cancer. I am also going to cover some ways you can help protect yourself from these things. •

• *Each main point is indicated by a roman numeral and is stated as one complete sentence.*

• *Subpoints are marked by uppercase letters. Be sure to check for appropriate subordination of all subpoints.*

BODY:

I. **Main Point 1:** Your risk for sunburn increases when you don't protect yourself adequately from the sun. •

  A. Sunburns happen from overexposure to the sun. •
    1. In a 2012 study, dermatologist Jennifer Lin and colleagues observed that among adolescents in the United States, about 83% reported at least one bad sunburn the previous summer.
    2. Only about 34% of adolescents reported sunscreen use (Lin, Eder, & Weinmann, 2012).

3. Sunburn doesn't discriminate by skin color.
   a. The Mayo Clinic website (2012) states that although lighter-skinned types may burn easily, darker-skinned types can also suffer sunburns. •
   b. All skin types are subject to deep skin damage due to overexposure to the sun (Mayo Clinic, 2012).

B. According to the National Library of Medicine (2011), "While the symptoms of sunburn are usually temporary . . . , the skin damage is often permanent and can have serious long-term health effects," and that "by the time the skin starts to become painful and red, the damage has been done."

• All supporting material is listed with proper points, including source citations.

(Transition: Sunburn is just the start of much larger issues of skin damage.) •

• Connectives are set off in parentheses. They also help show the relationship between main points.

II. **Main Point 2:** Another issue that can arise when you don't protect yourself well in the sun is premature aging.

A. Intrinsic aging is one type of skin aging.
   1. Intrinsic skin aging is related to natural biological aging.
   2. Intrinsically aged skin appears smooth, pale, and finely wrinkled.

B. Extrinsic aging (or photoaging) is the effect of a lifetime of UV exposure.
   1. According to Fitzpatrick Dermatology, "Many skin functions that decline with age show an accelerated decline in photoaged skin" (Gonzaga, 2009).
   2. Photoaged skin is characterized by coarse wrinkles, dark spots, and broken blood vessels.

(Transition: Although you might think that sunburns are temporary and aging skin is too far down the road to worry about, there is another damaging effect of the sun to your health.)

III. **Main Point 3:** Overexposure to the sun can contribute to skin cancer.

A. There are different kinds of skin cancer, and some are more aggressive than others.
   1. According to the American Cancer Society website (2013), more than 3.5 million cases of non-melanoma skin cancers are diagnosed in the United States each year. •
      a. These include basal- and squamous-cell carcinomas.
      b. These cancers develop on sun-exposed areas of the skin.
      c. These skin cancers are curable when caught early.
   2. Melanoma starts in the particular skin cells that produce our skin color, known as melanocytes.
   3. Melanoma accounted for about 75% of skin cancer deaths in 2012 (Lin et al.).

• In composing this speech, the speaker uses a variety of supporting materials, including statistics, examples, expert testimony, and stories.

B. I have had two family friends affected by skin cancer. •

• The speaker includes a personal story as supporting material to engage the audience.

(Transition: Given the potentially deadly effects of the sun, what can we do?)

• This speech uses four main points to develop the thesis. What organizational pattern does the speech follow?

IV. **Main Point 4:** There are several ways to protect yourself from the sun and its harmful effects. •

  A. Avoid sun exposure during hours of peak sun-ray intensity.

    1. The UV index is a measure of ultraviolet radiation from the sun.
    2. Here is a map of yesterday's UV index.

  B. If you're going to spend extended time in the sun, protect your skin by wearing sunscreen.

    1. Wear generous amounts of at least SPF 30 sunscreen.
    2. Apply 30 minutes before sun exposure to allow absorption.
    3. Remember to reapply, because it comes off in water and from sweat.

  C. You should also protect other exposed areas of your body.

    1. Wear UV-protective sunglasses.
    2. Wear lip balm with a high SPF.
    3. Wear a wide-brim hat.

  D. Even if you don't plan to spend time in the sun, develop the habit of wearing a daily lotion that has sunscreen in it.

    1. This is easy to do if you already put lotion on anyway.
    2. This simple change will ensure you get SPF protection every day.

• The conclusion summarizes the main points of the speech and is a final chance to leave the audience with a lasting impression about the topic.

CONCLUSION: •

I. Summary: Getting too much sun has negative and damaging effects on the body, but you can take simple, specific precautions to protect yourself from the sun's rays.

II. Summer is approaching, not to mention the fact that we live in Arizona, so do yourself a favor and start buying sunscreen and applying it when you are going to be in the sun.

III. You don't want to look older than you are or risk dying before your time.

• The last part of the outline is a properly formatted list of sources used for preparing the speech.

REFERENCES •

American Cancer Society (2013). Retrieved from http://www.cancer.org/cancer/cancercauses/sunanduvexposure/skin-cancer-facts

EPA. (n.d.). *UV index*. Retrieved from http://www2.epa.gov/sunwise/uv-index

Gonzaga, E. R. (2009, January). Role of UV light in photodamage, skin aging, and skin cancer. *American Journal of Clinical Dermatology 10*(S1), 19–24. Retrieved from Academic Search Premier.

Lin, J. S., Eder, M., & Weinmann, S. (2011, February). Behavioral counseling to prevent skin cancer: A systematic review for the U.S. Preventive Services Task Force. *Annals of Internal Medicine 154*(3), 190–201. Retrieved from Academic Search Premier.

Mayo Clinic. (2012). *Sunburn: Risk factors*. Retrieved from http://www.mayoclinic.com/health/sunburn/DS00964/DSECTION=risk-factors

National Library of Medicine. (2011, May 13). *Sunburn*. Retrieved from http://www.nlm.nih.gov/medlineplus/ency/article/003227.htm

Delivery Outline •

• The delivery outline uses phrases and keywords that the speaker can quickly reference to help guide the presentation.

INTRODUCTION:

I. "How many of you always protect yourselves when you know you are going to be in the sun for a significant amount of time?"

(Pause briefly)

II. Protecting yourself lessens your risk of skin damage and skin cancer.

III. Firsthand experience: two family friends died. Passionate about protection

(Maintain eye contact) •

• The notes in parentheses are reminders to stay focused on proper nonverbal and vocal delivery during the presentation. Time codes also help the speaker with pacing the speech.

IV. Living in AZ

V. Discuss how not protecting contributes to sunburn, premature aging, and skin cancer. Also go over some ways to protect yourself.

(1:00 minute)

BODY:

I. Sun exposure increases sunburn risk.
   A. Sunburn—overexposure to the sun
      1. Among adolescents in the U.S., about 83% had one bad sunburn (Lin, Eder, & Weinmann, 2012). •
      2. Only about 34% of adolescents reported sunscreen use (Lin et al.).
      3. Sunburn and skin color
         a. Lighter-skinned types burn easily; darker-skinned types can suffer sunburns (Mayo Clinic, 2012).
         b. All skin types suffer deep skin damage (Mayo Clinic, 2012).
   B. According to the National Library of Medicine (2011), "While the symptoms of sunburn are usually temporary . . . , the skin damage is often permanent and can have serious long-term health effects," and "by the time the skin starts to become painful and red, the damage has been done."

• The delivery outline includes source citation details so that the speaker gives proper credit to sources during the speech.

(Transition: Sunburn is just the start of much larger issues of skin damage.)

(Move to right side of room)
(3:00 minutes)

II. Another issue is premature aging.
   A. Intrinsic aging
      1. Intrinsic skin aging is natural.
      2. Appears smooth, pale, and finely wrinkled
   B. Extrinsic or photoaging
      1. According to Fitzpatrick Dermatology, "Many skin functions that decline with age show an accelerated decline in photoaged skin" (Gonzaga, 2009).
      2. Characterized by coarse wrinkles, dark spots, and broken blood vessels

(Transition: Although you might think that sunburns are temporary and aging skin is too far down the road to worry about, there is another damaging effect of the sun to your health.)

(Move to center of room)
(4:00 minutes)

III. Overexposure contributes to skin cancer.
   A. Different kinds of skin cancer; some are aggressive

   (Go slowly)

      1. According to the American Cancer Society website (2013), more than 3.5 million cases of non-melanoma skin cancers are diagnosed in the United States each year.
         a. Basal- and squamous-cell carcinomas
         b. Develop on sun-exposed areas of the skin
         c. Curable when caught early
      2. Melanoma starts in melanocytes.
      3. Melanoma—75% of skin cancer deaths in 2012 (Lin et al.)
   B. Two family friends affected by skin cancer

(Transition: Given the potentially deadly effects of the sun, what can we do?)

(Move to left of room)
(Maintain eye contact)
(5:00 minutes)

IV. Several ways to protect yourself

   (Move back to lectern)

   A. Avoid hours of peak sun-ray intensity.
      1. The UV index
      2. UV index map (Show map)
   B. Protect your skin by wearing sunscreen.

1. At least SPF 30 sunscreen (Show sunscreen container) •
2. Apply 30 minutes before exposure
3. Reapply

C. Protect other exposed areas of your body. (Show each object)
1. Wear UV-protective sunglasses.
2. Wear lip balm with a high SPF.
3. Wear a wide-brim hat.

D. Wear a daily SPF lotion. (Show everyday lotion container)
1. Already put lotion on anyway
2. Simple change ensures SPF protection.

(7:00 minutes)
(Brief pause)

• *Reminders reduce the chance of forgetting to display a presentation aid.*

CONCLUSION: •

I. Getting too much sun has negative and damaging effects on the body, but you can take specific, simple precautions to protect yourself from the sun's rays.

II. Summer is approaching.

(Brief pause)

III. You don't want to look older than you are or risk dying before your time.

• *Similar to the preparation outline, all three sections of the speech and connectives are marked to help the speaker stay organized and focused.*

REFERENCES:

American Cancer Society (2013). Retrieved from http://www.cancer.org/cancer/cancercauses/sunanduvexposure/skin-cancer-facts

EPA. (n.d.). *UV index*. Retrieved from http://www2.epa.gov/sunwise/uv-index

Gonzaga, E. R. (2009, January). Role of UV light in photodamage, skin aging, and skin cancer. *American Journal of Clinical Dermatology 10*(S1), 19–24. Retrieved from Academic Search Premier.

Lin, J. S., Eder, M., & Weinmann, S. (2011, February). Behavioral counseling to prevent skin cancer: A systematic review for the U.S. Preventive Services Task Force. *Annals of Internal Medicine 154*(3), 190–201. Retrieved from Academic Search Premier.

Mayo Clinic. (2012). *Sunburn: Risk factors*. Retrieved from http://www.mayoclinic.com/health/sunburn/DS00964/DSECTION=risk-factors

National Library of Medicine. (2011, May 13). *Sunburn*. Retrieved from www.nlm.nih.gov/medlineplus/ency/article/003227.htm

CHAPTER 14 REVIEW

CHAPTER RECAP

- Your **speech thesis** will guide the structure of your speech. Evolving from your *specific purpose statement*, it will inform your audience of your position on the topic and provide insight into your main points.
- The *body* of your speech contains your **main points**, which are backed up by your *supporting materials*.
- The *organizational pattern* you choose (**topical**, **chronological**, **spatial**, **cause-effect**, or **problem-solution**) will help your audience understand and follow your speech's main points.
- Both the *introduction* and the *conclusion* serve important purposes in a speech. These are moments when you have the opportunity to gain listeners' attention, disclose your thesis, establish credibility, connect to your audience, preview and summarize your main points, prepare listeners for the end of your speech, and make a final impression.
- Developing **preparation** and **delivery outlines** helps you plan the flow and logic of your speech and keeps you on task during the actual presentation, making you a more successful speaker.

LaunchPad

LaunchPad for *Choices & Connections* offers unique video scenarios and encourages self-assessment through adaptive quizzing. Go to **launchpadworks.com** to get access.

- LearningCurve adaptive quizzes
- Advance the Conversation video scenarios
- Video clips that illustrate key concepts

KEY TERMS

Composing, p. 344
Speech thesis, p. 344
Main point, p. 345
Subpoint, p. 347
Statistic, p. 348
Example, p. 348
Analogy, p. 349
Testimony, p. 349
Direct quotation, p. 349
Paraphrasing, p. 350
Topical pattern, p. 351
Chronological pattern, p. 351
Spatial pattern, p. 352
Cause-effect pattern, p. 352
Problem-solution pattern, p. 352
Connective, p. 352
Internal preview, p. 353
Internal summary, p. 353
Transitional phrase, p. 353
Signpost, p. 353
Preparation outline, p. 360
Delivery outline, p. 360
Principle of subordination, p. 361

POP QUIZ

Looking for more review questions? LearningCurve can help you master key concepts from this chapter. Go to **launchpadworks.com**

1. Which of the following is *not* a requirement of a speech thesis?
   a. It includes all your main points.
   b. It is one sentence.
   c. It is stated during your speech.
   d. It alerts the audience to your position.

2. When using statistics, it is important to
   a. give precise and detailed numbers.
   b. put the statistics in a meaningful context.
   c. use multiple examples each time.
   d. include the statistics throughout the speech.

3. You are giving a speech on how websites like Kickstarter have changed how small businesses raise funds. What would be the best organizational pattern to use?
   a. Spatial pattern
   b. Topical pattern
   c. Problem-solution pattern
   d. Cause-effect pattern

4. What is the best way to engage your listeners if they are already familiar with the information you are presenting?
   a. Include unrelated stories and jokes for a touch of humor.
   b. Spend more time on your presentation aids than on your supporting materials.
   c. Forgo any introduction, and get right to the body of the speech.
   d. Look for additional sources that present new testimony or examples.

5. Why might you create several drafts of your preparation outline?
   a. To include time codes to monitor pacing
   b. To eliminate any internal summaries
   c. To allow for revisions after practicing your speech
   d. To replace the organizational pattern

ACTIVITIES

For more activities, visit LaunchPad for *Choices & Connections* at **launchpadworks.com**

1 Speech Analysis

Find a professional speech that interests you. Try a TED talk (ted.com/talks), or search databases like Gifts of Speech (gos.sbc.edu) or American Rhetoric (americanrhetoric.com). In a brief paper, identify the speech thesis, its main points, and the organizational pattern. Additionally, analyze how well the speaker engages listeners through novelty, humor, stories, and presentation media.

2 Introduction Redo

Review the attention-getter used in the speech outline for "Protect the Largest Organ in Your Life" by Jessica Bordonaro on pages 364–369. Working with a group of classmates, brainstorm additional ways to gain listeners' attention if you were giving this speech. Choose one of the alternatives and present it to the class, explaining why you selected that one over the other ideas.

15

Delivering Your Speech

Executive Aria Finger places a high value on developing the public speaking skills of her employees. Every Wednesday her staff at DoSomething — a not-for-profit organization that mobilizes young people to take up social causes — spills into a big meeting room to pitch ideas.[1] The staff presents new projects, marketing strategies, or web designs, or proposes improvements. Presentations follow a standard format consisting of slides, recommendations, and lots of humor. Every speaker is expected to be engaging, upbeat, and persuasive.

Any employee can give a presentation at the Wednesday staff meetings, but they must be well prepared. After carefully composing their message, presenters dedicate themselves to practicing their presentations with a small group of coworkers. During practice, employees receive feedback about whether they are talking too fast or too slow. Coworkers point out slumping posture or hands slipping into pockets. Employees earn high praise when they maintain eye contact and avoid reading their speech notes. The time spent practicing gives employees a chance to determine how their audience will react to the message and to make any needed revisions prior to the actual presentation (Lorch, 2015).

Rehearsal also serves another useful purpose: employees discover that it calms nervousness about public speaking. The whole process is, as Lorch (2015) describes, "a crash course in public speaking." Even Aria Finger joins in with her employees by practicing and developing her own presentation skills right along with them. She is known to be an energetic and confident speaker who is "the master of long intentional pauses" that keep audiences' attention to her messages. Her enthusiasm for public speaking is infectious and helps set a positive example and a supportive communication climate for everyone at the company.

The company's devotion to practicing presentations and getting feedback translates into impactful presentations. Wednesday staff meetings are a mix of fun, high pressure, and "out-of-the-box" thinking, where employees tackle work challenges. The meeting presentations help DoSomething remain a leader in supporting social causes. The organization has reached over 4 million teens and young adults who organize social action projects related to homelessness, bullying, drug use, and a variety of other issues.

[1]Information in the chapter opener from Lorch (2015) and www.dosomething.org

Henry S. Dziekan III/Getty Images Entertainment/Getty Images

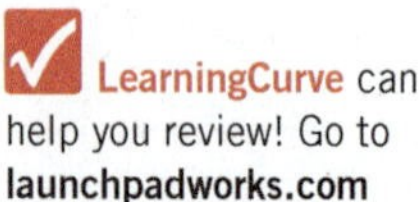
LearningCurve can help you review! Go to **launchpadworks.com**

DoSomething employees understand an essential requirement for improving their public-speaking skills: practice pays off. Given the considerable time you put into each step of the speech preparation process — *thinking* about your audience and specific speech purpose, *investigating* or researching your topic, and carefully *composing* the presentation — your speech will fall flat if you don't practice. That's why steps 4 and 5 — *rehearse* and *revise* — are important elements of your speech preparation. Only through rehearsing and revising can you get a sense of how to improve both your speech's content and your verbal and nonverbal skills in delivering it. (See Table 13.1 on page 317 for the Five Steps in Speech Preparation.) Such practice is key to engaging your audience during your speech delivery. In this chapter, you'll learn:

- How to deliver a speech effectively
- Ways to connect with your audience
- Ideas for managing speech anxiety
- The process for selecting and using presentation aids
- How to evaluate others' speeches and use feedback to improve your own presentation skills

Speech Delivery Modes

> **You can start step 4: rehearse by considering how you will actually deliver your speech. Will you have time to adequately prepare? How heavily (if at all) will you rely on notes? Will factors such as the setting, situation, or audience influence your presentation? Answering questions like these will help you determine your delivery style.**

Public speakers can rely on three primary modes of delivery. You might have to deliver your message when you have little to no time for preparation (impromptu); you might write out and then read or memorize an entire script (manuscript); or you might have a combination of both, in which you prepare your research and notes but do not plan every word you'll say in advance (extemporaneous).

Impromptu Speaking

Imagine that just as you arrive at a 25th anniversary dinner for your favorite aunt and uncle, your mother asks if you'll "say a few words" about the couple after dessert is served. You scan the room of more than 50 guests and nervously agree to do it. Responding to your mom's request requires **impromptu speaking** — making public remarks with little or no time for preparation or rehearsal.

Although daunting, there are ways you can handle impromptu speaking situations. First, anticipate as much as possible occasions where you could be asked to say something. If you know people will be making formal remarks at the anniversary dinner and you are especially close with your aunt and uncle, might you be expected to say a few words? Second, keep your message brief, and don't apologize for being unprepared. Third, identify a central point you want to make, and illustrate it with two or three supporting points to back you up. Fourth, restate your central point as your conclusion. If you have the time, compose a brief speaking outline to help keep you focused. For most impromptu situations, providing a small amount of information should satisfy your audience. No one expects you to give a long, detailed presentation on a moment's notice.

Because it's almost impossible to rehearse impromptu speeches, you can practice this type of speaking in other ways. Take advantage of opportunities that allow you to present your ideas in front of large groups, such as contributing to class discussions or work meetings. You'll gain experience thinking quickly on your feet, and grow more comfortable speaking on a moment's notice. Additionally, the Advance the Conversation video activity in Chapter 14 (pages 362–363) will help you develop your skills with a special type of impromptu speech known as an elevator speech.

Manuscript Speaking

Some occasions require **manuscript speaking**, in which your speech is based on a written text that you either read word for word or commit to memory. Manuscript speaking is necessary when exact word choice is critical. World leaders, for example, often speak from prepared texts in public. This helps them avoid saying something that could be misunderstood by listeners.

Manuscript speaking is appropriate in formal situations, such as political speeches, commencement addresses, and public ceremonies. Such occasions usually require a speaker to carefully craft a message using language that is finely polished, even poetic. This can be easier to do if the speech is written out in advance. Consider the following excerpt from Martin Luther King Jr.'s (1963) historic "I Have a Dream" speech:

> In a sense we have come to our nation's capital to cash a check. When the architects of our Republic wrote the magnificent words of the Constitution and the Declaration of Independence, they were signing a promissory note to which every American was to fall heir. This note was a promise that all men would be guaranteed the inalienable rights of life, liberty, and the pursuit of happiness.

Rather than using plain words to call for racial equality, Dr. King used vivid imagery ("we have come to our nation's capital to cash a check") to communicate America's responsibility for ending racial discrimination. Bringing that powerful image to his listeners' minds would have been more difficult

Manuscript speaking allows you to correctly state more intricate, emotional language and phrases, like Martin Luther King Jr. did in his "I Have a Dream" speech. When might you want to use a manuscript for your speeches?

Entertainment Pictures/Alamy Stock Photo

if Dr. King hadn't written out those exact words in advance. When using poetic language, constructing intricate metaphors, or delving into complicated matters, manuscript speaking allows you to get the details right.

But manuscript speaking also has drawbacks. For one thing, reading a written text reduces opportunities to maintain eye contact with your listeners. Or if you memorize your manuscript, you might sound stilted or lose your place, leading to embarrassing pauses or mistakes. Finally, manuscript speaking makes it difficult to adapt to your audience. If you sense your listeners need an additional example to understand a point you're making, it would be difficult to deviate from your script and provide that example. Using a manuscript should be reserved for formal occasions. For many classroom speeches, the extemporaneous delivery style is more appropriate.

Extemporaneous Speaking

Extemporaneous speaking includes elements of both manuscript and impromptu speaking. In this case, you create a preparation outline for your speech ahead of time, mapping out what you plan to cover (as in manuscript speaking). Then you reduce your preparation outline to a delivery outline that allows you to add or eliminate information as needed during your presentation (as in impromptu speaking). The resulting speech sounds more conversational than it would if you read from or memorized a manuscript. A *conversational tone* is similar to a casual conversation; it uses a natural, spoken language style rather than a formal, written language style, and the speaker exudes emotion and passion for the topic (Doetkott & Motley, 2009).

In most settings, an extemporaneous style of speaking is a great way to connect with your listeners. A well-prepared delivery outline allows you to focus on using familiar language, eye contact, gestures, and an engaging conversational style. Of course, these same qualities can be achieved in impromptu or manuscript speaking, but it can be challenging if you're speaking with little preparation, reciting a speech from memory, or reading from paper or a screen. With the extemporaneous mode, your speech will be a little bit different each time you deliver it. But if you've gone through the five steps of speech preparation beforehand, you can be confident that your speech will be successful each time.

Managing Your Speech Delivery

Step 4: rehearse isn't just about the delivery mode you will use. Practicing your delivery will help you feel more comfortable and confident, fostering a sense of closeness with your listeners and gaining their respect.

As founder of Girls Who Code, an organization that aims to close the gender gap in computing fields, Reshma Saujani gives speeches to inspire young girls to pursue careers in computer science as well as to gain financial support for her not-for-profit cause. It's not an easy message to deliver in a career field dominated by men. But Saujani commands attention by building connections with listeners and projecting confidence every time she speaks.

Saujani (2013) delivers speeches extemporaneously, maintaining steady eye contact with her listeners as she cites statistics showing that women are underrepresented in computer science careers. Her voice expresses genuine concern when she talks about women being "pushed away" from careers in science and math. Moving physically closer to her listeners, Saujani's facial expressions become animated as she tells stories about young girls whose lives have been transformed by Girls Who Code. Through a confident, poised, and engaging delivery, Saujani leaves listeners with a sense that she is addressing each of them individually—much like a conversation.

Audiences are motivated to listen closely when Saujani gives presentations because of two key elements in her delivery: immediacy and a powerful speech style. **Immediacy** is a sense of closeness that an audience feels toward a speaker (Mehrabian, 1972). You create immediacy by using everyday language and engaging nonverbal behaviors (e.g., eye contact or gestures). Communicators who show immediacy are often described as warm and approachable (Richmond, McCroskey, & Johnson, 2003). The other important element in speech delivery is the ability to present yourself and your message confidently. Known as a **powerful speech style**, these verbal

As founder of Girls Who Code, an organization that aims to close the gender gap in computing fields, lawyer and politician Reshma Saujani often speaks to groups large and small about the causes she believes in. Whether she is informing her audience about issues related to women in software development or persuading donors to fund her nonprofit organization, Saujani uses consistent eye contact to connect with her audience and project confidence.

John Minchillo/AP Images

and nonverbal behaviors gain the respect of your listeners (Fragale, 2006; Hosman, Huebner, & Siltanen, 2002). Because Saujani projects confidence and warmth in her delivery, audience members listen intently and trust what she says. To achieve the kind of positive impact Saujani does in her speeches, you will need to adopt an *oral language style* and learn the subtleties of language and nonverbal behaviors that give your language power.

Conveying Immediacy

You can create a sense of immediacy when delivering your speech by adopting an **oral language style** — using words that are similar to how people talk. An oral language style differs radically from a **written language style**, which is usually more formal and detailed. Consider the following examples:

> *Written language style:* "Although the word *sustainability* denotes a wide variety of concerns, many people restrict its meaning to the green movement. However, it is imperative that a broader meaning be embraced."
>
> *Oral language style:* "If you're like me, when you hear the word *sustainability*, you only think of things like energy conservation and recycling. But the word means so much more."

A written language style often comes from composing a manuscript speech or writing an overly detailed delivery outline. This results in a spoken presentation that sounds like a written paper. Listeners prefer the oral language style over the more formal tone of the written language style (Doetkott & Motley, 2009). An oral language style is evident in Saujani's speech, which has stories filled with personal pronouns like *I*, *we*, and *you*. She presents her message in a natural, conversational manner and creates a sense of immediacy with her audience.

However, immediacy isn't achieved through an oral language style alone. You also connect with your audience through *nonverbal behaviors*, such as vocal characteristics, eye contact, facial expressions, gestures and body posture, and personal space.

Vocal Characteristics. Your voice creates a sense of either closeness or distance with the audience. When delivering your speech, consider how the following three features will help you connect with listeners. First, your **vocal pitch** is the high and low registers of your voice. In ordinary conversation, your vocal pitch varies with your emotions. When you're excited, your pitch rises; when you're serious, your pitch lowers. While practicing your speech, mark sections of your delivery outline to show where your voice needs to convey emotion, such as when you are telling a story to illustrate a point or emphasizing an especially important statistic. This will help you vary your vocal pitch and give your audience a sense of how you feel about your topic.

Second, **vocal tone**—the richness and sound quality of your voice—also varies during natural conversations. For instance, your tone sounds different when you're discouraged than when you're optimistic. People who don't vary their vocal pitch and vocal tone during a conversation or public presentation are speaking in a **monotone**—which doesn't create a sense of immediacy. A monotone delivery bores an audience, giving the impression you don't care about what you are saying.

Third, **vocal rate**—how rapidly you speak—also determines immediacy. Ideally, public speakers deliver their messages at 140–175 words per minute. When speakers speak at a rate slower than 140 words per minute, audiences can quickly lose interest in the message. Don't worry too much about those exact numbers or counting your words. The real lesson is this: if you speak too rapidly, your listeners may miss something or feel exhausted trying to keep up. But if you speak too slowly, your audience's attention can begin to wander.

Eye Contact. In our discussion of nonverbal communication in Chapter 6, we explain how eye contact shows attention, interest, affection, and even aggression. During a presentation, eye contact signals your interest and desire to connect with your audience. You can do this by spending two to three seconds looking at listeners in one section of your audience, then spending the same amount of time looking at listeners in another section, and so on, throughout your speech. Be sure that you are establishing eye contact with listeners in every part of the room, including those sitting on the periphery of the room.

When managing your eye contact during a speech, watch out for two common mistakes: not making enough eye contact because you are too focused on reading your notes, or making eye contact with only those listeners who appear the most interested and supportive. In both instances, listeners who don't receive eye contact will feel ignored. Finally, if you are delivering an online presentation and no audience is physically present with you in the room, look straight at the camera, as though you were talking to a close friend. In televised political debates, candidates increase their chances of favorable ratings by gazing directly at the camera (Nagel, Maurer, & Reinemann, 2012).

Facial Expressions. Your audience can tell how strongly you feel about your message by observing your facial expressions. For example, you might smile with expressive eyes when making a humorous point. On the other hand, you would probably smile less and project a solemn look when telling a tragic story. In both cases, facial expressions reinforce your feelings about the message, strengthening the connection with your audience.

Facial expressions should naturally arise from your feelings about specific points you're making in the speech. As you compose your speech, take time to *critically self-reflect* (see Chapter 2) about your feelings related to the topic. This can help you become facially expressive as you deliver specific points during your speech. Keep in mind that a lack of facial expressiveness on your part — or worse, overly rehearsed or exaggerated expressions — will come across as insincere, unbelievable, or both.

Gestures and Body Posture. Your gestures and posture also reveal the intensity of your involvement with your topic and thus affect the degree of immediacy your audience feels. In everyday conversation, you naturally use your hands and move your body to help you describe something or tell a story. However, when you give a speech, nervousness can cause your gestures to be awkward, stilted, or even nonexistent. You may attempt to manage your nervousness through **adaptive gestures**, such as fidgeting, twirling your hair, or fiddling with your jewelry. Your posture may even stiffen, causing you to start swaying back and forth. Any of these changes can block you from creating a sense of immediacy with your audience. Folding your arms across your body or jingling your car keys sends the message that you're not engaged with your topic or your audience. Slumping over a lectern suggests that you're bored or tired — further eroding immediacy. Carefully monitor your gestures and posture to make sure you are producing *congruent messages*. As Chapter 6 explains, this happens when your verbal communication and nonverbal communication match. When rehearsing your speech, focus on proper posture and practice specific gestures, such as pointing, to emphasize main points or to reinforce your visual aids.

Personal Space. Presentations often involve the use of a lectern or simply occur at a physical distance known as *public space*. You may recall that public space exists when communicators are 12 or more feet apart (Chapter 6). Large physical distance between a speaker and the audience can reduce a sense of immediacy. But many of the nonverbal behaviors discussed earlier — such as varying your vocal pitch, maintaining eye contact, and practicing facial expressiveness — keep you connected with the audience even when you are physically far away.

Additionally, moving purposefully around the presentation space reduces the physical distance. When Reshma Saujani speaks to an audience, she walks out from behind the lectern to share success stories about Girls Who Code. Although you, too, will want to reduce the space between you and your listeners, there are three common pitfalls to avoid. First, move only to emphasize a key point or when transitioning to another point in your speech. Also, avoid distracting the audience by pacing back and forth. Finally, be aware of cultural norms related to personal space that may be specific to your audience. You don't want to be perceived as too pushy or too distant. It is important during your speech rehearsal to give attention to how you use personal space.

Projecting a Powerful Speech Style

During a presentation, your choice of language and other nonverbal behaviors can gain or lose the respect of your audience. Scholars have found that expressions of power enhance perceptions of a speaker's competence (Claeys & Cauberghe, 2014). Audiences will pay more attention if they respect you and will lose motivation to listen if they don't. You achieve a powerful speech style through the words you choose and the way you use your voice. Additionally, your dress and physical appearance will affect how the audience regards you and your message.

Language. A common mistake speakers make is to use **powerless language** during a speech — words that suggest they're uncertain about their message or themselves. Examples of powerless language include **hedging** — using words that lessen a message's impact, such as *sorta*, *kinda*, and *somewhat*. Such words can confuse an audience and suggest you're holding something back. **Disclaimers** — phrases that remove responsibility for the statement you're making — are another example. For instance, saying "I'm not an expert, but . . ." or "I could be wrong about this, but . . ." reduces your power. A final example is using unnecessary words — known as **intensifiers** — to overemphasize a point ("It was a *really, really* good movie" or "The decision to increase tuition was *so totally* wrong"). If you use a lot of powerless language while delivering a speech, you might be viewed as unlikable and fail to earn the respect of your audience (Holtgraves & Lasky, 1999).

Vocal Delivery. Your voice also projects confidence — or uncertainty — and influences how your audience perceives you. Consider your **vocal volume**, or how loudly or quietly you speak. Speaking too softly can make it hard for listeners to hear you and may cause them to doubt your confidence and credibility. Conversely, if you speak too loudly, your audience may see you as overbearing. You want to talk just loudly enough for people sitting in the back row to hear you.

Another important aspect of vocal delivery is to articulate words clearly and distinctly so that the audience can understand what you're saying. Poor **articulation** can erode how you are viewed because it can cause your audience to misunderstand what you're saying. Don't run through words ("Whaddayougonnado?" rather than "What are you going to do?") or drop the endings of words ("How's it goin'?" rather than "How's it going?"). Likewise, pay attention to your **pronunciation**, or the way you say words. Poor pronunciation — for example, saying "ambalance" instead of "ambulance" — may cause your audience to question your credibility.

ADVANCE THE CONVERSATION

THIS IS HOW I TALK

1 YOUR DILEMMA

Raised in the rural South, Mike never thought much about how he spoke until he enrolled at a university in the Midwest. After he moved to campus, Mike's roommates started teasing him about his accent, calling him "hick" and "redneck." Although he laughs it off, Mike has become self-conscious. Afraid of being stereotyped, he now rarely speaks up in class and dreads oral presentations. But his biggest concern is that he wants to be a lawyer, and attorneys do a lot of public speaking.

As you're leaving your political science class one day, Dr. Brenner calls you over to a conversation he's having with Mike about the college's mock trial team—a competitive activity where students simulate trial lawyers by delivering opening statements, questioning witnesses, and presenting closing statements. You've been on the mock trial team for a year and feel that you have benefited from it. You tell Mike that the team is great preparation for law school.

Mike looks unsure. "I don't like talking in front of people around here," he says. "They think I'm stupid 'cause of the way I talk." Dr. Brenner tells him that enrolling in a voice and diction class could help with his accent. Mike says, "I don't think it's right to change who I am. It'd be disrespecting my family. I'll probably just wind up going to law school back home anyway."

After Mike leaves, Dr. Brenner turns to you and says, "Will you talk to him and see if he'll reconsider?"

How would you describe Mike's point of view and feelings at this moment?

2 THE RESEARCH

Accents are a common basis for stereotypes. U.S. citizens consistently rate the South as a place where accented speech portrays residents as backward or uneducated (Preston, 1999; Preston, 2002). Even when a southern accent is perceived as friendly or polite, listeners may still question the speaker's competence. Such judgments aren't reserved solely for southerners, however; many non-native English speakers are also stereotyped if they have heavily accented speech (Burlage, Marafka, Parsons, & Milaski, 2004; Lev-Ari & Keysar, 2010).

Although such judgments are clearly wrong, they persist because accents signal cultural difference. In fact, accents may be more important than appearance in marking others as cultural *outgroupers* (Rakić, Steffens, & Mummendey, 2011). This is an important distinction because people feel less certain about and uncomfortable around those whom they judge as culturally different.

However, accents can create unfavorable judgments for another reason. Heavy accents can make it difficult to understand messages, leading listeners to question the speaker's credibility (Lev-Ari & Keysar, 2010). When an accent becomes a hindrance to being understood by others, pursuing a class or training to reduce these effects might be appropriate to consider.

Given the research, do you support Dr. Brenner's suggestion that Mike enroll in a voice and diction class? Why or why not?

3 YOUR OPPORTUNITY

Before you act, consider the facts of the situation, and think about the research on accented speech. Also, reflect on what you've learned so far about conveying immediacy (pp. 378–381) and projecting a powerful speech style (pp. 381–383).

Now it's your turn. Write a response to Mike.

Finally, avoid overusing **vocalized pauses and fillers** (*um, ah, you know*). Since these are common in ordinary conversation, your audience can tolerate occasional use of them. But researchers have found that frequent occurrence of such hesitations in a presentation leads to a negative impression of a speaker (Johnson & Vinson, 1990). If you need time to collect your thoughts about what you're going to say next, just pause briefly.

Dress and Physical Appearance. How you dress and your physical appearance can build or undermine the impression you make on an audience. If you want your audience to take you seriously, you should look the

DOUBLE TAKE

PROPER VS IMPROPER CLOTHING

What you wear when delivering a speech is more important than you might initially think. Improper dress risks being distracting or sending the message that you don't care. Of the speakers below, which one displays confidence and is more likely to capture an audience's attention?

skynesher/Getty Images

part. In addition to being properly groomed, this may mean not dressing as though you're headed to the beach, to sleep, or to the dance club. You'll also want to avoid chewing gum or wearing "noisy" jewelry, sunglasses, flip-flops, or a baseball cap during your presentation. In short, there should be nothing about your appearance that distracts the audience from listening to your speech. Look your best.

Start by matching your dress to what is appropriate for the occasion and your audience. In some situations, you may need to dress formally, whereas in others, a more casual appearance will be appropriate. For example, you might wear business attire when giving a presentation to college alumni at a fund-raising event, but you might choose more casual attire for delivering a speech in your communication class. A general rule of thumb is that you should dress slightly more formally than you expect your audience to dress.

Another consideration for determining how to dress is the speech topic. Shorts and a T-shirt could be proper attire for an informative speech about setting up a weekend campsite but would be completely inappropriate to wear for a persuasive speech about donating time to visit the elderly. Check with your instructor when in doubt about any special dress requirements for class assignments.

Managing Your Delivery in Online Speeches

As you progress through your college education and work life, you will increasingly face situations in which you will need to deliver an online presentation. For example, your sociology professor may require a video podcast, or your job could involve videoconferences with employees located around the world. In these and other situations, conveying immediacy and projecting a powerful speech style will ensure that your audience stays tuned in to your message. How? In addition to relying on the same language and nonverbal elements previously discussed, there are some specific things to keep in mind for online presentations.

Whether you are recording a video to post or streaming in real time, make sure the camera is properly adjusted. Focus the lens to a medium close-up shot to capture your upper torso and head. By doing so, your viewers will experience a more personal connection than they would if your image were too close or too far away. You should also keep your background free of visual distractions. Something as simple as a clock or a painting on the wall behind you can be distracting to listeners.

Be expressive with your face, eyes, and voice. Although this is clearly important for presentations where your audience will see you, it is also important for podcasts or any audio narrations you may do. Even if your audience can't see your facial expressions, using nonverbal communication will help your vocal expressiveness. If your audience can see you, avoid excessive gesturing and body movements that could be distracting.

When delivering a speech online, paying close attention to your surroundings, outside noise, and the camera angle is as important as your appearance and other delivery skills. What aspects of this speaker's setup for his online presentation were done well? What, if anything, could he improve?

Engaged facial expressions will convey nonverbal meaning to viewers.

Appropriate clothing helps establish credibility.

Check to make sure your head and upper torso appear on screen. You don't want to seem too far from audiences.

Could art on the walls behind him distract listeners?

Even if an area isn't seen, having a messy work surface could create noise during the speech.

To help keep your audience engaged, use presentation software and other visual aids. Well-designed and meaningfully integrated slides, for example, can help your audience understand complex ideas, especially statistical information. We cover more on how to use such software on page 390.

Of course, you'll still need to practice. A key part of any successful presentation, whether it's face-to-face or online, is rehearsal. It is especially important that you practice with any technology you might use to make sure you know how it works and are comfortable with it. Recording your practice also allows you to check and revise your camera setup, expressiveness, sound levels, and lighting quality.

Managing Speech Anxiety

> If you feel nervous while preparing for or while delivering a presentation, you're not alone. Everyone—from students to celebrities—experiences speech anxiety sometimes. The good news is that you can take concrete steps to manage the speech anxiety that you feel.

All the time you spend rehearsing can be undermined if nerves take over once you're in front of an audience. But being nervous about speaking in public, or **speech anxiety**, is common for many people because no one wants to lose face or become embarrassed in a public setting (Buss, 1980). Potentially adding to that fear are your own negative thoughts. As Chapter 2 discusses, *self-fulfilling prophecies* are predictions you make about interactions that lead you to communicate in ways that make those predictions come true. This can happen in any communication context, whether group, interpersonal, or public speaking. Studies have shown that people who experience high levels of anxiety about giving a speech often have thoughts such as "I'm really going to blow this!" or "I'm going to forget something" (Ayres, 1988; LeFebvre, LeFebvre, & Allen, 2018). Once you start thinking like this, it is more likely to happen.

Finding remedies for speech anxiety has long been a focus of research (McCroskey, 2009; Smith, Sawyer, & Behnke, 2005). Although there is no "magic pill" cure, there are several strategies to help reduce the nervousness associated with public speaking. If you experience speech anxiety, here are some suggestions to try:

- *Look for opportunities to speak up in large groups.* Make comments and ask questions whenever you're in a large group, such as a classroom, a forum, or a meeting. These experiences will gradually help reduce your feelings of self-consciousness when speaking in front of large groups.
- *Choose speech topics that matter to you.* If you can choose your speech topic, select a subject that you find interesting or important. This way, you'll be more focused on your message than on yourself, so you'll feel less nervous (Motley, 1990).
- *Conduct a situational analysis — that is, learn about the physical space where you will deliver the speech.* During the rehearsal step of your speech preparation, spend some time learning about your speech setting and equipment needs. You will feel more comfortable if you are familiar with the room setup. Trying to find a power outlet for your laptop just moments before the actual presentation can trigger nervousness. Conduct a situational analysis by planning for your physical settings before the actual presentation day (see Table 15.1).
- *Expect the unexpected.* Even if you conduct a thorough situational analysis, you can still be met with a last-minute surprise. Having to adapt to such surprises can magnify speech anxiety because you'll suddenly feel stressed. For example, how would you handle being unable to access your PowerPoint slides? Try to plan ahead for things that could go wrong (e.g., have more than one way to access your slides) so you won't have to make last-minute, under-pressure decisions. Anticipating "unexpected" events will help boost your confidence overall.
- *Know your introduction.* During the first few minutes of a speech, your nervousness peaks, since this is the time when your audience is the most attentive to you (Buss, 1980). Take time to rehearse exactly what your first few words are going to be as you greet your audience and begin your presentation.

- *Use visualization techniques.* If you've ever been involved in a competitive activity or sport, you know it can be helpful before a competition to quiet your mind and body and imagine yourself succeeding. Visualization is just as effective in reducing pre-speech jitters (Ayres & Ayres, 2003; Ayres & Hopf, 1987). To visualize a successful presentation, follow these steps: (1) relax your body through deep, concentrated breathing; (2) develop a vivid image of yourself confidently standing in front of your audience; (3) concretely imagine yourself giving the speech from start to finish, so that you see every moment of the presentation; and (4) visualize yourself getting praise from your audience and others after the speech (Ayres & Hopf, 1987). You can also watch videos of successful speakers and then substitute your own image for those speakers in a visualization session (Ayres, 2005).
- *Practice.* Students who have an intense fear of public speaking spend less time practicing and more time preparing their notes (Ayres, 1996). Although it's important to have well-prepared speaker notes, you must commit time to rehearsing with them. But just standing before

TABLE 15.1

SITUATIONAL ANALYSIS

1	2	3	4	5
Is the seating arrangement fixed or movable?	**Do you know how to control the room lighting?**	**Will there be a lectern in the room?**	**Will a microphone be used? Is it mobile? Do you know how to control its volume?**	**Do you know where the electrical power outlets are located? Will you need internet access?**
You may want to move chairs around to organize an activity or a small group discussion.	Knowing where light controls are and how they work is important if you need to dim the lights to make it easier to see media.	If you need a stand or a place for keeping your materials organized, you may need to make arrangements for it.	Depending on the size of your audience, you may need a microphone. If you don't want to be stuck behind a lectern, make sure you have a mobile microphone and that you know how it works.	Using any type of laptop or media requires that you have easy and reliable access to electrical power. You may also need to get online to show a video or website.

Sebra/Shutterstock

a mirror reciting your speech isn't practice. See pages 394–395, where we give advice on how to effectively practice and get feedback on your speech.

Finally, your enrollment in this class will provide experiences with public speaking. This will reduce its novelty and help you feel more confident when presenting.

Choosing and Using Presentation Aids

Incorporating visual support for your ideas will enhance your speech. Presentation aids not only help you keep your audience's attention but also help your audience understand complex points. But not just any image or slide will do. Selecting the right visuals and rehearsing with them is key to improving your delivery.

Neuroscientist Jill Bolte Taylor captivates her audiences when she brings out an actual human brain, with an attached spinal cord, in her presentations about the brain's remarkable capability to recover from certain injuries. But this display is no gimmick. Instead, Dr. Taylor uses this physical object to illustrate part of her powerful story about recovering from a massive stroke at the age of 37 (Taylor, 2008). Adding visuals or media (graphs, charts, physical objects, videos, and photographs) to speeches enhances interest for your listeners. In your own speeches, you'll want to use **presentation aids** — tools used to display the visuals you've selected to help explain or illustrate your points.

Types of Presentation Aids

In addition to common forms of presentation software, such as PowerPoint, Keynote, and Prezi, you can use whiteboards and flip charts, handouts, physical objects, posters, and video to present your speech's visual elements.

Whiteboards and Flip Charts. A whiteboard or flip chart allows you to write or show key ideas while you deliver your speech. For example, if you're describing a chemical formula, you can write it on a whiteboard or flip chart. Or if you solicit feedback from your audience — for example, as part of a real estate seminar asking them to call out the costs associated with renting an apartment — you can jot down their responses on a whiteboard or flip chart. Creating your visual aid as you present gives you the ability to interact with your audience: you have flexibility to address a specific audience's needs or produce a record of their responses. However, these tools have a few drawbacks. First, your writing must be neat and visible. It will frustrate your audience if they can't read your writing because it's messy or too small.

Second, while writing, you have to turn away from your listeners, breaking eye contact and reducing immediacy. To minimize the impact of this, stop talking while you're writing, then address your audience after you've finished writing. This way, you can make eye contact while you are talking, and the audience can always hear you.

Handouts. Suppose you're listening to a college official talk about how to apply for a particular scholarship on your campus. Wouldn't it be helpful if you had a handout of the steps to follow or the actual form that you need to complete? Handouts can help your listeners follow steps in a process or remember important information. But handouts can also present a major distraction during a presentation. For example, if you distribute handouts of PowerPoint slides just as you begin your speech, the listeners will probably start flipping through the handouts and may miss the opening of your presentation. If you decide to use handouts, give careful thought to how much information to put on them, and consider when would be the best point for distributing them.

Physical Objects. Sometimes it is easier to show your audience a prop, or a physical object that represents an idea in your speech. An advantage of using physical objects is that they can have more visual impact than a two-dimensional diagram or photograph. For example, the real human brain used by Dr. Taylor has greater impact than would diagrams alone. Physical objects provide a novel experience for your audience, giving them something to focus on beyond your words. If you decide to use physical objects, be sure to consider your presentation space. Will everyone be able to see your prop? Since passing an object around the room can be distracting, consider other options for displaying a small object. Can you walk it through the audience? Is a document camera available for projecting an image of the object on a screen? Of course, in a classroom setting, be sure to check with your instructor before bringing anything in. Most schools prohibit certain items on campus (weapons, alcohol, animals), and there may be other considerations that limit what you can display (such as certain plants or foods that some students may have allergies to).

Posters. Though increasingly rare in our digital age, posters are another form of presentation aid. (Students are likely to use posters for classroom speeches, especially if an instructor doesn't allow the use of PowerPoint.) The main advantage of using posters is that you're not dependent on electrical or technical support for your presentation—all you need is an easel or a wall for displaying them. Posters are usually best for displaying charts, graphs, or other visual information. If you choose to use posters in a speech, remember two things: First, make sure any information on the poster is large enough for the audience to see. Second, your poster should look neat and professional.

When film producer Laurie David saw former vice president Al Gore's slideshow on global warming, she was so inspired that she immediately contacted Gore to start a project that eventually became the 2006 documentary film *An Inconvenient Truth.* This documentary played a large role in driving the global conversation about climate change. Have you ever seen a presentation where the visuals enhanced the presentation and inspired you?

VALERY HACHE/AFP/Getty Images

When possible, use computer software to design the content so it is colorful and clear. Depending on the context of your speech, you may even consider having a print shop produce your poster.

Video. Speakers commonly include video clips in their presentations — either from websites like YouTube, Hulu, and Netflix or from content they create themselves. For example, some of our students shot video of their service-learning experiences at a Salvation Army family shelter and then used that as part of a group presentation. A major benefit of video is that — much like physical objects — it will grab your audience's attention. Yet effectively integrating video clips takes planning and practice. You must be sure that you can quickly access the required video clip. Few things create more of a distraction in a speech than when an audience has to watch a speaker try to locate a video on the web, fumble with equipment, or attempt to find the exact starting point on a video. Also, if you are using a clip that is streaming online, have a backup plan in case you lose internet access during your speech. Finally, make sure any clips you use are brief. Remember that a video clip is *supporting material* to help you illustrate a main point. It shouldn't take over the speech.

Presentation Software. Although PowerPoint has its critics, it is still widely used in academic, business, and military presentations. That's because presentation software — such as PowerPoint, Keynote, and Prezi — makes it easy to import graphics and achieve a highly professional, polished look on your slides. It can also help the audience follow your presentation by providing key points or summary information. But avoid letting presentation slides come between you and your listeners, thus undermining your immediacy or powerful speech style. The Advance the Conversation: Delivering a Speech video activity on pages 396–397 gives insight on how to successfully present with slides.

A common pitfall with presentation software is poor design. Do not bombard your audience with a steady stream of slides containing small text, hard-to-read fonts, too many bullet points, or overwhelming colors and images. Instead, use as few slides as possible; limit the use of text; and include relevant visuals, such as charts, graphs, or photos.

Tips for Using Presentation Aids

No matter what presentation aids you decide to use, keep the following tips in mind while preparing, rehearsing, and delivering your speech:

- *Know how to use your aids.* While composing and rehearsing your speech, spend time with the presentation aids you're going to be using—ideally, in the same setting where you'll be giving your presentation. You can damage your credibility by fumbling with equipment or not knowing how to properly handle any physical objects you've brought.
- *Prepare your audience for what they're about to see or hear.* Take time to introduce any slide or handout you present—especially if it contains complex information. For example, you should explain what a graph shows: "As this next graph will demonstrate, the number of students in federal subsidized school lunch programs has doubled over the past five years."
- *Thoroughly explain the information on a presentation aid.* Whether you're introducing a slide, a poster, or a video, don't rush your listeners through it. Take time to discuss the idea conveyed by the presentation aid.
- *Talk to your audience, not the medium.* Remember that you need to convey immediacy with your audience for them to pay attention. Don't talk with your back to your audience while writing on a whiteboard or looking at your slides on the screen. Such behaviors will make your audience feel disconnected.
- *Remove the presentation aid once you're done with it.* After you've made your point with a presentation aid, cover it up, remove it from the screen, or erase the image. You want your audience attending to *you* as you move to your next point, not mulling over a previous graph or image left up on the screen.
- *Have a backup plan.* You can never account for everything that could happen during your speech, but you should prepare alternatives in case your presentation aids fail. For example, what if a lightbulb in the projector burns out? Or the computer server is down? Or your marker runs out of ink? You always need to have a backup plan.

Evaluating Speeches and Managing Feedback

Rehearsing your speech is not a solitary activity. Getting feedback from others about your speech and delivery provides vital information you can use to complete the last part of your speech preparation—step 5: revise. You'll use feedback to make any necessary changes to the presentation, as well as to improve your public-speaking skills over the long term.

Imagine practicing your speech in front of a screen of avatars simulating an audience. While you're presenting, the avatars shift in their seat to indicate boredom or nod enthusiastically to show agreement with a point you're making. This may sound futuristic, but researchers at the University of California have created Cicero, an interactive virtual audience system that helps speakers rehearse and receive feedback on presentations (Belman, 2014).

Cicero is programmed to recognize the common characteristics of good and poor speech delivery. The avatars, just like a real audience, smile and sit forward when a speaker's delivery is engaging—when the speaker has a strong voice, purposeful gesturing, and sustained eye contact. When a speaker talks too softly or fails to maintain eye contact, the avatars will start to yawn and slouch. Now instead of rehearsing alone, speakers can practice in front of a simulated audience and get immediate feedback to improve their skills.

Even though it's unlikely you have access to technology like Cicero to practice your speech, you can enlist family, friends, or fellow classmates to help you rehearse and to provide feedback on your speech. Students who practice in front of a small audience are more likely to receive higher evaluations on their actual speech performance than those who practice alone or in front of a mirror (Smith & Frymier, 2006). By practicing in front of others, you can get feedback about your speech organization, content, and delivery. Using this information to make necessary changes to your speech outline and delivery is an important part of step 5: revise. But not all feedback is helpful. Feedback that is too general ("That was great!") or broadly critical ("You can do better") lacks details about what's working and what needs to change. Knowing how to give useful feedback and how to base your own revisions on the feedback others give you completes your speech preparation.

Giving Effective Feedback

Whether in your communication class, at work, or as a favor to a friend, you may be asked to give oral or written feedback on other people's presentations. Actively listening to and evaluating other speakers will improve your own public-speaking skills. But what should you listen for? Consider the checklist of elements regarding effective speech structure, content, and delivery in Figure 15.1 on page 393. These elements will help you give useful

FIGURE 15.1

GENERAL SPEECH CRITIQUE*

For each element, rate the speaker's use of the element on a scale of **1–3,** as defined below:

3 = Element was evident and very effective
2 = Element was there but could be revised for greater impact
1 = Element was not evident or ineffective

INTRODUCTION

When starting the speech, did the speaker — **Comments:**

____ **1.** gain attention through an interesting question, a story, or some other creative means?
____ **2.** provide appropriate background to the topic—including relevant definitions?
____ **3.** take steps to establish credibility?
____ **4.** clearly state the speech thesis and briefly preview the main points?

BODY

In developing the body of the speech, did the speaker — **Comments:**

____ **1.** identify and organize main points in a manner that was easy to follow?
____ **2.** use well-chosen examples, testimony, statistics, and other forms of support for main points?
____ **3.** integrate outside references, orally citing sources when appropriate?
____ **4.** choose appropriate and clear language; avoid unnecessary jargon?

CONCLUSION

When moving to the finish of the speech, did the speaker — **Comments:**

____ **1.** clearly indicate the speech was concluding by providing summary statements?
____ **2.** provide a final appeal or make a general point about the subject?
____ **3.** end the speech with a memorable statement?

PRESENTATION AIDS

When using presentation aids, did the speaker — **Comments:**

____ **1.** incorporate relevant and well-designed visual support (e.g., graphs and charts)?
____ **2.** effectively handle presentation aids, avoiding any distraction?

DELIVERY

During the speech, did the speaker — **Comments:**

____ **1.** use voice in a way appropriate to the topic by varying inflection, tone, and volume?
____ **2.** speak words clearly, with proper pronunciation and grammar?
____ **3.** physically move and gesture with purpose, avoiding distracting mannerisms?
____ **4.** establish and maintain eye contact with all areas of the room while making appropriate use of notes?
____ **5.** appear confident, poised, and in control of the situation; avoid rushing?

OVERALL EVALUATION

Considering the speech as a whole, did the speaker — **Comments:**

____ **1.** choose an appropriate topic and specific purpose statement?
____ **2.** adapt the topic to the audience throughout the speech?
____ **3.** meet the assignment requirements, including specified time limits?

*Note: This is just one example of a critique. Your instructor may use something different. This sample is meant to provide you with a sense of things to think about when evaluating your own or someone else's speech.

feedback while evaluating someone else's speech, as well as receive and use feedback from others on your own speeches.

Feedback is most useful when it's delivered soon after a rehearsal or the actual presentation and is specific — whether it's praise or criticism. Examples of useful feedback would include comments like "You maintained good eye contact with everyone in the audience" or "I would have been able to follow your ideas more easily if you had half the number of slides." When providing feedback to others, keep the following guidelines in mind:

1. *Make sure the recipient is ready to hear what you have to say.* Timing is everything when giving feedback. If a speaker has just finished a presentation (whether a rehearsal or real), the person may need a few minutes to collect his or her thoughts or take care of physical needs (e.g., getting a glass of water) before listening to what you have to say.
2. *Start with positive comments.* Find and articulate the strengths of the presentation in order to create some rapport with the speaker. This lays the groundwork for any constructive criticism that may follow.
3. *Use descriptive language.* Abstract or vague language creates misunderstanding ("You did a great job!"). It is usually best to point out specific things you saw and heard ("The story in your opener had vivid images that helped me see the people you were describing"). Although it's not easy to do, you will often need to point out problems with a speech to help the speaker improve. You'll especially want to use descriptive language when offering any *constructive criticism* ("You were pacing back and forth, and it was distracting" or "I didn't hear a preview of your main points").
4. *Don't overload the person with information.* People have a limit on how much they can process at a given time. Pick out the two or three things that are most important to say, and leave it at that.
5. *End on a positive note.* It's important to leave on good terms with the person. Make sure your closing offers hope or encouragement.

Using Feedback to Improve Your Speech Performance

Feedback is helpful during your speech rehearsal and after you have delivered your actual presentation. When practicing your speech, feedback will guide your revisions to the speech outline or your delivery. Making such changes is key to ensuring that your presentation is well received by the audience. Seeking out feedback after the actual presentation — perhaps from classmates or from your instructor — will support your development as a public speaker for your next class speech and throughout your life.

Of course, feedback is wasted if you don't act on it. But not all feedback will be useful. Seriously consider what advice you should take and what can be ignored. For example, does your introduction really need more punch? Is there a point where a graph would be more informative than a long list of statistics? Should you speak more slowly when telling a compelling story? Do you need to get out from behind the lectern more often during your talk? Make the changes you think need to be made prior to delivering your speech when it really counts.

After you've given the actual speech, ask for feedback from audience members or a trusted friend or colleague who sat in on the presentation. Their input can help you plan and practice for your next speech. If you video-record the speech, use the General Speech Critique form in Figure 15.1 to evaluate the recording and gather additional insights into how you can deliver a better speech the next time.

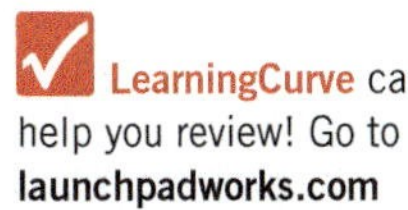

ADVANCE THE CONVERSATION
Video Activity

DELIVERING A SPEECH

The following scenario will enhance your ability to effectively manage your speech delivery. Visit LaunchPad at **launchpadworks.com** to get the full experience with video. As you watch the first video, recall what you've learned about effective delivery. Then complete the **Your Turn** prompts. Finally, watch the **Take Two!** video to explore how this scenario could have gone differently.

1 THE PROBLEM

Kate and two classmates are working together on a presentation for their food science class. The group splits the work into three sections, and Kate's portion will cover nutrition and fast food. Now the group is practicing their delivery together for the first time. One group member, Mirirai, surprises Kate by coming with a timer and announcing, "I'll time you, okay? Your section of the presentation should be about five minutes, right?" The other group member, Jason, nods and agrees: "More or less." Now Kate is nervous; she wasn't prepared to be timed. She begins delivering her section of the speech, using her speaking outline as a guide.

"Okay. There's a medical writer, Daniel DeNoon, who says that um . . . uh . . . nine out of ten Americans consume too much salt daily. Uh, salt is found in everything from, um, soft drinks to, uh, baked goods . . ."

"Hold on one sec. That was a little rough. I think maybe I made you nervous about the timing."

2 YOUR TURN

Observations. Reflect on how Kate delivered her section of the speech in this practice session by answering the following questions:

1. Do you agree with Mirirai that Kate's delivery was "a little rough"?
2. What did Kate do well? What can she improve on?

Discussion. In class or with a partner, share your thoughts about Kate's delivery and work to answer the following questions:

1. How might Kate's nervousness and use of vocal fillers affect her audience's understanding of the speech and perception of her as a speaker?
2. Do you think Mirirai gave effective feedback to Kate? Why or why not?

Conclusion. Based on your analysis, what advice would you give Kate to improve her delivery in this scenario?

3 TAKE TWO!

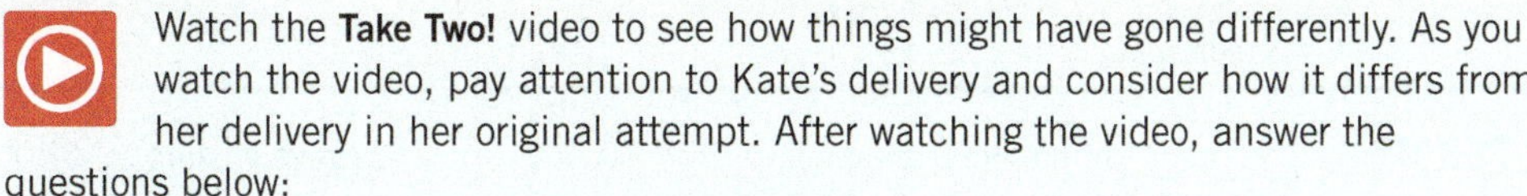

Watch the **Take Two!** video to see how things might have gone differently. As you watch the video, pay attention to Kate's delivery and consider how it differs from her delivery in her original attempt. After watching the video, answer the questions below:

1. What did Kate do differently in terms of her delivery? Identify specific examples.
2. In your opinion, is Kate's delivery in this video more effective than in the first video? Why or why not?

CHAPTER 15 REVIEW

CHAPTER RECAP

- There are three primary modes for delivering a speech: **impromptu**, **manuscript**, and **extemporaneous speaking**.
- Conveying **immediacy** and projecting a **powerful speech style** are ways to connect with your audience. Understanding these elements will help you with everything from adopting an **oral language style** and using appropriate nonverbal behaviors to choosing effective language, vocal delivery, and attire.
- **Speech anxiety** is a common experience, but you can manage it through a variety of strategies, such as conducting a situational analysis and rehearsing your delivery style.
- It is important to know how to use your **presentation aids**, to have a backup plan in case any technology fails, and to explain to the audience what they are about to see or hear.
- Learning how to give and receive competent feedback on public speeches will help you better prepare, rehearse, revise, and deliver your own presentations.

LaunchPad for *Choices & Connections* offers unique video scenarios and encourages self-assessment through adaptive quizzing. Go to **launchpadworks.com** to get access.

 LearningCurve adaptive quizzes

 Advance the Conversation video scenarios

 Video clips that illustrate key concepts

---

KEY TERMS

Impromptu speaking, p. 374
Manuscript speaking, p. 375
Extemporaneous speaking, p. 376
Immediacy, p. 377
Powerful speech style, p. 377
Oral language style, p. 378
Written language style, p. 378
Vocal pitch, p. 379
Vocal tone, p. 379
Monotone, p. 379
Vocal rate, p. 379
Adaptive gesture, p. 380
Powerless language, p. 381
Hedging, p. 381
Disclaimer, p. 381
Intensifier, p. 381
Vocal volume, p. 381
Articulation, p. 381
Pronunciation, p. 381
Vocalized pauses and fillers, p. 383
Speech anxiety, p. 385
Presentation aid, p. 388

POP QUIZ

Looking for more review questions? LearningCurve can help you master key concepts from this chapter. Go to **launchpadworks.com**

1. Whether you memorize a speech or read from a written version, manuscript speaking has several drawbacks, including
   a. lack of preparation time.
   b. reliance on a conversational tone.
   c. difficulty adapting to your audience.
   d. a depleted vocal rate.

2. Why do audience members prefer that speakers use an oral style of language?
   a. It sounds more like a written paper.
   b. It emphasizes nonverbal behaviors.
   c. It is more casual and conversational.
   d. It provides more detailed information.

3. Using a lot of over-the-top descriptions, such as "the absolutely best ever," is an example of
   a. disclaimers.
   b. intensifiers.
   c. hedging.
   d. vocalized pauses and fillers.

4. When you imagine yourself competently presenting and receiving praise, which strategy are you using to manage speech anxiety?
   a. Visualization techniques
   b. Creating a situational analysis
   c. Choosing topics that matter to you
   d. Knowing your introduction

5. Which of the following is *not* suggested as a guideline for providing speech feedback to others?
   a. Don't overload the person with information.
   b. Start with positive comments.
   c. Provide as much detailed information as possible.
   d. Make sure the participant is ready.

ACTIVITIES

For more activities, visit LaunchPad for *Choices & Connections* at **launchpadworks.com**

1 Slideshow

Choose a TED talk (available at www.ted.com/talks) on a subject that interests you. As you watch, note specific examples of presentation aids used by the speaker. Evaluate the speaker's use of presentation aids and how effectively the aids support the message. Share your findings with the class.

2 Practice, Feedback, Repeat

Arrange to rehearse your speech with a group of classmates (either in person or via video-recorded rehearsals). Using the General Speech Critique form in Figure 15.1, give feedback on the group's speeches. Then use the group's feedback to revise your own speech, and discuss your plan with the group.

16

Informative Speaking

Sitting in a village café drinking *malwa*, a local homemade brew, a group of Ugandan men are attending a lecture.[1] A health worker is explaining that women are more susceptible to malaria during pregnancy because their immune system is weakened. If a pregnant woman is infected with malaria—spread through the bite of mosquitoes—she and her child could become seriously ill and even die (World Health Organization, 2003). Though the village health clinics make this information available, most of the men don't know these facts. Why? As Christine Munduru of the Open Society Initiative for East Africa (OSIEA) explains, "When special meetings are held to educate people on health issues, the men don't go because they think health is something only the women should deal with" (Cumberland, 2010).

This practice prompted local scientists and health care workers to think of alternative ways to get important information distributed in the village. They decided to go where the village men *do* gather: the local bar. They began holding a series of casual discussions—known as Café Scientifique—to educate the men about health issues, as well as topics like agriculture and domestic violence. Conducted in the local language, the talks were a hit from the start. "It was amazing," says Munduru. "Nobody wanted to miss out. . . . We let the community take charge and choose the topics, although we guide them to make sure that they are balanced. We empower them with information then leave them to make their own decisions" (Cumberland, 2010).

While the Café Scientifique sessions are prospering in Uganda, the concept actually began in a wine bar in Leeds, England. Worried that people didn't know enough about modern scientific advancements, British television producer Duncan Dallas planned an informal session about Darwinism—a theory about how species evolve. Almost 50 people showed up and inspired Dallas to transform Café Scientifique into a worldwide movement. Also known as "science cafés," the idea is to provide "a place where, for the price of a cup of coffee or a glass of wine, anyone can come to explore the latest ideas in science and technology" (www.cafescientifique.org).

No matter where Café Scientifique events take place, the format is fairly consistent. Most talks are conducted in coffee shops, bars, or restaurants. A local scientist or technologist speaks for about 20 minutes about a topic of interest to listeners. Speakers focus their talks on simple main points, using everyday language that audience members can understand—even those with no scientific background (Dallas, 2006). After a talk, the speaker takes questions from the audience for about an hour. According to John Cohen, immunology professor at the University of Colorado and founder of a Café Scientifique in Denver, people can ask questions or just listen to scientists in a relaxed setting and learn something new (Sink, 2006). But the presenters also benefit—they learn how to competently communicate their research and ideas to the general public.

[1]Information from Cumberland (2010).

Betty Kituyi

SANTA LUCIA

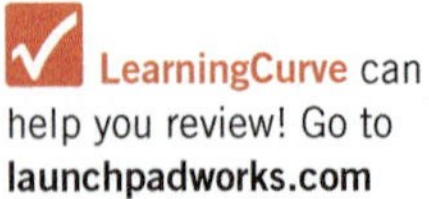
LearningCurve can help you review! Go to **launchpadworks.com**

The Café Scientifique presentations can also have unexpected outcomes. After listening to the malaria presentation, many Ugandan men—who ordinarily sleep alone under mosquito nets—gave the nets to their pregnant wives to protect them against mosquito bites. Informative speaking happens in a lot of different everyday settings. For example, in a college class, while at work, or elsewhere in your community, you could be asked to give a talk that's aimed at informing and enlightening an audience. Maybe you'll offer insights about a particular topic (why pregnant women are more susceptible to malaria), show how to do something (how to stain a piece of furniture), talk about an event or a person of interest (the story of Stan Lee's contribution to creating the Marvel universe), or explain the differences and similarities between several ideas or things (the distinguishing features of serif versus san serif fonts). When delivering an informative speech, you'll still follow the five steps for speech preparation that we discuss in Chapters 13, 14, and 15: think, investigate, compose, rehearse, and revise (see Table 13.1 on page 317). In addition, you'll consider the unique aspects of informative speeches. In this chapter, you'll learn:

- The functions and specific purposes of informative speeches
- Key differences between informative and persuasive speaking
- Four major types of informative speeches
- Guidelines for preparing informative speeches

What Is Informative Speaking?

Whenever you want to help your audience better understand a topic, you are speaking to inform. Many of the course lectures you attend (in person or online) fall into this category. But informative presentations also happen in other places, such as meetings at work, "how-to" demonstrations on YouTube, and even storytelling events.

Informative speeches educate your audience about a topic, demonstrate how something works, tell stories about events or people, or explain similarities and differences between things or ideas. The health care worker at the Ugandan village Café Scientifique gave an informative presentation that educated the audience about the risks of malaria during pregnancy.

Regardless of where you're delivering an informative speech (a local bar, a classroom, or a corporate boardroom) and how you're delivering it (face-to-face, via a podcast, or on YouTube), your first step is to *think* about how you'll adapt the talk to your audience. This includes determining your speech's function and specific purpose, and knowing how informative speeches differ from persuasive ones.

Functions of Informative Speeches

Informative presentations serve one of two functions. One function is to raise awareness about a topic for listeners (Rowan, 2003). For instance, suppose you're the treasurer of a youth soccer league. At monthly meetings,

you might give a routine financial report on the costs of running the league. Since board members are already familiar with these costs, your presentation simply functions to keep them up to date.

A second and different function for informative speeches is to provide an in-depth explanation of a topic (Rowan, 2003). Imagine that the soccer league received a large monetary donation. In this case, you'd probably prepare a presentation that gives board members detailed information about the gift—such as options for spending the money or investing it.

As you prepare an informative talk, ask yourself, Do I just want to raise my listeners' awareness about a topic? Or should I provide a deeper explanation so that they can better understand the issue? Your answer will depend on what you discover about your listeners' information needs during your audience analysis. As Chapter 13 explains, *audience analysis* is the process of identifying important characteristics about your listeners, and using this information to prepare your speech. Understanding your listeners' prior knowledge about the topic and other characteristics about them—such as their demographics and their attitudes, beliefs, and values—will help you determine your specific purpose.

Specific Purposes for Informative Speeches

After determining the information needs of your audience, it's time to write out your *specific purpose statement*, which is one complete sentence that summarizes your goal for the speech. As with any presentation, your specific purpose statement for an informative talk helps you narrow your topic. It also keeps you focused as you research and compose your speech. It will eventually form the basis for your *speech thesis*—the sentence that identifies the central idea of your presentation for your audience.

As you write your specific purpose statement, keep in mind what your audience already knows about your speech topic. By targeting your specific purpose to the audience's level of knowledge, you avoid **information overload**, which happens when the amount and nature of material exceeds listeners' ability to process it. For example, the health care workers in Uganda keep presentations about malaria at a basic level and avoid overwhelming the villagers with unnecessary medical jargon. When preparing your own speeches, use audience analysis to adapt your specific purpose statement to meet the information needs of your listeners.

You'll also want to focus the specific purpose statement on one central idea. Suppose you're assigned a 10-minute presentation on the Bauhaus movement for your art history class. Trying to cover the movement's impact on typography, architecture, and other art forms would be difficult to do in the assigned time. Instead, it would be better to narrow the topic to cover the movement's impact on just one area.

Whenever you're preparing an informative speech, start by writing a specific purpose statement appropriate to the audience and situation. Table 16.1 shows examples of specific purpose statements for a wide range

TABLE 16.1

SPECIFIC PURPOSE STATEMENTS FOR INFORMATIVE SPEECHES

ART HISTORY COURSE

General Assignment: Develop an oral presentation on an important movement in art history

Specific Purpose Statement: To inform my class on the impact of Bauhaus on typography.

SCOUT MEETING

General Assignment: Describe fund-raising responsibilities

Specific Purpose Statement: To explain who will do what to prepare for and conduct Saturday's Jamboree event.

EMPLOYEE MEETING

General Assignment: Update employees on changes to their health benefits

Specific Purpose Statement: To explain two major changes in the company's health benefits program.

RESEARCH CONFERENCE

General Assignment: Share your latest research findings with your colleagues

Specific Purpose Statement: To tell my listeners about the design and findings of my vaccine study.

INTRODUCTORY STATISTICS COURSE

General Assignment: Show class members that you understand the concept of standard deviation

Specific Purpose Statement: To demonstrate how to calculate a standard deviation.

CITY COUNCIL MEETING

General Assignment: Represent neighbors' views about traffic

Specific Purpose Statement: To identify five major concerns neighbors are expressing about traffic in our city.

VoodooDot/Shutterstock

of informative speech situations. A specific purpose statement brings clarity to your speech preparation. But sticking to the general purpose of informing rather than persuading an audience can be tricky if you don't understand how they differ.

Informative versus Persuasive Speaking

When you're writing your specific purpose statement, it can be easy to confuse informative speaking with persuasive speaking. Although both types of speeches are developed using the five steps in speech preparation, there are important differences between the two.

First, informative and persuasive speaking have different goals. When informing an audience, you want your listeners to understand the topic better. When you're giving a persuasive speech, the goal is to reinforce or change your listeners' attitudes—maybe even motivate them to take a particular action. Getting listeners to take an action or change their attitudes is not a primary goal of an informative speech.

Second, when preparing an informative talk, you must keep a neutral point of view as you *investigate* and *compose* your presentation. Suppose you are preparing an informative speech about animal testing in biomedical research. In this case, you would pull together information about the pros and cons of such research without taking a stand on the topic. But if you wanted to give a persuasive speech about animal testing in biomedical research, you would not only analyze the pros and cons but also take a position on the issue.

Maintaining a neutral stance when you're speaking informatively can be challenging—especially if your presentation is going to cover an issue that you feel strongly about. One way to remain neutral is to avoid making *motivational appeals* to your listeners' emotions, such as "If you care about cute, helpless, and innocent puppies. . . ." This does not mean you shouldn't try to connect with your audience by using interesting supporting materials. Instead, just keep reminding yourself that your purpose is to inform, not persuade. (Chapter 17 explains more about motivational appeals for persuasive speeches.)

Even though informative and persuasive presentations have distinct differences, they also have some similarities. For instance, when you're speaking to inform, you thoroughly *investigate* your topic and present the information in a balanced, neutral way. However, you still need to convince your audience that you're providing objective and credible information. Likewise, in persuasive speeches, you need to inform your listeners about the topic before you can try to persuade them to change their attitudes or practices. Given these similarities, the important thing to remember is to stay true to your speech's general purpose: informing or persuading.

Types of Informative Speeches

When determining your topic and specific purpose for an informative speech, you should also consider an additional aspect: your approach. Not all informative presentations work in the same way. Sometimes you may want to explain something or demonstrate how it works. Other times, you'll share a story about an event or draw comparisons between things.

Faced with an informative speech assignment in her communication course, Cheryl decided to talk about her Ta Moko. Often mistaken for a tattoo, a Ta Moko (or moko) is a permanent facial or body marking common

Whether you're speaking about a cultural practice, like the body markings of the Maori, or another informative topic, identifying what type of speech you'll give can help guide your work in the investigate and compose steps. As you consider your topic, think about whether you will focus on one type, or like Cheryl, combine types.

Tim Graham/Getty Images

to the Maori people of New Zealand. Having traveled to New Zealand three summers in a row, Cheryl developed an appreciation and affection for Maori culture. On her third trip, she had an artist create a Ta Moko on her right forearm. In *composing* her speech, Cheryl determined that her specific purpose was to inform her class about how a Ta Moko differs from a tattoo. To do this, she first defined the meaning of Ta Moko and explained its spiritual significance in Maori culture. She then compared and contrasted a Ta Moko and a tattoo. Finally, she explained the design and personal meaning of her own moko. During her six-minute presentation, Cheryl defined an important term (Ta Moko), described an object (the moko), compared it to a similar and well-known object (tattoo), and told a personal story.

Whether it's a classroom assignment or a work situation, there are various ways of making an informative presentation. Knowing what these are can help you make sound choices when you start *investigating* and *composing* an informative speech. In this chapter, we focus on the four most common types: expository, process or demonstration, narrative, and comparison/contrast. You might use one of these types as a primary way of presenting the information in your speech. For example, perhaps your instructor has assigned you an informative speech demonstrating a particular process. However, in most informative speaking situations outside the classroom, you may find yourself using a combination of the four types—as Cheryl did—to achieve your specific purpose.

Expository Presentations

When you *define* a term, *explain* a concept, or *describe* an object or a place to your audience, you are making an **expository presentation**. For instance, a museum guide enriches visitors' understanding of the art by defining relevant terms and describing painting techniques. In a meeting about salary increases, a manager defines "interest-based negotiation" and explains how it relates to pay raises. (See Table 16.2 on page 411 for examples of expository speech topics.)

When you're *composing* an expository presentation, you will apply many of the practices associated with this step of speech preparation, including choosing an appropriate organization pattern for your main points, and developing an introduction and a conclusion. A topical pattern is the most common way expository presentations are organized. You may recall from Chapter 14 that this organizational pattern breaks down main points into specific categories or subtopics. For example, if you're giving a speech about autism, you could organize the presentation like this:

Speech thesis: Scientific research is changing misconceptions about autism.

Main points:

I. *Autism* is a general term that reflects a range of pervasive developmental disorders, known as autism spectrum disorders (ASDs).

II. ASDs are characterized by abnormal social and communication behaviors.

III. Current research sheds some light on possible causes of ASDs.

You'll want to use clear, straightforward language in expository presentations. For instance, if you're talking about a complex, technical subject that's unfamiliar to your audience, don't use a lot of specialized vocabulary or acronyms. Also, remember that word meanings can vary widely. As Chapter 5 points out, life experiences and culture influence our understanding of language. Use your audience analysis to determine which words and types of examples would best help your listeners understand your points.

Process or Demonstration Presentations

In a **process or demonstration presentation**, you either explain how something works or show your audience how to do something. For example, an engineer might explain how fuel cells work. Or a training manager might show employees how to use the company's new web conferencing system. (Table 16.2 on page 411 includes additional examples of process or demonstration presentations.)

Since processes and activities take place over time, a chronological pattern is often the best organizational structure for this type of presentation. Help the audience follow the sequence by making frequent use of *signposts*, such as *First*, *Next*, and *The last step*. Here's an example of a process presentation organization:

Speech thesis: Creating a compost pile involves easy steps, using common household waste materials.

Main points:

I. First, select and prepare the right location in your yard for the compost pile.

II. Second, determine the types of household waste materials appropriate for composting.

III. Third, begin creating the compost pile by layering the waste materials to encourage proper decomposition.

IV. Fourth, be prepared to quickly address common problems in compost piles.

V. Finally, identify when the compost is ready for use.

In process or demonstration presentations, many speakers make the mistake of moving too quickly through each step. To avoid this, slow down the pace of your delivery by using *internal summaries* ("So as you can see from this step, most materials that wind up in your kitchen garbage disposal or recycle bin can be used in the compost pile"). This type of repetition also supports your listeners' ability to *remember* the information later (see Chapter 7 for a discussion of the listening process). Presentation aids, such as diagrams and objects, can further help your audience understand the steps you're describing. For example, a diagram showing how to choose a good location for your compost pile would enhance your verbal explanation. Finally, as with expository presentations, take the time to define unfamiliar terms and jargon so you don't confuse your audience.

Whenever you give a speech, listeners may have follow-up questions for you—asking for more information or wanting to further discuss or dispute a point. This type of question-and-answer session is common after a demonstration speech, when audience members may want clarification. For ideas on how to handle such situations, see the Advance the Conversation: Responding to Audience Questions video activity on pages 418–419.

Narrative Presentations

When you're describing an event or telling a story about a person, you're giving a **narrative presentation**. For example, you might report on your campus's annual Oktoberfest celebration to fulfill an oral presentation requirement for your history class. Or at a storytelling event you might share a story about childhood pranks you and your cousins played at family reunions. (See Table 16.2 for additional examples of narrative presentations.)

Cindy Ord/Getty Images

Perhaps even more compelling than her *Harry Potter* novels is the story of J. K. Rowling's rise from poverty to international success, with books for children as well as adults. Rowling's narrative speeches inform her audiences about her personal struggles and can inspire them to believe in their abilities. Have you ever heard a narrative speech that inspired you?

The best narrative presentations tell a good story that captures and holds listeners' interest and attention. A chronological pattern of organization usually works best for this kind of speech because it enables you to lay out a sequence of events. For example, suppose you're giving a speech about the Bonnaroo Music and Arts Festival. To provide an account of this event, you'd want to use vivid language while describing the people, the experience of camping for four days with thousands of strangers, and the intensity of the musical performances. Here's how your outline of main points might look:

Speech thesis: Convincing my friends to stay at the Bonnaroo festival paid off with an amazing surprise.

Main points:

I. Bonnaroo is one of the largest four-day music festivals in the United States.

II. After an exhausting day in the Tennessee heat, my friends were ready to go back to our campsite, but I convinced them to stay for the Earth Wind & Fire evening performance.

III. Imagine our surprise when the group invited Kendrick Lamar and Chance the Rapper to join them onstage to freestyle.

IV. Thanks to the easygoing, collaborative spirit of the festival, we experienced an amazing set of funk and rap music.

You'll also want to use language that draws your listeners into the sights, sounds, and emotions of the story (*heat, imagine, surprise*). The right nonverbal communication can further help you capture and hold your listeners' attention. Just observe the nonverbal skills of good storytellers, like those found on the Moth (http://themoth.org/stories). Their animated gestures and facial expressions, along with appropriate changes in vocal tone, pitch, and volume, engage listeners with the stories they're telling. Practice these same nonverbal skills when *rehearsing* your speech, and seek feedback to improve your delivery.

Comparison/Contrast Presentations

In some speaking situations, you'll be called on to present the similarities and differences between ideas, things, events, or people. In these cases, you'll be making a **comparison/contrast presentation**. For example, if you volunteer at the local science museum, you might explain the differences and similarities between bacterial and viral infections to visiting school groups. Or as the president of your parent-teacher organization, you might spell out the implications of purchasing playground equipment or a photocopier with the revenue generated from a recent fund-raiser.

When preparing this type of speech, start by identifying what you'll be comparing or contrasting. Stick to just a few things, so your audience can keep track of the comparisons. For example, at the science museum, you wouldn't want to compare and contrast 10 different types of bacteria and viruses. Instead, you would want to compare and contrast general differences and similarities.

A topical pattern of organization works well for most comparison/contrast speeches because it helps you focus on how the features or characteristics of the things you're comparing are similar and different. Consider the following outline for the speech examining the similarities and differences between bacterial and viral infections:

Speech thesis: Bacterial and viral infections have some similarities, but they also have important differences.

Main points:

I. Bacteria and viruses are spread in similar ways.

II. Both result in diseases of varying severity.

III. Bacteria are structurally different from viruses.

IV. Some bacteria are actually helpful to the body.

V. Treatments for bacterial and viral infections are different.

Other ways to compare and contrast are by talking about costs and benefits, advantages and disadvantages, or pros and cons related to different items. Table 16.2 shows more examples of comparison/contrast presentations.

TABLE 16.2

EXAMPLES OF INFORMATIVE PRESENTATIONS

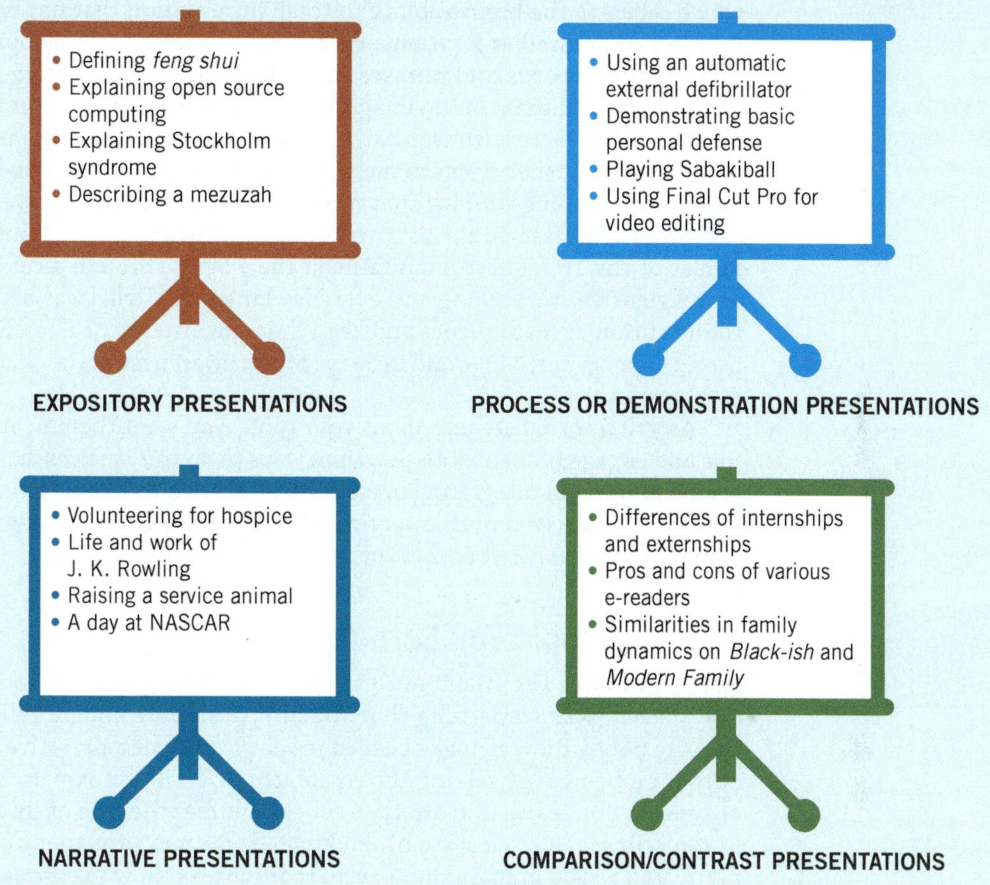

• Defining *feng shui*
• Explaining open source computing
• Explaining Stockholm syndrome
• Describing a mezuzah
EXPOSITORY PRESENTATIONS
• Using an automatic external defibrillator
• Demonstrating basic personal defense
• Playing Sabakiball
• Using Final Cut Pro for video editing
PROCESS OR DEMONSTRATION PRESENTATIONS
• Volunteering for hospice
• Life and work of J. K. Rowling
• Raising a service animal
• A day at NASCAR
NARRATIVE PRESENTATIONS
• Differences of internships and externships
• Pros and cons of various e-readers
• Similarities in family dynamics on *Black-ish* and *Modern Family*
COMPARISON/CONTRAST PRESENTATIONS

Introwiz1/Shutterstock.com

Guidelines for Informative Speaking

The type of informative speech you prepare is determined by the situation, your specific purpose, and the information needs of the audience. Although the type may vary, there are common guidelines competent speakers apply when preparing informative presentations.

Three-time U.S. Memory champion Nelson Dellis uses his expertise to keep audiences captivated during his speeches as he raises awareness about Alzheimer's.[2] Speaking onstage to a Chicago Ideas Week audience, Dellis

[2]Adapted from Dellis (2014).

demonstrated a technique for memorization known as the *method of loci,* which relies on the brain's ability to recall information that has been mentally linked to familiar locations. He asked the audience to memorize a list of 10 random words and phrases, including "rest" and "mango-par-bat," and then guided them on an imaginary journey around different locations on the stage, where each word or phrase was associated with a particular point. He then asked them to recite the list of random words and phrases from the beginning—which they did, without a hitch. Dellis revealed that each word or phrase on the list corresponded with a phonetic sound for the names of the 10 highest mountains in the world. Through a combination of imaginative storytelling and everyday language, Dellis was able to hold the attention of his audience and keep them involved as he demonstrated a useful memory technique and increased their awareness of the challenges of Alzheimer's.

As you inform listeners about your topic, you want them to stay attentive and engaged. Chapter 14 describes ways to do this, such as using appropriate humor and integrating presentation aids. Additionally, following the guidelines discussed in this section will keep your listeners engaged and help them remember your message for years to come.

Choose a Topic You Care About

When you have the freedom to choose your own topic for an informative speech, pick something that you are passionate about. Talk about a favorite hobby (how to make beaded jewelry), present a narrative about an outdoor adventure (walking the Appalachian Trail), or explain a concept or process you learned in another college course (the role of lie detectors in the criminal justice system). Picking a topic you care about keeps you motivated as you prepare the speech. (For more on how to choose a speech topic, see Chapter 13, pages 318–321.) It also helps you come across as more animated and enthusiastic in your speech delivery. When you care about your topic, it shows. If you seem bored by your topic, your audience will be, too.

Capture—and Hold—Your Listeners' Attention

Research on perception and listening reveals that people are highly selective in how they focus their attention. We tend to pay attention to messages that relate to our needs and interests (Fiske & Taylor, 1991). For example, if you're like most students, you perk up during a class lecture if your teacher says, "Listen up, people: what I'm covering now will be on the test." After all, it is in your best interest to do well on the test. But how do you create messages that connect with your listeners' interests?

Start with a compelling introduction to your speech. Explain how your audience will benefit from the information you're about to share ("Knowing

ADVANCE THE CONVERSATION

SOME THINGS ARE BETTER LEFT UNSAID

1 YOUR DILEMMA

As an active member of your campus, you serve as a representative to the college dean's advisory council. You also volunteer as a peer mentor, helping first-year students adjust to college. Given your popularity as a peer mentor, Dr. Dawkins—the dean—asks you to present a session called "Academic Survival Skills for Your First Semester" during new-student orientation.

Though you are honored, you are also nervous. You tell your friend Jack, "I'm freaking out. How will I keep the students interested? Dr. Dawkins wants me to present for 15 to 20 minutes."

"Just tell them what worked for you in your first semester," Jack says.

"I can't do that," you reply. "My first semester was a disaster! I was accused of plagiarizing a paper in my psych class. I didn't give proper credit for my sources ... I didn't know how to do it."

"So, did you fail the class?" Jack asks.

"No. I got an F on the paper. But I definitely learned to ask for help. The professor took me under her wing. I ended up passing the course, and I actually changed my major to psychology."

"Wow! That's a powerful lesson. Why don't you tell the students that story?" Jack suggests.

You're not sure. Dr. Dawkins will be there, and you don't want him to know about your embarrassing mistake. You also feel responsible to teach the first-year students how to *avoid* that kind of academic trouble.

How might the new students benefit from your personal story?

2 THE RESEARCH

Self-disclosure occurs in speeches when you share information about yourself that listeners wouldn't ordinarily know. Speakers often do this to bond with their listeners. In educational settings—like a new-student orientation—appropriate self-disclosure increases student motivation and liking for the instructor (Hill, Ah Yn, & Lindsey, 2008). Additionally, researchers have found that learning is promoted through the use of self-disclosure and stories to illustrate concepts (Downs, Javidi, & Nussbaum, 1988).

However, the kind of personal information you share matters. Researchers Pamela Lannutti and Elena Strauman (2006) found that students give high positive evaluations to teachers who self-disclose information that is positive and relevant to the lesson ("During my first week of college, I was so hyped that I was up and dressed by six o'clock every morning"). Such revelations help students see instructors as human. But there is a limit. Self-disclosing negative information (personal flaws, bad habits) or talking excessively about themselves causes students to view presenters unfavorably (Downs et al., 1988).

Given the research about self-disclosure, what risks do you take by including your personal narrative in the presentation?

3 YOUR OPPORTUNITY

Before deciding what to do, consider the facts of the situation, and think about the research on self-disclosure in academic settings. Also, reflect on what you've learned so far about informative speech preparation (pp. 402–405), narrative presentations (pp. 408–410), and capturing listeners' attention (pp. 412, 414).

Now it's your turn. Write out a response to Jack in which you explain whether or not you will include the personal story in your speech, and why.

the differences between face-to-face and online classes can help you decide which class format is better for you"). People will pay closer attention to your message when they know what's in it for them.

However, capturing your audience's attention during the introduction of your speech isn't all you need to do; you also need to hold their attention during the rest of your presentation. Develop your ideas by using supporting materials—such as interesting and relevant examples or stories—that relate to your audience members' lives and priorities. As you *compose* each main point of your speech, keep the following question in mind: How can I relate this point to my audience's physical, emotional, intellectual, or social priorities?

Use Everyday Language

Using an *oral language style* can make your informative presentation engaging. This style is similar to how people talk in everyday life instead of the formal language used in many written assignments. As Chapter 15 explains, adopting an oral language style creates a sense of immediacy with your audience. It helps people quickly understand what you're saying, and it makes your message more appealing. Consider the differences in the language of this main point for a speech on common chemicals found in the home:

> *Written language style:* "Biohazardous material exists in the kitchen cabinets of most U.S. households."
>
> *Oral language style:* "If you look in your kitchen cabinets tonight, you'll likely find some common biohazardous material."

Most audiences prefer to listen to an oral language style because it is more active, interesting, and common than a written language style. In addition to being easier on listeners' ears, an oral style of language helps you come across as personable and authentic to your audience.

Make Your Speech Understandable

When you're communicating ideas that are unfamiliar to your audience, it helps to connect those ideas to concepts or things that *are* familiar to them. For example, when Joe's children were preschoolers, he couldn't tell them he'd be home from work by four o'clock. They didn't know how to tell time yet, so "four o'clock" had no meaning for them. Instead, he'd say, "I'll be home when *Reading Rainbow* is over." Since *Reading Rainbow* was their favorite television program, this reference made a familiar connection in their minds. Similarly, you can use examples and stories to connect difficult concepts to your listeners' experiences and thus make those concepts easier to understand. Conservation biologist Dr. Rae Wynn-Grant is particularly

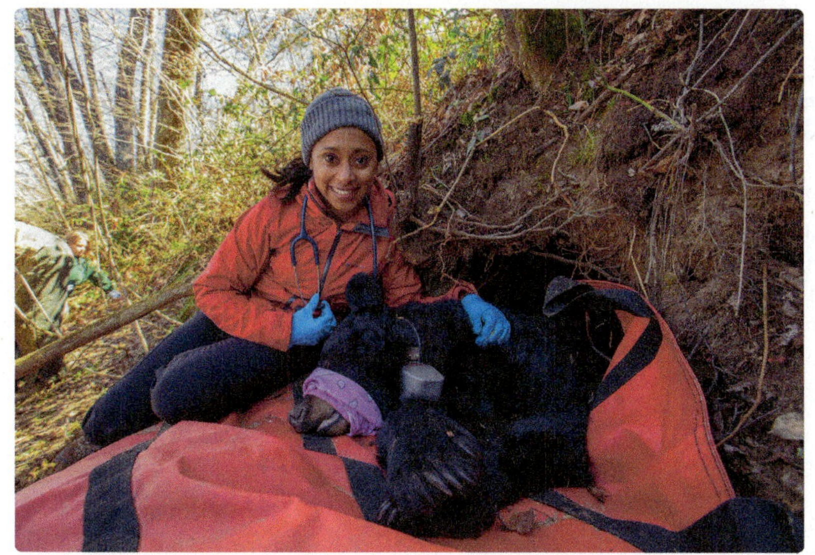

Peter R. Houlihan

Conservation biologist Dr. Rae Wynn-Grant uses her expertise and passion for wildlife to deliver clear, understandable presentations that captivate her audiences. What steps can you take to make sure your audience will be able to understand your speech?

effective at clarifying scientific ideas for her audiences. When describing her research on black bears, Dr. Wynn-Grant explains a commonly misunderstood idea about their name:

> One of my favorite things about black bears is also probably one of the trickiest things about black bears, and that is the name. The name *black bear* just delineates a species, so it makes us understand that they're separate from polar bears or panda bears . . . but black bears aren't always black. They can be a variety of colors. And the way I like to think about it is in comparison to human beings. We're all the same species, but we don't all have the same hair color. And it's the exact same thing with black bears. They can have a variety of colors. (Hayden Planetarium, 2017)

Dr. Wynn-Grant takes a simple idea her listeners will understand (variation of human hair color) to clarify confusion about the name *black bear.* She frequently uses such examples, stories, and demonstrations to convey complex scientific principles to general audiences who attend her lectures and speeches.

Help Your Audience Remember Your Message

One measure of an informative speech's success is whether your listeners remember it. A lot of things can interfere with an audience's ability to pay attention to—and retain—the information you share with them. For example, listeners may be distracted by outside *noise* during the speech—such as a phone or someone talking nearby. An overly warm or cool temperature in

FIGURE 16.1

HELP YOUR AUDIENCE REMEMBER YOUR MESSAGE

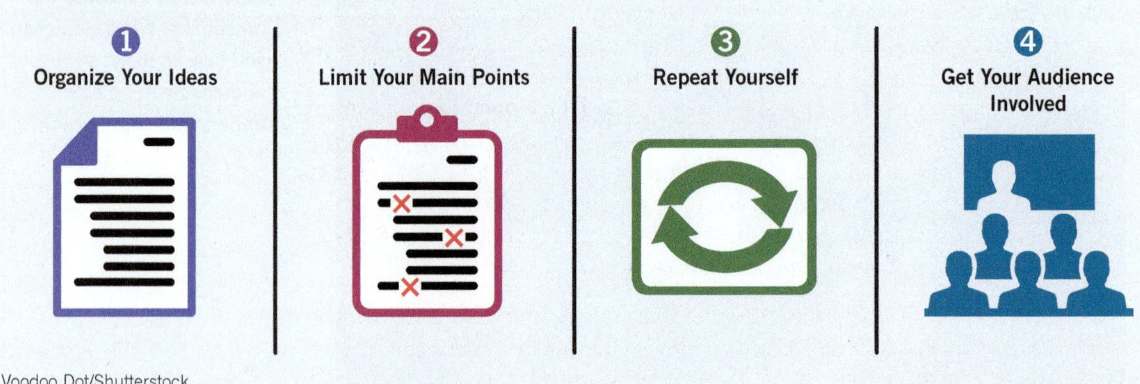

Voodoo Dot/Shutterstock

the room can be just as intrusive. Or listeners can simply get lost in their own thoughts or get sidetracked by other websites or apps if they are watching your speech online. To help your audience pay attention and remember your message, try the following strategies:

- *Organize your ideas.* When you show listeners how ideas go together, they'll be more likely to remember them. Consider this group of letters: PBSCBSESPNNBC. If you were to read these out loud to an audience, your listeners would find it difficult to remember them. But if you organized the letters into groupings that made sense to your audience—PBS, CBS, ESPN, NBC—the letters would become meaningful, and listeners would more easily retain them. Using *connectives* (*First*, *Next*) in your speech can further help your audience see how your main points are related.
- *Limit your main points.* As Chapter 14 discusses, *main points* are the key statements or principles that support the speech thesis (see pages 345–350). As you prepare your informative speech, try to limit your main points to between three and five. Too many more, and the audience (and you!) might have trouble following and remembering your line of thinking.
- *Repeat yourself.* Repeating information helps people retain it. While studying for a test, you probably go over the information several times to commit it to memory. Help your audience remember your main ideas by using the same basic principle of repetition. However, don't just say the same words over and over. Instead, illustrate a main point through different means. For instance, you can use a preview statement to introduce the point, increase the volume of your voice when explaining the point, reinforce the point through a visual aid, and then remind the audience of the point in your summary statement.

- *Get your audience involved.* People tend to remember things that they participate in. Think about your college classes. Which ones do you remember the most—the classes in which the teacher lectured in a monotone, or those that had lots of discussion and group work? Even with a large group, it's possible to still involve your audience. Nelson Dellis managed to get his listeners involved by asking them to recall the words and phrases after their journey story. To involve your listeners during an informative speech, ask for a volunteer to take part in a simple demonstration, or have listeners answer a simple question. These kinds of positive disruptions break up your speech and help your audience pay closer attention to your point—which makes it more likely that they'll remember your message.

To see how the principles and guidelines of informative speeches can come together, look over the transcript for the speech "Going Carbon Neutral on Campus" by Saundra Dixon on pages 420–423. A video of the speech is available online in LaunchPad for *Choices & Connections*. Visit **launchpadworks.com**

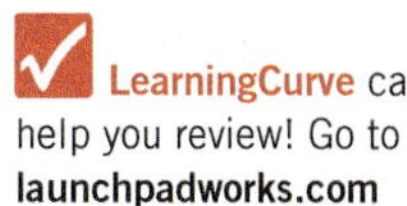

ADVANCE THE CONVERSATION
Video Activity

RESPONDING TO AUDIENCE QUESTIONS

The following scenario will enhance your ability to effectively manage a question-and-answer session after a speech. Visit LaunchPad at launchpadworks.com to get the full experience with video. As you watch the first video, recall what you've learned about citing sources in your speech. Then complete the **Your Turn** prompts. Finally, watch the **Take Two!** video to explore how this scenario could have gone differently.

1 *THE PROBLEM*

Jason delivers an informative speech to his communication class. Drawing on social science research, he explains why some online videos posted by ordinary people go viral and are seen by millions. After he concludes his speech, he has time to answer questions from the audience.

"Okay. I'm glad to take any questions if someone has something to ask. Kate?"

"You said there's research that predicts which videos are likely to go viral, right? Come on. Are you *really* telling me that scientists are actually making a study that someone singing with a plastic cup is going to be more popular than a cat playing piano? I don't believe it."

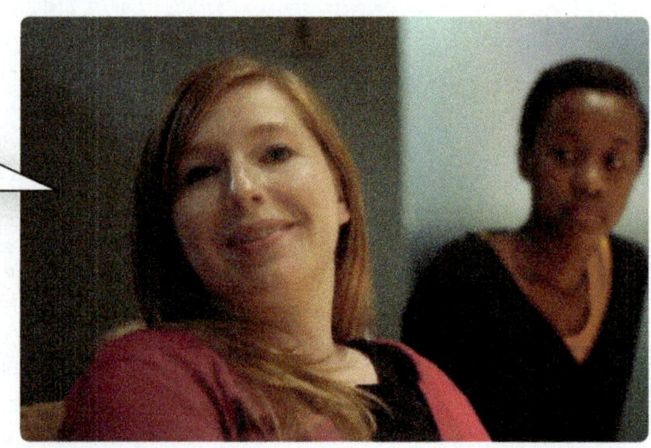

2 YOUR TURN

Observations. Reflect on how Jason and Kate communicated in this scenario by answering the following questions:

1. Which character do you identify with more in this situation? How would you feel if you were in their situation?
2. Where were the missed opportunities to practice competent communication?

Discussion. In class or with a partner, share your thoughts about the interaction between Jason and Kate and work to answer the following questions:

1. Could Kate have phrased her question more competently? If so, how?
2. How can Jason respond competently to Kate's question?

Conclusion. Choose one person in the scenario to offer your advice. Based on your analysis, what advice would you give to help them communicate competently in this scenario?

3 TAKE TWO!

Watch the **Take Two!** video to see one possible example of how things might have gone differently. As you watch the video, consider where the dialog reflects communication competence. After watching the video, answer the questions below:

1. Did Jason and/or the audience members take advantage of opportunities that they missed in the first scenario? Which ones?
2. Did their different actions result in a more productive question-and-answer session? Please explain.

Sample Informative Speech

• To watch a video of Saundra's first practice attempt at delivering this speech as well as her final, polished speech, go to launchpadworks.com

GOING CARBON NEUTRAL ON CAMPUS •

By Saundra Dixon

Throughout her speech, Saundra's nonverbal communication is expressive but appropriately restrained, fitting the serious nature of her topic.

"Climate change is real. It is happening right now. It is the most urgent threat facing our entire species, and we need to work collectively together and stop procrastinating." •

• Beginning the speech with a quote from Leonardo DiCaprio, a well-known actor and activist, effectively captures the audience's attention and gets them interested in the topic.

These words, from Leonardo DiCaprio in his 2016 Academy Awards acceptance speech, reflect the consensus of the worldwide scientific community, the Catholic Church, and the United States military. Human-caused climate change is indeed one of the greatest global challenges of our lifetimes. To address this challenge, colleges and universities are engaging in a range of actions to become carbon neutral.

During this presentation, I will explain the scope of the campus movement toward carbon neutrality. First I'll give a brief overview of carbon neutrality. Second, I'll describe what institutions of higher learning are doing to move toward carbon neutrality. Third, I'll share with you some specific means by which colleges and universities are attempting to achieve carbon neutrality. Led by student involvement, carbon neutrality at colleges of all sizes is one step in meeting the challenge of human-caused climate change. •

• In her preview statement, Saundra states her thesis and main points so that the audience knows what to expect from the rest of her speech.

To begin: What is carbon neutrality, and why is it important? • According to a 2014 assessment by the Intergovernmental Panel on Climate Change, it is 100 percent certain that the Earth's climate is warming, and 95 to 100 percent certain that human-caused activities are responsible for the warming. The United Nations Human Rights Council identifies climate change as an immediate and far-reaching human rights issue due to its likely impact on poor and marginalized countries. A 2016 study by the think tank Demos estimates that unchecked climate change will cost the millennial generation $8.8 trillion dollars in total lost lifetime income. •

• With this question, Saundra transitions smoothly from her introduction into the body of her speech.

• By citing data from authoritative sources, Saundra boosts her credibility.

These forecasts may sound bleak, but the good news is that steps can and are being taken to prevent these things from happening. This is where carbon neutrality comes in.

A quick pause to check her notes helps Saundra keep her speech focused and ensures she hits all her main points and examples.

Carbon neutrality means taking as much carbon-based pollution out of the atmosphere as we put in. We emit carbon in the form of carbon dioxide and methane gas, through activities like burning coal or natural gas for energy and dedicating large swaths of land to raising livestock. Reducing carbon output requires the use of renewable energy sources—like wind and solar—and altering habits of consumption, including eating a diet that is more plant based.

Carbon neutrality also requires that we offset or cancel out carbon-based pollution with such carbon-absorbing activities as, for example, preserving forests and wetlands. In other words, being carbon neutral means balancing the carbon equation and not causing additional carbon pollution. •

• *Saundra carefully defines **carbon neutrality**, a term that some audience members may not be familiar with. She uses an analogy—comparing carbon to an equation—to promote audience understanding.*

As I've mentioned, individuals can take steps to reduce carbon-based pollution, such as switching to renewable energy at home and eating a more plant-based diet. However, the biggest impacts will come from actions by groups and institutions, including colleges. If just one large school shifts to carbon neutrality, it can do more to reduce the impact of climate change than thousands of carbon-neutral individuals. •

• *Here Saundra approaches persuasive territory, yet still she mostly informs, rather than advocates. It is often acceptable for an informative speech to contain **some** persuasive elements, as long as the main purpose is to inform.*

In fact, many colleges in the United States and around the world are already taking big steps toward carbon neutrality. Over 500 U.S. colleges have signed the American College and University Presidents' Climate Commitment and have actively pledged to become carbon neutral by a specific date, which varies by school. According to Second Nature, the nonprofit organization overseeing this Climate Commitment, some colleges have already become 100 percent carbon neutral, such as College of the Atlantic, Green Mountain College, Colby College, and Middlebury College. •

• *Saundra supports her point with several examples of colleges that are achieving carbon neutrality.*

Those four schools have something in common: they are all relatively small liberal arts colleges, mostly located in rural areas. Some of the methods that these schools have successfully implemented to reduce carbon are difficult to scale up at larger schools. For example, Middlebury College uses a biomass gasification plant that superheats wood chips to create steam for heating, air conditioning, and hot water. The Middlebury campus in Vermont has a total enrollment of just over 2,500 students. The amount of wood chips that would be needed to power such a plant at a larger school would be prohibitive, forcing larger schools to seek other solutions to reduce their carbon footprint.

That's not to say that larger schools are getting left behind in the race for carbon neutrality. Colorado State University, a campus of over 30,000 students, is also home to a 30-acre field of solar panels—which the university claims generate enough electricity to power 949 homes—as well as a steam turbine that cuts the school's carbon emissions by 2,600 tons every year. Meanwhile, Stanford University successfully met its goal of reducing carbon emissions by 68 percent by the end of 2016 and pledged to meet even more ambitious emission goals in subsequent years. Finally, the entire 10-campus University of California system has pledged to become carbon neutral by 2025. Whether small or large, and whether early or recent adopters, colleges nationwide have begun doing their part to reduce their carbon outputs.

Saundra uses simple gestures and eye contact at appropriate moments to help her connect with her audience.

So far, we've seen that carbon neutrality is important and that there is a widespread commitment to moving toward carbon neutrality on college campuses. Let's look now at more specific ways in which students and administrators are achieving carbon neutrality. •

• *In this paragraph, Saundra uses an internal summary and an internal preview. She summarizes previous points and previews her next point, which helps audience members follow along.*

First and foremost, energy efficiency is the key to reducing emissions. Energy efficiency requirements for new buildings and retrofits for aging ones can go a long way toward this end. Colleges are switching to locally appropriate renewable energy, and some are even generating their own energy using solar arrays or wind farms. Additionally, administrators can choose to bring locally sourced food to campus dining halls, which cuts down on carbon emitted during food transportation. Speaking of transportation, another easy step that students can take is to use public transit and campus shuttles instead of personal cars whenever possible.

The other side of carbon neutrality is absorbing existing carbon emissions. To do this, some colleges are turning to offsite options. Preserving undeveloped land, for example, provides a natural system to absorb emissions. Meanwhile, purchasing carbon offsets pays for carbon-reducing projects elsewhere, such as reforestation, carbon dioxide or methane capture, and clean energy development. • For example, Green Mountain College partners with local energy company Native Energy and with the Seneca Meadows Landfill in upstate New York to obtain carbon offsets.

*• Saundra could have strengthened her speech by defining **carbon offsets**, a term that is likely unfamiliar to some audience members. Without such a definition, the audience may not fully understand her point about absorbing emissions.*

Perhaps the biggest barrier to carbon neutrality is the up-front cost. Building energy-efficient cafeterias, lecture halls, and dormitories isn't cheap, but it can be a smart business investment. In a 2015 *New York Times* commentary, journalist David Bornstein observed that the University of New Hampshire invested $600,000 in energy efficiency projects that resulted in $1.3 million in savings in just five years. • Colleges are finding ways to implement these projects not only because it saves the environment, but also because it saves them money in the long run.

*• Saundra supports her point with evidence from the **New York Times**, which she establishes as a credible source.*

Saundra shows a slide with a list of her supporting points to help her audience follow her discussion of how colleges are moving toward carbon neutrality.

Finally, students and administrators committed to carbon neutrality are taking other steps right now without spending a cent. Energy-saving competitions between dormitories on campus—like those sponsored by the nonprofit group Alliance to Save Energy—reduce energy costs, cut carbon emissions, and increase clean energy awareness and engagement among students. So do student groups tasked with turning off lights in unoccupied rooms, and coalitions between students, staff, and administration to reduce food waste. Schools are using all of these strategies as they to move toward carbon neutrality.

Today we've explored what carbon neutrality is and how it can be achieved. We learned about the steps college communities are taking to work towards carbon neutrality. • Human-caused climate change isn't just about our future. It is happening right now. As I've described today, so too are efforts by students and educators to curb it. Carbon neutrality—the balancing of carbon-based pollution with carbon absorption—can help to address human-caused climate change. In the words of Bob Best, Head of Energy and Sustainability at the investment management company JLL: "From students and faculty to parents and alumni, environmental

• By reminding her audience members what they have learned so far, Saundra signals the transition to her conclusion.

sustainability is now one of the pillars of a university's public image." • Colleges and universities recognize this reality and overwhelmingly support carbon neutrality initiatives. Through a mixture of emissions reduction and emissions capture, on- and offsite, small and large colleges have already been successful in moving toward a greener tomorrow.

• *Saundra includes a quotation in her conclusion. The quotation reinforces her thesis and helps make her conclusion memorable.*

REFERENCES

Bornstein, D. (2015, February 6). Investing in energy efficiency pays off. *New York Times.* Retrieved from https://opinionator.blogs.nytimes.com/2015/02/06/investing-in-energy-efficiency-pays-off/

Colorado State University. (n.d.). Sustainability in facilities management. Retrieved from https://www.fm.colostate.edu/sustain/energy.html

Core Writing Team. (2014). Climate change 2014 synthesis report. United Nations Intergovernmental Panel on Climate Change.

Demos. (2016, August 22). The price tag of being young: Climate change and millennials' economic future. Retrieved from http://www.demos.org/publication/price-tag-being-young-climate-change-and-millennials-economic-future

Jones Lang LaSalle. (2017, April 13). Carbon-neutral campus: Navigating the road to zero. Retrieved from http://www.us.jll.com/united-states/en-us/news/4487/lessons-for-higher-education-carbon-neutral-goals

Second Nature. (2018). Reporting platform. Retrieved from http://reporting.secondnature.org/institution/data/

Stanford University. (n.d.). Sustainable Stanford 2016–17 year in review. Retrieved from https://sustainability-year-in-review.stanford.edu/2017/

United Nations Human Rights Office of the High Commissioner. (n.d.). Human rights and climate change. Retrieved from http://www.ohchr.org/EN/Issues/HRAndClimateChange/Pages/HRClimateChangeIndex.aspx

Woodside, R. (2016, December 9). New England colleges demonstrate excellence. *Second Nature.* Retrieved from http://secondnature.org/2016/12/09/new-england-colleges-demonstrate-excellence/

SAMPLE SPEECH RESOURCES

There is a lot more to Saundra's speech than the transcript above. See how the whole speech came together by going to **launchpadworks.com**. There you will find:

1. Video of Saundra's speech "Going Carbon Neutral on Campus" (with closed captions available)
2. Video of Saundra's first practice attempt delivering the speech, so that you can see the improvements she made from practice to her final speech
3. Brief video clips highlighting specific techniques Saundra uses in her speech

CHAPTER 16 REVIEW

CHAPTER RECAP

- **Informative speeches** allow you to raise awareness about a topic or provide an in-depth explanation of a topic. Avoid **information overload** for your audience by considering how much information is possible to share with them.
- To maintain a focus on informing (instead of persuading), keep in mind your general purpose, and maintain a neutral point of view when preparing your presentation.
- The four most common types of informative speeches are **expository**, **process or demonstration**, **narrative**, and **comparison/contrast**. You may use one or more types to achieve your speech thesis.
- Delivering a successful informative speech includes following the five steps of speech preparation, but it is also important to focus on making your speech understandable and helping your audience remember key points.

LaunchPad

LaunchPad for *Choices & Connections* offers unique video scenarios and encourages self-assessment through adaptive quizzing. Go to **launchpadworks.com** to get access.

- LearningCurve adaptive quizzes
- Advance the Conversation video scenarios
- Video clips that illustrate key concepts
- Sample speech resources

KEY TERMS

Informative speech, p. 402
Information overload, p. 403
Expository presentation, p. 407
Process or demonstration presentation, p. 407
Narrative presentation, p. 408
Comparison/contrast presentation, p. 410

POP QUIZ

Looking for more review questions? **LearningCurve** can help you master key concepts from this chapter. Go to **launchpadworks.com**

1. If you are giving an informative speech about how to apply to the social work program on your campus, what function of informative speaking are you fulfilling?
   - **a.** In-depth explanation
   - **b.** Raising awareness
   - **c.** Audience analysis
   - **d.** Specific purpose
2. Which of the following is *not* a goal of informative speaking?
   - **a.** Improving listeners' understanding
   - **b.** Keeping a neutral point of view
   - **c.** Avoiding motivational appeals
   - **d.** Changing listeners' attitudes
3. Giving a speech about the different eras in internet development is an example of which type of presentation?
   - **a.** Expository presentation
   - **b.** Narrative presentation
   - **c.** Process or demonstration presentation
   - **d.** Comparison/contrast presentation
4. When giving an informative speech, using an oral style of language allows you to
   - **a.** be memorable.
   - **b.** target listeners' interests.
   - **c.** create immediacy.
   - **d.** use connotative meanings.
5. Using connectives in your speech will help you
   - **a.** limit your main points.
   - **b.** organize your ideas.
   - **c.** stay on message.
   - **d.** involve your listeners.

ACTIVITIES

For more activities, visit LaunchPad for *Choices & Connections* at **launchpadworks.com**

1 Show and Analyze

Watch a cooking show on the Food Network, like Rachael Ray's *30 Minute Meals* or Sunny Anderson's *Cooking for Real* (you can find episodes at www.foodnetwork.com, or use any how-to show you like). In a brief paper, identify specific strategies the host uses to explain the process of preparing a meal. Also, make note of how the guidelines for informative speaking are evident in the program.

2 Sharing Your Story

Identify a small object that has personal meaning for you (e.g., a photograph, tattoo, piece of jewelry, or family heirloom). Prepare a two- to three-minute narrative presentation that tells the story of the item's significance. Rehearse your presentation with a classmate, and get feedback to help you revise it. Then deliver the revised speech to your class, or video-record it for the course website.

17

Persuasive Speaking

On her 16th birthday, Malala Yousafzai did something extraordinary. She gave a speech to the United Nations (UN) about the right of every child in developing countries—especially girls—to 12 years of quality education.[1] Yousafzai's address to the UN was even more remarkable when you consider what had happened to her just nine months earlier in her native country of Pakistan. Two gunmen from the Taliban—an extremist group—boarded a school bus on which Yousafzai was riding and shot her, leaving her for dead.

Inspired by her father's work as a teacher and educational leader, Yousafzai learned early that formal schooling was a key to prosperity. She was a smart, confident, and exceptional student. But after the Taliban assumed control in the region of Pakistan where she lived, the extremist group banned girls from attending school. Just 11 years old at the time, Yousafzai protested by writing blogs, giving television interviews, and even giving a speech to a Pakistan press club titled "How Dare the Taliban Take Away My Basic Right to Education?" She quickly gained a high profile as an outspoken critic of the Taliban, and in response, the Taliban issued its death warrant on Yousafzai.

Miraculously, Yousafzai survived the gunshot wound to her head and became even more determined to advocate for children's education. Rather than appeal to her audience's emotion by seeking pity for what happened, Yousafzai showed strength of character and commitment to her purpose as she spoke to the UN General Assembly. At the beginning of her speech, she rejected any notion of personal revenge against the Taliban. Instead, she made clear her goal of advocating for children's right to education.

Yousafzai continued her speech by pointing out that terrorist groups fear educated citizens. She described recent attacks on students, teachers, and even medical workers. Using descriptive language, Yousafzai illustrated the difficulty of keeping schools open in some countries and demonstrated her broader commitment to human rights worldwide:

> Young girls have to do domestic labor and are forced to get married at an early age. Poverty, ignorance, injustice, racism and the deprivation of basic rights are the main problems faced by both men and women. (Yousafzai, 2013, p. 267)

After explaining the problem, Yousafzai asked the world leaders to ensure access to education for every child around the world. She described pens and books as "powerful weapons" against illiteracy, poverty, and terrorism. She concluded her speech by urging the leaders to see education as the only solution to peace and prosperity.

---

[1]Information in the chapter opener from Husain (2013).

AP Images/Sipa/Carlos Tischler

CHAPTER OUTLINE

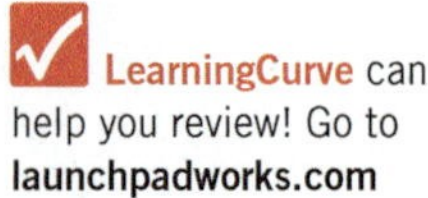
LearningCurve can help you review! Go to **launchpadworks.com**

Malala Yousafzai continues her work through a nonprofit named for her—the Malala Fund. Through speeches, social media campaigns, and personal outreach, she persuades policy makers and government officials to her cause. One social media campaign—#Booksnotbullets—produced 20,000 posts from around the world urging government leaders to invest $39 billion for primary and secondary education for all children (Leber, 2015). The Malala Fund has been improving access to schools in Pakistan, helping to educate Syrian refugees in Jordan and Lebanon, providing schooling for young girls in Kenya and Sierra Leone, and embarking on many other projects in developing countries. Yousafzai's persuasive leadership has commanded attention in unexpected ways as well. In 2014, she became the youngest person to be awarded the Nobel Peace Prize.

Yousafzai is using persuasive communication on a global stage to change a dire situation. To a much smaller degree, you communicate daily to try to influence others' attitudes, behaviors, and actions. For instance, on your way to work, you call a friend and try to persuade her to see the movie you want to see. At your job, you convince a coworker to cover your shift. Persuasive communications like these happen in a wide range of settings. In this chapter, we focus on **persuasive speeches**—those that reinforce or change listeners' attitudes and beliefs and possibly even motivate them to take action. These types of presentations may be an expectation of your job or your community involvement.

Persuasive speaking is notably different from coercion. **Coercion** involves using threats, manipulation, and even violence to force others to do something against their will. Any use of coercion is unethical. When you speak to persuade others, you provide your audience with accurate and honest information, giving them the freedom to choose whether to accept your message. In this chapter, you'll learn:

- The different types of persuasive propositions
- The importance of credibility in persuasive speaking
- How to organize a persuasive speech and support your claims
- Strategies for appealing to your audience's needs and emotions
- General guidelines for persuasive speaking

What Is Persuasive Speaking?

Persuasive speeches are unique because their goal is to change the audience's beliefs or behavior. When preparing such a presentation, consider the type of persuasive speech you'll give, what your specific purpose will be, and—most importantly—how to get your audience to believe what you have to say.

Throughout your academic, social, and professional life, you will be called on to prepare persuasive presentations. Your most immediate need, of course, is probably for this communication class. Luckily, you are already familiar with how to begin any speech assignment. To deliver a persuasive speech, follow the five steps for speech preparation discussed in Chapters 13, 14, and 15: think, investigate, compose, rehearse, and revise. (See Table 13.1 on page 317.) In addition, there are factors specific to persuasive speaking to keep in mind as you prepare.

Types of Persuasive Propositions

When *thinking* about the topic of your presentation, consider what type of proposition you want your listeners to accept. There are three types:

1. A **proposition of fact** establishes whether something is true or not ("Chocolate can reduce the onset of heart disease") or whether an event will or won't happen ("The polarity of the earth will be reversed by the year 3000").
2. A **proposition of value** urges a judgment on a topic ("Euthanasia is morally wrong") or explains why something is good or bad ("Here is why the Batman movies are better films than the Superman franchise").
3. A **proposition of policy** argues about whether an action should or should not be taken ("First-year students should be required to enroll in an academic success course").

Choosing which type of persuasive proposition you want the audience to accept helps you develop your speech thesis during the *composing* step of your preparation.

Audience Analysis for Persuasive Speeches

After determining your topic and persuasive proposition, the next part of the *thinking* step includes analyzing the attitudes your audience may have about your message. As Chapter 13 discusses, *audience analysis* is the process of identifying important characteristics about your listeners, and using this information to prepare your speech. Although you always want to know as much as possible about your audience, paying special attention to any strongly held *attitudes*, *beliefs*, and *values* is especially helpful when preparing a persuasive speech. Will the audience have favorable views toward your topic? Will they strongly oppose your position? Will they be undecided or uncommitted on the issue? Consider the answers to these questions while researching your topic and composing your speech; it will help you create persuasive main points and present your message ethically.

There is one more factor to consider about your listeners when preparing a persuasive speech: How motivated will they be to even pay attention?

Understanding the Elaboration Likelihood Model. In Chapter 7's discussion of the listening process, we explain how people go through stages of *understanding*, *interpreting*, and *evaluating* in order to judge the accuracy, interest, and relevance of the messages they hear. But scholars suggest that

Including the audience in your speech is a sure way to make sure they stay connected and attentive. Using personal pronouns—like *you* and *we*—instead of making general statements lets your audience know that your topic is being presented specifically to their interests. What other techniques could you use to encourage the central route to processing in your listeners?

Christopher Robbins/Media Bakery

audience members vary in their motivation and ability to process persuasive messages. Known as the **elaboration likelihood model**, this theory proposes that listeners who are intensely interested in your topic and can easily understand your presentation will put more effort into thinking about your persuasive message than will listeners who don't care about or don't understand your speech topic. Knowing how your audience will process your message will help when you're *composing* the presentation. There are two routes listeners take when processing persuasive messages: central and peripheral.

Audience members who are highly interested in your topic and who have the knowledge needed to understand your message will take a **central route** to processing your speech—meaning they'll pay more attention and carefully evaluate your points (Petty & Cacioppo, 1986). Consider medical doctors listening to a researcher trying to persuade them to try a new method for treating ovarian cancer. In such a high-stakes, professional setting, the audience members are highly motivated to pay attention, and they'll be comfortable with the complex information being presented. In this case, the researcher would want to emphasize medical study results, compose detailed supporting points for his or her main ideas, and plan time for audience questions.

Audiences who are less motivated about the topic or who don't have the time or knowledge needed to understand the information might take a **peripheral route** to processing your message (Petty & Cacioppo, 1986). This means they are not fully engaged with the speech. They may *selectively listen* for items of personal interest but miss your larger message and therefore not fully understand your speech thesis. Their attention may wane, or they may get easily distracted. Listeners who take a peripheral route to processing messages can be easily influenced by a speaker's expertise or emotional appeals, but any changes in attitudes and behaviors are often short lived (Petty, Barden, & Wheeler, 2002). For example, they might give a few dollars to a charity immediately after listening to an emotional appeal but not become regular contributors.

Using the Elaboration Likelihood Model. If your audience analysis indicates that most listeners may take a peripheral route to processing your message, there are ways to encourage them to use a central route. Suppose you're giving a presentation to persuade your classmates to embrace proper nutrition in their daily diet. But most of your classmates don't see proper nutrition as important and don't know a lot about the technical details related to nutrition (such as how it affects the body or long-term health consequences). Listeners are more likely to give considerable thought to a message when the topic is made personally relevant to them (Petty et al., 2002). Your speech introduction is the place to start building this awareness. As Chapter 14 explains, one function of the speech introduction is to *connect the topic to the needs and interests* of your audience. When introducing your speech, tell the audience how they will benefit from what you are about to say.

After the speech introduction, you can continue motivating the audience to use central route processing by composing a main point on the positive outcomes or benefits of accepting your speech thesis. For example, you could list the advantages of proper nutrition ("By eating healthier, you'll not only look better but also set a great example for your friends and family"). Additionally, you want to tell them what highly credible experts have said about the issue, so that they understand why good nutrition is something they should care about ("The National Institutes of Health points out that poor nutrition is a contributing factor in obesity, heart disease, and diabetes"). If you present personally relevant, logical, and well-supported messages, your listeners are more likely to process your message thoughtfully (Wagner & Petty, 2011). Later in this chapter, we cover more about how to organize and use logical reasoning in a persuasive speech.

Finally, researchers Wagner and Petty (2011) suggest that even small changes in language help listeners thoughtfully process persuasive messages. For example, using familiar words rather than technical words makes it easier to listen to a speech. Audience members become distracted and tune out when speakers use language that is hard to understand. Relying on personal pronouns ("*You* will feel great when *you* eat well") instead of impersonal pronouns ("*People* feel great when *they* eat well") encourages listeners to feel personally connected to your message and thus to take a central route in processing your speech (Wagner & Petty, 2011).

Specific Purposes for Persuasive Speeches. When it comes time to write the specific purpose statement for your persuasive speech, keep in mind that most persuasive presentations focus on one of three desired outcomes. First, your speech could *reinforce your audience's existing attitudes and beliefs*. Much like the inspiring and rousing speeches given at pep rallies ("This year we win it all!"), this focus is most effective when your listeners already support your position, and your specific purpose is to persuade them to "keep the faith." In this case, your specific purpose might be "To persuade my audience that we are the best team in the conference."

Second, if your listeners are uncommitted about your speech topic or if their attitudes and beliefs about the topic differ from yours, your desired outcome might be to *change your audience's attitudes and beliefs*. Let's say you're talking to an audience that doesn't care that much about sports, and you want to convince your listeners that your school's sports program matters. In this case, your specific purpose might be "To convince my audience that a successful sports team is good for student morale." Since some attitudes and beliefs are at the core of people's self-concept, such as religious and lifestyle choices, one speech won't likely change them. Later in this chapter, we consider how to keep your speech purpose realistic.

A third possible desired outcome is to *motivate your audience to take action*. This could include taking up a charitable cause, making a particular decision, or participating in a political action. If your audience is already convinced that successful sports teams improve student morale, your specific purpose could be "To persuade my audience to donate time or supplies to fund-raising efforts for new team uniforms."

Credibility in Persuasive Speeches

As a pediatrician and coinventor of the rotavirus vaccine, Dr. Paul Offit spends a lot of time talking with audiences about why it's important to vaccinate children against certain diseases (Wallace, 2009). During such occasions, he often meets people who disagree with his claim, usually because they believe that childhood vaccines may have unintended consequences—such as causing autism—and should therefore be avoided. This controversy, which has been raging for more than a decade, has passionate proponents on both sides.

Even though Offit believes that scientific research has shown no link between vaccinations and autism, he knows that some parents believe there's a connection. They place a lot of confidence in other sources, such as what they read online or hear other parents say about their own experiences. With so much competing information available, his audience members will have a range of existing knowledge about vaccines and possibly strong attitudes about the topic. Fully aware of the challenge, Offit carefully plans his speeches in order to persuade parents to vaccinate their children (Wallace, 2009).

A critical step for Offit is making sure his listeners find him credible. **Credibility** is an audience's perception of a speaker's trustworthiness and the validity of the information provided in the speech. If your listeners think you're credible, they are more likely to believe you. If they don't think you're credible, you'll find it difficult to persuade them. The importance of credibility in persuasive speaking can be traced all the way back to the ancient Greek philosopher Aristotle, who pointed out that a speaker's **ethos** (credibility) determines whether he or she can influence listeners (Cooper, 1960).

Certainly, a speaker needs more than credibility, or ethos, to be persuasive. According to Aristotle, speakers should also present the audience

UN Photo/Mark Garten/SIPA/Newscom

As a leader of the United Nations' HeForShe campaign for gender equality, actor Emma Watson spends a lot of time influencing audiences to support her cause. Part of her success is due to her ability to connect with audiences on a humane and passionate level, without relying on her celebrity status. How does someone's general character influence how you listen to her or him?

with good logical reasons (he called this *logos*) and make appeals to their emotions (*pathos*). These three elements—ethos, logos, and pathos—are known as **rhetorical proofs** (Cooper, 1960). Ethical and competent persuasive speeches will include all three forms of rhetorical proof. Later in the chapter, we consider principles and skills for using logical reasoning and emotional appeals in composing your speech.

But let's first look at ethos, or credibility. How exactly do listeners decide whether you're credible? They consider the three Cs: your character, competence, and charisma.

Character. You demonstrate **character** by showing your audience that you understand their needs, have their best interests in mind, and genuinely believe in your topic. This communicates that you are trustworthy. Another way to show character is by making it clear to your listeners what they stand to gain by hearing you out. How can you do all this? Determine what you and your audience have in common, and work that into your speech. Building this bridge to your audience conveys the message that you are all in this together.

Competence. When it comes to credibility, **competence** is the degree of expertise your audience thinks you have regarding your speech topic. Even if you're not an expert on the subject, you can still convey competence by thoroughly researching it.

One way to demonstrate competence is by using information from only those resources that pass the evaluation requirements discussed in Chapter 13. Your research sources should be highly credible, reliable (objective), and current. In addition, work any personal knowledge or experience you have regarding the topic into your speech. For example, if you want to persuade your listeners to get certified in cardiopulmonary resuscitation (CPR), tell them about your own CPR training experience. Finally, carefully organize and prepare your speech. Even the most knowledgeable, reputable speakers have a hard time looking competent if their material doesn't follow a logical sequence or if they jump around from point to point.

Charisma. Your **charisma** stems from how much warmth, personality, and dynamism your audience sees in you. Charismatic speakers engage their audience, even when presenting on topics that don't initially appeal to listeners. Although some people are more naturally outgoing and personable, anyone can work on strengthening their charisma. Even if you're usually more reserved, you can still practice behaviors that will help you engage with your audience and come across as charismatic. For instance, try varying the volume and pitch of your voice, establishing eye contact with audience members, and moving from behind the lectern and among your listeners if possible. As Chapter 15 describes, using such nonverbal communication skills in your delivery creates *immediacy*, or a sense of closeness, with your audience. This means they are more likely to view you as warm and approachable and be engaged by your presentation.

Organizing and Supporting Persuasive Speeches

Taking steps to establish credibility with your audience is important. But you can't rely only on your credibility to achieve your specific purpose. You also need to organize your points in a way that makes sense and give listeners evidence to support your claims.

Shortly after falling down a rabbit hole in the classic story *Alice in Wonderland*, Alice finds herself talking to the Cheshire Cat as she tries to make sense of the strange world she has found herself in:

> "What sort of people live about here?"
>
> "In *that* direction," the Cat said, waving its right paw round, "lives a Hatter: and in *that* direction," waving the other paw, "lives a March Hare. Visit either you like; they're both mad."
>
> "But I don't want to go among mad people," Alice remarked.
>
> "Oh, you can't help that," said the Cat: "we're all mad here. I'm mad. You're mad."
>
> "How do you know I'm mad?" said Alice.
>
> "You must be," said the Cat, "or you wouldn't have come here."
>
> Alice didn't think that proved it at all.
>
> —Lewis Carroll, *Alice in Wonderland*[2]

[2] Excerpted from Carroll (2013), p. 49.

Alice's encounter with the Cheshire Cat is just one of many conversations she has with unusual characters who pull her into loops of confusing logic. Though these characters try to get her to play by the absurd rules of their world, Alice demands stronger proof about why she should believe them.

If you want to be successful in persuading others, you must avoid twisted logic that leaves your listeners feeling like Alice. Even if you have a lot of credibility with your listeners, if you don't provide them with a clearly organized presentation and solid evidence, they may not accept what you have to say. The development of logical reasons for your position is what Aristotle referred to as **logos**.

Successful persuasive speeches have a clear organization and use logical reasoning to prove points. Without these two elements, you risk leaving audiences feeling as confused as Alice when she falls into Wonderland. How can you keep your audiences from feeling like they've entered another dimension?

AF Fotografie/Alamy Stock Photo

Organizing Persuasive Speeches

Chapter 14 discusses the five most common organizational patterns for composing a speech: topical, chronological, spatial, cause-effect, and problem-solution. A topical pattern is commonly used for organizing speeches based on *propositions of fact or value*. Take a look at Table 17.1 to see how a topical pattern would be applied to these two types of speech propositions.

In addition, the problem-solution pattern is a way to organize a speech based on a *proposition of policy* (you want the audience to take some action on your topic). A unique variation of the problem-solution approach is the **motivated sequence**—a five-step method for organizing a persuasive speech about a problem (Gronbeck, McKerrow, Ehninger, & Monroe, 1990).

To see how the motivated sequence can help you organize a persuasive speech, let's walk through the process using the following specific purpose: to persuade my audience to enroll in a cardiopulmonary resuscitation (CPR) course. (See Figure 17.1.)

Step 1: Attention. Introduce the topic to your audience, and give them a reason to listen. Recall from the discussion of the elaboration likelihood model that relating the topic to the needs and interests of the audience can help with this. Use the guidelines in Chapter 14 to compose an effective speech introduction that engages your listeners, discloses your speech thesis, establishes your credibility, and connects the topic to the audience.

TABLE 17.1

TOPICAL ORGANIZATION PATTERN FOR SPEECH OF FACT AND SPEECH OF VALUE

Fact	Value
Speech Thesis: Video gaming improves physical health by alleviating stress.	Speech Thesis: A child raised in a small town has a more enriched life than one raised in a large city.
I. Basic psychological principles exist within video game design. II. The challenges of playing release chemicals in the brain that have positive effects on emotions.	I. A developing child needs a sense of safety and belonging, as well as positive role models. II. A small town is safer than a large city. III. A small town provides a sense of community. IV. Positive role models are more easily accessible in a small town than in a large city.

Marish/Shutterstock

For example, "When I was hiking in Colorado last summer with my Uncle Bill, he suddenly collapsed. Thanks to my cardiopulmonary resuscitation (or CPR) training, I was able to help. This experience made me realize how important it is for all of us to know CPR; a situation like mine could happen to any of you." You can then preview the main points of the presentation as a transition to the body of the speech.

Step 2: Need. Clearly state the problem you want the audience to be concerned about as a main point. To highlight why knowing CPR is critical, you could say something like, "People die needlessly every year from cardiac arrest in the United States." Then use your research (statistical information, testimony, and other supporting materials) to show the audience why they should be concerned about the problem. Be sure that you're drawing from highly credible sources in your research.

Step 3: Satisfaction. Show the audience that the plan you are recommending is reasonable and that by supporting it, they can help solve or prevent the problem. For example, "CPR training is relatively easy to complete either here on campus or at other organizations, such as hospitals, fire departments, and

FIGURE 17.1

THE MOTIVATED SEQUENCE

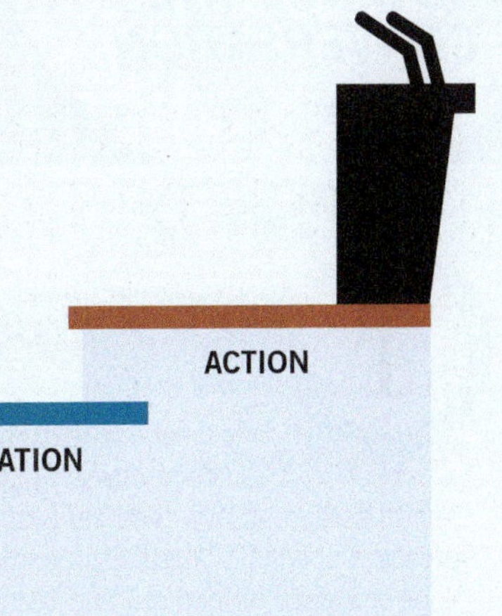

VoodooDot/Shutterstock

your local Red Cross." You could go on to explain the specifics of CPR training, including locations, costs, and what the training is like.

If you're taking on a large-scale problem in your speech that calls for complex solutions, focus on specific things your audience can do to help. When discussing inner-city deterioration, for example, you may try to persuade your audience to do one thing to help prevent it, such as eating at downtown restaurants instead of suburban restaurants. Don't just detail big problems without offering solutions.

Step 4: Visualization. Get your listeners to imagine the good things that can happen if the problem is fixed or the negative consequences if nothing is done. How you approach this step depends on what you've learned about your listeners through audience analysis. If you believe the audience will generally favor your position, focus on the positive results of taking action: "Learning CPR has many benefits, not the least of which is potentially saving lives."

If you think your audience is mostly uncommitted or undecided about your topic, you could focus on the negative consequences if listeners don't do anything about the problem: "If you're not CPR certified, you'll be unprepared to help if someone—your child, a colleague, a friend—goes into cardiac arrest." If you have time, you can emphasize the positive results of acting as well as the negative impact of doing nothing.

Step 5: Action. Summarize your main points, and challenge the audience to make a specific commitment. End your speech with a concise, powerful thought that leaves listeners reflecting about your overall message. You could close with a story, a rhetorical question, or a quotation, such as "Learn CPR. Save lives."

ADVANCE THE CONVERSATION

DO OR DIE: USING SCARE TACTICS TO PERSUADE OTHERS

1 YOUR DILEMMA

As a service-learning project, your life science class is planning a campus health-screening day. Medical professionals will offer blood pressure checks, diabetes screening, and vaccinations. Your professor formed student teams to organize the event, and you were assigned to the event-promotion team.

The team wants to create an event slogan that will appear in marketing materials on social media and on printed flyers. During your first team meeting, one member says, "I think we need a message that scares people. Something like, 'Don't be a zombie! Dying young is no joke. Attend the Health Fair.'" Two other group members immediately voice support for the idea.

But you see it differently. Since high school, your mother has encouraged you to have an annual physical exam. One routine test showed that you had a heart abnormality that was easily treated. This experience makes you believe the slogan should emphasize the positive benefits of health screenings rather than relying on fear tactics.

Should you self-disclose your experience to persuade the team toward a slogan that emphasizes the benefits of regular health exams?

2 THE RESEARCH

Communication scholars study how health professionals develop messages to maximize persuasive effect in health campaigns. One line of research looks at how the choice of positive or negative language influences receivers. Specifically, *gain-framed messages* use language that points out the benefits of taking care of your health (O'Keefe & Jensen, 2009). For example, a gain-framed message about health screening would be, "If you have regular health exams, you will have peace of mind." On the other hand, messages using language that emphasizes the cost of not following good health practices are known as *loss-framed messages* (O'Keefe & Jensen, 2009). A loss-framed message about health screening would be, "If you don't have regular health exams, you could die from a disease that could've been treated if it was caught earlier."

Gain-framed messages can be useful for encouraging preventive action to avoid "low-risk" problems, such as flossing to prevent tooth decay (Pavey & Churchill, 2014). But loss-framed references may be necessary when health professionals want to promote the importance of early detection for curbing serious disease (Pavey & Churchill, 2014). However, the persuasive impact of either type of message frame is affected by other factors, including individual differences. Specifically, receivers will respond differently to these appeals depending on their personality, motivational concerns about health, health history, and confidence in their ability to follow health recommendations (Covey, 2014).

What particular characteristics about your audience (e.g., age, gender, life experiences) are important to consider as you decide whether to use a gain- or a loss-framed approach for the slogan?

3 YOUR OPPORTUNITY

Before making a communication choice, consider the facts of the situation, and think about the research on gain-framed and loss-framed health messages. Also, reflect on what you've learned so far about the elaboration likelihood model (pp. 429–431), credibility (pp. 432–434), and the motivated sequence (pp. 435–437).

Now it's your turn. Write a response to your team in which you make a suggestion for the slogan. Be sure to indicate whether you will suggest a gain-framed or loss-framed slogan.

Reasoning for Persuasive Speeches

In addition to providing your audience with a clear structure for your speech, you need to develop a logical basis for each of your main points. During the *investigation* step of your speech preparation, you collect facts, expert testimony, and specific examples. To turn all that material into the logical basis for your speech, first identify patterns in your supporting materials, and then summarize those patterns into arguments that become the main points of your speech. This process is known as **reasoning**. So if your thesis is "Playing the right video games can enhance your brainpower," one of your main points (or arguments) might be "Video gaming strengthens spatial skills." Of course, it's not enough to just state the point; your audience expects you to prove it. This is where your research comes in. Use your research findings to back up your claim by citing studies and expert testimony that illustrate how video gaming improves students' spatial skills in educational settings.

There are many ways to use reasoning to support your ideas, but let's focus on the four most common ones: deductive, inductive, analogical, and cause-effect. (See Table 17.2 on page 440.)

Deductive Reasoning.

When you start with a generally held principle and then show how a specific instance relates to that principle, you're using **deductive reasoning**. Deductive reasoning typically has three elements: the **major premise**, or general statement you believe your audience will accept as true ("Honor students have disciplined study habits"); a **minor premise**, or specific instance of the general claim ("Ella is an honor student"); and a **conclusion** about the relationship between the two ideas ("Therefore, Ella must have disciplined study habits").

Of course, your audience may not readily accept a major premise that's very broad: "*All* honor students have disciplined study habits." It might be more realistic and believable to say that *most* honor students have disciplined study habits. Words like *most*, *probably*, and *likely* are **qualifiers**—language that indicates how certain you are about your major premise (Toulmin, 1958). Your audience will be more likely to consider your broader claims when you use qualifiers and provide additional evidence to support them.

Inductive Reasoning.

When you connect a set of specific, related facts to arrive at a more general conclusion, you're using **inductive reasoning**. For example, if a new friend is late meeting you for an evening out, you'll probably think nothing of it. But if it happens the next four or five times you get together, you'll probably conclude that your friend isn't capable of being on time. In a speech, you can use facts based on your personal observations or from the research you've compiled to arrive at a general conclusion.

When you're using inductive reasoning, avoid outdated or limited examples. For instance, suppose a speaker said, "I will never eat at that restaurant again, and you shouldn't either. Four years ago, they served me a soggy salad." If you heard this, you might think to yourself, "Well, that was four years ago. Things might have changed a lot at the restaurant since then. I'm not sure this person knows what he's talking about." Your audience is likely to recognize when you don't have enough adequate evidence to support your claim.

Analogical Reasoning. In Chapter 14, we discuss that when *composing* your speech, you can use *analogies*—comparisons of two unlike items—to support your points. Similarly, **analogical reasoning** supports a claim by drawing a comparison between two ideas or situations to show that what's true for one could be true for the other: "By following the town of Springfield's example of a comprehensive recycling program, we, too, could make our streets and alleys cleaner." Particularly for a speech of policy, this form of reasoning can demonstrate how your proposed solution has been successfully implemented elsewhere.

To use analogical reasoning, you'll need to show that the two things you're comparing have significant similarities. Making false or unrealistic comparisons is not ethical. To gauge similarities in the recycling example, you would want to ask yourself questions like, Is the population of Springfield similar to that of our city? Are the financial resources similar? Are citizens similarly interested in participating in a recycling program? If the things you're comparing are too different, you'll find it harder to convince your audience that your claim makes sense.

Cause-Effect Reasoning. When you use **cause-effect reasoning**, you draw a connection between two events or things and claim that one produced the

TABLE 17.2

USING REASONING TO SUPPORT YOUR IDEAS

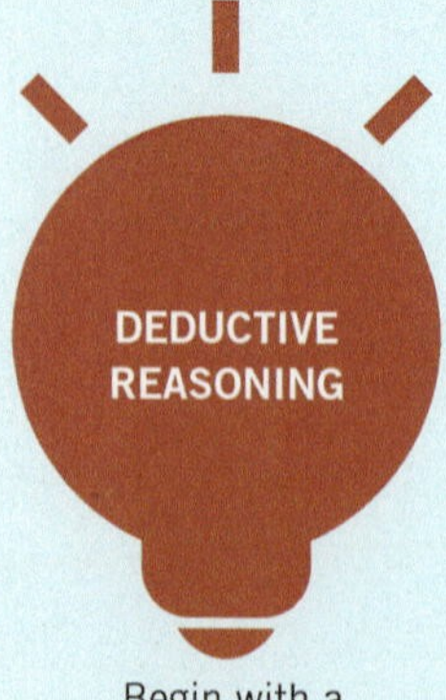

Begin with a generally held principle, and back it up with specific instances.

Use specific, related facts to arrive at a general conclusion.

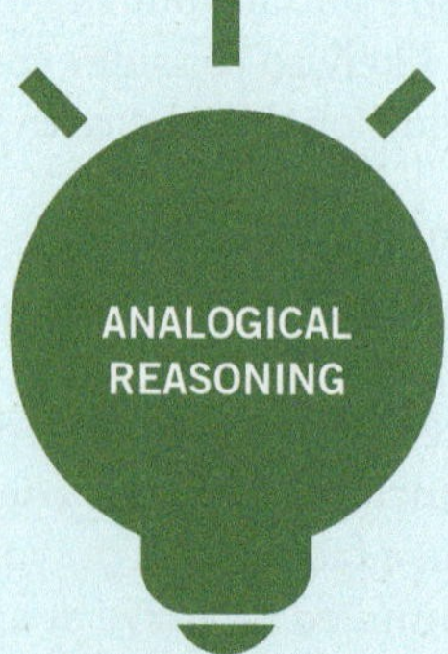

Draw a comparison between two ideas to show that their individual truths work in correlation.

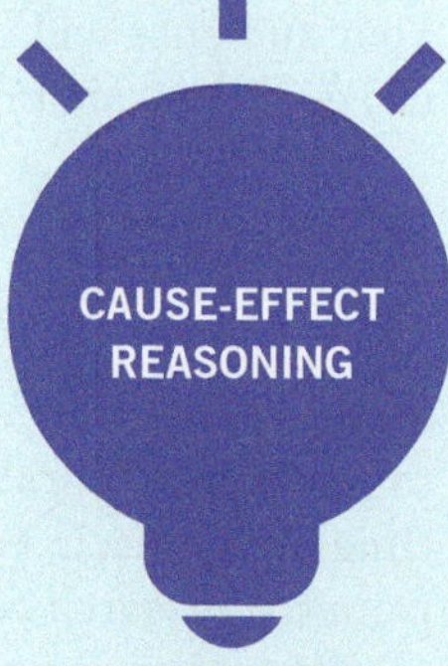

Claim that one thing caused another based on an evident connection you're able to draw between them.

popcic/Shutterstock

other. You can claim that effect Y was caused by X. For example, "An unnecessary number of human lives were lost [*effect*] during Hurricane Katrina because of a lack of timely and substantial response by the federal government [*cause*]." To reason from an effect to its cause, you have to work back in time. This type of claim is best suited for explaining why something occurred.

You can also claim that specific events or things will cause a particular effect in the future: "The use of performance-enhancing drugs can put someone at increased risk for cancer."

When using cause-effect reasoning, make sure your claims are based on causal relationships supported by the evidence found during the *investigation* step. You don't want to suggest a causal link when there isn't any solid evidence showing that such a link exists. For example, stating "It's going to rain tomorrow because I washed my car" is faulty causal reasoning. Cleaning your car doesn't *cause* rain. Reasoning errors like this are known as fallacies.

Avoiding Fallacies

One sure way to undermine your speech's organization and reasoning is by failing—much like the Cheshire Cat—to provide your listeners with a logical connection between the claims you're making and the facts. **Fallacies** are false claims—those that aren't true or are based on inadequate or inaccurate evidence. If you make false claims, not only will your listeners question your credibility but you will violate the ethical principle that says you're responsible for providing your audience with solid reasons to consider your position. Common fallacies you should avoid include the following:

- *Ad hominem arguments.* You attack a person rather than an idea: "Stephens never finished college. It's no wonder he's made such an insane proposal."
- *Hasty generalizations.* You make a bold claim based on limited evidence: "Four-wheeling is a safe sport. I ride a few times a year, and I've never had an accident."
- *Bandwagon appeals.* You claim that if others are doing what you're recommending, then it's a good course of action: "Many other colleges no longer place a high priority on SAT or ACT scores for admission, so our college should do the same."
- *Straw person claims.* You oversimplify or misrepresent the other side of a controversial topic to make your own case stronger: "Anyone who supports this proposed legislation has no respect for the U.S. Constitution."

To present a fallacy-free speech, thoroughly research and carefully compose your presentation. In addition, rehearse your presentation in front of others, and then ask them for feedback on the validity of your claims. If you think your claims may contain fallacies, conduct additional research to find evidence that strengthens your reasoning. Your listeners will ultimately decide whether to accept what you have to say, but if you provide them with well-developed reasons, they can make an informed choice.

Appealing to Your Audience's Needs and Emotions

Persuasion is more than just credibility and reasoning. Appealing to your listeners' emotions and encouraging them to experience strong feelings about your issue make it more likely that they will agree with you and follow your suggestions.

Imagine that you're watching your favorite show when a commercial for Save the Children comes on. There's a photo of an emaciated young girl, and a narrator says, "Only seven years old, Rokia lives a life of poverty and malnourishment in Mali, Africa. She isn't likely to see her 12th birthday. But you can be the difference in Rokia's life. Your contribution to Save the Children, an organization that helps children like Rokia, will ensure that she is well fed, is educated, and receives proper medical care." How persuasive would you find that argument? What about this one: imagine that there was no picture of Rokia, and the narrator said nothing about her life, only that "there are millions of African children who are victims of food shortage and disease." Which of the two announcements would be more likely to compel you to send money to Save the Children?

In a research study, participants who were given Rokia's personal story, along with her photograph, donated more money than those who had only received general information about what Save the Children does in Africa (Small, Loewenstein, & Slovic, 2007). What explains the difference? Simply put, it's easier to feel a sense of personal connection when you hear and see the specific struggles of a single person. Broad appeals and abstract language ("millions of African children need your help") often fail to make people feel the same kind of emotional connection and, as a result, are less persuasive.

Well-reasoned claims get your audience thinking about your message, but you also want them feeling something about your topic. Do you want them to experience compassion? Concern about their future well-being? A sense of urgency about solving a problem? During the *composing* step of your speech preparation, consider the needs of your listeners and the emotions you want them to experience. Then develop **motivational appeals**—explicit statements (examples, testimony, stories) that speak to these needs and feelings. Using motivational appeals in your speech encourages your audience to connect personally with your topic. As discussed earlier in this chapter, such appeals are what Aristotle called **pathos**.

Although motivational appeals enhance your persuasive message, remember to combine them with logical reasons for supporting your position. If your listeners think you're playing too heavily on their emotions, they may feel they're being manipulated, and you could lose credibility.

Connecting to Your Audience's Needs

According to psychologist Abraham Maslow, much of human behavior is motivated by the desire to meet basic life needs, known as the **hierarchy of needs** (Maslow, 1943; Greenfeld, 2017). If you're extremely hungry or

FIGURE 17.2

MASLOW'S HIERARCHY OF NEEDS

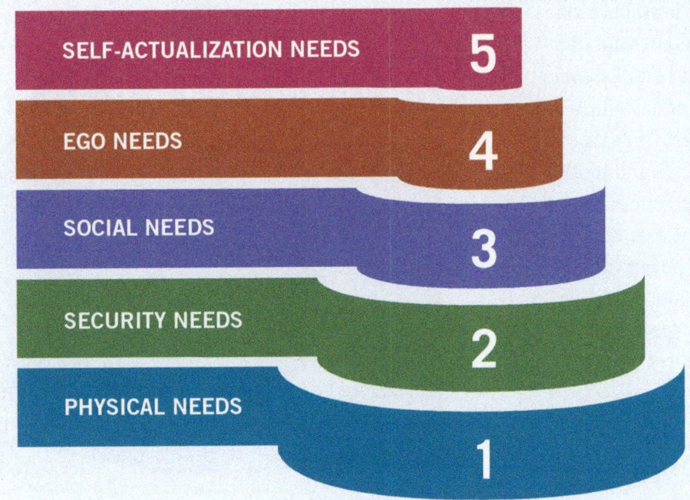

Naeblys/Shutterstock

tired, nothing matters to you except food or rest. Maslow suggested that such *physical needs* form the base of the hierarchy. Only after you've met your physical needs do you turn your attention to higher-level concerns—namely, *security needs* (avoiding harm and uncertainty), *social needs* (forming bonds with others), *ego needs* (having respect and admiration from others), and *self-actualization needs* (realizing your full potential). (See Figure 17.2.)

Maslow's framework is useful for planning motivational appeals for your speech. If you show your listeners how certain needs are in danger or how specific needs could be satisfied if they follow your call to action, you'll likely capture their attention. For example, suppose your presentation is encouraging your classmates to get a flu shot. To provide a motivational appeal, ask them, "Do you really want to get the flu just when you have to study for finals? If not, take a minute to get the shot—it won't take long, and it'll give you peace of mind." This would appeal to their security needs. Importantly, keep in mind that life needs will vary by culture (Greenfeld, 2017). For example, if you are speaking in a *collectivistic cultural* setting, your listeners may not be responsive to appeals based on ego needs.

Providing Testimony and Stories

As the study about Save the Children and the story of Rokia shows, listeners will pay more attention to a persuasive speech when you present relevant testimony from a person they can relate to or tell a compelling story about your topic. In composing your speech, consider how you can incorporate *testimony* (the words or experiences of others) or a personal story to make an emotional connection with your audience. In Chapter 14, we discuss how using such stories can help you capture and hold your audience's

Inspiring personal stories like astronaut Mae Carol Jemison's keep listeners engaged and wanting to know more. They can also inspire hope and motivation in audiences. What kinds of stories do you find the most powerful? How can you work them into your own speeches?

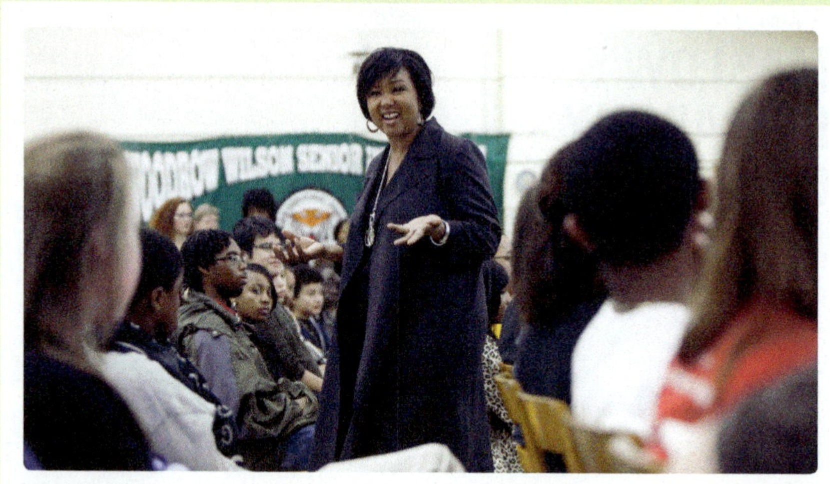

Brendan Hoffman/Getty Images

interest and attention while delivering your speech. A well-chosen story can also evoke powerful feelings in your listeners—such as pride, fear, anger, or hope. What feelings do you experience when reading this excerpt from a speech by NASA astronaut Mae Carol Jemison (2012)?

> When I was growing up in the 1960s on the south side of Chicago, I remember being so excited about space exploration! I wanted to be involved! But, there was always just one type of person in earth orbit or in Mission Control. And they did not look like me. Even though, as a country, we would proudly rally and root for the Space Program, so many of us felt as though we were left out. When I did finally fly in space, the first thing I saw from earth orbit was Chicago, my hometown. I was working on the mid-deck where there aren't many windows, and as we passed over Chicago, the commander called me up to the flight deck. It was such a significant moment, because ever since I was a little girl I had always assumed I would go into space. Looking out the window of that Space Shuttle, I thought if that little girl growing up in Chicago could see her older self now, she would have a huge grin on her face. (pp. 276–277)

Dr. Jemison, the first African American woman in space, tells a story that stirs optimism and hope in listeners: that they can overcome obstacles and achieve their dreams just like she did.

Using Descriptive Language

In Chapter 5 on verbal communication, we discuss how to use the *cooperative principle* to produce understandable messages. This means using language that is as informative, honest, relevant, and clear as required for a particular situation. When composing your speech, use the cooperative principle to ensure that your audience comprehends what you are saying.

In addition, you can make an emotional connection with your listeners by using language that's powerfully descriptive. Malala Yousafzai does this in her speech to the United Nations. When discussing the basis for some of the Taliban's actions, she could have just said, "The Taliban fears education." This matter-of-fact statement doesn't make the idea of "fear" real to her listeners. Instead, she told them about the Taliban's horrific, fear-based acts:

> The power of education frightens them. They are afraid of women. The power of the voice frightens them. This is why they killed 14 innocent students . . . and that is why they kill female teachers. That is why they are blasting schools every day because they were and they are afraid of change and equality that we will bring to our society. (Yousafzai, 2013, p. 266)

In her speech, Yousafzai took an abstract term—*fear*—and used descriptive language to convey vivid images. Picturing the loss of innocent lives would make her audience eager to help fund the education of children. As you compose your speech, think about how the use of descriptive language creates compelling images in your listeners' minds. The Advance the Conversation: Emotional Appeals video activity on pages 448–449 provides specific steps for developing emotional appeals in your speeches.

Guidelines for Persuasive Speaking

There's no doubt that persuading an audience is challenging. But careful preparation can lead to success. While preparing, composing, and delivering your speech, it is important to be realistic about what you're trying to accomplish and to maintain high ethical standards by giving your audience fair and objective information.

The unique goals of persuasive speeches—reinforcing or changing listeners' attitudes and beliefs, and possibly motivating them to take action—require that you keep in mind specific guidelines when preparing your presentation.

Establish Goodwill with Your Audience

When you show your listeners that you're genuinely concerned about their welfare, you're demonstrating *goodwill*. One way to demonstrate goodwill is to note in your speech's introduction how your topic relates to your audience ("I'm sure we are all concerned about the recent crime spree"). You can also show goodwill through the sincere expression of *empathy*—acknowledging emotions your audience may be experiencing ("I know that most of you are very worried, and some of you are outraged, by the increase in physical attacks in our community"). When you clearly demonstrate genuine concern for your listeners, they are more likely to pay attention to your message.

ESTABLISHING GOODWILL

Showing that you care about and can empathize with your audience creates a bond that keeps listeners focused on your message. This is important when delivering a speech in any context—whether among peers at work, at a fund-raising event, or in the classroom. How do you express to others that you have their best interest in mind?

(Counterclockwise from left) sanjeri/E+/Getty Images; Adam Crowley/Getty Images; KARIM SAHIB/AFP/Getty Images

If you are talking about a controversial issue, goodwill will be evident if you stay objective when preparing the speech. During your research phase, investigate all sides of the issue. This will give you a broad perspective on the topic. Not only will this help you compose your speech in a fair and informed way, but you'll also be able to anticipate and respond to questions from audience members. This shows goodwill because you can prove how you've thought about and prepared for your audience's reaction.

Keep Your Specific Purpose Realistic

Remember that you may not be able to effect change with one presentation. People don't easily abandon their deep-seated values or behaviors just by listening to a single speech. This is especially true with speeches of value and policy. Keep this in mind as you're developing your specific purpose. You might get better results by using the **foot-in-the-door technique**: asking your listeners to agree to a small action in the hope that you'll gain their compliance over time (Burger, 1999). For instance, rather than telling your listeners that they should eliminate all fast food from their diet, you may want to define a more realistic specific purpose: to persuade them to make healthy choices when ordering fast food.

Decide How to Present Your Issue

Many persuasive speeches center on controversial issues for which there are multiple viewpoints. If you choose such a topic for your speech, decide how you're going to deal with points of view that differ from your own. Will you acknowledge these opposing viewpoints in your speech, or will you ignore them? Consider two things when answering this question.

First, think about how much time you have for your presentation. If discussing opposing views about your topic means that you'll have to cut relevant arguments in support of your position, don't do it. Second, ask yourself if your audience will already be familiar with the opposing views. If not, introduce a main point that compares and contrasts the opposing views about your topic. When you expose your audience to opposing views, they are more likely to resist future attempts by others to change their minds (Banas & Rains, 2010).

Maintain High Ethical Standards

As in all communication situations, you must observe the highest ethical standards in preparing and delivering a persuasive message. How? Give your listeners valid and reliable information based on sound research. If you distort, withhold, or misrepresent the facts, you deprive listeners of the information they need and the ability to freely accept or reject your message. That's unethical and therefore incompetent.

To see how the principles and guidelines of persuasive speeches can come together, look over the transcript for the speech "Becoming a Socially Conscious Consumer" by Jacob Hahn on pages 450–453. A video of the speech is available online in LaunchPad for *Choices & Connections.* Visit **launchpadworks.com**

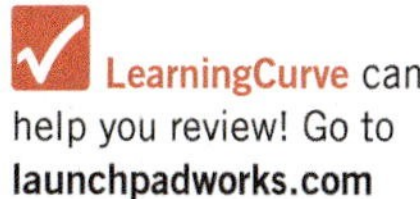

ADVANCE THE CONVERSATION
Video Activity

EMOTIONAL APPEALS

The following scenario will enhance your ability to use effective appeals to an audience's emotions in your speech. Visit LaunchPad at **launchpadworks.com** to get the full experience with video. As you watch the first video, recall what you've learned about using emotional appeals. Then complete the **Your Turn** prompts. Finally, watch the **Take Two!** video to explore how this scenario could have gone differently.

1 *THE PROBLEM*

Mirirai's final speech assignment is a persuasive one, and she decides to encourage her classmates to shop at local businesses. Since her parents own their own bakery, she feels very strongly about this issue. In addition to the arguments she developed from her research on the issue, she wants to inspire her audience to feel as passionate about local shopping as she does herself. She decides to appeal to her audience's emotions by including several references to her family bakery in her speech.

"At our bakery, we make breads that you just won't find at the grocery chain stores."

"You can go into the big grocery stores and never talk to a single person.... This would never happen in our bakery. After two or three visits, you'll be greeted by name. You become a part of the family."

2 YOUR TURN

Observations. Reflect on how Mirirai used personal examples and emotional appeals by answering the following questions:

1. Overall, do you think Mirirai's personal examples were effective in appealing to her audience's emotions?
2. What did Mirirai do well? What can she improve on?

Discussion. In class or with a partner, share your thoughts about Mirirai's emotional appeals and work to answer the following questions:

1. Do you think Mirirai's use of personal examples will affect her credibility with the audience? If so, do you think her credibility will be enhanced or diminished?
2. Can you think of any other strategies Mirirai might use to persuade her audience to care about local businesses? List them.

Conclusion. Based on your analysis, what advice would you give Mirirai regarding her emotional appeals in this scenario?

3 TAKE TWO!

Watch the **Take Two!** video to see how Mirirai might have used different strategies in her speech. As you watch the video, pay attention to the rhetorical techniques that Mirirai uses to appeal to her audience members' emotions. After watching the video, answer the questions below:

1. What techniques does Mirirai use to appeal to her audience members' emotions? Identify specific examples.
2. In your opinion, are Mirirai's emotional appeals in this version of her speech more effective or less effective than the personal examples she used in the first version? Why or why not?

Sample Persuasive Speech

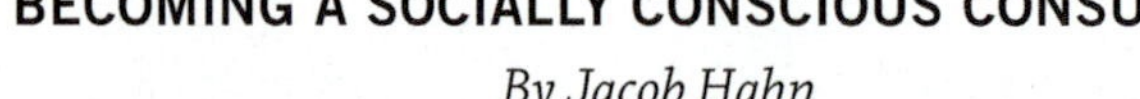

BECOMING A SOCIALLY CONSCIOUS CONSUMER •

By Jacob Hahn

• To watch a video of this speech and see Jacob's preparation and delivery outlines, go to launchpadworks.com

Through descriptive language and concerned facial expressions, Jacob conveys the emotional aspect of his speech topic.

It started with a few cracks in the wall. • But then, on April 24, 2013, it became the worst disaster in the history of the garment industry. According to BBC News, on that day the Rana Plaza garment factory in Dhaka, Bangladesh, completely collapsed, leading to the deaths of over 1,100 people.

• Jacob uses an event that gained a lot of media attention to immediately engage his audience. He also orally cites the source of his data to help build credibility. How else does Jacob demonstrate credibility throughout the speech?

Along with the bodies, bricks, and garments left in the rubble, questions remained about who was to blame for the tragedy. • Sure, there were the obvious culprits—the plaza owner, the construction company. But there were other suspects, too. What about the companies whose goods were manufactured there? As Emran Hossain and Dave Jamieson pointed out in their May 2, 2013, *Huffington Post* article, garment industry insiders partially blame Western retailers for the tragedy. They claim that it is retailer demand for low-priced labor that creates these poorly constructed and unsafe work factories, which then leads to disasters like the factory collapse.

• Jacob is using the motivated sequence to organize his speech. This section represents the Attention step, in which he gives his audience a reason to listen.

The thousands of miles that separate us from tragedies like this can make them seem unrelated to our everyday lives. But what if they are not? What if, by purchasing the products these companies make, individuals such as you and me are also somewhat responsible for what happened? •

• To make this topic relevant to his listeners, Jacob directly states how it relates to them. This enhances their interest and encourages them to take the central route to processing the speech message.

As we'll see today, there is evidence to support the idea that consumers and companies share a responsibility to ensure safer conditions for factory workers. This is why I encourage all of you to become socially conscious consumers and help convince companies to adopt ethical manufacturing standards. Being a socially conscious consumer means being aware of the issues communities face worldwide and actively trying to correct them. •

• Jacob's straightforward thesis statement tells his audience exactly what he wants them to take away from the speech.

To emphasize his point about the goods at the center of this issue, Jacob refers to the common types of clothing made in the factories.

Why would companies do business with factories that allow dangerous working conditions? • It's actually quite simple: Corporations want bigger profit margins. The cheaper the production costs, the more money they make when the product sells. And since consumers show more interest in buying lower-priced products than in thinking about how such items are produced, the pressure

• This is where Jacob begins the Need step of the motivated sequence.

is on to provide inexpensive goods. The only way to do this and still make money is to make the goods at the lowest cost possible.

But there is a way to break this cycle of cheap labor and deadly working conditions. You, me, all of us as consumers, must be willing to step up and take an active role in the system. • We can do this in two ways: first, we can pressure companies to improve working conditions for factory laborers, and second, we can pay fairer prices. • Some consumer groups are now signaling their willingness to do this, and corporations are responding.

• *Throughout the speech, Jacob uses personal pronouns to build goodwill with his audience. Using simple and familiar language also makes it easier to listen to his speech.*

• *As part of the Satisfaction step in the motivated sequence, Jacob explains how he plans to meet the needs discussed earlier.*

The force behind this new kind of partnership is called cause-related marketing. According to the *Financial Times*, *cause-related marketing* is when a company and a charity (or a consumer group) tackle a social or an environmental problem and create business value for the company at the same time. • In March 2012, the global marketing firm Nielsen conducted a worldwide study on consumer responses to cause-related marketing. The poll found that two-thirds of consumers around the world say they prefer to buy products and services from companies that give back to society. Nearly 50 percent of consumers said that they were, and I'm quoting here, "willing to pay more for goods and services from companies that are giving back."

• *Jacob introduces a new term by clearly defining it and orally citing a credible source for the definition.*

To connect with his audience, Jacob looks to different parts of the room throughout his speech, making sure that each listener feels included.

The fact that large numbers of consumers are concerned enough about fairness to pay more for products is key to solving the problems that surround the ethical manufacture of clothing. Corporations can appeal to this group of socially conscious consumers, as they are called, by addressing concerns about ethical manufacturing. What do corporations gain by meeting these concerns? It allows them to charge more for their products while also raising their profit margins and improving their brand image. This means that as socially conscious consumers, we can set the standards that corporations must meet if they wish to maximize their profit from our purchasing power.

You may find yourself asking, Can this actually work? • The answer is a simple yes. In both the food and the apparel industries, calls for changes in working conditions led to the now widely known nonprofit organization Fair Trade USA. According to its website, Fair Trade USA is an organization that seeks "to inspire the rise of the [socially] Conscious Consumer and eliminate exploitation" worldwide. If products are stamped with the Fair Trade logo, it means the farmers and workers who created those products were fairly treated and justly compensated through an internationally established price.

• *This brief question serves as a transitional phrase to the Visualization step of the motivated sequence, which helps the audience see how change is possible.*

Fair Trade USA made its mark in the food industry through its relationship to coffee production in third-world nations. Its success helped major companies such as Starbucks and Whole Foods recognize the strength of cause-related marketing: if you appeal to the high ethical standards of socially conscious consumers, they will pay more for your product. •

• From his audience analysis, Jacob learned that many of his classmates shop at and respect these two businesses. Thus, this example is very familiar to listeners.

Appealing to high ethical standards is often directly related to preventing tragedies like the one that occurred in Bangladesh. After the factory collapsed, the major apparel sellers faced intense criticism over their lax labor practices. In response, these companies are now much more interested in establishing their products as Fair Trade to meet socially conscious consumer standards. For example, as Jason Burke, Saad Hammadi, and Simon Neville report in the May 13, 2013, edition of the *Guardian*, major fashion chains like H&M, Zara, C&A, Tesco, and Primark have pledged to help raise the standards for working conditions. According to the article, they will be helping to "finance fire safety and building improvements in the factories they use in Bangladesh." •

• Jacob uses a direct quote here to support his point that things can change. The repetition of the opening example also makes the speech more coherent.

So, what exactly can you do to help bring about ethical labor practices within the clothing industry? The two steps I encourage you to take are these: become informed, and ask questions about what you're buying—whether it's shoes, a T-shirt, or any other type of apparel. •

• The Action step is the most important aspect of the motivated sequence. Jacob provides two clear ways his audience can participate and create actual change. Do you think he is proposing realistic actions for his audience to take? What other actions could he suggest?

Simple gestures, like counting off the two ways listeners can become socially conscious consumers, can help audience members follow along with the speech structure.

To be informed, go to websites such as fairtradeusa.org, thirdworldtraveler.com, and tenthousandvillages.com, which list and sell products from clothing manufacturers who have worked to meet the Fair Trade conditions. This list grows monthly, and by supporting these companies through your purchases, you can become a socially conscious consumer.

Additionally, ask questions of other retailers. Whether you shop online or at local retail stores, ask direct questions before purchasing clothes—for example, Where are your products made? Do you have proof of fair-trade practices? Where can I find this information before I make my purchase? Such questions define the socially conscious consumer, and they ensure that you will not be directly contributing to unsafe and unfair labor practices. •

• Jacob appeals to the ego needs of his audience by explaining how they can show concern for others when making purchases.

Although several factors contributed to the tragedy in Bangladesh, there is one clear way to help prevent future disasters: become a socially conscious consumer. By being informed and asking questions, you, too, can make a difference in the lives of workers around the world.

REFERENCES

BBC News. (2013, May 23). Bangladesh factory collapse probe uncovers abuses. *BBC*. Retrieved from www.bbc.co.uk/news/world-asia-22635409

Burke, J., Hammadi, S., & Neville, S. (2013, May 13). Fashion chains sign accord to help finance safety in Bangladesh factories. *The Guardian*. Retrieved from www.innovations.harvard.edu/news/2798331.html?p=1

Cheng, A. (2013, June 20). Market Watch: Fair trade fashion gaining momentum after Bangladesh incidents. Retrieved from www.fairtradeusa.org/press-room/in_the_news/marketwatch-fair-trade-fashion-gaining-momentum-after-bangladesh-incidents

Coffee. (n.d.). "Fair Trade" helps "free trade" work for the poor. Retrieved from www.fairtradeusa.org/products-partners/coffee

Financial Times Lexicon. (n.d.). Cause-related marketing. Retrieved from http://lexicon.ft.com/Term?term=cause_related-marketing

Hossain, E., & Jamieson, D. (2013, May 2). Bangladesh garment industry leader says blame for tragedies lies with Western retailers. *Huffington Post*. Retrieved from www.huffingtonpost.com/2013/05/02/bangladesh-garment-blame-retailers_n_3204245.html

Moore, B. (2011, November 1). Has campaigning for an ethical fashion industry had any impact? *The Guardian*. Retrieved from www.theguardian.com/environment/green-living-blog/2011/nov/01/campaigning-ethical-fashion-industry

Nielsen. (2012, March 27). The global, socially conscious consumer. Retrieved from www.nielsen.com/us/en/newswire/2012/the-global-socially-conscious-consumer.html

Nielsen. (2012, June 27). Successful brands care: The case for cause marketing. Retrieved from www.nielsen.com/us/en/newswire/2012/successful-brands-care-the-case-for-cause-marketing.html

SAMPLE SPEECH RESOURCES

There is a lot more to Jacob's speech than the transcript above. See how the whole speech came together by going to **launchpadworks.com**. There you will find:

1. Video of Jacob's speech "Becoming a Socially Conscious Consumer" (with closed captions available)
2. The preparation outline for Jacob's speech
3. The delivery outline for Jacob's speech
4. Brief video clips highlighting specific techniques Jacob uses in his speech

CHAPTER 17 REVIEW

CHAPTER RECAP

- There are three types of **persuasive propositions—fact**, **value**, and **policy**—which you can use to reinforce or change listeners' attitudes and beliefs, or encourage them to take action.
- Your **ethos**, or **credibility**, is what determines whether an audience views you as trustworthy. Failure to properly display your **character**, **competence**, and **charisma** can result in an ineffective speech.
- Using the **motivated sequence** will help you form a logical structure to your persuasive argument, but if you lack sound **reasoning**, listeners are less likely to believe your claims.
- **Motivational appeals** connect with an audience's needs and feelings. Also known as **pathos**, this is how you can get an audience emotionally involved with your topic.
- Considering the risk of **coercion**, it is especially important to maintain high ethical standards in persuasive speeches and to establish *goodwill* with your audience.

LaunchPad for *Choices & Connections* offers unique video scenarios and encourages self-assessment through adaptive quizzing. Go to **launchpadworks.com** to get access.

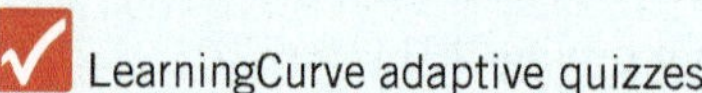

LearningCurve adaptive quizzes

Advance the Conversation video scenarios

Video clips that illustrate key concepts

Sample speech resources

KEY TERMS

Persuasive speech, p. 428
Coercion, p. 428
Proposition of fact, p. 429
Proposition of value, p. 429
Proposition of policy, p. 429
Elaboration likelihood model, p. 430
Central route, p. 430
Peripheral route, p. 430
Credibility, p. 432
Ethos, p. 432
Rhetorical proof, p. 433
Character, p. 433
Competence, p. 433
Charisma, p. 434
Logos, p. 435
Motivated sequence, p. 435
Reasoning, p. 439
Deductive reasoning, p. 439
Major premise, p. 439
Minor premise, p. 439
Conclusion, p. 439
Qualifier, p. 439
Inductive reasoning, p. 439
Analogical reasoning, p. 440
Cause-effect reasoning, p. 440
Fallacy, p. 441
Motivational appeal, p. 442
Pathos, p. 442
Hierarchy of needs, p. 442
Foot-in-the-door technique, p. 446

POP QUIZ

Looking for more review questions? **LearningCurve** can help you master key concepts from this chapter. Go to **launchpadworks.com**

1. Which type of proposition argues for a specific action—for example, persuading your audience to exercise at least three hours a week?
   - **a.** Proposition of fact
   - **b.** Proposition of policy
   - **c.** Proposition of value
   - **d.** Proposition of ethics
2. According to the elaboration likelihood model, when listeners already understand the content of a speech, they are more likely to take which approach to processing the message?
   - **a.** Peripheral route
   - **b.** Connected route
   - **c.** Central route
   - **d.** Direct route
3. When establishing ethos with an audience, creating a sense of immediacy can help with your
   - **a.** credibility.
   - **b.** charisma.
   - **c.** competence.
   - **d.** closeness.
4. Which of the following fallacies occurs if you argue that you deserve a Friday night off because a coworker also has it off?
   - **a.** Hasty generalization
   - **b.** Straw person claim
   - **c.** Ad hominem argument
   - **d.** Bandwagon appeal
5. Before convincing your audience to regularly volunteer at a local food bank, you may start by asking them to make a small donation or visit the website to learn more about the operation. This is known as
   - **a.** the foot-in-the-door technique.
   - **b.** a motivational appeal.
   - **c.** the hierarchy of needs.
   - **d.** displaying goodwill.

ACTIVITIES

For more activities, visit LaunchPad for *Choices & Connections* at **launchpadworks.com**

1 Identifying Rhetorical Proof

Find a persuasive speech online. This could be from a politician, a TED talk (www.ted.com), a commencement address, or even one of your own classmates. While listening to the speech, note effective uses of *ethos*, *logos*, and *pathos*, or times when they could have been used more effectively. Write a brief paper explaining the speech's thesis, your findings, and whether you found the speech persuasive.

2 As Seen on TV

Working in groups, use the motivated sequence on pages 435–437 to plan a two- to three-minute infomercial selling an imaginary service to your classmates. Base the infomercial on a service that college students might actually use (e.g., dating site, tutoring business, personal trainer, dog-sitting service). After preparing and rehearsing the infomercial, perform it in front of your class, or make a video and upload it to LaunchPad for *Choices & Connections* using the Macmillan Mobile Video app. Be prepared to explain how you incorporated each step in the motivated sequence.

APPENDIX
Interviewing

"What was the best mistake you made on the job? Why was it the best?"
"On a scale of 1–10, how weird are you?"[1]

If you ever interview for a job with Zappos—the online shoe, clothing, and accessories company—brace yourself for questions like these. Known for a unique culture that encourages workers to "create fun and a little weirdness," Zappos seeks to hire employees who embody the company's core values ("Zappos," n.d.). These include "delivering WOW through service," "embracing and driving change," and "being passionate and determined" ("Zappos," n.d.).

To identify prospective employees who personify these values, the Zappos hiring team conducts two types of interviews. In the initial interview—usually on the phone or at a job fair—team members evaluate candidates' job experience and skills, asking about work history, job-relevant abilities, and salary requirements. They also ask standard interview questions, such as, "What is your greatest strength?" and "Would you say you're more or less creative than the average person? Can you give me an example?"

People who make a good impression during the first interview are invited to Zappos's headquarters in Henderson, Nevada, for a second type of interview. At this point, the hiring team is interested in whether a candidate is a good fit for Zappos's company culture. Team members ask questions that explore the person's values and self-awareness, such as, "What would you say is the biggest misperception that people have of you?" (Bryant, 2010). Zappos CEO Tony Hsieh explains that such questions give interviewers a sense of how self-aware candidates are and of their honesty levels (Bryant, 2010).

But as with any interview, there's more to a Zappos meeting than just answering questions. The hiring team also pays attention to how candidates treat others and handle unexpected events, like meeting an employee who is wearing pajamas or bunny ears. That's typical at Zappos, where employees are known to be quirky. The team wants to know that new hires can adapt to such situations and that they don't take themselves too seriously (Gurchiek, 2011). Preparing for either interview type can be tricky, especially since you never know what you'll be asked or whom you will run into. But when interviews are well planned and have clear goals—like the ones at Zappos—they can be very useful and even surprisingly fun for both interviewers and interviewees.

[1]Information in the chapter opener from Hsieh (2010) unless otherwise specified.

Brad Swonetz/Redux Pictures

Zappos
.com
the web's most popular shoe store!®

APPENDIX OUTLINE

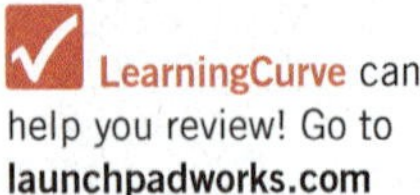

LearningCurve can help you review! Go to **launchpadworks.com**

Whether it's to get a job with Zappos or a job with any other company, developing competent interviewing skills will help you achieve your professional goals. But interviews aren't just for finding employment. You will use these skills in other communication situations—for example, interviewing someone as research for a presentation, as a way to explore a potential career path, or even to correspond with the public if you work in fields such as journalism or public relations. In this appendix, you'll learn:

- The different types of interviews
- Ways to plan interview topics and interview questions
- How to communicate competently during interviews
- Steps for preparing for and managing information and employment selection interviews
- Strategies for writing a résumé and cover letter

What Is Interviewing?

An interview is like a good conversation, filled with thoughtful questions and interesting answers. But an interview also has a structure and a defined purpose. Its success often depends on how carefully you plan it, including anticipating the topics that will be covered and the questions that will be asked.

Think about different situations in which you ask questions to get information from others. For example, to prepare a speech, you chat with an expert as part of your research on the topic. To write an article for the school paper, you meet with a school administrator. To make a hiring decision, you talk with a number of job applicants. In each of these situations, you are thoughtfully questioning, or interviewing, others. **Interviewing** is a planned and structured conversation between two or more persons that uses questions and answers to meet a specific purpose.

An interview is planned and structured because the participants have clearly defined roles and responsibilities. The **interviewer** determines the interview purpose, plans the questions, and manages the flow of the conversation. The success of an interview can depend on how well an interviewer prepares in advance. For example, before interviewing a school administrator for an article you're writing, you should think about the topics you want to discuss and create a list of relevant questions to ask.

The **interviewee** is the person answering the questions. However, this is not a passive activity. Interviewees must prepare for and actively participate in the interview, too. If the school administrator responds to your questions with one-word answers or shows little interest in being interviewed, you won't get the information you need for the article you're writing.

Many interviews are dyadic—that is, they involve two people. But some take place in small groups. For example, during a job interview, four team

DIFFERENT TYPES OF INTERVIEWS

Interviews are not limited to employment prospects. You may interview a grandparent to learn about your family history, collect information from witnesses, or talk to participants at a rally. All of these situations require you to ask questions in a succinct and thoughtful manner. When you have interviewed others, how did you plan for the interview purpose and protocol?

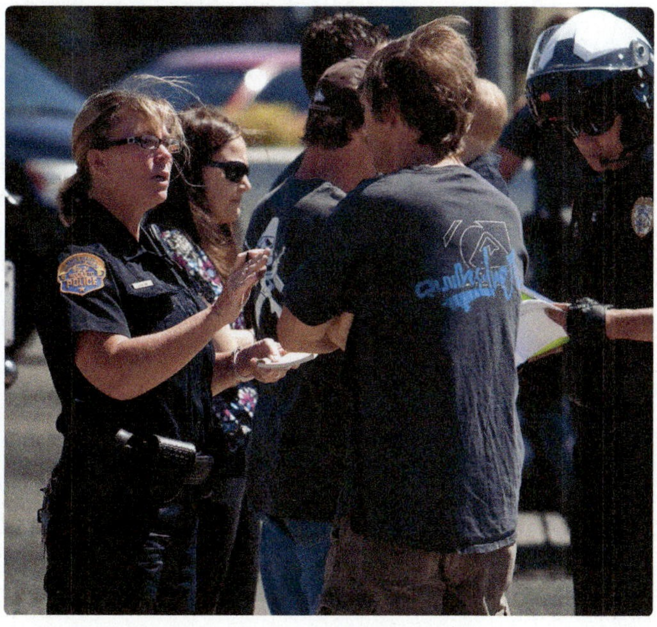

(Clockwise from top left) logoboom/Shutterstock; Modesto Bee/ZUMA Press Inc/Alamy Stock Photo; Richard Levine/Alamy Stock Photo

members might ask questions to one interviewee. Or a journalist may conduct a small group interview—meeting with multiple interviewees at the same time. Interviews can also occur in face-to-face settings or through mediated communication (such as by telephone or videoconferencing).

Types of Interviews

Although there are a variety of ways that interviews occur in public, personal, and professional settings, the two types you are most likely to encounter are information interviews and employment interviews.

Information interviews generate knowledge or understanding about a particular topic. For instance, marketing consultants use *focus groups* to interview customers about their experiences using a product or a service. Doctors ask their patients questions to learn about their medical histories. Information interviews can also help you prepare a speech. Interviewing other people about your topic helps you gather testimony and examples to use in your speech.

Employment interviews manage an organization's personnel. There are three kinds of employment interviews. **Selection interviews** determine whether applicants have the education, experience, and proper attitude required for a job. These interviews are the most common method employers use for making hiring decisions (Macan, 2009). Once a person is hired, employers use **performance or appraisal interviews** to evaluate his or her work and to set new goals. This kind of interview typically occurs once a year. Organizations use **exit interviews** to identify why an employee is leaving a job, and use the resulting insights to improve management practices. Since college students are most interested in learning how to interview for a job, this appendix focuses on selection interviews.

Because information interviews and employment selection interviews are used for different reasons, they require different approaches. In this appendix, you'll learn skills for communicating competently during both types of interviews. But the first step for both types is the same: preparation.

Preparing for an Interview

Preparing for an interview entails a number of steps for both the interviewer and the interviewee. An interviewer will need to define the purpose of the interview, develop an interview protocol, and determine questions to ask. If you're being interviewed, you'll want to anticipate the interview purpose as well as the types of questions you might be asked.

Defining Your Purpose. To prepare for an interview you'll be conducting, start by defining your purpose. This helps you identify what topics to cover. Imagine that you're preparing a persuasive speech about your school's spring break volunteer program. You might arrange to interview the dean of students to find out about volunteer opportunities, program requirements, and the benefits of doing community service. If you're interviewing job applicants, your purpose is to find the best candidate by exploring such topics as each applicant's work history and relevant experience (see Table A.1). Having a clear purpose for the interview gives focus to the topics that will be discussed.

If you're going to be interviewed, you should also take time beforehand to consider what topics might be covered so you can be prepared to answer questions. For instance, if you're going to be interviewed for a job, be ready to talk in depth about how you've successfully applied your skills in previous work settings.

Developing an Interview Protocol. When preparing to conduct an interview, you should also develop an **interview protocol**—a list of questions, written in a logical order, that guide the interview. Like a preparation outline for a speech, preparing an interview protocol in advance will show whether you are including all the topics you need and arranging them in a way that makes sense. For example, if you are interviewing a job candidate, you may want to start with general questions ("Tell me about your work history") before moving to more specific questions ("What project did you find most challenging?").

TABLE A.1

POSSIBLE INTERVIEW TOPICS

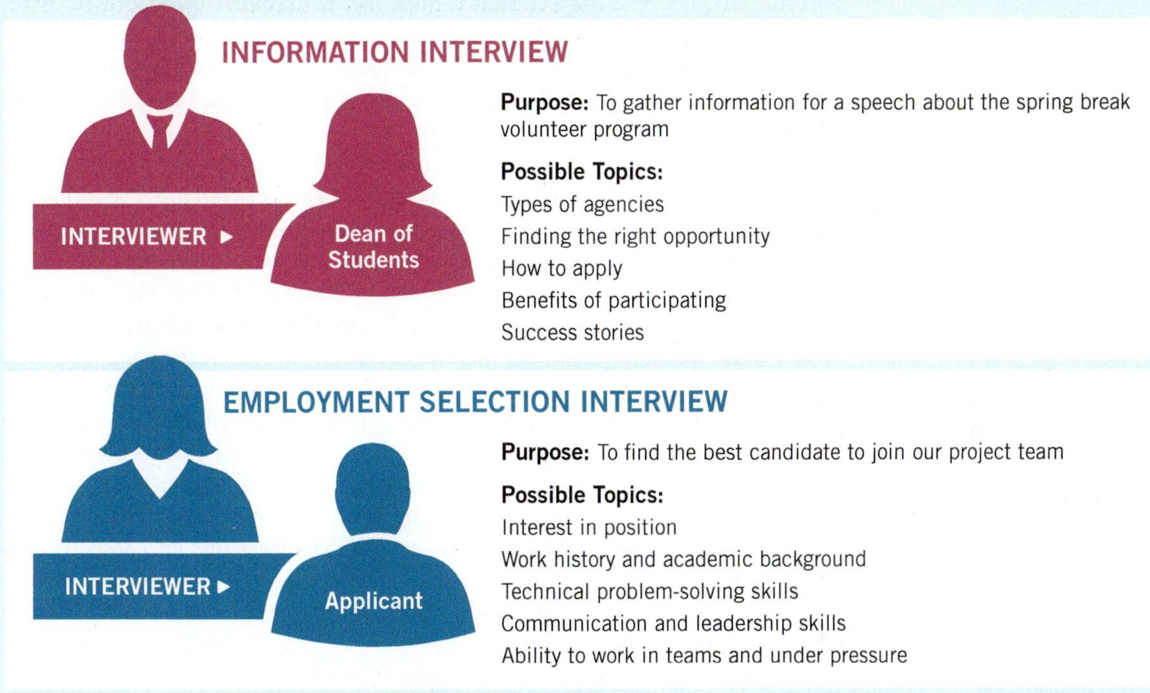

INFORMATION INTERVIEW

Purpose: To gather information for a speech about the spring break volunteer program

Possible Topics:
Types of agencies
Finding the right opportunity
How to apply
Benefits of participating
Success stories

EMPLOYMENT SELECTION INTERVIEW

Purpose: To find the best candidate to join our project team

Possible Topics:
Interest in position
Work history and academic background
Technical problem-solving skills
Communication and leadership skills
Ability to work in teams and under pressure

VoodooDot/Shutterstock

If you plan on asking highly specific or difficult questions, think about when to bring those up. Asking them too early in an interview could make the interviewee uncomfortable or confused. Depending on the type of interview, that could make it difficult to get the information you need. It's usually easier to start with less personal, or "safe," questions ("What did you like most about your last job?"), and then move on to questions about emotional or difficult topics ("What was your biggest mistake?").

When you are an interviewee, you should be responsive to the order of questions that you're asked. Allow the interviewer to ask each question in turn, and answer the question completely. Avoid *perceptual errors* by trying to second-guess where the interviewer is going with the questions. For example, you might be asked to discuss a time when you took a risk and failed (a common job-interview question). Don't jump to the conclusion that the interviewer is trying to eliminate candidates who make mistakes. Instead, clearly identify a time when you were not successful, and explain what you learned from the experience. If there are topics you had expected to cover in the interview but did not, respectfully ask the interviewer if you can address them at the end of the interview or follow up with an email.

Determining Questions to Ask. Questions are the heart of any interview. But not all questions have the same purpose. You can use questions to introduce a new topic, get clarification, or ask for additional details. Even the way you phrase a question influences the answers you get. So when you're developing your interview protocol, consider the different types of questions you can ask.

You can introduce topics or new areas within a topic by using **primary questions**. These questions guide the conversation and are written into the interview protocol. For example, "Dr. Ghent, let's talk about volunteer service and leadership. How does volunteering help students develop their leadership skills?"

You can follow up on answers given by an interviewee with **secondary questions**. These questions aren't usually written into the interview protocol; instead, they evolve out of the conversation. A secondary question can help you clarify vague answers ("When you say 'students increase their social intelligence,' what do you mean?") or probe further into a response ("Tell me more about your summer work as a lifeguard"). Often a secondary question is nothing more than a brief comment to encourage the interviewee to continue answering the question ("Then what happened?" or "How did you resolve that?"). To use secondary questions successfully, use *active listening skills* to ensure you understand the interviewee's answers. If you're preoccupied or distracted, you'll miss opportunities to clarify or probe answers further.

How you phrase a question can also affect the way interviewees answer. **Open questions** give interviewees a lot of freedom in formulating their responses. For example, "How do students benefit by volunteering during their spring break?" could be answered in any number of ways. On the other hand, **closed questions** usually require only a yes or no response, which limits the range of possible answers. For instance, "Can you operate a forklift?" Use open questions when you want to generate more detailed responses. Closed questions help you move quickly through topics during the interview and swiftly determine whether you've gathered critical information. If someone applying for a job as a forklift operator can't operate the equipment, you'd want to know that immediately.

To find out what the interviewee really thinks or feels about a topic, you can use **neutral questions** ("What do you think of the new bonus policy?"). **Leading questions** point the respondent to an answer you prefer ("Don't you think the new bonus policy is a great idea?"). For that reason, leading questions are generally less useful for finding out what an interviewee really thinks. Table A.2 provides examples of neutral and leading questions.

Knowing the different types of questions also helps when you're being interviewed. For example, you will want to provide an appropriate level of detail, including examples, when responding to an open question. On the other hand, the interviewer may not expect you to provide a long response to a closed question, like, "Do you have a driver's license?" As we discuss in the next section, listening carefully to the type of question being asked is important for providing satisfactory answers.

TABLE A.2

NEUTRAL AND LEADING QUESTIONS

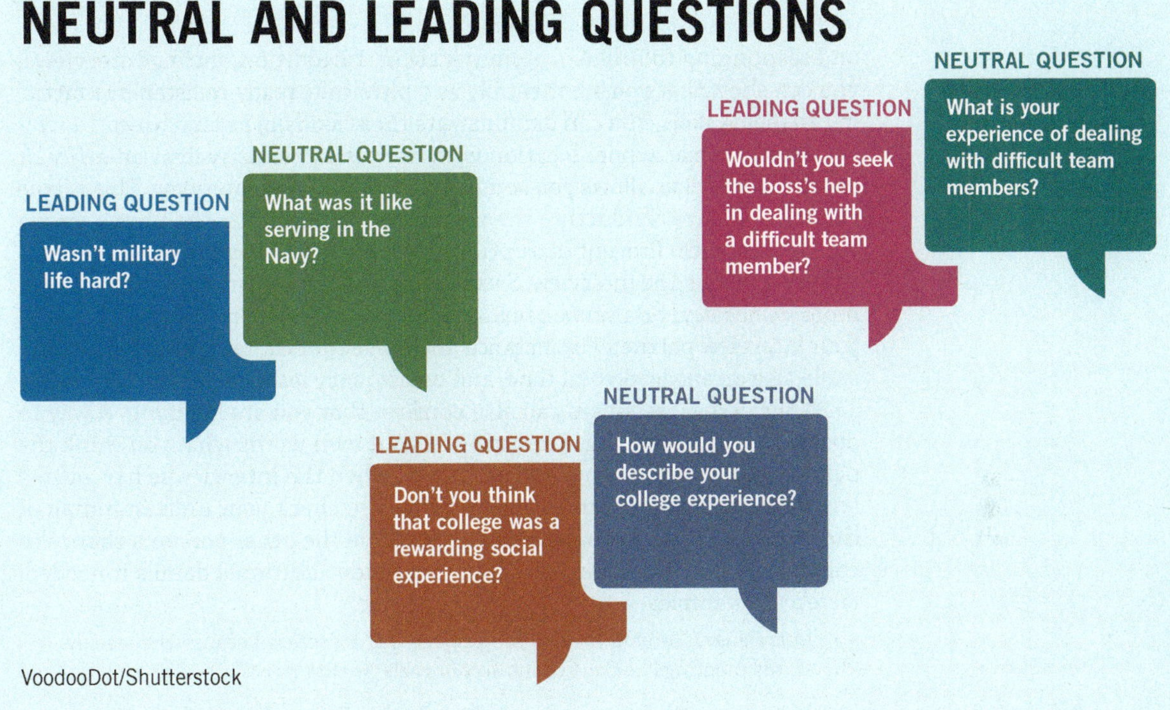

LEADING QUESTION
Wasn't military life hard?
NEUTRAL QUESTION
What was it like serving in the Navy?
LEADING QUESTION
Don't you think that college was a rewarding social experience?
NEUTRAL QUESTION
How would you describe your college experience?
LEADING QUESTION
Wouldn't you seek the boss's help in dealing with a difficult team member?
NEUTRAL QUESTION
What is your experience of dealing with difficult team members?

VoodooDot/Shutterstock

Essential Communication Skills for Interviewing

Regardless of your role—interviewer or interviewee—you create a relationship every time you take part in an interview. Just as with any interpersonal interaction you are a part of, the success of the interview depends on how well you communicate with your partner.

Although information and employment selection interviews have different purposes, you need the same essential communication skills to successfully manage either type. These include being an active listener; building rapport and demonstrating cooperation; and, if required, using mediated communication technologies competently.

Being an Active Listener

A successful interview requires both the interviewer and the interviewee to carefully listen to what is being said. As Chapter 7 explains, *listening* involves hearing, understanding, interpreting, evaluating, remembering, and responding to others' communication. In addition, during interviews, you can show that you are mentally and physically ready to listen by practicing **attending skills**. You can demonstrate these skills in several ways.

First, choose a quiet location with few distractions, such as an office or another room that allows you some privacy during the interview. This is true whether you are conducting the interview in person, on the phone, or via videoconference. Prevent disruptions by silencing your phone and not multitasking during the interview. Second, use nonverbal communication to promote *immediacy*, or a sense of closeness and involvement between you and your interview partner. For instance, make eye contact, face the other person, smile, use an engaged vocal tone, and occasionally lean toward him or her.

Your verbal responses can also confirm that you are listening. A way to do this is by **paraphrasing**—restating in your own words what you think the person said. Paraphrasing is most helpful when the interviewee has given a long and detailed answer because it helps you check your understanding of the response. When you paraphrase, you give the other person a chance to correct any misunderstandings and to provide additional details if needed. Here's an example:

> *Interviewer:* "So you believe the project was a success because the weekly status meetings held everyone accountable; is that right?"
>
> *Interviewee:* "Yes, the status meetings were one reason, but I also believe it was successful because . . ."

Interviewees can also use paraphrasing to check their understanding of something the interviewer asked ("So you want to know why some students aren't happy with their volunteer experience; is that right?").

Building Rapport and Demonstrating Cooperation

Since an interview is like a relationship, using interpersonal skills—such as establishing rapport and demonstrating cooperation—can help you participate in interviews more successfully.

Rapport building, or exchanging messages that create a bond and a positive first impression, helps you quickly set the tone for an interview. Studies show that even your opening handshake can strongly influence interviewers' impression of you during job interviews (Stewart, Dustin, Barrick, & Darnold, 2008). A friendly, upbeat greeting is key to establishing rapport. You'll also want to use the other person's name, know how the person prefers to be addressed (Dr. Flores or Julia), and pronounce the name correctly. Appropriate *self-disclosure*—revealing relevant private information about yourself—can also help build rapport. For example, early in the interview, find some common ground—family, sports, hobbies—and talk briefly about it. But keep these topics noncontroversial and appropriate.

In addition to building rapport, demonstrate cooperation. As Chapter 5 explains, applying Grice's *cooperative principle* means you make messages understandable by being informative, honest, relevant, and clear. Table A.3 explains how to use this principle during interviews.

TABLE A.3

USING GRICE'S COOPERATIVE PRINCIPLE IN AN INTERVIEW

Cooperative Principle	BE INFORMATIVE	BE HONEST	BE RELEVANT	BE CLEAR
Interviewer	Prepare an interview protocol. Clearly introduce yourself, and identify the interview purpose.	Ask secondary questions to clarify areas of confusion. Avoid asking leading questions.	Keep questions focused on the interview purpose.	Use appropriate and understandable language. Define jargon or specialized terms that the interviewee may not know.
Interviewee	Answer questions completely. Give specific examples to illustrate your points.	Provide truthful responses. Don't exaggerate or make false statements.	Give the necessary answers to questions. Avoid long-winded responses.	Use specific language in responding. Avoid vague or ambiguous words.

T-Kot/Shutterstock

Using Mediated Communication during Interviews

Many businesses use mediated communication technologies—such as videoconferencing or Skype—to conduct employment selection interviews. These technologies can help save time and travel costs, but they can also be challenging for interview participants. To ensure that your interview achieves its purpose, consider how to best use these technologies.

There are two forms of video interviews. *Synchronous video interviews* are done in real time, using Skype or other videoconferencing systems. In *asynchronous video interviews*, applicants record answers to questions provided to them in advance. The recorded video is then uploaded to a secure website, where employers can quickly view a number of applicants and determine whom to interview further. Organizations commonly use this tactic to reduce the cost and time of handling initial interviews (Kiger, 2010).

With synchronous and asynchronous video interviews, following certain steps will help you competently conduct or participate in the conversation. First, make sure you know how to use whatever equipment is involved. Take time to learn how the camera operates and how to use the related videoconferencing software. Second, test the equipment in the actual setting where you'll be conducting or recording the interview. Confirm that you have sufficient lighting and that the background is free of any visual or sound distractions. Third, practice your video delivery. Focus the camera to

DOUBLE TAKE

PROPER VS IMPROPER VIDEO INTERVIEWS

When you are interviewing via online videos, your dress, posture, and facial expressions, and even the room in the background, can all greatly impact the perceptions others have of you. Consider how seemingly small things make a big difference in the video interviews depicted below.

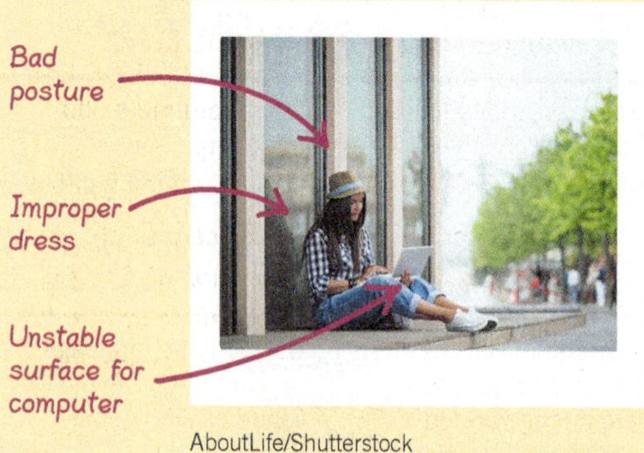

AboutLife/Shutterstock

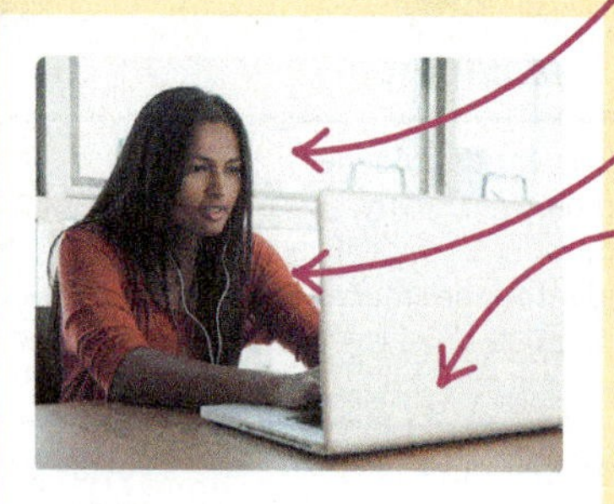

ImageSource/Superstock

a medium close-up shot, so that you capture your upper torso and head. Dress appropriately, and remember to maintain eye contact with the camera and vary your vocal expressiveness. In addition, minimize distracting gestures and be facially expressive. Finally, spend time rehearsing and recording yourself on video. Use the resulting feedback to adjust your delivery or appearance to create a good impression.

Information Interviewing

You might conduct information interviews for a variety of reasons: talking to an expert as research for a speech, or reaching out to a local nonprofit as part of a service-learning project. Or you might meet with someone who works at a company you want to learn more about. Careful preparation will help you get the most from these experiences.

When asked about her life, Kay Wang didn't want to share many details.[2] But as her son and granddaughter prodded her, she told tales of her adventures. Born and raised in China, she admits to being a disobedient child who often

[2]Information about Kay Wang from http://storycorps.org/animation/no-more-questions

Courtesy of StoryCorps

Through an animated version of Kay Wang's interview that StoryCorps created, you can hear the stories and memories that Wang shared with her son and granddaughter. Both the audio and animated copies of the interview provide her family with a lasting record of her life and allow the rest of us a glimpse at her feisty spirit. You can watch the animation of Wang's interview online at http://storycorps.org/animation/no-more-questions

lied to cut class and spend time with her boyfriends. After moving to the United States, her escapades continued. She worked as a detective for Bloomingdale's department store, catching shoplifters—including an unnamed famous designer. She was also a nurse and met her husband at a hospital, where he was a patient.

How do we know all this about Wang? Her family took her to a StoryCorps booth, where they could interview her and preserve the stories she told. StoryCorps is a nonprofit organization with permanent and mobile recording booths throughout the United States. Within these booths, people tell the ordinary and extraordinary stories of their lives. As one of the largest oral history projects in the United States, StoryCorps has a simple motto: "Listen. Honor. Share."

StoryCorps embodies its motto by encouraging friends, family members, coworkers, and romantic partners to interview each other. The goal of these conversations is to share and record the stories that participants consider important. To help them do that, StoryCorps provides participants with a trained facilitator who offers guidance on the types of questions to ask. Participants also receive instruction on how to listen, show respect to their interview partner, and take notes. Completed interviews are archived at the American Folklife Center at the Library of Congress. Some are even featured on NPR's *Morning Edition* or turned into animated shorts for the StoryCorps website.

Whether you're conducting an interview for StoryCorps or for your own interests, you will get the most out of an information interview if you carefully prepare for and manage it, like Kay Wang's family did.

Preparing for an Information Interview

Information interviews are conducted to gain knowledge or understanding about a particular topic. When you decide that you need to conduct an information interview—whether as part of your job hunt, for a speech, or even to explore certain interests—you can't just wing it. To prepare, start by conducting background research, identifying your purpose, and developing your interview protocol. Then you can actually set up the interview.

Conduct Background Research. Deciding whom you want to interview isn't always as easy as it sounds. The key is to select someone who has the relevant experience and knowledge to provide the information you need. For example, suppose your university recently enhanced the campus security system. A new text-message and email system now broadcasts all-campus alerts in the event of threats. You are preparing an informative speech to describe how the alert system works. At first, you consider interviewing a campus police officer, since the campus police normally enforce security protocols. However, the head of the university's information technology (IT) department might be an even better source of information since she selected the new system and will be in charge of implementing, operating, and maintaining it.

Identify Your Purpose. After conducting background research and selecting an individual to interview, it's time to identify your purpose: Why do you want to interview this particular person? What information are you hoping to gain? Framing your purpose in a focused rather than vague way will help you ask more specific questions, which will be more likely to get you the information you need. Consider the differences between the following information interview purposes:

- Vague: "I want to find out about the new campus-alert system."
- Focused: "I want to determine why the new system is better than the old one; how students and faculty can sign up for alerts; and how alerts are communicated to outside groups, such as students' parents and the media."

Imagine meeting with the head of the IT department and saying, "So, what can you tell me about the new campus-alert system?" She may respond with a lot of interesting information, and some of it may be just what you need. But some of it may *not* be what you need because you've asked a vague question. By having a focused purpose, you can ask specific questions, such as, "How is the new system better than the one we've been using?" which more likely gets you the information needed to fulfill your purpose.

Prepare Your Interview Protocol. As discussed earlier, an interview protocol is a written plan for the questions you will ask during the interview. Without a protocol, you could end up wasting your own and the interviewee's time.

Develop a protocol by coming up with a set of primary questions to introduce major topics and related areas. Write *open questions* that will lead to insightful and quality information ("What are the advantages of the new system?"). Make limited use of *closed questions* to gather important factual details ("What is the approximate annual cost of system maintenance?").

Request the Interview. Contact the person to request a meeting. Usually, email is the best way to do this, but you can also follow up with a phone call if necessary. Explain your purpose and how much time you will need to conduct the interview. Decide on a mutually agreeable date and time to meet, one that's convenient for the interviewee. Don't forget to confirm details, such as location (if meeting in person), telephone number (if phone based), or username and application (if web based). Most important, on the day of the interview, arrive/log in 5–10 minutes early, have your interview protocol in hand, and stick to the agreed-upon time frame.

Managing an Information Interview

Once you've been granted an information interview, you can manage it competently by building rapport, being engaged, and ending on a productive note.

Build Rapport. Open the interview by building rapport. Unless you're already well acquainted with the person, it's natural to be nervous. Chatting informally at first will help both of you feel more comfortable. During this time, provide the person with background about the interview purpose. If you want to video- or audio-record the session, ask for permission to do so.

Be Engaged. Apply *active listening skills* by asking follow-up questions to clarify the person's meaning or to get more information. Paraphrase lengthy answers to ensure that you understand what the interviewee has said. Take accurate notes, and capture any statement that you may later want to quote as part of a speech or a written document. If you are planning to use a quote, you may want to ask the interviewee to repeat the response so you can make sure your quote is precise and ethical.

End on a Productive Note. The process of ending an interview is known as **leave-taking**. Much like the conclusion to a speech, leave-taking indicates that the interview is about to finish. You can signal this through your final question, such as, "Is there anything I didn't ask about that you think I should know?" Or make a summary statement, such as "I very much appreciate your help. I now understand how the new system works." Making such summarizing questions and statements helps the person identify whether any important information has been left out, or whether some details need correcting. You can also use leave-taking to ask permission to get back in touch with any additional questions that might come up ("If I need to follow up, can I contact you at this number?"). Be sure to thank the person for his or her time, and follow up with a thank-you note.

Employment Selection Interviewing

Your best chance of getting the job of your dreams is to make an excellent impression during the employment selection interview. To do that, you'll need to prepare carefully for the interview and then skillfully manage the communication that unfolds during the interview.

It sounds cliché, but it's the little things that matter, especially when interviewing for a job. Whether it's face-to-face or through FaceTime, how you present yourself and communicate during a job interview can make or break your chances of getting hired. Corporate recruiters point out certain priority behaviors for creating a positive impression when interviewing: be on time, give a proper greeting, and present yourself neatly and organized (Tews, Frager, Citarella & Orndorff, 2018). Most importantly, silence your phone and keep it out of sight. This is true regardless of the type of job for which you are applying.

Even before you get to the job interview, you must take time to prepare. Following are some strategies for competently preparing for and managing an employment selection interview.

Preparing for an Employment Selection Interview

Whether you are looking for an internship or your first job, seeking a promotion, applying to a different company, or considering changing careers, you will need to prepare for employment selection interviews. This includes researching potential employers, developing your résumé and cover letter, reviewing your social media image, and planning your own questions for the interviewer. To learn even more about how to prepare for a job interview, check out sites like Monster.com or CareerBuilder.com, or visit your school's career services department.

Research Potential Employers. Learn as much as you can about the company that is interviewing you. Recruiters and hiring managers favor applicants who know something about the organization. This includes understanding what the enterprise does (what it produces and what industry it's in) and having a sense of how the job you're interviewing for fits into the company as a whole. Armed with this knowledge, you can speak more intelligently about how your experience and skills are a good fit for the job (Joyce, 2008).

If you saw the job listing in an advertisement or on the company's website, the posting probably included a job description. If the description is vague, try to get more details—for example, by contacting the company's human resources department. The more you understand the nature of the job, the better sense you'll have of whether you're a good fit for the position. The job description will also help you write a compelling cover letter and adapt your résumé (see pp. A-17 to A-19).

By researching the company, you can also prepare answers to questions that may come up during an interview. For example, the interviewer will likely ask you why you're interested in the job. "I just need a job" is not an acceptable answer; you need to explain how your experiences and skills make you a good fit for *that* job. (See Table A.4 for additional interview questions you should be ready to answer.) Also, think about what job-specific questions might come up during the interview. For instance, if you're interviewing for a programming position, the interviewer might ask you to describe your experience troubleshooting coding problems. Reviewing the job description will help you anticipate these questions and prepare responses.

Develop Your Résumé and Cover Letter. When you apply for a job, you typically submit a résumé. A **résumé** is a written summary of your education, work experience, and skills. Most employers require one of two types of résumés. The first type is the **chronological résumé**, which details the history of your education and work experience, beginning with the most recent. The second type is the **functional résumé**, which focuses on how your skills and experiences relate to the specific job you're applying for. This information is not in chronological order. See Figures A.1 and A.2 for samples of a chronological and a functional résumé. These samples show the basic categories and types of information résumés often include. However, there are a lot of opinions on what detailed content should be covered. Some recruiters say an objective statement is no longer necessary. Some advocate for disclosing a high GPA, while others say not to include one at all. When putting together your own résumés, research what is the acceptable standard in the industry to which you are applying.

Which type of résumé is more appropriate? We recommend preparing both types. Then you can decide which one to submit, depending on the job application requirements and your work history. For example, for employers that ask for a detailed work history, a chronological résumé is better. If you have a limited work history, a functional résumé may be the right choice, because it helps you emphasize job-relevant skills you've gained through your academic experience.

Many employers now expect you to submit your résumé electronically, either as an email attachment or uploaded to a website. This enables companies to scan résumés into a database and conduct keyword searches to quickly identify applicants with desirable experience and skills. For this reason, you will want to develop a searchable résumé that includes relevant keywords from the job description. Finally, some employers will allow or require you to submit other application materials, such as work samples, videos, or a portfolio of related classwork. In such cases, guidelines on formats, sizes, and submissions are likely to be provided. All these materials should be as carefully composed as any traditional résumé.

There are many good resources online that can help you create résumés, including Monster.com and CareerBuilder.com. You can also seek support at your college's career services department. Use these sources as well as your own research to carefully craft your application materials.

Résumés are often accompanied by a **cover letter**, which introduces you and highlights your qualifications for the job in question. (See Figure A.3.)

TABLE A.4

COMMONLY ASKED INTERVIEW QUESTIONS

- What behaviors or traits in coworkers do you find most difficult? How do you handle these?
- Give an example of a conflict you had with a coworker or boss. How did you handle it? What was the result?
- What educational and professional accomplishments do you hope to achieve in the next five years?

- What strengths and skills would you bring to this company?
- Describe a situation in which you've demonstrated competent leadership.
- Tell me about a time when something did not turn out well. What happened? Why do you think it happened? What did you learn from it?
- Why do you want to work for us?

- What makes you a good candidate for this job?
- What have you done to improve your knowledge and/or skills in the past year?
- What should I know about you that I cannot learn from reading your résumé?
- Provide an example of your work on a team. What was your role? What would others on the team say about your contribution?

- What would your coworkers say about what it's like to work with you?
- What would you describe as your biggest educational or work mistake? What happened? What did you learn from it?
- How do you manage stress?
- What is your greatest weakness?
- What has been your proudest accomplishment?

FIGURE A.1

CHRONOLOGICAL RÉSUMÉ

Jessica Garcia

124 Central Ave., Elgin, TX (512) 555-4621 JessieMGarcia@email.com

Objective *To use my digital media experience and skills to support the digital marketing goals of a business organization.*

Experience

Silver Onion Media, Austin, TX (January 2019–Present)

Social Media Intern

- Maintain daily updates to company's Facebook and Instagram accounts to help build brand awareness and customer loyalty.
- Create surveys and polls to gauge customer interest in relevant trends and topics. Report results to company's Marketing Director.

Bootstrap Youth Mentoring Project, Austin, TX (November 2018–Present)

Volunteer, Web Content Consultant

- Write articles and shoot video about program events.

The Accent, Austin, TX (September 2016–May 2018)

Reporter (Student Newspaper at Austin Community College)

- Wrote weekly articles on campus life; conducted interviews with faculty, staff, and students.
- Managed social events calendar in print edition and online version.
- Trained new reporters in the publication process.

Skills & Interests Maintain a personal blog documenting my travels and volunteer work: jessiesmarvels.blogspot.com; fluent in English and Spanish; proficient with Microsoft Office, Adobe Dreamweaver, InDesign, social media platforms

Education

University of Texas, Austin, Bachelor of Arts, Anticipated May 2020

Anticipated Summa Cum Laude honors
Major: Communication
Austin Community College, Associate Degree, 2018

References supplied upon request

FIGURE A.2

FUNCTIONAL RÉSUMÉ

Jessica Garcia

124 Central Ave., Elgin, TX (512) 555-4621 JessieMGarcia@email.com

Summary of Skills

Social Media Development

- Ability to apply communication theory in developing Facebook and Instagram presence for increasing brand awareness and customer loyalty.
- Maintain personal blog documenting travels and charitable work (jessiesmarvels.blogspot.com).

Digital Media and Survey Skills

- Proficient with Adobe Photoshop, Dreamweaver, InDesign, Zoomerang, and Survey Monkey. Portfolio of team-based Web design projects available.
- Ability to write survey questions gauging customer interest in relevant trends.
- Knowledge of Microsoft Excel for conducting descriptive data analysis.

Journalism and Creative Writing Skills

- Competent writer for both print and online publications. Recognized for feature-story writing. Trained student reporters for community college newspaper.

Communication and Team Skills

- Collaborate with others in developing web content for school and internships.
- Leader of service-learning project for nonprofit public relations course.
- Fluent in English and Spanish.

Summary of Work Experience

Silver Onion Media, Austin, TX (January 2019–Present)

- Social Media Intern

Bootstrap Youth Mentoring Project, Austin, TX (November 2018–Present)

- Volunteer, Web Content Consultant

The Accent, Austin, TX (September 2016–May 2018)

- Reporter (Student Newspaper at Austin Community College)

Education

University of Texas, Austin, Bachelor of Arts, Anticipated May 2020
Anticipated Summa Cum Laude honors
Major: Communication
Austin Community College, Associate Degree, 2018

References supplied upon request

FIGURE A.3

COVER LETTER

Jessica Garcia

124 Central Ave., Elgin, TX (512) 555-4621 JessieMGarcia@email.com

March 15, 2019

McKinney's Restaurant Group
Attn: Ms. Marianne Burton, Director of Marketing
2727 E. Rose Blvd., Suite 24B
Fort Worth, TX 76102

Dear Ms. Burton:

In response to your current posting on Monster.com, I am writing to apply for the position of digital marketing specialist with McKinney's Restaurant Group. I will be graduating this May from the University of Texas at Austin with a degree in Communication. Given the outstanding reputation of your restaurants, I would be delighted to contribute my digital media skills to your team of marketing professionals.

Your job posting states a desire to develop a social media presence with young adults and families. I could help you meet this goal. Currently as a social media intern for Silver Onion Media, I maintain its social media accounts. Since starting in January, I have increased Facebook followings by 15% and Instagram followings by 22%. Using Web analytics, I continue to identify new audiences to increase the online visibility of Silver Onion.

Additionally, my writing experience is notable. As a reporter for the student newspaper at Austin Community College, I increasingly gained responsibility for writing news and feature stories. Among my proudest achievements is receiving the Texas Community College Journalism Association's 2018 Best Feature Story award for my article "Homeless Scholar: The Real Education of Maya Rose."

Finally, your posting indicates a desire for a candidate who can collaborate with others in developing website content. Working in web design teams, my proficiency with Adobe Photoshop, Dreamweaver, and InDesign has helped solve difficult design challenges. I would be happy to share with you my portfolio of website content created in my courses and internships.

Enclosed is my résumé, including my contact address and phone number. I look forward to an opportunity to interview with you soon.

Respectfully,

Jessica Garcia

ADVANCE THE CONVERSATION

WELL . . . TO BE TOTALLY HONEST WITH YOU

1 YOUR DILEMMA

As a sports marketing major, you know how hard it is to land a job with a professional team. Now, sitting in the waiting area of the team's Chicago headquarters, you're about to interview for your dream job: an entry-level position in special events promotions.

Victoria Mines, special events coordinator, greets you and walks you to her office. An instant bond forms when you discover you both attended the same university. After reviewing your résumé, Victoria begins asking some of the exact questions you had anticipated. She nods approvingly to each of your responses. But then she asks a surprising question: "I notice on your résumé that you interned in special events for the Beaumont Scorpions. Will you describe that experience?"

You consider how to answer. You don't want to ruin the positive vibe with Victoria, but that internship was the worst. You answered phones, ran errands for the stadium manager, and worked the ticket booth. Frustrated by the lack of meaningful marketing experiences, you quit mid-season.

How do you feel when Victoria asks you about your previous internship?

2 THE RESEARCH

During an employment interview, you want to project a positive *face*, or view of yourself. As Chapter 2 explains, your *face* is actively created and presented through your communication with others. You create your face during interviews in one of three ways.

First, interviewees may *self-promote* by truthfully describing past work experiences using positive language ("I delivered outstanding service through sales and problem solving for guests"). Employers expect interviewees to use self-promotion when talking about work history and job-relevant skills (Swider, Barrick, Harris, & Stoverink, 2011). Second, interviewees may engage in slight *image creation*, which involves exaggerating or modifying some truth about past work experience. For example, saying "I coordinated ticket sales for the Scorpions" exaggerates your role working in the ticket booth. Third, job candidates may try to maintain positive face by creating a *false image* ("I planned an appreciation day for local firefighters"). Unlike slight image creation, which has some degree of truth, false image creation is lying (Swider et al., 2011).

Interviewers give high ratings to applicants who use self-promotion in interviews (Swider et al., 2011). But slight or false image creation can be costly. Exaggerating or creating a false face means that interviewees must pay careful attention to other answers in order to avoid contradicting them. This concentration often results in giving low-quality and less specific answers to questions in order to keep up the act, which then leads to poor interview performance (Swider et al., 2011).

What are the benefits and risks of choosing to maintain a positive face through self-promotion, exaggerating, or misrepresenting your internship?

3 YOUR OPPORTUNITY

Before you act, consider the facts of the situation and think about the research on managing impressions in an interview. Also, reflect on what you've learned so far about creating résumés (pp. A-15, A-17 to A-21), communication skills in interviewing (pp. A-7 to A-10), and managing employment selection interviews (pp. A-21 to A-25).

Now it's your turn. Write a response to Victoria's question about your previous internship.

Think of the cover letter as a persuasive message that expresses how your work experience and skills meet the employer's needs. Use vivid and descriptive language to direct the reader to key areas of your résumé that showcase your qualifications. Write different cover letters for each job you apply for, tailoring each letter to the position's specific needs. Conclude your cover letter by requesting an interview.

Remember that your résumé and cover letter are the first impression an employer will get of you as a potential employee. Make sure these documents truly convey your qualifications for the job. Ensure that they look good, too. Employers will spend just a few minutes reviewing them, so create professional-looking documents with clean, crisp formats. Use a readable font, such as Arial or Helvetica, and use active rather than passive voice to maintain readers' interest. Proofread carefully for proper spelling and grammar—careless mistakes will quickly place you in the rejection pile. Most important, keep both documents brief; each should be no more than one page long.

Review Your Social Media Image. If potential employers saw your Instagram or Twitter feed, what impressions would they form about you? Would they conclude that you're a serious, hardworking type, or that you mostly play paintball and hang out at the beach? As Chapter 4 on mediated communication points out, you create your *online face* through your social media activity: your posts, your email and usernames, and the comments others make about you.

Some employers check Google, LinkedIn, and social media sites to gather additional information about job applicants. They will more likely view you favorably if the images on these sites show you in a respectable setting (e.g., playing tennis rather than drinking at a party) and if others post positive comments about you (Hong, Tandoc, Kim, Kim, & Wise, 2012). Your email and usernames will also influence their impressions of you. If you don't already have at least one email address that includes your name, set one up and use it to correspond with potential employers. (For more on maintaining a positive online face, see Chapter 4, pp. 99–102.)

Develop Your Own Questions. Most employment selection interviewers conclude the interview by inviting the applicant to ask questions. This is another opportunity for you to demonstrate what you know about the company. Rather than saying "I can't think of anything," be prepared with a few questions. For example, you could ask about opportunities for advancement within the company, or inquire about some detail in the job description that wasn't covered during the interview. Avoid questions that you could easily answer by looking at the employer's website or other published material.

Managing an Employment Selection Interview

In addition to carefully preparing for a job interview, you'll make a good impression by communicating skillfully during the interview. Keys to successfully managing a job interview include dressing appropriately, understanding every question posed to you, dealing competently with any unlawful questions that arise, demonstrating positivity and optimism, and following up promptly and appreciatively.

Dress Appropriately. It may seem unfair, but interviewers will judge you by your clothes, hairstyle, body art, and other nonverbal behaviors. In one study of applicants for a university research-assistant position, students who dressed professionally for the interview were rated higher in social skills and considered more desirable for employment than those who were informally dressed (Gifford, Ng, & Wilkinson, 1985).

Because your appearance strongly influences how a prospective employer judges your abilities, you'll want to carefully plan your wardrobe for a selection interview—even if the interview will be conducted online or through video. If possible, visit the potential employer's work site or website to see how employees dress. You can also ask someone who's familiar with the business or someone in the company's human resources department. However, the standard rule is to dress in a professional manner.

Understand Every Question. Even when interviewers have prepared for the meeting, they may ask confusing or assumptive questions. Rather than just spouting out a response you are unsure of, take the time to clarify the question first. It is better to make sure you understand the question than to give an answer the interviewer thinks doesn't make sense. If the interviewer asks you a question that's unclear, ask him or her to repeat it or to clarify it.

You can also show that you understand a question by restating it or repeating a few key words in your response. For example:

> *Interviewer:* In this job, you will encounter demanding hotel guests who have little patience. What experience do you have dealing with difficult people?
>
> *You:* My experience in dealing with difficult people can be illustrated in three ways . . .

Deal Competently with Unlawful Questions. Federal and state laws exist to protect citizens from discrimination when applying for a job. It is illegal for employers to ask job applicants about things that are not relevant to the job, such as their age, sex, ethnicity, national origin, and religion. For example, an interviewer should not ask you any of the following questions:

- Where were you born?
- When were you born?
- What is your native language?

- Are you married?
- Do you have or plan to have children?
- Do you have reliable child care?
- Do you have any disabilities?
- Will you need to take time off for religious observances?

Employers *may* ask a question about religion, gender, age, or national origin if it relates to a **bona fide occupational qualification**—a characteristic essential to operating the business. For example, it's legal to ask "Are you over 21?" for a job that involves selling alcohol, "Can you speak Spanish or French?" if the job requires interacting with suppliers or consumers in specific languages, or "Can you lift a 50-pound box?" if the job calls for physical strength.

If you believe a question is unlawful, you'll need to decide how to respond. First, consider the motive behind the question. Is it an innocent mistake or malicious in intent? Second, think about how much you want the job. Though not legal or even fair, know that it might be risky to point out that a question is unlawful.

With these factors in mind, you could respond in a number of ways. You could answer briefly without elaborating. If the interviewer asks, "Is English your native language?" you may simply respond, "No." Or you could direct your answer to something that's relevant to the job. For instance, "I believe my Spanish-speaking skills would be an asset in serving many of your clients in South Texas." Finally, you could refuse to answer any question that you believe is unlawful or inappropriate. You can do this in a way that's assertive but polite. For example, "I don't believe my native language is important to my ability to do this job effectively."

Demonstrate Positivity and Optimism. During a job interview, you want to put your best foot forward. Interviewers expect you to do some self-promotion, including describing your job-related experiences positively, without misrepresenting your accomplishments (Swider et al., 2011). Focus on strengths you bring to the position. Your aim is to sell yourself by demonstrating how your experience and skills can meet the employer's needs.

Don't downplay or cover up negative work experiences. Instead, acknowledge a negative experience and emphasize what you learned from it. If you had a bad experience with a previous boss or job, be as diplomatic as possible in describing it. Criticizing your last boss will only make *you* look bad. Also anticipate questions about your weaknesses. When interviewers ask these types of questions, they are looking to see if you are self-aware and trying to improve. There may be times, however, when these types of questions may seem aggressive or overly stressful; the Advance the Conversation: Managing Stress Questions video activity on pages A-26 to A-27 considers additional skills necessary for responding competently.

FIGURE A.4

TIPS FOR PROFESSIONAL INTERVIEWING SUCCESS

Dr. Kelly Morrison is Professor of Communication Studies at the University of Alabama at Birmingham. She offers the following practical tips for success in an initial employment selection interview, based on her background in sales and years of preparing students for interviews:

KNOW AND PITCH YOURSELF

Know and be able to discuss your top three professional qualities. Many interviews open with "Tell me about yourself and why you're right for this job." Respond to these questions with your top three traits; for example, "I'm right for this job because I'm conscientious, hardworking, and creative . . ."

BACK IT UP

Be prepared to back up every claim you make about yourself with *specific* examples—that is, examples that detail particular events reflecting the traits you've described. If you claim "leadership ability," provide an example of your leadership—"I've been the president of several student organizations, for instance . . ."

KNOW YOUR AUDIENCE

Do your homework on the position, the company, and the industry. It is not uncommon for the interviewer to ask you, "Who is our chief competitor? Who is our CEO?" The internet is your best friend; research the company, competition, and industry ahead of time. This preparation may be the edge that sets you apart from others.

KNOW YOUR ROI

It costs companies time to recruit, interview, and train their workforce. With this in mind, you want to communicate your return-on-investment (ROI). The question to be prepared for is, "Why should I hire you instead of another candidate?" If you are interviewing on campus, the other candidates may have your major, your GPA, and similar student organization experiences. What, then, separates you? Be ready to answer this question with personal skill sets that you bring to the table that make you a more valuable investment than others.

BE PREPARED

Standard interview questions include "Why do you want this job?" and "What is your biggest weakness?" These questions probe your motives and whether or not you are self-reflective. Answer the first question in a way that demonstrates your desire to benefit the company, and in discussing your "weaknesses," be honest. Feel free to discuss weaknesses that you have since overcome or are cognizant of—for instance, "Sometimes I work too hard" or "I am too competitive."

Be ready for off-topic questions testing your ability to think on your feet. Questions of this type include "If you were a tree/animal/piece of furniture, what kind would you be?" and "What's your favorite book?"

Also be ready to ask the interviewer at least three questions. My favorite is, "What qualities do you think are most important for success in this job?" This is important for two reasons. First, if the qualities described are not ones that you currently possess, or care to possess, you may rethink whether or not you want to work for this company. Second, if you want the job but haven't yet described a quality that they list, you still have time to work it into the interview before it is over. Other useful questions include "Why is this position available?" "What is a typical day like?" and "Who will be training me for this position?"

CLOSE STRONG

A close consists of four things: thanking them for their time and information, reiterating why you are the best choice for the position, asking for the job, and confirming follow-up contact. Here is an example close: "Thank you so much for taking the time to meet with me today. I really appreciate your insight/candor/time . . . I believe I am the ideal candidate for this position because I have the qualities that you are looking for. . . . We talked about the importance of leadership and initiative and my experience in these areas. Additionally I have a background in ________ (fill in the blank with a quality and example that you have not yet identified). I would like to work for your company, and I want this position. When will you be making a decision?" (Listen to what they say here. They may say something like, "Well, we are just at the beginning of the process . . ."). DO NOT say something like, "Hope to hear from you soon." Instead, take control of the timeline by saying something like, "May I contact you in two weeks to see where you are in the process?"

Follow Up Promptly. Even after an interview, you'll need to continue making a positive impression as you follow up. For instance, if the interviewer asks for a list of references, send it within 24 hours. In addition to expressing appreciation at the end of the interview, send a follow-up email thanking the person for his or her time within 24 hours of the interview. While a handwritten note is optional as a personal touch, an email sent to your interviewer within 24 hours is critical (Tews et al., 2018). A gracious thank-you email includes specific details from the interview, such as why you continue to be interested in the job and why you think you are a good fit. If the hiring manager is trying to decide between you and another applicant, a skillfully crafted thank-you message will make you more memorable and could tip the scales in your favor. Even if you ultimately don't get the job, a memorable follow-up note may leave the door open for future interview opportunities at that company.

LearningCurve can help you review! Go to **launchpadworks.com**

ADVANCE THE CONVERSATION
Video Activity

MANAGING STRESS QUESTIONS

The following scenario will enhance your ability to navigate difficult questions in an employment selection interview. Visit LaunchPad at **launchpadworks.com** to get the full experience with video. As you watch the first video, recall what you've learned about interviewing. Then complete the **Your Turn** prompts. Finally, watch the **Take Two!** video to explore how this scenario could have gone differently.

1 THE PROBLEM

Hannah is interviewing for a new job that she is really excited about. The interviewer, Lynn, has hit her with a number of tough questions, but Hannah has kept calm and feels that she has given a strong answer to each question so far. Next, Lynn asks Hannah how her team members at her current job would describe her. Hannah is ready with a response for this question, too, and she answers with confidence.

"Fair-minded. Direct. I think they would also describe me as detail-oriented and open to suggestions and comments."

"So no issues? You make it sound like everyone on your team thinks you're just swell. I don't believe that."

2 YOUR TURN

Observations. Reflect on how Hannah and Lynn communicated in this scenario by answering the following questions:

1. How would you feel if you were in Hannah's situation?
2. Were there missed opportunities to practice competent communication? If so, what were they?

Discussion. In class or with a partner, share your thoughts about the interaction between Hannah and Lynn and work to answer the following questions:

1. Why do you think Lynn responded to Hannah's answer in this way?
2. Do you think Lynn should have responded differently? If so, how do you think she should have responded?

Conclusion. Based on your analysis, how would you advise Hannah to respond to Lynn's comment?

3 TAKE TWO!

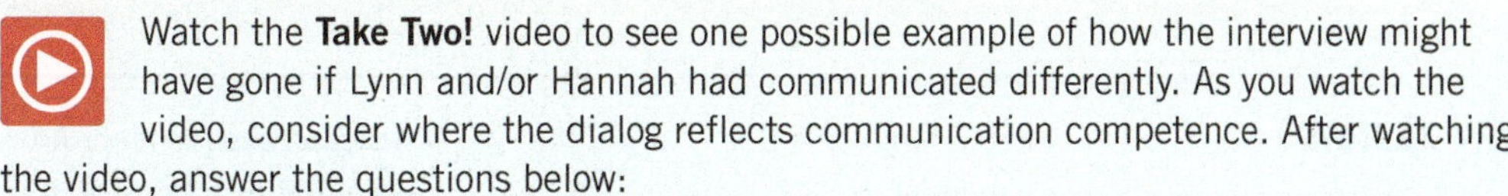

Watch the **Take Two!** video to see one possible example of how the interview might have gone if Lynn and/or Hannah had communicated differently. As you watch the video, consider where the dialog reflects communication competence. After watching the video, answer the questions below:

1. Did Lynn and/or Hannah take advantage of opportunities that they missed in the first scenario? Which ones?
2. Did their different actions result in a more productive interview? Please explain.

APPENDIX REVIEW

APPENDIX RECAP

- Whereas **employment interviews** are focused exclusively on workplace interactions, you can use **information interviews** in a variety of personal, school, and work situations.
- Developing an **interview protocol** will help you plan what topics to cover, what questions to ask, and the proper order for your questions. **Open questions** and **neutral questions** will help you get detailed responses.
- Using your **attending skills**, engaging in **rapport building**, demonstrating cooperation, and properly using mediated communication technologies will help you communicate competently during interviews.
- Some of the best things you can do to prepare for and manage information and employment interviews include doing your research, dressing appropriately, being engaged in the conversation, demonstrating positivity and optimism, and following up appropriately.
- When composing **résumés** and **cover letters** for **selection interviews**, craft each one to specifically highlight how your work experience and skills meet the employer's needs.

LaunchPad for *Choices & Connections* offers unique video scenarios and encourages self-assessment through adaptive quizzing. Go to **launchpadworks.com** to get access.

 LearningCurve adaptive quizzes

 Advance the Conversation video scenarios

KEY TERMS

Interviewing, p. A-2
Interviewer, p. A-2
Interviewee, p. A-2
Information interviews, p. A-3
Employment interviews, p. A-4
Selection interviews, p. A-4
Performance or appraisal interviews, p. A-4
Exit interviews, p. A-4
Interview protocol, p. A-4
Primary questions, p. A-6
Secondary questions, p. A-6
Open questions, p. A-6
Closed questions, p. A-6
Neutral questions, p. A-6
Leading questions, p. A-6
Attending skills, p. A-8
Paraphrasing, p. A-8
Rapport building, p. A-8
Leave-taking, p. A-13
Résumé, p. A-15
Chronological résumé, p. A-15
Functional résumé, p. A-15
Cover letter, p. A-15
Bona fide occupational qualification, p. A-23

POP QUIZ

Looking for more review questions? **LearningCurve** can help you master key concepts from this chapter. Go to **launchpadworks.com**

1. Before starting a new job, your previous employer asks you to meet and discuss why you are changing jobs. This is an example of which type of interview?

   a. Information interview
   b. Selection interview
   c. Appraisal interview
   d. Exit interview

2. You are interviewing a local artist for a research project and ask her, "How long have you been painting?" This is an example of which type of question?

   a. Open question
   b. Closed question
   c. Leading question
   d. Secondary question

3. In an interview, a good way to demonstrate that you have understood what the interviewer just said is to

   a. use paraphrasing.
   b. promote immediacy.
   c. build rapport.
   d. be informative.

4. If you don't have a lot of paid work experience but want to highlight your education and volunteer work, what type of résumé is best to use?

   a. Functional résumé
   b. Chronological résumé
   c. Scannable résumé
   d. Digital résumé

5. Which of the following is an example of a bona fide occupational qualification question?

   a. What is your date of birth?
   b. Do you have reliable child care?
   c. Are you available to work at night?
   d. What is your political affiliation?

ACTIVITIES

For more activities, visit LaunchPad for *Choices & Connections* at **launchpadworks.com**

1 Job Search Basics

Using a career website (Monster.com or CareerBuilder.com) or a specific company website, find an entry-level job posting that interests you, making sure it is appropriate for your work experience and qualifications. Then write a résumé and a cover letter for the position. Exchange your résumé and cover letter with a classmate, and get feedback on your documents.

2 What to Wear

Working in groups, use Google images (or a similar image search engine) to find examples of appropriate dress and appearance for an employment selection interview in a professional setting. Based on your findings, develop a list of recommendations for both men and women of appropriate employment interview attire and appearance. Share your results with the class.

Glossary

accommodation: (p. 244) Managing conflict by abandoning your own goals or actions and giving in to others' desires.

action-oriented listeners: (p. 175) those who like focused and organized information and want clear, to-the-point messages from others. Also known as *task-oriented listeners*.

actor-observer effect: (p. 48) The tendency to make external attributions regarding your own behaviors.

adaptive gesture: (p. 380) Movements that attempt to manage nervousness, such as fidgeting, twirling your hair, or fiddling with your jewelry.

adaptors: (p. 145) Touching gestures that serve a physical or psychological purpose, such as rubbing your chin when thinking about a tough question.

adjourning: (p. 266) The group developmental phase when members disband but first take time to evaluate and reflect on how well they accomplished the task and the quality of their relationships.

affect displays: (p. 153) Intentional or unintentional behaviors that depict actual or feigned emotion.

affective conflict: (p. 298) Disagreements stemming from interpersonal, gender, or cultural differences between members; power struggles; or simply bad feelings.

aggressive listening: (p. 179) Attending to what others say solely to find an opportunity to attack or criticize (also known as *ambushing*).

algebraic impression: (p. 50) An impression formed by analyzing the positive and negative things you learn about someone to calculate an overall impression, then updating this impression as you learn new information.

analogical reasoning: (p. 440) Supporting a claim by drawing a comparison between two ideas or situations to show that what's true for one could be true for the other.

analogy: (p. 349) A comparison between something familiar to your audience and an idea that is not familiar to them but that you want them to understand.

appropriateness: (p. 19) The degree to which your communication matches expectations regarding how people should communicate.

argumentativeness: (p. 274) A group member's willingness to take a stance on controversial issues and verbally refute others who disagree.

articulation: (p. 381) Presenting information clearly so that the audience can understand what you're saying.

artifacts: (p. 150) Objects you possess that influence how you see yourself and that you use to express your identity to others.

assurances: (p. 229) Messages that emphasize how much your relationship partners mean to you, point out how important the relationships are to you, and show that you see a secure future together.

asynchronous communication: (p. 96) Communication in which a time lapse exists between a message sent (as in email, voice mail, or a post to a social media site) and a response, if there is a response at all.

attending skills: (p. A-8) In an interview setting, the ability to show that you are mentally and physically ready to listen — choosing a quiet location with few distractions and using nonverbal communication to promote immediacy between you and your interview partner.

attitude: (p. 324) An evaluation that makes a person respond favorably or unfavorably toward an issue, a situation, or a person.

attribution: (p. 47) A rationale you create to explain the comments or behaviors of others.

attributional complexity: (p. 85) The ability to acknowledge that other people's behaviors have complex causes.

audience analysis: (p. 323) A process of identifying important characteristics about your listeners, and using this information to prepare your speech.

autocratic leadership style: (p. 290) A leadership style in which the leader directs others, telling them what to do.

avoidance: (p. 242) Approaching a conflict by ignoring it and not managing it.

avoiding: (p. 208) A stage in the coming-apart phase of a relationship when one or both partners decide that they can no longer be around each other and begin distancing themselves physically.

beautiful-is-good effect: (p. 196) The phenomenon that attractive people are often assumed to offer other valued resources, like competent communication skills, intelligence, and well-adjusted personalities.

belief: (p. 324) A conviction regarding what is true and untrue.

birds-of-a-feather effect: (p. 195) The notion that people seek romantic partnerships, close family involvements, friendships, and coworker relationships with those they see as similar to themselves.

bona fide occupational qualification: (p. A-23) A characteristic essential to operating a particular business, such as being of legal age to work in a store that sells alcohol.

bonding: (p. 206) In a relationship, a public ritual that announces to the world that you and your romantic partner have made a commitment to each other.

brainstorming: (p. 320) A creative problem-solving strategy that involves coming up with as many ideas as possible in a defined period of time.

butler lie: (p. 107) The type of deception people use to avoid conversation, prevent embarrassment, or simply be polite.

captive audience: (p. 325) Listeners who are required to attend the presentation.

cause-effect pattern: (p. 352) An organizational pattern that shows how events or forces will lead to (or did lead to) specific outcomes.

cause-effect reasoning: (p. 440) Drawing a connection between two events or things and claiming that one produced the other.

central route: (p. 430) The way audience members who are highly motivated to listen and who have the knowledge needed to understand your message will process your speech. These audience members pay more attention and carefully evaluate your points.

channel: (p. 6) The sensory dimension (sound, sight, or touch) along which communicators transmit information.

character: (p. 433) Showing your audience that you understand their needs, have their best interests in mind, and genuinely believe in your topic.

charisma: (p. 434) In speech delivery, the warmth, personality, and dynamism your audience sees in you.

chronological pattern: (p. 351) A pattern that organizes main points by time sequence or in a series of steps.

chronological résumé: (p. A-15) A résumé that details the history of your education and work experience, beginning with the most recent.

circumscribing: (p. 208) The stage of coming apart when you begin to restrict the quantity and quality of information you exchange in a relationship.

cisgender: (p. 64) Term used to describe individuals whose gender identity corresponds to the sex that they were assigned at birth.

closed questions: (p. A-6) Questions that require a yes or no response, which limits the range of possible answers.

co-cultural communication theory: (p. 75) The idea that the people who have more power within a society determine the dominant culture because they get to decide the prevailing views, values, and traditions of the society.

co-culture: (p. 75) A group comprising members of a society who don't conform to the language, values, lifestyle, or physical appearance of the dominant culture.

coercion: (p. 428) Communication that involves using threats, manipulation, and even violence to force others to do something against their will.

cohesive group: (p. 270) A group setting in which members like one another and have a sense of camaraderie.

collaboration: (p. 246) A way of approaching conflict by treating it as a mutual problem-solving challenge.

collectivistic culture: (p. 80) A culture that values the needs, goals, and views of the community or group above those of an individual. Collectivistic cultures also value the importance of belonging to groups that look after one another in exchange for loyalty.

communication: (p. 5) The process through which people use messages to generate meanings within and across contexts, cultures, channels, and media.

communication accommodation theory: (p. 83) The idea that people are especially motivated to adapt their communication when they seek social approval, wish to establish relationships with others, and view others' language use as appropriate.

communication apprehension: (p. 273) The fear or anxiety associated with real or anticipated communication with others.

communication climate: (p. 295) The emotional tone established within a group.

communication competence: (p. 19) The process of consistently communicating in ways that are appropriate, effective, and ethical.

communication privacy management theory: (p. 223) The idea that individuals create informational boundaries by carefully choosing the kind of private information they reveal and the people with whom they share it.

communication rules: (p. 224) Conditions governing what people can (and can't) talk about, how they can discuss such topics, and who else should have access to this information.

communication skills: (p. 23) Repeatable goal-directed behaviors and behavioral patterns that enable people to improve the quality of their interpersonal encounters and relationships.

companionate love: (p. 198) An intense form of liking defined by emotional investment and the close intertwining of two people's lives.

comparison/contrast presentation: (p. 410) A speech that presents the similarities and differences between ideas, things, events, or people.

competence: (p. 433) During public speeches, the degree of expertise your audience thinks you have regarding your speech topic.

competition: (p. 246) Confronting others and pursuing your own goals to the exclusion of theirs.

compose: (p. 317) The third step in the process of preparing a speech, in which you develop your speech structure and main ideas, arranging them into a coherent and engaging presentation, and plan any visual aids.

compromise: (p. 250) What happens when the parties involved in a conflict change their goals and actions to make them compatible.

concept map: (p. 320) A drawing showing connections among related ideas, which helps you expand on one idea with more specific topics.

conclusion: (p. 439) The third element in deductive reasoning, in which you show the relationship between your general (or major) premise and your specific (or minor) premise.

conflict: (p. 240) A communication process between people who perceive incompatible goals or interference in achieving their objective.

congruent messages: (p. 141) Messages in which the sender's verbal and nonverbal behaviors match.

connective: (p. 352) A word or phrase that links ideas together in a speech.

connotative meaning: (p. 119) The meaning you associate with a word based on your life experiences.

consensual validation: (p. 337) In evaluating your sources for a speech, this occurs when other sources agree with or use the same information you're considering using.

consensus: (p. 305) What occurs when all group members support a given course of action on a decision.

constitutive rules: (p. 119) Guidelines that define word meaning according to a particular language's vocabulary.

content-oriented listeners: (p. 175) Those who prefer to be intellectually challenged by messages. They enjoy hearing all sides of an argument and thoroughly evaluate what's been said before drawing conclusions.

contexts: (p. 6) Situations in which communication occurs. Context includes the physical locations, backgrounds, genders, ages, moods, and relationships of the communicators, as well as the time of day.

cooperative principle: (p. 123) The idea that you should make your verbal messages honest, relevant, and clear, as the situation requires.

cover letter: (p. A-15) A statement written by a job applicant that introduces him- or herself and highlights qualifications for the job in question.

credibility: (p. 432) An audience's perception of a speaker's trustworthiness and the validity of the information provided in the speech.

critical self-reflection: (p. 35) A special kind of self-awareness that focuses on evaluating and improving your communication.

cues-filtered-out model: (p. 96) Mediated communication in which many of the cues vital for making sense of messages (facial expressions, tone of voice) are not available, which makes mediated communication more difficult to understand than face-to-face communication.

culture: (p. 74) The established, coherent set of beliefs, attitudes, values, and practices shared by a large group of people.

cumulative annoyance: (p. 243) A result of avoiding conflict, in which your repressed resentment grows as your mental list of complaints about other people builds up.

cyberbullying: (p. 106) Persistent online harassment to exert power, cause social embarrassment, inflict emotional pain, or damage a person's reputation.

deception: (p. 130) The deliberate use of uninformative, untruthful, irrelevant, or vague language for the purpose of misleading others.

decision making: (p. 303) The process of making choices among alternatives.

deductive reasoning: (p. 439) The process of starting with a generally held principle and then showing how a specific instance relates to that principle.

defamation: (p. 133) Intentionally false communication that harms a person's reputation.

delivery outline: (p. 360) A set of notes that helps you keep track of your ideas while you're presenting your speech to an audience.

democratic leadership style: (p. 290) A leadership style in which the leader invites input from group members and encourages shared decision making.

demographics: (p. 323) Categorical groupings that make it easier to target people depending on their age, sex, education level, group memberships (religious or political associations), socioeconomic status, family status (single, married, divorced, partnered, with children or without), and cultural background.

denotative meaning: (p. 119) The literal, or dictionary, definition of a word, as agreed on by members of a culture.

dialect: (p. 120) A variation on language shared by a large group of people in a particular region or among members of a particular co-culture.

differentiating: (p. 208) In the first stage of coming apart in a relationship, the point at which the beliefs, attitudes, and values that distinguish you from your partner dominate your thoughts and communications.

digital deception: (p. 107) The act of sending messages that intentionally mislead or create a false belief in recipients.

direct quotation: (p. 349) In a speech, repeating the exact words a person said or wrote in order to make a point.

dirty secrets: (p. 254) Messages that are honest in content but have been kept hidden to protect someone's feelings.

disclaimer: (p. 381) A phrase that removes responsibility for the statement you're making.

display rules: (p. 82) Guidelines for when, where, and how to appropriately express emotion.

dominance: (p. 156) Interpersonal behaviors used to exert power or influence over others.

domination: (p. 249) What happens when one person or group of people get their way by influencing others to accommodate and abandon their goals.

dyadic: (p. 190) Involving pairs of people, or dyads.

effectiveness: (p. 20) The ability to use communication to accomplish self-presentation, instrumental, and relationship goals.

egocentric role: (p. 269) A role that occurs when one team member's communication disrupts the group's efforts.

elaboration likelihood model: (p. 430) A theory that proposes that listeners who are intensely interested in your topic and can easily understand your presentation will put more effort into thinking about your persuasive message than listeners who don't care about or understand your speech topic.

embarrassment: (p. 42) Feelings of shame, humiliation, and sadness that come when we lose face.

emblems: (p. 145) Gestures that symbolize a specific verbal meaning within a given culture, such as the "thumbs up" or the "V for victory" sign.

empathy: (p. 53) Understanding of another person's perspective and awareness of his or her feelings in an attempt to identify with that individual.

empathy deficit: (p. 105) The dramatic reduction in your ability to experience the other person's feelings during mediated communication.

empathy mindset: (p. 53) Beliefs about whether empathy is something that can be developed and controlled.

employment interviews: (p. A-4) Interviews that manage an organization's personnel.

escalation: (p. 246) A dramatic rise in emotional intensity and unproductive communication.

ethics: (p. 21) The set of moral principles that guide your behavior toward others. Ethical communication consistently displays respect, kindness, and compassion.

ethnocentrism: (p. 85) The belief that your own cultural beliefs, attitudes, values, and practices are superior to those of all other cultures.

ethos: (p. 432) A speaker's credibility, which, according to Greek philosopher Aristotle, determines whether he or she can influence listeners.

evaluating: (p. 168) Comparing newly received information against your past knowledge to check its accuracy and validity.

example: (p. 348) A specific reference that illustrates an idea.

exit interviews: (p. A-4) Interviews to identify why an employee is leaving a job. Resulting insights are used to improve management practices.

experimenting: (p. 206) A stage of coming together with someone that involves exchanging demographic information (e.g., names, college majors, hometowns).

expository presentation: (p. 407) A presentation that defines a term, explains a concept, or describes an object or a place to your audience.

extemporaneous speaking: (p. 376) Composing a preparation outline ahead of time (as in *manuscript speaking*) and then reducing your preparation outline to a brief speaking outline that allows you to add or eliminate information as needed during your presentation (as in *impromptu speaking*).

face: (p. 41) The positive self you want others to see and believe.

fallacy: (p. 441) A claim that isn't true or is based on inadequate or inaccurate evidence.

family: (p. 200) A network of people who share their lives over long periods of time and are bound by marriage, blood, or commitment; who consider themselves a family; and who share a significant history and anticipated future of functioning in a family relationship.

feedback: (p. 9) The verbal and nonverbal messages coming from recipients in response to messages from senders.

fields of experience: (p. 9) The beliefs, attitudes, values, and experiences that each participant brings to a communication event.

flaming: (p. 105) Saying vicious and aggressive things online that you would never say in person.

foot-in-the-door technique: (p. 446) A persuasive technique that involves asking your audience to agree to a small action in the hope that you'll gain their compliance over time.

formal role: (p. 267) An assigned position that a group member takes on by appointment or election.

forming: (p. 265) The group developmental phase in which members become acquainted with one another and seek to understand the task.

friendships: (p. 201) Voluntary interpersonal relationships characterized by intimacy and liking.

functional résumé: (p. A-15) A résumé that focuses on how your skills and experiences relate to the specific job you're applying for.

functional view of leadership: (p. 292) Considers the types of communication behaviors that help a group work toward its goal. If you volunteer to put together the slide deck for a group project presentation, you are providing useful task leadership.

fundamental attribution error: (p. 48) The tendency to attribute others' behaviors to internal rather than external forces.

gender: (p. 65) The set of social, psychological, and cultural attributes that characterize a person as male or female.

gender continuum: (p. 62) A way of viewing and understanding gender which emphasizes that individuals possess complex combinations of attributes traditionally thought of as masculine and feminine.

gender fluid: (p. 63) A type of gender identity in which an individual does not identify as being either male or female, and their leanings toward one gender or another may fluctuate.

gender identity: (p. 64) An individual's inner sense of being male, female, gender-fluid, gender-nonconforming, or gender-neutral.

gender polarization: (p. 62) A way of viewing and understanding gender which emphasizes a binary male-female construction of gender.

gender roles: (p. 67) The shared expectations for conduct and behaviors that are deemed appropriate for men and women as taught by society. These roles tend to be rigid and adhere to binary ideas about gender.

gender socialization: (p. 65) The process of cultural training by which individuals learn the gender norms that are expected of them in a society.

general purpose: (p. 319) When preparing a speech, your reason for giving the presentation.

gestalt: (p. 49) A general impression of a person that's either positive or negative.

group brainstorming: (p. 302) Occurs when a team focuses on generating as many ideas as possible to solve a defined problem, often integrated with step three of the structured problem-solving process.

group role: (p. 267) Also known as an *informal role*, a specific pattern of behavior and communication that a member of a group develops from interacting over time.

groupthink: (p. 297) A phenomenon that occurs when group members want to maintain harmony more than anything else and so avoid challenging one another's ideas.

halo effect: (p. 50) A tendency to positively interpret the behavior of a person for whom you have formed a positive Gestalt.

haptics: (p. 147) A nonverbal code that represents messages conveyed through touch.

hashtag activism: (p. 95) Using social media in a community-based fashion to heighten public awareness of important causes.

hearing: (p. 166) Physically processing the sound that others have produced, and mentally focusing your attention on it.

hedging: (p. 381) Using words that lessen a message's impact, such as *sorta*, *kinda*, and *somewhat*.

hierarchy of needs: (p. 442) A theory developed by psychologist Abraham Maslow that posits that much of human behavior is motivated by the desire to meet basic life needs.

high-context cultures: (p. 80) Cultures in which people use relatively vague and ambiguous language, and even silence, to convey important meanings. They talk indirectly, using hints or suggestions, and therefore don't feel the need to provide a lot of explicit information.

honesty: (p. 123) Sharing information you're certain about and never presenting information as true when you know it's false.

horn effect: (p. 50) A tendency to negatively interpret the behavior of a person for whom you have formed a negative Gestalt.

identity-based digital deception: (p. 107) The act of falsely misrepresenting an identity or gender by exaggerating or enhancing aspects of your identity online.

"I" language: (p. 124) Phrases that emphasize ownership of your feelings, opinions, and beliefs.

I-It: (p. 192) An interpersonal communication approach in which you regard people as objects to observe, that are there to be manipulated and exploited.

I-Thou: (p. 192) An interpersonal communication approach in which you consider an individual with an open mind, giving the person the same attention and respect you expect for yourself.

illustrators: (p. 145) Gestures used to accent or illustrate a verbal message.

immediacy: (p. 377) A sense of closeness that your audience feels toward you as a speaker.

impersonal communication: (p. 193) Exchanges that have a negligible perceived impact on your thoughts, emotions, behaviors, and relationships.

impression: (p. 49) A mental image of who a person is and how you feel about him or her.

impromptu speaking: (p. 374) The act of making public remarks with little or no time for preparation or rehearsal.

incongruent messages: (p. 141) Messages in which the sender's verbal and nonverbal behaviors contradict each other.

individualistic culture: (p. 80) A culture that values independence and personal goals over group goals.

inductive reasoning: (p. 439) Connecting a set of specific, related facts to arrive at a more general conclusion.

information interview: (p. 335) A meeting in which you ask questions to gain knowledge or understanding about a particular topic.

information overload: (p. 403) What happens when the amount and nature of material exceeds a listener's ability to process it.

informative speech: (pp. 319, 402) A speech that educates your audience about a topic, demonstrates how something works, tells a story about events or people, or explains similarities and differences between things or ideas.

ingroupers: (p. 46) People you consider fundamentally similar to you because they share your interests, beliefs, attitudes, and values.

initiating: (p. 205) A stage of coming together when you size up a new person to decide whether you want to get to know that person better.

instrumental goals: (p. 7) Practical objectives you want to achieve or tasks you want to accomplish.

integrating: (p. 206) A stage of coming together when your and your partner's personalities seem to blend.

integrative agreements: (p. 250) Creative solutions that enable all sides to keep and reach their original goals.

intensifier: (p. 381) An unnecessary word that overemphasizes a point, such as *really* and *totally*.

intensifying: (p. 206) A stage of coming together when you find yourself feeling strongly attracted to or interested in another person and begin to share more personal information about yourself.

interaction: (p. 6) The result of a series of messages exchanged between people, whether face-to-face or online.

interactive communication model: (p. 9) A model that views communication as a process involving senders and receivers but that is influenced by two additional factors: *feedback* and *fields of experience*.

intercultural communication: (p. 74) The communication you engage in when you interact with those who belong to a culture different from your own.

intercultural competence: (p. 84) The ability to communicate appropriately, effectively, and ethically with people from diverse backgrounds.

internal preview: (p. 353) A statement that signals to your audience what you are going to tell them before you actually do.

internal summary: (p. 353) A short review of information that you've discussed within a section of the speech.

interpersonal communication: (pp. 16, 190) A dynamic form of communication between two people in which the messages exchanged significantly influence their thoughts, emotions, behaviors, and relationships.

interpersonal relationships: (p. 194) The emotional, mental, and physical involvements that you forge with others through communication.

interpretation: (p. 46) The third step of the perception process, in which you assign meaning to the information you have selected.

interpreting: (p. 167) Identifying any implications (or connotative meanings) suggested in the person's words and considering what action the person is trying to perform.

interview protocol: (p. A-4) A list of questions, written in a logical order, that guide the interview.

interviewee: (p. A-2) The person at the interview who answers the question.

interviewer: (p. A-2) The person at the interview who determines the interview purpose, plans the questions, and manages the flow of the conversation.

interviewing: (p. A-2) A planned and structured conversation between two or more persons that uses questions and answers to meet a specific purpose.

intimacy: (pp. 155, 218) A feeling of closeness and bonding that exists between us and our relationship partners.

investigate: (p. 316) The second step in preparing a speech, in which you plan a research strategy, conduct research, and evaluate the resources found.

kinesics: (p. 144) Body movement communication that encompasses most of the cues people typically think of as nonverbal communication: facial expressions, eye contact, gestures, and postures.

kitchen sinking: (p. 246) A form of escalation in which combatants in a conflict hurl assorted accusations at each other that have little to do with the disagreement at hand.

laissez-faire leadership style: (p. 290) A leadership style in which the leader provides little direction or structure, leaving the group to maintain control of what happens.

leadership: (p. 288) The ability to influence and direct others to meet group goals.

leading questions: (p. A-6) Questions that point the respondent to an answer you prefer.

leave-taking: (p. A-13) The process of ending an interview, often signaled by asking the final question.

liking: (p. 198) A feeling of affection and respect that we often have for our friends, extended family members, and coworkers.

linear communication model: (p. 8) A depiction of communication as an activity in which information flows in one direction, from a starting point to an end point.

listening: (p. 166) The six-stage process of hearing, understanding, interpreting, evaluating, remembering, and responding to others' communication.

listening functions: (p. 170) The five general purposes that listening serves: to comprehend, to discern, to analyze, to appreciate, and to provide support.

listening style: (p. 175) An individual's habitual pattern of listening behaviors, which reflects one's attitudes, beliefs, and predispositions about listening.

logos: (p. 435) The development of logical reasons for your position.

loving: (p. 198) A more intense emotional connection consisting of intimacy, caring, and attachment.

low-context cultures: (p. 80) Cultures that are often individualistic, in which people tend not to presume that others share their beliefs, attitudes, and values. They strive to be informative, clear, and direct in their communication, and they openly express their views and try to persuade others to accept them.

main point: (p. 345) One of the key statements or principles that support your speech thesis and help your audience understand your message.

maintenance role: (p. 268) A role in which a group member communicates to build trusting and appreciative interpersonal relationships.

major premise: (p. 439) The general statement you believe your audience will accept as true.

manuscript speaking: (p. 375) A public speech that is based on a written text that you either read word for word or commit to memory.

mask: (p. 42) The public self designed to strategically veil the private self.

mass media: (p. 92) Mediated communication vehicles that involve the sending of messages from content creators to huge, relatively anonymous audiences.

mediated communication: (pp. 16, 92) Communication in which the communicators are separated, or "mediated," by some type of technological device.

meeting agenda: (p. 307) A structured, written outline that guides communication among meeting participants by showing which topics will be discussed, in what order, and (often) for how long.

meeting minutes: (p. 309) A written record of the discussion, actions, and decisions sent to everyone who attended, and to anyone who did not attend but needs to know what happened.

mere exposure effect: (p. 194) The phenomenon that you're more likely to pursue relationships with people with whom you have frequent contact, whether face-to-face or online.

message: (p. 6) The "package" of information transported during communication.

message-based digital deception: (p. 107) The manipulation of information with the intent of misleading recipients.
minor premise: (p. 439) A specific instance of a general claim.
misunderstanding: (p. 124) Misperceiving the meaning of another's verbal communication.
mnemonics: (p. 169) Devices that aid memory.
modality: (p. 6) Any form of exchanging communication messages, such as face-to-face interaction, photos, social media posts, texting, email, phone calls, or handwritten notes.
monotone: (p. 379) An unvarying vocal pitch and tone in conversation or public presentation.
motivated sequence: (p. 435) A five-step method for organizing a persuasive speech about a problem which appeals to an audience's attention, need to be concerned, satisfaction, ability to visualize the argument, and desire to take action.
motivational appeal: (p. 442) An explicit statement (an example, a story, or testimony) that speaks to the needs and feelings of your audience.
multitask: (p. 172) Shifting attention back and forth between many different tasks at once.
narrative presentation: (p. 408) A presentation that describes an event or tells a story about a person.
negative feedback: (p. 170) Using verbal and nonverbal cues to show that you're not listening to a speaker.
neutral questions: (p. A-6) Questions that do not point the respondent toward any specific answer.
noise: (p. 8) Distractions that change how the message is received. Noise may originate outside the communicators, as in poor phone reception.
nonverbal communication: (p. 140) The intentional or unintentional transmission of meaning through an individual's nonspoken physical and behavioral cues.
norming: (p. 266) The group developmental phase in which members agree about the plans for working toward the goal and who will do what.
norms: (p. 270) The expectations about behavior within a group.
online disinhibition: (p. 104) The ability to feel comfortable saying things—good and bad—online that you would never say to someone face-to-face.
online harassment: (p. 106) Mediated messages perceived by the recipient as disturbing, threatening, or obsessive.
open questions: (p. A-6) Questions that give interviewees a lot of freedom in formulating their responses.
oral language style: (p. 378) Using language that is similar to how people talk.
organization: (p. 45) The second step of the perception process, in which you structure the information you've received through your senses into a coherent pattern in your mind.
outgroupers: (p. 46) People you consider fundamentally different from you because of their beliefs, attitudes, and values.
paraphrasing: (pp. 350, A-8) Providing your own summary of another person's words or experience.
passionate love: (p. 198) A state of intense emotional and physical longing for union with another person.
pathos: (p. 442) Appeals to the audience's emotions, allowing them to connect personally with your topic.
people-oriented listeners: (p. 175) Those who view listening as an opportunity to establish bonds between themselves and others.
perception: (p. 44) The process of selecting, organizing, and interpreting information from your senses.
perception-checking: (p. 52) A five-step process to test your impressions of someone and to avoid errors in judgment. It involves reviewing your knowledge of the person, assessing attributions you've made, questioning your impressions, and sharing and checking your impressions with the person.
performance or appraisal interviews: (p. A-4) Usually annual reviews of an employee to evaluate his or her work and to set new goals.
performing: (p. 266) The group developmental phase in which members actually make the required contributions for completing the task. At this phase, group members' efforts are well coordinated and directed to achieving the goal.
peripheral route: (p. 430) The way audiences who are less motivated about the topic or who don't have the time or knowledge needed to understand the information may process your speech. They may selectively listen and are easily distracted.
persuasive speech: (pp. 319, 428) A speech that reinforces or changes listeners' attitudes and beliefs and may motivate them to take action.
plagiarism: (p. 331) The misrepresentation of others' works as your own, commonly occurring when you use someone else's exact words or summarize a unique idea without crediting the source.
positive feedback: (p. 170) Using verbal and nonverbal cues to show that you're listening and are comprehending specific comments.
positivity: (p. 228) A tactic in sustaining a healthy relationship by communicating in a cheerful and optimistic fashion, doing unsolicited favors, and giving unexpected gifts.
power: (pp. 75, 245) The ability to influence or control important resources, events, and people.
power distance: (p. 83) The degree to which people in a particular culture view the unequal distribution of power as acceptable.
powerful speech style: (p. 377) Using verbal and nonverbal behaviors to present yourself and your message confidently and thus gain the respect of your listeners.
powerless language: (p. 381) Words suggesting you're uncertain about your message or yourself.
prejudice: (p. 77) Stereotypes that reflect rigid attitudes, positive or negative, toward groups and their members.

prejudiced language: (p. 128) Speech that displays contempt, dislike, or disdain for a group or its members.

preparation outline: (p. 360) Details your presentation's overall structure and helps you plan the order, flow, and logic of your speech, ensuring there are no weaknesses or missing elements.

presentation aid: (p. 388) A tool used to display the visuals you've selected to help explain or illustrate your points.

primary groups: (p. 264) The individuals who meet your basic life, psychological, and social needs.

primary questions: (p. A-6) Questions that guide the conversation and are written into the interview protocol.

primary resources: (p. 332) Direct accounts, straight from the original source, such as scientific reports, firsthand descriptions of events, diary writings, photographs of events, congressional-hearing transcripts, and speech manuscripts.

principle of subordination: (p. 361) A practice in composing a preparation outline that ensures that you're making valid arguments and that your claims are well supported and logical.

problem-solution pattern: (p. 352) An organizational pattern that allows you to describe a problem and then present a solution that will help you motivate listeners to take action to address a challenge.

process or demonstration presentation: (p. 407) A presentation that explains how something works or shows the audience how to do something.

pronunciation: (p. 381) The way you say words.

proposition of fact: (p. 429) Establishes whether something is true or not or whether an event will or won't happen.

proposition of policy: (p. 429) Argues about whether an action should or should not be taken.

proposition of value: (p. 429) Urges a judgment on a topic or explains why something is good or bad.

proxemics: (p. 147) How close or far away you position yourself from others while communicating.

pseudo-conflict: (p. 243) The perception that there's a conflict between you and others when there really isn't.

pseudo-listening: (p. 179) Behaving as if you're paying attention though you're really not.

public communication: (p. 16) See *public speaking*.

public speaking: (p. 316) The process of preparing and delivering a message to an audience to achieve a specific purpose. Also known as *public communication*.

qualifiers: (p. 439) Language that indicates how certain you are about your major premise.

race: (p. 46) A classification of people based on common ancestry or descent that is judged almost exclusively by a person's physical features.

rapport building: (p. A-8) Exchanging messages that create a bond and a positive first impression that help you quickly set the tone for an interview.

reasoning: (p. 439) The act of turning all the material you've gathered into the logical basis for your speech, identifying patterns in your support materials, and summarizing those patterns into arguments that become the main points of your speech.

receiver: (p. 8) The person for whom a message is intended or to whom it is delivered.

reciprocal liking: (p. 195) When someone you're interested in makes it clear that he or she is also interested in you.

regulative rules: (p. 119) Guidelines that control how you use language.

regulators: (p. 145) Gestures used to help control turn taking during interpersonal encounters—for example, averting eye contact to avoid someone or zipping up book bags as a class to signal to a professor that the lecture should end.

rehearse: (p. 317) The fourth step in the process of preparing a speech, in which you practice a presentation on your own and in front of others, inviting feedback for improvements.

relational dialectics: (p. 223) Competing impulses and tensions that arise between ourselves and relational partners.

relational maintenance: (p. 228) Efforts that partners make to keep their relationship strong and ensure satisfaction from the relationship. They may show devotion by making time to talk, spending time together, and offering help or support to each other.

relationship goals: (p. 7) Building, maintaining, or terminating bonds with others through interpersonal communication.

remembering: (p. 169) Recalling stored information back into your conscious mind.

resources: (p. 194) The valued qualities people possess that compel us to pursue relationships with others.

responding: (p. 170) Communicating your attention and comprehension to the speaker.

résumé: (p. A-15) A written summary of your education, work experience, and skills.

revise: (p. 317) The fifth step in the process of preparing a speech, in which you adapt the speech based on the feedback you received while rehearsing.

rhetoric: (p. 13) The theory and practice of persuading others through speech.

rhetorical proof: (p. 433) One of the three elements of a speech that make it persuasive to an audience: credibility (ethos), good logical reasons (logos), and appeals to their emotions (pathos).

romantic relationships: (p. 197) Interpersonal involvements in which the participants perceive the bond as romantic.

secondary groups: (p. 264) People with whom you want to achieve specific goals or perform tasks, such as an event.

secondary questions: (p. A-6) Questions in an interview that evolve out of the conversation and can help you clarify vague answers.

secondary resources: (p. 333) Works that analyze and interpret primary resources, such as magazine articles, biographies, textbooks, and newspaper articles.

selection: (p. 45) The first step of *perception* that requires you to focus your attention on certain sights, sounds, tastes, touches, or smells in your environment.

selection interviews: (p. A-4) The kind of interviews that employers use to determine whether applicants have the education, experience, and proper attitude required for a job.

selective listening: (p. 179) Listening only to parts of a message (those that are the most interesting to the listener) and dismissing the rest.

self: (p. 34) The evolving blend of who you are, including your self-awareness, self-concept, and self-esteem.

self-awareness: (p. 34) The ability to view yourself as a unique person distinct from your surrounding environment and to reflect on your thoughts, feelings, and behaviors.

self-concept: (p. 35) Your overall idea of who you are based on the beliefs, attitudes, and values you have about yourself.

self-disclosure: (p. 217) Revealing private information about yourself to others.

Self-Discrepancy Theory: (p. 37) The idea that your self-esteem results from comparing two mental standards: your *ideal* self (the qualities you want to possess) and your *ought* self (the person you think others want you to be).

self-esteem: (p. 37) The overall value you assign to yourself.

self-fulfilling prophecies: (p. 37) Predictions you make about interactions that cause you to communicate in ways that make those predictions come true.

self-monitoring: (p. 20) The process of observing our own communication and the norms of the situation to make appropriate communication choices.

self-presentation goals: (p. 6) In interpersonal encounters, presenting yourself in certain ways so that others perceive you as you want them to.

self-serving bias: (p. 48) A tendency to credit yourself for successes by making an internal attribution.

Self-Verification Theory: (p. 37) The idea that you often choose your relational partners based on how well they support your self-concept.

sender: (p. 8) The individual who generates the information to be communicated, packages it into a message, and chooses one or more channels for sending it.

separation: (p. 249) What happens when one or more of the people involved in a conflict terminate communication.

sex: (p. 63) A category assigned at birth determined by anatomical and biological traits, such as external genitalia, internal reproductive organs, hormones, and sex chromosomes.

sexual orientation: (p. 39) An enduring emotional, romantic, sexual, or affectionate attraction to others that exists along a continuum from exclusive homosexuality to exclusive heterosexuality and that includes various forms of bisexuality.

shared leadership: (p. 288) Each group member having the capacity to influence and direct the group in achieving its goals.

signpost: (p. 353) A brief word—often, a number—that quickly introduces a new idea.

situational view of leadership: (p. 291) A view that maintains that effective leadership is determined by the group's readiness to take on a task, including its motivation and group members' experience and knowledge.

small group: (p. 262) Three or more interdependent persons who share a common identity and who communicate to achieve common goals or purposes.

small group communication: (p. 16) Communication that involves three or more interdependent persons who share a common identity (such as membership on a team) and who communicate to achieve common goals or purposes.

sniping: (p. 254) Communicating in a negative way and then leaving the encounter.

social bookmarking: (p. 331) Free web-based services that let you save, organize, and keep brief notes about your online resources.

social comparison: (p. 34) Observing and assigning meaning to others' behaviors and then comparing their behaviors to your own.

social exchange theory: (p. 194) The idea that you'll feel drawn to individuals who offer you substantial benefits (positive things you like and want) with few costs (negative things demanded of you in return).

social information processing theory: (p. 96) The idea that people communicating through social media compensate for the lack of nonverbal feedback by taking more care with choosing their words.

social loafing: (p. 269) A common egocentric group role in which one teammate relies on other members to do all the work.

social media: (p. 93) Communication vehicles that allow communicators to send and receive messages in real time or across time intervals in order to manage their personal and professional relationships.

social penetration theory: (p. 217) A model that suggests that you reveal information about yourself to others by peeling back, or penetrating, layers of yourself.

spatial pattern: (p. 352) An organizational pattern that shows listeners how things are related within a physical space.

special-occasion speech: (p. 319) A speech intended to entertain, celebrate, commemorate, or inspire. These include introducing someone at an event, accepting or giving an award, commemorating an event or a person, or giving a toast.

specific purpose statement: (p. 326) One complete sentence summarizing the goal of your speech.

speech anxiety: (p. 385) Being nervous about speaking in public.

speech thesis: (p. 344) One complete sentence that identifies the central idea of your presentation for your audience.

speech topic: (p. 319) The specific content you will present.

stagnating: (p. 208) The stage of coming apart in a relationship when communication between partners comes to a standstill because there are few safe topics to talk about.

statistic: (p. 348) A number that summarizes a formal observation about a phenomenon.

Stereotype Content Model: (p. 77) The idea that prejudice centers on two judgments made about others: how warm and friendly they are, and how competent they are. These judgments create two possible kinds of prejudice: benevolent and hostile.

stereotyping: (p. 51) Categorizing people into a social group and then evaluating them based on information you have related to the group.

storming: (p. 265) The group developmental phase in which members express different ideas about how to approach the task and who will take on leadership roles.

structural improvements: (p. 250) Clarifying rules that parties involved in a conflict use to change their relationship and improve the balance of power to prevent further disputes.

structured problem-solving approach: (p. 300) A problem-solving approach in which teams collect information on the nature and scope of the problem facing them, then systematically search for a solution.

style view of leadership: (p. 290) Focuses on the behaviors that leaders use to influence others.

submissiveness: (p. 156) The willingness to allow others to exert power over you.

subpoint: (p. 347) One of the specific principles derived from breaking down and further dividing main points to help you explain an idea more clearly.

substantive conflict: (p. 298) Disagreements about the group's tasks, procedures, or decision options.

sudden-death statements: (p. 254) Spontaneous declarations that the relationship is over, even though the people involved did not consider termination a possibility before the conflict.

supportive communication: (p. 231) Sharing messages that express emotional support and that offer personal assistance, such as telling a person of your sympathy or listening to someone without judging.

symbols: (p. 119) Items used to represent other things, ideas, or events.

synchronous communication: (p. 96) A back-and-forth exchange of messages that occurs in real time (by phone or instant message, for example), best for communicating difficult or complicated messages.

task role: (p. 268) A role that involves exchanging information about duties or goals important to your group.

terminating: (p. 208) The stage in ending a relationship when the partners come together for a final encounter to give a sense of closure and resolution.

testimony: (p. 349) A means of supporting a main point that relies on the words or experiences of others.

think: (p. 316) The first step in preparing a speech, in which you determine the purpose of your speech, choose the topic, and consider how to adapt it to your audience.

time-oriented listeners: (p. 176) Those who prefer brief, concise messages to save time.

topical pattern: (p. 351) A pattern that organizes main points into categories or subtopics.

traits view of leadership: (p. 289) Assumes that all talented leaders share certain personal and physical characteristics.

transactional communication model: (p. 10) A depiction of communication in which participants mutually influence one another's communication behavior.

transgender: (p. 64) Term used to describe individuals whose gender identity does not correspond to the sex that they were assigned at birth.

transitional phrase: (p. 353) A phrase that indicates that you're shifting to another point or idea.

trolling: (p. 106) Posting flame messages on purpose to start arguments online.

uncertainty avoidance: (p. 81) The degree to which a culture tolerates and accepts unpredictability.

understanding: (p. 167) Recognizing the literal (or denotative) meaning of the words the other person has said.

values: (p. 325) Strongly held beliefs that guide our behaviors.

verbal aggression: (p. 129) Using language to attack others' self-concepts—their appearance, behavior, or character—rather than their positions.

verbal communication: (p. 118) The use of spoken or written language to interact with others.

virtual small group: (p. 264) Any team of three or more people who communicate primarily through technology to achieve common goals.

vocal pitch: (p. 379) The high and low registers of your voice.

vocal rate: (p. 379) How rapidly you speak.

vocal tone: (p. 379) The richness and sound quality of your voice.

vocal volume: (p. 381) How loudly or quietly you speak.

vocalics: (p. 146) Vocal characteristics, such as tone, pitch, loudness, and speech rate, used to communicate nonverbal messages.

vocalized pauses and fillers: (p. 383) Words such as *um*, *ah*, and *you know* that create hesitations in the flow of your speech.

voluntary audience: (p. 326) Listeners who attend a presentation out of self-interest or to fulfill some personal need.

warranting value: (p. 99) The degree to which online information is supported by other people and outside evidence.

"we" language: (p. 125) Phrases that emphasize inclusion and enhance feelings of connection and similarity.

workplace relationships: (p. 202) Affiliations you have with professional peers, supervisors, subordinates, or mentors.

world-mindedness: (p. 84) The ability to practice and demonstrate acceptance and respect toward other cultures' beliefs, values, and customs.

written language style: (p. 378) Language that is more formal and detailed than an oral language style.

"you" language: (p. 124) Phrases that place the focus of attention and blame on others.

References

Acuna, K. (2018, Jun 18). The "Incredibles 2" villain was originally a lot different: Here's why it was changed. Retrieved from https://www.thisisinsider.com/incredibles-2-villain-originally-a-man-2018-6

Adelman, M. B., & Frey, L. R. (1994). The pilgrim must embark: Creating and sustaining community in a residential facility for people with AIDS. In L. R. Frey (Ed.), *Group communication in context: Studies of natural groups* (pp. 3–22). Hillsdale, NJ: Lawrence Erlbaum.

Afifi, T. D., & Steuber, K. (2010). The cycle of concealment model. *Journal of Social and Personal Relationships, 27*(8), 1019–1034.

Afifi, T. D., McManus, T., Hutchinson, S., & Baker, B. (2007). Inappropriate parental divorce disclosures, the factors that prompt them, and their impact on parents' and adolescents' well-being. *Communication Monographs, 74*(1), 78–102.

Afifi, T. D., McManus, T., Steuber, K., & Coho, A. (2009). Verbal avoidance and dissatisfaction in intimate conflict situations. *Human Communication Research, 35,* 357–383.

Allen, J. A., Sands, S. J., Mueller, S. L., Frear, K. A., Mudd, M., & Rogelberg, S. G. (2012). Employees' feelings about more meetings: An overt analysis and recommendations for improving meetings. *Management Research Review, 35*(5), 405–418. Retrieved from https://doi.org/10.1108/014091712112223

Allport, G. W. (1954). *The nature of prejudice.* Cambridge, MA: Addison-Wesley.

Altman, I., & Taylor, D. A. (1973). *Social penetration: The development of interpersonal relationships.* New York, NY: Holt, Rinehart & Winston.

American Psychological Association. (n.d.). Lesbian, gay, bisexual, transgender. Retrieved from https://www.apa.org/topics/lgbt/index.aspx

American Psychological Association. (2012). Guidelines for psychological practice with lesbian, gay, and bisexual clients. *American Psychologist, 67*(1), 10–42. doi:10.1037/a0024659

American Psychological Association. (2015). Guidelines for psychological practice with transgender and gender nonconforming people. *American Psychologist, 70*(9), 832–864.

Anderson, C. M., & Martin, M. M. (1999). The relationship of argumentativeness and verbal aggression to cohesion, consensus, and satisfaction in small groups. *Communication Reports, 12,* 21–31.

Anderson, N. H. (1981). *Foundations of information integration theory.* Orlando, FL: Academic Press.

Arasaratnam, L. A. (2006). Further testing of a new model of intercultural communication competence. *Communication Research Reports, 23,* 93–99.

Aron, A., Fisher, H., Strong, G., Acevedo, B., Riela, S., & Tsapelas, I. (2008). Falling in love. In S. Sprecher, A. Wenzel, & J. Harvey (Eds.), *Handbook of relationship initiation* (pp. 315–336). New York, NY: Psychology Press.

Aubert, B. A., & Kelsey, B. L. (2003). Further understanding of trust and performance in virtual teams. *Small Group Research, 34,* 575–618.

Ayres, J. (1988). Coping with speech anxiety: The power of positive thinking. *Communication Education, 37,* 289–296.

Ayres, J. (1996). Speech preparation processes and speech apprehension. *Communication Education, 45,* 228–235.

Ayres, J. (2005). Performance visualization and behavioral disruption: A clarification. *Communication Reports, 18,* 55–63.

Ayres, J., & Ayres, T. A. (2003). Using images to enhance the impact of visualization. *Communication Reports, 16,* 47–55.

Ayres, J., & Hopf, T. S. (1987). Visualization, systematic desensitization, and rational emotive therapy: A comparative evaluation. *Communication Education, 36,* 236–240.

Bailenson, J. N., Beall, A. C., Loomis, J., Blascovich, J., & Turk, M. (2005). Transformed social interaction, augmented gaze, and social influence in immersive virtual environments. *Human Communication Research, 31*(4), 511–537.

Banas, J. A., & Rains, S. A. (2010). A meta-analysis of research on inoculation theory. *Communication Monographs, 77,* 281–311.

Barker, L. L., & Watson, K. W. (2000). *Listen up.* New York, NY: St. Martin's Press.

Baumeister, R. F., & Leary, M. R. (1995). The need to belong: Desire for interpersonal attachments as a fundamental human motivation. *Psychological Bulletin, 117,* 497–529.

Baxter, L. A. (1990). Dialectical contradictions in relationship development. *Journal of Social and Personal Relationships, 7,* 69–88.

Baym, N. K. (2010). *Personal connections in the digital age.* Digital Media and Society Series. Malden, MA: Polity Press.

Beall, M. L. (2010). Perspectives on intercultural listening. In A. D. Wolvin (Ed.), *Listening and human communication in the 21st century* (pp. 225–238). Oxford, England: Blackwell.

Bell, B. S., & Kozlowski, S. W. J. (2002). A typology of virtual teams: Implications for effective leadership. *Group & Organization Management, 27,* 14–49.

Belman, O. (2014, December). A new way to practice what you preach. *USC News.* Retrieved from https://news.usc.edu/72003/a-new-way-to-practice-what-you-preach/

Benoit, P. J., & Benoit, W. E. (1990). To argue or not to argue. In R. Trapp & J. Schuetz (Eds.), *Perspectives on argumentation: Essays in honor of Wayne Brockriede* (pp. 55–72). Prospect Heights, IL: Waveland Press.

Berenson, T. (2015). The escape room: A Rubik's cube that locks the door behind you. *Time, 186*(8), 54–55.

Berger, C. R., & Bradac, J. J. (1982). *Language and social knowledge: Uncertainty in interpersonal relations.* London, England: Edward Arnold.

Berger, C. R., & Calabrese, R. J. (1975). Some explorations in initial interaction and beyond: Toward a developmental theory of interpersonal communication. *Human Communication Research, 1*, 99–112. doi:10.1111/j.1468-2958.1975.tb00258.x

Berscheid, E. (2002). Emotion. In H. H. Kelley et al. (Eds.), *Close relationships* (2nd ed., pp. 110–168). Clinton Corners, NY: Percheron Press.

Berscheid, E., & Regan, P. (2005). *The psychology of interpersonal relationships*. Upper Saddle River, NJ: Pearson Education.

Berscheid, E., & Walster, E. (1978). *Interpersonal attraction* (2nd ed.). Reading, MA: Addison-Wesley.

Bian, L., Leslie, S.-J., & Cimpian, A. (2017). Gender stereotypes about intellectual ability emerge early and influence children's interests. *Science, 355*, 389–391.

Bianconi, L. (2002). *Culture and identity: Issues of authenticity in another value system*. Paper presented at the XII Sietar-EU Conference, Vienna, Austria.

Birdwhistell, R. L. (1970). *Kinesics and context: Essays on body motion communication*. Philadelphia: University of Pennsylvania Press.

Bleidorn, W., Arslan, R. C., Denissen, J. J. A., Rentfrow, P. J., Gebauer, J. E., Potter, J., & Gosling, S. D. (2016). Age and gender differences in self-esteem: A cross-cultural window. *Journal of Personality and Social Psychology, 111*(3), 396–410.

Blum, R. W., Mmari, K., & Moreau, C. (2017). It begins at 10: How gender expectations shape early adolescence around the world. *Journal of Adolescent Health, 61*, S3–S4.

Bodenhausen, G. V., Macrae, C. N., & Sherman, J. W. (1999). On the dialectics of discrimination: Dual processes in social stereotyping. In S. Chaiken & Y. Trope (Eds.), *Dual process theories in social psychology* (pp. 271–290). New York, NY: Guilford Press.

Bodie, G. D., & Fitch-Hauser, M. (2010). Quantitative research in listening: Explication and overview. In A. D. Wolvin (Ed.), *Listening and human communication in the 21st century* (pp. 46–93). Oxford, England: Blackwell.

Bolden, C. F. (2015). Putting American boots on Martian soil. *Vital Speeches of the Day, 81*(7), 208–210.

Bondurant, T. (2015, October 2). Diamondbacks announcers' selfie shaming needlessly alienates younger fans. *SB Nation*. Retrieved from http://www.sbnation.com/mlb/2015/10/2/9437081/diamondbacks-announcers-selfie-video

Boon, S. D., Deveau, V. L., & Alibhai, A. M. (2009). Payback: The parameters of revenge in romantic relationships. *Journal of Social and Personal Relationships, 26*(6–7), 747–768.

Bornstein, R. F. (1989). Exposure and affect: Overview and meta-analysis of research, 1968–1987. *Psychological Bulletin, 106*, 265–289.

boyd, d. (2007, May 13). Social network sites: Public, private, or what? *Knowledge Tree*. Retrieved from http://www.danah.org/papers/KnowledgeTree.pdf

Braithwaite, D. O., Bach, B. W., Baxter, L. A., DiVerniero, R., Hammonds, J. R., Hosek, A. M., & Wolfe, B. M. (2010). Constructing family: A typology of voluntary kin. *Journal of Social and Personal Relationships, 27*(3), 388–407.

Brewer, M. B. (1999). The psychology of prejudice: Ingroup love or outgroup hate? *Journal of Social Issues, 55*, 429–444.

Brigman, G., Lane, D., Lane, D., Lawrence, R., & Switzer, D. (1999). Teaching children school success skills. *Journal of Educational Research, 92*(6), 323–329.

Bronner, S. (2015, June 18). Serena Williams: "I had to come to terms with loving myself." *Huffington Post*. Retrieved from http://www.huffingtonpost.com/2015/06/18/serena-williams-body-image_n_7599214.html

Brown, V. R., & Paulus, P. B. (2002). Making group brainstorming more effective: Recommendations from an associative memory perspective. *Current Directions in Psychological Science, 11*, 208–212.

Bryant, A. (2010, January 9). On a scale of 1 to 10, how weird are you? *New York Times*. Retrieved from www.nytimes.com/2010/01/10/business/10corner.html?_r=0

Bryant, G. A., & Fox Tree, J. E. (2005). Is there an ironic tone of voice? *Language and Speech, 48*, 257–277.

Brym, R. J., & Lenton, R. L. (2001). *Love online: A report on digital dating in Canada*. Retrieved from http://www.nelson.com/nelson/harcourt/sociology/newsociety3e/loveonline.pdf

Buber, M. (1965). *The knowledge of man: A philosophy of the interhuman*. New York, NY: Harper & Row.

Burger, J. M. (1999). The foot-in-the-door compliance procedure: A multiple-process analysis and review. *Personality and Social Psychology Review, 3*, 303–325.

Burgoon, J. K., Buller, D. B., & Woodall, W. G. (1996). *Nonverbal communication: The unspoken dialogue* (2nd ed.). New York, NY: McGraw-Hill.

Burgoon, J. K., & Dunbar, N. E. (2000). An interactionist perspective on dominance-submission: Interpersonal dominance as a dynamic, situationally contingent social skill. *Communication Monographs, 67*, 96–121.

Burgoon, J. K., & Hoobler, G. D. (2002). Nonverbal signals. In M. L. Knapp & J. A. Daly (Eds.), *Handbook of interpersonal communication* (3rd ed., pp. 240–299). Thousand Oaks, CA: Sage.

Burgoon, M. (1995). A kinder, gentler discipline: Feeling good about being mediocre. In B. R. Burleson (Ed.), *Communication yearbook* (Vol. 18, pp. 464–479). Thousand Oaks, CA: Sage.

Burlage, K., Marafka, J., Parsons, M., & Milaski, J. (2004). *Perception of speakers based on accent*. Paper presented at the 53rd annual convention of the International Communication Association, New Orleans, LA.

Burleson, B. R., & MacGeorge, E. L. (2002). Supportive communication. In M. L. Knapp & J. A. Daly (Eds.), *Handbook of interpersonal communication* (pp. 374–422). Thousand Oaks, CA: Sage.

Burleson, B. R., Metts, S., & Kirch, M. W. (2000). Communication in close relationships. In C. Hendrick & S. S. Hendrick (Eds.), *Close relationships: A sourcebook* (pp. 244–258). Thousand Oaks, CA: Sage.

Bushe, G. R., & Coetzer, G. H. (2007). Group development and team effectiveness: Using cognitive representations to measure group development and predict task performance and group viability. *Journal of Applied Behavioral Science, 43,* 184–212. doi:10.1177/0021886306298892

Buss, A. H. (1980). *Self-consciousness and social anxiety*. San Francisco, CA: W. H. Freeman.

Cain, S. (2013). *Quiet: The power of introverts in a world that can't stop talking.* New York, NY: Random House.

California Department of Education (n.d.). *Cesar E. Chavez.* Retrieved from http://chavez.cde.ca.gov

Cameron, D. (2009). *The myth of Venus and Mars: Do men and women really speak different languages?* New York, NY: Oxford University Press.

Campany, N., Dubinsky, R., Druskat, V. U., Mangino, M., & Flynn, E. (2007). What makes good teams work better: Research-based strategies that distinguish top-performing cross-functional drug development teams. *Organizational Development Journal, 25,* 179–186.

Campbell, R. G., & Babrow, A. S. (2004). The role of empathy in responses to persuasive risk communication: Overcoming resistance to HIV prevention messages. *Health Communication, 16,* 159–182.

Canary, D. J., Emmers-Sommer, T. M., & Faulkner, S. (1997). *Sex and gender differences in personal relationships.* New York, NY: Guilford Press.

Canary, D. J., & Hause, K. S. (1993). Is there any reason to research sex differences in communication? *Communication Quarterly, 41,* 129–144.

CareerBuilder. (2017). Number of employers using social media to screen candidates at all-time high, finds latest CareerBuilder study. Retrieved from https://www.prnewswire.com/news-releases/number-of-employers-using-social-media-to-screen-candidates-at-all-time-high-finds-latest-careerbuilder-study-300474228.html

Carlson (2015). *Marissa Mayer and the fight to save Yahoo!* New York: Twelve-Hatchette Book Group.

Carr, N. (2010). *The shallows: What the Internet is doing to our brains.* New York, NY: Norton.

Carroll, Lewis. (2013). *Alice in Wonderland* (3rd ed.; D. J. Gray, Ed.). New York, NY: Norton.

Carton, J. S., Kessler, E. A., & Pape, C. L. (1999). Nonverbal decoding skills and relationship well-being in adults. *Journal of Nonverbal Behavior, 23,* 91–100.

Castelli, L., Tomelleri, S., & Zogmaister, C. (2008). Implicit ingroup metafavoritism: Subtle preference for ingroup members displaying ingroup bias. *Personality and Social Psychology Bulletin, 34*(6), 807–818.

Catmull, E. (2014). *Creativity, Inc.: Overcoming the unseen forces that stand in the way of true inspiration.* New York, NY: Random House

Caughlin, J., & Golish, T. (2002). An analysis of the association between topic avoidance and dissatisfaction: Comparing perceptual and interpersonal explanations. *Communication Monographs, 69,* 275–296.

Caughlin, J. P., & Vangelisti, A. L. (2000). An individual difference explanation of why married couples engage in demand/withdraw patterns of conflict. *Journal of Social and Personal Relationships, 17,* 523–551.

Chaffee, S. H., & Metzger, M. J. (2001). The end of mass communication? *Mass Communication & Society, 4,* 365–379.

Chandra-Mouli, V., Plesons, M., Adebayo, E., Amin, A., Avni, M., Kraft, J. M., et al. (2017). Implications of the Global Early Adolescent Study's formative research findings for action and for research. *Journal of Adolescent Health, 61,* S5–S9.

Chen, G.-M. (1995). Differences in self-disclosure patterns among Americans versus Chinese: A comparative study. *Journal of Cross-Cultural Psychology, 26*(1). Retrieved from https://doi.org/10.1177/0022022195261006

Chen, G.-M., & Starosta, W. J. (1998). *Foundation of intercultural communication.* Boston, MA: Allyn and Bacon.

Chen, G.-M., & Starosta, W. J. (2005). *Foundation of intercultural communication.* Boston, MA: Allyn and Bacon.

Chesebro, J. L. (1999). The relationship between listening styles and conversational sensitivity. *Communication Research Reports, 16,* 233–238.

Cho, K. (2018, June 19). People are loving this photo of Colombian and Mexican soccer fans lifting an Egyptian fan at the World Cup. *BuzzFeed News.* Retrieved from https://www.buzzfeednews.com/article/kassycho/colombian-mexican-fans-lift-egyptian-fan-world-cup

Claeys, A. S., & Cauberghe, V. (2014). Keeping control: The importance of nonverbal expressions of power by organizational spokespersons in times of crisis. *Journal of Communication, 64,* 1160–1180.

Clark, R. A., & Delia, J. (1979). Topoi and rhetorical competence. *Quarterly Journal of Speech, 65,* 187–206.

Clarke, M. L. (1953). *Rhetoric at Rome: A historical survey.* London, England: Cohen and West.

Cleveland, J. N., Stockdale, M., & Murphy, K. R. (2000). *Women and men in organizations: Sex and gender issues at work.* Mahwah, NJ: Erlbaum.

Cochran, E. (2018). A call to cut back online addictions: Pitted against just one more click. *New York Times.* Retrieved from https://www.nytimes.com/2018/02/04/us/politics/online-addictions-cut-back-screen-time.html

Cooley, C. H. (1902). *Human nature and the social order.* New York, NY: Scribner.

Cooper, L. (1960). *The rhetoric of Aristotle: An expanded translation with supplementary examples for students of composition and public speaking.* Englewood Cliffs, NJ: Prentice Hall.

Costanzo, F. S., Markel, N. N., & Costanzo, R. R. (1969). Voice quality profile and perceived emotion. *Journal of Counseling Psychology, 16,* 267–270.

County of Los Angeles Public Library (n.d.). *About César E. Chávez.* Retrieved from http://www.colapublib.org/chavez/about.html

Coupland, N., Giles, H., & Wiemann, J. M. (Eds.). (1991). *Miscommunication and problematic talk.* Newbury Park, CA: Sage.

Covey, J. (2014). The role of dispositional factors in moderating message framing effects. *Health Psychology, 33*(1), 52–65.

Crosnoe, R., & Cavanagh, S. E. (2010). Families with children and adolescents: A review, critique, and future agenda. *Journal of Marriage and Family, 72,* 594–611.

Cross, S. E., & Madson, L. (1997). Models of the self: Self-construals and gender. *Psychological Bulletin, 122,* 5–37.

Culnan, M. J., & Markus, M. L. (1987). Information technologies. In F. M. Jablin, L. L. Putnam, K. H. Roberts, & L. W. Porter (Eds.), *Handbook of organizational communication: An interdisciplinary perspective* (pp. 420–443). Newbury Park, CA: Sage.

Cumberland, S. (2010). Life-saving learning around the drinking pot. *Bulletin of the World Health Organization, 88,* 721–722. doi:10.2471/BLT.10.011010

Dainton, M., & Stafford, L. (1993). Routine maintenance behaviors: A comparison of relationship type, partner similarity and sex differences. *Journal of Social and Personal Relationships, 10,* 255–271.

Dainton, M., Zelley, E., & Langan, E. (2003). Maintaining friendships throughout the lifespan. In D. J. Canary & M. Dainton (Eds.), *Maintaining relationships through communication: Relational, contextual, and cultural variations* (pp. 79–102). Mahwah, NJ: Erlbaum.

Dallas, D. (2006, July 28). Café Scientifique—Déjà vu. *Cell, 126*(2), 227–229. doi:10.1016/j.cell.2006.07.006

Davis, K. E., & Todd, M. L. (1985). Assessing friendship: Prototypes, paradigm cases, and relationship description. In S. Duck & D. Perlman (Eds.), *Understanding personal relationships: An interdisciplinary approach* (pp. 17–38). London, England: Sage.

Davis, M. H. (1994). *Empathy: A social psychological approach.* Madison, WI: Brown & Benchmark.

De Hoogh, A. H. B., Den Hartog, D. N., & Koopman, P. L. (2005). Linking the big five-factors of personality to charismatic and transactional leadership: Perceived dynamic work environment as a moderator. *Journal of Organizational Behavior, 26,* 839–865.

Delgado-Gaitan, C. (1993). Parenting in two generations of Mexican American families. *International Journal of Behavioral Development, 16,* 409–427.

Delia, J. G. (1972). Dialects and the effects of stereotypes on interpersonal attraction and cognitive processes in impression formation. *Quarterly Journal of Speech, 58,* 285–297.

Dellis, N. (2014, October). *The journey to improving memory* [Video file]. Edison Talks speech delivered at Chicago Ideas Week, Chicago, IL. Available at http://www.chicagoideas.com/video/776

DePaulo, B. M., Kirkendol, S. E., Kashy, D. A., Wyer, M. M., & Epstein, J. A. (1996). Lying in everyday life. *Journal of Personality and Social Psychology, 70,* 979–995.

DePaulo, B. M., Lindsay, J. J., Malone, B. E., Muhlenbruck, L., Charlton, K., & Cooper, H. (2003). Cues to deception. *Psychological Bulletin, 129*(1), 74–118.

Devine, P. G. (1989). Stereotypes and prejudice: Their automatic and controlled components. *Journal of Personality and Social Psychology, 56,* 5–18.

DeVito, M. A., Birnholtz, J., & Hancock, J. T. (2017). Platforms, people, and perception: Using affordances to understand self-presentation on social media. In *Proceedings of the 2017 ACM conference on computer supported cooperative work and social computing* (CSCW '17). Association for Computing Machinery, New York, NY, 740–754. doi:10.1145/2998181.2998192

Dewey, J. (1933). *How we think: A restatement of the relation of reflective thinking to the educative process* (Rev. ed.). Boston, MA: D. C. Heath.

Dey, R. (2010, October 18). *Leadership is key to success.* Retrieved from www.army.mil/-news/2010/10/18/46689-leadership-is-key-to-success/

Dindia, K., & Allen, M. (1992). Sex differences in self-disclosure: A meta-analysis. *Psychological Bulletin, 112,* 106–124.

Doetkott, R., & Motley, M. (2009, November 11). *Public speaking delivery styles: Audience preference and recollection.* Paper presented at the annual meeting of the NCA 95th Annual Convention, Chicago Hilton & Towers, Chicago, IL.

Donath, J. (1999). Identity and deception in the virtual community. In M. A. Smith & P. Kollock (Eds.), *Communities in cyberspace* (pp. 29–59). London, England: Routledge.

Donath, J., & boyd, d. (2004). Public displays of connection. *BT Technology Journal, 22,* 71–82.

Donohue, W. A., & Kolt, R. (1992). *Managing interpersonal conflict.* Newbury Park, CA: Sage.

Downs, V. C., Javidi, M. M., & Nussbaum, J. F. (1988). An analysis of teachers' verbal communication within the college classroom: Use of humor, self-disclosure, and narratives. *Communication Education, 37,* 127–141.

Drobnick, R. (2017). 5 ways men & women communicate differently. *Your Tango Experts for Psych Central.* Retrieved from https://psychcentral.com/blog/6-ways-men-and-women-communicate-differently/

Druskat, V., & Wolff, S. B. (2001). Building the emotional intelligence of groups. *Harvard Business Review, 79*(3), 81–90.

Duan, C., & Hill, C. E. (1996). The current state of empathy research. *Journal of Counseling Psychology, 43,* 261–274.

Dues, M., & Brown, M. (2004). *Boxing Plato's shadow: An introduction to the study of human communication.* Boston, MA: McGraw-Hill.

Eagly, A. H., Ashmore, R. D., Makhijani, M. G., & Longo, L. C. (1991). What is beautiful is good, but . . . : A meta-analytic review of research on the physical attractiveness stereotype. *Psychological Bulletin, 110,* 109–128.

Eagly, A. H., & Wood, W. (2012). Social role theory. In P. A. M. Van Lange, A. W. Kruglanski, & E. T. Higgins (Eds.), *Handbook of theories of social psychology* (pp. 458–476). Thousand Oaks, CA: Sage. http://dx.doi.org/10.4135/9781446249222.n49

Eagly, A. H., Wood, W., & Diekman, A. B. (2000). Social role theory of sex differences and similarities: A current appraisal. In T. Eckes & H. M. Trautner (Eds.), *The developmental social psychology of gender* (pp. 123–174). Mahwah, NJ: Erlbaum.

Edmondson, A. C., & Lei, Z. (2014). Psychological safety: The history, renaissance, and future of an interpersonal construct. *Annual Review of Organizational Psychology and Organizational Behavior, 1,* 23–43.

Educause (2007, June 7). 7 things you should know about Wikipedia. Retrieved from www.educause.edu/ELI/7ThingsYouShouldKnowAboutWikip/161666

Eisterhold, J., Attardo, S., & Boxer, D. (2006). Reactions to irony in discourse: Evidence for the least disruption principle. *Journal of Pragmatics, 38*, 1239–1256.

Ekman, P. (2003). *Emotions revealed. Recognizing faces and feelings to improve communication and emotional life*. New York, NY: Times Books.

Ekman, P., & Friesen, W. V. (1975). *Unmasking the face: A guide to recognizing emotions from facial clues*. Englewood Cliffs, NJ: Prentice Hall.

Ellison, N. B., Heino, R. D., & Gibbs, J. L. (2006). Managing impressions online: Self-presentation processes in the online dating environment. *Journal of Computer-Mediated Communication, 11*(2), 415–441.

Englehardt, E. E. (2001). Introduction to ethics in interpersonal communication. In E. E. Englehardt (Ed.), *Ethical issues in interpersonal communication: Friends, intimates, sexuality, marriage, and family* (pp. 1–27). Orlando, FL: Harcourt College.

Farrell, R. (2011, August 3). 23 traits of good leaders. *CNN.com*. Retrieved from www.cnn.com/2011/LIVING/08/03/good.leader.traits.cb/index.html

Febbraro, A. R., McKee, B., & Riedel, S. L. (2008, November). *Multinational military operations and intercultural factors* (NATO RTO Technical Report). Retrieved from http://ftp.rta.nato.int/public//PubFullText/RTO/TR/RTO-TR-HFM-120///$$TR-HFM-120-ALL.pdf

Felmlee, D., Orzechowicz, D., & Fortes, C. (2010). Fairy tales: Attraction and stereotypes in same-gender relationships. *Sex Roles, 62*, 226–240.

Felps, W., Mitchell, T. R., & Byington, E. (2006). How, when, and why bad apples spoil the barrel: Negative group members and dysfunctional groups. In B. M. Shaw (Ed.), *Research in organizational behavior: An annual series of analytical essays and critical reviews* (Vol. 27, pp. 175–222). Amsterdam, Netherlands: Elsevier.

Fenigstein, A., Scheier, M. F., & Buss, A. H. (1975). Public and private self-consciousness: Assessment and theory. *Journal of Consulting and Clinical Psychology, 43*, 522–527.

Fiske, S. T., Cuddy, A. J. C., Glick, P., & Xu, J. (2002). A model of (often mixed) stereotype content: Competence and warmth respectively follow from perceived status and competition. *Journal of Personality and Social Psychology, 82*, 878–902.

Fiske, S. T., & Taylor, S. E. (1991). *Social cognition* (2nd ed.). New York, NY: McGraw-Hill.

Floyd, K. (1999). All touches are not created equal: Effects of form and duration on observers' interpretations of an embrace. *Journal of Nonverbal Behavior, 23*, 283–299.

Floyd, K., & Burgoon, J. K. (1999). Reacting to nonverbal expressions of liking: A test of interaction adaptation theory. *Communication Monographs, 66*, 219–239.

Floyd, K., & Morman, M. T. (1999). The measurement of affectionate communication. *Communication Quarterly, 46*, 144–162.

Fontoura, M. (2014). Meet Niki Nakayama, one of the world's only female Kaiseki chefs. *Wall Street Journal*. Retrieved from http://www.wsj.com/articles/meet-niki-nakayama-one-of-the-worlds-only-female-kaiseki-chefs-1407509705

Forward, G. L., Czech, K., & Lee, C. M. (2011). Assessing Gibb's supportive and defensive communication climate: An examination of measurement and construct validity. *Communication Research Reports, 28*, 1–15.

Foss, S. K., Foss, K. A., & Trapp, R. (1991). *Contemporary perspectives in rhetoric* (2nd ed.). Prospect Heights, IL: Waveland Press.

Fox, J., & Vendemia, M. A. (2016). Selective self-presentation and social comparison through photographs on social networking sites. *Cyberpsychology, Behavior, and Social Networking, 19*(10), 593–600. Retrieved from https://doi.org/10.1089/cyber.2016.0248

Fox, K. R. (1992). Physical education and development of self-esteem in children. In N. Armstrong (Ed.), *New directions in physical education: Vol. 2. Towards a national curriculum* (pp. 33–54). Champaign, IL: Human Kinetics.

Fox, K. R. (1997). The physical self and processes in self-esteem development. In K. Fox (Ed.), *The physical self* (pp. 111–139). Champaign, IL: Human Kinetics.

Fragale, A. R. (2006). The power of powerless speech: The effects of speech style and task interdependence on status conferral. *Organizational Behavior and Human Decision Processes, 101*, 243–261.

Franco, J. (2013, December 26). The meaning of the selfie. *New York Times*. Retrieved from http://www.nytimes.com/2013/12/29/arts/the-meanings-of-the-selfie.html?_r=0

Frisby, B. N., & Westerman, D. (2010). Rational actors: Channel selection and rational choices in romantic conflict episodes. *Journal of Social and Personal Relationships, 27*, 970–981.

Galvin, K. M., Brommel, B. J., & Bylund, C. L. (2004). *Family communication: Cohesion and change* (6th ed.). New York, NY: Pearson.

Gangestad, S. W., & Snyder, M. (2000). Self-monitoring: Appraisal and reappraisal. *Psychological Bulletin, 126*, 530–555.

Garamone, J. (2011, January 3). *Mullen: Leaders key to nation's, military's future*. Retrieved from www.defense.gov/News/NewsArticle.aspx?ID=62303

Gettings, J. (2005). Civil disobedience: Black medalists raise fists for civil rights movement. Retrieved from http://www.infoplease.com/spot/mm-mexicocity.html

Giannakakis, A. E., & Fritsche, I. (2011). Social identities, group norms, and threat: On the malleability of ingroup bias. *Personality and Social Psychology Bulletin, 37*(1), 82–93.

Gibb, J. (1961). Defensive communications. *Journal of Communication, 11*, 141–148.

Gibbs, J. L., Ellison, N. B., & Heino, R. D. (2006). Self-presentation in online personals: The role of anticipated future interaction, self-disclosure, and perceived success in Internet dating. *Communication Research, 33*, 1–26.

Gifford, R., Ng, C. F., & Wilkinson, M. (1985). Nonverbal cues in the employment interview: Links between applicant qualities and interviewer judgments. *Journal of Applied Psychology, 70*, 729–736.

Giles, H., Coupland, N., & Coupland, J. (Eds.). (1991). *Contexts of accommodation: Developments in applied linguistics.* Cambridge, England: Cambridge University Press.

Giles, H., & Street, R. L. (1994). Communicator characteristics and behavior. In M. L. Knapp & G. R. Miller (Eds.), *Handbook of interpersonal communication* (2nd ed., pp. 103–161). Beverly Hills, CA: Sage.

Gleason, L. B. (1989). *The development of language.* Columbus, OH: Merrill.

Glenn, D. (2010, February 28). *Divided attention.* Retrieved from http://chronicle.com/article/Scholars-Turn-Their-Attention/63746/

Global Deception Research Team. (2006). A world of lies. *Journal of Cross-Cultural Psychology, 37*, 60–74.

Goffman, E. (1955). On facework: An analysis of ritual elements in social interaction. *Psychiatry, 18*, 319–345.

Goldstein, N. J., Vezich, I. S., & Shapiro, J. R. (2014). Perceived perspective-taking: When others walk in our shoes. *Journal of Personality and Social Psychology, 106*(6), 941–960. doi: 10.1037/a0036395

Goleman, D. (2007, February 20). Flame first, think later: New clues to e-mail misbehavior. *New York Times.* Retrieved from http://www.nytimes.com/2007/02/20/health/psychology/20essa.html

Golish, T. D. (2000). Changes in closeness between adult children and their parents: A turning point analysis. *Communication Reports, 13*, 79–97.

Goodwin, C. (1981). *Conversational organization: Interactions between speakers and hearers.* New York: Academic Press.

Gosling, S. D., Gaddis, S., & Vazire, S. (2007, March). *Personality impressions based on Facebook profiles.* Paper presented at the International Conference on Weblogs and Social Media, Boulder, CO.

Gottman, J. M., & Silver, N. (1999). *The seven principles for making marriage work.* New York, NY: Three Rivers Press.

Grant, A. M., Gino, F., & Hoffman, D. A. (2011). Reversing the extraverted leadership advantage: The role of employee productivity. *Academy of Management Journal, 54*, 528–550.

Gravois, J. (2005, April 8). Teach impediment. *Chronicle of Higher Education.* Retrieved from https://www.chronicle.com/article/Teach-Impediment/33613

Greenfeld, L. (2017). Approaching human nature—and needs—empirically, *Society, 54*(6), 510–511. Retrieved from https://doi.org/10.1007/s12115-017-0199-5

Grice, H. P. (1989). *Studies in the way of words.* Cambridge, MA: Harvard University Press.

Gronbeck, B. E., McKerrow, R. E., Ehninger, D., & Monroe, A. H. (1990). *Principles and types of speech communication* (11th ed.). Glenview, IL: Scott, Foresman/Little, Brown Higher Education.

Gruner, C. R. (1985). Advice to the beginning speaker on using humor—what the research tells us. *Communication Education, 34*, 142–147.

Gudykunst, W. B., & Kim, Y. Y. (2003). *Communicating with strangers: An approach to intercultural communication* (4th ed.). New York, NY: McGraw-Hill.

Gurchiek, K. (2011, June 21). Delivering HR at Zappos. Retrieved from www.weknownext.com/workplace/delivering-hr-at-zappos-hr-magazine-june-2011

Haas, S. M., & Stafford, L. (2005). Maintenance behaviors in same-sex and marital relationships: A matched sample comparison. *Journal of Family Communication, 5*, 43–60.

Hafner, J. (2017, March 13). Gender reveals: Insanely popular—And also outdated? *USA Today.* Retrieved from https://www.usatoday.com/story/news/nation-now/2017/

Hall, E. T. (1963). A system for the notation of proxemic behavior. *American Anthropologist, 65*, 1003–1026.

Hall, E. T. (1981). *The silent language.* New York, NY: Anchor/Doubleday.

Hall, E. T., & Hall, M. R. (1987). *Understanding cultural differences.* Yarmouth, ME: Intercultural Press.

Hall, J. A. (1998). How big are nonverbal sex differences? The case of smiling and sensitivity to nonverbal cues. In D. J. Canary & K. Dindia (Eds.), *Sex differences and similarities in communication: Critical essays and empirical investigations of sex and gender in interaction* (pp. 155–178). Mahwah, NJ: Erlbaum.

Hall, J. A., Carter, J. D., & Horgan, T. G. (2000). Gender differences in nonverbal communication of emotion. In A. H. Fischer (Ed.), *Gender and emotion: Social psychological perspectives* (pp. 97–117). Cambridge, England: Cambridge University Press.

Hall, J. A., Park, N., Song, H., & Cody, M. J. (2010). Strategic misrepresentation in online dating: The effects of gender, self-monitoring, and personality traits. *Journal of Social and Personal Relationships, 27*(1), 117–135.

Hammer, M. R., Bennett, M. J., & Wiseman, R. (2003). Measuring intercultural sensitivity: The intercultural development inventory. *International Journal of Intercultural Relations, 27*, 421–443.

Hancock, J. T. (2007). Digital deception: When, where and how people lie online. In K. McKenna, T. Postmes, U. Reips, & A. N. Joinson (Eds.), *Oxford handbook of Internet psychology* (pp. 287–301). Oxford, England: Oxford University Press.

Hancock, J. T., & Toma, C. L. (2009). Putting your best face forward: The accuracy of online dating photographs. *Journal of Communication, 59*, 367–386. doi:10.1111/j.1460-2466.2009.01420.x

Harkins, S. G. (1987). Social loafing and social facilitation. *Journal of Experimental Social Psychology, 23*, 1–18.

Hatfield, E. E., & Sprecher, S. (1986). *Mirror, mirror . . . the importance of looks in everyday life.* Albany: State University of New York Press

Hayden Planetarium. (2017, October 4). SciCafe: Humans and conflicts with bears, oh my! Retrieved from https://www.amnh.org/explore/videos/scicafe-lectures/scicafe-humans-and-conflicts-with-bears-oh-my

Hays, R. B. (1988). Friendship. In S. Duck (Ed.), *Handbook of personal relationships: Theory, research, and interventions* (pp. 391–408). Chichester, England: Wiley.

Heider, F. (1958). *The psychology of interpersonal relations.* New York, NY: Wiley.

Heino, R. D., Ellison, N. B., & Gibbs, J. L. (2010). Relationshopping: Investigating the market metaphor in online dating. *Journal of Social and Personal Relationships, 27*(4), 427–447.

Heisler, J. M., & Crabill, S. L. (2006). Who are "stinkybug" and "Packerfan4"? Email pseudonyms and participants' perceptions of demography, productivity, and personality. *Journal of Mediated Communication, 12,* 114–135.

Hemmings, K. H. (2007). *The Descendants.* New York, NY: Random House.

Hendrick, S. S., & Hendrick, C. (1992). *Romantic love.* Thousand Oaks, CA: Sage.

Hersey, P., & Blanchard, K. H. (1988). *Management and organizational behavior.* Englewood Cliffs, NJ: Prentice Hall.

Heslin, R. (1974, May). *Steps toward a taxonomy of touching.* Paper presented at the annual meeting of the Midwestern Psychological Association, Chicago, IL.

Hesse, D. (2015). Is a digitally connected world a better place? *Vital Speeches of the Day, 81*(5), 148–151.

Higgins, E. T. (1987). Self-discrepancy: A theory relating self and affect. *Psychological Review, 94,* 319–340.

Hill, J., Ah Yn, K., & Lindsey, L. (2008). *The interaction effect of teacher self-disclosure valence and relevance on student motivation, teacher liking, and teacher immediacy.* Conference Papers—National Communication Association, 1.

Hodgins, H. S., & Belch, C. (2000). Interparental violence and nonverbal abilities. *Journal of Nonverbal Behavior, 24,* 3–24.

Hofstede, G. (1991). *Cultures and organizations.* London, England: McGraw-Hill.

Hofstede, G. (2001). Culture's consequences: Comparing values, behaviors, institutions, and organizations across nations (2nd ed., pp. 79–123). Thousand Oaks, CA: Sage.

Hofstede, G. (2009). *The Hofstede Center, dimensions, uncertainty avoidance.* Retrieved from http://geert-hofstede.com/dimensions.html

Hofstede, G., Hofstede, G. J., & Minkov, M. (2010). *Cultures and organizations: Software for the mind* (3rd ed.). New York, NY: McGraw-Hill.

Holson, L. M. (2009, February 28). Putting a bolder face on Google. *New York Times.* Retrieved from http://www.nytimes.com/2009/03/01/business/01marissa.html?_r=4&adxnnl=1&src=tp&pagewanted=all&adxnnlx=1363061576-YzRRY641ZzY4fcuC6eA1AA

Holtgraves, T., & Lasky, B. (1999). Linguistic power and persuasion. *Journal of Language and Social Psychology, 18,* 196–205.

Honeycutt, J. M. (1999). Typological differences in predicting marital happiness from oral history behaviors and imagined interactions. *Communication Monographs, 66,* 276–291.

Hong, S., Tandoc, E., Jr., Kim, E. A., Kim, B., & Wise, K. (2012). The real you? The role of visual cues and comment congruence in perceptions of social attractiveness from Facebook profiles. *Cyberpsychology, Behavior, and Social Networking, 15,* 339–344. doi:10.1089/cyber.2011.0511

Horne, C. F. (1917). *The sacred books and early literature of the east: Vol. 2. Egypt.* New York, NY: Parke, Austin, & Lipscomb.

Hosman, L. A., Huebner, T. M., & Siltanen, S. A. (2002). The impact of power-of-speech style, argument strength, and need for cognition on impression formation, cognitive responses, and persuasion. *Journal of Language and Social Psychology, 21,* 361–379.

Hsieh, T. (2010). *Delivering happiness: A path to profits, passions, and purpose.* New York, NY: Business Plus.

Husain, M. (2013, October). Malala: The girl who was shot for going to school. BBC News. Retrieved from http://www.bbc.com/news/magazine-24379018

Hyde, J. S. (2005). The gender similarities hypothesis. *American Psychologist, 60,* 581–592.

Infante, D. (1995). Teaching students to understand and control verbal aggression. *Communication Education, 44,* 51–63.

Infante, D. A. (1987). Aggressiveness. In J. C. McCroskey & J. A. Daly (Eds.), *Personality and interpersonal communication* (pp. 157–192). Newbury Park, CA: Sage.

Infante, D. A., Chandler, T. A., & Rudd, J. E. (1989). Test of an argumentative skill deficiency model of interspousal violence. *Communication Monographs, 56,* 163–177.

Infante, D. A., & Rancer, A. S. (1982). A conceptualization and measure of argumentativeness. *Journal of Personality Assessment, 46,* 72–80.

Infante, D. A., & Wigley, C. J. (1986). Verbal aggressiveness: An interpersonal model and measure. *Communication Monographs, 53,* 61–69.

Institute of International Education. (2014, November 17). *Open Doors report on international educational exchange.* Retrieved from http://www.iie.org/Who-We-Are/News-and-Events/Press-Center/Press-Releases/2014/2014-11-17-Open-Doors-Data

Jackson, M. (2008). *Distracted: The erosion of attention and the coming dark age.* Amherst, NY: Prometheus Books.

Jacobs, S., Dawson, E. J., & Brashers, D. (1996). Information manipulation theory: A replication and assessment. *Communication Monographs, 63,* 70–82.

Jalongo, M. R. (2008). *Learning to listen, listening to learn: Building essential skills in young children.* Washington, DC: National Association for the Education of Young Children.

Janis, I. L. (1982). *Groupthink: Psychological studies of policy decisions and fiascoes* (2nd ed.). Boston, MA: Houghton Mifflin.

Janusik, L. A. (2002). Teaching listening: What do we do? What should we do? *International Journal of Listening, 16,* 5–39.

Jemison, M. C. (2012). If Title IX achieves its full potential. *Vital Speeches of the Day, 78*(9), 276.

Jenkins, J. A. (2017). Preparing for the 100-year life. *Vital Speeches of the Day, 83*(4), 120–124.

Jimenez, V., & McCornack, S. A. (2011, August). *Cross-cultural differences in immediacy behaviors of female friends.* Paper presented at the annual MSU McNair Fellowship conference, East Lansing, MI.

Johnson, A. J., Wittenberg, E., Villagran, M. M., Mazur, M., & Villagran, P. (2003). Relational progression as a dialectic: Examining turning points in communication among friends. *Communication Monographs, 70*(3), 230–249.

Johnson, C., & Vinson, L. (1990). Placement and frequency of powerless talk and impression formation. *Communication Quarterly, 38*, 325–333.

Johnson, D. W., & Johnson, F. P. (2008). *Joining together: Group theory and group skills* (10th ed.). New York, NY: Pearson.

Johnston, M. K. (2007). The influence of communication on group attraction during team activities. *Journal of Organizational Culture, Communication, and Conflict, 11*, 43–48.

Joinson, A. N. (2001, March/April). Self-disclosure in computer-mediated communication: The role of self-awareness and visual anonymity. *European Journal of Social Psychology, 31*, 177–192.

Jones, S. E., & LeBaron, C. D. (2002). Research on the relationship between verbal and nonverbal communication: Emerging integrations. *Journal of Communication, 52*, 499–521.

Jones, W., Bruce, H., Foxley, A., & Munat, C. F. (2006, November). *Planning personal projects and organizing personal information*. Paper presented at the Association for Information Science and Technology 2006 Annual Meeting, Austin, TX. Retrieved from http://kftf.ischool.washington.edu/docs/asist06.pdf

Jourard, S. M. (1964). *The transparent self*. New York, NY: Van Nostrand Reinhold.

Joyce, M. P. (2008). Interviewing techniques used in selected organizations today. *Business Communication Quarterly, 71*, 376–380. doi:10.1177/1080569908321427

JR. (2011). *The 2011 TED acceptance speech*. Retrieved from www.ted.com/talks/lang/en/jr_s_ted_prize_wish_use_art_to_turn_the_world_inside_out.html

Judge, T. A., Ilies, R., Bono, J. E., & Gerhardt, M. W. (2002). Personality and leadership: A qualitative and quantitative review. *Journal of Applied Psychology, 87*, 765–780.

Juncoa, R., & Cotten, S. R. (2012). No A 4 U: The relationship between multitasking and academic performance. *Computers & Education, 59*(2), 505–514. doi:10.1016/j.compedu.2011.12.023

Kagawa, N., & McCornack, S. A. (2004, November). *Collectivistic Americans and individualistic Japanese: A cross-cultural comparison of parental understanding*. Paper presented at the annual meeting of the National Communication Association, Chicago, IL.

Kapsin, K., & Hess, E. (2013, January 13). Engaging room design and distraction techniques comfort pediatric radiology patients, leading to less need for sedation, shorter wait times, higher satisfaction. Retrieved from https://innovations.ahrq.gov/profiles/engaging-room-design-and-distraction-techniques-comfort-pediatric-radiology-patients

Keck, K. L., & Samp, J. A. (2007). The dynamic nature of goals and message production as revealed in a sequential analysis of conflict interactions. *Human Communication Research, 33*, 27–47.

Keesing, R. M. (1974). Theories of culture. *Annual Review of Anthropology, 3*, 73–97.

Kellermann, K. (1989). The negativity effect in interaction: It's all in your point of view. *Human Communication Research, 16*, 147–183.

Kelley, H. H., & Thibaut, J. W. (1978). *Interpersonal relations: A theory of interdependence*. New York, NY: Wiley.

Kelley, T., & Kelley, D. (2012, November 20). Fighting the fears that block creativity. Retrieved from https://hbr.org/2012/11/fighting-the-fears-that-b

Kelley, T., & Littman, J. (2001). *The art of innovation: Lessons in creativity from IDEO, America's leading design firm*. New York, NY: Doubleday.

Kelly, A. E., & McKillop, K. J. (1996). Consequences of revealing personal secrets. *Psychological Bulletin, 120*, 450–465.

Kelly, L., Miller-Ott, A. E., & Duran, R. L. (2017). Sports scores and intimate moments: An Expectancy Violations Theory approach to partner cellphone behaviors in adult romantic relationships. *Western Journal of Communication, 81*(5), 619–640. doi:10.1080/10570314.2017.1299206

Kennedy, G. A. (1999). *Classical rhetoric and its Christian and secular tradition from ancient to modern times*. Chapel Hill: University of North Carolina Press.

Khatchadourian, R. (2011). In the picture: An artist's global experiment to help people be seen. *New Yorker*. Retrieved from www.newyorker.com/reporting/2011/11/28/111128fa_fact_khatchadourian#ixzz1x18s3xLj

Kiger, P. J. (2010, January 12). Webcam job interviews: How to survive and thrive. Retrieved from www.fastcompany.com/1508932/webcam-job-interviews-how-survive-and-thrive

King, M. L. (1963). *I have a dream . . .* Speech transcript from www.archives.gov/press/exhibits/dream-speech.pdf

Kingsley Westerman, C., & Westerman, D. (2010). Supervisor impression management: Message content and channel effects on impressions. *Communication Studies, 61*, 585–601.

Kirk, M. (March 25, 2013). Interview with Bennet Omalu. *PBS Frontline*. Retrieved from https://www.pbs.org/wgbh/pages/frontline/sports/league-of-denial/the-frontline-interview-dr-bennet-omalu/

Kirkman, B. L., Rosen, B., Gibson, C. B., Tesluk, P. E., & McPherson, S. O. (2002). Five challenges to virtual team success: Lessons from Sabre, Inc. *Academy of Management*. Retrieved from www.jstor.org/stable/4165869

Kirkpatrick, S. A., & Locke, E. A. (1991). Leadership: Do traits matter? *Academy of Management Executive, 5*(2), 48–60.

Klopf, D. W. (2001). *Intercultural encounters: The fundamentals of intercultural communication* (5th ed.). Englewood, CO: Morton.

Knapp, M. (1984). *Interpersonal communication and human relationships*. Boston, MA: Allyn and Bacon.

Knapp, M. L., Daly, J. A., Albada, K. F., & Miller, G. R. (2002). Background and current trends in the study of interpersonal communication. In M. L. Knapp & J. A. Daly (Eds.), *Handbook of interpersonal communication* (3rd ed., pp. 3–20). Thousand Oaks, CA: Sage.

Knapp, M. L., & Hall, J. A. (2002). *Nonverbal communication in human interaction* (5th ed.). Belmont, CA: Wadsworth/ Thomson Learning.

Koenig, A. M., Mitchell, A. A., Eagly, A. H., & Ristikari, T. (2011). Are leader stereotypes masculine? A meta-analysis of three research paradigms. *Psychological Bulletin, 137*, 616–642.

Kozlowski, S. W. J., & Bell, B. S. (2003). Work groups and teams in organizations. In W. C. Brown, D. R. Ilgen, & R. J. Klimoski (Eds.), *Handbook of psychology: Industrial and organizational psychology* (Vol. 12, pp. 333–375). London, England: Wiley.

Kozlowski, S. W. J., & Ilgen, D. R. (2006). Enhancing the effectiveness of work groups and teams. *Psychological Science in the Public Interest, 7*, 77–124.

Kramer, M. W. (2006). Shared leadership in a community theater group: Filling the leadership role. *Journal of Applied Communication Research, 34*, 141–162.

Krause, J. (2001). *Properties of naturally produced clear speech at normal rates and implications for intelligibility enhancement* (Unpublished doctoral dissertation). Massachusetts Institute of Technology, Cambridge, MA.

Kruger, J., Epley, N., Parker, J., & Ng, Z. (2005). Egocentrism over e-mail: Can we communicate as well as we think? *Journal of Personality and Social Psychology, 89*, 925–936.

Kubany, E. S., Richard, D. C., Bauer, G. B., & Muraoka, M. Y. (1992). Impact of assertive and accusatory communication of distress and anger: A verbal component analysis. *Aggressive Behavior, 18*, 337–347.

Kudoh, T., & Matsumoto, D. (1985). Cross-cultural examination of the semantic dimensions of body postures. *Journal of Personality and Social Psychology, 48*, 1440–1446.

Kuhn, J. L. (2001). Toward an ecological humanistic psychology. *Journal of Humanistic Psychology, 41*, 9–24.

LaFollette, H., & Graham, G. (1986). Honesty and intimacy. *Journal of Social and Personal Relationships, 3*, 3–18.

Lane, C., Brundage, C. L., & Kreinin, T. (2017). Why we must invest in early adolescence: Early intervention, lasting impact. *Journal of Adolescent Health, 61*, S10–S11.

Langdridge, D., & Butt, T. (2004). The fundamental attribution error: A phenomenological critique. *British Journal of Social Psychology, 43*, 357–369.

Lannutti, P. J., & Strauman, E. C. (2006). Classroom communication: The influence of instructor self-disclosure on student evaluations. *Communication Quarterly, 54*, 89–99.

Lea, M., & Spears, R. (1992). Paralanguage and social perception in computer-mediated communication. *Journal of Organizational Computing, 2*, 321–341.

Leaper, C., & Smith, T. E. (2004). A meta-analytic review of gender variations in children's language use: Talkativeness, affiliative speech, and assertive speech. *Developmental Psychology, 40*, 993–1027.

Leber, J. (2015, September). How teenage activist Malala Yousafzai is turning her fame into a movement. Retrieved from http://www.fastcoexist.com/3050372/how-teenage-activist-malala-yousafzai-is-turning-her-fame-into-a-movement

Ledbetter, C. (2015, October 19). Serena Williams named to *Harper's Bazaar* "Daring" list, says "I was born to do tennis." *Huffington Post*. Retrieved from http://www.huffingtonpost.com/entry/serena-williams-daring-list-harpers-bazaar_56250f15e4b02f6a900d05fc?utm_hp_ref=tw

LeFebvre, L., LeFebvre, L. E., & Allen, M. (2018). Training the butterflies to fly in formation: Cataloguing student fears about public speaking. *Communication Education, 67*(3), 348–362. doi:10.1080/03634523.2018.1468915

Lehmann-Willenbrock, N., Allen, J. A., & Kauffeld, S. (2013). A sequential analysis of procedural meeting communication: How teams facilitate their meetings. *Journal of Applied Communication Research, 41*, 365–388.

Lehrer, J. (2011, October 7). Steve Jobs: "Technology alone is not enough." *New Yorker.*

Lenhart, A., Ybarra, M., Zickuhr, K., & Price-Freeney, M. (2016, November 21). Online harassment, digital abuse, and cyberstalking in America. Center for Innovative Public Health Research. Retrieved from https://datasociety.net/output/online-harassment-digital-abuse-cyberstalking/

Lev-Ari, S., & Keysar, B. (2010). Why don't we believe non-native speakers? The influence of accent on credibility. *Journal of Experimental Social Psychology, 46*, 1093–1096. doi:10.1016/j.jesp.2010.05.025

Limon, M. S., & La France, B. H. (2005). Communication traits and leadership emergence: Examining the impact of argumentativeness, communication apprehension, and verbal aggressiveness in work groups. *Southern Communication Journal, 70*, 123–133.

Lin, R., van de Ven, N., & Utz, S. (2018). What triggers envy on social network sites? A comparison between shared experiential and material purchases. *Computers in Human Behavior, 85*, 271–281. Retrieved from https://doi.org/10.1016/j.chb.2018.03.049

Lippa, R. A. (2002). *Gender, nature, and nurture*. Mahwah, NJ: Erlbaum.

Littlejohn, S. W., & Foss, K. A. (2010). *Theories of human communication* (10th ed.). Long Grove, IL: Waveland Press.

Lohr, S. (2016). Civility in the age of artificial intelligence. *Vital Speeches of the Day, 82*(1), 8–12.

Lorch, J. (2015). Pitch, pleeeease: How xyz organizations make presenting a way of life. In N. Lubin & A. Ruderman (Eds.), *The XYZ Factor: The DoSomething.org guide to creating a culture of impact* (pp. 23–39). Dallas, TX: Ben Bella Books.

Luft, J. (1970). *Group processes: An introduction to group dynamics* (2nd ed.). Palo Alto, CA: National Press Books.

Lustig, M. W., & Koester, J. (2006). *Intercultural competence: Interpersonal communication across cultures* (5th ed.). Boston, MA: Allyn and Bacon.

Lynch, O. (2002). Humorous communication: Finding a place for humor in communication research. *Communication Theory, 12*, 423–445.

Macan, T. (2009). The employment interview: A review of current studies and directions for future research. *Human*

Resource Management Review, 19, 203–218. doi:10.1016/j.hrmr.2009.03.006

Ma-Kellams, C., Wang, M.C., & Cardiel, H. (2017). Attractiveness and relationship longevity: Beauty is not what it is cracked up to be. *Personal Relationships, 24*, 146–161. doi:10.1111/pere.12173

Malis, R. S., & Roloff, M. E. (2006). Demand/withdraw patterns in serial arguments: Implications for well-being. *Human Communication Research, 32*, 198–216.

Martinez, N. (2017, October 10). Men vs. women: Communication styles explained. *Huffington Post*. Retrieved from https://www.huffingtonpost.com/entry/men-vs-women-communication-styles-explained_us_59dc8d69e4b060f005fbd6ab

Mashek, D. J., & Aron, A. (2004). *Handbook of closeness and intimacy*. Mahwah, NJ: Erlbaum.

Maslow, A. H. (1943). A theory of human motivation. *Psychological Review, 50*, 370–396.

Matsumoto, D. (2006). Culture and nonverbal behavior. In V. Manusov & M. Patterson (Eds.), *Handbook of nonverbal communication*. Thousand Oaks, CA: Sage.

Mattioli, D. (2008, June 10). Next on the agenda: Kisses from Honey Bunny. *WSJ.com*.

Mayer, D. M. (2018, October 18). How men get penalized for straying from masculine norms. *Harvard Business Review*. Retrieved from https://hbr.org/2018/10/how-men-get-penalized-for-straying-from-masculine-norms

McCornack, S. A. (2008). Information manipulation theory: Explaining how deception works. In L. A. Baxter & D. O. Braithwaite (Eds.), *Engaging theories in interpersonal communication: Multiple perspectives*. Thousand Oaks, CA: Sage.

McCornack, S. A., & Levine, T. R. (1990). When lies are uncovered: Emotional and relational outcomes of discovered deception. *Communication Monographs, 57*, 119–138.

McCornack, S. A., Morrison, K., Paik, J. E., Wisner, A., & Zhu, X. (2014). Information manipulation theory 2 (IMT2): A propositional theory of deceptive discourse production. *Journal of Language and Social Psychology, 33*(4), 348–377.

McCroskey, J. C. (2009). Communication apprehension: What have we learned in the last four decades? *Human Communication, 12*, 157–171.

McCroskey, J. C., & Andersen, J. F. (1976). The relationship between communication apprehension and academic achievement among college students. *Human Communication Research, 3*, 73–81.

McCroskey, J. C., Daly, J. A., & Sorensen, G. (1976). Personality correlates of communication apprehension: A research note. *Human Communication Research, 2*, 376–380.

McCroskey, J. C., & Teven, J. J. (1999). Goodwill: A reexamination of the construct and its measurement. *Communication Monographs, 66*, 90–103.

McEwan, B., Babin Gallagher, B., & Farinelli, L. (2008, November). *The end of a friendship: Friendship dissolution reasons and methods*. Paper presented at the annual meeting of the National Communication Association, San Diego, CA.

Medina, J. (2008). *Brain rules: 12 principles for surviving and thriving at work, home, and school*. Seattle, WA: Pear Press.

Mehrabian, A. (1972). *Nonverbal communication*. Chicago, IL: Aldine-Atherton.

Menegatos, L., Lederman, L. C., & Hess, A. (2010). Friends don't let Jane hook up drunk: A qualitative analysis of participation in a simulation of college drinking-related decisions. *Communication Education, 59*, 374–388.

Miller, G. R., & Steinberg, M. (1975). *Between people: A new analysis of interpersonal communication*. Chicago, IL: Science Research Associates.

Miller, L., Hefner, V., & Scott, A. (2007, May). *Turning points in dyadic friendship development and termination*. Paper presented at the annual meeting of the International Communication Association, San Francisco, CA.

Miller-Ott, A. E., & Kelly, L. (2015). The presence of cellphones in romantic partner face-to-face interactions: An Expectancy Violation Theory approach. *Southern Communication Journal, 80*(4), 253–270. doi:10.1080/1041794X.2015.1055371

Miller-Ott, A. E., & Kelly, L. (2017). A politeness theory analysis of cell-phone usage in the presence of friends. *Communication Studies, 68*, 190–207. Retrieved from https://doi.org/10.1080/10510974.2017.1299024

Milne, A. A. (1926). *Winnie-the-Pooh*. New York, NY: E.P. Dutton.

Milne, A. A. (1928). *The house at Pooh Corner*. New York, NY: E.P. Dutton.

Milne, J. (2007). *The page at Pooh Corner*. Retrieved from www.pooh-corner.org/index.shtml

Mooney, J. (2015, June 15). OITNB's Ruby Rose schools us on gender fluidity. Retrieved from https://www.elle.com/culture/movies-tv/a28865/ruby-rose-oitnb/

Morgeson, F. P., DeRue, D. S., & Karam, E. P. (2010). Leadership in teams: A functional approach to understanding leadership structures and processes. *Journal of Management, 36*, 5–39. doi:10.1177/0149206309347376

Motley, M. T. (1990). Public speaking anxiety qua performance anxiety: A revised model and an alternative therapy. *Journal of Social Behavior & Personality, 5*, 85–104.

Mulac, A., Incontro, C. R., & James, M. R. (1985). Comparison of the gender-linked language effect and sex role stereotypes. *Journal of Personality and Social Psychology, 49*, 1098–1109.

Munro, K. (2002). Conflict in cyberspace: How to resolve conflict online. In J. Suler (Ed.), *The psychology of cyberspace*. Retrieved from http://www-usr.rider.edu/~suler/psycyber/conflict.html

Myers, D. G. (2000). Wealth, well-being, and the new American dream. *Center for a New American Dream*. Retrieved from www.davidmyers.org/Brix?pageID=49

Myers, D. G. (2002). *The pursuit of happiness: Discovering the pathway to fulfillment, well-being, and enduring personal joy*. New York, NY: HarperCollins.

Myers, D. G. (2004, Summer). The secret to happiness. *Yes!* 13–16.

Myers, D. G. (2013). Happiness. Excerpted from *Psychology* (10th ed.). New York, NY: Worth.

Myers, S. A., & Anderson, C. M. (2008). *The fundamentals of small group communication.* Thousand Oaks, CA: Sage.

Nagel, F., Maurer, M., & Reinemann, C. (2012). Is there a visual dominance in political communication? How verbal, visual, and vocal communication shape viewers' impressions of political candidates. *Journal of Communication, 62*, 833–850.

National Communication Association. (1999). *NCA credo for ethical communication.* Retrieved from http://www.natcom.org

National Foundation for American Policy. (2017). Declining international student enrollment at U.S. universities and its potential impact. Retrieved from https://nfap.com/wp-content/uploads/2018/02/Decline-in-International-Student-Enrollment.NFAP-Policy-Brief.February-2018-2.pdf

Neimeyer, R. A., & Mitchell, K. A. (1988). Similarity and attraction: A longitudinal study. *Journal of Social and Personal Relationships, 5*, 131–148.

Neuliep, J. W., & McCroskey, J. C. (1997). The development of a U.S. and generalized ethnocentrism scale. *Communication Research Reports, 14*, 385–398.

New Media and Marketing. (2017, August 22). Men and women communicate differently. Retrieved from http://www.newmediaandmarketing.com/men-women-communicate-differently/

Nosko, A., Wood, E., & Molema, S. (2010). All about me: Disclosure in online social networking profiles: The case of Facebook. *Computers in Human Behavior, 26*, 406–418.

Nunamaker, J. F., Jr., Reinig, B. A., & Briggs, R. O. (2009). Principles for effective virtual teamwork. *Communications of the ACM, 52*(4), 113–117.

Oetzel, J. G., & Ting-Toomey, S. (2003). Face concerns in interpersonal conflict: A cross-cultural empirical test of the face negotiation theory. *Communication Research, 30*, 599–624. doi:10.1177/0093650203257841

Oetzel, J., Ting-Toomey, S., Matsumoto, T., Yokochi, Y., Pan, X., Takai, J., & Wilcox, R. (2001). Face and facework in conflict: A cross-cultural comparison of China, Germany, Japan, and the United States. *Communication Monographs, 68*, 235–258.

Ohbuchi, K., & Sato, K. (1994). Children's reactions to mitigating accounts: Apologies, excuses, and intentionality of harm. *Journal of Social Psychology, 134*, 5–17.

Ohio State University. (2018). Is that selfie edited? Why it may matter for women viewers: Perceptions of photo editing affect thin ideal internalization. *ScienceDaily.* Retrieved from www.sciencedaily.com/releases/2018/09/180926140739.htm

O'Keefe, D. J., & Jensen, J. D. (2009). The relative persuasiveness of gain-framed and loss-framed messages for encouraging disease detection behaviors: A meta-analytic review. *Journal of Communication, 59*, 296–316.

Ophir, E., Nass, C. I., & Wagner, A. D. (2012). Cognitive control in media multitaskers. *Proceedings of the National Academy of Sciences.*

Orbe, M. P. (1998). *Constructing co-cultural theory: An explication of culture, power, and communication.* Thousand Oaks, CA: Sage.

Osborn, A. F. (1953). *Applied imagination: Principles and procedures of creative thinking.* New York, NY: Charles Scribner's Sons.

Oyamot, C. M., Fuglestad, P. T., & Snyder, M. (2010). Balance of power and influence in relationships: The role of self-monitoring. *Journal of Social and Personal Relationships, 27*(1), 23–46. doi:10.1177/0265407509347302

Park, H. S., & Guan, X. (2006). The effects of national culture and face concerns on intention to apologize: A comparison of the USA and China. *Journal of Intercultural Communication Research, 35*(3), 183–204.

Parks, M. R. (1994). Communicative competence and interpersonal control. In M. L. Knapp & G. R. Miller (Eds.), *Handbook of interpersonal communication* (2nd ed., pp. 589–620). Beverly Hills, CA: Sage.

Parks, M. R., & Adelman, M. B. (1983). Communication networks and the development of romantic relationships: An expansion of uncertainty reduction theory. *Human Communication Research, 10*, 55–79.

Parks, M. R., & Floyd, K. (1996). Making friends in cyberspace. *Journal of Communication, 46*, 80–97.

Patterson, M. L. (1983). *Nonverbal behavior: A functional perspective.* New York, NY: Springer-Verlag.

Patterson, M. L. (1988). Functions of nonverbal behavior in close relationships. In S. W. Duck (Ed.), *Handbook of personal relationships* (pp. 41–56). New York, NY: Wiley.

Patterson, M. L. (1995). A parallel process model of nonverbal communication. *Journal of Nonverbal Behavior, 19*, 3–29.

Pavey, L., & Churchill, S. (2014). Promoting the avoidance of high-calorie snacks: Priming autonomy moderates message framing effects. *PLOS One* 9(7). doi:10.1371/journal.pone.0103892

Payne, M. J., & Sabourin, T. C. (1990). Argumentative skill deficiency and its relationship to quality of marriage. *Communication Research Reports, 7*, 121–124.

Pearce, C. L., & Conger, J. A. (Eds.). (2002). *Shared leadership: Reframing the hows and whys of leadership.* Thousand Oaks, CA: Sage.

Pennebaker, J. W. (1997). *Opening up: The healing power of expressing emotions.* New York, NY: Guilford Press.

Peterson, D. R. (2002). Conflict. In H. H. Kelley et al. (Eds.), *Close relationships* (2nd ed., pp. 360–396). Clinton Corners, NY: Percheron Press.

Petronio, S. (2000). The boundaries of privacy: Praxis of everyday life. In S. Petronio (Ed.), *Balancing the secrets of private disclosures* (pp. 37–49). Mahwah, NJ: Erlbaum.

Petronio, S., & Caughlin, J. P. (2006). Communication privacy management theory: Understanding families. In D. O. Braithwaite & L. A. Baxter (Eds.), *Engaging theories in family communication: Multiple perspectives* (pp. 35–49). Thousand Oaks, CA: Sage.

Pettegrew, L. S., & Day, C. (2015). Smart phones and mediated relationships: The changing face of relational communication. *Review of Communication, 15*, 122–139.

Petty, R. E., Barden, J., & Wheeler, S. E. (2002). The elaboration likelihood model of persuasion: Health promotions that yield sustained behavior change. In R. J. DiClemente, R. A. Crosby, & M. C. Kegler (Eds.), *Emerging theories in health promotion practice* (pp. 71–99). San Francisco, CA: Jossey-Bass.

Petty, R. E., & Cacioppo, J. T. (1986). The elaboration likelihood model of persuasion. In L. Berkowitz (Ed.), *Advances in experimental social psychology* (Vol. 19, pp. 123–205). New York, NY: Academic Press.

Phillips, K. W. (2014, September 16). How diversity makes us smarter. *Scientific American*. Retrieved from http://www.scientificamerican.com/article/how-diversity-makes-us-smarter/#comment-3D37A78A-D0C0-48BF-88AD44F57AA0B8B8

Piaget, J. (1926). *Language and thought of the child.* (M. Gabain, Trans.). London, England: Routledge & Kegan Paul.

Planalp, S., & Honeycutt, J. M. (1985). Events that increase uncertainty in personal relationships. *Human Communication Research, 11*, 593–604.

Preston, D. R. (1999). Language myth #17: They speak really bad English Down South and in New York City. In L. Bauer & P. Trudgill (Eds.), *Language myths* (pp. 139–149). New York, NY: Penguin Books.

Preston, D. R. (2002). Language with an attitude. In J. K. Chambers, P. Trudgill, & N. Schilling-Estes (Eds.), *The handbook of language variation and change* (pp. 40–66). Oxford, England: Blackwell.

Primack, B. A., Shensa, A., Sidani, J. E., Whaite, E. O., Lin, L. Y., Rosen, D., et al. (2017). Social media use and perceived social isolation among young adults in the U.S. *American Journal of Preventive Medicine, 53*(1), 1–8. doi:10.1016/j.amepre.2017.01.010

Pruitt, D. G., & Carnevale, P. J. (1993). *Negotiation in social conflict.* Monterey, CA: Brooks-Cole.

Przybylski, A. K., & Weinstein, N. (2012). Can you connect with me now? How the presence of mobile communication technology influences face-to-face conversation quality. *Journal of Social and Personal Relationships, 30*(3), 237–246.

Purdy, M., & Newman, N. (1999, March). *Listening and gender: Characteristics of good and poor listeners.* Paper presented to the International Listening Association, Albuquerque, NM.

Quan-Haase, A., & Young, A. L. (2010). Uses and gratifications of social media: A comparison of Facebook and instant messaging. *Bulletin of Science Technology & Society, 30*, 350–361.

Rahim, M. A. (2002). Toward a theory of managing organizational conflict. *International Journal of Conflict Management, 13*, 206–235.

Rainey, V. P. (2000, December). The potential for miscommunication using email as a source of communications. *Transactions of the Society for Design and Process Science, 4*, 21–43.

Rainie, L., & Tancer, B. (2007, April 24). *Wikipedia users*. Retrieved from http://pewinternet.org/Reports/2007/Wikipedia-users.aspx

Rakić, T., Steffens, M. C., & Mummendey, A. (2011). Blinded by the accent! The minor role of looks in ethnic categorization. *Journal of Personality and Social Psychology, 100*, 16–29. doi:10.1037/a0021522

Ramasubramanian, S. (2010). Testing the cognitive-affective consistency model of intercultural attitudes: Do stereotypical perceptions influence prejudicial feelings? *Journal of Intercultural Communication Research, 39*(2), 105–121.

Ramirez-Sanchez, R. (2008). Marginalization from within: Expanding co-cultural theory through the experience of the Afro punk. *Howard Journal of Communications, 19*, 89–104.

Rawlins, W. K. (1992). *Friendship matters: Communication, dialectics, and the life course*. New York, NY: Aldine de Gruyter.

Redden, E. (2017, November 13). New international enrollments decline. *Inside Higher Ed.* Retrieved from https://www.insidehighered.com/news/2017/11/13/us-universities-report-declines-enrollments-new-international-students-study-abroad

Reik, T. (1972). *A psychologist looks at love*. New York, NY: Lancer.

Reis, H. T., & Patrick, B. C. (1996). Attachment and intimacy: Component processes. In E. T. Higgins & A. W. Kruglanski (Eds.), *Social psychology: Handbook of basic principles* (pp. 523–563). New York, NY: Guilford Press.

Reis, H. T., & Shaver, P. (1988). Intimacy as an interpersonal process. In S. W. Duck (Ed.), *Handbook of personal relationships* (pp. 367–389). New York, NY: Wiley.

Rice, L. (2011, March 15). *The Bachelor* creator on his long-running franchise: "The romance space is ours." *Entertainment Weekly.* Retrieved from http://insidetv.ew.com/2011/03/15/the-bachelor-creator-ashley-h/

Richmond, V. P., McCroskey, J. C., & Johnson, A. D. (2003). Development of the nonverbal immediacy scale (NIS): Measures of self- and other-perceived nonverbal immediacy. *Communication Quarterly, 51*, 504–517.

Ridge, R. D., & Berscheid, E. (1989, May). *On loving and being in love: A necessary distinction.* Paper presented at the annual convention of the Midwestern Psychological Association, Chicago, IL.

Riela, S., Rodriguez, G., Aron, A., Xu, X., & Acevedo, B. P. (2010). Experiences of falling in love: Investigating culture, ethnicity, gender, and speed. *Journal of Social and Personal Relationships, 27*, 473–493.

Riggio, R. E. (2006). Nonverbal skills and abilities. In V. Manusov & M. Patterson (Eds.), *Handbook of nonverbal communication*. Thousand Oaks, CA: Sage.

Rochat, P. (2003). Five levels of self-awareness as they unfold early in life. *Consciousness and Cognition, 12*, 717–731.

Rodell, B. (2013, October 13). N/naka review: Japanese formalism flawlessly executed in palms. *LA Weekly*. Retrieved from http://www.laweekly.com/restaurants/n-naka-review-japanese-formalism-flawlessly-executed-in-palms-2694350

Rodrick, S. (2013, June 18). Serena Williams: The great one. *Rolling Stone*. Retrieved from http://www.rollingstone.com/culture/news/serena-williams-the-great-one-20130618

Roethlisberger, F. J., & Dickson, W. J. (1939). *Management and the worker.* Cambridge, MA: Harvard University Press.

Roloff, M. E., & Soule, K. P. (2002). Interpersonal conflict: A review. In M. L. Knapp & J. A. Daly (Eds.), *Handbook of interpersonal communication* (3rd ed., pp. 475–528). Thousand Oaks, CA: Sage.

Romano, N. C., Jr., & Nunamaker, J. F., Jr. (2001). Meeting analysis: Findings from research and practice. In *Proceedings of the 34th annual Hawaii international conference on system sciences*. Retrieved from www.computer.org/csdl/proceedings/hicss/2001/0981/01/index.html

Rosen, L. D., Carrier, L. M., & Cheever, N. A. (2013). Facebook and texting made me do it: Media-induced task-switching while studying. *Computers in Human Behavior, 29*, 948–958. doi:10.1016/j.chb.2012.12.001

Rowan, K. (2003). Informing and explaining skills: Theory and research on informative communication. In J. O. Green and B. R. Burleson (Eds.), *Handbook of Communication and Social Interaction* (pp. 403–438). Mahwah, NJ: Lawrence Erlbaum.

Rubin, R. (2018). Box office: "Incredibles 2" shatters records with heroic $180 million opening. Retrieved from https://variety.com/2018/film/news/incredibles-2-box-office-record-opening-1202849209/

Rubin, Z. (1973). *Liking and loving: An invitation to social psychology*. New York, NY: Holt, Rinehart & Winston.

Rui, J. R., & Stefanone, M. (2013). Strategic image management online. *Information, Communication & Society*. Retrieved from http://dx.doi.org/10.1080/136118X.2013.763834

Sager, K. L., & Gastil, J. (1999). Reaching consensus on consensus: A study of the relationships between individual decision-making styles and use of the consensus decision rule. *Communication Quarterly, 47*, 67–79.

Sager, K. L., & Gastil, J. (2006). The origins and consequences of consensus decision making: A test of the social consensus model. *Southern Communication Journal, 71*, 1–24.

Saujani, R. (2013, October). *You cannot be what you cannot see* [Video file]. Speech delivered at the Chicago Ideas Week Tech Summit, Chicago, IL. Available at https://www.chicagoideas.com/videos/483

Saul, S. (2017, November 13). Fewer foreign students are coming to U.S., survey shows. *New York Times*. Retrieved from https://www.nytimes.com/2017/11/13/us/fewer-foreign-students-coming-to-us.html

Sawyer, K. (2007). *Group genius: The creative power of collaboration*. New York, NY: Basic Books.

Schmitt, D. P. & Buss, D. M. (2001). Human mate poaching: Tactics and temptations for infiltrating existing mateships. *Journal of Personality and Social Psychology, 80*, 894–917. Retrieved from http://dx.doi.org/10.1037/0022-3514.80.6.894

Schramm, W. (Ed.). (1954). *The process and effects of mass communication*. Urbana: University of Illinois Press.

Schumann, K., Zaki, J., & Dweck, C. S. (2014). Addressing the empathy deficit: Beliefs about the malleability of empathy predict effortful responses when empathy is challenging. *Journal of Personality and Social Psychology, 107*(3), 475–493. doi:10.1037/a0036738

Schutz, A. (1999). It was your fault! Self-serving biases in autobiographical accounts of conflicts in married couples. *Journal of Social and Personal Relationships, 16*, 193–208.

Searle, J. (1965). What is a speech act? In M. Black (Ed.), *Philosophy in America* (pp. 221–239). Ithaca, NY: Cornell University Press.

Seattle Poetry Slam. (2013). *Ed Mabrey*. Retrieved from http://seattlepoetryslam.org/?p=598

Seguin, R. (2017). Becoming visible: Insights for working women from the women of *Hidden Figures*. *Vital Speeches of the Day, 83*(10), 304–306.

Seider, B. H., Hirschberger, G., Nelson, K. L., & Levenson, R. W. (2009). We can work it out: Age differences in relational pronouns, physiology, and behavior in marital conflict. *Psychology and Aging, 24*(3), 604–613.

Shannon, C. E., & Weaver, W. (1949). *The mathematical theory of communication*. Urbana: University of Illinois Press.

Shedletsky, L. J., & Aitken, J. E. (2004). *Human communication on the Internet*. Boston, MA: Pearson Education/Allyn and Bacon.

Shelton, J. N., Trail, T. E., West, T. V., & Bergsieker, H. B. (2010). From strangers to friends: The interpersonal process model of intimacy in developing interracial friendships. *Journal of Social and Personal Relationships, 27*(1), 71–90.

Shibley Hyde, J., Bigler, R. S., Joel, D., Chucky Tate, C., & van Anders, S. M. (2018). The future of sex and gender in psychology: Five challenges to the gender binary. *American Psychologist*. Retrieved from http://dx.doi.org/10.1037/amp0000307

Sias, P. M., & Cahill, D. J. (1998). From co-workers to friends: The development of peer friendships in the workplace. *Western Journal of Communication, 62*, 273–300.

Sias, P. M., & Perry, T. (2004). Disengaging from workplace relationships: A research note. *Human Communication Research, 30*, 589–602.

Sias, P. M., Drzewiecka, J. A., Meares, M., Bent, R., Konomi, Y., Ortega, M., & White, C. (2008). Intercultural friendship development. *Communication Reports, 21*(1), 1–13.

Sidibe, M. (2014, September). The simple power of hand-washing. TED@Unilever. Retrieved from https://www.ted.com/talks/myriam_sidibe_the_simple_power_of_hand_washing

Siebdrat, F., Hoegl, M., & Ernst, H. (2009). How to manage virtual teams. *MIT Sloan Management Review, 50*(4), 63–68.

Sillars, A. L. (1980). Attributions and communication in roommate conflicts. *Communication Monographs, 47*, 180–200.

Sillars, A., Roberts, L. J., Leonard, K. E., & Dun, T. (2000). Cognition during marital conflict: The relationship of thought and talk. *Journal of Social and Personal Relationships, 17*, 479–502.

Sillars, A., Smith, T., & Koerner, A. (2010). Misattributions contributing to empathic (in)accuracy during parent-adolescent conflict discussions. *Journal of Social and Personal Relationships, 27*(6), 727–747.

Silverstein, M., & Giarrusso, R. (2010). Aging and family life: A decade review. *Journal of Marriage and Family, 72*, 1039–1058.

Silvia, P. (2008). Interest—The curious emotion. *Current Directions in Psychological Science, 17*, 57–60.

Sink, M. (2006, February 21). Science comes to the masses (you want fries with that?). *New York Times* (Late Edition [East Coast]), p. F3. Retrieved from ProQuest National Newspapers Core (Document ID: 990692051).

Small, D. A., Loewenstein, G., & Slovic, P. (2007). Sympathy and callousness: The impact of deliberative thought on donations to identifiable and statistical victims. *Organizational Behavior and Human Decision Processes, 102*, 143–153.

Smith, C. D., Sawyer, C. R., & Behnke, R. R. (2005). Physical symptoms of discomfort associated with worry about giving a public speech. *Communication Reports, 18*, 31–41.

Smith, G., & Anderson, K. J. (2005). Students' ratings of professors: The teaching style contingency for Latino/a professors. *Journal of Latinos and Education, 4*, 115–136.

Smith, J. S., LaFrance, M., Knol, K. H., Tellinghuisen, D. J., & Moes, P. (2015). Surprising smiles and unanticipated frowns: How emotion and status influence gender categorization. *Journal of Nonverbal Behavior, 39*, 115–130.

Smith, T. E., & Frymier, A. B. (2006). Get "real": Does practicing speeches before an audience improve performance? *Communication Quarterly, 54*, 111–125.

Snyder, M. (1974). Self-monitoring of expressive behavior. *Journal of Personality and Social Psychology*, 30, 526–537.

Socha, T. J. (1997). Group communication across the life span. In L. R. Frey & J. K. Barge (Eds.), *Managing group life: Communicating in decision-making groups* (pp. 3–28). Boston, MA: Houghton Mifflin.

Sommer, R. (1965). Further studies of small group ecology. *Sociometry, 28*, 337–348.

Soto, J. A., Levenson, R. W., & Ebling, R. (2005). Cultures of moderation and expression: Emotional experience, behavior, and physiology in Chinese Americans and Mexican Americans. *Emotion, 5*, 154–165.

Spears, R., Postmes, T., Lea, M., & Watt, S. E. (2001). A SIDE view of social influence. In J. P. Forgas & K. D. Williams (Eds.), *Social influence: Direct and indirect processes* (pp. 331–350). Philadelphia, PA: Psychology Press/ Taylor and Francis Group.

Spender, D. (1990). *Man made language*. London, England: Pandora Press.

Spitzberg, B. H., & Cupach, W. R. (1984). *Interpersonal communication competence*. Beverly Hills, CA: Sage.

Spitzberg, B. H., & Cupach, W. R. (2002). Interpersonal skills. In M. L. Knapp & J. A. Daly (Eds.), *Handbook of interpersonal communication* (3rd ed., pp. 564–611). Thousand Oaks, CA: Sage.

Sporer, S. L., & Schwandt, B. (2006). Paraverbal indicators of deception: A meta-analytic synthesis. *Applied Cognitive Psychology, 20*(4), 421–446.

Sprecher, S. (2001). A comparison of emotional consequences of and changes in equity over time using global and domain-specific measures of equity. *Journal of Social and Personal Relationships, 18*, 477–501.

Stafford, L. (2010). Measuring relationship maintenance behaviors: Critique and development of the revised relationship maintenance behavior scale. *Journal of Social and Personal Relationships, 28*, 278–303.

Stafford, L., Dainton, M., & Haas, S. (2000). Measuring routine and strategic relational maintenance: Scale revision, sex versus gender roles, and the prediction of relational characteristics. *Communication Monographs, 67*, 306–323.

Statistics Canada, Government of Canada. (2012). Portrait of families and living arrangements in Canada. Retrieved from http://www12.statcan.ca/census-recensement/2011/as-sa/98-312-x/98-312-x2011001-eng.cfm

Stewart, G. L., Dustin, S. L., Barrick, M. R., & Darnold, T. C. (2008). Exploring the handshake in employment interviews. *Journal of Applied Psychology, 93*, 1139–1146.

Stiff, J. B., Dillard, J. P., Somera, L., Kim, H., & Sleight, C. (1988). Empathy, communication, and prosocial behavior. *Communication Monographs, 55*, 198–213.

Streek, J. (1980). Speech acts in interaction: A critique of Searle. *Discourse Processes, 3*, 133–154.

Suler, J. (2004). The online disinhibition effect. *Cyberpsychology & Behavior, 7*, 321–326.

Sumner, William G. (1906). *Folkways*. Boston, MA: Ginn.

Swann, W. B., Jr., Chang-Schneider, C., & Angulo, S. (2007). Self-verification in relationships as an adaptive process. In J. Wood, A. Tesser, & J. Holmes (Eds.), *Self and Relationships*. New York, NY: Psychology Press.

Swann, W. B., Jr., Hixon, J. G., & De La Ronde, C. (1992). Embracing the bitter truth: Negative self-concepts and marital commitment. *Psychological Science, 3*, 118–121.

Swann, W. B., Jr., & Pelham, B. W. (2002). Who wants out when the going gets good? Psychological investment and preference for self-verifying college roommates. *Journal of Self and Identity, 1*, 219–233.

Swider, B. W., Barrick, M. R., Harris, T. B., & Stoverink, A. C. (2011). Managing and creating an image in the interview: The role of interviewee initial impressions. *Journal of Applied Psychology, 96*, 1275–1288.

Tardy, C. H. (2000). Self-disclosure and health: Revising Sidney Jourard's hypothesis. In S. Petronio (Ed.), *Balancing the secrets of private disclosures* (pp. 111–122). Mahwah, NJ: Erlbaum.

Tardy, C., & Dindia, K. (1997). Self-disclosure. In O. Hargie (Ed.), *The handbook of communication skills*. London, England: Routledge.

Tavernise, S. (2011, May 26). Married couples are no longer a majority, Census finds. *New York Times*. Retrieved from https://www.nytimes.com/2011/05/26/us/26marry.html

Taylor, J. B. (2008, February). *My Stroke of Insight*. [Video file]. Speech delivered at a TED talk. Available at https://www.ted.com

TED.com (n.d.). *The TED Prize*. Retrieved from www.ted.com/prize

Teo, T. M. S. (2005). *Cross-cultural leadership: A military perspective (NSSC7)*. Kingston, Ontario, Canada: Canadian Forces College.

Teven, J. J. (2008). An examination of perceived credibility of the 2008 presidential candidates: Relationships with believability, likeability, and deceptiveness. *Human Communication, 11*, 383–400.

Teven, J. J., & Hanson, T. L. (2004). The impact of teacher immediacy and perceived caring on teacher competence and trustworthiness. *Communication Quarterly, 52*, 39–53.

Tews, M. J., Frager, K., Citarella, A. I., & Orndorff, R. M. (2018). What is etiquette today? Interviewing etiquette for today's college student. *Journal of Advances in Education Research, 3*(3), 166–175. doi:10.22606/jaer.2018.33005

Thomas, L. T., & Levine, T. R. (1994). Disentangling listening and verbal recall: Related but separate constructs? *Human Communication Research, 21*, 103–127.

Timmerman, C. E., & Scott, C. R. (2006). Virtually working: Communicative and structural predictors of media use and key outcomes in virtual work teams. *Communication Monographs, 73*, 108–136, doi:10.1080/03637750500534396. A previous version of this work was presented as a Top 3 Paper in the Organizational Communication Division at the International Communication Association Annual Conference, New Orleans, LA (May 2004).

Ting-Toomey, S. (1997). Managing intercultural conflicts effectively. In L. A. Samovar & R. E. Porter (Eds.), *Intercultural communication: A reader* (pp. 392–403). Belmont, CA: Wadsworth.

Ting-Toomey, S. (1999). *Communicating across cultures*. New York, NY: Guilford Press.

Ting-Toomey, S. (2005). The matrix of face: An updated face-negotiation theory. In W. B. Gudykunst (Ed.), *Theorizing about intercultural communication* (pp. 211–234). Thousand Oaks, CA: Sage.

Toulmin, S. (1958). *The uses of argument*. Cambridge, England: Cambridge University Press.

Tovares, A. V. (2010). All in the family: Small stories and narrative construction of a shared family identity that includes pets. *Narrative Inquiry, 20*(1), 1–19.

Tuckman, B. (1965). Developmental sequence in small groups. *Psychological Bulletin, 63*, 384–399.

Tuckman, B. W., & Jensen, M. A. C. (1977). Stages of small-group development revisited. *Group & Organization Studies, 2*(4), 419–427.

Turner, J. C., Hogg, M. A., Oakes, P. J., Reicher, S. D., & Wetherell, M. S. (1987). *Rediscovering the social group: A self-categorization theory.* Cambridge, MA: Basil Blackwell.

U.S. Census Bureau (2017). Current population survey, annual social and economic supplements, 1994 to 2017: Figure SHP-1a percent of married couple families that have a stay at home parent (couples with children under 15). Retrieved from https://www.census.gov/content/dam/Census/library/visualizations/time-series/demo/families-and-households/shp-1a.pdf

U.S. Department of Defense. (2016). Transgender policy. Retrieved from https://www.defense.gov/News/Special-Reports/0616_transgender-policy/

Utz, S. (2010). Show me your friends and I will tell you what type of person you are: How one's profile, number of friends, and type of friends influence impression formation on social network sites. *Journal of Computer-Mediated Communication,* 15, 314–335.

Van der Nagel, E. (2017). From usernames to profiles: The development of pseudonymity in Internet communication. *Internet Histories, 1*(4), 312–331. Retrieved from https://doi.org/10.1080/24701475.2017.1389548

Vaterlaus, J. M., Barnett, K., Roche, C., & Young, J. A. (2016). "Snapchat is more personal": An exploratory study on Snapchat behaviors and young adult interpersonal relationship. *Computers in Human Behavior, 62*, 594–601. Retrieved from https://doi.org/10.1016/j.chb.2016.04.029

Vazire, S., & Gosling, S. D. (2004). E-Perceptions: Personality impressions based on personal websites. *Journal of Personality and Social Psychology, 87*, 123–132.

Verduyn, P., Ybarra, O., Résibois, M., Jonides, J., & Kross, E. (2017). Do social network sites enhance or undermine subjective well-being? A critical review. *Social Issues and Policy Review, 11*, 274–302. doi:10.1111/sipr.12033

Wagner, B. C., & Petty, R. E. (2011). The elaboration likelihood model of persuasion: Thoughtful and non-thoughtful social influence. In D. Chadee (Ed.), *Theories in social psychology* (pp. 96–116). Oxford, England: Wiley-Blackwell.

Walker, C. M., Sockman, B. R., & Koehn, S. (2011). An exploratory study of cyberbullying with undergraduate university students. *TechTrends, 55*(2), 31–38.

Wallace, A. (2009). How panicked parents skipping shots endanger us all. *Wired*. Retrieved from https://www.wired.com/2009/10/ff-waronscience/

Walther, J. B. (1992). Interpersonal effects in computer-mediated interaction: A relational perspective. *Communication Research, 19*, 52–90.

Walther, J. B. (2007). Selective self-presentation in computer-mediated communication: Hyperpersonal dimensions of technology, language, and cognition. *Computers in Human Behavior, 23*(5), 2538–2557. Retrieved from https://doi.org/10.1016/j.chb.2006.05.002

Walther, J. B., & Parks, M. R. (2002). Cues filtered out, cues filtered in: Computer-mediated communication and relationships. In M. L. Knapp & J. A. Daly (Eds.), *Handbook of interpersonal communication* (pp. 529–563). Thousand Oaks, CA: Sage.

Walther, J., Van Der Heide, B., Hamel, L. M., & Shulman, H. C. (2009). Self-generated versus other-generated statements and impressions in computer-mediated communication: A test of warranting theory using Facebook. *Communication Research, 36*, 229–253.

Walther, J., Van Der Heide, B., Kim, S. Y., Westerman, D., & Tong, S. T. (2008). The role of friends' appearance and behavior on evaluations of individuals on Facebook: Are we known by the company we keep? *Human Communication Research, 34*, 28–49.

Watercutter, A. (2013, February 4). How Oreo won the marketing super bowl with a timely blackout ad on Twitter. *Wired.* Retrieved from www.wired.com/underwire/2013/02/oreo-twitter-super-bowl/

Waterman, A. (1984). *The psychology of individualism*. New York, NY: Praeger.

Watzlawick, P., Beavin, J. H., & Jackson, D. D. (1967). *Pragmatics of human communication: A study of interactional patterns, pathologies, and paradoxes.* New York, NY: Norton.

Weisz, C., & Wood, L. F. (2005). Social identity support and friendship outcomes: A longitudinal study predicting who will be friends and best friends 4 years later. *Journal of Social and Personal Relationships, 22*(3), 416–432.

Wendt, H., Euwema, M. C., & van Emmerik, I. J. H. (2009). Leadership and team cohesiveness across cultures. *Leadership Quarterly, 20*, 358–370.

West, C., & Zimmerman, D. H. (1987). Doing gender. *Gender & Society, 1*, 125–151.

Whalen, J. M., Pexman, P. M., & Gill, A. J. (2009). "Should Be Fun—Not!" Incidence and marking of nonliteral language in e-mail. *Journal of Language and Social Psychology, 28*, 263–280.

Wheeless, L. R. (1978). A follow-up study of the relationships among trust, disclosure, and interpersonal solidarity. *Human Communication Research, 4*, 143–145.

White, J. (2010, September 28). Workplace bullying: Recognize and prevent it. *CIO insight.* Retrieved from http://www.cioinsight.com/c/a/Latest-News/Workplace-Bullying-Recognize-and-Prevent-It-884670/

White, K., & Hwang, K. (2015, October 9). ASU sorority sisters appear on "Ellen" show. *AZCentral.* Retrieved from http://www.azcentral.com/story/entertainment/television/2015/10/09/asu-sorority-sisters-ellen-degeneres-show/73675812/

Whorf, B. L. (1952). *Collected papers on metalinguistics*. Washington, DC: Department of State, Foreign Service Institute.

Wiemann, J. M. (1977). Explication and test of a model of communicative competence. *Human Communication Research, 3*, 195–213.

Wilmot, W. W., & Hocker, J. L. (2010). *Interpersonal conflict* (8th ed.). Boston, MA: McGraw-Hill.

Wilson, T. D. (2002). *Strangers to ourselves: Discovering the adaptive unconscious.* Cambridge, MA: Harvard University Press.

Wolak, J., Mitchell, K., & Finkelhor, D. (2006). *Online victimization of youth: Five years later*. Alexandria, VA: National Center for Missing and Exploited Children.

World Health Organization. (2003). *Lives at risk: Malaria in pregnancy*. Retrieved from www.who.int/features/2003/04b/en

Wu, D. Y. H., & Tseng, W. (1985). Introduction: The characteristics of Chinese culture. In W. Tseng & D. Y. H. Wu (Eds.), *Chinese culture and mental health* (pp. 3–13). Orlando, FL: Academic Press.

Yoshimura, S. (2007). Goals and emotional outcomes of revenge activities in interpersonal relationships. *Journal of Social and Personal Relationships, 24*(1), 87–98.

Yousafzai, M. (2013). Let us wage a glorious struggle. *Vital Speeches of the Day, 79*(9), 266–267.

Zacchilli, T. L., Hendrick, C., & Hendrick, S. S. (2009). The romantic partner conflict scale: A new scale to measure relationship conflict. *Journal of Social and Personal Relationships, 26*, 1073–1096.

Zandan, N. (2018, May 18). Behind the scenes: My TED experience. Retrieved from https://medium.com/tedx-experience/behind-the-scenes-my-ted-experience-8137c3f34d91

Zappos family core values. (n.d.). Retrieved from http://about.zappos.com/our-unique-culture/zappos-core-values

Zell, E., Strickhouser, J. E., Lane, T. N., & Teeter, S. R. (2016). Mars, Venus, or Earth? Sexism and the exaggeration of psychological gender differences. *Sex Roles, 75*, 287–300.

Zong, J., Batalova, J., & Hallock, J. (2018, February 28). Frequently requested statistics on immigrants and immigration in the United States. Migration Policy Institute. Retrieved from https://www.migrationpolicy.org/article/frequently-requested-statistics-immigrants-and-immigration-united-states

Acknowledgments

The Credo of the National Communication Association. Reprinted with permission of the NCA.

Adapted with permission from American Psychological Association & National Association of School Psychologists. (2015) *Resolution on gender and sexual orientation diversity in children and adolescents in schools.* Retrieved from http://www.apa.org/about/policy/orientation-diversity.aspx.

Index

Pop Quiz Answers

Chapter 1

1. B (p. 5)
2. C (p. 7)
3. A (p. 10)
4. B (p. 21)
5. A (p. 23)

Chapter 2

1. A (p. 37)
2. B (p. 42)
3. D (p. 48)
4. C (p. 50)
5. B (p. 54)

Chapter 3

1. B (p. 63)
2. C (p. 65)
3. D (p. 75)
4. B (p. 80)
5. B (p. 84)

Chapter 4

1. B (p. 96)
2. D (p. 100)
3. C (p. 105)
4. A (p. 105)
5. D (p. 110)

Chapter 5

1. C (p. 119)
2. B (p. 123)
3. A (p. 125)
4. D (p. 129)
5. D (p. 131)

Chapter 6

1. D (p. 143)
2. A (p. 145)
3. A (p. 150)
4. C (p. 156)
5. B (p. 159)

Chapter 7

1. A (p. 168)
2. C (p. 170)
3. D (p. 172)
4. C (p. 175)
5. A (p. 180)

Chapter 8

1. C (p. 192)
2. D (p. 196)
3. A (p. 200)
4. A (p. 202)
5. B (p. 206)

Chapter 9

1. B (p. 219)
2. A (p. 224)
3. C (p. 226)
4. C (p. 228)
5. D (p. 218)

Chapter 10

1. A (p. 243)
2. D (p. 246)
3. B (p. 250)
4. B (p. 254)
5. C (p. 254)

Chapter 11

1. B (p. 268)
2. C (p. 270)
3. A (p. 272)
4. C (p. 280)
5. D (p. 281)

Chapter 12

1. C (p. 290)
2. C (p. 293)
3. B (p. 297)
4. D (p. 303)
5. A (p. 306)

Chapter 13

1. D (p. 319)
2. C (p. 325)
3. A (p. 328)
4. D (p. 330)
5. B (p. 338)

Chapter 14

1. A (p. 346)
2. B (p. 350)
3. D (p. 354)
4. D (p. 356)
5. C (p. 362)

Chapter 15

1. C (p. 376)
2. C (p. 378)
3. B (p. 381)
4. A (p. 387)
5. C (p. 394)

Chapter 16

1. B (p. 402)
2. D (p. 405)
3. A (p. 407)
4. C (p. 414)
5. B (p. 416)

Chapter 17

1. B (p. 435)
2. C (p. 430)
3. B (p. 434)
4. D (p. 441)
5. A (p. 446)

Appendix

1. D (p. A-4)
2. B (p. A-6)
3. A (p. A-8)
4. A (p. A-15)
5. C (p. A-23)

Your Video Choices

launchpadworks.com

LaunchPad offers superior video content organized to work seamlessly with the printed textbook. Go to LaunchPad for *Choices & Connections,* Third Edition, to find the **Advance the Conversation** video scenarios; **Sample Speech Resources**, which complement the speeches in the book and include speech video clips and full-length speech videos; and **Key Term Videos** located in More Resources. Here is a list of the videos and where their concepts appear in the text.